*For Private Circulation only.*

List of British Officers taken prisoner in the various Theatres of War between August, 1914, and November, 1918.

*Compiled from Records kept by Messrs. COX & Co.'s Enquiry Office, at Harrington House, Craig's Court, Charing Cross, London, S.W. 1.*

The Naval & Military Press Ltd

Published by
**The Naval & Military Press Ltd**
Unit 10 Ridgewood Industrial Park,
Uckfield, East Sussex,
TN22 5QE England
Tel: +44 (0) 1825 749494
Fax: +44 (0) 1825 765701
www.naval-military-press.com
www.military-genealogy.com
www.militarymaproom.com

*In reprinting in facsimile from the original, any imperfections are inevitably reproduced and the quality may fall short of modern type and cartographic standards.*

## CONTENTS.

| | PAGE. |
|---|---|
| CONTENTS ... ... ... ... ... ... ... ... ... ... ... | 3 |
| PREFATORY NOTE ... ... ... ... ... ... ... ... ... ... | 5 |
| AEGEAN GROUP ... ... ... ... ... ... ... ... ... ... ... | 187 |
| ARGYLL AND SUTHERLAND HIGHLANDERS ... ... ... ... | 112 |
| ARMY CHAPLAINS DEPARTMENT ... ... ... ... ... ... ... | 135 |
| ARMY CYCLISTS CORPS ... ... ... ... ... ... ... ... ... | 116 |
| AUSTRALIAN FORCE ... ... ... ... ... ... ... ... ... ... | 136 |
| BALKAN FORCE ... ... ... ... ... ... ... ... ... ... ... | 187 |
| BEDFORDSHIRE REGIMENT ... ... ... ... ... ... ... ... | 45 |
| BLACK WATCH ... ... ... ... ... ... ... ... ... ... ... | 73 |
| BORDER REGIMENT ... ... ... ... ... ... ... ... ... ... | 68 |
| CAMBRIDGESHIRE REGIMENT ... ... ... ... ... ... ... ... | 126 |
| CAMERON HIGHLANDERS ... ... ... ... ... ... ... ... ... | 107 |
| CAMERONIANS (SCOTTISH RIFLES) ... ... ... ... ... ... | 59 |
| CANADIAN FORCE ... ... ... ... ... ... ... ... ... ... ... | 138 |
| CHESHIRE REGIMENT ... ... ... ... ... ... ... ... ... ... | 54 |
| COLDSTREAM GUARDS ... ... ... ... ... ... ... ... ... ... | 18 |
| CONNAUGHT RANGERS ... ... ... ... ... ... ... ... ... ... | 111 |
| DARDANELLES ... ... ... ... ... ... ... ... ... ... ... | 178 |
| DEVONSHIRE REGIMENT ... ... ... ... ... ... ... ... ... | 36 |
| DORSETSHIRE REGIMENT ... ... ... ... ... ... ... ... ... | 71 |
| DRAGOONS ... ... ... ... ... ... ... ... ... ... ... | 8 |
| DRAGOON GUARDS ... ... ... ... ... ... ... ... ... ... ... | 8 |
| DUKE OF CORNWALL'S LIGHT INFANTRY ... ... ... ... ... | 66 |
| DURHAM LIGHT INFANTRY ... ... ... ... ... ... ... ... | 99 |
| EAST AFRICA ... ... ... ... ... ... ... ... ... ... ... | 189 |
| EASTERN THEATRE OF WAR ... ... ... ... ... ... ... ... | 178 |
| EAST KENT REGIMENT (BUFFS) ... ... ... ... ... ... ... | 22 |
| EAST LANCASHIRE REGIMENT ... ... ... ... ... ... ... | 63 |
| EAST SURREY REGIMENT ... ... ... ... ... ... ... ... ... | 65 |
| EAST YORKSHIRE REGIMENT ... ... ... ... ... ... ... ... | 43 |
| ESSEX REGIMENT ... ... ... ... ... ... ... ... ... ... ... | 75 |
| GLOUCESTER REGIMENT ... ... ... ... ... ... ... ... ... | 61 |
| GRENADIER GUARDS ... ... ... ... ... ... ... ... ... ... | 17 |
| GORDON HIGHLANDERS ... ... ... ... ... ... ... ... ... | 105 |
| HAMPSHIRE REGIMENT ... ... ... ... ... ... ... ... ... | 69 |
| HEREFORDSHIRE REGIMENT ... ... ... ... ... ... ... ... | 131 |
| HERTFORDSHIRE REGIMENT ... ... ... ... ... ... ... ... | 131 |
| HIGHLAND LIGHT INFANTRY ... ... ... ... ... ... ... ... | 103 |
| HOUSEHOLD BATTALION ... ... ... ... ... ... ... ... ... | 8 |
| HOUSEHOLD BRIGADE (CAVALRY) ... ... ... ... ... ... | 8 |
| HUSSARS ... ... ... ... ... ... ... ... ... ... ... | 9 |
| INDIAN ARMY ... ... ... ... ... ... ... ... ... ... ... | 143 |
| IRISH GUARDS ... ... ... ... ... ... ... ... ... ... ... | 18 |
| KING EDWARD'S HORSE ... ... ... ... ... ... ... ... ... | 9 |
| KING'S LIVERPOOL REGIMENT ... ... ... ... ... ... ... | 31 |
| KING'S OWN ROYAL LANCASTER REGIMENT ... ... ... ... | 23 |
| KING'S OWN SCOTTISH BORDERERS ... ... ... ... ... ... | 58 |
| KING'S OWN YORKSHIRE LIGHT INFANTRY ... ... ... ... | 85 |
| KING'S ROYAL RIFLE CORPS ... ... ... ... ... ... ... ... | 90 |
| KING'S SHROPSHIRE LIGHT INFANTRY ... ... ... ... ... | 86 |
| KUT GARRISON ... ... ... ... ... ... ... ... ... ... ... | 182 |
| LANCASHIRE FUSILIERS ... ... ... ... ... ... ... ... ... | 50 |
| LANCERS ... ... ... ... ... ... ... ... ... ... ... | 9 |
| LEICESTERSHIRE REGIMENT ... ... ... ... ... ... ... ... | 45 |
| LEINSTER REGIMENT ... ... ... ... ... ... ... ... ... | 112 |
| LINCOLNSHIRE REGIMENT ... ... ... ... ... ... ... ... ... | 35 |
| LONDON REGIMENT ... ... ... ... ... ... ... ... ... ... | 126 |
| LOYAL NORTH LANCS. ... ... ... ... ... ... ... ... ... | 79 |

|   |   | PAGE. |
|---|---|---|
| Machine Gun Corps | ... | 116 |
| Manchester Regiment | ... | 94 |
| Mesopotamia | ... | 180 |
| Middlesex Regiment | ... | 87 |
| Monmouthshire Regiment | ... | 126 |
| M.O.R.C.—U.S.A. | ... | 135 |
| Newfoundland Regiment | ... | 141 |
| New Zealand Force | ... | 141 |
| Norfolk Regiment | ... | 34 |
| Northamptonshire Regiment | ... | 81 |
| North Staffordshire Regiment | ... | 97 |
| Northumberland Fusiliers | ... | 24 |
| Oxfordshire and Buckinghamshire Light Infantry | ... | 75 |
| Palestine | ... | 178 |
| Persian Gulf | ... | 180 |
| Rifle Brigade | ... | 114 |
| Royal Air Force | ... | 146 |
| Royal Army Medical Corps | ... | 131 |
| Royal Army Service Corps | ... | 131 |
| Royal Berkshire Regiment | ... | 82 |
| Royal Dublin Fusiliers | ... | 113 |
| Royal Engineers | ... | 16 |
| Royal Field Artillery | ... | 10 |
| Royal Fusiliers | ... | 30 |
| Royal Garrison Artillery | ... | 15 |
| Royal Guernsey Light Infantry | ... | 135 |
| Royal Inniskillen Fusiliers | ... | 59 |
| Royal Irish Fusiliers | ... | 110 |
| Royal Irish Regiment | ... | 47 |
| Royal Irish Rifles | ... | 108 |
| Royal Munster Fusiliers | ... | 113 |
| Royal Naval Air Service | ... | 176 |
| Royal Naval Division | ... | 143 |
| Royal Scots | ... | 19 |
| Royal Scots Fusiliers | ... | 53 |
| Royal Sussex Regiment | ... | 69 |
| Royal Warwickshire Regiment | ... | 28 |
| Royal Welsh Fusiliers | ... | 56 |
| Royal West Kent Regiment | ... | 83 |
| Royal West Surrey Regiment (Queen's) | ... | 21 |
| Scots Guards | ... | 18 |
| Seaforth Highlanders | ... | 104 |
| Sherwood Foresters (Notts and Derby) | ... | 77 |
| Somerset Light Infantry | ... | 38 |
| South African Force | ... | 141 |
| South Lancashire Regiment | ... | 71 |
| South Staffordshire Regiment | ... | 70 |
| South Wales Borderers | ... | 57 |
| Staff | ... | 7 |
| Suffolk Regiment | ... | 37 |
| Tank Corps | ... | 124 |
| Welsh Regiment | ... | 72 |
| West African Force | ... | 189 |
| West Riding Regiment (Duke of Wellington's) | ... | 67 |
| West Yorkshire Regiment | ... | 39 |
| Wiltshire Regiment | ... | 93 |
| Worcestershire Regiment | ... | 62 |
| Yeomanry | ... | 10 |
| Yorkshire Regiment | ... | 48 |
| York and Lancaster Regiment | ... | 98 |

ALPHABETICAL INDEX TO NAMES AT END OF BOOK.

# PREFATORY NOTE.

MESSRS. COX & Co.'s Enquiry Office was opened in September, 1914, in a small room lent by Lord Harrington in his house adjoining the Bank in Craig's Court.

It was instituted for the purpose of giving general advice and information regarding the wounded to the relatives of officers of the original Expeditionary Force

In consequence of the unparalleled strain placed on the Casualty Department at the War Office, and of the conditions existing in France at the beginning of the War, Messrs. COX & Co.'s organization was found to be of considerable benefit in obtaining fuller details of individual cases and also in conveying messages to and from wounded officers still in hospital in France.

A system was also built up of obtaining all available information regarding officers reported "missing"; and this gradually came to be the principal work of the Enquiry Office, who had the great pleasure of being able to give, in a very large number of cases, the first news of the safety of missing officers.

This information was obtained in various ways, but chiefly by means of the fact that a missing officer's cheque was often the first intimation of his being a Prisoner of War, and that all cheques cashed by officer prisoners in Germany passed through the hands of Messrs. COX & Co. Careful records were kept from the beginning, drawn from official and other sources, of all Prisoners of War, and it is from these records that the following list is compiled. As the Army grew, so did the work of the Enquiry Office, and, early in 1915, Lord Harrington kindly allowed Messrs. COX & Co. the use of his large Music Room at Harrington House, and in these two rooms the work was carried on until the end.

The organization was extended, as necessity arose, to every theatre of War in which British or Colonial Troops were engaged, and through Messrs. COX & Co.'s representatives in all parts of the world, information could be had, which in many cases would have been otherwise unobtainable.

Between September 8th, 1914, and February 1st, 1919, the Enquiry Office was never closed to the public for a single day.

*JUNE, 1919.*

# List of British Officers taken prisoner in the various Theatres of War between August, 1914, and November, 1918.

## (1) WESTERN THEATRE OF OPERATIONS.

### STAFF.

| Name. | | Missing. | Interned. | Rapatriated. |
|---|---|---|---|---|
| H. G. ROBERTSON. | Staff Surgeon. | 30/10/14 | | 1/7/15 |
| Lieut. C. J. GAGE-BROWN | Interpreter att. 1st Life Guards. | 6/11/14 | Holland 24/2/18 | 22/1/19 |
| Lieut. H. MARTIN. | Intelligence Corps. | —/14 | Holland 6/2/18 | 23/9/18 |
| Lieut. F. H. BEVAN. | Intelligence Corps. | —/14 | Holland 6/2/18 | 23/10/18 |
| Lieut. T. BREEN. | Intelligence Corps. | —/14 | | |
| Lieut. H. LE GRAND | Intelligence Corps. | —/15 | Switzerland 30/5/16 | 23/12/18 |
| Brig.-Gen. C. D. BRUCE. | 27th Infantry Bde. | 26/9/15 | Holland 19/4/18 | —/4/19 |
| Capt. P. ROSE. | 63rd Infantry Bde. | —/15 | | 9/12/16 |
| Lt.-Col. Hon. H. NAPIER | General Staff. | —/16 | | |
| Brig.-Gen. H. S. L. RAVENSHAW. | | 4/12/17 | | 18/12/18 |
| Capt. F. H. D. VICKERMAN. | | 4/12/16 | | 14/12/18 |
| Capt. J. BROADWOOD. | 35th Infantry Bde. | 30/11/17 | | 29/11/18 |
| Capt. F. B. RYAN. | R.A.M.C. att. R.E. H.Q. | 30/11/17 | | 23/2/18 |
| Capt. G. PEIRSON. | 48th Infantry Bde. | —/3/17 | | 23/2/18 |
| Brig.-Gen. V. T. BAILEY. | 142nd Infantry Bde. | 23/3/18 | | 30/12/18 |
| Brig.-Gen. F. S. DAWSON. | S. Africans att. H.Q. | 24/3/18 | | 30/12/18 |
| Capt. R. BEVERLEY. | S. Africans att. H.Q. | 24/3/18 | | 25/12/18 |
| 2/Lieut. E. A. F. BATTY. | Intelligence att. 41st Infantry Bde. | 24/3/18 | | 25/12/18 |
| Lt.-Col. C. O. PLACE | 36th Infantry Division | 26/3/18 | | 8/12/18 |
| Brig.-Gen. E. H. BELLINGHAM. | 118th Infantry Bde. | 28/3/18 | | —/12/18 |
| Bde.-Major F. H. GUNNER. | 39th Division. | 28/3/18 | | 31/12/18 |
| Major P. C. VELLACOTT. | 23rd Infantry Bde. | 28/3/18 | | 31/12/18 |
| Capt. J. P. CUTHBERT. | 42nd Infantry Bde. | 4/4/18 | | 25/12/18 |
| Brig.-Gen. J. K. DICK CUNYNGHAN | 152nd Infantry Bde. | 12/4/18 | | 13/12/18 |
| Capt. H. P. M. BERNEY FICKLIN. | 152nd Infantry Bde. | 12/4/18 | | 3/12/18 |
| Capt. W. DRUMMOND. | 152nd Infantry Bde. | 12/4/18 | | 2/12/18 |
| 2/Lieut. F. E. FAIRBANK | H.Q. | 25/4/18 | | 1/12/18 |
| Brig.-Gen. H. REES. | 50th Division. | 27/5/18 | | —/12/18 |
| Capt. A. S. WIMBLE. | 24th Infantry Bde. | 27/5/18 | | 25/12/18 |
| Capt. C. JENNINGS. | 7th Infantry Bde. | 27/5/18 | | 6/12/18 |
| 2/Lieut. R. M. RUSTON. | R.F.A. att. Divisional H.Q. | 4/6/18 | | 16/12/18 |
| Lieut. J. L. OUTRAN | Interpreter | —/18 | | 1/12/18 |
| Brig.-Gen. C. E. BRADLEY | | —/16 | Holland | 24/2/18 |
| 2/Lieut. J. A. THIN | 5th Corps Cavalry | 22/3/17 | | 14/12/18 |

## 1st LIFE GUARDS.

| Name. | Missing. |  | Interned. | Repatriated. |
|---|---|---|---|---|
| Lieut. C. J. GAGE-BROWN. | 6/11/14 | Holland | 24/2/18 | 22/1/19 |

## 2nd LIFE GUARDS.

| | | | | |
|---|---|---|---|---|
| Capt. H. C. S. ASHTON. | 19/10/14 | Holland | 6/2/18 | 18/11/18 |
| Lieut. K. R. PALMER. | 19/10/14 | Holland | 6/2/18 | 18/11/18 |

## ROYAL HORSE GUARDS.

| | | | | |
|---|---|---|---|---|
| Lieut. A. J. CAMPBELL. | | | | 19/12/18 |

## HOUSEHOLD BATTALION.

| | | | | |
|---|---|---|---|---|
| 2/Lt. B. M. GREENHILL. | 3/5/17 | | | 4/12/18 |

## DRAGOONS.

### 1st (Royal).

| | | | | |
|---|---|---|---|---|
| Capt. H. JUMP. | 30/12/14 | Switzerland | 9/12/17 | 9/12/18 |

### 2nd (Scots Greys).

| | | | | |
|---|---|---|---|---|
| Capt. H. ESTCOURT. | 4/12/15 | Switzerland | 5/12/17 | 23/12/18 |

### 6th (Inniskilling).

| | | | | |
|---|---|---|---|---|
| 2/Lt. A. M. NIALL. | 1/12/17 | | | 31/12/18 |
| Lieut. F. K. PRIDEAUX-BRUNE. | 23/3/18 | | | 12/10/18 |

## DRAGOON GUARDS.

### 4th (Royal Irish).

| | | | | |
|---|---|---|---|---|
| *Capt. A. Fitz. G. RAMSAY. | 11/9/14 | Holland | 24/2/18 | |
| Capt. Sir A. HICKMAN. | 11/9/14 | Holland | 29/12/17 | 17/11/18 |
| Lieut. O. SANDERSON. | 11/9/14 | Switzerland | 9/12/17 | 24/3/18 |
| Capt. H. GURNEY. | | | | –/12/18 |

### 5th (Princess Charlotte of Wales's).

| | | | | |
|---|---|---|---|---|
| Lieut. M. B. BURROWS. | 2/9/14 | Holland | 6/2/18 | 18/11/18 |

### 6th (Carabiniers).

| | | | | |
|---|---|---|---|---|
| Lieut. R. H. H. JONES. | 10–11/10/18 | | | 18/11/18 |

### 7th (Princess Royal's).

| | | | | |
|---|---|---|---|---|
| Capt. J. MONTGOMERY. | 24/8/14 | Holland | 5/1/18 | 22/11/18 |

*Attached from 22nd Indian Cavalry.

## HUSSARS.

### 4th (Queen's Own).

| Name. | Missing. | Interned. | | Repatriated. |
|---|---|---|---|---|
| Lieut. D. BIBBY. | 16/9/14 | Holland | 29/12/17 | 22/11/18 |
| Lieut. B. B. FAULKNER. | 17/10/14 | Holland | 6/2/18 | 22/11/18 |

### 7th (Queen's Own).

| | | | | |
|---|---|---|---|---|
| Major P. L. E. WALKER. | 27/10/18 | | | 10/1/19 |

### 8th (King's Royal Irish).

| | | | | |
|---|---|---|---|---|
| Capt. P. S. ALEXANDER. | 22/3/18 | | | 28/11/18 |
| 2/Lt. J. P. ROBINSON. | 22/3/18 | | | –/11/18 |

### 11th (Prince Albert's Own).

| | | | | |
|---|---|---|---|---|
| Lieut. H. E. TALBOT. | 19/10/14 | Switzerland | 19/12/16 | –/12/17 |
| Lieut. W. H. JAGGERS. | 21/3/18 | | | –/11/18 |

### 15th (The King's).

| | | | | |
|---|---|---|---|---|
| Lieut. J. C. ROGERSON. | 10/9/14 | Holland | 6/2/18 | 16/11/18 |
| 2/Lt. W. J. PICKERING. | 21/3/18 | | | 11/12/18 |
| Capt. J. GODMAN. | 22/3/18 | | | 14/12/18 |
| Lieut. W. J. M. LOWE. | 22/3/18 | | | |

### 18th (Queen Mary's Own).

| | | | | |
|---|---|---|---|---|
| Lieut. G. FIRTH. | 20/10/14 | Holland | 6/2/18 | 18/11/18 |

### 19th (Queen Alexandra's Own Royal).

| | | | | |
|---|---|---|---|---|
| Lieut. W. G. HORNE. | 3/9/14 | Holland | 5/1/18 | 22/11/18 |
| Lieut. Sir C. W. CAYZER. | 8/10/18 | | | –/12/18 |
| Lieut. J. S. COCKBURN. | 8/10/18 | | | 13/12/18 |

### 20th.

| | | | | |
|---|---|---|---|---|
| Lieut. J. T. UPTON. | 10/9/14 | Holland | 6/2/18 | 18/11/18 |

## LANCERS.

### 5th (Royal Irish).

| | | | | |
|---|---|---|---|---|
| Capt. Hon. I. J. L. HAY. | | Holland | 5/1/18 | 18/11/18 |
| Capt. J. A. T. RICE. | 26/3/18 | (Died 14/4/18 at Cugny). | | |

### 9th (Queen's Royal).

| | | | | |
|---|---|---|---|---|
| Lieut. R. G. PEEK. | 29/8/14 | | | 13/9/17 |
| Lieut. C. W. NORMAN. | 30/10/14 | Holland | 24/2/18 | 24/11/18 |
| Lieut. F. S. CROSSLEY. | 30/11/14 | Holland | 6/2/18 | 23/10/18 |
| Lieut. E. JOICEY. | 21/11/17 | | | 25/12/18 |
| Lieut. S. G. BROCKWELL. | 9/8/18 | | | 13/12/18 |

### 12th (Prince of Wales's Royal).

| | | | | |
|---|---|---|---|---|
| Major P. J. BAILEY. | 11/9/14 | Switzerland | 9/12/17 | 6/12/18 |
| Lieut. R. L. MOORE. | 12/9/14 | Switzerland | 12/8/16 | –/9/17 |

### 16th (The Queen's).

| | | | | |
|---|---|---|---|---|
| Capt. G. E. BELLVILLE. | 11/9/14 | Switzerland | 12/8/16 | 11/9/17 |
| Lieut. J. J. RYAN. | 21/2/15 | Holland | 1/3/18 | 23/10/18 |

### 21st (Empress of India's).

| | | | | |
|---|---|---|---|---|
| Capt. G. N. REYNOLDS. | 30/10/14 | Holland | 24/2/18 | 4/1/19 |
| Capt. Hon. B. F. R. ROBERTSON. | 30/10/14 | Switzerland | 30/5/16 | 17/9/17 |

## KING EDWARD'S HORSE.

| | | | | |
|---|---|---|---|---|
| 2/Lt. J. F. BRAKELL. | 31/7/17 | | | 23/12/18 |
| Lieut. D. G. LAURENSON. | 9/4/18 | | | 13/12/18 |
| Lieut. R. O'HALLORAN-GILES. | 9/4/18 | (Died) | | |
| Lieut. Ian STEIN. | 9/4/18 | | | 10/12/18 |

## YEOMANRY.
### Buckinghamshire.

| Name. | Missing. | Interned. | Repatriated. |
|---|---|---|---|
| Major C. E. G. GOETZ. | | | 23/12/18 |

### Derbyshire.

| | | | |
|---|---|---|---|
| Major W. WILSON. | 27/3/18 | | 29/11/18 |

### Essex.

| | | | |
|---|---|---|---|
| †Lieut. G. MORGAN. | 28/4/18 | | –/12/18 |

### Northumberland (Hussars).

| | | | |
|---|---|---|---|
| Lieut. I. A. PATTERSON. | 22/8/18 | | –/12/18 |

## ROYAL FIELD ARTILLERY.

| Name | Missing | Interned | Repatriated |
|---|---|---|---|
| Capt. I. L. SMYTHE. | | | –/11/18 |
| 2/Lt. R. F. GORE-BROWN. | | Switzerland 9/12/17 | 24/3/18 |
| Lieut. D. HILL. | | Switzerland 30/5/16 | 14/9/17 |
| Capt. C. J. F LEECH. | –/8/14 | Holland 22/1/18 | 12/2/19 |
| Capt. P. LYSTER. | 24/8/14 | Holland 29/12/17 | 23/9/18 |
| Lt.-Col. C. STEVENS. | 27/8/14 | Switzerland 9/12/17 | 9/12/18 |
| Major A. C. R. NUTT. | 27/8/14 | Switzerland 27/12/17 | 23/12/18 |
| Major R. E. BIRLEY. | 5/9/14 | Switzerland 30/5/16 | 14/9/17 |
| Major A. R. BAYLY. | 10/9/14 | Switzerland 9/12/17 | –/2/19 |
| Lieut. A. STEWART-COX. | 10/9/14 | Holland 22/1/18 | 4/10/18 |
| Lieut. E. A. SPENCER. | 10/9/14 | Holland 5/1/18 | 18/11/18 |
| 2/Lt. R. W. McLEOD. | 10/9/14 | Holland 6/2/18 | 18/11/18 |
| Lieut. J. STANFORD. | 10/9/14 | Holland 5/1/18 | 14/11/18 |
| Lieut. J. E. YOUNGER. | 10/9/14 | Holland 5/1/18 | 18/11/18 |
| Major G. H. F. TAILYOUR. | 10/9/14 | Holland 5/1/18 | 23/10/18 |
| Major E. H. JONES. | 10/9/14 | Switzerland 12/8/16 | 14/9/17 |
| Lieut. E. L. ARMITAGE. | 26/9/14 | Holland 5/1/18 | 17/11/18 |
| Lieut. Michael ABRAHAM. | 11/11/14 | Switzerland 12/8/16 | 14/6/18 |
| 2/Lt. H. C. HINWOOD. | 15/3/15 | Switzerland 27/12/17 | 24/3/18 |
| Lieut. A. COULSON. | 9/5/15 | Holland 23/3/18 | 18/11/18 |
| Lieut. J. A. DONNELLY. | 10/5/15 | | 1/1/19 |
| Capt. F. H. PRICHARD. | 2/6/15 | Holland –/6/15 | 2/6/15 |
| Lieut. K. W. POWER. | 26/9/15 | Holland 10/4/18 | 18/11/18 |
| 2/Lt. F. W. LONG. | 4/6/16 | (*Died* 28/6/16). | |
| 2/Lt. H. F. DENHAM-SMITH. | 18/11/16 | Switzerland 27/12/17 | 24/3/18 |
| Capt. A. T. SLOAN. | 25/2/17 | | 12/11/18 |
| *Lieut. B. P. LUSCOMBE. | 10/7/17 | | 14/12/18 |
| 2/Lt. C. L. NICHOLS. | 10/7/17 | | 17/12/18 |
| 2/Lt. H. TOWNSEND. | 10/7/17 | | 14/12/18 |
| 2/Lt. H. G. E. DURNFORD. | 5/8/17 | | 9/11/18 |
| Capt. C. B. DARLEY. | 30/11/17 | | 14/12/18 |
| *Lieut. L. GOLDSTEIN. | 30/11/17 | | 18/12/18 |
| Lieut. H. MAYNARD. | 30/11/17 | | 3/12/18 |
| *Lieut. J. G. LOMAX. | 30/11/17 | | 29/11/18 |
| 2/Lt. J. R. ANNANDALE. | 30/11/17 | | 17/12/18 |
| *2/Lt. R. H. GRIBBLE. | 30/11/17 | | 17/12/18 |
| 2/Lt. K. S. PATTERSON. | 30/11/17 | (*Died* 6/12/17). | |
| 2/Lt. H. J. WINDER. | 1/12/17 | | 27/11/18 |
| Capt E. C. HAGEN. | 1/12/17 | | 25/12/18 |

\* Attached T.M.B.    † Attached Divisional Artillery.

## ROYAL FIELD ARTILLERY—continued.

| Name. | Missing. | Interned. | Repatriated. |
|---|---|---|---|
| Lieut. H. S. ANDERSON. | 16/1/18 | | 14/12/18 |
| Major W. R. CUNLIFFE. | –/3/18 | | 19/1/19 |
| Capt. W. V. DAWSON. | –/3/18 | | 29/11/19 |
| †Lieut. R. MacARTHUR. | –/3/18 | | 1/1/19 |
| 2/Lt. F. G. J. RASMUSSON. | –/3/18 | | 29/11/18 |
| 2/Lt. T. STUART. | –/3/18 | | 1/12/18 |
| 2/Lt. Pat GORDON. | –/3/18 | | –/12/18 |
| 2/Lt. G. G. R. PATON. | 20/3/18 | | 28/11/18 |
| Major A. F. M. RIECKE. | 21/3/18 | | 6/12/18 |
| Major E. T. DOBBIE. | 21/3/18 | | 14/12/18 |
| Major Cleveland KEYES. | 21/3/18 | (*Died* 24/3/18). | |
| Major R. H. FARREN. | 21/3/18 | | 18/12/18 |
| Major R. V. MAUDSLAY. | 21/3/18 | | 17/12/18 |
| *Capt. R. E. GUDGEON. | 21/3/18 | (*Died* 2/4/18 at Stendal). | |
| *Capt. A. D. BOLLAM. | 21/3/18 | | 4/12/18 |
| *Capt. J. W. WHITAKER. | 21/3/18 | | 18/12/18 |
| *Lieut. C. A. FELL. | 21/3/18 | | 2/12/18 |
| *Lieut. Wm. HORSFIELD. | 21/3/18 | | 14/12/18 |
| *Lieut. R. M. HAMMOND. | 21/3/18 | (*Died* 20/5/18 at Hoilbronn). | |
| *Lieut. B. D. M. BREWER. | 21/3/18 | | 11/12/18 |
| *Lieut. E. C. ROSE. | 21/3/18 | | 17/12/18 |
| *Lieut. T. K. MEIKLE. | 21/3/18 | | 1/12/18 |
| Lieut. J. M. COUPER. | 21/3/18 | (*Died* 4/4/18 at Friedrichsfeld). | |
| Lieut. W. H. F. BIRD. | 21/3/18 | | 29/11/18 |
| Lieut. F. A. HODGES. | 21/3/18 | | 5/1/19 |
| Lieut. W. H. CROWDER. | 21/3/18 | | 19/12/18 |
| Lieut T. A. B. COPESTAKE. | 21/3/18 | | 8/12/18 |
| Lieut. E. T. SCOTT. | 21/3/18 | | 18/12/18 |
| Lieut. Hugh G. LE RAY. | 21/3/18 | | 14/12/18 |
| Lieut. H. R. Dale HARRIS. | 21/3/18 | | 6/12/18 |
| ‡Lieut. N. E. TYNDALE-BISCOE. | 21/3/18 | | 10/12/18 |
| Lieut. P. H. GIBBONS. | 21/3/18 | | 28/11/18 |
| Lieut. L. HANNAN. | 21/3/18 | | 18/12/18 |
| Lieut. E. N. GODFREY. | 21/3/18 | | 17/12/18 |
| ‡2/Lt. G. D. CASTELLI. | 21/3/18 | | 25/12/18 |
| 2/Lt. G. K. STANLEY. | 21/3/18 | | 14/12/18 |
| 2/Lt. J. HOLLIDAY. | 21/3/18 | | 18/12/18 |
| 2/Lt. G. GREENWOOD | 21/3/18 | | 13/12/18 |
| 2/Lt. Robert HALL. | 21/3/18 | | 1/12/18 |
| 2/Lt. T W. W. GOODRIDGE. | 21/3/18 | | 14/12/18 |
| 2/Lt. E. GOSMORE. | 21/3/18 | | 4/12/18 |
| 2/Lt. J. HUTCHISON. | 21/3/18 | | 8/12/18 |
| 2/Lt. R. HOWL. | 21/3/18 | | 11/12/18 |
| 2/Lt. R. F. TROWER. | 21/3/18 | | 18/12/18 |
| Lieut. E. V. GOODMAN. | 21/3/18 | | 29/11/18 |
| 2/Lt. C. F. TOD. | 21/3/18 | | 11/12/18 |
| 2/Lt. R. C. MacKIE. | 21/3/18 | | 13/1/19 |
| 2/Lt. I. MEO. | 21/3/18 | | 11/12/18 |
| 2/Lt. W. G. MITCHELL. | 21/3/18 | | 11/12/18 |
| 2/Lt. D. de E. STRICKLAND. | 21/3/19 | | –/12/18 |
| 2/Lt. J. L. SPITE. | 21/3/18 | | 11/12/18 |
| 2/Lt. S. W. BALL. | 21/3/18 | | 18/12/18 |
| 2/Lt. A. TRUSLER. | 21/3/18 | | 11/12/18 |
| 2/Lt. H. SNODGRASS. | 21/3/18 | | 14/12/18 |

\* Attached T.M.B.     † Attached from East Lancs.
‡ R.H.A.

## ROYAL FIELD ARTILLERY—continued.

| Name. | Missing. | Interned. | Repatriated. |
|---|---|---|---|
| 2/Lt. J. A. BROWN. | 21/3/18 | | 12/12/18 |
| 2/Lt. D'A. J. LANGNER. | 21/3/18 | | 28/11/18 |
| 2/Lt. A. N. RAWES. | 21/3/18 | | 1/12/18 |
| 2/Lt. E. C. A RUNNELS-MOSS. | 21/3/18 | (Died 9/7/18 at Mainz). | |
| 2/Lt. R. U. NUTTER. | 21/3/18 | | 2/12/18 |
| 2/Lt. R. G. W. NORRISH. | 21/3/18 | | 18/12/18 |
| 2/Lt. G. W. CARR. | 21/3/18 | | 29/11/18 |
| 2/Lt. J. H. DAVIES. | 21/3/18 | | 18/12/18 |
| 2/Lt. W. F. LONGDON. | 21/3/18 | | 11/12/18 |
| 2/Lt. R. E. R. LUFF. | 21/3/18 | | 2/12/18 |
| 2/Lt. F. B. JONES. | 21/3/18 | | —/12/18 |
| 2/Lt. C. W. BROOKFIELD. | 21/3/18 | | 18/12/18 |
| 2/Lt. W. E. BOLTON. | 21/3/18 | | 18/12/18 |
| 2/Lt. H. A. BLUNDELL. | 21/3/18 | | 6/12/18 |
| 2/Lt. J. B. BENNETT. | 21/3/18 | | 5/1/19 |
| 2/Lt. J. S. WOOD. | 21/3/18 | | —/12/18 |
| 2/Lt. E. B. WALLER. | 21/3/18 | | 18/12/18 |
| 2/Lt. D. WADDELL. | 21/3/18 | | 25/12/18 |
| 2/Lt. A. K. ROBERTS. | 21/3/18 | | 10/12/18 |
| 2/Lt. Hon. E. F. FRENCH. | 21/3/18 | (Died —/11/18 at Mainz). | |
| 2/Lt. J. L. ELLIS. | 21/3/18 | | 28/11/18 |
| 2/Lt. J. R. EDWARDS. | 21/3/18 | | 14/12/18 |
| 2/Lt. J. DODDS. | 21/3/18 | | 29/11/18 |
| 2/Lt. T. H. DAVIES. | 21/3/18 | | 18/12/18 |
| 2/Lt. W. F. N. CHURCHILL. | 21/3/18 | | 14/12/18 |
| 2/Lt. E. S. PONT. | 21/3/18 | | 6/12/18 |
| 2/Lt. G. P. PITTAR. | 21/3/18 | | 11/12/18 |
| 2/Lt. G. H. PHILIP. | 21/3/18 | | 11/12/18 |
| 2/Lt. R. M. PATTERSON | 21/3/18 | | 25/12/18 |
| 2/Lt. J. C. L. PARSONS. | 21/3/18 | | 11/12/18 |
| 2/Lt. E. G. PARFITT. | 21/3/18 | | 11/12/18 |
| *2/Lt. J. H. YARDLEY. | 21/3/18 | | 18/12/18 |
| *2/Lt. R. F. TODD. | 21/3/18 | | 14/12/18 |
| *2/Lt. A. W. HUMPHREYS. | 21/3/18 | | 17/12/18 |
| *2/Lt. B. L. WILKINSON. | 21/3/18 | | 28/11/18 |
| *2/Lt. J. H. GRAY. | 21/3/18 | | 5/1/19 |
| 2/Lt. W. G. DARNELL. | 22/3/18 | | 6/1/19 |
| 2/Lt. C. S. DAWNEY. | 22/3/18 | | 27/11/18 |
| 2/Lt. H. W. N. FANE. | 22/3/18 | | 28/11/18 |
| 2/Lt. R. G. M. JONES. | 22/3/18 | | 2/12/18 |
| 2/Lt. E. R. B. REYNOLDS. | 22/3/18 | | 3/1/19 |
| 2/Lt. W. MARLOW. | 22/3/18 | | 18/12/18 |
| 2/Lt. C. M. H. HICKS. | 22/3/18 | | 16/12/18 |
| 2/Lt. M. J. HARKER. | 22/3/18 | | 11/12/18 |
| 2/Lt. G. J. R. MacAULAY. | 23/3/18 | | 18/12/18 |
| 2/Lt. W. A. WILLIAMS. | 23/3/18 | | 17/12/18 |
| 2/Lt. F. W. LEWIS. | 23/3/18 | | 17/12/18 |
| Lieut. R. REEVES. | 25/3/18 | | 14/12/18 |
| †2/Lt. K. McBRYDE. | 25/3/18 | | 25/12/18 |
| 2/Lt. J. H. SWANN. | 25/3/18 | | 18/12/18 |
| 2/Lt. R. R. GREEN. | 24–28/3/18 | | 17/12/18 |
| 2/Lt. J. TODD. | 27/3/18 | | 31/12/18 |
| Lieut. C. B. ROWE-EVANS. | 28/3/18 | | 17/12/18 |
| Lieut. A. STROUDLEY. | 28/3/18 | | —/1/19 |
| 2/Lt. D. S. D. NICHOLL. | 28/3/18 | | 25/12/18 |

* Attached T.M.B.     † Attached from A.S.C.

## ROYAL FIELD ARTILLERY—continued.

| Name. | Missing. | Interned. | Repatriated. |
|---|---|---|---|
| 2/Lt. A. J. GOING. | 28/3/18 | | 25/12/18 |
| 2/Lt. J. R. HALL. | 28/3/18 | | 17/12/18 |
| 2/Lt. J. W. STONEMAN. | 28/3/18 | | 1/12/18 |
| 2/Lt. J. WILKIE. | 28/3/18 | | 17/12/18 |
| 2/Lt. W. H. PEARCE. | 28/3/18 | (Died 24/4/18 at Le Cateau). | |
| *2/Lt. A. M. URQUGART. | 29/3/18 | | 10/12/18 |
| Capt. J. H. HUDSON. | 4/4/18 | | 1/1/19 |
| Major J. N. RITCHIE. | 9/4/18 | | 17/12/18 |
| Lieut. L. G. A. CUST. | 9/4/18 | | 1/12/18 |
| Lieut. W. R. BOOTH. | 9/4/18 | | 29/11/18 |
| Lieut. G. HULL. | 9/4/18 | | 3/12/18 |
| 2/Lt. H. S. THOMPSON. | 9/4/18 | | 18/12/18 |
| *2/Lt. L. H. MAYNARD. | 9/4/18 | | 11/12/18 |
| 2/Lt. Andrew SALLEY. | 9/4/18 | | 14/1/19 |
| 2/Lt. F. McN. JACKSON. | 9/4/18 | | 1/12/18 |
| *2/Lt. P. A. McEWEN. | 9/4/18 | | 5/12/18 |
| 2/Lt. J. R. WALKER. | 9/4/18 | | 29/11/18 |
| 2/Lt. E. McGEACHY. | 9/4/18 | | 29/11/18 |
| Capt. W. J. BROOKS. | 10/4/18 | | 1/12/18 |
| *Lieut. N. V. WATSON. | 10/4/18 | | 18/12/18 |
| *2/Lt. W. E. GREEN. | 10/4/18 | | 25/12/18 |
| Lieut. W. E. HUNTER. | 11/4/18 | | 8/12/18 |
| Lt.-Col. F. FLEMING. | 12/4/18 | | 14/12/18 |
| *2/Lt. T. R. SCOTT, M.C. | 24/4/18 | | 1/12/18 |
| 2/Lt. J. BRAILSFORD. | 24/4/18 | | 18/12/18 |
| 2/Lt. G. M. O. DAVY. | 25/4/18 | | 2/12/18 |
| 2/Lt. K. R. BLACKWELL. | 25/4/18 | | 29/11/18 |
| Lieut. W. E. STRICKLAND. | 26/4/18 | | –/12/18 |
| 2/Lt. George LORD. | 26/4/18 | | 18/12/18 |
| Lieut. A. B. THOMSON. | 10/5/18 | | –/12/18 |
| 2/Lt. H. R. WHITEMAN. | 25/5/18 | | –/12/18 |
| Major G. J. NANTES. | 26/5/18 | | 13/12/18 |
| Major H. G. FISHER, D.S.O. | 27–31/5/18 | | 30/12/18 |
| Capt. E. A. PALMER. | 27–31/5/18 | | 31/12/18 |
| Lieut. E. H. THOMAS. | 27–31/5/18 | | 26/12/18 |
| Lieut. D. C. OWEN. | 27–31/5/18 | | 31/12/18 |
| *2/Lt. A. J. MACK. | 27–31/5/18 | | 23/10/18 |
| *2/Lt. W. F. KEATING. | 27–31/5/18 | | 30/12/18 |
| 2/Lt. E. F. BRYAN. | 27–31/5/18 | | 2/1/19 |
| 2/Lt. M. de la P. BERESFORD. | 27–31/5/18 | | 31/12/18 |
| 2/Lt. K. HOLME-BARNETT. | 27–31/5/18 | | 30/12/18 |
| 2/Lt. M. C. HULLAH. | 27–31/5/18 | | –/12/18 |
| 2/Lt. I. S. NICOL. | 27–31/5/18 | | 30/12/18 |
| 2/Lt. J. W. HART. | 27–31/5/18 | | 25/12/18 |
| Colonel E. V. SARSON. | 27/5/18 | | –/12/18 |
| Lt.-Col. F. B. MOSS-BLUNDELL. | 27/5/18 | | 24/12/18 |
| Major A. P. EVERSHED, M.C. | 27/5/18 | | –/12/18 |
| Major N. SOUTHERN. | 27/5/18 | | 31/12/18 |
| Major G. CHAPMAM. | 27/5/18 | | 9/1/19 |
| Major D. C. WILSOR, D.S.O. | 27/5/18 | | –/1/19 |
| Major Hon. G. BOSCAWEN. | 27/5/18 | (Died 7/6/18 at Liesse). | |
| Major W. H. H. HUTCHINSON. | 27/5/18 | | 21/12/18 |
| Major W. GOLDING. | 27/5/18 | | 25/12/18 |
| Capt. C. B. GOLDING, M.C. | 27/5/18 | | 31/12/18 |
| Capt. J. E. HUMBERSTONE. | 27/5/18 | | –/12/18 |

* Attached T.M.B.

## ROYAL FIELD ARTILLERY—continued.

| Name. | Missing. | Interned. | Repatriated. |
|---|---|---|---|
| Capt. L. F. STEMP. | 27/5/18 | | 14/12/18 |
| Capt. B. K. BARTON. | 27/5/18 | | 30/12/18 |
| Capt. E. DARLING, M.C. | 27/5/18 | | 31/12/18 |
| Capt. A. L. CHANTRILL. | 27/5/18 | | –/12/18 |
| Lieut. C. O. FRANK. | 27/5/18 | | 22/1/19 |
| Lieut. A. D. ROBERTS. | 27/5/18 | | 14/12/18 |
| Lieut. G. E. PATTON. | 27/5/18 | | –/12/18 |
| Lieut. W. W. WHYTE. | 27/5/18 | | –/12/18 |
| Lieut. A. BOSTOCK. | 27/5/18 | | –/12/18 |
| Lieut. R. J. BARDSLEY. | 27/5/18 | | –/12/18 |
| Lieut. A. S. WITHERINGTON. | 27/5/18 | | –/12/18 |
| Lieut. J. MacLEOD. | 27/5/18 | | 14/12/18 |
| Lieut. E. G. ATTENBOROUGH. | 27/5/18 | | –/12/18 |
| Lieut. C. M. HARVEY. | 27/5/18 | | 14/12/18 |
| Lieut. H. R. HORNSBY. | 27/5/18 | | 31/12/18 |
| Lieut. J. P. HUTCHINSON. | 27/5/18 | | 31/12/18 |
| Lieut. T. M. GATHERAL. | 27/5/18 | | 31/12/18 |
| Lieut. W. S. GALL. | 27/5/18 | | 13/12/18 |
| Lieut. E. D. TUDHOPE. | 27/5/18 | | 30/12/18 |
| 2/Lt. D. H. THOMPSON. | 27/5/18 | | –/1/19 |
| 2/Lt. K. M. GOODENOUGH. | 27/5/18 | | 25/12/18 |
| 2/Lt. C. E. HOLLIDAY. | 27/5/18 | | 25/12/18 |
| 2/Lt. F. J. HODDER. | 27/5/18 | | 25/12/18 |
| 2/Lt. W. GRAHAM. | 27/5/18 | | 13/12/18 |
| 2/Lt. G. W. PARKES. | 27/5/18 | | 30/12/18 |
| 2/Lt. A. O. STANDEN. | 27/5/18 | | 23/12/18 |
| 2/Lt. W. T. MERCER. | 27/5/18 | | 26/12/18 |
| 2/Lt. F. L. MAYNARD. | 27/5/18 | | 14/12/18 |
| 2/Lt. I. H. WHITE. | 27/5/18 | | 25/12/18 |
| *2/Lt. W. E. WHITE. | 27/5/18 | | –/12/18 |
| 2/Lt. R. WILSON. | 27/5/18 | | 26/12/18 |
| 2/Lt. H. W. ABEY. | 27/5/18 | | –/12/18 |
| 2/Lt. H. BULLING. | 27/5/18 | | 30/12/18 |
| 2/Lt. W. JOYES. | 27/5/18 | | –/12/18 |
| 2/Lt. E. J. CURPHEY. | 27/5/18 | | 2/1/19 |
| 2/Lt. B. V. CROAL. | 27/5/18 | | 25/12/18 |
| 2/Lt. D. H. COSTAR. | 27/5/18 | | 2/1/19 |
| 2/Lt. E. G. CLEMSON. | 27/5/18 | | |
| 2/Lt. W. E CLARKE | 27/5/18 | | 26/12/18 |
| *2/Lt. E. H. B. CLARK. | 27/5/18 | | 31/12/18 |
| 2/Lt. C. W. CARTER. | 27/5/18 | | 13/12/18 |
| 2/Lt. S. R. K. REAKES. | 27/5/18 | | 31/12/18 |
| 2/Lt. A. H. PULLIN. | 27/5/18 | | 31/12/18 |
| 2/Lt. T. POWELL. | 27/5/18 | | 13/12/18 |
| 2/Lt. G. W. PARKES. | 27/5/18 | | 30/12/18 |
| *Capt. S. R. C. PLIMSOLL. | 29/5/18 | | 11/12/18 |
| 2/Lt. R. M. RUSTON. | 4/6/18 | | 16/12/18 |
| 2/Lt. J. E. ELLIOTT. | 2/9/18 | | 8/12/18 |
| 2/Lt. J. A. SYKES. | 2/9/18 | | 8/12/18 |
| 2/Lt. J. C. D. SCARLETT. | 6/9/18 | | 13/12/18 |
| 2/Lt. A. H. P. WILKES. | 10/10/18 | | 15/12/18 |
| 2/Lt. H. R. VERNON. | 24/10/18 | | 27/11/18 |

* Attached T.M.B.

## ROYAL GARRISON ARTILLERY.

| Name. | Missing. | Interned. | Repatriated. |
|---|---|---|---|
| Capt. F. E. FRYER. | –/4/15 | Holland –/4/15 | –/8/18 |
| 2/Lt. A. W. PURNELL. | 14/11/17 | (*Died* –/11/17) | |
| Major H. WHITTINGHAM. | 30/11/17 | Holland 30/4/18 | 18/8/18 |
| Lieut. A. H. FLINT. | 30/11/17 | | 3/12/18 |
| Lieut. George SISSON. | 30/11/17 | (*Died* 20/12/17). | |
| Lieut. E. J. EDWARD. | 30/11/17 | | 2/12/18 |
| 2/Lt. H. L. H. FISHER. | 30/11/17 | | 2/12/18 |
| 2/Lt. O. J. B. COLE. | 30/11/17 | | 14/12/18 |
| 2/Lt. A. C. STIRLING. | 30/11/17 | | 18/12/18 |
| 2/Lt. F. E. S. JAMES. | 30/11/17 | | 5/12/18 |
| 2/Lt. P. S. GURNEY. | 30/11/17 | | 17/12/18 |
| 2/Lt. J. WOODS. | 30/11/17 | | 2/12/18 |
| 2/Lt. G. W. H. POTTER. | 30/11/17 | | 17/12/18 |
| 2/Lt. G. N. PHILLIPS. | 30/11/17 | | 17/12/18 |
| 2/Lt. J. A. BROWN. | 30/11/17 | | –/12/18 |
| Lieut. T. H. N. BATTLE. | 21/3/18 | | 25/12/18 |
| Lieut. J. A. G. STUART. | 21/3/18 | | 14/12/18 |
| 2/Lt. A. FINLAYSON. | 21/3/18 | | 18/12/18 |
| 2/Lt. C. R. CHADWICK. | 21/3/18 | | 1/12/18 |
| 2/Lt. J. F. MacGREGOR. | 21/3/18 | | 4/12/18 |
| 2/Lt. A. E. CURTIS. | 21/3/18 | | 18/12/18 |
| 2/Lt. A. D. HEGGIE. | 21/3/18 | | 6/12/18 |
| 2/Lt. C. H. MAPP. | 21/3/18 | | 29/11/18 |
| 2/Lt. L. K. ROBINSON. | –/3/18 | | 18/12/18 |
| †Lieut. G. M. G. FARMER. | 21/3/18 | | 29/11/18 |
| 2/Lt. K. W. SAWREY. | 21/3/18 | | 29/11/18 |
| 2/Lt. J. L. CRAIG. | 21/3/18 | | 1/12/18 |
| 2/Lt. H. ALLSOP. | 21/3/18 | | 11/12/18 |
| 2/Lt. B. W. F. BRETON. | 21/3/18 | | 18/12/18 |
| 2/Lt. K. C. BOSWELL. | 21/3/18 | | –/11/18 |
| 2/Lt. J. H. BENEDICTUS. | 21/3/18 | | 4/12/18 |
| *2/Lt. D. WATKINS. | 21/3/18 | | 18/12/18 |
| 2/Lt. W. A. COCHRANE. | 21/3/18 | | 18/12/18 |
| Lieut. R. A. LEE. | 22/3/18 | | 25/12/18 |
| 2/Lt. H. L. GUMMER. | 22/3/18 | | 8/12/18 |
| 2/Lt. W. M. HORSEMAN. | 22/3/18 | | 18/12/18 |
| 2/Lt. F. N. FLEMING. | 28/3/18 | (*Died* –/6/18 at Pforzheim). | |
| Capt. J. H. HUDSON. | 4/4/18 | | 1/1/19 |
| Major A. M. STEPHEN. | 9/4/18 | | –/12/18 |
| Lieut. A. CAYLEY. | 9/4/18 | | 16/12/18 |
| *Lieut. F. B. KIRBY. | 9/4/18 | | 17/12/18 |
| 2/Lt. G. C. VEYSEY. | 9/4/18 | | 30/11/18 |
| 2/Lt. F. GARNETT. | 9/4/18 | | 18/12/18 |
| 2/Lt. C. E. GATES. | 9/4/18 | | 29/11/18 |
| 2/Lt. G. F. GLENN. | 9/4/18 | | 29/11/18 |
| 2/Lt. P. N. GLEAVE. | 9/4/18 | | 29/11/18 |
| 2/Lt. R. P. M. BROWN. | 9/4/18 | | 1/12/18 |
| 2/Lt. S. ROGERS. | 9/4/18 | | 18/12/18 |
| 2/Lt. J. G. NOLAN. | 10/4/18 | | 25/12/18 |
| 2/Lt. A. G. HUTCHEON. | 25/4/18 | | 1/12/18 |
| 2/Lt. F. S. KILBURN. | 25/4/18 | | –/12/18 |
| Capt. F. H. WATTS. | 27/5/18 | | 28/12/18 |
| ‡Capt. H. R. FRENCH. | 27/5/18 | | 13/12/18 |
| 2/Lt. E. G. HOLMES. | 27/5/18 | | –/12/18 |

\* Attached T.M.B.      † Attached from A.S.C.
‡ Attached from 7th Dragoon Guards.

**ROYAL GARRISON ARTILLERY**—continued.

| Name. | Missing. | Interned. | Repatriated. |
|---|---|---|---|
| 2/Lt. S. J. LANGFORD. | 27/5/18 | | –/12/18 |
| 2/Lt. W. J. G. STONE. | 27/5/18 | | 13/12/18 |
| 2/Lt. R. WILSON. | 27/5/18 | | 26/12/18 |
| Capt. A. Scott RUSSELL. | | | 16/11/18 |

**ROYAL ENGINEERS.**

| Name. | Missing. | Interned. | Repatriated. |
|---|---|---|---|
| Lieut. O. BALFOUR. | 25/8/14 | Holland 5/1/18 | |
| Capt. A. PARIS. | | Switzerland –/11/17 | 9/12/18 |
| Lieut. R. C. WELLS. | | Holland 6/2/18 | 18/11/18 |
| 2/Lt. C. ELLINGER. | | Holland 30/4/18 | 18/11/18 |
| Lieut. A. F. DAY. | | Holland 29/12/17 | 21/1/19 |
| Lieut. C. M. G. URE. | 5/10/15 | Holland 19/4/18 | 18/11/18 |
| 2/Lt. R. N. MONTGOMERY. | 23/4/17 | | –/1/19 |
| Capt. D. S. THORNE. | 31/7/17 | | 3/1/19 |
| 2/Lt. J. N. TINNISWOOD. | 12/9/17 | | 6/12/18 |
| Lieut. F. G. HARNESS. | 30/11/17 | | 17/12/18 |
| Lieut. A. F. NEAL. | 30/11/17 | | 27/11/18 |
| Major A. F. G. RUSTON. | 30/11/17 | | 17/12/18 |
| 2/Lt. W. A. LOWE. | 30/11/17 | | 3/12/18 |
| 2/Lt. P. NEILL. | 30/11/17 | | 17/12/18 |
| Capt. L. C. HALL. | 30/11/17 | | 3/12/18 |
| Lieut. C. H. S. HAYGARTH. | | | –/12/18 |
| Capt. C. J. R. GREENWOOD. | | | 23/11/18 |
| 2/Lt. W. S. BEAUMONT. | | | 17/12/18 |
| Capt. W. LEGG. | –/3/18 | | 25/12/18 |
| Capt. C. LAYCOCK. | 21/3/18 | | 25/12/18 |
| Lieut. W. HULSE. | 21/3/18 | | 29/11/18 |
| Lieut. J. E. HENSHAW. | 21/3/18 | | 10/12/18 |
| Lieut. G. BRANDON. | 21/3/18 | | 28/11/18 |
| Lieut. W. DRAKE. | 21/3/18 | | –/12/18 |
| Lieut. G. P. H. WATSON. | 21/3/18 | | 30/12/18 |
| 2/Lt. J. B. LONGMUIR. | 21/3/18 | | 23/9/18 |
| 2/Lt. J. W. ENGLISH. | 21/3/18 | | –/12/18 |
| *2/Lt. A. L. HUSBAND. | 21/3/18 | | 29/11/18 |
| 2/Lt. R. A. MacDONALD. | 21/3/18 | | 18/12/18 |
| Major E. L. V. DAKIN. | 22/3/18 | | 8/1/19 |
| Capt. N. J. C. FARMER. | 22/3/18 | | 13/12/18 |
| Lieut. E. C. MAXWELL. | 22/3/18 | | 30/12/18 |
| Lieut. K. C. BARRELL. | 22/3/18 | | 29/11/18 |
| Lieut. R. C. TOTTENHAM. | 22/3/18 | | 28/11/18 |
| 2/Lt. J. McCARTHY. | 22/3/18 | | 17/12/18 |
| 2/Lt. T. E. MORGAN. | 22/3/18 | | 13/12/18 |
| 2/Lt. C. K. ROYLANCE | 22/3/18 | | 2/12/18 |
| Lieut. I. W. SMITH. | 23/3/18 | | 11/12/18 |
| Lieut. R. L. GOLDSMITH. | 23/3/18 | | 29/11/18 |
| Major W. F. BRUCE. | 24/3/18 | | 29/11/18 |
| 2/Lt. M. SWALES. | 24/3/18 | | 5/12/18 |
| 2/Lt. W. G. HOLE. | 24/3/18 | | 2/12/18 |
| Lieut. J. LOGAN. | 26/3/18 | | 25/12/18 |
| Lieut. E. L. PARKES. | 26/3/18 | | 18/12/18 |
| 2/Lt. P. M. HEPTINSTALL. | 26/3/18 | | 26/11/18 |
| Lieut. R. E. WALSH. | 27/3/18 | | 29/11/18 |
| 2/Lt. Robert HARLAND. | 28/3/18 | | 18/12/18 |
| 2/Lt. John POPE. | 28/3/18 | | 2/1/19 |
| Capt. E. M. BESLEY. | 30/3/18 | | 3/12/18 |

* Attached from Durham Light Infantry.

## ROYAL ENGINEERS—continued.

| Name. | Missing. | Interned. | Repatriated. |
|---|---|---|---|
| Lieut. C. A. BORASTON. | 30/3/18 | | 17/12/18 |
| Lieut. G. I. SINCLAIR. | 30/3/18 | | 11/12/18 |
| *2/Lt. W. F. WELSBY. | 9/4/18 | | 4/12/18 |
| Capt. J. ELLMANN. | 10/4/18 | | 8/12/18 |
| 2/Lt. W. A. WILKEN. | 11/4/18 | | 4/12/18 |
| 2/Lt. S. C. MOSS. | 11/4/18 | | –/12/18 |
| 2/Lt. John R. WALLACE. | 11/4/18 | | 29/11/18 |
| 2/Lt. A. H. TIBBOTTS. | 12/4/18 | | 6/12/18 |
| 2/Lt. A. K. ROBINSON. | 12/4/18 | | 11/12/18 |
| Lieut. B. L. RIGDEN. | 17/4/18 | | 13/12/18 |
| Lieut. B. E. REES. | 18/4/18 | | 18/12/18 |
| Lieut. T. MARSLAND. | 18/4/18 | | 17/12/18 |
| Major E. C. HILLMAN, M.C. | 27/5/18 | | 17/12/18 |
| Major A. G. RAINSFORD-HANNAY. | 27/5/18 | | –/12/18 |
| Major John W. LLOYD. | 27/5/18 | | 19/1/19 |
| Capt. Jack R. GRANT, M.C. | 27/5/18 | | 17/12/18 |
| Capt. F. J. SLATTERY. | 27/5/18 | | 31/12/18 |
| Lieut. H. J. HOGG. | 27/5/18 | | 31/1/19 |
| Lieut. E. W. YOUNG. | 27/5/18 | | 31/12/18 |
| Lieut. T. R. RUSSELL. | 27/5/18 | | 25/12/18 |
| ‡Lieut. D. V. L. CRADDOCK. | 27/5/18 | | 30/12/18 |
| Lieut. R. H. REAY. | 27/5/18 | | 25/12/18 |
| Lieut. P. BURR. | 27/5/18 | | 17/12/18 |
| 2/Lt. C. A. KENNEDY. | 27/5/18 | | 25/12/18 |
| 2/Lt. W. L. LAX. | 27/5/18 | | 13/12/18 |
| 2/Lt. Alan. ATKINSON. | 27/5/18 | | –/12/18 |
| 2/Lt. H. F. SHARP. | 27/5/18 | | –/12/18 |
| 2/Lt. R. H. WALMSLEY. | 27/5/18 | | 21/1/19 |
| †2/Lt. P. H. WOODING. | 27/5/18 | | 13/12/18 |
| 2/Lt. W. F. GARDNER. | 27/5/18 | | 14/12/18 |
| Lieut. R. G. GODSON. | 28/5/18 | | 11/12/18 |
| 2/Lt. A. H. FENNELL. | 29/5/18 | | 17/12/18 |
| Lieut. N. D. McKAY. | 6/8/18 | | 10/1/19 |
| Lieut. W. W. RUSSELL. | 22/8/18 | | 13/12/18 |
| Lieut. T. DAVIES. | 30/9/18 | | 29/11/18 |

## GRENADIER GUARDS.

### 1st Battalion.

| Name. | Missing. | Interned. | | Repatriated. |
|---|---|---|---|---|
| Lt.-Col. M. EARLE. | 29/10/14 | Switzerland | 30/5/16 | 15/9/17 |
| Lieut. C. G. GOSCHEN. | 24/12/14 | | | –/6/16 |
| 2/Lt. C. CRUTTENDEN. | 25/8/18 | | | 13/12/18 |

### 3rd Battalion.

| Lieut. C. S. ROWLEY. | 27/9/15 | Holland | –/4/18 | 21/1/19 |
|---|---|---|---|---|

### 4th Battalion.

| Lieut. M. D. THOMAS. | 12/4/18 | | 18/12/18 |
|---|---|---|---|
| Lieut. G. C. BURT. | 13/4/18 | | 18/12/18 |
| Lieut. C. C. S. RODNEY. | 13/4/18 | | 1/12/18 |
| Lieut. P. H. COX. | 13/4/18 | | 18/12/18 |
| 2/Lt. G. P. PHILIPS. | 13/4/18 | | 6/1/19 |

\* Attached from King's Liverpool Regiment.

† Attached from Rifle Brigade.

‡ Attached from 9th Durhams.

## COLDSTREAM GUARDS.

### 1st Battalion.

| Name. | Missing. | Interned. | | Repatriated. |
|---|---|---|---|---|
| Capt. E. CHRISTIE-MILLER. | 3/11/14 | Holland | 24/2/18 | 12/1/19 |
| Capt. J. E. GIBBS. | 22/11/14 | Holland | 24/2/18 | 2/1/19 |
| Lieut. R. J. WAVELL-PAXTON. | 29/11/14 | Holland | 24/2/18 | 2/1/19 |
| 2/Lt. J. S. ALISON. | 29/11/14 | Holland | 24/2/18 | 27/11/18 |
| 2/Lt. J. H. McNEILE. | 22/12/14 | Holland | 1/3/18 | 18/11/18 |
| *Capt. C. K. HUTCHISON. | 25/1/15 | Switzerland | –/11/17 | 23/12/18 |
| 2/Lt. H. N. CLIFTON. | 25/1/15 | (Died 1/2/15). | | |
| 2/Lt. O. STYLE. | 26/9/15 | | | 22/11/18 |
| Capt. G. H. SMITH. | 16/10/18 | | | |

### 3rd Battalion.

| Name. | Missing. | Interned. | | Repatriated. |
|---|---|---|---|---|
| Capt. Hon. R. O. D. KEPPEL. | 26/8/14 | Holland | 5/1/18 | 18/11/18 |
| Capt. J. A. C. WHITAKER. | 13/4/18 | | | 18/12/18 |
| Capt. R. P. ELWES. | 13/4/18 | | | 1/12/18 |
| Lieut. V. N. ROWSELL. | 13/4/18 | | | 24/12/18 |
| 2/Lt. C. O. LEADBITTER. | 13/4/18 | | | 13/12/18 |
| 2/Lt. W. A. MILLAR. | 13/4/18 | | | 23/10/18 |
| 2/Lt. A. M. CARR. | 13/4/18 | | | 30/11/18 |
| 2/Lt. J. ASHBY. | 13/4/18 | | | 1/12/18 |

## SCOTS GUARDS.

### 1st Battalion.

| Name. | Missing. | Interned. | | Repatriated. |
|---|---|---|---|---|
| Major E. Y. VAN DER WEYER. | 31/10/14 | Holland | 24/2/18 | 18/11/18 |
| Capt. B. G. JOLLIFFE. | 29/11/14 | Switzerland | –/11/17 | 8/12/18 |
| Lieut. R. FITZROY. | 29/11/14 | Holland | 6/2/18 | 7/9/18 |
| 2/Lt. G. E. V. CRUTCHLEY. | 25/1/15 | Holland | 1/3/18 | 18/11/18 |

### 2nd Battalion.

| Name. | Missing. | Interned. | | Repatriated. |
|---|---|---|---|---|
| 2/Lt. Lord GARLIES. | 27/9/14 | Switzerland | 9/12/17 | 8/12/18 |
| Lt.-Col. R. G. I. BOLTON. | 27/10/14 | Switzerland | 9/12/17 | 6/12/18 |
| Major Earl of STAIR. | 27/10/14 | | | 13/9/17 |
| Capt. C. V. FOX. | 27/10/14 | | (Escaped) | –/7/17 |
| Capt. Hon. J. COKE. | 27/10/14 | Holland | 24/2/18 | 18/11/18 |
| Lieut. E. B. TRAFFORD. | 27/10/14 | Holland | 24/2/18 | 24/2/18 |
| Lieut. R. STEUART-MENZIES. | 27/10/14 | Holland | 24/2/18 | 7/9/18 |
| Lieut. Lord G. GROSVENOR. | 28/10/14 | Holland | 24/2/18 | 23/9/18 |
| Capt. Sir F. L. FITZWYGRAM. | 17/5/15 | Holland | 10/4/18 | 26/12/18 |

### 3rd Battalion.

| Name. | Missing. | Interned. | | Repatriated. |
|---|---|---|---|---|
| Major A. C. MORRISON-BELL. | 25/1/15 | Switzerland | 5/12/17 | 28/11/18 |

## IRISH GUARDS.

### 2nd Battalion.

| Name. | Missing. | Interned. | | Repatriated. |
|---|---|---|---|---|
| 2/Lt. B. O'D. MANNING. | 13/9/17 | | | 23/12/18 |
| 2/Lt. W. G. REA. | 27/11/17 | | | 14/12/18 |
| Lieut. M. R. FITZGERALD. | 13/4/18 | (Died 19/4/18). | | |

### 3rd Battalion.

| Name. | Missing. | Interned. | | Repatriated. |
|---|---|---|---|---|
| Lord C. H. SETTRINGTON. | 13/4/18 | | | 1/12/18 |

* Attached from Royal Scots.

## ROYAL SCOTS.

### 1st and 2nd Battalions.

| Name. | Missing. | Interned. | | Repatriated. |
|---|---|---|---|---|
| Lt.-Col. H. McMICKING. | 26/8/14 | Switzerland | 9/12/17 | 23/3/18 |
| Major G. S. TWEEDIE. | 3/9/14 | Holland | 29/12/17 | Returned for Duty. |
| Capt. A. F. GRAHAM-WATSON. | 10/9/14 | Holland | 22/1/18 | 18/11/18 |
| Lieut. C. SCARISBRICK. | 10/9/14 | Holland | 22/1/18 | 24/1/19 |
| 2/Lt. C. D. MAYO. | 25/9/15 | Holland | 10/4/18 | 18/11/18 |
| 2/Lt. D. PEASE. | 26/9/15 | | | 22/11/18 |
| Capt. D. KININMONTH. | 12/4/18 | | | 1/12/18 |
| Capt. J. HENDERSON. | 12/4/18 | | | 1/12/18 |
| Lieut. A. ROBERTSON. | 12/4/18 | | | 18/12/18 |
| 2/Lt. R. C. WILKIE. | 12/4/18 | | | 13/12/18 |
| 2/Lt. R. MURCHISON. | 12/4/18 | | | 18/12/18 |
| 2/Lt. A. E. W. McLACHLAN. | 12/4/18 | | | 6/1/19 |
| 2/Lt. James TODD. | 12/4/18 | | | 18/12/18 |

### 4th Battalion.

| Name. | Missing. | Interned. | Repatriated. |
|---|---|---|---|
| *2/Lt. F. B. MOFFATT. | 21/3/18 | | 29/11/18 |
| 2/Lt. G. R. FORRESTER. | 23/3/18 | | 29/11/18 |

### 7th Battalion.

| Name. | Missing. | Interned. | Repatriated. |
|---|---|---|---|
| Lieut. W. F. R. MacARTNEY. | 21/9/18 | | –/11/18 |

### 8th Battalion.

| Name. | Missing. | Interned. | Repatriated. |
|---|---|---|---|
| Major J. A. TODD. | 12/4/18 | | 17/12/18 |
| Capt. A. D. JONES. | 12/4/18 | | 17/12/18 |
| Lieut. A. MUNRO. | 12/4/18 | | –/12/18 |
| 2/Lt. A. M. WHITE. | 12/4/18 | | –/12/18 |

### 9th Battalion.

| Name. | Missing. | Interned. | | Repatriated. |
|---|---|---|---|---|
| Lieut. N. MacDONALD. | 16/6/15 | Holland | 10/4/18 | 22/1/19 |
| 2/Lt. D. WALLACE. | 24/3/18 | (*Died* 18/4/18 at Guise). | | |

### 11th Battalion.

| Name. | Missing. | Interned. | | Repatriated. |
|---|---|---|---|---|
| Lieut. G. L. BRANDER. | 26/9/15 | Holland | 10/4/18 | 15/12/18 |
| Lieut. H. C. MEIN. | 21/3/18 | | | 30/12/18 |
| 2/Lt. W. L. DOUGLAS. | 21/3/18 | | | 25/12/18 |
| 2/Lt. C. L. CHEYNE. | 23/3/18 | (*Died* 21/4/18 at Hammerstein). | | |
| Lieut. J. J. MANN. | 25/7/18 | | | 14/12/18 |

### 12th Battalion.

| Name. | Missing. | Interned. | Repatriated. |
|---|---|---|---|
| Capt. J. BROADWOOD. | 30/11/17 | | 29/11/18 |
| 2/Lt. T. G. NICHOLSON. | 23/3/18 | | 13/12/18 |
| 2/Lt. H. G. COLQUHOUN. | 24/3/18 | | 18/12/18 |
| 2/Lt. A. M. YOUNG. | 25/3/18 | | 29/11/18 |
| Capt. G. S. P. McMEEKEN. | 26/3/18 | (doubtful). | |
| Lieut. G. MIDDLEMAS. | 26/3/18 | | 29/11/18 |
| 2/Lt. D. C. COCHRANE. | 25/4/18 | | 29/11/18 |
| 2/Lt. A. CROW. | 25/4/18 | | 6/12/18 |
| Capt. H. E. SANDERSON. | 26/4/18 | | 2/12/18 |
| Capt. W. R. DAWSON. | 26/4/18 | | 3/12/18 |
| 2/Lt. R. A. SCOTT. | 26/4/18 | | 29/11/18 |
| 2/Lt. J. MILLAR. | 26/4/18 | | –/12/18 |
| 2/Lt. C. H. SUTHERLAND. | 29/9/18 | | 29/12/18 |
| 2/Lt. H. S. DRIVER. | 1/10/18 | | 26/12/18 |

* Attached T.M.B.

## ROYAL SCOTS—continued.

### 13th Battalion.

| Name. | Missing. | Interned. | Repatriated. |
|---|---|---|---|
| Lieut. G. N. DOBBIE. | 1/8/17 | | 17/12/18 |
| 2/Lt. W. T. LOW. | 1/8/17 | | 25/12/18 |
| 2/Lt. J. GIBSON. | 1/8/17 | Switzerland 27/12/17 | 7/12/18 |
| 2/Lt. J. S. AITKEN. | 1/8/17 | | 14/12/18 |
| 2/Lt. L. W. GUTHRIE. | 22/3/18 | | 25/12/18 |
| Lieut. J. V. R. MITCHELL. | 28/3/18 | | 26/12/18 |
| Lieut. A. A. FARQUHARSON. | 28/3/18 | | 18/12/18 |
| 2/Lt. J. HOBBS. | 28/3/18 | | 18/12/18 |
| 2/Lt. J. S. McGREGOR. | 28/3/18 | | 13/12/18 |
| 2/Lt. S. C. CUMMING | 28/3/18 | | 18/12/18 |
| 2/Lt. W. A. MATHIESON. | 28/3/18 | | 18/12/18 |

### 15th Battalion.

| Name. | Missing. | Interned. | Repatriated. |
|---|---|---|---|
| Capt. L. S. ROBSON. | 28/4/17 | | 6/12/18 |
| Lieut. J. D. FERGUSON. | 28/4/17 | | 17/12/18 |
| 2/Lt. J. R. FISHER. | 28/4/17 | | 31/12/18 |
| 2/Lt. M. WARREN. | 28/4/17 | | 6/12/18 |
| 2/Lt. G. A. STEWART. | 28/4/17 | | 7/1/18 |
| 2/Lt. J. E. V. CHUBB. | 22/10/17 | | 3/12/18 |
| 2/Lt. A. B. B. DOWIE. | 21/3/18 | | –/12/18 |
| Capt. W. MILNE. | 22/3/18 | | 18/12/18 |
| Capt. S. J. BROWN. | 22/3/18 | | 17/12/18 |
| Lieut. J. R. KINNES. | 22/3/18 | | 18/12/18 |
| Lieut. A. T. McLAREN. | 22/3/18 | | 11/12/18 |
| 2/Lt. R. ANDREW. | 22/3/18 | | 18/12/18 |
| 2/Lt. J. R. L. SMITH. | 22/3/18 | | 11/12/18 |
| 2/Lt. J. MATHESON. | 22/3/18 | | 11/12/18 |
| Capt. E. B. PALMER. | 10/4/18 | | 19/12/18 |
| Capt. N. BIDDOLPH. | 10/4/18 | | 25/12/18 |
| *Capt. E. B. NICHOLSON. | 11/4/18 | | 25/12/18 |

### 16th Battalion.

| Name. | Missing. | Interned. | Repatriated. |
|---|---|---|---|
| Capt. A. WHYTE. | 1/7/16 | Switzerland 27/12/17 | 14/6/18 |
| 2/Lt. R. M. PRINGLE. | 2/7/16 | Holland 15/6/18 | 23/10/18 |
| †2/Lt. C. W. WOOD. | 20/7/16 | Holland 15/6/18 | 21/1/19 |
| Capt. Hon. M. C. H. BOWES-LYON. | 28/4/17 | | 29/11/18 |
| 2/Lt. W. D. HOWAT. | 28/4/17 | | 6/12/18 |
| 2/Lt. G. H. HENDERSON. | 28/4/17 | Switzerland 27/12/17 | 9/12/18 |
| 2/Lt. F. M. DUFF. | 28/4/17 | | 6/12/18 |
| 2/Lt. G. H. DALGETY. | 28/4/17 | Switzerland 27/12/17 | 9/12/18 |
| Capt. R. B. EVANS. | 22/10/17 | | 27/11/18 |
| Capt. C. J. LAMBERT. | 22/3/18 | | 28/11/18 |
| Lieut. P. M. MacANDREW. | 22/3/18 | | 28/11/18 |
| Major A. E. WARR. | 9/4/18 | | 28/11/18 |
| 2/Lt. A. ROBINSON. | 9/4/18 | | 1/12/18 |
| 2/Lt. H. TONATHY. | 9/4/18 | | 11/12/18 |
| Capt. H. W. RAWSON. | 10/4/18 | (*Died* 22/4/18). | |
| 2/Lt. W. LAWRIE. | 10/4/18 | | 25/12/18 |
| 2/Lt. W. C. MOLLOY. | 11/4/18 | (*Died* 10/5/18 at Ingolstadt). | |

### 17th Battalion.

| Name. | Missing. | Interned. | Repatriated. |
|---|---|---|---|
| 2/Lt. A. I. GRANT. | 30/9/18 | | 28/11/18 |

* Attached T.M.B.  † Attached M.G.C.

## ROYAL WEST SURREY REGIMENT.
### 1st and 2nd Battalions.

| Name. | Missing. | Interned. | | Repatriated. |
|---|---|---|---|---|
| Capt. H. F. H. MASTER. | 25/10/14 | | | 13/9/17 |
| Capt. E. de L. BARTON. | 29/10/14 | Holland | 6/2/18 | 31/8/18 |
| Capt. C. E. SOAMES. | 29/10/14 | Holland | 24/2/18 | 18/11/18 |
| Lieut. W. GREEN. | 29/10/14 | Holland | 6/2/18 | 18/11/18 |
| 2/Lt. J. M. ROSE-TROUP. | 29/10/14 | Holland | 24/2/18 | 18/11/18 |
| Lieut. C. ELLIOT. | 31/10/14 | Holland | 24/2/18 | 23/9/18 |
| Capt. W. H. ALLEYNE. | 7/11/14 | Holland | 24/2/18 | 18/8/18 |
| 2/Lt. C. J. ROUGHT. | 18/12/14 | Holland | 24/2/18 | 18/11/18 |
| 2/Lt. E. A. WALMISLEY. | 18/12/14 | | | 11/9/17 |
| Capt. R. C. G. FOSTER. | 14/3/17 | | | 14/12/18 |
| 2/Lt. C. R. SMITH. | 14/3/17 | | | 30/12/18 |
| Capt. F. S. BALL. | 23/4/17 | Holland | 15/6/18 | 23/10/18 |
| Capt. R. BRODHURST-HILL. | 23/4/17 | | | 2/12/18 |
| Capt. F. GODFREY. | 23/4/17 | | | 30/12/18 |
| 2/Lt. O. V. BOTTON. | 23/4/17 | | | 6/12/18 |
| 2/Lt. J. HOLLIDAY. | 23/4/17 | | | 30/12/18 |
| 2/Lt. G. P. S. JACOB. | 23/4/17 | | | 6/1/18 |
| 2/Lt. R. S. WALKER. | 23/4/17 | | | 20/12/18 |
| Lieut. W. F. CLENSHAW. | 25/9/17 | | | 13/12/18 |
| 2/Lt. H. M. THOMPSON. | 23/4/17 | | | 7/1/19 |

### 6th Battalion.

| | | | | |
|---|---|---|---|---|
| Lieut. M. G. L. WALLICH. | 3/7/16 | | | 15/12/18 |

### 7th Battalion.

| | | | | |
|---|---|---|---|---|
| Capt. J. S. WALTER. | 19/11/16 | (Shot while escaping –/6/18). | | |
| 2/Lt. C. G. BROWN. | 19/11/16 | Holland | 15/4/18 | 20/7/18 |
| 2/Lt. J. E. RUSSELL. | 19/11/16 | (Died 23/11/16). | | |
| 2/Lt. R. W. E. SHEATHER. | 27/2/17 | | | 6/12/18 |
| 2/Lt. P. E. THORN. | 27/2/17 | | | 27/11/18 |
| 2/Lt. H. W. VAUGHAN. | 27/2/17 | | | 7/1/18 |
| 2/Lt. A. A. BROOKES. | 21/3/18 | | | 18/12/18 |
| 2/Lt. A. OGDEN. | 21/3/18 | | | 18/12/18 |
| Capt. T. C. FILBY. | 23/3/18 | | | 28/11/18 |
| Lieut. W. R. COHEN. | 23/3/18 | | | 28/11/18 |
| Lieut. A. L. HAIG. | 23/3/18 | | | 2/12/18 |
| 2/Lt. E. V. BATTEN. | 23/3/18 | | | 18/12/18 |
| 2/Lt. A. F. A. HAY. | 23/3/18 | | | 18/12/18 |
| 2/Lt. W. G. PHIPPS. | 23/3/18 | | | 11/12/18 |

### 8th Battalion.

| | | | | |
|---|---|---|---|---|
| Lieut. L. G. DUKE. | 26/9/15 | | | 18/11/18 |
| 2/Lt. P. G. BURGESS. | 26/9/15 | (Died 13/10/15). | | |
| 2/Lt. C. P. BURNLEY. | 19/3/16 | Holland | 30/4/18 | 18/11/18 |
| 2/Lt. J. E. DAY. | 25/7/17 | | | 17/12/18 |
| Capt. R. D. C. HIGHTON. | 21/3/18 | | | 29/11/18 |
| Lieut. C. W. H. P. WAUD. | 21/3/18 | | | 28/11/18 |
| Lieut. E. J. YOUNG. | 21/3/18 | | | 28/12/18 |
| 2/Lt. C. J. DUGGINS. | 21/3/18 | | | 28/11/18 |
| 2/Lt. P. E. MAY. | 21/3/18 | | | 28/11/18 |
| 2/Lt. S. A. MARTIN. | 21/3/18 | | | 29/11/18 |
| 2/Lt. A. C. NYE. | 21/3/18 | | | 29/11/18 |
| 2/Lt. C. L. PIESSE. | 21/3/18 | | | 17/12/18 |
| 2/Lt. W. P. TOMLEY. | 21/3/18 | | | 28/11/18 |
| 2/Lt. D. C. EVANS. | 22/3/18 | | | 28/11/18 |
| *Capt. C. P. HAWARD. | 9/8/18 | | | 17/12/18 |
| Capt. A. E. WHEATLEY. | 9/8/18 | | | 6/1/19 |

\* Attached from Middlesex Regiment.

## ROYAL WEST SURREY REGIMENT. continued.
### 10th Battalion.

| Name. | Missing. | Interned. | Repatriated. |
|---|---|---|---|
| 2/Lt. J. A. C. RECORD. | 23/3/18 | | 28/12/18 |
| Lieut. J. Y. SCOTT. | 24/3/18 | (*Died* at Cassel 26/7/18). | |
| 2/Lt. C. C. BRATTLE. | 24/3/18 | | 26/12/18 |
| 2/Lt. W. FENWICK. | 24/3/18 | (*Died* at Ohligs 5/4/18). | |
| 2/Lt. H. S. PAYNE. | 24/3/18 | | 12/10/18 |

### 11th Battalion.

| Name. | Missing. | Interned. | Repatriated. |
|---|---|---|---|
| †Colonel R. OTTER. | 23/3/18 | | 8/12/18 |
| Capt. G. D. HENDERSON. | 23/3/18 | | 2/12/18 |
| Lt. A. E. CLARET. | 23/3/18 | | 2/12/18 |
| 2/Lt. L. T. M. ALLEN. | 23/3/18 | | 13/12/18 |
| 2/Lt. R. S. BROWN. | 23/3/18 | | 25/12/18 |
| 2/Lt. E. W. SPENCER. | 23/3/18 | | 2/12/18 |

## EAST KENT REGIMENT.
### (Buffs).
### 1st and 2nd Battalions.

| Name. | Missing. | Interned. | | Repatriated. |
|---|---|---|---|---|
| Capt. H. E. WARD. | 2/11/14 | | | 15/12/18 |
| Lieut. A. L. D. RYDER. | 16/2/15 | | | 18/12/18 |
| 2/Lt. E. F. D. STRETTELL. | 16/2/15 | Holland | 2/3/18 | 25/12/18 |
| 2/Lt. E. W. P. HAYMAN. | 16/2/15 | Holland | 6/2/18 | 4/10/18 |
| Capt. F. W. TOMLINSON. | 21/4/15 | Switzerland | 9/12/17 | 9/6/18 |
| Lieut. L. H. SMITH. | 21/4/15 | Holland | 23/3/18 | 31/8/18 |
| Lieut. G. R. HOWE. | 3/5/15 | Holland | 23/3/18 | 15/1/19 |
| 2/Lt. G. E. A. STEGGALL. | 26/9/15 | Holland | 19/4/18 | 18/11/18 |
| Capt. J. V. R. JACKSON. | 30/9/15 | | | 13/9/17 |
| 2/Lt. T. F. HARRINGTON. | 28/6/17 | | | 3/12/18 |
| 2/Lt. H. S. WOTTON. | 21/3/18 | | | 4/12/18 |

### (Buffs).
### 3rd Battalion.

| Name. | Missing. | Interned. | | Repatriated. |
|---|---|---|---|---|
| Capt. A. R. JACKSON. | | Holland | 24/2/18 | 7/9/18 |
| *2/Lt. D. J. DAVISON. | 21/3/18 | | | 17/12/18 |

### 6th Battalion.

| Name. | Missing. | Interned. | | Repatriated. |
|---|---|---|---|---|
| Lieut. A. E. GRANT. | 3/5/17 | Holland | 30/4/18 | 18/8/18 |
| 2/Lt. E. A. KING. | 3/5/17 | | | 6/12/18 |
| Capt. L. P. CAUSTON. | 30/11/17 | | | 2/1/19 |
| Lieut. W. F. BEAVAN. | 30/11/17 | | | 17/12/18 |
| 2/Lt. W. R. TAYLOR. | 30/11/17 | | | 11/12/18 |
| 2/Lt. T. C. FILLERY. | 30/11/17 | | | 8/12/18 |
| 2/Lt. A. E. W. SANDBACH. | 30/11/17 | | | 19/5/18 |
| 2/Lt. W. T. STEVENS. | 30/11/17 | | | 5/12/18 |

### 7th Battalion.

| Name. | Missing. | Repatriated. |
|---|---|---|
| 2/Lt. N. G. BLAKE. | 3/5/17 | 17/12/18 |
| 2/Lt. J. E. M. KNIGHT. | 12/10/17 | 13/12/18 |
| Capt. D. GRANT. | 21/3/18 | 2/12/18 |
| Capt. H. FINE. | 21/3/18 | 18/12/18 |
| Capt. W. E. CHANT. | 21/3/18 | 2/12/18 |
| Lieut. L. H. KENNETT. | 21/3/18 | 18/12/18 |

† Attached from Norfolk Regiment.    * Attached T.M.B.

## EAST KENT REGIMENT—continued.
### 7th Battalion—continued.

| Name. | Missing. | Interned. | | Repatriated. |
|---|---|---|---|---|
| Lieut. G. W. CAMERON. | 21/3/18 | | | 29/11/18 |
| 2/Lt. H. F. DANA. | 21/3/18 | | | 18/12/18 |
| 2/Lt. F. C. WINTER. | 21/3/18 | | | 29/11/18 |
| 2/Lt. L. W. MARTIN. | 21/3/18 | | | 18/12/18 |
| 2/Lt. S. A. HARVEY. | 21/3/18 | | | –/12/18 |
| Capt. H. TUPPER. | 5/8/18 | | | 24/12/18 |
| Lieut. H. S. WATSON. | 6/8/18 | | | –/12/18 |
| Lieut. R. H. PLUMB. | 6/8/18 | | | 26/12/18 |
| Lieut. J. W. BRYANT. | 6/8/18 | | | 16/1/19 |
| †2/Lt. A. G. BROWN. | 6/8/18 | | | 29/11/18 |

### 8th Battalion.

| Name | Missing | Interned | | Repatriated |
|---|---|---|---|---|
| Major G. W. WARDEN. | 26/9/15 | Switzerland | 9/12/17 | 24/3/18 |
| Major D. F. ROBINSON. | 26/9/15 | Holland | 10/4/18 | 1/11/18 |
| Capt. F. W. WATSON. | 26/9/15 | Switzerland | 9/12/17 | 9/12/18 |
| Capt. W. D. JOHNSON. | 26/9/15 | | | 11/9/17 |
| Lieut. T. H. TAYLOR. | 26/9/15 | Holland | 10/4/18 | 18/11/18 |
| Lieut. B. H. PICKERING. | 26/9/15 | (*Died* 1/12/15 at Cologne). | | |
| Lieut. F. D. MONTGOMERIE. | 26/9/15 | Holland | 10/4/18 | 12/10/18 |
| Lieut. S. VAUGHAN. | 26/9/15 | Holland | 10/4/18 | 18/11/18 |
| 2/Lt. R. B. CARROW. | 26/9/15 | Holland | 10/4/18 | 18/11/18 |

### 10th Battalion.

| Name | Missing | Interned | | Repatriated |
|---|---|---|---|---|
| Lieut. F. D. WILKINSON. | 21/9/18 | | | 3/12/18 |

## KING'S OWN ROYAL LANCASTER REGIMENT.
### 1st and 2nd Battalions.

| Name | Missing | Interned | | Repatriated |
|---|---|---|---|---|
| Lieut. C. G. S. IRVINE. | 10/9/14 | Holland | 5/1/18 | 16/11/18 |
| Lieut. A. S. D. B. DOUGLAS. | –/–/14 | Switzerland | 30/5/16 | 26/12/17 |
| Lieut. J. A. BEVAN. | 21/10/14 | Holland | 6/2/18 | 18/11/18 |
| Lieut. J. H. C. COULSTON. | 21/10/14 | Switzerland | 12/8/16 | 30/11/17 |
| Capt. C. W. GROVER. | 10/5/15 | Holland | 23/3/18 | 19/12/18 |
| Lieut. F. H. ELLIS. | 10/5/15 | | | 13/9/17 |
| Lieut. A. D. SEDDON. | 10/5/15 | Holland | 10/4/18 | 18/11/18 |
| 2/Lt. A. O. D. TAYLOR. | 10/5/15 | Holland | 23/3/18 | 18/11/18 |
| 2/Lt. N. N. HART. | 17/11/17 | | | 27/11/18 |
| *2/Lt. P. J. ALLAN. | 28/3/18 | (*Died* 22/5/18 at Hamburg). | | |
| 2/Lt. P. S. ROBERTSHAW. | 18/4/18 | | | 13/12/18 |
| 2/Lt. J. S. NEVARD. | 18/4/18 | | | 18/12/18 |
| 2/Lt. A. W. WALL. | 18/4/18 | | | 18/12/18 |
| Capt. H. J. T. De CARTERET. | 22/10/14 | Holland | 2/3/18 | 22/11/18 |

### 4th Battalion.

| Name | Missing | Interned | | Repatriated |
|---|---|---|---|---|
| Capt. W. G. PEARSON. | 16/6/15 | | | –/9/17 |
| Capt. H. A. BROCKLEBANK. | 31/7/17 | | | 14/12/18 |
| 2/Lt. G. FIELD. | 20/11/17 | | | 23/2/18 |
| Lieut. A. S. LATHAM. | 9/4/18 | | | 10/12/18 |
| 2/Lt. H. THREADGOLD. | 9/4/18 | | | 8/12/18 |
| 2/Lt. E. D. OSGOOD. | 9/4/18 | | | 11/12/18 |
| 2/Lt. R. A. TAYLOR. | 9/4/18 | | | 11/12/18 |
| 2/Lt. W. HOLMES. | 9/4/18 | | | 18/12/18 |
| 2/Lt. W. McANDREW. | 9/4/18 | | | 18/12/18 |

† Attached from Royal West Kent Regiment.
* Attached T.M.B.

## KING'S OWN ROYAL LANCASTER REGIMENT—continued.
### 5th Battalion.

| Name. | Missing. | Interned. | Repatriated. |
|---|---|---|---|
| *2/Lt. K. St. C. H. TOOVEY. | 30/11/17 | (*Died* –/10/18 at Frankfort). | |
| 2/Lt. E. STAINTON. | 30/11/17 | | 3/12/18 |
| 2/Lt. W. HARRISON. | 30/11/17 | | 25/12/18 |
| 2/Lt. J. E. FISHER. | 30/11/17 | | 19/5/18 |
| Capt. O. G. HUNT. | 9/4/18 | | 29/11/18 |
| 2/Lt. A. J. WHITE. | 9/4/18 | | 8/12/18 |
| 2/Lt. W. YOUNG. | 9/4/18 | | 8/12/18 |
| 2/Lt. F. BUCKLEY. | 9/4/18 | | 8/12/18 |
| 2/Lt. G. STEEL. | 9/4/18 | | 10/12/18 |
| 2/Lt. B. PERCIVAL. | 9/4/18 | | 11/12/18 |
| 2/Lt. G. CONHEENY. | 9/4/18 | (*Killed* 5/12/18 at Stralsund). | |
| 2/Lt. H. J. WARBRICK. | 11–12/4/18 | | 28/11/18 |
| 2/Lt. J. ALEXANDER. | 22/4/18 | | –/11/18 |
| 2/Lt. W. McE. YACOMENI. | 22/4/18 | | 29/11/18 |
| 2/Lt. H. F. WOODCOCK. | 10/7/18 | | 13/12/18 |
| 2/Lt. J. MANN. | 30/8/18 | | 8/12/18 |
| 2/Lt. M. SWINBURNE. | 30/8/18 | (doubtful). | |
| †2/Lt. F. A. DANSON. | 28/9/18 | | 29/11/18 |

### 7th Battalion.

| | | | |
|---|---|---|---|
| Capt. H. G. DAVIES. | 31/7/17 | Switzerland | 13/5/18 |

### 8th Battalion.

| | | | |
|---|---|---|---|
| 2/Lt. H. C. BROWN. | 18/8/16 | Holland 12/10/18 | 18/11/17 |
| Capt. W. C. SKERRETT. | 28/3/18 | | 10/12/18 |
| Capt. A. HOLLAND. | 28/3/18 | | 28/11/18 |
| 2/Lt. W. CROMPTON. | 28/3/18 | | 28/11/18 |
| 2/Lt. R. M. RAE. | 28/3/18 | | 28/11/18 |
| 2/Lt. S. G. GODDARD. | 12/4/18 | | 4/12/18 |

### 11th Battalion.

| | | | |
|---|---|---|---|
| 2/Lt. J. C. BESWICK. | 21/4/17 | (*Died* 22/4/17 at Cambrai). | |

## NORTHUMBERLAND FUSILIERS.
### 1st Battalion.

| Name. | Missing. | Interned. | Repatriated. |
|---|---|---|---|
| Capt. H. O. SUTHERLAND. | 16/9/14 | Switzerland 12/8/16 | 11/9/17 |
| Lieut. D. CONDON. | 1/11/14 | (*Died* –/8/17). | |
| Capt. G. O. SLOPER. | 16/6/15 | Holland 16/5/18 | 18/11/18 |
| Capt. W. R. ALLEN. | 28/3/18 | | 25/12/18 |
| 2/Lt. E. I. LAWRENCE. | 28/3/18 | | –/12/18 |
| 2/Lt. J. RICHARDS. | 28/3/18 | (*Died* at Ferin 30/3/18). | |
| 2/Lt. H. P. MULLEN. | 28/3/18 | | –/12/18 |
| 2/Lt. J. C. THOMPSON. | 28/3/18 | | 18/12/18 |
| Lieut. D. STORY. | 22/8/18 | | 13/12/18 |

### 2nd Battalion.

| | | | | |
|---|---|---|---|---|
| 2/Lt. W. TAYLOR. | 9/5/15 | Holland | 10/4/18 | 5/12/18 |
| Lt.-Col. S. H. ENDERBY. | 11/5/15 | Holland | 23/3/18 | 17/11/18 |
| Capt. R. T. K. AULD. | 11/5/15 | Holland | 23/3/18 | 18/11/18 |
| Capt. B. E. S. MAHON. | 11/5/15 | Holland | 10/4/18 | |
| 2/Lt. F. B. A. CARDEW. | 11/5/15 | Holland | 23/8/18 | 23/11/18 |
| 2/Lt. V. C. HARDY. | 11/5/15 | Holland | 10/4/18 | 21/1/19 |

\* Attached T.M.B.    † Attached from Loyal North Lancs.

## NORTHUMBERLAND FUSILIERS—continued.

### 3rd Battalion.

| Name. | Missing. | Interned. | Repatriated. |
|---|---|---|---|
| *2/Lt. J. SOWERBY. | 27/5/18 | | 14/12/18 |

### 4th Battalion.

| Name. | Missing. | Interned. | Repatriated. |
|---|---|---|---|
| Capt. W. B. HICKS. | 26/3/18 | | 1/12/18 |
| 2/Lt. A. N. LAWSON. | 10/4/18 | | 18/12/18 |
| Capt. C. G. GASSON. | 27/5/18 | | 30/12/18 |
| Capt. R. ALLEN. | 27/5/18 | | 25/12/18 |
| Capt. A. WILLIS. | 27/5/18 | | 1/12/18 |
| Lieut. F. J. IVES. | 27/5/18 | | 9/1/19 |
| Lieut. J. J. HOLME. | 27/5/18 | | –/12/18 |
| 2/Lt. H. E. FINDLEY. | 27/5/18 | | –/12/18 |
| 2/Lt. J. W. MARSDEN. | 27/5/18 | | 17/12/18 |
| 2/Lt. W. L. McLEAN. | 27/5/18 | | 17/12/18 |
| 2/Lt. A. H. ROYLE. | 27/5/18 | | 30/12/18 |
| 2/Lt. F. PEDDIE. | 27/5/18 | | 1/1/19 |
| 2/Lt. J. A. McINTYRE. | 27/5/18 | | 17/12/18 |
| 2/Lt. W. J. MAXFIELD. | 27/5/18 | | 21/1/19 |
| Lieut. F. H. BEDFORD. | 28/5/18 | | –/12/18 |
| 2/Lt. H. R. REES. | 28/5/18 | | –/12/18 |
| Lieut. H. H. HARRISON. | 14/6/18 | | 30/12/18 |

### 5th Battalion.

| Name. | Missing. | Interned. | Repatriated. |
|---|---|---|---|
| 2/Lt. T. A. CROFTS. | 22/3/18 | | 25/12/18 |
| 2/Lt. W. H. J. MARKHAM. | 22/3/18 | (*Died* at Belleglise 27/3/18). | |
| Capt. F. W. GRINLING. | 9/4/18 | | 25/12/18 |
| Lieut. J. W. LOUGH. | 10/4/18 | | –/12/18 |
| Capt. G. BRANFOOT. | 11/4/18 | | 25/12/18 |
| Lt. R. G. SMITH. | 11/4/18 | | 29/11/18 |
| Lieut. P. GRAHAM. | 11/4/18 | | 25/12/18 |
| Capt. H. G. DODDS. | 27/5/18 | | –/1/19 |
| 2/Lt. R. H. QUINE. | 27/5/18 | | –/12/18 |
| †2/Lt. R. T. DENNIS. | 27/5/18 | (*Died* 19/12/18 at Wimereux). | |
| 2/Lt. G. E. D. BURBIDGE. | 27/5/18 | | –/12/18 |
| 2/Lt. A. E. BROWN. | 27/5/18 | | 18/12/18 |
| 2/Lt. S. WEATERTON. | 27/5/18 | | –/12/18 |

### 6th Battalion.

| Name. | Missing. | Interned. | Repatriated. |
|---|---|---|---|
| Lieut. C. A. BALDEN. | 22/3/18 | | 28/11/18 |
| Lieut. G. A. OSWALD. | 22/3/18 | | 12/10/18 |
| Lieut. S. MORPETH. | 10/4/18 | | 29/11/18 |
| Lieut. A. THOMPSON. | 12/4/18 | | 28/11/18 |
| Lt.-Col. E. TEMPERLEY. | 27/5/18 | | 25/12/18 |
| Capt. H. GRAHAM. | 27/5/18 | | 26/12/18 |
| Capt. R. E. M. HEANLEY. | 27/5/18 | | 25/12/18 |
| Capt. J. G. GARRARD. | 27/5/18 | | 21/1/19 |
| Lieut. J. WATSON. | 27/5/18 | | –/12/18 |
| Lieut. J. W. CRAKE. | 27/5/18 | | 25/12/18 |
| Lieut. W. M. McLARE. | 27/5/18 | | 6/1/19 |
| Lieut. C. O. MARSHALL. | 27/5/18 | | 14/12/18 |
| Lieut. H. V. RUSSELL. | 27/5/18 | | 18/12/18 |
| 2/Lt. W. R. DODD. | 27/5/18 | | –/12/18 |
| ‡2/Lt. A. E. GLANVILLE. | 27/5/18 | | 8/12/18 |
| 2/Lt. J. GRAY. | 27/5/18 | | 2/1/19 |
| 2/Lt. J. S. STOKOE. | 27/5/18 | | –/12/18 |

\* Attached T.M.B.     † Attached from R. Irish Rifles.
‡ Attached from R. Dublin Fus.

## NORTHUMBERLAND FUSILIERS—continued.

### 6th Battalion—continued.

| Name. | Missing. | Interned. | Repatriated. |
|---|---|---|---|
| 2/Lt. A. S. TAYLOR. | 27/5/18 | | 30/12/18 |
| *2/Lt. T. R. LEES. | 27/5/18 | | 18/12/18 |
| *2/Lt. H. R. B. BELLERBY. | 27/5/18 | | 25/12/18 |
| †2/Lt. A. P. ANDERSON. | 27/5/18 | | —/12/18 |

### 8th Battalion.

| | | | |
|---|---|---|---|
| 2/Lt. C. TOLKIEN. | 27/5/18 | | 18/12/18 |

### 9th Battalion.

| | | | |
|---|---|---|---|
| 2/Lt. H. E. WOODS. | 23/4/17 | (*Died*). | |
| 2/Lt. L. W. FEATHERSTONE. | 9/4/18 | | 18/12/18 |

### 12th and 13th Battalions.

| | | | |
|---|---|---|---|
| 2/Lt. C. R. M. GREENFIELD. | 25/1/18 | | 17/12/18 |
| 2/Lt. B. E. ASTBURY. | 26/1/18 | | 17/12/18 |
| Major G. WHITE. | 21/3/18 | | 17/12/18 |
| Capt. J. McKINNON. | 21/3/18 | | —/1/19 |
| Capt. J. O. BYRNE. | 21/3/18 | | 10/12/18 |
| Lieut. A. P. HARROWER. | 21/3/18 | (*Died* at Roisel 26/3/18). | |
| Lieut. F. L. SMART. | 21/3/18 | | 14/12/18 |
| 2/Lt. A. WILLIAMSON. | 21/3/18 | | 18/12/18 |
| 2/Lt. R. H. COMLEY. | 21/3/18 | | 2/12/18 |
| 2/Lt. H. L. JOHNSON. | 21/3/18 | | —/12/18 |
| 2/Lt. G. COPELAND. | 21/3/18 | | 5/12/18 |
| 2/Lt. H. F. DODD. | 21/3/18 | | 17/12/18 |
| 2/Lt. G. H. R. DOMAN. | 21/3/18 | (*Died* at Ostrove 11/6/18). | |
| 2/Lt. J. RICHARDSON. | 21/3/18 | | 12/10/18 |
| ‡Capt. J. R. SHORT. | 22/3/18 | | 8/12/18 |
| Capt. C. R. LINGWOOD. | 16/4/18 | | 13/12/18 |
| Lieut. J. R. RITZEMA. | 16/4/18 | | 11/12/18 |
| 2/Lt. H. V. GATESHILL. | 16/4/18 | | 18/12/18 |
| 2/Lt. W. BRIGHAM. | 16/4/18 | | 11/12/18 |
| 2/Lt. G. W. LACEY. | 16/4/18 | | 25/12/18 |
| 2/Lt. H. W. DICKINSON. | 16/4/18 | (*Died* 9/8/18). | |
| Lieut. J. N. HALL. | 27/5/18 | | 25/12/18 |
| Lieut. E. R. BRAIN. | 27/5/18 | | 25/12/18 |
| Lieut. I. W. MAKEPEACE. | 27/5/18 | | 17/12/18 |
| 2/Lt. P. J. PASCOE. | 27/5/18 | | —/12/18 |
| 2/Lt. B. H. CLARKE. | 27/5/18 | | —/1/19 |
| 2/Lt. D. GEGGIE. | 27/5/18 | | 25/12/18 |
| 2/Lt. J. B. JACKSON. | 27/5/18 | | —/1/19 |
| 2/Lt. W. C. DICKINSON. | 27/5/18 | | 26/12/18 |
| 2/Lt. R. E. FISHER. | 27/5/18 | | 10/12/18 |

### 13th Battalion.

| | | | |
|---|---|---|---|
| Capt. F. J. REIDY. | 16/6/17 | | 2/1/19 |
| 2/Lt. A. INGLE. | 16/6/17 | | 6/12/18 |
| 2/Lt. S. J. KERR. | 16/6/17 | | 6/12/18 |

\* Attached from R. Irish Rifles.
† Attached from Durham Light Infantry.
‡ Attached from Yorkshire Regiment.

## NORTHUMBERLAND FUSILIERS—continued.
### 14th Battalion.

| Name. | Missing. | Interned. | Repatriated. |
|---|---|---|---|
| 2/Lt. J. E. HENDERSON. | 22/3/18 | (*Died*). | |
| 2/Lt. T. D. LAWSON. | 22/3/18 | | 18/12/18 |
| 2/Lt. J. P. SOWERBY. | 23/3/18 | | 1/12/18 |
| 2/Lt. M. S. BRYCE. | 27/5/18 | | –/12/18 |
| 2/Lt. F. T. DAVIS. | 27/5/18 | | –/12/18 |
| 2/Lt. S. B. MILNE. | 27/5/18 | | –/12/18 |
| 2/Lt. J. PARSONS. | 27/5/18 | | 30/12/18 |
| Capt. S. A. HOLMAN. | 28/5/18 | | 20/12/18 |
| Capt. C. E. MAYNARD. | 28/5/18 | | –/1/19 |
| 2/Lt. L. LANGLEY. | 28/5/18 | | –/12/18 |
| 2/Lt. A. GIBSON. | 28/5/18 | | –/12/18 |

### 17th Battalion.

| Name. | Missing. | Interned. | Repatriated. |
|---|---|---|---|
| 2/Lt. E. TURNBULL. | 10/4/18 | | 18/12/18 |

### 20th Battalion.

| Name. | Missing. | Interned. | Repatriated. |
|---|---|---|---|
| 2/Lt. T. P. CONOLLY. | 3/7/16 | Holland 16/5/18 | 2/12/18 |
| 2/Lt. H. SEARS. | 22/10/17 | | 3/12/18 |

### 22nd Battalion.

| Name. | Missing. | Interned. | Repatriated. |
|---|---|---|---|
| 2/Lt. D. A. ROGERS. | 22/10/17 | | 3/12/18 |
| Lieut. J. H. FAULDER. | 21/3/18 | | 1/12/18 |
| Lieut. A. E. CARTER. | 21/3/18 | | 29/11/18 |
| 2/Lt. F. G. OLIVER. | 21/3/18 | | 1/12/18 |
| 2/Lt. N. C. HENRY. | 21/3/18 | | 8/12/18 |
| 2/Lt. J. H. GRANT. | 21/3/18 | | 18/12/18 |
| 2/Lt. N. DAVIDSON. | 21/3/18 | | 18/12/18 |
| 2/Lt. B. PEACOCK. | 21/3/18 | | 11/12/18 |
| 2/Lt. J. ROBINSON. | 21/3/18 | | 11/12/18 |
| Lieut. J. H. NICHOLSON. | 11/4/18 | | 25/12/18 |
| Capt. A. W. D. MARK. | 13/4/18 | | 13/12/18 |
| 2/Lt. R. L. NISBET. | 13/4/18 | | 29/11/18 |
| 2/Lt. G. M. GIBSON. | 3/9/18 | | 13/12/18 |

### 23rd Battalion.

| Name. | Missing. | Interned. | Repatriated. |
|---|---|---|---|
| 2/Lt. A. A. MORRIS. | 29/4/17 | | 14/12/18 |
| Lt.-Col. G. CHARLTON. | 21/3/18 | | 28/11/18 |
| Capt. W. M. DODDS. | 21/3/18 | (*Died* at Posen). | 14/10/18 |
| Capt. S. H. MATTHEWS. | 21/3/18 | | 2/12/18 |
| Capt. J. T. V. WIGGANS. | 21/3/18 | | 2/12/18 |
| Capt. G. A. BROWN. | 21/3/18 | | 28/11/18 |
| Lieut. S. J. WILLMOTT. | 21/3/18 | | 29/11/18 |
| Lieut. W. WATSON. | 21/3/18 | | 1/12/18 |
| Lieut. A. R. LIDDELL. | 21/3/18 | | 11/12/18 |
| 2/Lt. H. J. WILSON. | 21/3/18 | | 18/12/18 |
| 2/Lt. W. R. T. COLE. | 21/3/18 | | 1/12/18 |
| 2/Lt. J. C. RODGER. | 21/3/18 | | 11/12/18 |
| 2/Lt. W. L. BOWMAN. | 21/3/18 | | 18/12/18 |
| 2/Lt. W. BOYD. | 21/3/18 | | 11/1/19 |
| 2/Lt. A. LAMBERT. | 21/3/18 | | 18/12/18 |
| 2/Lt. H. H. DAVIES. | 21/3/18 | | 27/11/18 |
| 2/Lt. G. R. JEFFERSON. | 21/3/18 | | –/12/18 |
| Capt. A. MORLIDGE. | 11/4/18 | | 3/12/18 |
| 2/Lt. J. P. HUGHES. | 12/4/18 | | –/12/18 |
| 2/Lt. A. N. THOMPSON. | 12/4/18 | | 3/12/18 |
| 2/Lt. L. F. LEATHARD. | 12/4/18 | | 3/12/18 |
| 2/Lt. S. F. EGAN. | 13/4/18 | | 1/12/18 |

## NORTHUMBERLAND FUSILIERS—continued.
### 24th Battalion.

| Name. | Missing. | Interned. | Repatriated. |
|---|---|---|---|
| 2/Lt. R. G. LENNARD. | 20/4/17 | (Died). | |

### 25th Battalion.

| | | | |
|---|---|---|---|
| Lt.-Col. N. LEITH-HAY-CLARK. | 21/3/18 | Switzerland 21/10/18 | 9/12/18 |
| Capt. F. McKELLEN. | 21/3/18 | | 10/12/18 |
| Capt. J. G. KIRKUP. | 21/3/18 | | 10/12/18 |
| 2/Lt. T. H. TAYLOR. | 21/3/18 | | 1/12/18 |
| 2/Lt. F. A. HARRISON. | 21/3/18 | | 18/12/18 |
| 2/Lt. G. C. SNOWDON. | 21/3/18 | | 8/12/18 |
| Lieut. G. HARDY. | 11/4/18 | | 1/12/18 |

### 26th Battalion.

| | | | |
|---|---|---|---|
| Lieut. P. A. GAMBLE. | 21/3/18 | | –/1/19 |

## ROYAL WARWICKSHIRE REGIMENT.
### 1st and 2nd Battalions.

| | | | |
|---|---|---|---|
| Lieut. C. F. MAUNSELL. | 26/8/14 | Switzerland 9/12/17 | 6/12/18 |
| Major R. MEIKLEJOHN. | 4/9/14 | Switzerland 30/5/16 | 24/3/18 |
| Lieut. C. H. J. CHICHESTER-CONSTABLE. | 4/9/14 | | 1/1/19 |
| Capt. J. B. B. MACKY. | 25/9/14 | Switzerland 9/12/17 | 23/12/18 |
| Capt. P. E. BESANT. | 30/9/14 | Switzerland 9/12/17 | 14/6/18 |
| Major D. A. L. DAY. | 1/10/14 | Holland 22/1/18 | 18/11/18 |
| Capt. J. H. W. KNIGHT-BRUCE. | 1/10/14 | | 11/9/17 |
| Capt. E. G. SYDENHAM. | 20/10/14 | Switzerland 27/12/17 | 14/6/18 |
| Capt. N. B. F. COLLINS. | 23/10/14 | Holland 6/2/18 | 22/11/18 |
| Lieut. J. METCALFE. | 23/10/14 | Holland 6/2/18 | 27/11/18 |
| Lieut. G. H. R. B. SOMERVILLE. | 3/10/14 | | 9/4/18 |
| Capt. J. M. LUCAS. | 31/10/14 | Holland 24/2/18 | 18/11/18 |
| Capt. E. M. ONSLOW. | 31/10/14 | Holland 7/10/18 | 15/10/18 |
| Capt. H. W. OZANNE. | 31/10/14 | Holland 24/2/18 | 21/11/18 |
| Capt. A. J. PECK. | 31/10/14 | Holland 24/2/18 | 21/5/18 |
| Major P. J. FOSTER. | 31/11/14 | Switzerland 9/12/17 | 9/12/18 |
| Capt. I. A. BROWN. | 31/11/14 | | 26/12/18 |
| Capt. J. B. HADDON. | 18/12/14 | Holland 24/2/18 | 18/11/18 |
| 2/Lt. P. F. W. HERBAGE. | 26/9/15 | | 18/11/18 |
| 2/Lt. G. S. M. NATHAN. | 3/5/17 | | 11/1/19 |
| 2/Lt. J. PARKER. | 3/5/17 | | 4/1/19 |
| 2/Lt. A. H. WILLES. | 3/5/17 | | 31/12/18 |
| 2/Lt. P. H. HORSLEY. | 9/8/18 | | 17/12/18 |
| 2/Lt. J. E. C. GUEST. | 9/9/18 | (Died). | |

### 5th Battalion.

| | | | |
|---|---|---|---|
| *Capt. F. W. BLANCHARD. | 3/12/17 | (Died 26/1/18). | |
| Capt. H. P. CHURCHOUSE. | 3/12/17 | | 17/12/18 |
| 2/Lt. A. W. BARNES. | 3/12/17 | | 19/1/19 |
| 2/Lt. R. T. HARRIS. | 3/12/17 | | 17/12/18 |
| 2/Lt. A. E. WINTER. | 3/12/17 | | 18/12/18 |
| 2/Lt. A. A. C. BROWN. | 15/6/18 | | 20/11/18 |
| Capt. E. P. Q. CARTER. | 15/6/18 | | 12/11/18 |
| Capt. J. B. FLORENCE. | 15/6/18 | | 12/11/18 |

### 2/5th Battalion.

| | | | |
|---|---|---|---|
| †Capt. G. W. S. HOPKINS. | 23/3/18 | | 3/12/18 |

* Attached from D.C.L.I.    † Attached T.M.B.

## ROYAL WARWICKSHIRE REGIMENT—continued.

### 2/6th Battalion.

| Name. | Missing. | Interned. | Repatriated. |
|---|---|---|---|
| Capt. F. AYRE. | 21/3/18 | | 1/12/18 |
| Capt. A. PHELPS. | 22/3/18 | | –/12/18 |
| 2/Lt. J. W. CROFT. | 22/3/18 | | 29/11/18 |
| 2/Lt. F. HARDY. | 22/3/18 | | 25/12/18 |
| Capt. F. J. BREEDON. | 14/4/18 | | 2/12/18 |
| Capt. B. K. PARSONS. | 14/4/18 | | 2/12/18 |
| 2/Lt. H. G. CHELLINGWORTH. | 4/4/18 | | 3/12/18 |
| 2/Lt. T. T. HAWORTH. | 14/4/18 | | 13/12/18 |
| *2/Lt. R. H ATTWELL. | 29/6/18 | | 29/11/18 |
| 2/Lt. A. E. CLARKE. | 2/7/16 | (*Died* at Cologne 9/7/16). | |

### 2/7th Battalion.

| Name. | Missing. | Interned. | Repatriated. |
|---|---|---|---|
| 2/Lt. R. H. ADAMS. | 22/3/18 | | 25/12/18 |
| 2/Lt. W. CROOK. | 22/3/18 | | 29/11/18 |
| Capt. G. L. GRAHAM. | 23/3/18 | (*Died* at Seboncourt 11/4/18). | |
| 2/Lt. H. V. DAVIES. | 23/3/18 | | 1/12/18 |
| 2/Lt. A. R. JONES. | 23/3/18 | (*Died*). | |
| 2/Lt. W. J. MOON. | 23/3/18 | | 30/12/18 |
| Lieut. H. N. SMITH. | 24/3/18 | | 13/12/18 |

### 8th Battalion.

| Name. | Missing. | Interned. | Repatriated. |
|---|---|---|---|
| Capt. G. C. FIELD. | 26/6/16 | Switzerland 8/12/17 | 14/6/18 |
| Lieut. F. A. BRETTELL. | 1/7/16 | | 24/3/18 |
| 2/Lt. H. S. TOOGOOD. | 27/8/16 | | 18/12/18 |

### 2/8th Battalion.

| Name. | Missing. | Interned. | Repatriated. |
|---|---|---|---|
| †Lieut. F. G. LEIGH. | 22/3/18 | | 19/12/18 |

### 10th Battalion.

| Name. | Missing. | Interned. | Repatriated. |
|---|---|---|---|
| Capt. A. B. O'DONNELL. | 17/8/16 | | 23/10/18 |
| Capt. J. R. GRIBBLE. | 23/3/18 | (*Died* at Mainz 25/11/18). | |
| Lieut. J. G. H. MANDER. | 23/3/18 | | 25/12/18 |
| 2/Lt. H. L. KEENE. | 23/3/18 | | 26/12/18 |
| 2/Lt. C. G. BAGLEY. | 23/3/18 | | 1/12/18 |
| Capt. S. St. G. S. KINGDON. | 10/4/18 | | 1/1/19 |
| Capt. C. MARTINEAU. | 10/4/18 | (*Died* at Kortryk 5/5/18). | |
| Lieut. R. ASTON. | 10/4/18 | | 13/12/18 |

### 11th Battalion.

| Name. | Missing. | Interned. | Repatriated. |
|---|---|---|---|
| Capt. J. W. GRIFFIN. | 22/3/18 | | –/12/18 |

### 14th Battalion.

| Name. | Missing. | Interned. | Repatriated. |
|---|---|---|---|
| 2/Lt. J. P. IVENS. | 25/6/17 | | 2/1/19 |
| Lieut. F. C. ILETT. | | | 1/12/18 |

### 15th Battalion.

| Name. | Missing. | Interned. | Repatriated. |
|---|---|---|---|
| 2/Lt. E. C. HOBSON. | 9/5/17 | | 20/5/17 |
| 2/Lt. A. H. THORPE. | 25/10/17 | | 5/12/18 |
| Capt. A. C. COLDICOTT. | 28/6/18 | (*Died* at Dortmund 16/8/18). | |

### 16th Battalion.

| Name. | Missing. | Interned. | Repatriated. |
|---|---|---|---|
| 2/Lt. G. ELTHAM. | 27/℅/17 | Switzerland 29/12/17 | 23/12/18 |
| Lieut. G. H. HADLEY. | 14/4/17 | | 29/11/18 |
| 2/Lt. J. E. GOPSILL. | 9/10/17 | | 14/12/18 |

\* Attached from Suffolk Regiment.
† Attached T.M.B.

## ROYAL FUSILIERS.
### 1st and 2nd Battalions.

| Name. | Missing. | Interned. | | Repatriated. |
|---|---|---|---|---|
| Lieut. F. A. SAMPSON. | 26/8/14 | Holland | 5/1/18 | 23/9/18 |
| Capt. Mowbray COLE. | 14/9/14 | (Died). | | |
| Lieut. R. W. JACKSON. | 20/10/14 | Holland | 24/2/18 | 22/1/19 |
| Lieut. L. C. RUSSELL. | 1/7/16 | (Escaped) | | 30/11/17 |
| 2/Lt. A. HEDGES. | 1/7/16 | Switzerland | –/12/16 | 11/9/17 |
| 2/Lt. W. W. LINE. | 30/11/17 | | | 27/11/18 |
| 2/Lt. W. DIMMOCK. | 30/11/17 | | | 17/12/18 |
| 2/Lt. W. R. SPIKESMAN. | 21–25/3/18 | | | 28/11/18 |
| Capt. G. A. JONES. | 22/3/18 | | | –/11/18 |
| 2/Lt. S. W. WALLIS. | 22/3/18 | | | 11/12/18 |
| 2/Lt. W. T. GOULD. | 11/4/18 | | | 31/12/18 |

### 3rd Battalion.

| Name. | Missing. | Interned. | | Repatriated. |
|---|---|---|---|---|
| Lieut. J. A. BREWSTER. | 25/5/15 | Switzerland | 12/8/16 | 11/9/17 |
| 2/Lt. T. ROBERTSON. | 25/5/15 | Holland | 10/4/18 | 30/12/18 |

### 5th Battalion.

| Name. | Missing. | Interned. | | Repatriated. |
|---|---|---|---|---|
| Capt. R. S. SCHOLEFIELD. | 25/9/15 | Switzerland | 19/12/16 | 13/9/17 |

### 7th Battalion.

| Name. | Missing. | Interned. | | Repatriated. |
|---|---|---|---|---|
| 2/Lt. W. R. TRICKER. | 30/12/17 | | | 27/11/18 |
| 2/Lt. G. W. MARPLE. | 30/12/17 | | | 27/11/18 |
| 2/Lt. H. R. POOLEY. | 30/12/17 | | | 27/11/18 |
| 2/Lt. H. M. P. PHELPS. | 30/12/17 | | | 17/12/18 |
| 2/Lt. G. R. J. DUCKWORTH. | 25/3/18 | | | 19/12/18 |
| 2/Lt. S. W. DUNTHORNE. | 25/3/18 | | | 25/12/18 |
| 2/Lt. R. W. POLLARD. | 25/3/18 | | | 29/11/18 |
| 2/Lt. A. E. V. BUDGE. | 4/4/18 | | | 25/12/18 |
| *Lieut. S. H. YOUNG. | 26/8/18 | | | 13/12/18 |
| Lieut. A. W. WHITLOCK. | 27/8/18 | | | 18/12/18 |

### 8th Battalion.

| Name. | Missing. | Interned. | | Repatriated. |
|---|---|---|---|---|
| Col. N. B. ELLIOTT-COOPER. | 30/11/17 | (Died 11/2/18). | | |
| Capt. F. W. GADE. | 30/11/17 | | | 31/12/18 |
| Lieut. W. CARMICHAEL. | 30/11/17 | | | 3/12/18 |
| 2/Lt. G. F. PARFECT. | 30/11/17 | | | 25/12/18 |
| 2/Lt. D. A. B. FRY. | 30/11/17 | | | 25/12/18 |
| 2/Lt. G. F. STEARNE. | 30/11/17 | | | 3/12/18 |
| 2/Lt. C. PATERSON. | 7/10/16 | | | 18/12/18 |

### 9th Battalion.

| Name. | Missing. | Interned. | | Repatriated. |
|---|---|---|---|---|
| Lieut. T. B. JONES. | 3/5/17 | | | 31/12/18 |
| 2/Lt. H. H. BROOKER. | 21/11/17 | Holland | 30/4/18 | 23/11/18 |
| 2/Lt. A. V. EDWARDS. | 30/11/17 | | | 3/12/18 |
| 2/Lt. A. H. ELLIOTT. | 30/11/17 | | | 17/12/18 |
| 2/Lt. S. POTTER. | 30/11/17 | | | 17/12/18 |

### 10th Battalion.

| Name. | Missing. | Interned. | | Repatriated. |
|---|---|---|---|---|
| 2/Lt. S. J. THOMPSON. | 14/9/18 | | | 9/12/18 |

### 11th Battalion.

| Name. | Missing. | Interned. | | Repatriated. |
|---|---|---|---|---|
| 2/Lt. W. H. PRIOR. | 3/5/17 | | | 1/1/19 |
| Lieut. H. R. CRESSY. | 10/8/17 | | | 14/12/18 |
| 2/Lt. G. W. H. ROGERS. | 10/8/17 | | | 14/12/18 |
| 2/Lt. G. A. RENDLE. | 10/8/17 | | | 19/12/18 |
| Major G. DEKIN. | 23/3/18 | | | 18/12/18 |
| Capt. G. S. PEARCY. | 23/3/18 | | | 10/12/18 |

* Attached 17th L.T.M.B.
† Attached from Royal Sussex Regiment.

## ROYAL FUSILIERS—continued.
### 11th Battalion—continued.

| Name. | Missing. | Interned. | | Repatriated. |
|---|---|---|---|---|
| 2/Lt. W. R. ROE. | 3/5/17 | (*Died* at Henn Lenglet 11/5/17). | | |
| Capt. H. W. BROOKLING. | 23/3/18 | | | 1/12/18 |
| 2/Lt. G. WILCOX. | 23/3/18 | | | –/12/18 |
| 2/Lt. G. M. GIBBS. | 23/3/18 | | | 18/12/18 |
| 2/Lt. E. JAMES. | 23/3/18 | | | –/12/18 |
| 2/Lt. J. P. CRUIKSHANK. | 23/3/18 | | | 18/12/18 |
| 2/Lt. A. H. MATTHEWS. | 23/3/18 | | | 18/12/18 |

### 12th Battalion.

| Name. | Missing. | Interned. | | Repatriated. |
|---|---|---|---|---|
| 2/Lt. C. H. L. SKEET. | 25/9/15 | Holland | 19/4/18 | 18/11/18 |
| 2/Lt. J. EASTON. | 26/9/15 | Holland | 19/4/18 | 18/11/18 |

### 13th Battalion.

| Name. | Missing. | Interned. | | Repatriated. |
|---|---|---|---|---|
| 2/Lt. L. E. SHORMAN. | 30/9/17 | | | 13/12/18 |
| *2/Lt. T. W. SENIOR. | 23/10/18 | | | 8/12/18 |

### 21st Battalion.

| Name. | Missing. | Interned. | | Repatriated. |
|---|---|---|---|---|
| Capt. R. H. WHITTINGTON. | 1/2/16 | Holland | 19/4/18 | 18/11/18 |

### 22nd Battalion.

| Name. | Missing. | Interned. | | Repatriated. |
|---|---|---|---|---|
| 2/Lt. J. H. E. ELLISON. | 17/2/17 | | | 30/12/18 |
| †2/Lt. J. W. IRELAND. | 25/3/18 | | | 18/12/18 |

### 23rd Battalion.

| Name. | Missing. | Interned. | | Repatriated. |
|---|---|---|---|---|
| 2/Lt. C. H. DEACON. | 17/2/17 | | | 17/12/18 |
| 2/Lt. F. K. HADDEN. | 16/4/17 | | | 4/12/18 |
| 2/Lt. E. E. PENGILLEY. | 3/5/17 | | | 14/12/18 |
| 2/Lt. C. D. ROWE. | 23/3/18 | | | 11/12/18 |
| Major N. A. LEWIS. | 25/3/18 | | | 25/12/18 |
| Capt. H. A. NICHOLSON. | 25/3/18 | | | 18/12/18 |
| Lieut. R. J. EVANS. | 25/3/18 | | | 13/12/18 |
| Lieut. J. LEIGHTON. | 25/3/18 | | | 1/12/18 |
| Lieut. N. THORNHILL. | 25/3/18 | | | 30/12/18 |
| 2/Lt. H. WILLIAMS. | 25/3/18 | | | 2/12/18 |
| 2/Lt. J. F. MANCE. | 25/3/18 | | | 18/12/18 |
| 2/Lt. H. D. BIRD. | 25/3/18 | | | 23/9/18 |
| 2/Lt. G. S. B. ANDREW. | 25/3/18 | | | 18/12/18 |
| 2/Lt. W. H. RITCHIE. | 25/3/18 | | | 18/12/18 |
| 2/Lt. P. PIPER. | 25/3/18 | | | 31/12/18 |
| 2/Lt. C. PEARCE. | 7/9/18 | | | 8/12/18 |

### 24th Battalion.

| Name. | Missing. | Interned. | | Repatriated. |
|---|---|---|---|---|
| 2/Lt. G. C. CLIFFORD. | 29/4/17 | | | 6/12/18 |
| Lieut. A. WING. | 24/3/18 | | | 3/1/19 |
| 2/Lt. H. W. H. MOORE. | | | | 18/12/18 |
| 2/Lt. S. C. LAMBERT. | 25/3/18 | | | 18/12/18 |
| 2/Lt. R. W. WINKWORTH. | 25/3/18 | | | 18/12/18 |

## LIVERPOOL REGIMENT.
### 1st Battalion.

| Name. | Missing. | Interned. | | Repatriated. |
|---|---|---|---|---|
| Capt. F. L. KING. | 8/8/16 | Holland | 12/10/18 | 21/1/19 |
| Lieut. T. P. BREMNER. | 8/8/16 | Holland | 12/10/18 | 22/11/18 |
| Lieut. W. B. MOORHEAD. | 8/8/16 | Holland | 12/10/18 | 22/11/18 |
| 2/Lt. C. R. D. BUSTARD. | 8/8/16 | Holland | 12/10/18 | 9/12/18 |
| 2/Lt. H. W. SHAPTON. | 30/11/17 | | | 3/12/18 |

\* Attached from Northumberland Fusiliers.
† Attached T.M.B.

## LIVERPOOL REGIMENT—continued.
### 1st Battalion—continued.

| Name. | Missing. | Interned. | Repatriated. |
|---|---|---|---|
| 2/Lt. A. H. ALEXANDER. | 30/11/17 | | 23/12/18 |
| 2/Lt. T. BOX. | 30/11/17 | | 17/12/18 |
| 2/Lt. J. DICKINSON. | 30/11/17 | | 25/12/18 |
| 2/Lt. J. H. S. GIBSON. | 30/11/17 | | 17/12/18 |
| *Lieut. S. J. HENDRY. | 24/3/18 | | –/12/18 |
| 2/Lt. G. H. EDWARDS. | 24/3/18 | | 25/12/18 |
| Lieut. F. L. CHEETHAM. | 27/9/18 | | 28/11/18 |

### 4th Battalion.

| Name. | Missing. | Interned. | Repatriated. |
|---|---|---|---|
| 2/Lt. S. THOMPSON. | 15/4/18 | | –/12/18 |
| Capt. D. H. PACK. | 16/4/18 | | 18/12/18 |
| †2/Lt. A. O. WARD. | 16/4/18 | | 25/12/18 |
| 2/Lt. J. SPENCER. | 16/4/18 | | 25/12/18 |
| 2/Lt. S. E. BIRKUMSHAW. | 16/4/18 | | 30/12/18 |
| 2/Lt. J. F. MARRION. | 16/4/18 | | 1/12/18 |
| 2/Lt. L. COLLINGS. | 16/4/18 | | 18/12/18 |
| 2/Lt. C. NEWMAN. | 16/4/18 | | 25/12/18 |
| 2/Lt. F. WHEELER. | 16/4/18 | | 25/12/18 |
| Lieut. W. J. KENDALL. | 26/4/18 | | 18/12/18 |

### 5th Battalion.

| Name. | Missing. | Interned. | Repatriated. |
|---|---|---|---|
| 2/Lt. H. F. STEWART. | 22/11/16 | | 6/1/19 |
| Lieut. T. W. SAUNDERS. | 8/4/18 | | 11/12/18 |
| Capt. E. S. FORSTER. | 9/4/18 | | 11/12/18 |
| Capt. G. B. EDWARDS. | 9/4/18 | | 8/12/18 |
| 2/Lt. R. W. FOULKES. | 9/4/18 | | 11/12/18 |
| 2/Lt. F. W. HARKIN. | 9/4/18 | | 11/12/18 |
| 2/Lt. K. R. A. ALLBON-BENNETT. | 9/4/18 | | 11/12/18 |
| 2/Lt. R. H. RICHARDS. | 9/4/18 | | 11/12/18 |
| 2/Lt. W. B. LEITHEAD. | 9/4/18 | | 11/12/18 |
| 2/Lt. J. A. NICHOLSON. | 9/4/18 | | 11/12/18 |
| 2/Lt. E. CLARK. | 9/4/18 | | 28/11/18 |
| 2/Lt. M. B. JONES. | 9/4/18 | | 25/12/18 |
| 2/Lt. F. M. KNIVETON. | 9/4/18 | | 11/12/18 |
| 2/Lt. F. WHITEHEAD. | 9/4/18 | | 11/12/18 |
| 2/Lt. P. GRUNDY. | 9/4/18 | | 29/11/18 |
| 2/Lt. F. W. FIRMINGER. | 3/5/18 | | 29/11/18 |

### 6th Battalion.

| Name. | Missing. | Interned. | Repatriated. |
|---|---|---|---|
| Capt. G. D. TYSON. | 30/11/17 | | 13/12/18 |
| Lieut. V. R. BOWERS. | 30/11/17 | | 4/12/18 |
| Lieut. R. R. STEWART. | 30/11/17 | | 6/1/19 |
| 2/Lt. E. S. ROGERS. | 30/11/17 | | 25/12/18 |
| 2/Lt. C. V. WATTS. | 30/11/17 | | 29/11/18 |
| 2/Lt. W. R. SMITH. | 30/11/17 | | 25/12/18 |
| 2/Lt. H. J. SHEPPARD. | 30/11/17 | | 3/12/18 |
| 2/Lt. W. K. DAVY. | 30/11/17 | | 2/12/18 |
| 2/Lt. C. F. COLE. | 30/6/18 | | 18/12/18 |

### 7th Battalion.

| Name. | Missing. | Interned. | Repatriated. |
|---|---|---|---|
| 2/Lt. G. TAYLOR. | 23/3/18 | | 6/12/18 |
| Lieut. S. B. POOLE. | 9/4/18 | | 25/12/18 |
| 2/Lt. W. P. SMART. | 16/6/18 | | –/12/18 |
| 2/Lt. E. JONES. | 29/9/18 | | 13/12/18 |

* Attached from Border Regiment. † Attached from Devonshire Regiment.

## LIVERPOOL REGIMENT—continued.

### 8th Battalion.

| Name. | Missing. | Interned. | | Repatriated. |
|---|---|---|---|---|
| Capt. E. M. MURPHY. | 8/8/16 | Holland | 12/10/18 | 21/1/19 |
| Lieut. W. D. N. LILLEY. | 8/8/16 | (*Died* 11/8/16 at St. Quentin). | | |
| Lieut. W. DUNCAN. | 8/8/16 | | Escaped | 16/2/18 |
| 2/Lt. H. WHITESIDE. | 8/8/16 | | | 22/11/18 |
| 2/Lt. J. A. SISSON. | 8/8/16 | Holland | 12/10/18 | 25/11/18 |
| 2/Lt. R. BURROW. | 8/8/16 | Holland | 12/10/18 | 22/11/18 |
| 2/Lt. C. B. J. COLLISON. | 8/8/16 | Holland | 12/10/18 | 21/1/19 |
| 2/Lt. W. N. SPARGO. | 8/8/16 | | | 11/9/17 |
| 2/Lt. B. MALLINSON. | 22/2/17 | | | 6/1/19 |
| Lieut. E. F. G. ORCHARD. | 31/7/17 | (*Died*). | | |
| 2/Lt. C. W. VICK. | 20/11/17 | | | 13/12/18 |
| 2/Lt. P. A. R. GEORGE. | 20/11/17 | | | 13/12/18 |
| 2/Lt. R. A. DAVIES. | 22/11/17 | | | 3/12/18 |
| 2/Lt. F. A. FREE. | 22/12/17 | | | 29/11/18 |
| *Capt. W. B. DOWSON. | 21/3/18 | | | 10/12/18 |
| 2/Lt. O. P. CASEY. | 31/3/18 | | | 2/1/19 |

### 10th Battalion.

| Name. | Missing. | | Repatriated. |
|---|---|---|---|
| Capt. J. R. WILLIAMS. | 10/8/16 | (*Died* 13/8/16 at St. Quentin). | |
| 2/Lt. G. R. HUGHES. | 11/10/17 | | 13/12/18 |
| Capt. A. T. SALVIDGE. | 30/11/17 | | 28/11/18 |
| Lieut. S. F. VELHO. | 30/11/17 | | 25/12/18 |
| 2/Lt. G. L. DICKSON. | 30/11/17 | | 3/12/18 |
| 2/Lt. J. D. GULICH. | 30/11/17 | | 27/11/18 |
| *2/Lt. H. M. LOCKE. | 30/11/17 | | 17/12/18 |
| †2/Lt. W. GARROW. | 30/11/17 | | 3/12/18 |
| 2/Lt. F. H. LOWE. | 30/11/17 | | 15/11/18 |
| 2/Lt. A. MANTLE. | 30/11/17 | | 17/12/18 |
| 2/Lt. I. A. STEWART. | 30/11/17 | | 3/12/18 |

### 11th Battalion.

| Name. | Missing. | Repatriated. |
|---|---|---|
| Lieut. J. E. ACHESON. | 23/3/18 | 18/12/18 |

### 12th Battalion.

| Name. | Missing. | Repatriated. |
|---|---|---|
| 2/Lt. J. BELL. | 30/11/17 | 14/12/18 |
| 2/Lt. C. D. TAYLOR. | 30/11/17 | 27/11/18 |
| 2/Lt. F. L. MULLIS. | 30/11/17 | 3/12/18 |
| 2/Lt. C. M. SWATMAN. | –/3/18 | 18/12/18 |
| 2/Lt. G. M. GATHERAL. | 21/3/18 | 25/12/18 |
| Capt. J. E. B. PLUMMER. | 21/3—3/4/18 | 16/12/18 |
| Lieut. F. W. BUDD. | 21/3—3/4/18 | 29/11/18 |
| Lieut. J. S. MIDDLETON. | 21/3—3/4/18 | 2/1/19 |
| 2/Lt. J. O'N. KENNEDY. | 21/3—3/4/18 | 12/10/18 |

### 13th Battalion.

| Name. | Missing. | Repatriated. |
|---|---|---|
| ‡2/Lt. McC. DALY. | 3/5/17 | 6/12/18 |
| 2/Lt. A. RICHARDS. | 28/8/17 | 14/12/18 |
| 2/Lt. A. CHALLIS. | 23/3/18 | –/12/18 |
| Lieut. B. W. GRAY. | 28/3/18 | 18/12/18 |
| §2/Lt. C. J. ALLISON. | 28/3/18 | 2/12/18 |
| 2/Lt. H. HALEY. | 28/3/18 | 2/1/19 |
| 2/Lt. A. R. TETLOW. | 28/3/18 | 25/12/18 |
| 2/Lt. W. S. LITTLE. | 28/3/18 | 2/1/19 |
| 2/Lt. S. MITCHELL. | 28/3/18 | 11/12/18 |
| Capt. S. T. J. PERRY. | 31/8/18 | 10/12/18 |

\* Attached T.M.B.     † Attached from Cameron Highlanders.
‡ Attached from K.O.R.L.     § Attached from Household Battalion.

## LIVERPOOL REGIMENT—continued.

### 17th Battalion.

| Name. | Missing. | Interned. | Repatriated. |
|---|---|---|---|
| Lieut. E. S. ASHCROFT. | 1/5/18 | (*Died* 12/5/18 at Lauwe). | |
| 2/Lt. A. H. ELLIS. | 2/5/18 | | 6/12/18 |

### 18th Battalion.

| | | | |
|---|---|---|---|
| Capt. E. B. BEAZLEY. | 18/10/16 | Switzerland 9/12/17 | 14/6/18 |
| Capt. F. M. SHEARD. | 21/3/18 | (*Died* 2/4/18 at Bohain). | |
| *2/Lt. S. HOPE. | 21/3/18 | | 11/12/18 |
| 2/Lt. A. E. BARLOW. | 23/3/18 | | 18/12/18 |
| 2/Lt. A. G. COX. | 23/3/18 | | 18/12/18 |

### 19th Battalion.

| | | | |
|---|---|---|---|
| Lt.-Col. J. N. PECK. | 22/3/18 | | 18/12/18 |
| Capt. H. T. WILLMER. | 22/3/18 | | 10/12/18 |
| Lieut. J. C. MUIR. | 22/3/18 | | –/12/18 |
| 2/Lt. L. D. OWEN. | 22/3/18 | | 18/12/18 |
| 2/Lt. J. ROSS. | 22/3/18 | | 29/11/18 |
| 2/Lt. A. BRADBURY. | 22/3/18 | | 11/12/18 |
| 2/Lt. J. P. KING. | 22/3/18 | | 28/11/18 |
| 2/Lt. G. P. KING. | 22/3/18 | | 28/11/18 |

### 20th Battalion.

| | | | | |
|---|---|---|---|---|
| Lieut. G. W. LAMB. | 30/7/16 | Holland | 15/6/18 | 18/11/18 |
| 2/Lt. H. K. BUSH. | 30/7/16 | Holland | 15/6/18 | 22/11/18 |
| 2/Lt. A. E. WILSON. | 30/7/16 | | (Escaped) | 12/5/18 |
| 2/Lt. H. DERBYSHIRE. | 24/3/18 | | | 25/12/18 |

### 25th Battalion.

| | | | |
|---|---|---|---|
| 2/Lt. S. B. CARSON. | 9/10/18 | | 8/12/18 |
| 2/Lt. T. E. GEORGE. | 10/10/18 | | –/11/18 |

## NORFOLK REGIMENT.

### 1st and 2nd Battalions.

| | | | | |
|---|---|---|---|---|
| Capt. R. REDDIE. | 24/8/14 | | Escaped | 4/8/17 |
| Lieut. J. OAKES. | 24/8/14 | Holland | 29/12/17 | 17/11/18 |
| Lieut. G. PAGET. | 11/9/14 | Holland | 29/12/17 | 17/11/18 |
| Lieut. A. REEVE. | 11/9/14 | Holland | 29/12/17 | 17/11/18 |
| Lieut. G. P. BURLTON. | 4/6/16 | (*Died* 5/6/16). | | |
| Lieut. O. S. D. WILLS. | 26/3/18 | | | 1/12/18 |

### 7th Battalion.

| | | | |
|---|---|---|---|
| 2/Lt. W. G. FERGUSON. | 2/8/17 | | 29/11/18 |
| 2/Lt. D. C. WHITE. | 14/10/17 | | 3/12/18 |
| Capt. K. R. POTTER. | 30/11/17 | | 14/12/18 |
| Lieut. W. G. COLLINS. | 30/11/17 | (*Died* 21/1/18 at Hamburg). | |
| 2/Lt. G. D. SUMMERS. | 30/11/17 | | 17/12/18 |
| 2/Lt. H. E. A. PAYNE. | 30/11/17 | | 2/1/19 |
| ‡Lt.-Col. E. T. REES. | 27/3/18 | | –/1/19 |
| 2/Lt. W. H. BARTER. | 27/3/18 | | 25/12/18 |
| §2/Lt. A. C. L. HILL. | 27/3/18 | | 18/12/18 |
| §2/Lt. H. P. HOPTON. | 27/3/18 | | 18/12/18 |
| §2/Lt. H. J. PHELPS. | 27/3/18 | | –/12/18 |
| 2/Lt. E. G. U. CLARK. | 27/3/18 | | –/1/19 |
| 2/Lt. F. A. HAYLOCK. | 27/3/18 | | 18/12/18 |

\* Attached T.M.B.
† Attached from Northants Regiment.
‡ Attached from South Wales Borderers. § Attached from Royal Warwicks.

## NORFOLK REGIMENT—continued.
### 9th Battalion.

| Name. | Missing. | Interned. | Repatriated. |
|---|---|---|---|
| 2/Lt. F. T. BURTON. | 21/3/18 | | 29/11/18 |
| 2/Lt. J. R. C. LANE. | 21/3/18 | | 2/12/18 |
| 2/Lt. R. L. PERCIVAL. | 21/3/18 | | 29/11/18 |
| Capt. J. W. HOWLETT. | 13/4/18 | | 18/12/18 |
| 2/Lt. C. J. W. TRENDELL. | 16/4/18 | | 18/12/18 |

## LINCOLNSHIRE REGIMENT.
### 1st and 2nd Battalions.

| Name. | Missing. | Interned. | | Repatriated. |
|---|---|---|---|---|
| Capt. F. C. ROSE. | 23/8/14 | Switzerland | 9/12/17 | 9/12/18 |
| Major C. TOOGOOD. | 10/9/14 | Holland | 5/1/18 | 23/9/18 |
| Lieut. F. R. BRISLEE. | 4/3/16 | Holland | 30/4/18 | –/11/18 |
| 2/Lt. W. C. C. COX. | 4/3/17 | | | 30/12/18 |
| *Capt. L. Coleman SMITH. | 16/8/17 | | | 25/12/18 |
| 2/Lt. S. J. BUSTON. | 16/1/18 | | | 25/12/18 |
| †2/Lt. F. G. COLE. | 21/3/18 | | | 17/12/18 |
| †2/Lt. C. E. WILLCOX. | 22/3/18 | | | 17/12/18 |
| †2/Lt. R. H. STAFFORD. | 22/3/18 | | | 17/12/18 |
| 2/Lt. R. O. EDWARDS. | 22/3/18 | | | 18/12/18 |
| 2/Lt. W. A. CROFT. | 16/4/18 | | | 11/12/18 |
| Lt.-Col. R. BASTARD. | 27/5/18 | | | –/1/19 |
| Capt. H. MARSHALL. | 27/5/18 | | | 25/12/18 |
| Capt. J. T. PRESTON. | 27/5/18 | | | 25/12/18 |
| Lieut. G. R. HOLLIDAY. | 27/5/18 | | | 30/12/18 |
| Lieut. G. MATSON. | 27/5/18 | | | –/1/19 |
| Lieut. H. G. CALDER. | 27/5/18 | | | 11/1/19 |
| 2/Lt. J. HIGGINS. | 27/5/18 | | | 11/1/19 |
| 2/Lt. L. J. TURNER. | 27/5/18 | | | –/12/18 |
| 2/Lt. S. G. SOLE. | 27/5/18 | | | 2/1/19 |
| 2/Lt. C. RACE. | 27/5/18 | | | –/12/18 |
| 2/Lt. E. L. JONES. | 27/5/18 | | | 18/12/18 |
| 2/Lt. B. W. PYE. | 27/5/18 | | | –/1/19 |
| 2/Lt. R. W. OSGERBY. | 27/5/18 | | | –/12/18 |
| 2/Lt. F. DONELL. | 27/5/18 | | | –/1/19 |
| 2/Lt. V. NOCTON. | 27/5/18 | | | –/1/19 |
| 2/Lt. A. R. BRADDY. | 27/5/18 | | | 2/1/19 |
| 2/Lt. M. D. GRIEVE. | 27/5/18 | | | –/12/19 |
| 2/Lt. R. W. HARTLEY. | 29/5/18 | | | 13/12/18 |
| Lieut. H. W. FIRTH. | 17/8/18 | | | 10/12/18 |

### 3rd Battalion.

| Name. | Missing. | Interned. | | Repatriated. |
|---|---|---|---|---|
| Capt. R. F. PESKETT. | | Switzerland | 24/12/16 | 11/9/17 |

### 4th Battalion.

| Name. | Missing. | Interned. | Repatriated. |
|---|---|---|---|
| 2/Lt. J. W. E. JOHNSON. | 6/12/17 | | 13/12/18 |
| 2/Lt. C. BLAMIRES. | –/3/18 | | 18/12/18 |

### 5th Battalion.

| Name. | Missing. | Interned. | Repatriated. |
|---|---|---|---|
| 2/Lt. R. W. ALSTON. | 11/4/17 | | 1/1/19 |
| 2/Lt. F. L. ROSE. | 3/10/17 | | 27/11/18 |
| Capt. E. R. J. HETT. | 21/3/18 | | 18/12/18 |
| 2/Lt. W. G. ALLEN. | 21/3/18 | | –/12/18 |
| 2/Lt. F. SHARPE. | 21/3/18 | | 11/12/18 |
| 2/Lt. F. R. GIBBONS. | 21/3/18 | | 18/12/18 |
| 2/Lt. A. J. ELSTON. | 21/3/18 | | 18/12/18 |
| Lieut. P. E. COTTIS. | 27/3/18 | | 11/12/18 |
| Capt. B. H. CHALLENOR. | 31/3/18 | | 18/12/18 |
| Lieut. W. G. FENTON. | 15/4/18 | | 29/11/18 |
| 2/Lt. J. C. MYERS. | 15/4/18 | | 28/1/19 |

\* Attached from South Staffs.   † Attached from Royal Warwicks.

## LINCOLNSHIRE REGIMENT—continued.

### 7th Battalion.

| Name. | Missing. | Interned. | Repatriated. |
|---|---|---|---|
| Capt. E. de G. CARR. | 23/3/18 | | 6/12/18 |
| Capt. H. C. F. WOTHERSPOON. | 24/3/18 | | 29/11/18 |
| *Lieut. L. A. E. E. HOMMERT. | 24/3/18 | | 11/12/18 |

### 8th Battalion.

| Name. | Missing. | Interned. | Repatriated. |
|---|---|---|---|
| Capt. L. D. McN. DAVIS. | 25/9/15 | Holland 10/4/18 | 18/11/18 |
| Lieut. M. A. HALL. | 25/9/15 | Switzerland 9/12/17 | 7/12/18 |
| Lieut. J. W. REYNOLDS. | 25/9/15 | Switzerland 30/5/16 | 14/9/17 |
| Lieut. G. W. PARKER. | 25/9/15 | (*Died* 29/5/16). | |
| 2/Lt. E. C. Van SOMERAN. | 25/9/15 | Holland 10/4/18 | 18/11/18 |
| 2/Lt. J. H. ALCOCK. | 25/9/15 | Holland 10/4/18 | 18/11/18 |
| Lieut. L. D. EDWARDS. | 16/11/16 | Holland 9/4/18 | 16/8/18 |
| 2/Lt. B. W. GREGORY. | 28/4/17 | | 6/12/18 |
| 2/Lt. N. M. TIMPSON. | 1/8/17 | | –/12/18 |

### 9th Battalion.

| Name. | Missing. | Interned. | Repatriated. |
|---|---|---|---|
| 2/Lt. N. G. WOODROW. | 10/4/18 | | 10/12/18 |

### 10th Battalion.

| Name. | Missing. | Interned. | Repatriated. |
|---|---|---|---|
| Lieut. E. de L. W. ROEBUCK. | 28/4/17 | | 17/12/18 |
| 2/Lt. J. S. HILL. | 28/4/17 | | 31/12/18 |
| 2/Lt. H. J. LODGE. | 28/4/17 | | 6/12/18 |
| 2/Lt. A. R. MacKAY. | 10/4/18 | | 1/12/18 |
| Lieut. W. S. ABBOTT. | 10/4/18 | | 18/12/18 |

## DEVONSHIRE REGIMENT.

### 1st and 2nd Battalions.

| Name. | Missing. | Interned. | Repatriated. |
|---|---|---|---|
| 2/Lt. A. R. ABELL. | 23/4/17 | (*Died* 10/6/17). | |
| 2/Lt. J. L. GREGORY. | 25/11/17 | | 6/11/18 |
| 2/Lt. C. E. CARPENTER. | 22/3/18 | | 1/12/18 |
| 2/Lt. R. TADMAN. | 24/3/18 | | 18/12/18 |
| 2/Lt. W. J. HANNAM. | 26/3/18 | | 11/12/18 |
| 2/Lt. W. E. DYSON. | 24/4/18 | | 29/11/18 |
| Capt. U. B. BURKE. | 27/5/18 | | 23/10/18 |
| *Capt. G. O. OPENSHAW. | 27/5/18 | (*Died* 9/8/18). | |
| *Capt. James MILNER. | 27/5/18 | | 6/12/18 |
| *Capt. F. H. MILLMAN. | 27/5/18 | | 30/12/18 |
| *Capt. S. H. COX. | 27/5/18 | | –/12/18 |
| *Capt. E. A. MILLAR. | 27/5/18 | | 30/12/18 |
| Capt. W. L. CLEGG. | 27/5/18 | | 9/12/18 |
| Capt. J. A. FERGUSSON. | 27/5/18 | | 30/12/18 |
| Lieut. A. E. RUTLEDGE. | 27/5/18 | | –/12/18 |
| Lieut. T. OERTON. | 27/5/18 | | 31/12/18 |
| ‡Lieut. F. E. HARRIS. | 27/5/18 | | 13/12/18 |
| *2/Lt. W. L. BARRETT. | 27/5/18 | | 14/12/18 |
| 2/Lt. R. F. B. HILL. | 27/5/18 | | 31/12/18 |
| 2/Lt. W. T. CROSS. | 27/5/18 | | 31/12/18 |
| 2/Lt. W. CANDLER. | 27/5/18 | | –/12/18 |
| 2/Lt. F. MALKIN. | 27/3/18 | | 17/12/18 |
| 2/Lt. W. C. MAUNDER. | 27/5/18 | | –/1/19 |
| 2/Lt. C. WREFORD. | 27/5/18 | | –/12/18 |
| 2/Lt. R. LAMBERT. | 27/5/18 | | 31/12/18 |
| 2/Lt. A. M. HARVEY. | 27/10/18 | | –/2/19 |

\* Attached from A.S.C.
● Attached Portuguese Mission.
‡ Attached from South Staffs.

## DEVONSHIRE REGIMENT—continued.

### 7th Battalion.

| Name. | Missing. | Interned. | Repatriated. |
|---|---|---|---|
| *Lieut. J. N. HURRELL. | 21/3/18 | | 2/12/18 |

### 8th Battalion.

| | | | |
|---|---|---|---|
| 2/Lt. G. A. DREW. | 26/10/17 | | 3/12/18 |
| 2/Lt. W. J. REED. | 26/10/17 | (D.ed at Kortryk 28/10/17). | |

### 9th Battalion.

| | | | |
|---|---|---|---|
| 2/Lt. H. E. B. DICKSON. | | Switzerland 27/12/17 | 24/3/18 |
| 2/Lt. B. W. BLIGHT. | 26/10/17 | | 2/7/18 |
| 2/Lt. W. G. EVANS. | 26/10/17 | | -/1/19 |
| 2/Lt. W. T. SANDERS. | 26/10/17 | | 16/12/18 |

## SUFFOLK REGIMENT.

### 1st and 2nd Battalions.

| Name | Missing | Interned | Repatriated |
|---|---|---|---|
| Capt. E. PEARSON. | 9/9/14 | Holland 22/1/18 | 18/11/18 |
| Lieut. V. G. M. PHILLIPS. | 9/9/14 | Holland 29/12/17 | 22/11/18 |
| Major S. BARNARDISTON. | 10/9/14 | Holland 5/1/18 | 15/12/18 |
| Major E. C. DOUGHTY. | 10/9/14 | | 13/9/17 |
| Major A. PEEBLES. | 10/9/14 | | 13/9/17 |
| Major F. T. WILSON. | 10/9/14 | Holland 5/1/18 | 30/11/18 |
| Capt. W. M. CAMPBELL. | 10/9/14 | | -/4/17 |
| Capt. L. HEPWORTH. | 10/9/14 | (Died 10/3/17) | |
| Capt. A. CUTBILL. | 10/9/14 | Holland 22/1/18 | 21/12/18 |
| Capt. E. ORFORD. | 10/9/14 | | 13/9/17 |
| Lieut. E. H. W. BACKHOUSE. | 10/9/14 | Holland 22/1/18 | 21/1/19 |
| Lieut. F. C. BERRILL. | 10/9/14 | Holland 5/1/18 | 18/11/18 |
| Lieut. N. A. BITTLESTON. | 10/9/14 | Holland 22/1/18 | 18/11/18 |
| Lieut. T. GEORGE | 10/9/14 | Holland 5/1/18 | 15/2/19 |
| Lieut. R. G. HARVEY. | 10/9/14 | Holland 22/1/18 | 23/9/18 |
| Lieut. J. B. MORGAN. | 10/9/14 | | -/8/16 |
| Lieut. C. B. NICHOLLS. | 10/9/14 | Holland 22/1/18 | 14/1/19 |
| 2/Lieut. H. P. JAMES | 10/9/14 | Holland 29/12/17 | 10/12/18 |
| 2/Lieut. A. F. KEMBLE. | | Holland 10/4/18 | 23/10/18 |
| Lieut. P. CARTHEW. | 15/9/14 | Holland 22/1/18 | 18/11/18 |
| Lieut. H. BIGGS. | 16/12/14 | Holland 1/3/18 | ret. for duty |
| Colonel W. B. WALLACE. | 10/5/15 | Holland 23/3/18 | 18/11/18 |
| Capt. F. MOYSEY. | 10/5/15 | Holland 1/3/18 | 27/11/18 |
| Lieut. C. AINSLEY. | 10/5/15 | Holland 23/3/18 | 22/11/18 |
| Lieut. F. V. C. PEREIRA. | | Holland 22/1/18 | 18/11/18 |
| 2/Lt. K. H. E. CAYLEY. | 10/5/15 | Holland 23/3/18 | 18/11/18 |
| 2/Lt. D. COX. | 10/5/15 | (Died 31/5/15) | |
| 2/Lt. A. G. B. PATTEN. | 21/7/16 | | 22/11/18 |
| 2/Lt. H. W. WRIGHT. | 13–15/11/16 | | 18/12/18 |
| 2/Lt. K. M. DINGLEY. | 13–15/11/16 | | 18/12/18 |
| Capt. W. L. SIMPSON. | 22/3/18 | | 10/12/18 |
| 2/L. H. J. BAYLIS | 23/3/18 | | 29/11/18 |
| Capt. L. J. BAKER. | 28/3/18 | | 2/12/18 |
| †Lieut. D. U. STONEHOUSE. | 28/3/18 | | 25/12/18 |
| 2/Lt. A. H. WARD. | 28/3/18 | | 29/11/18 |
| 2/Lt. H. W. WHITE. | 28/3/18 | | 11/12/18 |
| 2/Lt. E. H. HAMMONDS. | 29/8/18 | | 28/11/18 |

\* Attached T.M.B.  † Attached from Norfolk Regiment.

## SUFFOLK REGIMENT—Continued.
### 7th Battalion.

| Name. | Missing. | Interned. | Repatriated. |
|---|---|---|---|
| Major P. S. WALKER. | 30/11/17 | | 11/1/19 |
| Capt. L. A. G. BOWEN. | 30/11/17 | | 3/12/18 |
| Capt. J. W. HAUGHTON. | 30/11/17 | | 3/12/18 |
| 2/Lt. H. W. CROOK. | 30/11/17 | | 2/12/18 |
| 2/Lt. J. C. DABBS. | 30/11/17 | | 3/12/18 |
| *2/Lt. H. F. T. HAMILTON. | 30/11/17 | | 3/12/18 |
| 2/Lt. T. HAWKINS. | 30/11/17 | | 17/12/18 |
| 2/Lt. C. G. POULTER. | 30/11/17 | (Died 6/3/18) | |
| 2/Lt. W. E. TEAGER. | 30/11/17 | | 27/11/18 |
| 2/Lt. H. THOMSON. | 30/11/17 | | 27/11/18 |

### 9th Battalion.

| Name. | Missing. | Interned. | Repatriated. |
|---|---|---|---|
| 2/Lt. H. L. FRAMPTON. | 22/3/18 | | 17/12/18 |

### 11th Battalion.

| Name. | Missing. | Interned. | Repatriated. |
|---|---|---|---|
| 2/Lt. W. A. MUDD. | 28/4/17 | | 1/1/19 |
| 2/Lt. J. M. HARMER. | 28/4/17 | | 1/1/19 |
| 2/Lt. F. W. BENNETT. | 22/3/18 | | 18/12/18 |
| Capt. L. H. RODWELL. | 6/4/18 | | 18/12/18 |
| 2/Lt. R. S. SHEPHERD. | 10/4/18 | | 2/12/18 |
| 2/Lt. G. S. KEIGHTLEY. | 13/4/18 | | 1/12/18 |
| 2/Lt. J. A. SIMMONS. | 13/4/18 | | 18/12/18 |
| 2/Lt. G. C. LLOYD. | 15/4/18 | | 18/12/18 |

### 12th Battalion.

| Name. | Missing. | Interned. | Repatriated. |
|---|---|---|---|
| 2/Lt. K. PEARCE. | 24/11/17 | | 3/6/18 |
| Capt. R. ENGLAND. | 22/3/18 | | 18/12/18 |
| Lieut. G. HOPKINS. | 22/3/18 | | 18/12/18 |
| Lieut. H. C. MATHEW. | 22/3/18 | | 28/11/18 |
| 2/Lt. J. A. BLANCH. | 22/3/18 | | 18/12/18 |
| 2/Lt. S. E. CLARKE. | 22/3/18 | | 1/12/18 |
| 2/Lt. G. HALLSMITH. | 22/3/18 | | 8/12/18 |
| 2/Lt C. H. HITCHCOCK. | 22/3/18 | | 10/12/18 |
| 2/Lt. G. T. TAYLOR. | 22/3/18 | | 18/12/18 |
| 2/Lt. E. L. TURNER. | 22/3/18 | | 18/12/18 |
| 2/Lt. A. J. WELLS. | 22/3/18 | | 18/12/18 |

## SOMERSET LIGHT INFANTRY.
### 1st and 2nd Battalions.

| Name. | Missing. | Interned. | | Repatriated. |
|---|---|---|---|---|
| Lieut. J. G. SWAYNE. | 26/8/14 | Holland | 22/1/18 | returned on duty. |
| Capt. A. HARGREAVES. | 6/9/14 | | | 11/9/17 |
| Capt. J. BRODERIP. | 25/9/14 | Holland | 22/1/18 | 24/12/18 |
| Lieut. J. C. W. MACBRYAN. | 25/9/14 | Holland | 22/1/18 | 18/11/18 |
| Lieut. G. B. PHILBY. | 25/9/14 | Holland | 22/1/18 | 21/12/18 |
| Lieut. J. TAYLOR. | 25/9/14 | Holland | 22/1/18 | 18/11/18 |
| 2/Lt. K. G. G. DENNYS. | 19/12/14 | | | 11/9/17 |
| 2/Lt. H. W. V. TILLEY. | 1/7/16 | Holland | 16/5/18 | 23/9/18 |
| Lieut. Godwin NEWTON. | | | | 18/12/18 |

\* Attached from Norfolk Regiment.
† Attached Trench Mortar Battery.

## SOMERSET LIGHT INFANTRY—continued.
### 6th Battalion.

| Name. | Missing. | Interned. | Repatriated. |
|---|---|---|---|
| Capt. H. S. BURRINGTON. | 21/3/18 | | 10/12/18 |
| Capt. H. E. MAKINS. | 21/3/18 | | 31/12/18 |
| *Capt. J. YELLOWLEES. | 21/3/18 | | 10/12/18 |
| †Lieut. H. F. BOYCE. | 21/3/18 | | 8/12/18 |
| Lieut. A. E. COTTRELL. | 21/3/18 | | 29/11/19 |
| Lieut. R. G. C. DRAKE. | 21/3/18 | | 18/12/18 |
| Lieut. I. A. ESTRIDGE. | 21/3/18 | | 10/12/18 |
| Lieut. F. A. LEIVERS. | 21/3/18 | | 10/12/18 |
| Lieut. W. A. N. THATCHER. | 21/3/18 | | 10/12/18 |
| 2/Lt. F. G. BURGESS. | 21/3/18 | | 11/12/18 |
| 2/Lt. A. C. V. HOSTLER. | 21/3/18 | | 11/12/18 |
| 2/Lt. W. D. SCOTT. | 21/3/18 | | 11/12/18 |
| 2/Lt. A. STAFFORD. | 21/3/18 | | 11/12/18 |
| 2/Lt. R. J. TUCKER. | 21/3/18 | | 11/12/18 |
| 2/Lt. T. F. TWIST. | 21/3/18 | | 11/12/18 |
| 2/Lt. W. J. WILCE. | 21/3/18 | | 18/12/18 |

### 7th Battalion.

| Name. | Missing. | Interned. | Repatriated. |
|---|---|---|---|
| 2/Lt. R H. FRYE. | 15/6/17 | | 6/12/18 |
| Capt. A. A. ANDREWS. | 30/11/17 | | 15/12/18 |
| 2/Lt. W. B. PAUL. | 30/11/17 | | 9/5/18 |
| Capt. H. A. FOLEY. | 21/3–3/4/18 | | 1/12/18 |
| Lieut. R. ANDERSON. | 21/3–3/4/18 | | 28/12/18 |
| 2/Lt. H. A. COPE. | 21/3–3/4/18 | | 25/12/18 |
| 2/Lt. H. J. DUNCAN. | 21/3–3/4/18 | | –/12/18 |
| 2/Lt. T. MITCHELL. | 21/3–3/4/18 | | 25/12/18 |
| †2/Lt. F. PALMER. | 21/3–3/4/18 | | 18/12/18 |
| 2/Lt. H. M. SQUIBB. | 21/3–3/4/18 | | 2/12/18 |
| Capt. G. D. J. McMURTRIE. | 23/3/18 | | 1/12/18 |
| 2/Lt. T. W. R. ELLIS. | 8/4/18 | | 25/12/18 |
| 2/Lt. D. C. J. CONSTABLE. | 29/6/18 | | 16/12/18 |

### 8th Battalion.

| Name. | Missing. | Interned. | Repatriated. |
|---|---|---|---|
| Major W. H. NICHOLS. | 26/9/15 | (*Died* 15/10/15) | |
| †2/Lt. W. E. HAYES. | 5/4/18 | | 2/12/18 |
| 2/Lt. P. J. JONES. | 5/4/18 | | –/1/19 |
| 2/Lt. S. T. DYTE. | 5/4/18 | | 25/12/18 |

### 12 Battalion.

| Name. | Missing. | Interned. | Repatriated. |
|---|---|---|---|
| Capt. F. EDBROOKE. | 1–11/9/18 | | 29/11/18 |

## WEST YORKSHIRE REGIMENT.
### 1st and 2nd Battalions.

| Name. | Missing. | Interned. | | Repatriated. |
|---|---|---|---|---|
| Capt. P. LOWE. | 20/9/14 | Switzerland | 19/1/17 | 13/9/17 |
| Capt. K. S. S. HENDERSON. | 20/9/14 | Holland | 6/2/18 | 18/11/18 |
| Capt. H. HARINGTON. | 20/9/14 | Holland | 6/2/18 | 22/11/18 |
| Capt. E. F. GRANT-DALTON. | 20/9/14 | Holland | 6/2/18 | 1/11/18 |
| Lieut. B. RATCLIFFE. | 20/9/14 | (Escaped) | | –/4/17 |
| Lieut. W. H. LANGRAN. | 20/9/14 | Holland | 1/1/19 | 4/1/19 |
| Lieut. P. FRYER. | 20/9/14 | Holland | 6/2/18 | 14/1/19 |
| Lieut. L. A. DAVIES. | 20/9/14 | Holland | 6/2/18 | 24/1/19 |
| Lieut. J. PARISH. | 31/1/16 | Holland | 30/2/18 | 22/11/18 |
| Lieut. W. E. H. SPICER. | 17/4/17 | | | 1/1/19 |
| 2/Lt. J. EXLEY. | 16/8/17 | | | 6/12/18 |

* Attached from Durham Light Infantry.    † Attached from Devonshire Regiment.

## WEST YORKSHIRE REGIMENT—Continued.

### 1st Battalion.

| Name. | Missing. | Interned. | Rapatriated. |
|---|---|---|---|
| Lt.-Col. A. M. BOYALL. | 21/3/18 | | 28/11/18 |
| Major H. A. W. COLE-HAMILTON | 21/3/18 | | 18/12/18 |
| Capt. W. C. NEWSTEAD. | 21/3/18 | | 17/12/18 |
| Capt. J. F. WALLACE. | 21/3/18 | | 17/12/18 |
| Lieut. J. R. BEE. | 21/3/18 | | 29/11/18 |
| Lieut. P. E. ADAMS. | 21/3/18 | | 29/11/18 |
| Lieut. G. SERGEANT. | 21/3/18 | | 13/12/18 |
| 2/Lt. H. SALMONS. | 21/3/18 | (Died 1/4/18). | |
| 2/Lt. A. E. H. PARROTT. | 21/3/18 | | 10/12/18 |
| 2/Lt. P. D. STEWART. | 21/3/18 | | 2/12/18 |
| 2/Lt. G. W. SMITH. | 21/3/18 | | 3/12/18 |
| 2/Lt. F. HODGES. | 21/3/18 | | 29/11/18 |
| 2/Lt. A. W. FRENCH. | 21/3/18 | | –/12/18 |
| 2/Lt. J. LITTLEWOOD. | 22/3/18 | | 17/12/18 |
| Capt. E. AMBLER. | 24/3/18 | | 29/11/18 |
| 2/Lt. E. BROOKS. | 16/4/18 | | 3/12/18 |
| Lieut. A. J. DOYLE. | 9/8/18 | | 23/10/18 |

### 2nd Battalion.

| Name. | Missing. | Interned. | Rapatriated. |
|---|---|---|---|
| 2/Lt. W. H. DE VOIL. | 27/3/18 | | 18/12/18 |
| Lieut. T. L. FIELDER. | 24/4/18 | | 29/11/18 |
| 2/Lt. H. PRESTON. | 24/4/18 | | 30/12/18 |
| 2/Lt. E. St. B. STUART-KELSO. | 24/4/18 | | 29/11/18 |
| 2/Lt. W. SMITH. | 24/4/18 | | 3/12/18 |
| 2/Lt. E. JOWETT. | 24/4/18 | | 29/11/18 |
| 2/Lt. S. S. L. JACKSON. | 24/4/18 | | 29/11/18 |
| 2/Lt. K. K. MAKIN. | 24/4/18 | | 25/12/18 |
| Major F. H. TOUNSEND. | 27/5/18 | | 25/12/18 |
| Lieut. N. O. TUCKER. | 27/5/18 | | 13/12/18 |
| Lieut. G. W. HALL. | 27/5/18 | | 25/12/18 |
| 2/Lt. H. WIGGINS. | 27/5/18 | | 13/12/18 |
| 2/Lt. V. R. SCOTT. | 27/5/18 | | 31/12/18 |
| 2/Lt. H. J. RIGBY. | 27/5/18 | | 6/12/18 |
| 2/Lt. J. W. MARSDEN. | 27/5/18 | | 13/12/18 |
| 2/Lt. W. B. GERRITY. | 27/5/18 | | 17/12/18 |
| *2/Lt. J. W. GARDNER. | 27/5/18 | | 25/12/18 |
| 2/Lt. D. G. GARBUTT. | 27/5/18 | | –/12/18 |

### 5th Battalion.

| Name. | Missing. | Interned. | Rapatriated. |
|---|---|---|---|
| 2/Lt. H. WILCOX. | 3/5/17 | | 29/11/18 |
| Lieut. P. CHEESMAN. | 25/4/18 | | 17/12/18 |
| Lieut. A. D. CLUBB. | 25/4/18 | | 29/11/18 |
| Lieut. J. SAYES. | 25/4/18 | | –/12/18 |
| 2/Lt. S. R. MARDON. | 25/4/18 | | 29/11/18 |
| 2/Lt. J. HATTON. | 25/4/18 | | 11/12/18 |
| 2/Lt. C. R. FIRTH. | 25/4/18 | | 9/11/18 |
| 2/Lt. R. BLACKER. | 25/4/18 | | 3/12/18 |
| 2/Lt. J. W. DUNNINGTON. | 25/4/18 | | 2/12/18 |
| Lieut. J. V. BATTERSBY-HARFORD. | 29/4/18 | | 1/12/18 |

### 6th Battalion.

| Name. | Missing. | Interned. | Rapatriated. |
|---|---|---|---|
| 2/Lt. S. Senior SMITH. | 2/3/17 | Holland 7/5/18 | 22/11/18 |
| 2/Lt. F. COOKSON. | 14/4/18 | | 18/12/18 |
| Capt. F. W. WHITTAKER. | 25/4/18 | | 2/12/18 |
| Capt. J. S. GORDON. | 25/4/18 | | 2/12/18 |

* Attached T.M.B.

## WEST YORKSHIRE REGIMENT—continued.
### 6th Battalion—continued.

| Name. | Missing. | Interned. | Repatriated. |
|---|---|---|---|
| Capt. G. SANDERS. | 25/4/18 | | 26/12/18 |
| Lieut. E. BELDON. | 25/4/18 | | —/12/18 |
| Lieut. H. W. ROBINSON. | 25/4/18 | | 29/11/18 |
| Lieut. T. L. SHIELD. | 25/4/18 | | —/12/18 |
| *2/Lt. H. E. JOWETT. | 25/4/18 | | 25/12/18 |
| 2/Lt. F. SUGDEN. | 25/4/18 | | 2/12/18 |
| 2/Lt. C. N. PEPPER. | 25/4/18 | | 2/12/18 |
| 2/Lt. G. MATTHEWS. | 25/4/18 | (*Died* 2/7/18 at Cologne). | |
| 2/Lt. W. E. WARNER. | 25/4/18 | | 11/12/18 |
| 2/Lt. W. C. WHITING. | 25/4/18 | | 2/12/18 |
| 2/Lt. F. E. FAIRBANK. | 25/4/18 | | 1/12/18 |
| 2/Lt. T. BAIRSTOW. | 25/4/18 | | 12/10/18 |
| 2/Lt. B. ARCHER. | 25/4/18 | | 2/12/18 |
| Capt. W. N. MOSSOP. | 28/4/18 | (*Died* 8/5/18 at Ghent). | |

### 7th Battalion.

| Name. | Missing. | Interned. | Repatriated. |
|---|---|---|---|
| 2/Lt. C. C. FRANK. | 1/7/16 | Holland 16/5/18 | 23/9/18 |
| 2/Lt. A. L. H. CLELAND. | 12/5/17 | | 14/12/18 |
| Capt. C. L. FOULDS. | —/3/18 | | 17/12/18 |
| 2/Lt. L. W. METCALFE. | 21/3/18 | | 2/12/18 |
| 2/Lt. W. J. JEHU. | 14/4/18 | | 2/12/18 |
| Capt. E. ROBERTS. | 16/4/18 | | 2/12/18 |
| Lieut. R. W. HORSFALL. | 16/4/18 | | 3/12/18 |
| 2/Lt. G. J. NYE. | 16/4/18 | | 14/12/18 |
| 2/Lt. E. O. PANTING. | 16/4/18 | | 29/11/18 |
| 2/Lt. J. WILSON. | 16/4/18 | | 4/12/18 |
| 2/Lt. A. CHANDLER. | 25/4/18 | | 5/12/18 |
| †2/Lt. T. CHAPMAN. | 25/4/18 | | 31/12/18 |
| Lt.-Col. H. D. BOUSFIELD. | 28/4/18 | | 29/11/18 |

### 8th Battalion.

| Name. | Missing. | Interned. | Repatriated. |
|---|---|---|---|
| Lieut. G. K. WILL. | 3/9/16 | (*Died* 11/9/16 at Velu) | |
| Lieut. V. TANSLEY. | 3/5/17 | | 3/12/18 |
| 2/Lt. W. D. MUIRHEAD. | 3/5/17 | Holland 7/5/18 | 19/7/18 |
| Lieut. E. PEPPER. | 24/5/18 | | 3/1/19 |
| 2/Lt. J. D. PORTEOUS. | | | —/12/18 |
| †2/Lt. W. R. WORRALL. | 27/5/18 | | 13/12/18 |
| 2/Lt. F. O. LAMB. | 28/7/18 | | 8/12/18 |
| ‡2/Lt. F. AXE. | 27/9/18 | | 29/11/18 |
| 2°Lt. W. I. WHITTELL. | 27/9/18 | | —/11/18 |
| 2/Lt. R. L. A. TINGLE. | 27/9/18 | | 28/11/18 |
| 2/Lt. C. E. CROFT. | 27/9/18 | | 28/12/18 |

### 9th Battalion.

| Name. | Missing. | Interned. | Repatriated. |
|---|---|---|---|
| Lieut. G. W. HOLLOWAY. | 11/8/16 | Holland 12/10/18 | 19/11/18 |
| 2/Lt. J. W. TOWNSEND. | 15/12/17 | | 23/12/18 |
| 2/Lt. R. B. WALKER. | 5/11/18 | | —/11/18 |
| 2/Lt. F. G. MARSDEN. | 5/11/18 | | 5/1/19 |

### 10th Battalion.

| Name. | Missing. | Interned. | Repatriated. |
|---|---|---|---|
| 2/Lt. C. E. B. BERNARD. | 1/7/16 | Holland 16/5/18 | 25/11/18 |
| 2/Lt. M. COUCHMAN. | 14/9/16 | | 18/12/18 |
| Lt.-Col. P. R. O. A. SIMNER. | 25/3/18 | | 24/12/18 |
| Lieut. F. A. SHURROCK. | 25/3/18 | | 17/12/18 |
| Lieut. F. D. DAMS. | 21/4/18 | | 18/12/18 |
| Lieut. E. G. ADDINGTON. | 24/8/18 | | 13/12/18 |

*Attached 146/T.M.B.  ‡Attached from East Yorkshire Regiment.
†Attached T.M.B.

## WEST YORKSHIRE REGIMENT—continued.

### 12th Battalion.

| Name. | Missing. | Interned. | | Repatriated. |
|---|---|---|---|---|
| Capt. H. G. S. BRANCH. | 25/9/15 | Holland | 10/4/18 | 18/11/18 |
| 2/Lt. E. L. SHAWCROSS. | 26/9/15 | Holland | 10/4/18 | 18/11/18 |
| *Capt. R. H. T. SMITH. | 30/11/17 | | | 27/11/18 |
| *Lieut. E. K. G. PIROUET. | 12/12/17 | | | 27/11/18 |
| Lieut. A. J. DAVIS. | 12/12/17 | | | 14/12/18 |
| 2/Lt. T. H. ENGLISH. | 12/12/17 | | | 3/12/18 |
| 2/Lt. C. A. MONKS. | 12/12/17 | | | 14/12/18 |
| 2/Lt. R. LEACH. | 12/12/17 | | | 3/12/18 |

### 13th Battalion.

| Name. | Missing. | Interned. | Repatriated. |
|---|---|---|---|
| 2/Lt. T. S. PATTISON. | 13/11/16 | | 18/12/18 |

### 14th Battalion.

| Name. | Missing. | Interned. | | Repatriated. |
|---|---|---|---|---|
| 2/Lt. J. H. BIRKINSHAW. | 11/7/16 | Holland | 15/6/18 | 22/11/18 |
| 2/Lt. L. S. WALTON. | 28/7/16 | Holland | 15/6/18 | 2/1/19 |

### 15th Battalion.

| Name. | Missing. | Interned. | | Repatriated. |
|---|---|---|---|---|
| Lieut. A. H. RILEY. | 3/5/17 | Holland | 24/2/18 | 23/2/18 |
| 2/Lt. R. S. TATE. | 3/5/17 | | | 14/12/18 |
| †Lt.-Col. C. C. H. TWISS. | 27/3/18 | | | 25/12/18 |
| 2/Lt. B. WILLEY. | 27/3/18 | | | 13/12/18 |
| 2/Lt. E. KEIGHLEY. | 27/3/18 | | | 23/12/18 |
| 2/Lt. J. G. PEDLEY. | 27/3/18 | | | 25/12/18 |
| ‡2/Lt. A. W. ROBERTS. | 27/3/18 | (Died 18/12/18) | | |
| 2/Lt. E. G. STEVENS. | 27/3/18 | | | 11/12/18 |
| 2/Lt. R. H. SMITH. | 27/3/18 | | | 11/12/18 |
| 2/Lt. J. H. CLEGG. | 12/14/18 | | | 13/12/18 |
| 2/Lt. W. STRONG. | 27/4/18 | | | 31/12/18 |
| 2/Lt. G. WEATHERILL. | 18/9/18 | | | 29/11/18 |

### 16th Battalion.

| Name. | Missing. | Interned. | Repatriated. |
|---|---|---|---|
| Capt. O. ILLINGWORTH | 3/5/17 | | 2/12/18 |
| Lieut. E. CROWTHER. | 3/5/17 | | 31/12/18 |
| 2/Lt. E. G. BANTOCK. | 3/5/17 | | 4/1/19 |
| 2/Lt. G. L. TUCKER. | 3/5/17 | | 31/12/18 |
| 2/Lt. N. PARKER. | 3/5/17 | | 4/1/19 |
| 2/Lt. L. ASHWORTH. | 3/5/17 | | 7/1/18 |

### 17th Battalion.

| Name. | Missing. | Interned. | | Repatriated. |
|---|---|---|---|---|
| 2/Lt. O. DAY. | 30/8/17 | (*Died* at Candry 3/9/17). | | |
| Lieut. J. C. ACHESON. | 31/8/17 | Holland | 30/4/18 | 18/8/18 |
| 2/Lt. N. ODDY. | 31/8/17 | | | –/1/19 |
| 2/Lt. R. D. FITZPATRICK. | 31/8/17 | | | 14/12/18 |

### 18th Battalion.

| Name. | Missing. | Interned. | | Repatriated. |
|---|---|---|---|---|
| Lieut. A. HOWARTH. | 27/7/16 | Holland | 15/6/18 | 22/11/18 |
| 2/Lt. R. W. CLARKSON. | 3/5/17 | | | 19/4/18 |
| 2/Lt. N. H. PRIDAY. | 3/5/17 | | | 6/12/18 |
| 2/Lt. O. H. STAFF. | 3/5/17 | Switzerland | 27/12/17 | 6/12/18 |

### 20th Battalion.

| Name. | Missing. | Interned. | | Repatriated. |
|---|---|---|---|---|
| Lieut. L. C. WATSON. | 28/7/16 | Holland | 15/6/18 | 27/11/18 |

\* Attached from A.S.C.
† Attached from East Yorkshire Regiment.     ‡ Attached from Durham L.I.

## EAST YORKSHIRE REGIMENT.

### 1st Battalion.

| Name. | Missing. | Interned. | Repatriated. |
|---|---|---|---|
| Capt. C. L. MacMAHON. | 22/3/18 | | 25/12/18 |
| 2/Lt. N. E. GASSON. | 22/3/18 | | 13/1/19 |
| 2/Lt. G. R. WARE. | 17/4/18 | | 11/12/18 |
| Capt. W. F. SLEATH. | 24/4/18 | | 2/12/18 |
| Capt. F. L. BALL. | 24/4/18 | | –/12/18 |
| 2/Lt. W. E. WHITLEY. | 24/4/18 | | 31/12/18 |
| 2/Lt. A. TATLOW. | 24/4/18 | | 6/12/18 |
| 2/Lt. H. T. STEPHENS. | 24/4/18 | | 2/12/18 |
| 2/Lt. S. COVERDALE. | 24/4/18 | | 2/12/18 |
| 2/Lt. Lt. S. A. FARMER. | 24/4/18 | | 2/12/18 |
| 2/Lt. E. H. HARDY. | 24/4/18 | | 29/11/18 |
| 2/Lt. P. WALLIS. | 24/4/18 | | –/12/18 |
| 2/Lt. G. W. WISBEY. | 24/4/18 | | 2/12/18 |
| 2/Lt. F. A. TOOGOOD. | 24/4/18 | | –/12/18 |
| 2/Lt. T. G. MAYHEW. | 24/4/18 | | 1/12/18 |
| Capt. E. B. ROBINSON. | 26/4/18 | | 2/12/18 |
| *Lieut. O. GREENWOOD. | 27/5/18 | | –/1/19 |
| 2/Lt. A. D. ROBINSON. | 27/5/18 | | 6/1/19 |
| 2/Lt. B. WAHL. | 27/5/18 | | 28/12/18 |
| 2/Lt. P. L. WRIGHT. | 27/5/18 | | 6/1/19 |
| 2/Lt. A. J. BOARDMAN. | 27/5/18 | | –/12/18 |
| *2/Lt. N. SPEEDY. | 27/5/18 | | 25/12/18 |
| *Lieut. K. E. BLACK. | 10/9/18 | | 29/11/18 |
| *Lieut. H. H. SCOBY. | 10/9/18 | | 13/12/18 |
| 2/Lt. J. WALKER. | 10/9/18 | | 29/11/18 |
| 2/Lt. F. O. RIDEOUT. | 10/9/18 | | 29/11/19 |

### 4th Battalion.

| Name. | Missing. | Interned. | Repatriated. |
|---|---|---|---|
| 2/Lt. B. V. HILDYARD. | 23/4/17 | | 31/12/18 |
| 2/Lt. F. STEVENSON. | 23/4/17 | | 30/12/18 |
| 2/Lt. W. C. WALGATE. | 23/4/17 | | 30/12/18 |
| 2/Lt. R. DUGGLEBY. | 27/6/17 | Switzerland 27/12/17 | 24/3/18 |
| Capt. T. J. MORRILL. | 28/6/17 | | 2/1/19 |
| 2/Lt. F. LINSLEY. | 28/6/17 | | 6/12/18 |
| Lieut. G. T. HOLLIS. | 22/3/18 | | 25/12/18 |
| 2/Lt. H. NEEDHAM. | 22/3/18 | | 2/1/19 |
| 2/Lt. C. R. INGHAM. | 22/3/18 | | 17/12/18 |
| 2/Lt. R. E. HATFIELD. | 22/3/18 | | 28/11/18 |
| 2/Lt. G. F. STEPHENSON. | 23/3/18 | | 12/10/18 |
| 2/Lt. S. B. WILSON. | 25/3/18 | | 18/12/18 |
| 2/Lt. C. W. PRETTY. | 26/3/18 | | 8/12/18 |
| Capt. C. M. SLACK. | 8/4/18 | | 28/11/18 |
| 2/Lt. R. THOMPSON. | 8–17/4/18 | | 28/11/18 |
| 2/Lt. A. T. WOODCOCK. | 8–17/4/18 | (*Died 4/6/18 at Cologne*). | |
| Major H. B. JACKSON. | 10/4/18 | | –/12/18 |
| †Major H. R. HASLETT. | 27/5/18 | | 18/12/18 |
| Capt. E. JOHNSON. | 27/5/18 | | –/12/18 |
| Capt. E. LAVERACK. | 27/5/18 | | 6/12/18 |
| ‡Lieut. E. WILLISON. | 27/5/18 | | 28/1/19 |
| Lieut. W. E. HEWAT. | 27/5/18 | | 31/12/18 |
| Lieut. C. S. JOHNSON. | 27/5/18 | | 31/12/18 |
| †Lieut. J. F. STEVENSON. | 27/5/18 | | –/12/18 |
| †Lieut. P. S. MURRAY. | 27/5/18 | | 31/12/18 |
| †2/Lt. T. K. DIGBY. | 27/5/18 | | 21/1/19 |

*Attached from Yorkshire Regiment. †Attached from Royal Irish Rifles.
‡Attached from Durham L.I.

## EAST YORKSHIRE REGIMENT—continued.
### 4th Battalion—continued.

| Name. | Missing. | Interned. | Repatriated. |
|---|---|---|---|
| †2/Lt. A. McB. SMITH. | 27/5/18 | | —/12/18 |
| †2/Lt. A. G. V. MARSH. | 27/5/18 | | 18/12/18 |
| †2/Lt. B. C. BINER. | 27/5/18 | (Died 21/7/18). | |
| 2/Lt. H. R. HOLLIS. | 27/5/18 | | 31/12/18 |
| 2/Lt. D. G. DANN. | 27/5/18 | | 31/12/18 |
| 2/Lt. J. W. CAMPBELL. | 27/5/18 | | 13/12/18 |
| 2/Lt. E. C. BROWN. | 27/5/18 | | —/12/18 |
| 2/Lt. S. F. BASTOW. | 27/5/18 | | —/12/18 |
| 2/Lt. W. J. WALKER. | 27/5/18 | | —/12/18 |
| 2/Lt. W. C. WADDINGTON. | 27/5/18 | (Died 3/7/18 at Cassel). | |
| 2/Lt. A. V. THRUSTLE. | 27/5/18 | | —/12/18 |

### 5th Battalion.

| Name. | Missing. | Interned. | Repatriated. |
|---|---|---|---|
| Capt. C. F. DICKINSON. | 9/4/18 | | 18/12/18 |

### 6th Battalion.

| Name. | Missing. | Interned. | Repatriated. |
|---|---|---|---|
| *Capt. F. W. LAWE. | 10/4/18 | | 1/12/18 |

### 7th Battalion.

| Name. | Missing. | Interned. | Repatriated. |
|---|---|---|---|
| 2/Lt. W. CLARKSON. | 23/2/16 | | 14/12/18 |
| Capt. J. HIRST. | 24/3/18 | | —/12/18 |
| Lieut. N. GIBSON. | 24/3/18 | | 18/12/18 |
| 2/Lt. H. F. ALLEN. | 25/3/18 | | 25/12/18 |
| 2/Lt. E. G. PICKERING. | 25/3/18 | | 25/12/18 |

### 8th Battalion.

| Name. | Missing. | Interned. | Repatriated. |
|---|---|---|---|
| 2/Lt. J. M. LAMB. | 15/3/17 | | 4/1/19 |
| 2/Lt. G. F. BUCKLAND. | 26/9/17 | Switzerland 3/8/18 | 6/12/18 |

### 10th Battalion.

| Name. | Missing. | Interned. | Repatriated. |
|---|---|---|---|
| Capt. S. E. JONES. | 27/2/17 | Switzerland 27/12/18 | 24/3/18 |
| Lieut. D. R. MORRISH. | 3/5/17 | | 19/12/18 |
| 2/Lt. L. M. BUTT. | 3/5/17 | | 31/12/18 |
| 2/Lt. G. AKESTER. | 3/5/17 | | 17/12/18 |
| Lieut. J. H. LAWES. | 3/11/17 | | 3/12/18 |
| 2/Lt. A. F. W. MARSHALL. | 15/8/18 | (Died 26/9/18 at Karlsruhe). | |

### 11th Battalion.

| Name. | Missing. | Interned. | Repatriated. |
|---|---|---|---|
| 2/Lt. R. WOOLCOTT. | 3/5/17 | Switzerland 27/12/17 | 9/12/18 |
| 2/Lt. E. WRIGHT. | 27/3/18 | | 25/12/18 |
| 2Lt. R. F. PITZ. | 27/3/18 | | 29/11/18 |
| Capt. H. A. C. FITZPATRICK. | 10/4/18 | | 18/12/18 |
| Major C. W. WAITE. | 12/4/18 | (Died 31/1/19). | —/12/18 |
| Major L. A. CATTLEY. | 12/4/18 | | 29/12/18 |
| Lieut. F. G. NICHOLS. | 12/4/18 | | 31/12/18 |
| Lieut. G. SUTHRIEN. | 12/4/18 | | 31/12/18 |
| Lieut. C. GOUGH. | 8/9/18 | | |
| ‡2/Lt. G. W. KOPLIK. | 28/9/18 | | 13/12/18 |

### 12th Battalion.

| Name. | Missing. | Interned. | Repatriated. |
|---|---|---|---|
| 2/Lt. C. FENWICK. | 3/5/17 | | 4/1/19 |
| 2/Lt. E. P. COOPER. | 3/5/17 | Switzerland 24/4/18 | 9/12/18 |

\* Attached Portuguese Mission.     † Attached from Royal Irish Rifles.
‡ Attached T.M.B.

## EAST YORKSHIRE REGIMENT—continued.
### 13th Battalion.

| Name. | Missing. | Interned. | Repatriated. |
|---|---|---|---|
| Capt. R. M. WOOLLEY. | 13/11/16 | | 6/1/19 |
| 2/Lt. C. CLOVER. | 13/11/16 | | 6/1/19 |
| 2/Lt. E. G. BRINDLEY. | 13/11/16 | | 18/12/18 |
| 2/Lt. W. J. LUCAS. | 10/4/18 | | 25/12/18 |

### 15th Battalion.

| Name. | Missing. | Interned. | Repatriated. |
|---|---|---|---|
| 2/Lt. F. CAIRNS. | 18/9/18 | | 8/12/18 |

## BEDFORDSHIRE REGIMENT.
### 1st and 2nd Battalions.

| Name. | Missing. | Interned. | | Repatriated. |
|---|---|---|---|---|
| Lieut. W. WAGSTAFF. | 9/9/14 | Holland | 22/1/18 | 18/11/18 |
| Capt. A. B. LEMON. | 14/11/14 | Holland | 24/2/18 | 18/11/18 |
| Lieut. C. POPE. | 14/11/14 | Holland | 24/1/18 | 18/11/18 |
| 2/Lt. I. T. M. COLLINS. | 28/7/17 | | | 3/6/18 |
| 2/Lt. F. E. THOMPSON. | 21/3/18 | | | 11/12/18 |
| Capt. F. W. PARKER. | 23/3/18 | | | 1/12/18 |
| 2/Lt. W. R. SHAW. | 23/3/18 | | | 14/12/18 |
| Lieut. C. HAYWOOD. | 25/3/18 | | | 15/12/18 |
| Capt. G. A. ANSTEE. | 28/3/18 | | | 1/12/18 |
| *Lieut. H. W. H. DRUITT. | 26/4/18 | | | 28/11/18 |
| *2/Lt. A. H. CHANDLER. | 26/4/18 | | | 3/12/18 |
| Lieut. A. H. BAKER. | 9/5/18 | | | 6/12/18 |
| Lieut. A. F. WOODFORD. | 6/8/18 | | | –/12/18 |
| Lieut. D. D. WARREN. | 6/8/18 | | | –/12/18 |
| 2/Lt. R. W. SMITH. | 21/9/18 | | | 8/12/18 |

### 4th Battalion.

| Name. | Missing. | Repatriated. |
|---|---|---|
| 2/Lt. V. B. SHOTT. | 11/2/17 | 15/12/18 |
| Lieut. F. A. GIRLING. | 23/3/16 | 23/10/18 |
| 2/Lt. MAX KRUGER. | 23/3/18 | 29/11/18 |
| 2/Lt. E. M. L. GREEN. | 24/3/18 | 25/12/18 |
| 2/Lt. R. G. COWELL. | 25/3/18 | –/12/18 |

### 5th Battalion.

| Name. | Missing. | Repatriated. |
|---|---|---|
| Lieut. E. W. HASTINGS. | 27/8/18 | 13/12/18 |

### 6th Battalion.

| Name. | Missing. | Repatriated. |
|---|---|---|
| Lieut. J. H. A. LOVE. | 28/4/17 | 30/12/18 |

### 7th Battalion.

| Name. | Missing. | Repatriated. |
|---|---|---|
| 2/Lt. E. J. F. SCOTT. | 28/4/17 | 6/12/18 |
| 2/Lt. R. A. STILES. | 22/3/18 | 29/11/18 |

## LEICESTERSHIRE REGIMENT.
### 1st Battalion.

| Name. | Missing. | Repatriated. |
|---|---|---|
| Capt. J. H. JOHN. | 21/3/18 | 29/11/18 |
| Capt. F. E. SHELTON. | 21/3/18 | 29/11/18 |
| Lieut. S. C. LAWRENCE. | 21/3/18 | 4/12/18 |
| Lieut. A. C. ANSELL. | 21/3/18 | 17/12/18 |
| Lieut. J. O. VESSEY. | 21/3/18 | 17/12/18 |
| 2/Lt. T. C. A. CLARKE. | 21/3/18 | 18/12/18 |
| 2/Lt. C. H. WATSON. | 21/3/18 | 18/12/18 |
| 2/Lt. M. MILLS. | 21/3/18 | 29/11/18 |
| 2/Lt. A. N. BAGSHAW. | 21/3/18 | 25/12/18 |
| 2/Lt. L. W. E. RUSSELL. | –/3/18 | (*Died* 1/11/18 at Mainz). |

*Attached from 2nd Wiltshire Regiment.

## LEICESTERSHIRE REGIMENT—continued.

### 4th Battalion.

| Name. | Missing. | Interned. | Repatriated. |
|---|---|---|---|
| Capt. F. S. PARR. | 11–13/10/15 | Holland  —/4/18 | 18/11/18 |
| Lieut. L. B. LAMBIE. | 22/4/17 | | 14/12/18 |
| Capt. P. K. BLUNT. | 24/3/18 | | 2/12/18 |
| Capt. G. B. WILLIAMS. | 25/3/18 | | 1/12/18 |
| Lieut. C. D. BROWN. | 25/3/18 | | 25/12/18 |
| 2/Lt. E. ROBERTS. | 25/3/18 | | 1/12/18 |
| 2/Lt. A. G. RALEIGH. | 25/3/18 | | 29/11/18 |

### 5th Battalion.

| Name. | Missing. | Interned. | Repatriated. |
|---|---|---|---|
| Lieut. L. H. PEARSON. | 6/8/18 | | 19/1/19 |

### 6th Battalion.

| Name. | Missing. | Interned. | Repatriated. |
|---|---|---|---|
| 2/Lt. M. J. S. DYSON. | 21/3/18 | | 18/12/18 |
| *2/Lt. B. L. ASQUITH. | 21/3/18 | | 17/12/18 |
| Lieut. W. E. MAJOR. | 22/3/18 | | 11/12/18 |
| 2/Lt. J. H. SMEDLEY. | 22/3/18 | | 28/11/18 |
| 2/Lt. N. S. HOGGARTH. | 22/3/18 | (*Died* 30/5/18 at Cassel). | |
| 2/Lt. E. G. LANE-ROBERTS. | 22/3/18 | | 18/12/18 |
| Capt. G. B. F. RUDD. | 27/4/18 | | 18/12/18 |
| 2/Lt. P. J. STRONG. | 27/4/18 | | 18/12/18 |
| †2/Lt. A. F. CLARK. | 27/5/18 | | —/12/18 |
| †2/Lt. C. W. MARTEN. | 27/5/18 | | 14/12/18 |
| Lieut. W. T. STEVENS. | 28/5/18 | | 3/1/19 |
| 2/Lt. W. A. BAGULEY. | 28/5/18 | | 6/1/19 |
| ‡Lt.-Col. M. C. MARTYN. | 25/8/18 | | 13/12/18 |

### 7th Battalion.

| Name. | Missing. | Interned. | Repatriated. |
|---|---|---|---|
| 2/Lt. W. STUBBS. | 22/3/18 | | 11/12/18 |
| 2/Lt. B. J. S. DODRIDGE. | 22/3/18 | | 28/11/18 |
| 2/Lt. C. G. SCARFE. | 22/3/18 | | 17/12/18 |
| 2/Lt. W. WOOD. | 22/3/18 | | 17/12/18 |
| 2/Lt. W. WATKINSON. | 22/3/18 | | 11/12/18 |
| 2/Lt. W. HOWITT. | 22/3/18 | | —/12/18 |
| 2/Lt. A. D. GODFREY. | 24/3/18 | | 25/12/18 |
| Capt. H. H. HEMPHILL. | 27/5/18 | | —/12/18 |
| Capt. W. A. EVANS. | 27/5/18 | | —/12/18 |
| Lieut. J. S. SHARPE. | 27/5/18 | | 31/12/18 |
| 2/Lt. J. ROYLE. | 27/5/18 | | 6/1/19 |
| 2/Lt. St. G. REDHEAD. | 27/5/18 | | 3/1/19 |
| *2/Lt. A. W. ACOCKS. | 27/5/18 | | 25/12/18 |
| *2/Lt. F. N. MORGAN. | 27/5/18 | | 2/1/19 |
| 2/Lt. F. B. STEVENSON. | 27/5/18 | | 31/12/18 |
| 2/Lt. H. J. CRESSWELL. | 27/5/18 | | 2/1/19 |
| 2/Lt. J. H. BONSHOR. | 27/5/18 | | 2/1/19 |

### 8th Battalion.

| Name. | Missing. | Interned. | Repatriated. |
|---|---|---|---|
| 2/Lt. F. W. H. CLARKE. | 3/5/17 | | 2/1/19 |
| 2/Lt. W. HARRIS. | 3/5/17 | | 31/12/18 |
| 2/Lt. E. B. PITTS. | 3/5/17 | (*Died* 17/5/17 at Bouchain). | |
| 2/Lt. E. H. BONE. | 20/3/18 | | 18/12/18 |
| 2/Lt. S. HOBSON. | 21/3/18 | | 18/12/18 |
| Lt.-Col. A. T. LE M. UTTERSON. | 22/3/18 | | 18/12/18 |

*Attached from Manchesters.     †Attached from Gloucesters.
‡Attached from Sherwood Foresters.

## LEICESTERSHIRE REGIMENT.—continued.
### 8th Battalion.

| Name. | Missing. | Interned. | Repatriated. |
|---|---|---|---|
| **Capt. R. M. R. DAVISON. | 22/3/18 | | 11/12/18 |
| 2/Lt. H. M. JACKSON. | 22//318 | | 11/12/18 |
| 2/Lt. H. JASPER. | 26/5/18 | | 5/12/18 |
| Capt. W. S. MURPHY. | 27/5/18 | | 2/1/19 |
| Lieut. A. HALKYARD. | 27/5/18 | | 25/12/18 |
| Lieut. E. H. WRIGGLESWORTH. | 27/5/18 | | 6/1/19 |
| *Lieut. W. SEAMAN. | 27/5/18 | | 26/12/18 |
| 2/Lt. C. S. DEARMAN. | 27/5/18 | | 6/1/19 |
| 2/Lt. A. H. T. CROWSON. | 27/5/18 | | 2/1/19 |
| 2/Lt. H. CARDALL. | 27/5/18 | | 2/1/19 |
| 2/Lt. E. W. ROGERSON. | 27/5/18 | | 11/12/18 |
| 2/Lt. A. E. RAYNER. | 27/5/18 | | 6/1/19 |
| 2/Lt. H. H. METTERS. | 27/5/18 | | 31/12/18 |
| 2/Lt. F. LARDER. | 27/5/18 | | 31/12/18 |
| 2/Lt. W. HANDFORD. | 27/5/18 | | -/12/18 |
| 2/Lt. J. H. GREEN. | 27/5/18 | | -/12/18 |
| 2/Lt. F. HARPER. | 27/5/18 | | 2/1/19 |

### 9th Battalion.

| Name. | Missing. | Interned. | Repatriated. |
|---|---|---|---|
| Capt. H. E. MILBURN. | 3/5/17 | | 16/1/19 |
| 2/Lt. E. E. RAWLINGS. | 3/5/17 | | 17/12/18 |

### 11th Battalion.

| Name. | Missing. | Interned. | Repatriated. |
|---|---|---|---|
| Lieut. A. L. HICKS. | 21/3/18 | (*Died* 4/4/18 at Auberchicourt). | |

## ROYAL IRISH REGIMENT.
### 1st and 2nd Battalions.

| Name. | Missing. | Interned. | | Repatriated. |
|---|---|---|---|---|
| Lieut. C. G. MAGRATH. | 24/8/14 | Holland | 6/2/18 | -/-/18 |
| Lieut. A. E. B. ANDERSON. | 24/8/14 | Holland | 6/2/18 | 18/11/18 |
| Capt. J. B. GEORGE. | 10/9/14 | | | 11/9/17 |
| Capt. J. FITZGERALD. | 10/9/14 | Holland | 6/2/18 | 19/7/18 |
| Capt. G. ELLIOTT. | 10/9/14 | Holland | 22/1/18 | 18/11/18 |
| Lieut. R. E. G. PHILLIPS. | 10/9/14 | | | 13/9/17 |
| Lieut. A. FRAZER. | 10/9/14 | Holland | 6/2/18 | 22/11/18 |
| Lieut. C. F. T. O'B. FFRENCH. | 10/9/14 | Holland | 29/12/17 | 18/11/18 |
| Lieut. H. G. O. DOWNING. | 10/10/14 | | | 13/9/17 |
| Capt. J. A. SMITHWICK. | 19/10/14 | | | 24/8/15 |
| | | (*Died* 10/11/15 in England). | | |
| Capt. G. O. E. FURNELL. | 19/10/14 | Switzerland | 9/12/17 | 14/6/18 |
| Lieut. K. FOULKES. | 19/10/14 | Switzerland | 27/12/17 | 2/6/18 |
| 2/Lt. W. E. BREDIN. | 19/10/14 | Holland | 6/2/18 | 18/11/18 |
| 2/Lt. T. NICHOLSON. | 19/10/14 | Holland | 6/2/18 | 16/8/18 |
| 2/Lt. J. MCLOUGHLIN. | 19/10/14 | Holland | 6/2/18 | 18/11/18 |
| Capt. M. C. C. HARRISON. | 20/11/14 | | | 13/9/17 |
| Capt. E. D. HANLEY. | 21/5/15 | | | 14/9/17 |
| Lieut. A. R. ROYALL. | 3/9/16 | | | 13/9/17 |
| 2/Lt. J. P. CORCORAN. | 30/10/16 | Holland | 15/4/18 | 2/7/18 |
| *Lieut. E. G. LEE. | 9/4/17 | | | 14/12/18 |
| Capt. A. S. PIM. | 21/3/18 | | | 14/12/18 |
| Lieut. H. JORDAN. | 21/3/18 | | | -/12/18 |
| Lieut. V. W. F. HICKS. | 21/3/18 | | | 28/11/18 |
| Lieut. J. A. MOUAT-BIGGS. | 21/3/18 | (*Died* 22/3/18 at Clary). | | |
| Lieut. W. J. ROCHE. | 21/3/18 | | | 5/12/18 |
| Lieut. J. J. DONOVAN. | 21/3/18 | | | 14/12/18 |

** Attached from North Staffs.
*Attached from A.S.C.

## ROYAL IRISH REGIMENT—continued.
### 1st and 2nd Battalions.

| Name. | Missing. | Interned. | Repatriated. |
|---|---|---|---|
| Lieut. V. FARQUHARSON-HICKS. | 21/3/18 | | 28/11/18 |
| *2/Lt. C. H. SMITH. | 21/3/18 | | 18/12/18 |
| **2/Lt. W. N. ABBOTT. | 21/3/18 | | 18/12/18 |
| 2/Lt. J. M. TERRY. | 21/3/18 | | 14/12/18 |
| 2/Lt. J. G. MAHAFFY. | 21/3/18 | | 28/11/18 |
| 2/Lt. J. T. FARRELL. | 21/3/18 | | 28/11/18 |
| 2/Lt. L. O'KEEFE. | 21/3/18 | | 3/12/18 |
| 2/Lt. J. BAILEY. | 21//318 | | |
| *2/Lt. M. MULCAHY. | 22/3/18 | | 25/12/18 |
| 2/Lt. W. R. SIMMONS. | 25/8/18 | | 5/1/19 |

### 6th Battalion.

| Name. | Missing. | Interned. | Repatriated. |
|---|---|---|---|
| 2/Lt. R. J. KELLY. | 21/8/16 | | 7/1/18 |

### 7th Battalion.

| Name. | Missing. | Interned. | Repatriated. |
|---|---|---|---|
| Major J. D. MORROGH. | 21/3/18 | | 15/12/18 |
| Major FELIX CALL. | 21/3/18 | | 17/12/18 |
| Capt. A. C. PATMAN. | 21/3/18 | | 2/12/18 |
| Capt. P. N. SMITH. | 21/3/18 | | 14/12/18 |
| *Capt J. M. WARDELL. | 21/3/18 | | 6/12/18 |
| *Lieut. W. S. BARRETT. | 21/3/18 | | 3/12/18 |
| *Lieut. J. S. MATTHEWS. | 21/3/18 | | 14/12/18 |
| Lieut. P. J. GIBSON. | 21/3/18 | | –/12/18 |
| *2/Lt. A. B. HADDEN. | 21/3/18 | | 14/12/18 |
| *2/Lt. J. A. WATTS. | 21/3/18 | | 20/12/18 |
| *2/Lt. R. CONWAY. | 21/3/18 | | 25/12/18 |
| 2/Lt. H. J. JONES. | 21/3/18 | (*Died* 29/3/18 at Bertry). | |
| 2/Lt. H. E. ROBINSON. | 21/3/18 | | 17/12/18 |
| 2/Lt. C. J. BAILEY. | 21/3/18 | | 8/12/18 |
| 2/Lt. R. W. M. HENDERSON. | 17/9/18 | | 28/11/18 |

### 8th Battalion.

| Name. | Missing. | Interned. | Repatriated. |
|---|---|---|---|
| Capt. T. BEDELL-SIVWRIGHT. | 5/9/18 | | 28/11/18 |
| Lieut. S. RIVERS. | 5/9/18 | | 29/11/18 |
| †Lieut. A. PATERSON. | 5/9/18 | | 29/11/18 |

## YORKSHIRE REGIMENT.
### 1st and 2nd Battalions.

| Name. | Missing. | Interned. | | Repatriated. |
|---|---|---|---|---|
| Capt. R. LEDGARD. | 10/9/14 | Holland | 5/1/18 | 12/11/18 |
| Capt. W. WORSLEY. | 30/10/14 | Holland | 24/2/18 | 22/1/19 |
| Lieut. R. H. MIDDLEDITCH. | 30/10/14 | Switzerland | 12/8/16 | 9/12/18 |
| Lieut. A. C. BENTLEY. | 26/9/15 | | | 6/1/19 |
| Lieut. W. GRAY. | 26/9/15 | Holland | 19/4/18 | 18/11/18 |
| 2/Lt. J. C. McINTYRE. | 26/9/15 | (*Died*). | | |

### 2nd Battalion.

| Name. | Missing. | Interned. | Repatriated. |
|---|---|---|---|
| 2/Lt. J. J. COWNLEY. | 21/3/18 | | 29/11/18 |
| 2/Lt. G. F. LOCKWOOD. | 21/3/18 | | 29/11/18 |
| 2/Lt. W. VASEY. | 21/3/18 | | 18/12/18 |
| 2/Lt. J. W. WALKER. | 21/3/18 | | 13/12/18 |
| 2/Lt. N. MORANT. | 22/3/18 | (*Died* 27/3/18 at St. Quentin). | |
| 2/Lt. C. A. BARKER. | 23/3/18 | | 11/12/18 |
| ‡Lieut. E. R. HARBOUR. | 25/4/18 | | 3/12/18 |
| Capt. C. DAVISON. | 8/5/18 | | 1/12/18 |
| 2/Lt. J. E. HIBBERT. | 8/5/18 | | 13/12/18 |
| Lieut. F. TENNEY. | 6/11/18 | | 11/12/18 |

*Attached from South Irish Horse.
‡Attached T.M.B.
†Attached from Northumberland Fusiliers.
**Attached from 3rd Connaught Rangers.

## YORKSHIRE REGIMENT—Continued.

### 4th Battalion.

| Name. | Missing. | Interned. | Repatriated. |
|---|---|---|---|
| Capt. A. R. POWEYS. | 23/3/18 | | 29/11/18 |
| 2/Lt. W. THORNTON. | 25/3/18 | | 25/12/18 |
| Major L. NEWCOMBE. | 27/5/18 | | 30/12/18 |
| Capt. A. L. GORING. | 27/5/18 | | 30/12/18 |
| Capt. R. M. HOWES. | 27/5/18 | | 30/12/18 |
| Lieut. H. R. B. BAILEY. | 27/5/18 | | —/12/18 |
| Lieut. R. GATES. | 27/5/18 | | 14/12/18 |
| Lieut. C. K. KELK. | 27/5/18 | | —/12/18 |
| Lieut. G. C. W. MacKAY. | 27/5/18 | | 13/12/18 |
| Lieut. V. W. W. S. PURCELL. | 27/5/18 | | —/12/18 |
| Lieut. T. A. ROBSON. | 27/5/18 | | 13/12/18 |
| Lieut. J. C. STORY. | 27/5/18 | | 13/12/18 |
| 2/Lt. A. W. APPLEBY. | 27/5/18 | | —/12/18 |
| 2/Lt. A. E. BEDFORD. | 27/5/18 | | 25/12/18 |
| 2/Lt. H. A. CLIDERO. | 27/5/18 | | 13/12/18 |
| 2/Lt. J. H. DERRETT. | 27/5/18 | | 25/12/18 |
| *2/Lt. J. A. A. FLYNN. | 27/5/18 | | 14/12/18 |
| 2/Lt. G. A. GREEN. | 27/5/18 | | 18/12/18 |
| 2/Lt. W. R. HOLMES. | 27/5/18 | | —/12/18 |
| 2/Lt. C. W. STIRK. | 27/5/18 | | —/12/18 |
| 2/Lt. H. E. WEBB. | 27/5/18 | | 13/12/18 |

### 5th Battalion.

| Name. | Missing. | Interned. | Repatriated. |
|---|---|---|---|
| 2/Lt. G. F. ROGERS. | 24/4/17 | | 2/1/19 |
| Lieut. A. HEPTON. | 22/3/18 | (*Died* 13/4/18 at St. Quentin). | |
| †Lieut. H. P. GREGORY. | 25/3/18 | | 1/12/19 |
| 2/Lt. W. N. PEARSON. | 25/3/18 | | 29/12/18 |
| 2/Lt. A. H. STRONG. | 26/3/18 | | 13/12/18 |
| Lieut. W. H. ALLIS. | 8–17/4/18 | | 25/12/18 |
| Lieut. J. G. CROSS. | 9/4/18 | | 1/12/18 |
| 2/Lt. T. A. WILLIAMS. | 12/4/18 | | 11/12/18 |
| Capt. H. G. AMIS. | 27/5/18 | | 26/12/18 |
| Capt. G. A. MAXWELL. | 27/5/18 | | 30/12/18 |
| Capt. G. MOSELEY. | 27/5/18 | | 30/12/18 |
| Capt. G. THOMPSON. | 27/5/18 | | 1/1/19 |
| Capt. E. H. WEIGHILL. | 27/5/18 | | 14/12/18 |
| Capt. A. S. WOOD. | 27/5/18 | | 30/12/18 |
| Lieut. G. W. COOPER. | 27/5/18 | | 30/12/18 |
| Lieut. H. W. KNIGHT. | 27/5/18 | | 1/1/19 |
| Lieut. E. A. LISTER. | 27/5/18 | | —/12/18 |
| Lieut. W. PATTERSON. | 27/5/18 | | —/12/18 |
| Lieut. C. B. R. REES. | 27/5/18 | | —/12/18 |
| Lieut. G. H. SMITH. | 27/5/18 | | 30/12/18 |
| Lieut. J. H. E. WINSTON. | 27/5/18 | | —/12/18 |
| 2/Lt. J. M. ATKINSON. | 27/5/18 | | —/12/18 |
| 2/Lt. F. BARROWCLIFF. | 27/5/18 | | —/12/18 |
| *2/Lt. T. J. CAVANAGH. | 27/5/18 | | 25/12/18 |
| *2/Lt. R. J. CHARTERS. | 27/5/18 | | 25/12/18 |
| 2/Lt. C. L. KING. | 27/5/18 | | —/12/18 |
| 2/Lt. P. LAWSON. | 27/5/18 | | —/12/18 |
| 2/Lt. H. T. ROBSON. | 27/5/18 | | —/12/18 |
| 2/Lt. L. RYMER. | 27/5/18 | | 30/12/18 |

*Attached from Royal Irish Rifles.
†Attached T.M.B.

## YORKSHIRE REGIMENT—Continued.

### 6th Battalion.

| Name. | Missing. | Interned. | Repatriated. |
|---|---|---|---|
| 2/Lt. W. A. BOOT. | 27/9/16 | | 4/1/19 |

### 10th Battalion.

| | | | |
|---|---|---|---|
| 2/Lt. F. E. STOKELD. | 7/5/18 | | 25/12/18 |

### 11th Battalion.

| | | | |
|---|---|---|---|
| 2/Lt. O. R. AGERSKOW. | 12/4/18 | | 18/12/18 |

### 12th Battalion.

| | | | |
|---|---|---|---|
| 2/Lt. H. D'A. CHAMPNEY. | 9/4/18 | (*Died* 29/4/18). | |
| Lieut. J. BINNS. | 11/4/18 | | 25/12/18 |

### 13th Battalion.

| | | | |
|---|---|---|---|
| 2/Lt. R. LANGLEY. | 27/9/16 | | 18/12/18 |
| Capt. J. H. G. BAYLES. | 23/11/17 | | 24/12/18 |
| 2/Lt. W. HARDWICK. | 23/11/17 | | 14/12/18 |
| 2/Lt. P. R. THOMPSON. | 23/11/17 | | 19/5/18 |
| Capt. R. G. De QUETTEVILLE. | 10/4/18 | | 28/11/18 |
| Lieut. L. G. COLLINS. | 10/4/18 | | –/12/18 |

## LANCASHIRE FUSILIERS.

### 1st and 2nd Battalions.

| | | | | |
|---|---|---|---|---|
| Capt. J. A. DAVENPORT. | 26/8/14 | Holland | 22/1/18 | 27/11/18 |
| Lieut. F. F. CORBETT-WINDER. | 25/9/14 | Holland | 22/1/18 | 18/11/18 |
| 2/Lt. H. S. CARTER. | 20/2/16 | Holland | 19/4/18 | 21/5/18 |
| Lieut. A. V. DAVIES. | 1/7/16 | Holland | 7/10/18 | 22/11/18 |
| 2/Lt. W. O. BOLTON. | 12/10/16 | | | 18/12/18 |
| 2/Lt. G. St. J. WRIGHT. | 3/5/17 | | | 4/1/19 |
| 2/Lt. J. H. STOTT. | 3/5/17 | | | 4/1/19 |
| 2/Lt. O. JAMES. | 3/5/17 | | | 29/11/18 |
| *2/Lt. J. ALLEN. | 3/5/17 | | | 29/11/18 |
| 2/Lt. E. J. TOWNLEY. | 31/5/17 | Switzerland | 27/12/17 | 24/3/18 |
| 2/Lt. A. M. THOMPSON. | 11/7/17 | (*Died* 31/7/17 at Douai). | | |
| Lieut. C. CARMODY. | 30/11/17 | | | 17/12/18 |
| Capt. J. H. SPENCER. | 12/4/18 | (*Died* 15/7/18 at Limburg). | | |
| 2/Lt. L. TAYLOR. | 12/4/18 | | | –/12/18 |
| 2/Lt. F. W. GOODWIN. | 13/4/18 | | | 29/12/18 |
| †2/Lt. C. V. LONGLAND. | 8/8/18 | | | 17/12/18 |

### 3rd Battalion.

| | | | |
|---|---|---|---|
| Lieut. J. R. WILKINSON. | 3/9/14 | (*Died* 20/5/16 at Gradenfrei). | |

### 5th Battalion.

| | | | | |
|---|---|---|---|---|
| 2/Lt. H. M. AINSCOW. | 28/6/16 | Holland | 16/5/18 | 4/10/18 |
| Lieut. R. YOUNG. | 31/7/17 | | | 14/12/18 |
| 2/Lt. V. A. TELFER. | 31/7/17 | | | 6/12/18 |
| 2/Lt. S. KIRKPATRICK. | 20/11/17 | (*Died* –/10/18 at Saarbrucken). | | |
| 2/Lt. C. J. LEWIS. | 21/3/18 | | | 3/12/18 |
| Capt. G. GRAY. | 26/3/18 | | | 8/12/18 |
| ‡Lieut. G. NICHOLSON. | 26/3/18 | | | 5/12/18 |
| 2/Lt. A. WALLACE. | 26/3/18 | | | 29/11/18 |
| 2/Lt. P. PLATT. | 26/3/18 | | | 1/12/18 |

*Attached from 1/5 South Lancs. †Attached from Lincolns.
‡Attached from York and Lancaster Regiment.

## LANCASHIRE FUSILIERS —Continued.

### 6th Battalion.

| Name. | Missing. | Interned. | Repatriated. |
|---|---|---|---|
| 2/Lt. F. C. NOXON. | 6/9/17 | | 17/12/18 |
| Major W. WIKE. | 21/3/18 | | 18/12/18 |
| Capt. J. L. LEE. | 21/3/18 | | 18/12/18 |
| Capt. F. A. H. BEALEY. | 21/3/18 | (*Died* at Bad Colberg). | |
| Lieut. E. ORMEROD. | 21/3/18 | | 10/12/18 |
| 2/Lt. I. SKENE. | 21/3/18 | (*Died* 13/4/18 at Valenciennes). | |
| 2/Lt. H. T. SMITH. | 21/3/18 | | 5/12/18 |
| 2/Lt. C. R. CURTIS. | 21/3/18 | | 5/12/18 |
| 2/Lt. V. DELANEY. | 21/3/18 | | 1/12/18 |
| 2/Lt. D. R. MacKAY. | 21/3/18 | | 18/12/18 |
| 2/Lt. H. HEWITT. | 21/3/18 | | 29/11/18 |
| Lieut. C. GRAY. | | | –/12/18 |
| Capt. L. M. ROBINSON. | 22/3/18 | | 10/12/18 |
| 2/Lt. C. H. VINES. | 27/3/18 | | 1/12/18 |
| Capt. J. F. U. GRIFFIN. | 6/9/17 | | 11/1/19 |

### 7th Battalion.

| Name. | Missing. | Interned. | Repatriated. |
|---|---|---|---|
| *Capt. S. E. REID. | 21/3/18 | | 5/12/18 |
| Capt. K. L. KIRK. | 21/3/18 | | 6/12/18 |
| Lieut. K. MUDIE. | 21/3/18 | | 2/12/18 |
| Lieut. C. H. KELSALL. | 21/3/18 | | 3/12/18 |
| 2/Lt. D. W. HOWARD. | 21/3/18 | | 18/12/18 |
| 2/Lt. B. FURRELL. | 21/3/18 | | 17/12/18 |
| 2/Lt. H. PALMER. | 21/3/18 | | 3/1/19 |
| 2/Lt. S. MARSHALL. | 21/3/18 | | |
| 2/Lt. H. W. CULLEN. | 21/3/18 | | 2/12/18 |
| 2/Lt. D. MARSHALL. | 21/3/18 | | 10/12/18 |
| 2/Lt. F. A. BROWN. | 21/3/18 | | 2/12/18 |
| 2/Lt. J. G. ANDERSON. | 21/3/18 | | 29/11/18 |
| 2/Lt. H. W. WALTON. | 21/3/18 | | 2/12/18 |
| 2/Lt. E. PHILLIPSON. | 21/3/18 | | 29/11/18 |
| 2/Lt. H. ROSS. | 21/3/18 | (*Died* 8/4/18 at Le Cateau). | |
| Lieut. H. N. APPLEFORD. | 26/3/18 | | 12/10/18 |
| †Lt.-Col. E. A. S. GELL. | 27/3/18 | | 25/12/18 |
| 2/Lt. A. G. CRUMP. | 27/3/18 | | 13/12/18 |

### 8th Battalion.

| Name. | Missing. | Interned. | Repatriated. |
|---|---|---|---|
| 2/Lt. J. C. COLLINGE. | 4/10/17 | (*Died* 25/10/17 at Hamburg). | |
| 2]Lt. G. E. POWELL. | 9/10/17 | | 3/12/18 |
| 2/Lt. J. C. J. TOOMER. | 2/2/18 | | 25/12/18 |
| ‡Lt.-Col. H. G. ROBERTS. | 21/3/18 | | 6/12/18 |
| †Lt.-Col. A. E. STOKES-ROBERTS. | 21/3/18 | | 11/1/19 |
| Major T. J. BIDDOLPH. | 21/3/18 | | –/11/18 |
| Capt. J. EDGAR. | 21/3/18 | | 2/12/18 |
| Capt. R. S. MORLEY. | 21/3/18 | | 9/12/18 |
| Capt. R. L. BUSBY. | 21/3/18 | | 29/11/18 |
| Lieut. G. H. YAPP. | 21/3/18 | | 2/12/18 |
| Lieut. J. A. HOLDSWORTH. | 21/3/18 | (*Died* 17/6/18 at Zwickau). | |
| Lieut. E. S. ELLWOOD. | 21/3/18 | | 10/12/18 |
| Lieut. H. HASTINGS. | 21/3/18 | | 3/12/18 |
| 2/Lt. G. LOFTHOUSE. | 21/3/18 | | 14/12/18 |
| 2/Lt. H. TYE. | 21/3/18 | | 3/12/18 |

*Attached from K.S.L.I.   †Attached from Royal Fusiliers.
‡Attached from South Lancs.   §Attached from Worcesters.

## LANCASHIRE FUSILIERS—Continued.
### 8th Battalion—continued.

| Name. | Missing. | Interned. | Repatriated. |
|---|---|---|---|
| 2/Lt. J. HOWARTH. | 21/3/18 | | 29/11/18 |
| 2/Lt. E. J. DUNN. | 21/3/18 | | 2/12/18 |
| 2/Lt. H. M. NEWTON. | 21/3/18 | | 17/12/18 |
| 2/Lt. C. E. PALK. | 21/3/18 | | 2/12/18 |
| *2/Lt. A. A. SIMPSON. | 21/3/18 | | 2/12/18 |
| 2/Lt. C. C. MOORE. | 21/3/18 | | 1/11/18 |
| 2/Lt. R. W. MABBETT. | 21/3/18 | | 2/12/18 |
| 2/Lt. J. BARLOW. | 21/3/18 | | 29/11/18 |
| 2/Lt. T. O. BOWEN. | 21/3/18 | | 2/12/18 |
| 2/Lt. G. MASSEY. | 26/3/18 | | 25/12/18 |
| 2/Lt. R. TOWERS. | 27/3/18 | | 18/12/18 |
| Capt. H. THRUSH. | 5/4/18 | | 29/11/18 |
| Lieut. J. H. RICK. | 5/4/18 | | —/12/18 |
| 2/Lt. J. G. LYMER. | 5/4/18 | | 29/11/18 |

### 9th Battalion.

| Name. | Missing. | Interned. | Repatriated. |
|---|---|---|---|
| Capt. E. H. DAVIES. | 28–30/9/16 | Holland 12/8/18 | 18/12/18 |
| 2/Lt. H. W. POTTER. | 28–30/9/16 | | 18/12/18 |

### 10th Battalion.

| Name. | Missing. | Interned. | Repatriated. |
|---|---|---|---|
| 2/Lt. G. BELL. | 1/2/17 | | 28/11/18 |
| Capt. A. J. BARROW. | 23/3/18 | (Died 24/6/18 at Cassel). | |
| 2/Lt. G. J. CUNNINGHAM. | 26/3/18 | | 25/12/18 |
| Lieut. C. MANSBRIDGE. | 4/6/18 | | 8/12/18 |
| 2/Lt. H. L. HEELIS. | 4/6/18 | | 21/1/19 |
| Capt. I. SANKEY. | 25/8/18 | | 28/11/18 |

### 11th Battalion.

| Name. | Missing. | Interned. | Repatriated. |
|---|---|---|---|
| 2/Lt. J. ADAMSON. | 23/12/17 | | 27/11/18 |
| 2/Lt. J. PORTEUS. | 23/3/18 | | 11/12/18 |
| 2/Lt. E. E. SHARP. | 23/3/18 | | 31/12/18 |
| Lt.-Col. E. C. de R. MARTIN. | 10/4/18 | | 11/1/19 |
| *Lt.-Col. G. P. POLLITT. | 27/5/18 | | 24/12/18 |
| Capt. C. M. NEWMAN. | 27/5/18 | | 24/12/18 |
| Lieut. F. EYRE. | 27/5/18 | | 14/12/18 |
| 2/Lt. E. A. NORTH. | 27/5/18 | | —/12/18 |
| †2/Lt. W. DALE. | 27/5/18 | | 14/12/18 |
| †2/Lt. D. R. AUTY. | 27/5/18 | | 13/1/19 |
| †2/Lt. G. A. BROADBENT. | 27/5/18 | | 18/12/18 |
| †2/Lt. J. W. BOTTOMLEY. | 27/5/18 | | 25/12/18 |
| †2/Lt. J. H. SMITH. | 27/5/18 | | —/12/18 |
| †2/Lt. F. H. GRAHAM. | 28/5/18 | | 31/12/18 |
| †2/Lt. J. A. PIGHILLS. | 28/5/18 | (Died 29/5/18 at Rheims). | |

### 15th Battalion.

| Name. | Missing. | Interned. | Repatriated. |
|---|---|---|---|
| ‡2/Lt. L. DE LOZEY. | 2/11/18 | | 9/12/18 |
| 2/Lt. E. H. EDWARDS. | 2/11/18 | | —/12/18 |
| 2/Lt. J. A. CLARK. | 2/11/18 | | 11/12/18 |
| 2/Lt. F. R. CROCKFORD. | 3/11/18 | | 4/12/18 |

### 16th Battalion.

| Name. | Missing. | Interned. | Repatriated. |
|---|---|---|---|
| 2/Lt. N. H. ANDERTON. | 11/3/16 | Holland 30/4/18 | 18/11/18 |
| Capt. F. F. WAUGH. | 3/7/18 | | —/12/18 |
| 2/Lt. N. J. GILLMORE. | 13/9/18 | | 16/12/18 |

*Attached T.M.B.
†Attached from R.E.
‡Attached from North Staffs.

## LANCASHIRE FUSILIERS—Continued.
### 17th Battalion.

| Name. | Missing. | Interned. | Repatriated. |
|---|---|---|---|
| Capt. J. M. COWAN. | 25/8/16 | | 18/12/18 |
| 2/Lt. E. C. WEBSTER. | 12/4/18 | | 1/12/18 |

### 18th Battalion.

| | | | |
|---|---|---|---|
| 2/Lt. P. TORRANCE. | 22/10/17 | | 5/11/18 |
| 2/Lt. L. G. WILSON. | 25/3/18 | | 4/12/18 |
| Lieut. H. B. ALMOND. | 1/6/18 | | 19/12/18 |

### 19th Battalion.

| | | | |
|---|---|---|---|
| Major J. AMBROSE-SMITH. | 25/4/18 | | 8/12/18 |
| Capt. H. W. HUXLEY. | 25/4/18 | | 8/12/18 |
| Lieut. H. B. CARTWRIGHT. | 25/4/18 | | –/12/18 |
| Lieut. F. R. MUTCH. | 25/4/18 | | 31/12/18 |
| Lieut. L. N. MIDDLETON. | 25/4/18 | | 11/12/18 |
| Lieut. R. MARRIOTT. | 25/4/18 | | 6/12/18 |
| 2/Lt. H. W. SMITH. | 25/4/18 | | 6/12/18 |
| 2/Lt. S. BELCHER. | 25/4/18 | | 4/12/18 |
| 2/Lt. J. BALL. | 25/4/18 | | 29/11/18 |
| 2/Lt. E. J. WILSON. | 25/4/18 | | 18/12/18 |
| 2/Lt. M. WALKER. | 25/4/18 | | 29/11/18 |
| 2/Lt. J. CROSBIE. | 25/4/18 | | –/12/18 |

### 20th Battalion.

| | | | |
|---|---|---|---|
| 2/Lt. H. BAKER. | 2/10/16 | | 30/12/18 |

### 23rd Battalion.

| | | | |
|---|---|---|---|
| 2/Lt. M. J. HENDERSON. | 8/8/18 | | 17/12/18 |
| 2/Lt. P. FARRELL. | 8/8/18 | | 18/12/18 |
| 2/Lt. G. S. CHARLTON. | 27/9/18 | | 8/12/18 |

## ROYAL SCOTS FUSILIERS.
### 1st Battalion.

| Name. | Missing. | Interned. | | Repatriated. |
|---|---|---|---|---|
| Capt. T. A. ROSE. | 10/9/14 | (*Died*). | | |
| Capt. R. W. S. STIVEN. | 10/9/14 | (*Died* –/9/15 at Mainz). | | |
| Lieut. Cecil GRAVES. | 10/9/14 | Holland | 5/1/18 | 15/12/18 |
| Major A. H. McGREGOR. | 30/10/14 | Switzerland | 9/12/17 | 24/3/18 |
| Capt. A. LE GALLAIS. | 30/10/14 | Switzerland | 9/12/17 | 9/12/18 |
| Capt. J. FLEETWOOD. | 8/11/14 | Holland | 24/2/18 | 28/11/18 |
| Capt. R. M. BURGOYNE. | 30/11/14 | Switzerland | 27/12/17 | 14/6/18 |
| Lieut. E. P. O. BOYLE. | 30/11/14 | Holland | 24/2/18 | 14/12/18 |
| Lieut. J. L. BOWEN. | 30/11/14 | Switzerland | 9/12/17 | 14/6/18 |
| Capt. F. JUDGE. | 15/12/14 | Holland | 24/2/18 | 23/9/18 |
| 2/Lt. A. G. LOCHHEAD. | 13/11/16 | | | 18/12/18 |
| 2/Lt. P. DOBIE. | 22/3/17 | | | 7/1/18 |
| 2/Lt. A. P. ORR. | 29/3/18 | | | 5/1/19 |
| 2/Lt. W. McMINN. | 10/4/18 | | | 1/12/18 |
| Capt. R. G. FERGUSON. | 18/5/18 | (*Died* 11/6/18 at Habourdin). | | |
| 2/Lt. R. A. GERSTENBERG. | 18/9/18 | | | 8/12/18 |

## ROYAL SCOTS FUSILIERS—continued.

### 2nd Battalion.

| Name. | Missing. | Interned. | | Repatriated. |
|---|---|---|---|---|
| Lieut. H. STEWART. | 30/10/14 | Switzerland | 9/12/17 | 14/6/18 |
| Lt.-Col. A. G. BAIRD-SMITH. | 14/12/14 | Holland | 24/2/18 | 17/11/18 |
| 2/Lt. P. McHUGH. | 1/8/16 | Holland | 17/6/18 | 22/11/18 |
| 2/Lt. J. McA. C. GRACIE. | 1/8/16 | Switzerland | 27/12/17 | 24/3/18 |
| 2/Lt. G. H. SLAUGHTER. | 1/8/16 | Switzerland | 9/12/17 | 24/3/18 |
| 2/Lt. G. DICEY. | 23/4/17 | | | 4/12/18 |
| 2/Lt. A. R. DOUGALL. | 25/3/18 | | | 25/12/18 |
| 2/Lt. W. TEMPLETON. | 26/3/18 | | | 18/12/18 |
| Lieut. F. W. FRANCIS. | 9/4/18 | | | 18/12/18 |

### 6th Battalion.

| Name. | Missing. | Interned. | | Repatriated. |
|---|---|---|---|---|
| Capt. G. ROBERTSON. | 25/9/15 | Holland | 10/4/18 | 18/11/18 |
| Capt. A. B. PURVES. | 25/9/15 | (*Died* 8/11/15 at Cologne). | | |
| 2/Lt. A. R. CARR. | 12/8/16 | Holland | 12/10/18 | 21/1/19 |

### 6/7th Battalion.

| Name. | Missing. | Interned. | | Repatriated. |
|---|---|---|---|---|
| 2/Lt. T. SMILLIE. | 21/3/18 | | | 2/12/18 |
| 2/Lt. E. McQUAID. | 21/3/18 | | | 19/12/18 |
| 2/Lt. G. P. CROCKETT. | 30/3/18 | | | 2/12/18 |
| 2/Lt. N. B. FIFE. | 21/4/18 | | | –/12/18 |

### 7th Battalion.

| Name. | Missing. | Interned. | | Repatriated. |
|---|---|---|---|---|
| 2/Lt. A. WEIR. | 21/3/18 | | | 2/12/18 |

## CHESHIRE REGIMENT.

### 1st and 2nd Battalions.

| Name. | Missing. | Interned. | | Repatriated. |
|---|---|---|---|---|
| Lt.-Col. D. C. BOGER. | 24/8/14 | Holland | 29/12/17 | 23/9/17 |
| Capt. W. G. R. ELLIOT. | 31/8/14 | Holland | 29/12/17 | 30/11/18 |
| Capt. A. J. L. DYER. | 31/8/14 | Holland | 29/12/17 | 31/12/18 |
| Capt. C. J. JOLLIFFE. | 31/8/14 | | | 13/9/17 |
| Capt. E. A. JACKSON. | 31/8/14 | Switzerland | 9/12/17 | 24/3/18 |
| Major B. CHETWYND-STAPYLTON. | 4/9/14 | Holland | 29/12/17 | 23/10/18 |
| Capt. B. E. MASSY. | 4/9/14 | Holland | 5/1/18 | 18/11/18 |
| Capt. C. A. K. MATTERSON. | 4/9/14 | Holland | 5/1/18 | 13/11/18 |
| Capt. C. H. RANDALL. | 4/9/14 | Holland | 29/12/17 | 4/10/18 |
| Capt. V. TAHOURDIN. | 10/9/14 | Switzerland | 9/12/17 | 14/6/18 |
| Capt. W. L. E. DUGMORE. | 11/9/14 | Holland | 29/12/17 | 18/8/18 |
| Lieut. W. L. STEWART. | 11/9/14 | Holland | 6/2/18 | 18/11/18 |
| Lieut. R. H. BOLTON. | 11/9/14 | Holland | 29/12/17 | 23/11/18 |
| Lieut. T. FAIRWEATHER. | 11/9/14 | Holland | 29/12/17 | 17/11/18 |
| Capt. S. BUTTERWORTH. | 12/10/14 | Holland | 6/2/18 | 18/11/18 |
| Major F. YOUNG. | 13/10/14 | | | 13/9/17 |
| Capt. H. N. HARRINGTON. | 13/10/14 | Switzerland | 9/12/17 | 14/6/18 |
| Lieut. W. THOMAS. | 13/10/14 | Holland | 29/12/17 | 22/11/18 |
| Capt. L. A. FORSTER. | 22/10/14 | (*Died*). | | |
| Capt. J. L. SHORE. | 22/10/14 | Switzerland | 9/12/17 | 4/3/19 |
| Lieut. G. W. LEICESTER. | 22/10/14 | Holland | 24/2/18 | 18/11/18 |
| Lieut. G. S. JACOBS. | 4/11/14 | Holland | 29/12/17 | 12/12/18 |
| Capt. E. R. HARBORD. | 13/11/14 | Switzerland | 9/12/17 | 24/3/18 |
| Lieut. B. V. HAYES-NEWINGTON. | 11/5/15 | Holland | 23/3/18 | 8/2/19 |
| Lieut. H. FORMAN. | 11/5/15 | | | 18/11/18 |
| Lieut. W. A. WARD. | 11/5/15 | | | 1/11/18 |
| *2/Lt. A. Q. ROBINSON. | 28/6/18 | | | 3/12/18 |

*Attached from Worcesters.

## CHESHIRE REGIMENT—Continued.

### 4th Battalion.

| Name. | Missing. | Interned. | Repatriated. |
|---|---|---|---|
| Lieut. H. R. WALL. | 10/4/18 | | 2/12/18 |

### 5th Battalion.

| | | | |
|---|---|---|---|
| Lieut. T. MOULTON. | 17/5/18 | | 31/12/18 |

### 6th Battalion.

| | | | |
|---|---|---|---|
| 2/Lt. S. KING. | 31/7/17 | | 19/7/18 |
| 2/Lt. G. B. JORDAN. | 27/5/18 | | 18/12/18 |

### 7th Battalion.

| | | | |
|---|---|---|---|
| 2/Lt. J. C. JONES. | 25/10/18 | | 24/11/18 |
| 2/Lt. A. BRADLEY. | 25/10/18 | | 24/11/18 |
| 2/Lt. W. W. DAVIES. | 25/10/18 | | 1/12/18 |

### 9th Battalion.

| | | | |
|---|---|---|---|
| Capt. J. A. BAIRD. | | | 18/12/18 |
| 2/Lt. G. H. VERITY. | 25/3/18 | | 26/12/18 |
| Lieut. G. W. DAY. | 31/5/18 | | 7/9/18 |

### 10th Battalion.

| | | | |
|---|---|---|---|
| *Lt.-Col. W. E. WILLIAMS. | 11/4/18 | | 29/11/18 |
| Capt. G. C. MEREDITH. | 11/4/18 | | 29/11/18 |
| Lieut. E. J. SAUNDERS. | 12/4/18 | | 29/11/18 |
| †2/Lt. H. G. EVANS. | 12/4/18 | | 1/12/18 |
| 2/Lt. E. M. GIBSON. | 26/4/18 | | 8/12/18 |
| 2/Lt. K. B. RALSTON. | 26/4/18 | | 12/10/18 |
| 2/Lt. S. A. ELLIS. | 27/5/18 | | 1/12/18 |
| 2/Lt. H. J. HOLLAMBY. | 27/5/18 | | 13/12/18 |
| ‡2/Lt. P. COOKSON. | 27/5/18 | | 13/12/18 |
| ‡2/Lt. W. P. HUNTER. | 27–30/5/18 | | 6/1/19 |

### 11th Battalion.

| | | | |
|---|---|---|---|
| 2/Lt. H. H. OWEN. | 22/3/18 | | 11/12/18 |
| 2/Lt. A. H. D. DUTTON. | 22/3/18 | | 29/11/18 |
| 2/Lt. E. F. BYRON. | 22/3/18 | | 29/11/18 |
| Lieut. E. C. DIXON. | 23/3/18 | | 29/11/18 |
| Lieut. A. H. KISSACK. | 23/3/18 | | 1/12/18 |
| §Lieut. W. A. WILLIAMS. | 23/3/18 | | 18/12/18 |
| 2/Lt. W. R. JONES. | 23/3/18 | | 11/12/18 |
| 2/Lt. J. W. FOSTER. | 23/3/18 | | 18/12/18 |
| 2/Lt. R. S. COOLE. | 23/3/18 | | 5/1/19 |
| 2/Lt. W. M. BARRY. | 23/3/18 | | 18/12/18 |
| Lieut. F. W. HARVEY. | 10/4/18 | | 29/11/18 |
| Lieut. J. A. SNAPE. | 10/4/18 | | 13/12/18 |
| Lieut. C. A. BEARD. | 10/4/18 | | 31/12/18 |
| 2/Lt. A. TAYLOR. | 10/4/18 | | 25/12/18 |
| 2/Lt. F. HAMMOND. | 10/4/18 | | 18/12/18 |
| Capt. C. de Witte WOODYER. | 27/5/18 | | |
| Lieut. H. R. CARSON. | 27/5/18 | | –/12/18 |
| 2/Lt. W. RYDEN. | 27/5/18 | | 26/12/18 |
| 2/Lt. A. MAYOR. | 27/5/18 | | 13/12/18 |
| 2/Lt. J. S. BURGOYNE. | 27/5/18 | | 25/12/18 |
| 2/Lt. A. W. BYTHEWAY. | 27/5/18 | | 18/12/18 |
| 2/Lt. C. F. M. BARRETT. | 27/5/18 | | 22/12/18 |
| Capt. H. M. WILKINSON. | 28/5/18 | | 14/12/18 |

*Attached from Middlesex.  †Attached from R. W. Kents.  ‡Attached from Manchesters.
§Attached from Liverpools.

## CHESHIRE REGIMENT—Continued.
### 15th Battalion.

| Name. | Missing. | Interned. | Repatriated. |
|---|---|---|---|
| Major H. F. A. Le MESURIER. | 24/3/18 | | 1/1/19 |
| Capt. E. W. BIGLAND. | 24/3/18 | | 25/12/18 |
| Capt. V. G. BARNETT. | 24/3/18 | | 13/12/18 |
| Lieut. D. W. MILLS. | 24/3/18 | | 11/12/18 |
| 2/Lt. E. H. BANN. | 24/3/18 | | 11/12/18 |
| 2/Lt. A. CHUCK. | 24/3/18 | | 25/12/18 |
| 2/Lt. T. YOUNG. | 24/3/18 | | 25/12/18 |
| *2/Lt. A. J. C. WALTERS. | 10/4/18 | | 29/11/18 |

## ROYAL WELSH FUSILIERS.
### 1st Battalion.

| Name | Missing | Interned | | Repatriated |
|---|---|---|---|---|
| Capt. E. SKAIFE. | 20/10/14 | Holland | 24/2/18 | 18/8/18 |
| Capt. SMYTHE OSBORNE. | 20/10/14 | Holland | 6/2/18 | 29/12/18 |
| Lieut. Hon. R. BINGHAM. | 20/10/14 | Holland | 24/2/18 | 14/1/19 |
| Lieut. H. COURAGE. | 20/10/14 | Holland | 6/2/18 | 18/11/18 |
| Lieut. C. G. H. PEPPE. | 20/10/14 | Holland | 24/2/18 | 22/1/19 |
| Lieut. R. E. HINDSON. | 23/10/14 | Holland | 6/2/18 | 18/11/18 |
| 2/Lt. E. WODEHOUSE. | 30/10/14 | Holland | 6/2/18 | 18/11/18 |
| Lieut. B. C. H. POOLE. | 8/11/14 | Holland | 24/2/18 | 18/11/18 |
| Lieut. D. M. BARCHARD. | –/–/14 | Holland | 6/2/18 | 22/11/18 |

### 2nd Battalion.

| Name | Missing | Interned | | Repatriated |
|---|---|---|---|---|
| Lieut. A. M. G. EVANS. | 30/10/14 | Holland | 24/2/18 | 22/1/19 |
| 2/Lt. J. D. M. RICHARDS. | 27/5/17 | Switzerland | 27/12/17 | 24/3/18 |
| 2/Lt. J. A. SOAMES. | 5/5/17 | | | 7/1/18 |
| 2/Lt. C. P. CRABTREE. | 1/9/18 | | | 28/11/18 |
| 2/Lt. D. JONES. | 1/9/18 | | | 8/12/18 |
| Lieut. E. C. TUNNICLIFFE. | 1/9/18 | | | 11/12/18 |
| 2/Lt. T. ROWLAND. | 27/3/17 | | | 8/1/17 |

### 4th Battalion.

| Name | Missing | | | Repatriated |
|---|---|---|---|---|
| Capt. P. R. FOULKES-ROBERTS. | 23/3/18 | | | 28/11/18 |
| Lieut. O. P. T. N. BLAKE. | 24/3/18 | | | 1/12/18 |

### 9th Battalion.

| Name | Missing | | | Repatriated |
|---|---|---|---|---|
| 2/Lt. R. E. SMITH. | 23/3/18 | | | 11/12/18 |
| Lieut. W. O. H. ELLIS. | 24/3/18 | | | 17/12/18 |
| Capt. J. M. WARDLAW. | 10/4/18 | | | 8/12/18 |
| 2/Lt. W. B. BEDDOW. | 10/4/18 | | | 18/12/18 |
| 2/Lt. A. C. CLOUGH. | 10/4/18 | | | 17/12/18 |
| 2/Lt. G. H. WEBB. | 10/4/18 | | | 29/11/18 |
| †Capt. S. DARVELL. | 30/5/18 | | | 14/12/18 |
| Capt. J. R. WILLIAMS. | 30/5/18 | | | 14/12/18 |
| Lieut. R. S. R. PITTARD. | 30/5/18 | | | –/12/18 |
| Lieut. A. WYNNE. | 30/5/18 | | | –/12/18 |
| 2/Lt. L. JONES. | 30/5/18 | | | 11/1/19 |
| 2/Lt. E. C. THOMAS. | 30/5/18 | | | 11/1/19 |
| 2/Lt. S. WATKINS. | 30/5/18 | | | 28/12/18 |

*Attached from South Lancashire.
†Attached from Denbighshire Yeomanry.

## ROYAL WELSH FUSILIERS—Continued.

### 13th Battalion.

| Name. | Missing. | Interned. | Repatriated. |
|---|---|---|---|
| 2/Lt. D. O. JONES. | 10/3/18 | | 25/12/18 |

### 14th Battalion.

| | | | |
|---|---|---|---|
| 2/Lt. C. PARKER. | 19/9/18 | (Died). | 25/10/18 |
| 2/Lt. B. LAW. | 7/10/18 | | 29/11/18 |

### 15th Battalion.

| | | | |
|---|---|---|---|
| Lieut. L. C. NEWMAN. | 21/12/18 | (Died). | |

### 16th Battalion.

| | | | |
|---|---|---|---|
| Lieut. P. A. ROBERTS. | 2/12/16 | | 7/1/19 |
| 2/Lt. J. RICHARDS. | 18/9/18 | | |
| 2/Lt. G. E. YOUNG. | 18/9/18 | | 2/12/18 |

### 18th Battalion.

| | | | |
|---|---|---|---|
| Capt. E. W. BISHOP. | 15/11/16 | | 18/12/18 |
| 2/Lt. S. T. JONES. | | | 18/11/18 |

### 25th Battalion.

| | | | |
|---|---|---|---|
| Lieut. H. L. MORGAN. | 21/9/18 | | 8/12/18 |

## SOUTH WALES BORDERERS.

### 1st and 2nd Battalions.

| | | | |
|---|---|---|---|
| *Lieut. G. W. PHILLIMORE. | 5/4/16 | | 12/11/18 |
| Lieut. C. DAVIDSON. | 20/5/16 | Holland 30/4/18 | 22/1/19 |
| Capt. J. C. B. TRAGETT. | 3/12/17 | | 18/8/18 |
| 2/Lt. H. EDWARDS. | 3/12/17 | | 17/12/18 |
| 2/Lt. D. R. WINDSOR. | 3/12/17 | | 17/12/18 |
| 2/Lt. T. J. JORDAN. | 13/12/17 | | 25/12/18 |

### 2nd Battalion.

| | | | |
|---|---|---|---|
| Major D. H. S. SOMERVILLE. | 11/4/18 | | 28/11/18 |
| Capt. E. A. LLOYD. | 11/4/18 | | 25/12/18 |
| Capt. J. B. STERNDALE-BENNETT. | 11/4/18 | | 25/12/18 |
| Lieut. W. F. PAGE. | 11/4/18 | | 25/12/18 |
| 2/Lt. F. H. BEES. | 11/4/18 | | —/1/19 |
| 2/Lt. S. F. HEARDER. | 11/4/18 | | 18/12/18 |
| 2/Lt. J. S. LEWIS. | 11/4/18 | | 18/12/18 |
| †2/Lt. W. PARRY. | 11/4/18 | | 18/12/18 |
| 2/Lt. J. PEMBERTON. | 11/4/18 | | 18/12/18 |
| 2/Lt. G. F. SMITH. | 11/4/18 | | 18/12/18 |
| †2/Lt. F. T. WILLIAMS. | 11/4/18 | | 25/12/18 |

### 6th Battalion.

| | | | |
|---|---|---|---|
| ‡Lieut. H. DAVIES. | 27/5/18 | | 17/12/18 |
| †2/Lt. G. CARLYLE. | 28/5/18 | | 14/12/18 |
| 2/Lt. H. R. MURRAY. | 28/5/18 | | 18/12/18 |

### 11th Battalion.

| | | | |
|---|---|---|---|
| §2/Lt. H. E. GRIFFITHS. | 11/4/18 | | 18/12/18 |

*Attached from Highland L.I.  †Attached from Welsh Regiment.
‡Attached from Royal Welsh Fusiliers.  §Attached from Entrenching Battery.

## SOUTH WALES BORDERERS—Continued.
### 12th Battalion.

| Name. | Missing. | Interned. | Repatriated. |
|---|---|---|---|
| 2/Lt. E. O. DAVIES. | 24/11/17 | | 17/12/18 |

## K.O. SCOTTISH BORDERERS.
### 1st and 2nd Battalions.

| Name | Missing | Interned | Repatriated |
|---|---|---|---|
| Capt. H. COBDEN. | 26/8/14 | Holland 22/1/1 | 18/11/18 |
| Lieut. R. P. M. BELL. | 26/8/14 | Holland 5/1/18 | 2/1/19 |
| Capt. R. JOYNSON. | 27/8/14 | Holland 22/1/18 | 18/11/18 |
| Lt.-Col. C. M. STEPHENSON. | 10/9/14 | Switzerland 28/12/16 | 24/3/18 |
| Lieut. W. N. SHEWEN. | 10/9/14 | Holland 5/1/18 | 20/12/18 |
| Major A. E. HAIG. | 10/9/14 | Holland 22/1/18 | 23/10/18 |
| Capt. E. W. MacDONALD. | | Holland 11/8/18 | 7/9/18 |
| Lieut. T. F. TEELING. | | Holland 22/1/18 | 23/10/18 |
| 2/Lt. A. C. RANKINE. | 13/12/16 | | 14/12/18 |
| 2/Lt. N. MacLEOD. | 28/1/17 | | 14/12/18 |
| 2/Lt. U. A. BOND. | 11/4/18 | | 18/12/18 |
| Capt. R. M. SHORTER. | 11/4/18 | | 17/12/18 |
| 2/Lt. W. C. TAYLOR. | 11/4/18 | | 25/12/18 |
| 2/Lt. A. W. ROBB. | 11/4/18 | | 11/12/18 |
| 2/Lt. E. C. J. CROFTS. | 11/4/18 | (*Died* 28/4/18 at Langensalza). | |
| 2/Lt. W. R. COX. | 18/9/18 | | 28/11/18 |

### 4th Battalion.

| Name | Missing | Interned | Repatriated |
|---|---|---|---|
| Lieut. L. T. O'HANLON. | 18/9/18 | | 29/11/18 |
| 2/Lt. D. L. SCOTT. | 3/10/18 | | 28/11/18 |

### 6th Battalion.

| Name | Missing | Interned | Repatriated |
|---|---|---|---|
| 2/Lt. J. S. FRANKLIN. | 26/9/15 | | 11/9/17 |
| 2/Lt. A. D. McKERRELL. | 1/4/17 | | 30/12/18 |
| 2/Lt. G. K. GREENAWAY. | 3/5/11 | | 5/1/19 |
| *Capt. H. W. SAMSON. | 3/5/17 | | 2/12/18 |
| 2/Lt. J. H. NELSON. | 3/5/17 | Switzerland 27/12/17 | 14/6/18 |
| 2/Lt. J. MABEN. | 22/3/18 | | 29/11/18 |
| 2/Lt. J. R. MASSON. | 26/3/18 | | 25/12/18 |
| 2/Lt. J. D. STARK. | 15/4/18 | (*Died* 3/9/18 at Cologne). | |
| 2/Lt. George PENMAN. | 25/4/18 | | 14/12/18 |
| 2/Lt. P. ORMISTON. | 25/4/18 | | 29/11/18 |
| 2/Lt. W. E. LIVINGSTONE. | 25/4/18 | | 29/11/18 |
| 2/Lt. A. D. ARCHIBALD. | 25/4/18 | | 29/11/18 |
| Capt. H. J. WILKIE. | 25/4/18 | | 29/12/18 |
| 2/Lt. A. G. FARQUHARSON. | 25/4/18 | | −/11/18 |
| 2/Lt. P. J. SPARKES. | 16/10/18 | | 13/12/18 |

*Attached from Royal Scots.

### 7th Battalion.

| Name | Missing | Interned | Repatriated |
|---|---|---|---|
| Capt. T. BLACKBURN. | 26/9/15 | | 13/9/17 |
| 2/Lt. W. M. HONEYMAN. | 23/7/18 | | −/12/18 |

### 8th Battalion.

| Name | Missing | Interned | Repatriated |
|---|---|---|---|
| 2/Lt. H. G. MITCHELL. | 26/9/15 | Switzerland 9/12/17 | 9/12/18 |
| Lieut. P. M. ROSS. | 26/9/15 | | 18/11/18 |

## CAMERONIANS.
### (Scottish Rifles.)
#### 1st and 2nd Battalions.

| Name. | Missing. | Interned. | Repatriated. |
|---|---|---|---|
| Capt. A. R. MacALLAN. | | Switzerland 12/8/16 | 13/9/17 |
| *Capt. A. ARMSTRONG. | 22/8/17 | | —/12/18 |
| 2/Lt. H. D. GRANT. | 24/3/18 | | 8/12/18 |
| †Capt. P. J. BOOTH. | 25/3/18 | | 2/12/18 |
| Capt. A. W. F. STEWART. | 25/3/18 | | 1/12/18 |
| Capt. M. MALLACE. | 25/3/18 | | 1/12/18 |
| Lieut. W. B. THOMAS. | 25/3/18 | | —/12/18 |
| 2/Lt. J. E. MacKAY. | 25/3/18 | | —/12/18 |
| Lt.-Col. F. G. W. DRAFFEN. | 9/5/18 | | 1/12/18 |
| Lieut. A. G. ROBB. | 9/5/18 | (*Died* 20/5/18 at Hanover). | |

#### 5/6th Battalions.

| | | | |
|---|---|---|---|
| 2/Lt. A. ANDERSON. | 24/10/18 | | 8/12/18 |

#### 6th Battalion.

| | | | |
|---|---|---|---|
| 2/Lt. D. C. CALDWELL. | 19/8/18 | | 13/12/18 |

#### 9th Battalion.

| | | | |
|---|---|---|---|
| 2/Lt. J. R. KAY. | 28/12/16 | | 17/12/18 |
| Capt. A. L. BROWN. | 3/5/17 | | 17/12/18 |
| Lieut. T. A. NEILSON. | 23/3/18 | | 29/11/18 |
| 2/Lt. R. O. LOCKHEAD. | 2/7/18 | | 17/12/18 |

#### 10th Battalion.

| | | | |
|---|---|---|---|
| Leiut. A. FLEMING. | 1/8/17 | | 6/12/18 |
| Lieut. H. J. ROBISON. | 19/8/18 | | 11/12/18 |
| Lieut. G. M. DREW. | 19/8/18 | | 29/11/18 |
| 2/Lt. L. McK. EWEN. | 21/12/17 | | 3/12/18 |

## ROYAL INNISKILLING FUSILIERS.
### 1st Battalion.

| Name. | Missing. | Interned. | Repatriated. |
|---|---|---|---|
| Lieut. S. W. AITCHISON. | 19/5/17 | | —/12/18 |
| ‡2/Lt. J. CLANCY. | 19/5/17 | Switzerland 27/12/17 | 7/12/18 |
| Capt. J. McMECHAN. | 21/3/18 | | 25/12/18 |
| Lieut. S. McCONNELL. | 21/3/18 | | 28/11/18 |
| 2/Lt. F. S. MARCHANT. | 21/3/18 | | 18/12/18 |
| 2/Lt. C. GREGG. | 21/3/18 | | —/12/18 |
| Lt.-Col. J. N. CRAWFORD. | 22/3/18 | | 3/1/19 |
| Capt. E. E. J. MOORE. | 22/3/18 | | 1/12/18 |
| Capt. T. H. COCKBURN-MERCER. | 22/3/18 | | 11/1/19 |
| Lieut. B. L. GRIGGS. | 22/3/18 | | 18/12/18 |
| Lieut. W. G. BAKER. | 22/3/18 | | 25/12/18 |
| 2/Lt. S. S. HUNTER. | 22/3/18 | | 25/12/18 |
| 2/Lt. J. P. ROBINSON. | 22/3/18 | | 17/12/18 |
| ₤/Lt. W. PRICE. | 22/3/18 | | 29/11/18 |
| 2/Lt. R. B. McCONNELL. | 22/3/18 | | 25/12/18 |
| Capt. G. W. WILLOCK. | 23/3/18 | | 18/12/18 |

*Attached T.M.B.  †Attached from Royal Scots Fusiliers.
‡Attached from Munster Fusiliers.

## ROYAL INNISKILLING FUSILIERS—Continued.

### 2nd Battalion.

| Name. | Missing. | Interned. | Repatriated. |
|---|---|---|---|
| Capt. E. R. LLOYD. | —/—/14 | (*Died* at Cambrai). | |
| Lieut. I. R. F. MILLER. | 11/9/14 | (*Died* 8/3/15). | |
| Lieut. C. F. BEVERLAND. | 23/11/16 | (*Died* 4/12/16 at Pronville). | |
| 2/Lt. D. H. O'HARA. | 27/2/17 | | 18/12/18 |
| Capt. J. A. S. HOPKINS. | 21/3/18 | | 1/12/18 |
| Capt. R. M. VAUGHAN. | 21/3/18 | | 10/12/18 |
| Capt. R. M. BOYLE. | 21/3/18 | | 8/12/18 |
| Capt. C. C. MILLER. | 21/3/18 | | 29/11/18 |
| Lieut. W. V. MORONY. | 21/3/18 | | 18/12/18 |
| Lieut. F. W. DAVIDSON. | 21/3/18 | | 1/12/18 |
| 2/Lt. F. CINNAMOND. | 21/3/18 | (*Died* 13/11/18 at Graudenz). | |
| 2/Lt. S. B. McCONNELL. | 21/3/18 | | —/12/18 |
| 2/Lt. G. WATSON. | 21/3/18 | | 28/11/18 |
| 2/Lt. J. F. O'BRIEN. | 21/3/18 | | 2/12/18 |
| 2/Lt. P. HENNESSY. | 21/3/18 | | 18/12/18 |
| 2/Lt. G. M. BURKE. | 21/3/18 | | 20/12/18 |
| *Lt.-Col. Lord A. K. FARNHAM. | 21/3/18 | | 17/12/18 |
| Lieut. J. H. WHERRY. | 21–29/3/18 | | 17/12/18 |
| †Lieut. C. J. ARMSTRONG. | 21–29/3/18 | | 10/12/18 |
| ‡Lieut. T. H. BIRD. | 21–29/3/18 | | —/12/18 |
| ‡2/Lt. D. R. CLARK. | 21–29/3/18 | | 18/12/18 |
| ‡2/Lt. J. D. McCULLOUGH. | 21–29/3/18 | | 18/12/18 |
| 2/Lt. F. C. WILLIAMS. | 21–29/3/18 | | 29/11/18 |
| 2/Lt. R. B. W. IRWIN. | 21–29/3/18 | | 14/12/18 |
| 2/Lt. J. M. J. MARTIN. | 24/3/18 | | 17/12/18 |
| Major E. F. EAGAR. | 29/3/18 | | 29/11/18 |

### 7th Battalion.

| Name. | Missing. | Interned. | Repatriated. |
|---|---|---|---|
| 2/Lt. H. W. RUDDOCK. | 16/8/17 | Switzerland 24/4/18 | 9/12/18 |
| 2/Lt. J. FISHER. | 16/8/17 | | 6/1/19 |
| 2/Lt. J. T. FLANAGAN. | 16/8/17 | | 18/12/18 |
| Capt. H. P. McKENNA. | 21/3/18 | | 28/11/18 |
| Capt. D. H. MORTON. | 16/8/17 | | 3/12/18 |

### 7/8th Battalion.

| Name. | Missing. | Interned. | Repatriated. |
|---|---|---|---|
| Major V. H. PARR. | 21/3/18 | | 2/1/19 |
| §Capt. L. W. L. LEADER. | 21/3/18 | | —/12/18 |
| Capt. L. W. P. YATES. | 21/3/18 | | 16/1/19 |
| Lieut. E. W. McKEGNEY. | 21/3/18 | | 11/12/18 |
| Lieut. W. J. A. H. AUCHINLECK. | 21/3/18 | | 13/12/18 |
| 2/Lt. T. J. STACK. | 21/3/18 | | 3/12/18 |
| 2/Lt. J. G. O'NEILL. | 21/3/18 | | 23/9/18 |
| †2/Lt. J. W. BURKE. | 1/9/18 | | 16/12/18 |

### 8th Battalion.

| Name. | Missing. | Interned. | Repatriated. |
|---|---|---|---|
| 2/Lt. J. L. CHARLESWORTH. | 16/8/17 | | 9/12/18 |

### 9th Battalion.

| Name. | Missing. | Interned. | Repatriated. |
|---|---|---|---|
| Capt. A. B. DOUGLAS. | 6/12/17 | | 6/1/19 |
| Lieut. J. F. PARKHOUSE. | 21/3/18 | | 29/11/18 |
| 2/Lt. J. F. R. DARBYSHIRE. | 21–29/3/18 | | 29/11/18 |
| 2/Lt. H. H. MURDOCH. | 21–29/3/18 | | 1/12/18 |
| 2/Lt. J. A. GIBSON. | 23/3/18 | (*Died* 24/9/18 at Trier). | |
| Lieut. G. M. K. MARTIN. | 2/10/18 | | —/12/18 |

*Attached from Irish Horse.     †Attached from Royal Irish Fusiliers.
‡Attached from Royal Munster Fusiliers.     §Attached from Connaught Rangers.

## ROYAL INNISKILLING FUSILIERS—Continued.
### 10th Battalion.

| Name. | Missing. | Interned. | Repatriated. |
|---|---|---|---|
| 2/Lt. J. H. SHANNON. | 1/7/16 | | 13/9/17 |

## GLOUCESTERSHIRE REGIMENT.
### 1st and 2nd Battalions.

| Name. | Missing. | Interned. | | Repatriated. |
|---|---|---|---|---|
| Capt. A. F. CHAPMAN. | 29/10/14 | Switzerland | | 24/3/18 |
| Capt. D. A. GREENSLADE. | 29/11/14 | Holland | 24/2/18 | 18/11/18 |
| Lieut. C. F. L. TEMPLER. | 22/12/14 | Escaped | | –/9/17 |
| Capt. J. A. CAUNTER. | | Escaped | | –/6/17 |
| Major R. CONNOR. | | Exchanged | | –/8/17 |
| Lieut. P. P. KING. | 23/3/18 | | | –/12/18 |
| 2/Lt. I. SYKES. | 23/3/18 | | | 6/1/19 |
| Capt. R. F. RUBINSTEIN. | 15/6/18 | | | –/11/18 |

### 4th Battalion.

| Name. | Missing. | Interned. | | Repatriated. |
|---|---|---|---|---|
| Lieut. C. M. COOTE. | 24/7/16 | Holland | –/6/16 | 22/11/18 |
| Capt. W. R. HUTCHINGS. | 3/12/17 | | | 27/11/18 |
| Lieut. W. G. SHIPWAY. | 3/12/17 | | | 3/12/18 |
| 2/Lt. F. R. RAWLINGS. | 3/12/17 | | | 3/12/18 |

### 5th Battalion.

| Name. | Missing. | Interned. | | Repatriated. |
|---|---|---|---|---|
| 2/Lt. F. W. HARVEY. | 19/8/16 | Holland | 12/10/18 | 21/1/19 |
| *2/Lt. F. G. L. WOOSTER. | 29/8/17 | | | 20/12/18 |
| Lieut. R. HOWELL. | 22/3/18 | (*Died* 30/5/18 at Heilbronn). | | |
| 2/Lt. T. E. MONDAY. | 22/3/18 | | | 18/12/18 |
| Lieut. A. F. BARNES. | 23/3/18 | | | 15/12/18 |
| 2/Lt. R. A. FOTHERGILL. | 23/3/18 | | | 25/12/18 |
| 2/Lt. W. PETTIGREW. | 15/6/18 | | | –/11/18 |
| 2/Lt. R. R. E. ELCOCK. | 15/6/18 | | | –/11/18 |
| 2/Lt. J. THOMAS. | 15/6/18 | | | 21/11/18 |
| †2/Lt. J. J. OVENSTONE. | 15/6/18 | | | –/11/18 |

### 6th Battalion.

| Name. | Missing. | Interned. | | Repatriated. |
|---|---|---|---|---|
| 2/Lt. E. B. CLARKE. | 22/8/16 | Holland | 12/10/18 | 22/11/18 |
| ‡Capt. H. B. GOULDING. | 3/12/17 | | | 22/3/18 |
| 2/Lt. G. M. SHEPPARD. | 3/12/17 | | | 1/1/19 |
| 2/Lt. K. G. GURNEY. | 3/12/17 | (*Died* 17/12/17 at Selvigny). | | |

### 8th Battalion.

| Name. | Missing. | Interned. | Repatriated. |
|---|---|---|---|
| 2/Lt. E. A. SQUIRE. | 25/2/17 | | 14/12/18 |
| 2/Lt. F. J. R. GARLAND. | 25/2/17 | | 14/12/18 |
| Capt. M. A. JAMES. | 23/3/18 | | 25/12/18 |
| Lieut. S. H. WATSON. | 23/3/18 | | 25/12/18 |
| 2/Lt. A. W. SHUBROOK. | 23/3/18 | | 17/12/18 |
| 2/Lt. G. ELLIS. | 23/3/18 | | 18/12/18 |
| Capt. F. H. BOWLES. | 10/4/18 | | 2/12/18 |
| 2/Lt. H. COOPER. | 10/4/18 | | 18/12/18 |
| 2/Lt. R. W. NORRIS. | 10/4/18 | | 25/12/18 |
| 2/Lt. D. W. VICK. | 10/4/18 | | 29/11/18 |
| 2/Lt. C. MARFELL. | 10/4/18 | | 13/12/18 |
| 2/Lt. J. B. W. HUGHES. | 22/9/18 | | 23/1/19 |

*Attached from Norfolk Yeomanry.
†Attached from Dorsets.
‡Attached from R.A.M.C.

## GLOUCESTERSHIRE REGIMENT—Continued.

### 12th Battalion.

| Name. | Missing. | Interned. | Rapatriated. |
|---|---|---|---|
| Lieut. R. J. FITZGERALD. | 8/5/17 | Escaped | –/10/17 |
| 2/Lt. W. J. G. ABBOTT. | 25/6/18 | | 29/11/18 |

### 13th Battalion.

| | | | |
|---|---|---|---|
| Lieut. F. C. BRIGHT. | 23/3/18 | | 18/12/18 |
| Capt. G. M. HELE. | 26/4/18 | | 29/11/18 |
| Capt. F. E. A. BERGER-WHEELER. | 26/4/18 | | 29/11/18 |
| Lieut. A. C. BAKER. | 26/4/18 | | 31/12/18 |
| Lieut. F. B. WHITTALL. | 26/4/18 | | 29/11/18 |
| 2/Lt. D. D. HERRING. | 26/4/18 | | 29/11/18 |
| 2/Lt. J. S. PAWSEY. | 26/4/18 | | 2/12/18 |
| 2/Lt. L. C. FARR. | 26/4/18 | | 29/11/18 |
| 2/Lt. F. S. SMITH. | 26/4/18 | | 29/11/18 |

## WORCESTERSHIRE REGIMENT.

### 1st Battalion.

| | | | |
|---|---|---|---|
| Capt. R. C. MARSHALL. | 27/5/18 | | 17/12/18 |
| *Capt. A. B. PRATT. | 27/5/18 | | 8/12/18 |
| †Lieut. T. G. MARTIN. | 27/5/18 | | 31/12/18 |
| Lieut. F. PERCY. | 27/5/18 | | –/12/18 |
| Lieut. F. RODMAN. | 27/5/18 | | –/12/18 |
| Lieut. R. B. BERRY. | 27/5/18 | | 21/12/18 |
| 2/Lt. W. KELLY. | 27/5/18 | | 13/12/18 |
| 2/Lt. A. P. EDGAR. | 27/5/18 | | 13/12/18 |

### 2nd Battalion.

| | | | |
|---|---|---|---|
| Capt. T. F. V. MATTHEWS. | 13/4/18 | | 18/12/18 |
| Lieut. C. W. V. PEAKE. | 13/4/18 | | 1/12/18 |
| 2/Lt. A. HURLEY. | 13/4/18 | | 29/11/18 |
| ‡Major E. J. DONALDSON. | 15/4/18 | | –/1/18 |
| 2/Lt. H. O. TREDWELL. | 15/4/18 | | 18/12/18 |
| 2/Lt. F. J. D. GUNSTON. | 15/4/18 | (Died 14/7/18). | |

### 3rd Battalion.

| | | | |
|---|---|---|---|
| Capt. C. V. BERESFORD. | 10/9/14 | Switzerland –/8/16 | 13/9/17 |
| 2/Lt. A. E. FRYER. | 25/12/17 | | 27/11/18 |
| 2/Lt. E. H. JONES. | 25/12/17 | | 27/11/18 |
| 2/Lt. C. LATHAM. | 28/3/18 | | 11/12/18 |
| Lieut. H. U. RICHARDS. | –/4/18 | | –/11/18 |
| Capt. E. A. HUMPHRIES. | 27/5/18 | | 11/1/19 |
| 2/Lt. R. O. GOOLDEN. | 27/5/18 | | 25/12/18 |
| 2/Lt. V. B. WASLEY. | 27/5/18 | | 31/12/18 |
| 2/Lt. E. V. MATTHEWS. | 27/5/18 | | 11/1/19 |
| Lieut. W. E. J. WILL. | 28/5/18 | | –/12/18 |
| 2/Lt. W. H. TODHUNTER. | 28/5/18 | | –/12/18 |
| 2/Lt. A. J. SINCLAIR. | 28/5/18 | | 19/1/19 |
| Lieut. A. S. ABRAHALL. | 5/9/18 | | 23/1/19 |

### 4th Battalion.

| | | | |
|---|---|---|---|
| 2/Lt. T. C. HAMBLING. | 5/5/16 | Holland 30/4/18 | 24/12/18 |
| 2/Lt. G. E. OVERBURY. | 20/10/16 | | 18/12/18 |
| 2/Lt. W. H. PITT. | 23/4/17 | Holland 30/10/18 | 23/11/18 |

*Attached from Leinsters. †Attached from Manchesters.
‡Attached from Lovats Scouts.

## WORCESTERSHIRE REGIMENT—Continued.

### 5th Battalion.

| Name. | Missing. | Interned. | | Repatriated. |
|---|---|---|---|---|
| Capt. E. G. WILLIAMS. | 31/10/14 | Switzerland | 9/12/17 | 24/3/18 |

### 7th Battalion.

| Name. | Missing. | Repatriated. |
|---|---|---|
| 2/Lt. J. WHALE. | 26/8/17 | 14/12/18 |
| *Lieut. W. E. VACHER. | 22/3/18 | 14/12/18 |
| 2/Lt. F. C. PERRETT. | 27/5/18 | 13/12/18 |

### 8th Battalion.

| Name. | Missing. | Repatriated. |
|---|---|---|
| 2/Lt. E. W. WELLS. | 21/3/19 | 25/12/18 |
| Major H. W. DAVIES. | 22/3/18 | 4/12/18 |
| Capt. A. T. BUTLER. | 22/3/18 | 14/12/18 |
| Capt. S. A. GODSALL. | 22/3/18 | 14/12/18 |
| 2/Lt. J. A. GREAVES. | 22/3/18 | 27/11/18 |
| 2/Lt. C. C. HAFFIELD. | 22/3/18 | –/12/18 |
| 2/Lt. W. G. JONES. | 22/3/18 | 14/12/18 |
| 2/Lt. T. A. LANDRETH. | 22/3/18 | –/12/18 |
| 2/Lt. W. RUNDLE. | 22/3/18 | 25/12/18 |
| 2/Lt. C. H. THOMAS. | 22/3/18 | 31/12/18 |
| 2/Lt. J. G. PLAYER. | 22/3/18 | 4/12/18 |
| 2/Lt. E. A. BROWN. | 22/3/18 | 14/12/18 |
| 2/Lt. P. C. RUSHTON. | 22/3/18 | 14/12/18 |
| 2/Lt. W. RADFORD. | 22/3/18 | 6/12/18 |
| 2/Lt. C. W. LAWRENCE. | 27/3/18 | 28/11/18 |
| 2/Lt. V. C. H. SPENCELAYH. | 27/3/18 | 11/12/18 |
| 2/Lt. R. J. BURTON. | 14/4/18 | (Died 15/4/18 at Kortryk). |
| Capt. C. R. PAWSEY. | 2/8/18 | –/11/18 |
| 2/Lt. A. G. GRANGER. | 3/8/18 | –/11/18 |
| Lieut. R. S. MILLER. | 23/10/18 | 16/12/18 |

### 10th Battalion.

| Name. | Missing. | Repatriated. |
|---|---|---|
| 2/Lt. F. I. SMITH. | 21/3/18 | 23/9/18 |
| 2/Lt. O. J. SHORT. | 24/3/18 | (Died 3/4/18 at Peruwelz). |
| Capt. G. M. IRELAND-BLACKBURNE. | 10/4/18 | –/11/18 |
| Capt. A. M. DICKINSON. | 10/4/18 | 25/12/18 |
| 2/Lt. P. E. THOMPSON. | 10/4/18 | 1/12/18 |
| †Capt. H. STREET. | 30/5/18 | (Died 1/6/18 at Brouille). |

## EAST LANCASHIRE REGIMENT.
### 1st and 2nd Battalions.

| Name. | Missing. | Interned. | | Repatriated. |
|---|---|---|---|---|
| Capt. C. F. HARGREAVES. | 14/9/14 | Holland | 6/2/18 | 21/1/19 |
| Major E. R. COLLINS. | 17/9/14 | | | 9/12/18 |
| Lieut. Kenneth HOOPER. | 19/9/14 | Holland | 22/1/18 | 18/11/18 |
| 2/Lt. C. S. DODWELL. | 10/4/15 | Holland | 10/4/18 | 18/11/18 |
| Capt. G. MacK. SMITH. | 14/5/15 | Switzerland | 27/12/17 | 9/12/18 |
| 2/Lt. W. H. T. HILPERN. | 14/5/15 | Holland | 10/4/18 | 18/11/18 |
| Capt. M. G. BROWNE. | 1/7/16 | Holland | 16/5/18 | 16/12/18 |
| Capt. C. WADDINGTON. | 18/10/16 | | | 18/12/18 |
| Capt. A. N. SCOTT. | 18/10/16 | | | 18/12/18 |
| Lieut. Mark QUAYLE. | 18/10/16 | | | 23/10/18 |
| 2/Lt. J. M. WILKS. | 18/10/16 | | | 18/12/18 |

*Attached 183/L.T.M.B.
†Attached from South Lancs Regiment.

## EAST LANCASHIRE REGIMENT—Continued.

### 1st and 2nd Battalions.—continued.

| Name. | Missing. | Interned. | Repatriated. |
|---|---|---|---|
| 2/Lt. J. C. THOMPSON. | 10/4/17 | | 4/1/19 |
| 2/Lt. S. T. MARTIN. | 21/3/18 | | 11/12/18 |
| Lieut. E. F. G. CHAPMAN. | 24/3/18 | | 8/12/18 |
| 2/Lt. H. E. ROBERTS. | 24/3/18 | | 19/1/19 |
| 2/Lt. B. H. RIDGARD. | 10/4/18 | | 11/12/18 |
| Lieut. W. E. MILWARD. | 11/4/18 | | 3/12/18 |
| 2/Lt. J. ROWBOTTOM. | 11/4/18 | | 18/12/18 |
| *2/Lt. E. L. FORD. | 12/4/18 | | 18/12/18 |
| 2/Lt. E. H. BURR. | 24/4/18 | | 3/12/18 |
| Lt.-Col. G. E. M. HILL. | 27/5/18 | | –/12/18 |
| *Lieut. H V. SAMPSON. | 27/5/18 | | 23/12/18 |
| Lieut. R PHILLIPS. | 27/5/18 | | 31/12/18 |
| †2/Lt. W. YELLAND. | 27/5/18 | | 13/12/18 |
| †2/Lt. G. FLETCHER. | 27/5/18 | | –/12/18 |
| †2/Lt. D. A. ROPER. | 27/5/18 | | –/12/18 |
| 2/Lt. T. SHERIDAN. | 27/5/18 | | 31/12/18 |
| 2/Lt. G. H. HOWARTH. | 27/5/18 | | 31/12/18 |
| *2/Lt. J. P. HAYLEY. | 27/5/18 | | –/12/18 |
| *2/Lt. F. J. COTTON. | 28/5/18 | | 30/12/18 |
| 2/Lt. W. A. LAUDERDALE. | 28/5/18 | | 31/12/18 |
| *2/Lt. A. ROBINSON. | 28/5/18 | | 31/12/18 |

### 4th Battalion.

| Name. | Missing. | Interned. | Repatriated. |
|---|---|---|---|
| Capt. A. D. S. A. FLETCHER. | 21/3/18 | | 2/12/18 |
| Capt. H. A. MELLOWES. | 21/3/18 | | 2/12/18 |
| ‡Capt. R. CALEY. | 21/3/18 | | 28/11/18 |
| ‡Lieut. D. B. ROBERTSON. | 21/3/18 | | 28/11/18 |
| Lieut. H. A. RILEY. | 21/3/18 | | 4/12/18 |
| Lieut. E. M. SPICER. | 21/3/18 | | 14/12/18 |
| †Lieut. P. A. PHILLIPS. | 21/3/18 | | 29/11/18 |
| 2/Lt. V. L. W. BROWN. | 21/3/18 | | –/12/18 |
| 2/Lt. R. J. BARR. | 21/3/18 | | 18/12/18 |
| 2/Lt. A. E. QUAINTRELL. | 21/3/18 | | 29/11/18 |
| 2/Lt. H. W. VICCARS. | 21/3/18 | | 2/12/18 |
| 2/Lt. W. E. EADIE. | 21/3/18 | | 3/12/18 |
| 2/Lt. J. W. H. CRAIG. | 21/3/18 | | 29/11/18 |
| 2/Lt. J. C. MacDONALD. | 29/3/18 | | 17/12/18 |

†Attached from 23rd Londons.   †Attached T.M.B.

### 5th Battalion.

| Name. | Missing. | Interned. | Repatriated. |
|---|---|---|---|
| 2/Lt. N. J. HOWITT. | 28/1/18 | | 17/12/18 |
| 2/Lt. F. W. BROWN. | 21/3/18 | | –/12/18 |
| 2/Lt. H. H. MASSEY. | 21/3/18 | | 13/12/18 |
| 2/Lt. L. PINDER. | 21/3/18 | | 2/12/18 |
| 2/Lt. A. K. HORN. | 21/3/18 | | 17/12/18 |
| 2/Lt. V. H. JOHNSTON. | 21/3/18 | | –/12/18 |
| 2/Lt. E. B. OSBORNE. | 21/3/18 | (*Died* 1/4/18 at Le Cateau). | |
| 2/Lt. G. V. MARSH. | 22/3/18 | | 11/12/18 |

### 8th Battalion.

| Name. | Missing. | Interned. | Repatriated. |
|---|---|---|---|
| 2/Lt. W. POWELL. | 14/8/17 | | 17/12/18 |
| ‡2/Lt. J. H. CALVERT. | 22/3/18 | | 18/12/18 |

*Attached from Lancashire Fusiliers.   †Attached from Manchesters.
‡Attached from South Lancs.   §Attached 15th Entrenching Battalion.

## EAST LANCASHIRE REGIMENT—Continued.
### 11th Battalion.

| Name. | Missing. | Interned. | Repatriated. |
|---|---|---|---|
| 2/Lt. F. J. WILD. | 8/3/17 | | 6/12/18 |
| Capt. C. H. MALLINSON. | 4/12/17 | (*Died* –/6/18 at Ingolstadt). | |
| 2/Lt. E. TYER. | 27/3/18 | | 31/12/18 |
| 2/Lt. H. D. WALMSLEY. | 5/9/18 | | 8/12/18 |
| 2/Lt. J. MARSHALL. | 5/9/18 | | 8/12/18 |
| 2/Lt. T. C. ATKINSON. | 5/9/18 | | 29/11/18 |

## EAST SURREY REGIMENT.
### 1st and 2nd Battalions.

| Name. | Missing. | Interned. | Repatriated. |
|---|---|---|---|
| Capt. F. A. BOWRING. | –/–/14 | Holland 6/2/18 | 18/11/18 |
| Capt. R. CAMPBELL. | 10/9/14 | Holland 29/12/17 | 16/11/18 |
| Lieut. W. G. MORRITT. | 10/9/14 | (*Killed* while escaping 27/6/17). | |
| Capt. R. J. HILLIER. | 8/5/17 | | 17/12/18 |
| 2/Lt. S. WINDEBANK. | 8/5/17 | | 6/12/18 |
| 2/Lt. E. A. WEEKS. | 8/5/17 | | 6/12/18 |
| 2/Lt. W. C. ROSER. | 8/5/17 | | 6/12/18 |
| 2/Lt. E. G. NEAME. | 8/5/17 | | 6/12/18 |
| 2/Lt. G. S. HEARN. | 8/5/17 | (*Died* 12/5/17). | |

### 3rd Battalion.

| Name. | Missing. | Interned. | Repatriated. |
|---|---|---|---|
| 2/Lt. W. G. PRICE. | 9/4/18 | | 10/12/18 |

### 7th Battalion.

| Name. | Missing. | Interned. | Repatriated. |
|---|---|---|---|
| 2/Lt. J. A. ROSS. | 12/8/16 | Holland 12/10/18 | 6/12/18 |
| 2/Lt. J. L. McNAUGHTON. | 3/5/17 | | 31/12/18 |
| 2/Lt. F. W. GEE. | 3/5/17 | | 31/12/18 |
| 2/Lt. P. WARBURTON. | 3/5/17 | | 31/12/18 |
| Lt.-Col. R. H. BALDWIN. | 30/11/17 | | 30/12/18 |
| Capt. C. B. LITTLE. | 30/11/17 | | 3/12/18 |
| Capt. K. ANNS. | 30/11/17 | | 14/12/18 |
| 2/Lt. H. M. BINSTEAD. | 30/11/17 | | 3/12/18 |
| *2/Lt. E. E. W. BOWEN. | 30/11/17 | | 17/12/18 |
| 2/Lt. H. BUCK. | 9/4/18 | | 8/12/18 |

### 8th Battalion.

| Name. | Missing. | Interned. | Repatriated. |
|---|---|---|---|
| Capt. J. R. ACKERLEY. | 3/5/17 | Switzerland 27/12/17 | 23/12/18 |
| Capt. C. J. LONERGAN. | 3/5/17 | | 18/8/18 |
| 2/Lt. G. S. FACER. | 3/5/17 | | –/11/18 |
| 2/Lt. L. H. PEARSE. | 3/5/17 | Switzerland 27/12/17 | 23/12/18 |
| 2/Lt. J. F. McMILLAN. | 3/5/17 | | 6/12/18 |
| 2/Lt. H. T. SMITH. | 23/3/18 | | –/12/18 |
| Lieut. A. R. TOD. | 4/4/18 | (*Died* 18/4/18 at Caix). | |

### 9th Battalion.

| Name. | Missing. | Interned. | Repatriated. |
|---|---|---|---|
| Capt. B. FENWICK. | 26/9/15 | Holland 10/4/18 | 7/12/18 |
| Capt. C. E. BARNETT. | 26/9/15 | (*Died* 1/10/15 at Douai). | |
| Capt. W. B. BIRT. | 26/9/15 | (*Died* 18/4/16 at Cologne). | |
| Lieut. J. W. S. SEATON. | 21/3/18 | | 11/12/18 |
| 2/Lt. A. E. CLARE. | 21/3/18 | | 11/12/18 |
| 2/Lt. B. BISHOP. | 22/3/18 | | 18/12/18 |
| 2/Lt. R. B. CRABB. | 22/3/18 | | 18/12/18 |
| 2/Lt. A. F. ORCHARD. | 23/3/18 | | 25/12/18 |
| Lieut. M. S. BLOWER. | 25/3/18 | | –/12/18 |

*Attached T.M.B.

## EAST SURREY REGIMENT—continued.
### 9th Battalion—continued.

| Name. | Missing. | Interned. | Repatriated. |
|---|---|---|---|
| 2/Lt. W. S. AUSTIN. | 25/3/18 | | 25/12/18 |
| Major C. A. CLARK. | 26/3/18 | | 25/12/18 |
| Capt. G. W. WARRE-DYMOND. | 26/3/18 | | –/11/18 |
| 2/Lt. W. H. BABER. | 16/10/18 | | 11/12/18 |
| *2/Lt. A. C. NILSON. | 16/10/18 | | 11/12/18 |

### 12th Battalion

| | | | |
|---|---|---|---|
| 2/Lt. L. H. JENNINGS. | 5/8/17 | | 25/12/18 |
| 2/Lt. F. A. SAMUELS. | 5/8/17 | | 31/12/18 |
| Lieut. L. DAWSON. | 25/3/18 | | 29/11/18 |
| 2/Lt. R. C. JOHNS. | 25/3/18 | | 13/10/18 |

### 13th Battalion.

| | | | |
|---|---|---|---|
| Lieut. F. W. LANHAM. | 26/11/17 | | 2/12/18 |
| Lieut. R. H. HARKER. | 26/11/17 | | 3/12/18 |
| †Major W. G. WEST. | 9/4/18 | | 31/12/18 |
| Capt. F. S. AINGER. | 9/4/18 | | 11/12/18 |
| Capt. C. E. LINGE. | 9/4/18 | | 9/12/18 |
| Lieut. H. W. ALLASON. | 9/4/18 | | 10/12/18 |
| Lieut. L. W. PINNICK. | 9/4/18 | | 29/11/18 |
| Lieut. W. A. MORRIS. | 9/4/18 | | 10/12/18 |
| 2/Lt. R. R. WEBB. | 9/4/18 | | 18/12/18 |
| 2/Lt. W. B. PARKER. | 9/4/18 | | –/11/18 |
| 2/Lt. J. A. V. CANT. | 9/4/18 | | 3/12/18 |
| 2/Lt. H. E. BLATCH. | 9/4/18 | | 31/12/18 |

## DUKE OF CORNWALL'S LIGHT INFANTRY.
### 1st and 2nd Battalions

| Name | Missing | Interned | | Repatriated |
|---|---|---|---|---|
| Major Paul PETAVEL. | 10/9/14 | | | 7/1/18 |
| Lieut. W. M. RICHARDSON. | 10/9/14 | Holland | 5/1/18 | 4/10/18 |
| Capt. F. H. SPAN. | 21/10/14 | Holland | 24/2/18 | 18/11/18 |
| Lieut. C. H. RUSSEL. | 21/10/14 | Holland | 6/2/18 | 29/1/19 |
| Lieut. H. S. LEVERTON. | 21/10/14 | Holland | 6/2/18 | 18/11/18 |
| Capt. E. E. BARROW. | 30/11/14 | Holland | 24/2/18 | 18/11/18 |
| 2/Lt. F. R. NORTH. | 24/7/16 | Holland | 15/6/18 | 26/11/18 |
| 2/Lt. H. M. SMAIL. | 23/4/17 | | | 13/1/19 |
| Lieut. J. L. A. CRAVEN. | 15/4/18 | | | 18/12/18 |
| 2/Lt. G. B. ROBSON. | 20/8/18 | | | 13/12/18 |
| 2/Lt. B. D. JOHNSTONE. | 21/8/18 | | | 13/12/18 |

### 5th Battalion

| | | | |
|---|---|---|---|
| 2/Lt. H. A. BLACKLOCK. | 12/4/18 | | 13/12/18 |
| 2/Lt. P. L. MALTON. | 20/8/18 | (*Died* –/–/18 at Lille). | |

### 6th Battalion.

| | | | |
|---|---|---|---|
| Lieut. R. M. PADDISON. | 4/4/17 | | 14/12/18 |
| *Lieut. A. DOWNING. | 21/3/18 | | 18/12/18 |

*Attached T.M.B.
†Attached from Sherwood Foresters.

## DUKE OF CORNWALL'S LIGHT INFANTRY—continued.

### 7th Battalion.

| | | | | |
|---|---|---|---|---|
| Lieut. R. F. WHITELEY. | 30/11/17 | | | 27/11/18 |
| Lieut. H. RICKARD. | 30/11/17 | Switzerland | —/4/18 | 6/12/18 |
| 2/Lt. WM. KING. | 21/3/18 | (*Died* 26/6/18). | | |
| *Lt.-Col. H. G. R. BURGES-SHORT. | 24/3/18 | | | 25/12/18 |
| †Lieut. S. RUNDLE. | 18/4/18 | (*Died* 30/4/18 at Rouvin). | | |

## WEST RIDING REGIMENT.

### 1st and 2nd Battalions.

| | | | | |
|---|---|---|---|---|
| Lieut. O. PRICE. | 7/9/14 | Holland | 29/12/17 | 7/1/19 |
| Lt.-Col. J. A. GIBBS. | 10/9/14 | Holland | 29/12/17 | 16/8/18 |
| Capt. E. JENKINS. | 10/9/14 | Holland | 29/12/17 | 3/1/19 |
| Lieut. M. C. B. K. YOUNG. | 10/9/14 | Holland | 29/12/17 | 17/2/19 |
| Major E. N. TOWNSEND. | 19/9/14 | Switzerland | 9/12/17 | 9/12/18 |
| 2/Lt. H. G. HENDERSON. | 8/11/14 | | | 11/9/17 |
| Lieut. R. O'D. CAREY. | 10/11/14 | Holland | 24/2/18 | 1/1/19 |
| Lieut. J. BENNETT. | 16/11/14 | Holland | 24/2/18 | 18/11/18 |
| Lieut. E. B. DAVIS. | 5/5/15 | Holland | 23/3/18 | 18/11/18 |
| Lieut. G. W. OLIPHANT. | | Holland | 29/12/17 | 22/1/19 |
| 2/Lt. G. H. BEYFUS. | 6/5/15 | | | 14/12/18 |
| Capt. K. E. CUNNINGHAM. | 3/5/17 | (*Died*). | | |
| 2/Lt. J. F. RHODES. | 3/5/17 | | | 6/12/18 |
| 2/Lt. A. H. LARCOMBE. | 3/5/17 | | | 16/1/19 |
| 2/Lt. W. REES. | 3/5/17 | | | 31/12/18 |
| 2/Lt. S. A. BELSHAW. | 3/5/17 | | | 4/1/19 |
| 2/Lt. J. D. V. MACKINTOSH. | 3/5/17 | | | 7/1/18 |
| 2/Lt. G. D. JOHNSTON. | 10/10/17 | | | 6/12/18 |
| ‡Lieut. S. WALLER. | 15/4/18 | | | 1/12/18 |

### 4th Battalion.

| | | |
|---|---|---|
| †2/Lt. J. MAUDE. | 20/7/18 | 14/1/19 |

### 5th Battalion.

| | | | |
|---|---|---|---|
| 2/Lt. N. E. BENTLEY. | 6/2/17 | | 2/1/19 |
| Capt. G. E. GLOVER. | 3/5/17 | | 6/1/19 |
| 2/Lt. T. W. M. HUTTON. | 3/5/17 | | 6/12/18 |
| 2/Lt. G. T. DARWENT. | 3/5/17 | | 4/1/19 |
| 2/Lt. T. C. JACOBS. | 3/5/17 | | 17/12/18 |
| §2/Lt. E. G. MACKENZIE. | 20/1/18 | | 17/12/18 |
| 2/Lt. A. CAWTHRA. | 28/3/18 | | 6/12/18 |
| Lieut. E. R. STORRY. | 22/7/18 | | 11/1/19 |
| Capt. W. GRANTHAM. | 11/10/18 | (*Died* 30/11/18 at Gottingen). | |

### 6th Battalion

| | | |
|---|---|---|
| Capt. W. K. LAW. | 3/5/17 | 7/1/18 |
| 2/Lt. G. F. SWABY. | 25/4/18 | 18/12/18 |

### 7th Battalion.

| | | |
|---|---|---|
| Capt. J. L. WATSON. | 11/10/18 | 11/1/18 |

*Attached from Som. L.I.  †Attached from A.S.C.
‡Attached from D.C.L.I.  §Attached from West Yorks.

**WEST RIDING REGIMENT—Continued.**

### 9th Battalion.

| Name. | Missing. | Interned. | Repatriated. |
|---|---|---|---|
| 2/Lt. H. S. FORD. | 13/8/17 | | 2/1/19 |

### 13th Battalion.

| | | | |
|---|---|---|---|
| 2/Lt. H. E. L. PRIDAY. | 14/10/18 | | 16/12/18 |

## BORDER REGIMENT.
### 1st and 2nd Batts.

| | | | |
|---|---|---|---|
| Capt. H. SLEIGH. | | Holland 24/2/18 | 18/11/18 |
| 2/Lt. H. T. THOMPSON. | 14/8/17 | | 14/12/18 |
| 2/Lt. J. W. ROBSON. | 19/11/17 | | 3/12/18 |
| 2/Lt. W. COE. | 11/4/18 | | 13/12/18 |
| 2/Lt. J. W. LITTLE. | 29/10/18 | | –/11/18 |
| 2/Lt. A. EMSLIE. | 29/10/18 | | –/12/18 |

### 5th Battalion.

| | | | |
|---|---|---|---|
| Lieut. E. L. FLEMING. | | | 18/12/18 |
| 2/Lt. T. H. ARNOTT. | | | 29/11/18 |
| 2/Lt. W. D. BROWN. | | | 3/12/18 |
| *2/Lt. A. G. CROLL. | –/3/18 | | 2/1/19 |
| 2/Lt. F. ROBERTSON. | –/3/18 | (*Died* 3/12/18 at Mainz). | |
| Capt. J. N. FRANKS. | 21/3/18 | | 29/11/18 |
| Lieut. A. T. POTTER. | 21/3/18 | | 29/11/18 |
| Lieut. J. S. TURNBULL. | 21/3/18 | | 28/11/18 |
| 2/Lt. C. H. CORBETT. | 21/3/18 | | 3/12/18 |
| Capt. O. J. FEETHAM. | 22/3/18 | | 3/12/18 |
| Lieut. N. GRAHAM. | 24/3/18 | | 18/12/18 |

### 7th Battalion.

| | | | |
|---|---|---|---|
| 2/Lt. H. L. MORGAN. | 2/11/16 | | 18/12/18 |
| 2/Lt. R. G. BIRD. | 21/3/18 | | 5/1/19 |
| Lieut. H. S. TUCKETT. | 20/10/18 | | 16/12/18 |

### 8th Battalion.

| | | | |
|---|---|---|---|
| †Capt. A. MISCAMPBELL. | 27/5/18 | | 26/12/18 |
| Lieut. H. LANSLEY. | 27/5/18 | | 2/1/19 |
| 2/Lt. J. BROWN. | 27/5/18 | | –/12/18 |
| 2/Lt. D. PHILIP. | 27/5/18 | | –/12/18 |
| 2/Lt. C. SPENCE. | 27/5/18 | | –/12/18 |
| 2/Lt. G. SUTCLIFFE. | 27/5/18 | | –/12/18 |
| 2/Lt. W. T. THORNTON. | 27/5/18 | | –/1/19 |

### 11th Battalion.

| | | | |
|---|---|---|---|
| Capt. W. A. WELSH. | 18/11/16 | | –/1/19 |
| 2/Lt. H. N. SPENCE. | 18/11/16 | | 17/12/18 |
| 2/Lt. J. G. NIXON. | 18/11/16 | | |
| 2/Lt. D. W. BRADY. | 18/11/16 | | 17/12/18 |
| 2/Lt. JOHN CHERRY. | 10/7/17 | | 17/12/18 |
| Lieut. G. W. N. ROWSELL. | 10/7/17 | | 16/8/18 |
| 2/Lt. J. B. A. HOPE. | 10/7/17 | | 17/12/18 |
| 2/Lt. W. Y. FERNIE. | 10/7/17 | | 2/1/19 |
| ‡2/Lt. F. J. RIDGWAY. | 10/7/17 | | 14/12/18 |

\*Attached from Durham L. I.  
†Attached from A.S.C.  ‡Attached T.M.B.

## ROYAL SUSSEX REGIMENT.
### 1st and 2nd Battalions.

| Name. | Missing. | Interned. | Repatriated. |
|---|---|---|---|
| 2/Lt. J. J. RUSSELL. | | Switzerland 12/8/16 | −/10/17 |
| 2/Lt. A. J. HUTCHINS. | 21/3/18 | (*Died* 22/3/18 at Pithem) | |
| Lieut. A. H. SMART. | 27/3/18 | | 29/11/18 |

### 7th Battalion.

| | | | |
|---|---|---|---|
| 2/Lt. C. F. ROLFE. | 4/8/16 | Switzerland 27/12/17 | 9/12/18 |
| 2/Lt. A. D. BULLOCK. | 25/7/17 | | 17/12/18 |

### 9th Battalion.

| | | | |
|---|---|---|---|
| Capt. H. BURY. | 26/9/15 | | 11/9/17 |
| Capt. F. T. GODMAN. | 26/9/15 | (*Died* 12/10/17 at Holzminden) | |
| 2/Lt. T. R. KIRKPATRICK. | 26/9/15 | Holland 10/4/18 | 20/11/18 |
| Capt. H. SAXON. | 21/3/18 | | 11/12/18 |
| Lieut. W. E. PALING. | 21/3/18 | | 10/12/18 |
| 2/Lt. C. CLERIHEW. | 22/3/18 | | −/12/18 |
| Capt. N. E. YOUNG. | 25/3/18 | | 14/12/18 |

### 11th Battalion.

| | | | |
|---|---|---|---|
| 2/Lt. C. H. CONWAY. | 31/7/17 | | 3/1/19 |
| 2/Lt. J. W. GIBBS. | 21/3/18 | | 3/12/18 |
| 2/Lt. H. ETHERTON. | 22/3/18 | | 31/12/18 |
| Capt. C. LAPWORTH. | 24/3/18 | | 25/12/18 |
| 2/Lt. A. R. NORRIS. | 24/3/18 | | 21/1/19 |
| 2/Lt. E. C. PIPER. | 26/3/18 | | 3/12/18 |
| *2/Lt. A. W. NEALE. | 30/3/18 | | 31/12/18 |
| Lieut. H. V. BADCOCK. | 26/4/18 | | 31/12/18 |
| 2/Lt. C. A. VORLEY. | 3/9/16 | (*Died* at Cauldry 13/9/16). | |

### 12th Battalion.

| | | | |
|---|---|---|---|
| 2/Lt. J. R. ARDILL. | 30/6/16 | Holland 16/5/18 | 22/11/18 |
| 2/Lt. F. W. MOYLE. | 30/6/16 | | −/11/18 |
| 2/Lt. S. H. SWALLOW. | 30/6/16 | Holland 16/5/18 | 23/10/18 |

### 13th Battalion.

| | | | |
|---|---|---|---|
| Capt. C. G. WALTER. | 22/3/18 | | −/12/18 |
| Lieut. R. L. J. CLEAN. | 22/3/18 | | −/12/18 |
| 2/Lt. E. LEVETT. | 22/3/18 | | 17/12/18 |
| 2/Lt. L. G. WHISTLER. | 22/3/18 | | 28/11/18 |
| 2/Lt. S. W. COWAN. | 22/3/18 | | 14/12/18 |
| 2/Lt. R. A. LUSTY. | 26/3/18 | | 18/12/18 |
| Lieut. H. C. HARVEY. | 26/4/18 | | 29/11/18 |
| 2/Lt. L. H. STOTT. | 26/4/18 | | 3/12/18 |
| 2/Lt. F. J. SOUTHERN. | 26/4/18 | | 29/11/18 |

### 16th Battalion.

| | | | |
|---|---|---|---|
| Lieut. H. T. TRIGGS. | 21/9/18 | | −/12/18 |

## HAMPSHIRE REGIMENT.
### 1st and 2nd Battalions.

| | | | |
|---|---|---|---|
| Major N. W. BARLOW. | 2/9/14 | Switzerland 9/12/17 | 8/12/18 |
| Capt. N. BAXTER. | 10/9/14 | Holland 5/1/18 | 22/11/18 |
| Lt. Col. S. JACKSON. | 13/9/14 | Switzerland 19/1/17 | 14/9/17 |
| Lieut. S. HALLS. | 14/9/14 | Holland 5/1/18 | −/−/18 |
| Lieut. J. LE HUNTE. | 16/9/14 | Switzerland 9/12/17 | 9/12/18 |

*Attached T.M.B.

## HAMPSHIRE REGIMENT—continued.
### 1st and 2nd Battalions—continued.

| Name. | Missing. | Interned. | Repatriated. |
|---|---|---|---|
| Lieut. G. T. ROSE. | 25/9/14 | Holland 22/1/18 | 18/11/18 |
| Capt. N. C. ROBERTSON. | 23/4/17 | (*Died* 20/6/17) | |
| Lieut. P. A. CORNISH. | 23/4/17 | | 4/12/18 |
| 2/Lt. J. B. SIMONDS. | 23/4/17 | | 31/12/18 |
| 2/Lt. H. W. RENSHAW. | 28/3/18 | | 18/12/18 |
| 2/Lt. J. R. POUNCEY. | 15/6/18 | | 8/12/18 |

### 11th Battalion.

| Name. | Missing. | Interned. | Repatriated. |
|---|---|---|---|
| *2/Lt. H. S. ROOTS. | 21/3/18 | | 17/12/18 |
| 2/Lt. R. F. COURTIER. | 22/3/18 | | 2/1/19 |
| Major T. P. THYNE. | 29/3/18 | | –/12/18 |
| Major C. J. HAZARD. | 29/3/18 | | –/1/19 |
| 2/Lt. J. SMITH. | 29/3/18 | | 18/12/18 |

### 14th Battalion.

| Name. | Missing. | Interned. | Repatriated. |
|---|---|---|---|
| Lieut. R. SIMPSON. | 3/9/16 | | 18/12/18 |
| 2/Lt. J. S. HAYDON. | 3/9/16 | | 3/1/19 |
| 2/Lt. D. McL. TEW. | 3/9/16 | | 18/12/18 |

### 15th Battalion.

| Name. | Missing. | Interned. | Repatriated. |
|---|---|---|---|
| 2/Lt. R. E. MARTIN. | 5/8/17 | | 4/12/18 |

## SOUTH STAFFORDSHIRE REGIMENT.
### 1st and 2nd Battalions.

| Name. | Missing. | Interned. | Repatriated. |
|---|---|---|---|
| Capt. O. DE TRAFFORD. | 20/10/14 | Holland 24/2/18 | 18/11/18 |
| Lieut. C. Boys ADAMS. | 20/10/14 | Holland 6/2/18 | 22/11/18 |
| Lieut. R. R. RILEY. | 20/10/14 | Holland 24/2/18 | 18/11/18 |
| Lieut. H. WILLOUGHBY. | 31/10/14 | Holland 6/2/18 | 18/11/18 |
| Lieut. W. FOSTER. | | (*Died* 14/11/14 at Frankfort). | |
| 2/Lt. T. W. DOKE. | 11/1/17 | | 14/12/18 |
| 2/Lt. E. R. OXLADE. | 17/2/17 | | 29/11/18 |
| Lieut. W. A. DICKINS. | 28/3/17 | | 14/12/18 |
| Capt. W. A. SIMMONDS. | 28/4/17 | | 3/1/19 |
| 2/Lt. C. W. BLOOMFIELD. | 28/4/17 | | 6/12/18 |
| 2/Lt. V. HIELD. | 26/10/17 | Holland 30/4/18 | 7/9/18 |
| 2/Lt. A. E. CAUNT. | 24/3/18 | | –/12/18 |
| 2/Lt. A. T. JACKSON. | 24/3/18 | | 18/12/18 |
| 2/Lt. S. J. BUCKLEY. | 24/3/18 | (*Died*) | |
| 2/Lt. F. W. M. LAMBERT. | 24/3/18 | | 25/12/18 |
| 2/Lt. E. D. ROBERTS. | 24/3/18 | | 11/12/18 |
| 2/Lt. M. J. QUILL. | 24/3/18 | | 11/12/18 |
| Capt. E. O. KAY. | 25/3/18 | | 25/12/18 |
| 2/Lt. J. W. MILLAR. | 25/3/18 | | 25/12/18 |
| Capt. E. H. PAYNE. | 24/3/18 | | 10/12/18 |

### 4th Battalion.

| Name. | Missing. | Interned. | Repatriated. |
|---|---|---|---|
| 2/Lt. S. G. WHITAKER. | 23/4/17 | Switzerland 27/12/17 | 23/12/18 |
| 2/Lt. S. K. MOREY. | 9/4/18 | | 30/12/18 |
| 2/Lt. A. P. WALKER. | 9/4/18 | | 19/12/18 |
| †Lt.-Col. L. H. K. FINCH. | 11/4/18 | | 6/12/18 |
| Capt. A. H. NUTT. | 26/4/18 | | 14/12/18 |
| Capt. H. R. WEBB. | 26/4/18 | (*Died* 7/3/18 at Deinye). | |
| ‡2/Lt. L. PARAMORE. | 27/5/18 | | 6/1/19 |
| 2/Lt. A. St. LEDGER. | 27/5/18 | | 5/1/19 |

*Attached from Royal Dublin Fusiliers.
†Attached from Cheshire Regiment.
‡Attached T.M.B.

## SOUTH STAFFORDSHIRE REGIMENT—continued.
### 5th Battalion.

| Name. | Missing. | Interned. | Repatriated. |
|---|---|---|---|
| 2/Lt. H. W. GREGORY. | 21/3/18 | | 18/12/18 |
| 2/Lt. R. BAXTER. | 21/3/18 | | 18/12/18 |
| 2/Lt. J. W. WRIGHT. | 12/10/18 | | 5/1/19 |

### 6th Battalion.

| Name. | Missing. | Interned. | Repatriated. |
|---|---|---|---|
| 2/Lt. A. DOWNES. | 26/4/17 | | 3/12/18 |
| Capt. C. E. L. WHITEHOUSE. | 21/3/18 | | 13/12/18 |
| Capt. W. A. JORDAN. | 21/3/18 | | 9/12/18 |
| Capt. W. S. LYNES. | 21/3/18 | | 1/12/18 |
| Capt. W. A. ADAM. | 21/3/18 | | 29/11/18 |
| Lieut. L. J. SHELTON. | 21/3/18 | | 4/12/18 |
| Lieut. R. G. BOYCOTT. | 21/3/18 | | –/11/18 |
| Lieut. W. T. BUTLER. | 21/3/18 | | 30/12/18 |
| 2/Lt. T. A. GOUGH. | 21/3/18 | | 11/12/18 |
| 2/Lt. J. A. GEYTON. | 21/3/18 | | 20/12/18 |
| 2/Lt. H. P. BUNN. | 21/3/18 | | –/12/18 |
| 2/Lt. J. H. HICKMAN. | 21/3/18 | | 2/1/19 |
| 2/Lt. C. HAWORTH. | 21/3/18 | | 29/11/18 |
| 2/Lt. H. E. SHIPTON. | 21/3/18 | | 11/12/18 |
| 2/Lt. F. W. SPIBEY. | 21/3/18 | | 11/12/18 |
| 2/Lt. G. A. YATES. | 21/3/18 | | 19/12/18 |
| 2/Lt. J. BONSHOR. | 21/3/18 | (*Died* 26/7/18 at Stendal). | |

## DORSETSHIRE REGIMENT.
### 1st and 2nd Battalions.

| Name. | Missing. | Interned. | | Repatriated. |
|---|---|---|---|---|
| Lieut. G. A. BURNAND. | 24/8/14 | Holland | 5/1/18 | 17/11/18 |
| Lieut. W. LEISHMAN. | 10/9/14 | Holland | 29/12/17 | 16/11/18 |
| Capt. C. F. M. MARGETTS. | 14/9/14 | Holland | 5/1/18 | 18/11/18 |
| 2/Lt. C. WELLS. | 14/9/14 | Holland | 24/2/18 | 4/10/18 |
| Capt. A. CLUTTERBUCK. | 13/10/14 | Holland | 6/2/18 | –/11/18 |
| Capt. A. S. FRASER. | 13/10/14 | Switzerland | 12/8/17 | 11/9/17 |
| Capt. J. KELSALL. | 13/10/14 | Holland | 6/2/18 | 18/11/18 |
| Lieut. L. GRANT-DALTON. | 13/10/14 | Holland | 6/2/18 | 14/1/19 |
| Capt. H. BEVERIDGE. | 22/10/14 | Holland | 24/2/18 | –/11/18 |
| Lieut. C. H. WOODHOUSE. | 22/10/14 | Holland | 10/4/18 | 18/11/18 |
| *2/Lt. W. E. EDWARDS. | 2/10/18 | | | 28/11/18 |
| 2/Lt. H. B. RATHBORNE. | 2/10/18 | | | 28/12/18 |

### 5th Battalion.

| Name. | Missing. | | | Repatriated. |
|---|---|---|---|---|
| 2/Lt. K. S. B. BATEMAN. | 11/1/17 | | | –/12/18 |
| 2/Lt. R. L. STATHAM. | 9/4/18 | | | –/11/18 |

### 6th Battalion.

| Name. | Missing. | | | Repatriated. |
|---|---|---|---|---|
| Lieut. E. L. B. LART. | 25/3/18 | | | 25/8/18 |

## SOUTH LANCASHIRE REGIMENT.
### 1st and 2nd Battalions.

| Name. | Missing. | Interned. | | Repatriated. |
|---|---|---|---|---|
| Major G. EWART. | 10/9/14 | Holland | 29/12/17 | 1/2/19 |
| Lieut. F. BERRY. | 30/9/14 | Holland | 29/12/17 | returned for duty. |
| Lieut. H. G. W. IRWIN. | 10/9/14 | | | 13/9/17 |
| Lieut. J. ICKE. | 10/9/14 | Holland | 22/1/18 | 1/11/18 |

*Attached from Gloucesters.

## SOUTH LANCASHIRE REGIMENT—continued.
### 1st and 2nd Battalions—continued.

| Name. | Missing. | Interned. | | Repatriated. |
|---|---|---|---|---|
| *Lieut. H. T. D. MEREDITH. | –/–/14 | Switzerland | –/8/16 | 24/3/18 |
| Capt. F. M. COLVILLE. | 21/10/14 | Holland | 6/2/18 | 23/10/18 |
| Lieut. A. F. THORP. | 21/10/14 | Holland | 6/2/18 | 18/11/18 |
| 2/Lt. W. G. CLARK. | 21/10/14 | Holland | 24/2/18 | 18/11/18 |
| Capt. K. H. O. R. SADGROVE. | 22/3/18 | | | 10/12/18 |
| Lieut. A. C. GOSDEN. | 22/3/18 | | | 22/12/18 |
| 2/Lt. L. G. MARTHEWS. | 22/3/18 | (Died 22/4/18 at Achen). | | |
| †Capt. A. C. DEVLIN. | 27/5/18 | | | 2/1/19 |
| 2/Lt. G. PARKIN. | 27/5/18 | | | 11/12/18 |
| 2/Lt. W. NAPIER. | 28/5/18 | | | 13/12/18 |
| 2/Lt. R. W. SIMPSON. | 2/6/18 | | | 13/12/19 |

### 4th Battalion.

| Name. | Missing. | Interned. | | Repatriated. |
|---|---|---|---|---|
| Lieut. E. E. TOWLER. | 28/8/18 | | | 11/12/18 |

### 5th Battalion.

| Name. | Missing. | Interned. | | Repatriated. |
|---|---|---|---|---|
| 2/Lt. H. GAMBLE. | 24/10/15 | Holland | 9/4/18 | 23/9/18 |
| 2/Lt. S. R. SMITH. | 22/4/18 | | | 23/12/18 |
| Lt.-Col. C. P. JAMES. | 30/11/17 | | | 27/11/18 |
| Capt. F. B. F. HARGREAVES. | 30/11/17 | | | 27/11/18 |
| Capt. H. G. WHITAKER. | 30/11/17 | | | 17/12/18 |
| Capt. J. SHUFFLEBOTHAM. | 30/11/17 | | | 3/12/18 |
| Capt. E. R. McLEOD. | 30/11/17 | | | 17/12/18 |
| Lieut. P. PLOWMAN. | 30/11/17 | | | 25/12/18 |
| Lieut. V. T. THIERENS. | 30/11/17 | | | 14/12/18 |
| ‡2/Lt. E. KITCHEN. | 30/11/17 | | | 17/12/18 |
| ‡2/Lt. L. B. TAYLOR. | 30/11/17 | | | 17/12/18 |
| 2/Lt. D. DE PENNINGTON. | 30/11/17 | | | 17/12/18 |
| §2/Lt. F. H. FRANCIS. | 30/11/17 | | | 14/12/18 |
| 2/Lt. W. DICKINSON. | 30/11/17 | | | 3/12/18 |
| 2/Lt. A. E. EMBERSON. | 30/11/17 | | | 17/12/18 |
| 2/Lt. H. C. INGHAM. | 30/11/17 | | | 17/12/18 |
| 2/Lt. F. V. CLIFFE. | 30/11/17 | | | 25/12/18 |
| 2/Lt. J. G. HALL. | 30/12/17 | | | 24/12/18 |
| 2/Lt. E. G. GIBSON. | 27/5/18 | | | 25/12/18 |
| 2/Lt. A. S. LATTA. | 22/10/18 | | | 8/12/18 |
| 2/Lt. J. C. O. COCKING. | 10/4/17 | (Died). | | 24/9/17 |

### 11th Battalion.

| Name. | Missing. | Interned. | | Repatriated. |
|---|---|---|---|---|
| 2/Lt. R. CARR. | 23/10/18 | | | 30/12/18 |

## WELSH REGIMENT.
### 1st and 2nd Battalions.

| Name. | Missing. | Interned. | | Repatriated. |
|---|---|---|---|---|
| Major L. I. O. ROBINS. | 14/9/14 | | | 13/9/17 |
| Capt. T. MARSHALL. | 21/10/14 | Holland | 24/2/18 | 12/10/18 |
| 2/Lt. A. LEACH. | 21/10/14 | Holland | 24/2/18 | 18/11/18 |
| Lieut. E. M. DOUGLAS. | 20/2/15 | Holland | 1/3/18 | 8/1/19 |
| Major A. G. PROTHERO. | 26/9/15 | Holland | 10/4/18 | 23/9/18 |
| Lieut. E. W. PIDDUCK. | 26/9/15 | Holland | 10/4/18 | 18/11/18 |
| 2/Lt. A. N. HAZELL. | 2/10/15 | Switzerland | 19/12/16 | 11/9/17 |
| Capt. C. E. H. JAMES. | 21/5/16 | Holland | 30/4/18 | 29/1/19 |
| 2/Lt. E. C. MCGROARTY. | 26/7/16 | Switzerland | 9/12/17 | 22/12/18 |
| 2/Lt. L. C. GARBETT. | 12/5/18 | | | 18/12/18 |

*Attached from Liverpool Regiment.    †Attached T.M.B.
‡Attached from Somerset L.I.    §Attached from Buffs.

## WELSH REGIMENT—Continued.

### 3rd Battalion.

| Name. | Missing. | Interned. | Repatriated. |
|---|---|---|---|
| 2/Lt. T. C. S. HUSS. | | | 28/11/18 |

### 9th Battalion.

| Name. | Missing. | Interned. | Repatriated. |
|---|---|---|---|
| Lieut. E. EMBLEM. | 23/3/18 | | 29/11/18 |
| 2/Lt. H. W. THOMPSON. | 25/3/18 | | 13/12/18 |
| Major E. W. BROAKES. | 30/5/18 | | —/12/18 |
| Capt. T. SUGRUE. | 30/5/18 | | 1/1/19 |
| Capt. D. H. THOMAS. | 30/5/18 | | 1/1/19 |
| Lieut. F. M. ST. H. EVANS. | 30/5/18 | | 14/12/18 |
| 2/Lt. J. BODYCOMBE. | 30/5/18 | | 16/1/19 |
| 2/Lt. J. EVANS. | 30/5/18 | | 17/12/18 |
| 2/Lt. T. E. NOBLE. | 30/5/18 | | 31/12/18 |
| 2/Lt. G. WILLIAMS. | 30/5/18 | | 30/12/18 |

### 14th Battalion.

| Name. | Missing. | Interned. | Repatriated. |
|---|---|---|---|
| Capt. J. S. STRANGE. | 10/5/18 | | 18/12/18 |

### 15th Battalion.

| Name. | Missing. | Interned. | Repatriated. |
|---|---|---|---|
| 2/Lt. D. I. REES. | 10/5/18 | | 23/10/18 |

### 17th Battalion.

| Name. | Missing. | Interned. | Repatriated. |
|---|---|---|---|
| Lieut. W. J. MOULD. | 24/11/17 | | 25/12/18 |
| 2/Lt. F. S. J. McK. LEWIS. | 25/11/17 | | 27/11/18 |

### 18th Battalion.

| Name. | Missing. | Interned. | Repatriated. |
|---|---|---|---|
| Capt. T. G. WHITE. | 9/4/18 | | 18/12/18 |
| Lieut. E. V. EVANS. | 9/4/18 | | 10/12/18 |
| Lieut. J. S. G. HACKNEY. | 9/4/18 | | 23/9/18 |
| Lieut. R. O. OWEN. | 9/4/18 | | 13/12/18 |
| Lieut. J. I. RICHARDS. | 9/4/18 | | —/12/18 |
| Lieut. O. SALISBURY. | 9/4/18 | | 23/9/18 |
| Lieut. G. I. TURNBULL. | 9/4/18 | (*Died* at Lille). | |
| 2/Lt. D. M. DAVIES. | 9/4/18 | | 2/12/18 |
| 2/Lt. W. P. GARNER. | 9/4/18 | | |
| *2/Lt. G. OWENS. | 9/4/18 | | 29/11/18 |
| 2/Lt. C. S. THOMAS. | 9/4/18 | | 25/12/18 |
| 2/Lt. J. C. TUCKER. | 9/4/18 | | 25/12/18 |
| 2/Lt. W. M. WILLIAMS. | 9/4/18 | | 1/12/18 |
| 2/Lt. J. C. HILL. | 9/4/18 | | 2/12/18 |

### 24th Battalion.

| Name. | Missing. | Interned. | Repatriated. |
|---|---|---|---|
| Lieut. H. C. WATKINS. | 21/9/18 | (*Died* at Le Cateau 23/10/18). | |

## BLACK WATCH.

### 1st and 2nd Battalions.

| Name. | Missing. | Interned. | | Repatriated. |
|---|---|---|---|---|
| Capt. A. D. CAMPBELL KROOK. | 29/11/14 | Holland | 24/2/18 | 4/10/18 |
| 2/Lt. L. MACLEOD. | 2/11/15 | Holland | —/4/18 | 18/11/18 |
| Capt. R. K. ARBUTHNOT, M.C. | 18/4/18 | | | 29/11/18 |
| Lieut. G. T. KIRKCALDY. | 18/4/18 | | | 6/12/18 |
| Lieut. J. C. STEPHEN. | 18/4/18 | | | 18/12/18 |
| Lieut. D. C. STEWART-SMITH. | 18/4/18 | | | 13/12/18 |
| 2/Lt. R. M. HUME. | 18/4/18 | | | —/1/19 |
| 2/Lt. P. W. MACKAY. | 18/4/18 | | | 13/12/18 |
| 2/Lt. R. W. RAMSAY. | 18/4/18 | | | 1/12/18 |
| †2/Lt. M. JAMESON. | 18/4/18 | | | 18/12/18 |

*Attached from Royal Welsh Fusiliers.    †Attached from A.S.C.

## BLACK WATCH—continued.

### 4th Battalion.

| Name. | Missing. | Interned. | Repatriated. |
|---|---|---|---|
| Capt. C. M. COUPER. | 26/9/15 | (*Died* 28/9/15 at Sainghain). | |
| Capt. O. MOODIE. | 26/9/15 | Switzerland 9/12/17 | |
| 2/Lt. G. A. ANDERSON. | 12/4/18 | | 1/12/18 |

### 4/5th Battalion.

| | | | |
|---|---|---|---|
| Lieut. J. D. STEWART. | 22/3/18 | | 1/1/19 |
| 2/Lt. D. McNICOL. | 22/3/18 | | 25/12/18 |
| Lieut. W. L. GILLIES. | 23/3/18 | | 17/12/18 |
| Lieut. J. F. McL. WILKIE. | 26/3/18 | | –/12/18 |
| 2/Lt. G. R. FARRAR. | 26/4/18 | | 6/12/18 |
| 2/Lt. W. K. M GREGOR. | 28/7/18 | | 13/12/18 |
| 2/Lt. T. C. BELL. | 21/8/18 | | 13/12/18 |

### 5th Battalion.

| | | | |
|---|---|---|---|
| Capt. J. M. R. KEILLER. | 23/3/18 | | 18/12/18 |
| Lieut. G. W. YOUNG. | | (*Died* 8/4/18). | |

### 6th Battalion.

| | | | |
|---|---|---|---|
| Capt. J. LINDSAY, M.C. | 21/3/18 | | 19/12/18 |
| Capt. D. CABLE. | 21/3/18 | | 29/12/18 |
| Lieut. J. PATRICK. | 21/3/18 | | 18/12/18 |
| 2/Lt. A. REID. | 21/3/18 | | 18/12/18 |
| 2/Lt. N. A. LAUGHLAND. | 21/3/18 | | 18/12/18 |
| 2/Lt. H. S. GUTHRIE. | 21/3/18 | (*Died* 31/3/18 at Bouchain). | |
| 2/Lt. C. C. MACINTYRE. | 22/3/18 | | 11/12/18 |
| 2/Lt. W. ROBSON. | 11/4/18 | | 2/12/18 |

### 7th Battalion.

| | | | |
|---|---|---|---|
| Capt. D. S. GREIG. | 21/3/18 | | 19/12/18 |
| Capt. A. M. MOODIE. | 21/3/18 | | 10/12/18 |
| Lieut. T. W. BERRY. | 21/3/18 | | 29/11/18 |
| Lieut. J. R. GORDON. | 21/3/18 | | –/12/18 |
| Lieut. J. MACLENNAN. | 21/3/18 | | 3/1/19 |
| 2/Lt. A. KERR. | 21/3/18 | | 18/12/18 |
| 2/Lt. J. HISLOP. | 21/3/18 | | 11/12/18 |
| Lieut. A. L. MILLER. | 22/3/18 | | 25/12/18 |
| 2/Lt. I. K. MACKINTOSH. | 22/3/18 | | 10/12/18 |
| 2/Lt. A. M. SIMPSON. | 22/3/18 | | 18/12/18 |
| 2/Lt. J. McCRACKEN. | 27/3/18 | | 11/12/18 |

### 8th Battalion.

| | | | |
|---|---|---|---|
| Lieut. T. D. SHAW-MACLAREN. | 22/3/18 | | –/11/18 |
| 2/Lt. J. B. POLLOCK. | 22/3/18 | | 29/11/18 |
| 2/Lt. H. F. C. GOVAN. | 23/3/18 | | 11/12/18 |
| 2/Lt. G. R. B. HENDERSON. | 24/3/18 | | 25/12/18 |

### 9th Battalion.

| | | | |
|---|---|---|---|
| 2/Lt. E. P. M. WALCOTT. | 28/3/18 | | –/12/18 |
| 2/Lt. W. A. FORREST. | 28/3/18 | | 29/11/18 |
| 2/Lt. R. B. ANDERSON. | 10/4/18 | | 2/12/18 |

*Attached from American Red Cross.

## OXFORDSHIRE AND BUCKINGHAMSHIRE LIGHT INFANTRY.
### 1st and 2nd Battalions.

| Name. | Missing. | Interned. | Repatriated. |
|---|---|---|---|
| Lieut. G. T. BUTTON. | 25/9/14 | Switzerland 27/12/17 | 9/12/18 |
| Capt. P. GODSAL. | 8/10/14 | (Escaped) | –/4/17 |
| Capt. D. T. BARNES. | 25/3/18 | | –/12/18 |

### Bucks Battalion.

| | | | |
|---|---|---|---|
| Capt. G. G. JACKSON. | 21/7/16 | | 1/11/18 |
| *2/Lt. H. F. HORNE. | 30/3/18 | | 1/12/18 |

### 4th Battalion.

| | | | |
|---|---|---|---|
| 2/Lt. T. W. F. GUILDFORD. | 28/2/17 | | 1/1/19 |
| 2/Lt. C. B. HUNT. | 28/2/17 | | 18/12/18 |
| Capt. G. V. ROWBOTHAM. | 21/3/18 | | 2/12/18 |
| Capt. K. E. BROWN. | 21/3/18 | (Died 12/4/18 at Hautmont). | |
| Capt. C. E. P. FORESHEW. | 21/3/18 | | 14/12/18 |
| †Lieut. R. OSTLER. | 21/3/18 | | 2/12/18 |
| 2/Lt. C. H. WALLINGTON. | 21/3/18 | | 14/12/18 |
| 2/Lt. G. SHELLEY. | 21/3/18 | | –/12/18 |
| 2/Lt. J. C. CUNNINGHAM. | 21/3/18 | | 14/12/18 |
| 2/Lt. C. C. HALL. | 21/3/18 | | –/12/18 |
| 2/Lt. V. C. GRAY. | 21/3/18 | | –/12/18 |
| 2/Lt. R. G. H. GOUGH. | 21/3/18 | | 14/12/18 |
| 2/Lt. P. J. SIMMS. | 21/3/18 | | 14/12/18 |
| 2/Lt. C. H. LEACH. | 21/3/18 | | 14/12/18 |
| 2/Lt. E. LITTLE. | 21/3/18 | | 14/12/18 |
| 2/Lt. F. A. NAYLOR. | 21/3/18 | | 14/12/18 |
| Major H. J. BENNETT. | 30/3/18 | | –/12/18 |
| 2/Lt. H. G. LEDGER. | 6/4/18 | | 1/12/18 |
| 2/Lt. G. A. ROWLERSON. | 13/9/18 | | 13/12/18 |
| 2/Lt. P. E. CRADDOCK. | 29/9/18 | | 29/11/18 |

### 5th Battalion.

| | | | |
|---|---|---|---|
| 2/Lt. R. J. RICHARDS. | 3/5/17 | (Died 12/5/17 at Ferin). | |
| ‡Lieut. W. A. RAMSAY. | 21/3/18 | | 11/12/18 |
| 2/Lt. F. J. COLLINGE. | 21/3/18 | | 8/12/18 |
| Lieut. E. C. COOK. | 21–23/3/18 | | 1/12/18 |
| 2/Lt. R. G. CRESWELL. | 21–23/3/18 | | 10/12/18 |
| Capt D. J. BANKS. | 23/3/18 | | 10/12/18 |
| Capt. H. MONEY. | 23/3/18 | | –/12/18 |
| 2/Lt. H. M. GRAY. | 29/3/18 | | 25/12/18 |
| Major A. M. LABOUCHERE. | 4/4/18 | (Died 30/4/18 at Valenciennes). | |
| Lieut. L. V. D. OWEN. | 4/4/18 | | 3/12/18 |

### 6th Battalion.

| | | | |
|---|---|---|---|
| §2/Lt. A K. STANDAGE. | 10/4/18 | | 1/12/18 |

## ESSEX REGIMENT.
### 1st and 2nd Battalions.

| Name | Missing. | Interned. | Returned for Duty. |
|---|---|---|---|
| Lieut. G. DALE. | –/–/14 | Holland 24/2/18 | |
| 2/Lt. J. P. PEARCE. | 21/10/14 | Holland 6/2/18 | 1/11/18 |
| 2/Lt. A. L. PIPER. | 14/4/17 | Holland –/4/18 | 19/7/18 |
| 2/Lt. G. D. TURK. | 14/4/17 | (Died 23/6/17). | |

*Attached Entrenching Batt.     †Attached from A.S.C.
‡Attached T.M.B.     §Attached Portuguese Corps.

## ESSEX REGIMENT—continued.

### 1st and 2nd Battalions—continued.

| Name. | Missing. | Interned. | Repatriated. |
|---|---|---|---|
| Capt. O. W. HORNE. | 3/5/17 | | 6/12/18 |
| Lieut. C. J. T. F. HOPEGOOD. | 20/11/17 | | 29/11/18 |
| 2/Lt. F. HAVILL. | 21/3/18 | | 18/12/18 |
| Capt. B. C. N. WILLMOTT. | 28/3/18 | | 10/12/18 |
| Lieut. H. L. HUGHES. | 28/3/18 | | 18/12/18 |
| 2/Lt. L. H. PULFER. | 28/3/18 | | 11/12/18 |
| 2/Lt. E. A. PATTERSON. | 28/3/18 | | 13/12/18 |
| 2/Lt. M. S. CLAYDON. | 28/3/18 | | 11/12/18 |
| 2/Lt. G. B. ARNOLD. | 28/3/18 | | 11/12/18 |
| 2/Lt. F C. YOUNG. | 28/3/18 | | 25/12/18 |
| *2/Lt. W. HOPWOOD. | 28/3/18 | | 8/12/18 |
| 2/Lt. S. STORER. | 19/4/18 | | 1/12/18 |
| †2/Lt. W. R. FITCH. | 27/5/18 | | 26/12/18 |

### 9th Battalion.

| Name. | Missing. | Interned. | Repatriated. |
|---|---|---|---|
| 2/Lt. V. C. H. YOUNG. | 17/3/17 | | 14/12/18 |
| 2/Lt. S. A. CLARK. | 11/7/17 | | 13/5/18 |
| †Capt. C. COLLINS. | 30/11/17 | | 27/11/18 |
| Capt. E. R. CAPPER. | 30/11/17 | (*Died* 8/12/17 at Coblenz). | |
| Lieut. H. S. COPE. | 27/3/18 | | 26/12/18 |
| Lieut. H. E. D. ELLIOTT. | 27/3/18 | | 25/12/18 |
| ‡2/Lt. T. W. BETTS. | 18/9/18 | | 14/12/18 |
| 2/Lt. S. G. LOWSON. | 18/9/18 | | 29/11/18 |

### 10th Battalion.

| Name. | Missing. | Interned. | Repatriated. |
|---|---|---|---|
| §2/Lt. G. M. TURNER. | 30/11/17 | | 14/12/18 |
| 2/Lt. J. G. CULVER. | 21/3/18 | | 19/1/19 |
| Lieut. J. P. AMPS. | 23/3/18 | | 27/11/18 |
| ‖Lieut. A. H. GALLIE. | 23/3/18 | | 1/12/18 |
| Lieut. P. C. CLEALL. | 8/8/18 | (*Died* 26/8/18 at Longavesnes). | |
| 2/Lt. A. WOODS. | 8/8/18 | | 8/12/18 |

### 11th Battalion.

| Name. | Missing. | Interned. | Repatriated. |
|---|---|---|---|
| Major J. L. DAVIES. | 26/9/15 | (*Died*). | |
| Lieut. B. L. MIDDLETON. | 26/9/15 | Holland  —/4/18 | 24/1/19 |
| Lieut. P. E. DALE. | 26/9/15 | | 12/5/18 |
| Capt. J. S. MARKS. | 21/3/18 | | —/12/18 |
| Capt. W. F. MARTINSON. | 21/3/18 | | 19/1/19 |
| Capt. G. SIMPSON. | 22/3/18 | | 29/11/18 |
| 2/Lt. R. V. BULLEN. | 22/3/18 | | 3/12/18 |
| 2/Lt. H. J. WIDGERY. | 12/10/18 | | 13/12/18 |

### 13th Battalion.

| Name. | Missing. | Interned. | Repatriated. |
|---|---|---|---|
| 2/Lt. C. C. N. MARSHALL. | 14/11/16 | | 7/1/18 |
| 2/Lt. H. P. TURNER. | 28/4/17 | | 6/12/18 |
| 2/Lt. A. C. LEECH. | 28/4/17 | | 7/1/19 |
| 2/Lt. W. FREEMAN. | 28/4/17 | | 17/12/17 |
| Capt. H. T. JESSOP. | 29/11/17 | | 18/12/18 |
| Lieut. J. D. ROBINSON. | 29/11/17 | | 25/12/18 |
| 2/Lt. E. L. CORPS. | 29/11/17 | | 31/12/18 |
| †2/Lt. R. J. TREBILCO. | 30/11/17 | | 6/1/19 |
| 2/Lt. C. W. PHILLIPS. | 2/12/17 | | 25/12/18 |
| 2/Lt. V. E. BLOOMFIELD. | 21/3/18 | | 27/11/18 |

*Attached from Liverpools.  †Attached T.M.B.
‡ Attached from Hunts Cyclists.  §Attached from Glasgow Yeomanry.
‖Attached 35/T.M.B.

## SHERWOOD FORESTERS.
### 1st and 2nd Battalions.

| Name. | Missing. | Interned. | | Repatriated. |
|---|---|---|---|---|
| Capt. W. DRURY-LOWE. | 20/10/14 | Holland | 6/2/18 | 18/11/18 |
| Capt. W. H. WILKIN. | 20/10/14 | Holland | 6/2/18 | 18/11/18 |
| Lieut. T. E. DAVEY. | 20/10/14 | Holland | 6/2/18 | 18/11/18 |
| Lieut. G. EDWARDS | 20/10/14 | Holland | 6/2/18 | 17/11/18 |
| Lieut. T. HUDSON. | 20/10/14 | Switzerland | 9/12/17 | 9/12/18 |
| Lieut. R. G. S. MAY. | 20/10/14 | Holland | 6/2/18 | 19/1/19 |
| Lieut. C. SCHNEIDER | 20/10/14 | Holland | 6/2/18 | 18/11/18 |
| Lieut. A. TROOPS | 20/10/14 | Holland | 6/2/18 | Returned for Duty |

### 1st Battalion.

| Name. | Missing. | Interned. | Repatriated. |
|---|---|---|---|
| Lieut. R. W. ROUNDS. | 25/3/18 | | 25/12/18 |
| 2/Lt. J. T. SIDDONS. | 25/3/18 | | -/1/19 |
| 2/Lt. W. GREENSMITH. | 26/3/18 | | -/12/18 |
| *Capt. E. B. GREENSMITH. | 27/5/18 | | 25/12/18 |
| Capt. C. HARRISON. | 27/5/18 | | -/12/18 |
| Capt. J. F. MENZIES. | 27/5/18 | | 30/12/18 |
| *Lieut. J. E. M. WALKER. | 27/5/18 | | 30/12/18 |
| 2/Lt. W. E. BROWN. | 27/5/18 | | -/12/18 |
| 2/Lt. T. E. INMAN. | 27/5/18 | | -/12/18 |
| 2/Lt. A. NEILD. | 27/5/18 | | 13/12/18 |
| 2/Lt. FitzD. SEVERN. | 27/5/18 | | 30/12/18 |
| 2/Lt. D. M. START. | 29/5/18 | | 13/12/18 |
| 2/Lt. G. W. WEBB. | 29/5/18 | | 13/12/18 |

### 2nd Battalion.

| Name. | Missing. | Interned. | Repatriated. |
|---|---|---|---|
| Capt. N. H. BEEDHAM. | 21/3/18 | | 13/12/18 |
| Capt. L. H. FINCH. | 21/3/18 | | 14/1/19 |
| Capt. T. THORNTON. | 21/3/18 | | 18/12/18 |
| 2/Lt. E. BOOTHROYD | 21/3/18 | (*Died* 20/4/18 at Aachen). | |
| 2/Lt. G. S. W. PROFIT | 21/3/18 | | 17/12/18 |
| 2/Lt. H. STIRLAND. | 21/3/18 | | -/12/18 |
| 2/Lt. H. G. TAYLOR. | 21/3/18 | | 29/11/18 |

### 5th Battalion.

| Name. | Missing. | Interned. | | Repatriated. |
|---|---|---|---|---|
| Lieut. M. S. FRYAR. | 1/7/16 | | | 22/11/18 |
| Capt. F. H. M. LEWES. | 2/7/16 | (*Died*). | | |
| 2/Lt. T. F. C. DOWNMAN. | 2/7/16 | | | 15/12/18 |
| 2/Lt. H. H. LILLY. | 2/7/16 | Holland | 15/5/18 | |
| 2/Lt. W. T. GREENFIELD. | 30/6/17 | | | 6/12/18 |

### 2/5th Battalion.

| Name. | Missing. | Interned. | Repatriated. |
|---|---|---|---|
| Lt.-Col. H. R. GADD. | 21/3/18 | | 8/12/18 |
| Capt. F. E. ANDREWS. | 21/3/18 | | |
| Capt. R. J. CASE. | 21/3/18 | | 1/12/18 |
| Capt. H. WATERHOUSE. | 21/3/18 | | 25/12/18 |
| Lieut. R. E. A. GRONER. | 21/3/18 | | 20/12/18 |
| Lieut. T. L. HILL. | 21/3/18 | | 2/1/19 |
| Lieut. F. H. SUTHERLAND. | 21/3/18 | | 30/12/18 |
| 2/Lt. H. E. BARKER. | 21/3/18 | | 18/12/18 |
| 2/Lt. A. H. CHAMBERS. | 21/3/18 | | 13/12/18 |
| 2/Lt. L. De MAUNY. | 21/3/18 | | 11/12/18 |
| 2/Lt. S. E. GRAYSTON. | 21/3/18 | | 29/11/18 |
| 2/Lt. W. HAGUE. | 21/3/18 | (*Died* 31/3/18 at Mons). | |
| *2/Lt. A. C. HARRIS. | 21/3/18 | | 15/2/19 |

*Attached T.M.B.

## SHERWOOD FORESTERS—continued.

### 2/5th Battalion—continued.

| Name. | Missing. | Interned. | Repatriated. |
|---|---|---|---|
| 2/Lt. J. W. JAGO. | 21/3/18 | | 21/12/18 |
| 2/Lt. P. A. MURPHY. | 21/3/18 | | 29/11/18 |
| 2/Lt. H. C. PICKTHALL. | 21/3/18 | | 29/11/18 |
| 2/Lt. A. E. SILVERWOOD. | 21/3/18 | | 13/12/18 |
| 2/Lt. A. J. SMITH. | 21/3/18 | | 29/11/18 |
| 2/Lt. R. STONE. | 21/3/18 | | 14/12/18 |
| 2/Lt. C. M. WRIGHT. | 21/3/18 | | 18/12/18 |
| 2/Lt. G. A. MIDDLEMISS. | 23/3/18 | | 1/12/18 |

### 6th Battalion.

| Name. | Missing. | Interned. | Repatriated. |
|---|---|---|---|
| 2/Lt. T. O. COLLES. | 7/4/17 | | 9/12/18 |
| 2/Lt. S. M. JOHNSON. | 21/3/18 | | –/14/18 |
| 2/Lt. H. NUTTALL. | 22/3/18 | | 29/11/18 |

### 2/6th Battalion.

| Name. | Missing. | Interned. | Repatriated. |
|---|---|---|---|
| *Col. H. S. HODGKIN. | 21/3/18 | | 1/12/18 |
| Major A. C. CLARKE. | 21/3/18 | | 29/12/18 |
| †Capt. H. P. GREAVES. | 21/3/12 | | 18/12/18 |
| Capt. S. A. ROGERS. | 21/3/18 | (Died). | |
| Lieut. A. G. F. ELLWOOD. | 21/3/18 | | 29/11/18 |
| ‡Lieut. F. P. FOSTER. | 21/3/18 | | 5/12/18 |
| 2/Lt. L. W. ALLEN. | 21/3/18 | | 17/12/18 |
| 2/Lt. H. C. BARHAM. | 21/3/18 | | 1/12/18 |
| 2/Lt. R. B. BRACE. | 21/3/18 | | 13/12/18 |
| 2/Lt. W. A. COTTON. | 21/3/18 | | 11/12/18 |
| 2/Lt. C. G. HASLAM. | 21/3/18 | | 18/12/18 |
| 2/Lt. H. HICKMAN. | 21/3/18 | | 11/12/18 |
| §2/Lt. P. E. JACKSON. | 21/3/18 | | 29/12/18 |
| 2/Lt. G. V. MIDDLETON. | 21/3/18 | | 31/12/18 |
| 2/Lt. S. C. RAYMENT. | 21/3/18 | | 29/12/18 |
| 2/Lt. C. STARK. | 21/3/18 | | 1/12/18 |
| 2/Lt. W. H. V. WOODROW. | 21/3/18 | | 11/12/18 |

### 7th Battalion.

| Name. | Missing. | Interned. | Repatriated. |
|---|---|---|---|
| Lieut. J. M. McBAIN. | 1/7/16 | (Died 9/7/16). | |
| Capt. C. GASCOYNE. | 2/4/17 | (Died 8/5/17). | |
| ‖Lt.-Col. W. S. N. TOLLER. | 21/3/18 | | 8/12/18 |
| Capt. A. S. BRIGHT. | 21/3/18 | | 23/9/18 |
| Capt. F. PRAGNELL. | 21/3/18 | | 29/11/18 |
| Capt. W. PRITCHETT. | 21/3/18 | | 17/12/18 |
| Lieut. F. H. CLARK. | 21/3/18 | | 29/11/18 |
| Lieut. R. B. EMMETT. | 21/3/18 | | 18/12/18 |
| Lieut. J. E. HARTSHORN. | 21/3/18 | | 26/12/18 |
| Lieut. C. F. PARRY. | 21/3/18 | | 31/12/18 |
| ‖Lieut. E. WRIGHTON. | 21/3/18 | | 10/12/18 |
| 2/Lt. T. ALLEN. | 21/3/18 | | 25/12/18 |
| 2/Lt. G. A. BREACH. | 21/3/18 | | 29/11/18 |
| 2/Lt. F. G. ELLIS. | 21/3/18 | | 3/12/18 |
| 2/Lt. G. L. THORPE. | 21/3/18 | | 25/12/18 |
| 2/Lt. A. P. WARD. | 21/3/18 | | 29/11/18 |
| 2/Lt. J. F. BISHOP. | 1/4/16 | | 18/11/18 |

*Attached from Dragoon Guards.     ‡Attached from Derby Yeomanry.
†Attached T.M.B.     §Attached from S. Notts. Hussars.
‖ Attached from Leicester Regiment.

## SHERWOOD FORESTERS—continued.

### 8th Battalion.

| Name. | Missing. | Interned. | | Repatriated. |
|---|---|---|---|---|
| 2/Lt. R. T. SKINNER. | 23/4/17 | | | 1/1/19 |

### 9th Battalion.

| | | | | |
|---|---|---|---|---|
| 2/Lt. F. J. ARCHER. | 19/12/17 | | | 3/12/18 |

### 10th Battalion.

| | | | | |
|---|---|---|---|---|
| Capt. E. T. R. CARLYON. | 16/2/16 | Switzerland | 19/12/16 | 6/12/18 |
| Lieut. P. KNOX-SHAW. | 16/2/16 | Holland | 19/4/18 | 18/11/18 |
| Lieut. E. A. TOLLEMACHE. | 16/2/16 | Holland | 10/4/18 | 18/11/18 |
| 2/Lt. R. MILWARD. | 16/2/16 | Holland | 19/4/18 | 23/10/18 |
| Lt.-Col. L. GILBERT. | 23/4/17 | | | 18/12/18 |
| Lieut. R. A. PAGE. | 23/3/18 | | | 18/12/18 |
| Lieut. T. C. NUGENT. | 21/4/18 | | | 3/1/19 |

### 12th Battalion.

| | | | | |
|---|---|---|---|---|
| 2/Lt. E. N. TAYLOR. | 21/3/18 | | | 11/12/18 |
| Capt. W. J. ASHER. | 28/3/18 | | | -/12/18 |

### 15th Battalion.

| | | | | |
|---|---|---|---|---|
| Capt. R. W. AINSWORTH. | 31/5/16 | Holland | 19/4/18 | 29/12/18 |
| 2/Lt. E. WARBURTON. | 25/10/16 | Switzerland | 9/12/17 | 24/3/18 |
| 2/Lt. J. S. BECKETT. | 24/3/18 | Switzerland | 25/9/18 | 7/12/18 |
| 2/Lt. F. HEMSTOCK. | 24/3/18 | | | 17/12/18 |
| 2/Lt. J. KEELING. | 24/3/18 | | | 1/12/18 |
| 2/Lt. C. J. McDONNELL. | 24/3/18 | | | 1/12/18 |
| 2/Lt. M. H. STEPHENSON. | 24/3/18 | | | -/12/18 |
| 2/Lt. H. J. WICKENDEN. | 25/3/18 | | | 25/12/18 |
| Lieut. T. WILLIAMSON. | 20/10/18 | | | 13/12/18 |
| 2/Lt. J. F. POWELL. | 20/10/18 | | | 12/12/18 |

### 16th Battalion.

| | | | | |
|---|---|---|---|---|
| 2/Lt. F. NURSE. | 30/3/18 | | | 18/12/18 |
| 2/Lt. H. B. BUSWELL. | 21/3/18 | | | 2/12/18 |

## LOYAL NORTH LANCASHIRE REGIMENT.

### 1st and 2nd Battalions.

| Name. | Missing. | Interned. | | Repatriated. |
|---|---|---|---|---|
| 2/Lt. C. E. WALLIS. | 14/9/14 | | | 13/9/17 |
| Capt. A. COLLEY. | 2/11/14 | | | 13/9/17 |
| Lieut. D. GARDEN. | 2/11/14 | Holland | 24/2/18 | 18/11/18 |
| Lieut. J. GRIFFITH. | 2/11/14 | Holland | 24/2/18 | 11/1/19 |
| Capt. G. T. BODY. | 22/12/14 | (*Died*). | | |
| Lieut. S. H. BATTY-SMITH. | 22/12/14 | Holland | 23/8/18 | 22/11/18 |
| 2/Lt. L. G. GILLILAND. | 22/12/14 | *Escaped.* | | -/4/17 |
| Lieut. F. R. C. BARRETT. | 10/7/17 | | | 6/12/18 |
| 2/Lt. S. E. MATTHEWS. | 10/7/17 | Holland | 15/4/18 | 19/7/18 |
| Lieut. E. GLADDING. | 18/4/18 | | | -/11/18 |
| 2/Lt. C. G. CLARIDGE. | 18/4/18 | | | 25/12/18 |
| 2/Lt. H. E. SMITH. | 18/4/18 | | | 6/1/19 |
| *2/Lt. E. H. NORMAN. | 18/4/18 | | | 18/12/18 |
| *Capt. A. HARRISON. | 27/5/18 | | | 5/1/19 |
| 2/Lt. H. J. McCOVEY. | 2/10/18 | | | -/11/18 |

*Attached T.M.B.

## LOYAL NORTH LANCASHIRE REGIMENT—continued.

### 4th Battalion.

| Name. | Missing. | Interned. | | Repatriated. |
|---|---|---|---|---|
| 2/Lt. J. F. HOLDEN. | 8/8/16 | Holland | 12/10/18 | 22/11/18 |
| 2/Lt. O. H. DUCKSBURY. | 8/8/16 | Holland | 12/10/18 | 22/11/18 |
| 2/Lt. C. RIGBY. | 31/7/17 | | | 2/1/19 |
| 2/Lt. D. H. McSWEENY. | 31/7/17 | | | 17/12/18 |
| 2/Lt. H. S. HOLDEN, | 31/7/17 | | | 3/12/18 |
| 2/Lt. G. H. VARAH. | 10/4/18 | | | 2/12/18 |
| *2/Lt. E. IVES. | 2/10/18 | | | 13/12/18 |
| 2/Lt. W. G. E. TAYLOR. | 13/10/18 | | | 13/12/18 |
| 2/Lt. G. A. BLOUNT. | 22/10/18 | | | –/12/18 |
| 2/Lt. JAMES CHAMBERS. | 22/10/18 | | | 8/12/18 |

### 5th Battalion.

| Name. | Missing. | Interned. | | Repatriated. |
|---|---|---|---|---|
| Capt. R. K. G. MARSEILLE | 6/7/17 | Switzerland | 27/12/17 | 24/3/18 |
| Capt. T. A. BARTER. | 30/11/17 | | | 17/12/18 |
| 2/Lt. C. A. BRYAN. | 30/11/17 | | | 27/11/18 |
| 2/Lt. C. B. WRAY. | 30/11/17 | | | 2/12/18 |
| 2/Lt. W. WADWORTH. | 30/11/17 | | | 14/12/18 |
| †2/Lt. C. A. ROBERTSON. | 30/11/17 | | | 17/12/18 |
| 2/Lt. W. MARSDEN. | 30/11/17 | | | 14/12/18 |
| 2/Lt. H. N. HOBSON. | 30/11/17 | | | 14/12/18 |
| 2/Lt. E. N. O. WEIGHILL. | 30/11/17 | | | 19/5/18 |
| ‡2/Lt. W. H. INCE. | 22/3/18 | | | 14/12/18 |
| ‡2/Lt. N. ENTWISLE. | 11/4/18 | | | 1/12/18 |
| 2/Lt. H. WHITEHEAD. | 18/4/18 | | | 18/12/18 |
| 2/Lt. A. W. KITCH. | 13/9/18 | | | 8/12/18 |
| Lieut. J. FORSHAW. | 1/10/18 | | | –/1/19 |

### 8th Battalion.

| Name. | Missing. | Repatriated. |
|---|---|---|
| *Lieut. G. W. TOLLETT. | 12/4/18 | 2/12/18 |

### 9th Battalion.

| Name. | Missing. | Repatriated. |
|---|---|---|
| 2/Lt. R. WILSON. | 21/3/18 | 2/12/18 |
| 2/Lt. F. N. SCOTT. | 22/3/18 | 11/12/18 |
| 2/Lt. G. HOLT. | 23/3/18 | 11/12/18 |
| 2/Lt. H. S. A. BRIEN. | 23/3/18 | 4/12/18 |
| Capt. R. J. P. HEWETSON. | 27/5/18 | (Died –/7/18 at Beaurieux). |
| Capt. P. R. SHIELDS. | 27/5/18 | 6/12/18 |

### 10th Battalion.

| Name. | Missing. | Repatriated. |
|---|---|---|
| Capt. P. BEE. | 22/3/18 | 2/12/18 |
| Lieut. B. W. PEACHEY. | 22/3/18 | 14/12/18 |
| 2/Lt. A. W. BELLIS. | 22/3/18 | 2/12/18 |
| 2/Lt. J. F. MILLS. | 22/3/18 | 18/12/18 |
| 2/Lt. F. B. HEWITT. | 22/3/18 | 6/12/18 |
| 2/Lt. J. A. JACKSON. | 22/3/18 | 25/12/18 |
| 2/Lt. C. H. LAW. | 22/3/18 | 14/12/18 |
| 2/Lt. E. WRIGLEY. | 22/3/18 | 25/12/18 |
| †Lieut. F. HAYES. | | 14/12/18 |

*Attached from Yorkshire Regiment. †Attached from Manchester Regiment.
‡Attached Entrenching Battalion.

## NORTHAMPTONSHIRE REGIMENT.

### 1st and 2nd Battalions.

| Name. | Missing. | Interned. | | Repatriated. |
|---|---|---|---|---|
| 2/Lt. H. F. W. BARNETT. | 20/7/16 | Holland | 15/6/18 | 21/9/19 |
| 2/Lt. T. E. BOURDILLON. | 22/7/16 | Holland | 15/6/18 | 19/11/18 |
| 2/Lt. B. J. F. WYLDE. | 26/4/17 | | | 30/12/18 |
| Lt.-Col. Hon. D. P. TOLLEMACHE. | 10/7/17 | | | 4/12/18 |
| Capt. C. CHISHOLM. | 10/7/17 | | | 6/12/18 |
| Capt. E. R. C. AYLETT. | 10/7/17 | | | 6/12/18 |
| Lieut. G. R. C. D. LINDLEY. | 10/7/17 | | | 6/12/18 |
| Lieut. J. H. A. WOOD. | 10/7/17 | | | 6/12/18 |
| Lieut. T. C. BLANDFORD. | 10/7/17 | | | 17/12/18 |
| 2/Lt. E. C. AIRTH. | 10/7/17 | | | 6/12/18 |
| 2/Lt. N. H. V. COGILL. | 10/7/17 | | | 17/12/18 |
| 2/Lt. A. R. McANALLY. | 10/7/17 | | | 6/12/18 |
| 2/Lt. E. H. JONES. | 10/7/17 | | | 17/12/18 |
| 2/Lt. R. P. NEEDHAM. | 10/7/17 | | | 17/12/18 |
| 2/Lt. J. L. JENNINGS. | 10/7/17 | | | 17/12/18 |
| 2/Lt. J. BOSTON. | 10/7/17 | | | 17/12/18 |
| 2/Lt. R. L. COWLEY. | 10/7/17 | | | 17/12/18 |
| 2/Lt. R. C. SAXTON. | 10/7/17 | | | 14/12/18 |
| 2/Lt. C. E. BORROW. | 10/7/17 | | | 2/1/19 |
| Lieut. R. MACPHERSON. | 24/3/18 | | | 18/12/18 |
| Lieut. J. E. JARVIS. | 26/3/18 | | | 1/12/18 |
| Lieut. W. GILLITT. | 26/3/18 | | | 1/12/18 |
| *Lieut. L. L. L. LEMAN. | 26/3/18 | | | 17/12/18 |
| †2/Lt. B. E. DAVEY. | 26/3/18 | | | 18/12/18 |
| 2/Lt. J. CALDWELL. | 20/4/18 | | | 1/12/18 |
| ‡Capt. J. HANDLEY. | 27/5/18 | | | 14/1/19 |
| Capt. A. M. WILLIAMS. | 27/5/18 | | | 16/1/19 |
| Lieut. G. M. EDMONDS. | 27/5/18 | | | 14/12/18 |
| Lieut. W. H. DENTON. | 27/5/18 | | | 26/12/18 |
| Lieut. J. S. DENTON. | 27/5/18 | | | 26/12/18 |
| *Lieut. C. H. TOLLEMACHE. | 27/5/18 | | | 13/12/18 |
| Lieut. W. H. SHAW. | 27/5/18 | | | 30/12/18 |
| 2/Lt. H. JONES. | 27/5/18 | | | 31/12/18 |
| 2/Lt. L. A. JOSLAND. | 27/5/18 | | | —/12/18 |
| 2/Lt. J. T. HIGSON. | 27/5/18 | (Died 8/8/18). | | |
| 2/Lt. J. L. HUTTON. | 27/5/18 | | | 31/12/18 |
| §2/Lt. H. GRIFFIN. | 27/5/18 | | | —/12/18 |
| §2/Lt. E. G. PARTRIDGE. | 27/5/18 | | | 31/12/18 |
| 2/Lt. W. H. KENNEDY. | 27/5/18 | | | 26/12/18 |
| 2/Lt. S. E. FARBON. | 27/5/18 | | | 31/12/18 |
| 2/Lt. M. V. EYDEN. | 27/5/18 | | | —/12/18 |

### 5th Battalion.

| Name. | Missing. | Interned. | Repatriated. |
|---|---|---|---|
| 2/Lt. H. J. WATT. | 30/11/17 | | 27/11/18 |

### 6th Battalion.

| Name. | Missing. | Interned. | Repatriated. |
|---|---|---|---|
| 2/Lt. A. B. SWAIN. | 17/2/17 | Switzerland 27/12/17 | 24/3/18 |
| Capt. H. C. GRACE. | 10/8/17 | (Died 2/9/17 at Courtrai). | |
| Lieut. D. I. GOTCH. | 23/3/18 | | 18/12/18 |
| 2/Lt. A. C. HERRING. | 23/3/18 | | 18/12/18 |
| 2/Lt. I. McNALLY. | 23/3/18 | | 18/12/18 |

*Attached from A.S.C.
†Attached from Middlesex Regiment.   ‡Attached from Essex Regiment.
§Attached from South Staffs Regiment.

## NORTHAMPTONSHIRE REGIMENT—continued.
### 6th Battalion.

| Name. | Missing. | Interned. | Repatriated. |
|---|---|---|---|
| *2/Lt. G. W. GREEN. | 23/3/18 | | 18/12/18 |
| *2/Lt. E. P. PARRISH. | 23/3/18 | | 11/12/18 |
| *2/Lt. C. W. CASWELL. | 5/4/18 | | 11/12/18 |
| 2/Lt. M. WEBBER. | 31/8/18 | | 28/11/18 |
| †Lieut. H. G. TEBB. | 21/9/18 | | 11/12/18 |

### 7th Battalion.

| Name. | Missing. | Interned. | Repatriated. |
|---|---|---|---|
| 2/Lt. L. J. P. LAYCOCK. | 13/7/17 | (*Died*). | |
| 2/Lt. F. COMPTON. | 25/3/18 | | 18/12/18 |

## ROYAL BERKSHIRE REGIMENT.
### 1st and 2nd Battalions.

| Name. | Missing. | Interned. | Repatriated. |
|---|---|---|---|
| Major A. S. TURNER. | 10/9/14 | Holland 5/1/18 | 16/11/18 |
| Capt. D. A. MacGREGOR. | 9/5/15 | (*Died* 15/8/15 at Hanover). | |
| 2/Lt. A. E. HENLEY. | 3/5/17 | Holland 30/4/18 | 19/7/18 |
| 2/Lt. G. R. THRELFELL. | 16/8/17 | | 14/12/18 |
| 2/Lt. S. M. LOUDAN. | 16/8/17 | | 6/12/18 |
| 2/Lt. A. E. BERRY. | 16/8/17 | | 7/1/18 |
| 2/Lt. E. L. THOMPSON. | 16/8/17 | | 14/12/18 |
| 2/Lt. A. C. URRY. | 24/3/18 | | 25/12/18 |
| 2/Lt. H. T. L. WOOSTER. | 24/3/18 | | 28/12/18 |
| Capt. H. A. CURTIS. | 25/3/18 | | 12/10/18 |
| 2/Lt. A. E. FARMER. | 25/3/18 | | 1/12/18 |
| ‡Lt.-Col. J. A. A. GRIFFIN. | 27/5/18 | | 25/12/18 |
| §Capt. C. W. FOWLER. | 27/5/18 | | 1/11/19 |
| Capt. A. D. CLARE. | 27/5/18 | | 25/12/18 |
| Capt. R. WHITTAKER. | 27/5/18 | | 3/1/19 |
| Lieut. R. B. GILLIAT. | 27/5/18 | (*Died* 28/5/18 at Sevigny). | |
| ‖Lieut. Oscar WILD. | 27/5/18 | | 25/12/18 |
| ‖Lieut. R. de C. McDONNELL. | 27/5/18 | | 31/12/18 |
| ‖Lieut. E. S. HAIGHTON. | 27/5/18 | | 25/12/18 |
| 2/Lt. W. VAUGHAN. | 27/5/18 | | –/12/18 |
| **2/Lt. G. S. HALLEY. | 27/5/18 | | –/12/18 |
| ** 2/Lt. R. B. HADDOW. | 27/5/18 | | 31/12/18 |
| **2/Lt. H. E. FLIGHT. | 27/5/18 | | 21/12/18 |
| ††2/Lt. C. D. WILLIAMS. | 27/5/18 | | –/12/18 |
| ‡‡2/Lt. J. M. BENNETT. | 27/5/18 | | –/12/18 |
| 2/Lt. W. A. UPTON. | 27/5/18 | | 25/12/18 |
| 2/Lt. C. A. N. BOSTON. | 21/9/18 | | 28/11/18 |
| 2/Lt. S. H. OSWELL. | 21/9/18 | | 6/12/18 |
| Lieut. A. J. EASTMAN. | 14/10/18 | | 11/12/18 |

### 2/4th Battalion.

| Name. | Missing. | Interned. | Repatriated. |
|---|---|---|---|
| 2/Lt. J. LAWRENCE. | 21/3/18 | | 11/1/19 |
| 2/Lt. J. TULLETT. | 21/3/18 | | –/12/18 |
| §§2/Lt. G. W. DE ST. LEGIER. | 21/3/18 | | 14/12/18 |
| ‖Capt. G. HINCHLIFFE. | 28/3/18 | | 28/12/18 |
| Lieut. H. W. FRY. | 11/5/18 | | –/12/18 |

*Attached from Middlesex Regiment.     †Attached from Herts Regiment.
‡Attached from Lincolns.     §Attached from R.A.M.C.
‖Attached from Manchesters.
**Attached from Hants.     ††Attached from Worcs.     ‡‡Attached from Sussex.
§§Attached from Devons.

## ROYAL BERKSHIRE REGIMENT—continued.

### 5th Battalion.

| Name. | Missing. | Interned. | | Repatriated. |
|---|---|---|---|---|
| 2/Lt. R. HAYWOOD. | 3/7/16 | Holland | 16/5/18 | 22/11/18 |
| 2/Lt. C. P. HOLLOWAY. | 3/7/16 | Holland | 16/5/18 | 22/11/18 |
| 2*Lt. F. C. R. HILL. | 30/11/17 | | | 2/1/19 |
| 2/Lt. H. SCHOFIELD. | 30/11/17 | | | 2/1/19 |
| 2/Lt. E. JONES. | 30/11/17 | | | 25/12/18 |
| *2/Lt. W. BARKER. | 5/4/18 | | | 18/12/18 |
| 2/Lt. B. MILES. | 5/4/18 | | | 11/12/18 |
| 2/Lt. P. L. HOWARD. | 24/6/18 | | | -/12/18 |

### 7th Battalion.

| | | | | |
|---|---|---|---|---|
| 2/Lt. W. L. HAILE. | 22/3/18 | | | 17/12/18 |

### 8th Battalion.

| | | | | |
|---|---|---|---|---|
| Capt. C. GENTRY-BIRCH. | 21/3/18 | | | 28/11/18 |
| Capt. D. J. FOOTMAN. | 21/3/18 | | | 28/11/18 |
| Capt. H. R. FENNER. | 21/3/18 | | | 18/12/18 |
| Lieut. E. J. MECEY. | 21/3/18 | | | 18/12/18 |
| Lieut. C. F. R. BLAND. | 21/3/18 | | | 28/11/18 |
| Lieut. G. R. GOODSHIP. | 21/3/18 | | | 28/11//8 |
| Lieut. N. LANGSTON. | 21/3/18 | | | 28/11/18 |
| *2/Lt. T. H. ROBERTS. | 21/3/18 | | | 28/11/18 |
| 2/Lt. E. F. JOHNSON. | 21/3/18 | | | 28/11/18 |
| 2/Lt. G. CAPES. | 21/3/18 | | | 16/12/18 |
| 2/Lt. W. V. HEALE. | 21/3/18 | | | 1/12/18 |
| 2/Lt. W. C. A. HANNEY. | 21/3/18 | | | 18/12/18 |
| 2/Lt. J. R. McMULLEN. | 21/3/18 | | | 28/11/18 |
| *2/Lt. A. G. WILLIAMS. | 26/3/18 | | | 17/12/18 |

### 9th Battalion.

| | | | | |
|---|---|---|---|---|
| 2/Lt. J. A. V. WOOD. | 14/11/16 | | | -/12/18 |

## ROYAL WEST KENT REGIMENT.

### 1st and 2nd Battalions.

| | | | | |
|---|---|---|---|---|
| Capt. G. D. LISTER. | 23/8/14 | Switzerland | 9/12/17 | 14/6/18 |
| Lieut. A. A. CHITTY. | -/-/14 | Switzerland | 12/9/16 | 11/9/17 |
| 2/Lt. H. E. FRY. | 26/10/17 | | | 13/5/18 |
| Capt. A. M. CAMPBELL. | -/-/16 | | | -/-/18 |

### 6th Battalion.

| | | | | |
|---|---|---|---|---|
| Capt. G. A. L. HATTON. | 3/7/16 | Holland | 16/5/18 | 18/11/18 |
| Lieut. H. B. ANTILL. | 3/5/17 | | | 6/12/18 |
| 2/Lt. L. PYRKE. | 3/5/17 | Switzerland | 27/12/17 | 9/12/18 |
| 2/Lt. E. N. ALLEN. | 3/5/17 | | | 6/12/18 |
| 2/Lt. L. W. BROWNING. | 3/5/17 | | | 6/12/18 |
| 2/Lt. H. HIBBETT. | 3/5/17 | | | 6/12/18 |
| 2/Lt. E. J. W. ELY. | 3/5/17 | | | 17/12/18 |
| Capt. W. B. HODSON-SMITH. | 30/11/17 | Holland | 30/4/18 | 18/8/18 |
| Lieut. S. G. WRIGHT. | 30/11/17 | | | 5/12/18 |
| Lieut. S. E. ROBERTS. | 30/11/17 | | | 3/12/18 |
| 2/Lt. V. S. LEATHER. | 30/11/17 | | | 5/12/18 |
| 2/Lt. M. W. J. SWALLOW. | 30/11/17 | | | 2/12/18 |
| 2/Lt. W. S. NEWSHOLME. | 30/11/17 | | | 11/12/18 |
| 2/Lt. J. W. LOWE. | 30/11/17 | | | 27/11/18 |
| 2/Lt. J. E. ABEL. | 30/11/17 | (*Died* 22/12/17 at Sevigny). | | |

*Attached from Worcs.

## ROYAL WEST KENT REGIMENT—continued.

### 7th Battalion.

| Name. | Missing. | Interned. | Repatriated. |
|---|---|---|---|
| Lieut. C. S. STEVENSON. | 19/11/16 | | 26/12/18 |
| 2/Lt. K. G. FRYER. | 19/11/16 | | 17/12/18 |
| *Lt.-Col. J. D. CROSTHWAITE. | 21/3/18 | | 3/1/19 |
| Capt. E. WATTS. | 21/3/18 | | 29/11/18 |
| Capt. A. GODLY. | 21/3/18 | | 2/12/18 |
| Lieut. P. B. WHITROW. | 21/3/18 | | 5/12/18 |
| Lieut. A. A. EASON. | 21/3/18 | | 3/12/18 |
| 2/Lt. W. F. DRAIN. | 21/3/18 | | 8/12/18 |
| 2/Lt. S. H. WEBB. | 21/3/18 | (*Died* 26/3/18 at Ribemont). | |
| 2/Lt. E. V. SAWYER. | 21/3/18 | | 18/12/18 |
| 2/Lt. B. VAUGHAN. | 21/3/18 | | 13/12/18 |
| 2/Lt. G. M. HEAPHY. | 21/3/18 | | 25/12/18 |
| 2/Lt. H. LYNCH-WATSON | 21/3/18 | | 11/12/18 |
| †2/Lt. J. A. HORTON. | 21/3/18 | | –/12/18 |
| 2/Lt. G. T. M. LEWIS. | 21/3/18 | | 27/11/18 |
| 2/Lt. H. P. RIMINGTON. | 21/3/18 | | 29/11/18 |
| 2/Lt. W. U. C. TAYLOR. | 21/3/18 | | 5/12/18 |
| ‡2/Lt. J. H. BENTLEY. | 4/4/18 | | 18/12/18 |

### 8th Battalion.

| Name. | Missing. | Interned. | Repatriated. |
|---|---|---|---|
| Col. E. VANSITTART. | 26/9/15 | | 13/9/17 |
| Major J. C. CHILLINGWORTH. | 26/9/15 | Switzerland 27/12/17 | 17/12/18 |
| Capt. C. de C. MIDDLETON. | 26/9/15 | Switzerland 27/12/17 | 12/6/18 |
| Capt. C. A. HUTCHINSON. | 26/9/15 | | 13/9/17 |
| Lieut. R. M. OLD. | 26/9/15 | Holland 10/4/18 | 22/11/18 |
| 2/Lt. N. S. ELL. | 26/9/15 | (Exchanged) | 7/12/15 |
| 2/Lt. J. S. CRIGHTON. | 3/2/18 | | 25/1/19 |
| Capt. C. R. H. ALLWORTH. | 21/3/18 | | 10/12/18 |
| 2/Lt. H. W. BEATTIE. | 21/3/18 | | 28/11/18 |
| 2/Lt. J. BOWSKILL. | 21/3/18 | | –/11/18 |
| 2/Lt. C. D. WHITBOURN. | 21/3/18 | | 29/11/18 |
| 2/Lt. E. LEVEY. | 21/3/18 | | 29/11/18 |
| 2/Lt. D. C. M. OLIVER. | 21/3/18 | | 25/12/18 |

### 9th Battalion.

| Name. | Missing. | Interned. | Repatriated. |
|---|---|---|---|
| 2/Lt. A. L. HART. | 30/11/17 | | 25/12/18 |

### 10th Battalion.

| Name. | Missing. | Interned. | Repatriated. |
|---|---|---|---|
| Capt. F. W. ROBERTS. | 21/9/17 | (*Died*). | |
| 2/Lt. F. C. RENNELLS. | 22/3/18 | | 11/12/18 |
| Lt.-Col. A. C. CORFE. | 23/3/18 | | 18/12/18 |
| Major A. J. JIMENEZ. | 23/3/18 | | 18/12/18 |
| Capt. C. F. HALL. | 23/3/18 | | 29/11/18 |
| Capt. F. W. WAYDELIN. | 23/3/18 | | 18/12/18 |
| §Lieut. L. E. HALE. | 23/3/18 | | 29/11/18 |
| Lieut. L. A. PANCHAUD. | 23/3/18 | | 10/12/18 |
| 2/Lt. F. C. VASS. | 23/3/18 | | 1/12/18 |
| 2/Lt. J. R. PHILLIPS. | 23/3/18 | | 25/12/18 |
| 2/Lt. B. E. LONG. | 23/3/18 | | 25/12/18 |
| 2/Lt. R. H. CHANDLER. | 23/3/18 | | 1/12/18 |

*Attached from 1st Londons. †Attached T.M.B. ‡Attached from Gloucester Regiment.
§Attached from Scottish Rifles.

## KING'S OWN YORKSHIRE LIGHT INFANTRY.

### 1st and 2nd Battalions.

| Name. | Missing. | Interned. | | Repatriated. |
|---|---|---|---|---|
| Lt.-Col. R. C. BOND. | 10/9/14 | Holland | 5/1/18 | 27/11/18 |
| Capt. W. E. GATACRE. | 10/9/14 | Holland | 5/1/18 | 18/11/18 |
| Capt. A. R. KEPPEL. | 10/9/14 | Holland | 5/1/18 | returned for duty. |
| Capt. A. C. G. LUTHER. | 10/9/14 | Holland | 6/2/18 | 18/11/18 |
| Capt. L. SIMPSON. | 10/9/14 | Holland | 5/1/18 | 18/11/18 |
| Lieut. T. BUTT. | 10/9/14 | | | 11/9/17 |
| Lieut. H. D. HIBBERT. | 10/9/14 | Holland | 22/1/18 | 18/11/18 |
| Lieut. C. H. RAWDON. | 10/9/14 | Holland | 5/1/18 | 18/11/18 |
| Lieut. T. REYNOLDS. | 10/9/14 | Holland | 5/1/18 | 18/11/18 |
| Lieut. W. H. UNETT. | 10/9/14 | Holland | 5/1/18 | 18/11/18 |
| Lieut. G. C. WYNNE. | 10/9/14 | | | 18/2/18 |
| Capt. C. H. ACKROYD. | 10/10/14 | Holland | 5/1/18 | 21/1/19 |
| *Capt. T. H. CLEMSON. | 27/10/14 | Holland | 24/2/18 | 18/11/18 |
| 2/Lt. J. B. NOEL. | 30/10/14 | Holland | 5/1/18 | 18/11/18 |
| Lieut. W. BATEMAN. | 10/5/15 | Holland | 23/3/18 | 18/11/18 |
| 2/Lt. J. A. ARMITAGE. | 18/11/16 | Switzerland | 27/12/17 | 14/6/18 |
| 2/Lt. R. F. CORLETT. | 18/11/16 | | | 4/1/19 |
| 2/Lt. A. RYLETT. | 18/11/16 | Holland | 20/4/18 | 18/8/18 |
| 2/Lt. A. L. WESTWOOD. | 18/11/16 | | | 28/11/18 |

### 4th Battalion.

| Name | Missing | Interned | | Repatriated |
|---|---|---|---|---|
| Capt. C. H. PLACKETT. | 5/7/16 | Holland | 16/5/18 | 18/11/18 |
| Capt. W. M. WILLIAMSON. | 6/7/16 | Holland | 15/6/18 | 21/1/19 |
| Lieut. J. C. PLEWS. | 23/7/16 | Holland | 15/6/18 | returned for duty. |
| †2/Lt. H. W. SAMPSON. | 14/4/18 | | | 2/12/18 |

### 2/4th Battalion.

| Name | Missing | | | Repatriated |
|---|---|---|---|---|
| Capt. A. E. PILLEY. | 27/3/18 | | | 25/12/18 |
| 2/Lt. D. O. C. MAGGS. | 27/3/18 | | | 18/12/18 |
| 2/Lt. H. W. SPINK. | 27/3/18 | | | 2/12/18 |
| Capt. G. L. HUDSON. | 28/3/18 | | | –/12/18 |
| ‡2/Lt. J. W. POWNALL. | 28/3/18 | | | 25/12/18 |

### 5th Battalion.

| Name | Missing | | | Repatriated |
|---|---|---|---|---|
| Lieut. R. GRIGG. | 27/3/18 | | | 2/12/18 |
| Capt. B. A. BEACH. | 28/3/18 | | | 29/11/18 |
| Capt. E. ROBERTS. | 28/3/18 | | | 29/11/18 |
| §Capt. A. D. THOMSON. | 28/3/18 | | | 3/12/18 |
| †2/Lt. R. APPLETON. | 28/3/18 | | | 29/11/18 |
| 2/Lt. W. IBBOTT. | 28/3/18 | | | 2/12/18 |
| 2/Lt. B. P. JENKINSON. | 28/3/18 | | | 6/12/18 |
| 2/Lt. H. G. NORTHEY. | 28/3/18 | | | 2/12/18 |
| †2/Lt. T. WELDON. | 28/3/18 | | | 2/12/18 |
| 2/Lt. A. H. FEHR. | 14/4/18 | | | 2/12/18 |

### 6th Battalion.

| Name | Missing | | | Repatriated |
|---|---|---|---|---|
| **2/Lt. G. B. JUBB. | 21/3/18 | | | 14/12/18 |

*Attached from Dorset Regiment.
†Attached from K.O.R. Lanc. Regiment.
‡Attached from W. Yorks Regiment.
§Attached from A.S.C.
**Attached T.M.B.

## KING'S OWN YORKSHIRE LIGHT INFANTRY—continued.

### 7th Battalion.

| Name. | Missing. | Interned. | Repatriated. |
|---|---|---|---|
| Capt. R. CLIBBORN. | 23/9/16 | | 18/12/18 |
| 2/Lt. C. ELLIS. | 18/10/17 | | 6/12/18 |
| 2/Lt. J. D. AITKEN. | 24/4/18 | | 25/12/18 |

### 9th Battalion.

| Name. | Missing. | Interned. | Repatriated. |
|---|---|---|---|
| Lieut. J. F. LITTLEDALE. | 23/3/18 | | 11/12/18 |
| Lieut. D. EVANS. | 23/3/18 | | —/12/18 |
| 2/Lt. H. HUTSON. | 23/3/18 | (*Died* at Villers Fancon) | 26/3/18 |
| 2/Lt. J. MAGIN. | 23/3/18 | | 2/1/19 |
| Capt. G. F. ELLENBERGER. | 27/5/18 | | 25/12/18 |
| Lieut. F. P. NILEN. | 27/5/18 | | —/12/18 |
| 2/Lt. R. H. L. DAVIS. | 27/5/18 | | —/1/19 |
| 2/Lt. J. W. DORE. | 27/5/18 | | —/1/19 |
| 2/Lt. F. A. MARSDEN. | 27/5/18 | | —/1/19 |
| 2/Lt. C. E. SCOTT. | 27/5/18 | | 25/12/18 |
| 2/Lt. C. E. TAYLOR. | 27/5/18 | | 30/12/18 |

### 10th Battalion.

| Name. | Missing. | Interned. | Repatriated. |
|---|---|---|---|
| *2/Lt. R. J. CARLESS. | 22/8/18 | | 5/1/19 |

### 12th Battalion.

| Name. | Missing. | Interned. | Repatriated. |
|---|---|---|---|
| Lieut. L. FORSDIKE. | 13/4/18 | | 18/12/18 |
| Lieut. J. R. WILSON. | 13/4/18 | | 18/12/18 |
| 2/Lt. J. B. CLARKE. | 13/4/18 | | 13/12/18 |

## KING'S SHROPSHIRE LIGHT INFANTRY.

### 1st Battalion.

| Name. | Missing. | Interned. | Repatriated. |
|---|---|---|---|
| Lt.-Col. H. M. SMITH. | 21/3/18 | | 17/12/18 |
| †Major H. P. OSBORNE. | 21/3/18 | | 1/1/19 |
| Capt. E. BIRD. | 21/3/18 | | 25/12/18 |
| Capt. J. DEEDES. | 21/3/18 | | 19/12/18 |
| Lieut. B. E. CRAIGIE. | 21/3/18 | | 18/12/18 |
| ‡Lieut. G. P. LLOYD. | 21/3/18 | | 2/12/18 |
| Lieut. N. V. WEBBER. | 21/3/18 | | —/12/18 |
| †Lieut. A. C. WELBOURNE. | 21/3/18 | | 29/11/18 |
| 2/Lt. H. W. D. EVANS. | 21/3/18 | | —/12/18 |
| 2/Lt. A. W. LEPPER. | 21/3/18 | | 13/12/18 |
| 2/Lt. W. H. MORRIS. | 21/3/18 | | 9/1/19 |
| 2/Lt. L. A. T. SPEER. | 21/3/18 | | 2/12/18 |
| 2/Lt. C. VAN HUMBEECK. | 21/3/18 | | 2/12/18 |
| †2/Lt. S. G. WHITE. | 21/3/18 | | 17/12/18 |
| 2/Lt. M. H. WRIGHT. | 21/3/18 | | 25/12/18 |

### 2nd Battalion.

| Name. | Missing. | Interned. | Repatriated. |
|---|---|---|---|
| Capt. H. G. BRYANT. | 27/4/15 | (*Died* —/5/15). | |
| 2/Lt. R. du B. EVANS. | 27/4/15 | Switzerland 19/12/16 | 6/12/18 |
| 2/Lt. F. W. VOELKER. | 27/4/15 | Holland 23/3/18 | 18/11/18 |
| 2/Lt. T. S. LANYON. | 7/12/17 | | 18/12/18 |

*Attached from K. Shrop. L.I.
†Attached from Middlesex Regiment.      ‡Attached from Herefordshire Regiment.

## KING'S SHROPSHIRE LIGHT INFANTRY—continued

### 4th Battalion.

| Name. | Missing. | Interned. | Repatriated. |
|---|---|---|---|
| Capt. C. E. R. LITT. | | | 27/11/18 |
| Lieut. F. J. K. SMITH. | 25/3/18 | | 8/12/18 |
| 2/Lt. R. H. FRANCIS. | 25/3/18 | | -/1/19 |
| 2/Lt. J. SANDERSON. | 25/3/18 | | 21/1/19 |

### 6th Battalion.

| Name. | Missing. | Interned. | Repatriated. |
|---|---|---|---|
| 2/Lt. J. P. SHAW. | 3/9/16 | | 18/12/18 |
| 2/Lt. D. T. FOULDS. | 21/3/18 | | 18/12/18 |
| *2/Lt. L. S. MUNN. | 21/3/18 | | 18/12/18 |
| Capt. M. J. HELLIER. | 22/3/18 | | 18/12/18 |
| †Capt. F. A. H. STANIER. | 22/3/18 | | 14/12/18 |
| *Lieut. C. C. KELLY. | 22/3/18 | | -/12/18 |
| 2/Lt. W. BULLOCK. | 22/3/18 | | 18/12/18 |
| ‡2/Lt. De W. HOWARD. | 22/3/18 | | 18/12/18 |
| ‡2/Lt. C. H. KING. | 22/3/18 | | 1/12/18 |
| 2/Lt. A. M. A. LYLE. | 22/3/18 | | 19/12/18 |
| 2/Lt. G. R. MATHER. | 22/3/18 | | 18/12/18 |
| Capt. T. MILLYARD. | 24/3/18 | | 23/10/18 |
| Capt. R. H. BANKS. | 28/3/18 | | 18/12/18 |

### 7th Battalion.

| Name. | Missing. | Interned. | Repatriated. |
|---|---|---|---|
| 2/Lt. G. V. JONES. | 28/3/18 | (*Died* at Duisburg 24/4/18). | |

### 10th Battalion.

| Name. | Missing. | Interned. | Repatriated. |
|---|---|---|---|
| 2/Lt. A. F. McEWEN. | 22/8/18 | | 8/12/18 |

## MIDDLESEX REGIMENT.

### 1st to 4th Battalions.

| Name. | Missing. | Interned. | | Repatriated. |
|---|---|---|---|---|
| Capt. H. A. CARTWRIGHT. | 3/9/14 | | | 16/8/18 |
| Capt. L. J. GRAHAM-TOLER. | 3/9/14 | | | 1/1/19 |
| Capt. L. F. SLOANE-STANLEY. | 10/9/14 | Holland | 29/12/17 | 22/12/18 |
| Capt. L. H. O. JOSEPHS. | 10/9/14 | Holland | 29/12/17 | 22/11/18 |
| Capt. H. E. L. GLASS. | 10/9/14 | Switzerland | 9/12/17 | 21/1/19 |
| Lieut. E. R. RUSHTON. | 10/9/14 | Holland | 29/12/17 | 18/11/18 |
| Lieut. G. C. DRUCE. | 10/9/14 | Holland | 29/12/17 | 18/11/18 |
| Capt. H. F. SPENCE. | 11/9/14 | Switzerland | 27/12/17 | 24/3/18 |
| 2/Lt. B. G. HORROCKS. | 21/10/14 | | | 17/12/18 |
| Major W. H. C. DAVY. | -/-/14 | | | Exchange 17/2/15 |
| 2/Lt. F. E. BEACHAMP. | 31/7/17 | | | 10/12/18 |
| 2/Lt. W. S. BERTIOLI. | 25/9/17 | | | 6/12/18 |
| 2/Lt. J. C. OLIVER. | 24/3/18 | | | 18/12/18 |
| §2/Lt. F. S. PENFOLD. | 24/3/18 | | | 18/12/18 |
| Lieut. E. FRAYNE. | 25/3/18 | (*Died*). | | |
| 2/Lt. J. L. WENN. | 27/3/18 | | | 18/12/18 |
| 2/Lt. J. R. S. CHAPMAN. | 27/3/18 | | | 18/12/18 |
| Lieut. H. E. WHITE. | 28/3/18 | | | 1/12/18 |
| 2/Lt. H. CAWDRON. | 28/3/18 | | | 8/12/18 |
| 2/Lt. P. H. E. FAIRCLOUGH. | 1/4/18 | | | 18/12/18 |
| §Capt. H. C. KILLINGBACK. | 9/4/18 | | | 10/12/18 |
| **Lieut. W. J. FRANCIS. | 24/4/18 | | | 1/12/18 |
| **Lieut. J. H. F. HARVEY. | 24/4/18 | | | 29/11/18 |
| **2/Lt. A. H. PALIN. | 24/4/18 | | | 15/12/18 |
| **2/Lt. J. G. MORTON. | 24/4/18 | | | 29/11/18 |
| †2/Lt. S. SLAVITZ. | 24/4/18 | | | 29/11/18 |
| †2/Lt. H. HOWARTH. | 24/4/18 | | | 16/12/18 |

*Attached from Herefordshire Regiment.  †Attached from Shropshire Yeomanry.
‡Attached from Berkshire Regiment.
§Attached T.M.B.  **Attached from Gloucester Regiment.

## MIDDLESEX REGIMENT—continued.
### 1st to 4th Battalions—continued.

| Name. | Missing. | Interned. | Repatriated. |
|---|---|---|---|
| 2/Lt. F. POND. | 24/4/18 | | –/11/18 |
| 2/Lt. F. W. STAFFORD. | 24/4/18 | | 29/11/18 |
| 2/Lt. F. D. AITKEN. | 24/4/18 | | 29/11/18 |
| Major C. A. S. PAGE. | 27/5/18 | | 12/10/18 |
| Capt. H. L. McILWAINE. | 27/5/18 | | –/12/18 |
| Capt. T. C. MANDERS. | 27/5/18 | | 6/12/18 |
| Capt. W. G. S. JONES. | 27/5/18 | | 31/12/18 |
| Capt. S. F. DEL COURT. | 27/5/18 | | 19/1/19 |
| 2/Lt. A/Capt. L. WANSTALL. | 27/5/18 | | 13/12/18 |
| Lieut. R. GREIG. | 27/5/18 | | 13/12/18 |
| Lieut. R. D. HORNBY. | 27/5/18 | | –/12/18 |
| Lieut. G. D. HARVEY-SAMUEL. | 27/5/18 | | 2/1/19 |
| Lieut. J. E. MAYNARD. | 27/5/18 | | 17/12/18 |
| 2/Lt. W. J. MARTIN. | 27/5/18 | | 13/1/19 |
| 2/Lt. H. T. BYE. | 27/5/18 | | –/12/18 |
| 2/Lt. C. S. LEWIS. | 27/5/18 | | 30/12/18 |
| 2/Lt. J. H. MARKS. | 27/5/18 | | 17/12/18 |
| 2/Lt. C. T. M. HALL. | 27/5/18 | | –/12/18 |
| 2/Lt. J. HAYER. | 27/5/18 | | 13/12/18 |
| 2/Lt. G. OEHL. | 27/5/18 | | 11/1/19 |
| 2/Lt. A. N. OVERELL. | 27/5/18 | | 30/12/18 |
| 2/Lt. S. F. CORNWELL. | 27/5/18 | | 25/12/18 |
| 2/Lt. T. F. COLLINGWOOD. | 27/5/18 | | 8/12/18 |
| 2/Lt. W. O. PEARSON. | 27/5/18 | | 30/12/18 |
| 2/Lt. C. E. CADE. | 24/10/18 | | 8/12/18 |

### 6th Battalion.

| Name. | Missing. | Interned. | Repatriated. |
|---|---|---|---|
| Lieut. A. B. W. ALLISTONE. | 10/9/14 | Switzerland 13/2/17 | 9/12/18 |

### 7th Battalion.

| Name. | Missing. | Interned. | Repatriated. |
|---|---|---|---|
| Capt. J. W. CATER. | 3/5/17 | (Died 9/7/17 at Cassel). | |
| 2/Lt. F. A. PEARSON. | 26/8/18 | | 28/11/18 |

### 8th Battalion.

| Name. | Missing. | Interned. | Repatriated. |
|---|---|---|---|
| Lieut. E. B. BUDDEN. | | Holland 5/1/18 | 18/11/18 |
| Lieut. H. BROUGH. | 31/5/15 | (Exchanged) | 26/8/15 |
| Capt. G. W. TREMLETT. | 19/5/17 | Switzerland 27/12/17 | 7/12/18 |
| Capt. H. C. VAUX. | 30/11/17 | | 14/12/18 |
| Lieut. W. S. SIMPSON. | 30/11/17 | Switzerland 2/10/18 | 25/12/18 |
| Lieut. G. D. DOWTY. | 30/11/17 | | 14/12/18 |
| Lieut. J. E. BAYLISS. | 30/11/17 | | 28/11/18 |
| Lieut. V. L. H. MEYERS. | 30/11/17 | | 6/12/18 |
| 2/Lt. C. J. N. JEFFREYS. | 30/11/17 | | 4/12/18 |
| 2/Lt. C. R. BIRD. | 30/11/17 | | 14/12/18 |
| 2/Lt. R. W. SMART. | 30/11/17 | | 14/12/18 |
| 2/Lt. C. H. JACKSON. | 30/11/17 | | 3/12/18 |
| 2/Lt. F. C. W. LAGDEN. | 15/5/18 | | 31/12/18 |

### 12th Battalion.

| Name. | Missing. | Interned. | Repatriated. |
|---|---|---|---|
| Capt. F. G. SKINNER. | 3/5/17 | | 20/1/18 |
| Capt. H. PERKS. | 3/5/17 | Holland 15/4/18 | 20/7/18 |
| Lieut. F. S. HEARD. | 3/5/17 | | 3/1/19 |
| *Capt. H. F. PEARSON. | 24/3/18 | | 29/11/18 |

*Attached Entrenching Battalion.

## MIDDLESEX REGIMENT—continued.

### 13th Battalion.

| | | | | |
|---|---|---|---|---|
| Lieut. C. E. HARMAN. | 27/9/15 | Holland | 10/4/18 | 22/11/18 |
| 2/Lt. A. R. HAYFORD. | 22/3/18 | | | 25/12/18 |

### 16th Battalion.

| | | | |
|---|---|---|---|
| Capt. E. W. HALL. | 1/7/16 | | 11/9/17 |
| Capt. F. S. COCKRAM. | 1/7/16 | Switzerland 27/12/17 | 9/12/18 |
| 2/Lt. R. F. MICHELMORE. | 1/7/16 | (*Died* 7/7/16 at Velu). | |
| Lieut. L. J. LUFFINGHAM. | 31/5/17 | | 17/12/18 |
| 2/Lt. D. S. B. STARNES. | 31/5/17 | | 17/12/18 |
| 2/Lt. T. W. LANE. | 30/11/17 | | 1/1/19 |

### 17th Battalion.

| | | | |
|---|---|---|---|
| Lieut. E. W. MARCHANT. | 13–15/11/16 | | 14/12/18 |
| 2/Lt. A. M. MURRAY. | 13–15/11/16 | | 18/12/18 |
| 2/Lt. C. KOOP. | 13–15/11/16 | Switzerland 9/12/17 | 23/12/18 |
| 2/Lt. C. FLINT. | | | 14/12/18 |
| 2/Lt. E. S. KING. | 21/1/17 | | 17/12/18 |
| Capt. E. PARFITT. | 28/4/17 | (*Died* 28/5/17 at Kempton). | |
| Lieut. J. H. K. SEBRIGHT. | 28/4/17 | | 3/1/19 |
| 2/Lt. P. G. CARRUTHERS. | 28/4/17 | | 2/1/19 |
| Lieut. H. W. SANDERS. | 5/6/17 | | 7/12/18 |

### 19th Battalion.

| | | |
|---|---|---|
| Major O. S. PRATT. | 24/3/18 | 8/12/18 |

### 20th Battalion.

| | | |
|---|---|---|
| Lieut. W. WELLS. | 22/3/18 | 11/12/18 |
| 2/Lt. E. T. HOOPER. | 22/3/18 | 25/12/18 |
| Capt. E. D. SAMUEL. | 9/4/18 | 9/12/18 |
| Lieut. H. P. CRITTALL. | 9/4/18 | 18/12/18 |
| 2/Lt. A. R. HULLS. | 9/4/18 | 11/12/18 |
| 2/Lt. J. A. ROLLS. | 9/4/18 | 11/12/18 |
| 2/Lt. T. W. R. FAIRALL. | 9/4/18 | 28/11/18 |
| 2/Lt. R. D. STEINBERG. | 9/4/18 | 29/11/18 |
| 2/Lt. L. W. FREEMAN. | 9/4/18 | 8/12/18 |
| 2/Lt. G. F. WHITBREAD. | 9/4/18 | 13/12/18 |
| 2/Lt. F. IZOD. | 9/4/18 | 29/11/18 |
| 2/Lt. H. G. BAYLIS. | 9/4/18 | 9/12/18 |
| 2/Lt. T. S. MOORE. | 9/4/18 | 5/12/18 |
| Major F. R. HILL. | 10/4/18 | 17/12/18 |
| Capt. L. PRICE. | 10/4/18 | 23/12/18 |
| Lieut. D. O. LIGHT. | 10/4/18 | 10/12/18 |

### 21st Battalion.

| | | | |
|---|---|---|---|
| *2/Lt. A. S. T. SMURTHWAITE. | 28/8/17 | | 14/12/18 |
| Capt. H. J. SKILL. | 24/3/18 | (*Died* 7/4/18). | |
| Capt. J. H. DALGARNO. | 9/4/18 | | 11/12/18 |
| Capt. A. P. HEARD. | 9/4/18 | | –/1/19 |
| 2/Lt. G. HENDERSON. | 9/4/18 | | 18/12/18 |
| 2/Lt. P. M. BESTER. | 9/4/18 | | 11/12/18 |
| 2/Lt. E. J. CONYNHAM. | 9/4/18 | | 18/12/18 |
| 2/Lt. R. L. SEARS. | 9/4/18 | | 2/1/19 |
| 2/Lt. C. H. SULLENS. | 9/4/18 | | –/12/18 |
| Capt. R. C. SHEEN. | 11/4/18 | | 10/12/18 |

* Attached T.M.B.

## MIDDLESEX REGIMENT—continued.
### 23rd Battalion.

| Name. | Missing. | Interned. | Repatriated. |
|---|---|---|---|
| Capt. B. T. FOSS. | 23/3/18 | | 29/11/18 |

## KING'S ROYAL RIFLE CORPS.
### 1st to 4th Battalions.

| Name | Missing | Interned | Repatriated |
|---|---|---|---|
| Capt. W. P. LYNES. | | | 8/10/16 |
| | | (Died at Q.A.M. Hosp. | 14/10/16) |
| Lieut. J. F. E. GOAD. | 31/10/14 | Holland 24/2/18 | 21/1/19 |
| Lieut. T. WADNER. | 1/11/14 | Holland 24/2/18 | 14/1/18 |
| Lieut. A. M. WAKEFIELD-SAUNDERS. | 2/11/14 | Holland 24/2/18 | 16/11/18 |
| Lieut. C. F. SCHOON. | 2/11/14 | Holland 24/2/18 | 5/1/18 |
| Lieut. S. LUCAS. | 2/11/14 | Holland 24/2/18 | 15/10/18 |
| Lieut. G. V. H. GOUGH. | 2/11/14 | Holland 24/2/18 | 18/11/18 |
| 2/Lt. R. RICHARDS. | 2/11/14 | Holland 24/2/18 | 18/11/18 |
| 2/Lt. C. H. REYNARD. | 2/11/14 | | 18/9/17 |
| 2/Lt. K. H. Wodehouse WARD. | 14/3/15 | Switzerland 12/8/16 | 13/9/17 |
| 2/Lt. J. S. POOLE. | 9/5/15 | | –/11/16 |
| 2/Lt. M. B. HOPE. | 9/5/15 | Holland 10/4/18 | 18/11/18 |
| 2/Lt. H. CHEVIS. | 10/7/17 | | 2/1/19 |
| Capt. W. L. CLINTON. | 10/7/17 | (Died at Belgrade | 22/11/18). |
| Lieut. W. H. E. GOTT. | 10/7/17 | | 3/12/18 |
| Lieut. H. J. F. MILLS. | 10/7/17 | | 4/12/18 |
| Lieut. A. PINNOCK. | 10/7/17 | | 1/1/19 |
| 2/Lt. A. SIMPSON. | 10/7/17 | | 7/12/18 |
| 2/Lt. H. J. LINDSAY. | 10/7/17 | | 14/12/18 |
| 2/Lt. D. H. TAYLOR. | 10/7/17 | | 7/12/18 |
| 2/Lt. R. MADELEY. | 10/7/17 | | 17/12/18 |
| *Lieut. C. E. S. S. ECCLES. | 21/3/18 | | 25/12/18 |
| Lt.-Col. H. M. GOSLING. | 23/3/18 | | 4/12/18 |
| 2/Lt. H. M. BARNET. | 24/3/18 | (Died at Langensalza | 21/4/18). |
| 2/Lt. O. L. MARLOW. | 19/9/18 | | 2/12/18 |

### 7th Battalion.

| Name | Missing | Repatriated |
|---|---|---|
| Capt. W. BORTHWICK. | 21/3/18 | 12/12/18 |
| Lieut. W. L. SANDERS. | 21/3/18 | 18/12/18 |
| 2/Lt. C. ALLEN. | 21/3/18 | 11/12/18 |
| 2/Lt. H. M. DAY. | 21/3/18 | 11/12/18 |
| 2/Lt. H. A. JACKSON. | 21/3/18 | 18/12/18 |
| 2/Lt. H. J. RATHBONE. | 21/3/18 | 8/12/18 |
| Lt.-Col. J. G. BIRCH. | 22/3/18 | 2/12/18 |

### 8th Battalion.

| Name | Missing | Repatriated |
|---|---|---|
| Capt. J. W. LESLEY. | 3/5/17 | 31/12/18 |
| 2/Lt. H. M. COOK. | 3/5/17 | 30/12/18 |
| 2/Lt. H. H. LIDDLE. | 3/5/17 | 7/1/18 |
| Major N. E. BARBER. | 21/3/18 | –/12/18 |
| Major R. L. BOWEN. | 21/3/18 | 6/12/18 |
| Capt. P. M. POPE. | | 2/12/18 |
| Capt. C. L. DOMVILLE. | 21/3/18 | 6/12/18 |
| †Capt. W. J. REYNOLDS. | 21/3/18 | 6/12/18 |
| Capt. F. G. SCOTT. | 21/3/18 | 14/12/18 |

*Attached T.M.B.   †Attached from London Regiment.

## KING'S ROYAL RIFLE CORPS.—continued.
### 8th Battalion—continued.

| Name. | Missing. | Interned. | Repatriated. |
|---|---|---|---|
| *Lieut. F. B. ADAMS. | 21/3/18 | | 25/12/18 |
| †Lieut. A. J. BELL. | 21/3/18 | | 3/1/19 |
| ‡Lieut. J. E. GIBSON. | 21/3/18 | | 11/12/18 |
| 2/Lt. J. D. K. BEIGHTON. | 21/3/18 | | 6/12/18 |
| §2/Lt. L. C. BUTLER. | 21/3/18 | | 14/12/18 |
| 2/Lt. E. BUTTIFANT. | 21/3/18 | | 6/12/18 |
| **2/Lt. F. G. W. CONNON. | 21/3/18 | | 6/12/18 |
| 2/Lt. D. S. FORSYTH. | 21/3/18 | | -/12/18 |
| 2/Lt. W. S. P. GOW. | 21/3/18 | | 6/12/18 |
| 2/Lt. P. JOHNSON. | 21/3/18 | | -/12/18 |
| ‡‡P2/Lt. C. RAYNER. | 21/3/18 | | 11/12/18 |
| **2/Lt. R. ROBERTSON. | 21/3/18 | | 10/12/18 |
| 2/Lt. S. R. C. SHARP. | 21/3/18 | | 6/12/18 |
| 2/Lt. W. STUART. | 21/3/18 | | 6/12/18 |
| 2/Lt. G. TUXFORD. | 21/3/18 | | 6/12/18 |
| 2/Lt. P. J. JEFFREYS. | 4/4/18 | | 18/12/18 |

### 9th Battalion.

| Name. | Missing. | Interned. | Repatriated. |
|---|---|---|---|
| Lt.-Col. C. H. HOWARD-BURY. | | | -/12/18 |
| Capt. E. R. VICKERS. | 21/3/18 | | 10/12/18 |
| Capt. R. P. GRAHAM. | 21/3/18 | | 4/12/18 |
| Capt. H. M. GRIFFITH. | 21/3/18 | | 10/12/18 |
| Capt. R. T. RIDLEY. | 21/3/18 | | 10/12/18 |
| Lieut. A. J. D'ALTON. | 21/3/18 | | 10/12/18 |
| 2/Lt. C. G. BAKER. | 21/3/18 | | 11/12/18 |
| 2/Lt. E. H. V. BURGESS. | 21/3/18 | | 11/12/18 |
| 2/Lt. J. S. CHOWN. | 21/3/18 | | 11/12/18 |
| 2/Lt. L. S. DAGG. | | | 11/12/18 |
| 2/Lt. L. G. MACKIE. | 21/3/18 | | 11/12/18 |
| 2/Lt. R. R. MITCHELL. | 21/3/18 | | 11/12/18 |
| 2/Lt. P. D. ROGERS. | 21/3/18 | | 11/12/18 |
| **2/Lt. A. F. PARSONS. | 21/31/8 | | 11/12/18 |
| 2/Lt. W. E. ROOKE. | 21/3/18 | | 11/12/18 |
| 2/Lt. P. J. WHITE. | 21/3/18 | | 18/12/18 |

### 10th Battalion.

| Name. | Missing. | Interned. | | Repatriated. |
|---|---|---|---|---|
| 2/Lt. R. D. EVANS. | 14/8/16 | Holland | 12/10/18 | 22/12/18 |
| Capt. H. C. H. ILLINGWORTH. | 28/2/17 | Switzerland | 9/12/17 | 18/12/18 |
| Capt. R. L. JONES. | 10/8/17 | | | 11/1/19 |
| ‖2/Lt. J. M. LOVATT. | 12/8/17 | | | 25/12/18 |
| Capt. F. G. FISON. | 30/11/17 | | | 9/12/18 |
| Lieut. E. G. PRIOR. | 30/11/17 | | | 14/12/18 |
| 2/Lt. J. HUNTER. | 30/11/17 | | | 28/11/18 |
| 2/Lt. A. MACKENZIE. | 30/11/17 | | | 27/11/18 |
| 2/Lt. J. T. KING. | 30/11/17 | | | 3/12/18 |
| 2/Lt. N. A. MACLEAN. | 30/11/17 | | | 17/12/18 |
| 2/Lt. W. E. PRISTO. | 30/11/17 | | | 25/12/18 |
| 2/Lt. P. B. DIPLOCK. | 30/11/17 | | | 2/12/18 |
| 2/Lt. J. J. LEE. | 30/11/17 | | | 15/1/19 |
| 2/Lt. C. M. PENNEY. | 30/11/17 | | | 4/12/18 |

*Attached from Liverpool Regiment.
†Attached from A.S.C.
‡Attached from Scottish Rifles.
§Attached from Manchester Regiment.
**Attached from London Regiment.
††Attached T.M.B.
‖Attached from Dorset Regiment.
‖Attached from N. Staffs.

## KING'S ROYAL RIFLE CORPS.—continued.

### 11th Battalion.

| Name. | Missing. | Interned. | Repatriated. |
|---|---|---|---|
| Capt. C. N. BARLOW. | 30/11/17 | | 13/5/18 |
| Lieut. C. P. E. De PARAVICINI. | 30/11/17 | | 25/12/18 |
| 2/Lt. G. P. LOWE. | 30/11/17 | | 3/12/18 |
| 2/Lt. W. P. MORRIS. | 30/11/17 | (*Died* at Rouen 20/12/18). | |
| 2/Lt. J. S. PORTEOUS. | 30/11/17 | | 25/12/18 |
| 2/Lt. R. READER. | 30/11/17 | | 17/12/18 |
| 2/Lt. G. H. WILLIS. | 30/11/17 | | 17/12/18 |
| 2/Lt. A. G. E. TAYLOR. | 30/11/17 | | 3/12/18 |
| Capt. J. A. WATT. | 30/11/17 | | 9/12/18 |
| *Lieut. L. E. JAMES. | 23/3/18 | | 18/12/18 |
| 2/Lt. E. C. GRIFFITHS. | 24/3/18 | | 18/12/18 |
| †P2/Lt. A. J. SUTTERS. | 24/3/18 | | 3/12/18 |
| Capt. C. G. WEBB. | 25/3/18 | | 3/12/18 |
| 2/Lt. B. JOHNSTON. | 29/3/18 | (*Died*). | |

### 12th Battalion.

| Name. | Missing. | Interned. | Repatriated. |
|---|---|---|---|
| 2/Lt. H. PRATT. | 19/2/16 | Holland 7/10/18 | 22/11/18 |
| Lieut. W. L. WARD-DAVIS. | 21/3/18 | | 4/12/18 |
| 2/Lt. J. C. CALDWELL. | 21/3/18 | | –/12/18 |
| 2/Lt. P. SMITTEN. | 21/3/18 | | 31/12/18 |
| Lt.-Col. L. G. MOORE. | 23/3/18 | | –/12/18 |
| 2/Lt. W. H. TAYLOR. | 25/3/18 | | 29/11/18 |
| 2/Lt. J. W. EVERETT. | 29/3/18 | (*Died* at Beaufort 12/4/18). | |
| Capt. A. N. CRANSWICK. | 31/3/18 | | 10/12/18 |

### 13th Battalion.

| Name. | Missing. | Interned. | Repatriated. |
|---|---|---|---|
| 2/Lt. A. J. WIGGETT. | 8/3/16 | (Died 15/3/16). | |

### 16th Battalion.

| Name. | Missing. | Interned. | Repatriated. |
|---|---|---|---|
| Capt. A. B. BERNARD. | 23/4/17 | (*Died* at Munster 4/5/17). | |
| Capt. L. E. FRANCIS. | 12/4/18 | | 25/12/18 |
| 2/Lt. R. H. M. LEA. | 13/4/18 | | –/12/18 |
| 2/Lt. W. SULLIVAN. | 13/4/18 | | 2/12/18 |
| Capt. C. H. CORK. | 14/4/18 | | 4/12/18 |
| Lieut. E. F. SARGENT. | 15/4/18 | | 25/12/18 |
| 2/Lt. L. J. GOLDSACK. | 15/4/18 | | 23/9/18 |
| 2/Lt. J. E. RICHES. | 15/4/18 | | 6/1/19 |
| Lieut. C. E. HOWARD. | 16/4/18 | | 2/12/18 |
| 2/Lt. H. W. H. CONSIDINE. | 16/4/18 | | 25/12/18 |
| 2/Lt. R. W. EDWARDS. | 16/4/18 | | 4/12/18 |
| 2/Lt. J. HANNAY. | 16/4/18 | | –/12/18 |
| 2/Lt. W. H. McLEAN. | 16/4/18 | | 4/12/18 |
| 2/Lt. G. S. HOGAN. | 24/9/18 | | 16/12/18 |
| 2/Lt. A. H. VILLIERS. | 12/10/18 | | 18/12/18 |

### 17th Battalion.

| Name. | Missing. | Interned. | Repatriated. |
|---|---|---|---|
| ‡Capt. A. W. HARVEY. | 22/3/18 | (*Died* at Walincourt 27/3/18). | |
| 2/Lt. W. McINTYRE. | 22/3/18 | | 25/12/18 |
| 2/Lt. J. P. BUNCE. | 29/3/18 | | 6/1/19 |
| 2/Lt. T. J. G. EASTMAN. | 30/3/18 | | –/12/18 |

### 18th Battalion.

| Name. | Missing. | Interned. | Repatriated. |
|---|---|---|---|
| Lieut. F. W. PARISH. | 14/6/16 | Holland 30/4/18 | 22/11/18 |
| Capt. J. B. GRAY. | 24/3/18 | | 2/12/18 |
| 2/Lt. G. CALDER. | 24/3/18 | | 3/12/18 |
| 2/Lt. J. A. HARRIS. | 24/3/18 | | 18/12/18 |
| 2/Lt. H. J. PICKUP. | 24/3/18 | | 10/12/18 |
| 2/Lt. G. RICHARDSON. | 24/3/18 | | 11/12/18 |

*Attached from London Regiment. †Attached from T.M.B.
‡Attached from Scottish Rifles.

## KING'S ROYAL RIFLE CORPS—continued.

### 18th Battalion—continued.

| Name. | Missing. | Interned. | Repatriated. |
|---|---|---|---|
| 2/Lt. E. P. W. SHEPHEARD. | 24/3/18 | | —/12/18 |
| 2/Lt. C. T. UREN. | 24/3/18 | | 2/12/18 |
| 2/Lt. W. A. F. BINNS. | 11/8/18 | | 13/12/18 |
| Lieut. S. PYE. | 22/10/18 | | 8/12/18 |
| 2/Lt. E. J. HACKING. | 22/10/18 | | —/12/18 |

### 20th Battalion.

| | | | |
|---|---|---|---|
| Lieut. C. W. YOUNG. | 2/10/18 | | 28/11/18 |

### 21st Battalion.

| | | | |
|---|---|---|---|
| Lieut. J. A. BEARN. | 21/3/18 | | 2/12/18 |

## WILTSHIRE REGIMENT.

### 1st and 2nd Battalions.

| Name. | Missing. | Interned. | | Repatriated. |
|---|---|---|---|---|
| Lieut. W. LODER-SYMONDS. | 10/9/14 | | | 14/3/18 |
| | | *(Killed* 30/5/18 at Thetford). | | |
| Major J. R. WYNDHAM. | 24/10/14 | Holland | 24/2/18 | 31/8/18 |
| Capt. A. W. TIMMIS. | 24/10/14 | Holland | 24/2/18 | 20/11/18 |
| Capt. R. SMITH. | 24/10/14 | Holland | 24/2/18 | 18/11/18 |
| Capt. C. H. E. MOORE. | 24/10/14 | Holland | 24/2/18 | 18/11/18 |
| Lieut. R. P. ROGERS. | 24/10/14 | Switzerland | 9/12/17 | 6/12/18 |
| Lieut. H. B. ROSE. | 27/10/14 | Holland | 24/2/18 | 18/11/18 |
| Lieut. J. H. WAND-TETLEY. | 27/10/14 | Holland | 24/2/18 | 19/11/18 |
| Lieut. F. B. RILEY. | 27/10/14 | Holland | 24/2/18 | 15/9/18 |
| Lieut. K. J. P. OLIPHANT. | 27/10/14 | Holland | 24/2/18 | 17/11/18 |
| Lieut. H. W. C. LLOYD. | 27/10/14 | (Escaped) | | —/1/17 |
| 2/Lt. W. MARTIN. | 27/10/14 | Holland | 24/2/18 | Returned for duty. |
| Lieut. M. R. WATSON. | 29/10/14 | Holland | 24/2/18 | 20/12/18 |
| Capt. E. L. HENSLOW. | 8/11/14 | Holland | 24/2/18 | 29/1/19 |
| Capt. R. CULVER. | 1/11/14 | Holland | 24/2/18 | 18/11/18 |
| Lt.-Col. J. N. FORBES. | 24/11/14 | Holland | 6/2/18 | —/—/18 |
| Major C. LAW. | 24/11/14 | Holland | 24/2/18 | 8/2/19 |
| Capt. G. LE HUQUET. | 24/11/14 | Holland | 24/2/18 | 18/11/18 |
| Capt. H. F. CODDINGTON. | 24/11/14 | Holland | 24/2/18 | 1/11/18 |
| Lieut. A. K. BLECKLY. | 24/11/14 | Switzerland | —/12/17 | 7/12/18 |
| Lieut. E. L. BETTS. | 24/11/14 | Holland | 24/2/18 | 18/11/18 |
| Lieut. C. H. R. BARNES. | 24/11/14 | Holland | 6/2/18 | 18/11/18 |
| Lieut. D. A. ANSTED. | 24/11/14 | Holland | 24/2/18 | 21/11/18 |
| Lieut. A. S. HOOPER. | 24/11/14 | Holland | 20/12/17 | 18/11/18 |
| 2/Lt. G. P. OLDFIELD. | 24/11/14 | Holland | 24/2/18 | 21/1/19 |
| 2/Lt. F. RYLANDS. | 14/1/15 | Holland | 24/2/18 | Returned for duty. |
| Capt. A. E. STICKINGS. | 16/6/15 | | | 11/9/17 |
| 2/Lt. H. G. DEHN. | 9/7/16 | Switzerland | 9/12/17 | 14/6/18 |
| 2/Lt. C. H. BLAKE. | 15/12/16 | | | 17/12/18 |

### 1st Battalion.

| | | | |
|---|---|---|---|
| 2/Lt. S. C. SMITH. | 24/3/18 | | 11/12/18 |
| 2/Lt. A. V. S. GRANT. | 24/3/18 | | 23/9/18 |
| Capt. F. SMITH. | 10/4/18 | | 25/12/18 |
| 2/Lt. S. J. PARKER. | 11/4/18 | | 29/11/18 |
| Lt.-Col. S. S. OGILVIE. | 12/4/18 | | 4/12/18 |
| Capt. C. H. G. THOMAS. | 12/4/18 | | 9/1/19 |
| Lt.-Col. E. K. B. FURZE. | 27/5/18 | | 21/12/18 |
| Capt. J. F. ARNOTT. | 27/5/18 | | 18/12/18 |
| Lieut. H. C. REID. | 27/5/18 | | 18/12/18 |
| 2/Lt. J. B. STANLEY. | 27/5/18 | | —/12/18 |
| 2/Lt. S. T. DOWSON. | 15/8/18 | | 13/12/18 |
| 2/Lt. D. H. DAVIES. | 30/8/18 | (*Died* at Gottingen 18/11/18 |

## WILTSHIRE REGIMENT—continued.
### 2nd Battalion.

| Name. | Missing. | Interned. | Repatriated. |
|---|---|---|---|
| Lt.-Col. A. V. P. MARTIN. | 21/3/18 | | 6/12/18 |
| Capt. L. C. MAKEHAM. | 21/3/18 | | 6/12/18 |
| Lieut. R. M. P. BEAVEN. | 21/3/18 | | -/12/18 |
| Lieut. S. S. MILLER. | 21/3/18 | | 6/12/18 |
| 2/Lt. J. F. F. McQUEEN. | 21/3/18 | | 6/12/18 |
| 2/Lt. C. D. BAKER. | 21/3/18 | | -/12/18 |
| 2/Lt. R. H. EDWARDS. | 21/31/8 | | 6/12/18 |
| 2/Lt. E. W. APPS. | 21/3/18 | | 6/12/18 |
| 2/Lt. P. E. KING-SMITH. | 21/3/18 | | 14/12/18 |
| 2/Lt. B. M. IVISON. | 21/3/18 | | 14/12/18 |
| 2/Lt. H. J. HULBERT. | 21/3/18 | | 25/12/18 |
| 2/Lt. A. R. MOORE. | 21/3/18 | | 6/12/18 |
| Lieut. F. J. LONDON. | 24/3/18 | | 10/12/18 |
| Lieut. C. L. USHER. | 28/3/18 | (*Died* 23/4/18). | |
| 2/Lt. F. J. E. SPENCER. | 26/4/18 | | 9/11/18 |
| Lt. T. W. GLYNN. | 21/3/18 | | 6/12/18 |

### 6th Battalion.

| Name. | Missing. | Interned. | Repatriated. |
|---|---|---|---|
| Lieut. E. E. PEGGE. | 22/3/18 | | 10/12/18 |
| *Lieut. M. G. SUMNER. | 23/3/18 | | 28/11/18 |
| Lieut. S. H. WILLIAMS. | 24/3/18 | | 25/12/18 |
| Lieut. J. STOGDEN. | 24/3/18 | | 10/12/18 |
| Lieut. L. R. MILLERSHIP. | 24/3/18 | | 11/12/18 |
| 2/Lt. A. G. AUSTIN. | 24/3/18 | | 18/12/18 |
| Capt. N. L. FLOWER. | 25/3/18 | | 13/1/19 |
| *2/Lt. D. B. CAMPBELL. | 25/3/18 | | -/1/19 |
| Capt. G. C. H. KENT. | 10/4/18 | | 25/12/18 |
| *Lieut. B. M. KNOWLES. | 10/4/18 | | -/12/18 |
| †2/Lt. P. G. HART. | 10/4/18 | | 25/12/18 |
| Capt. W. M. AUSTIN. | 11/4/18 | | -/12/18 |

## MANCHESTER REGIMENT.
### 1st and 2nd Battalions.

| Name. | Missing. | Interned. | | Repatriated. |
|---|---|---|---|---|
| Capt. C. MORLEY. | 30/8/14 | | | 13/9/17 |
| Lieut. R. F. G. BURROWS. | 30/8/14 | Holland | 5/1/18 | 18/11/18 |
| 2/Lt. R. T. MILLER. | 3/9/14 | Switzerland | 12/8/16 | 23/3/18 |
| Capt. G. P. WYMER. | 10/9/14 | Holland | 22/1/18 | 18/8/18 |
| 2/Lt. W. BUTLER. | | | | 2/1/19 |
| Capt. B. L. ERSKINE. | 18/11/16 | | | 5/1/19 |
| Lieut. M. R. DAVIDSON. | 18/11/16 | | | 1/1/19 |
| 2/Lt. G. B. GRIFFIN. | 18/11/16 | | | 1/1/19 |
| 2/Lt. E. E. J. HENDERSON. | 18/11/16 | | | 17/12/18 |
| 2/Lt. N. F. HARLEY. | 18/11/16 | | | 17/12/18 |
| 2/Lt. F. HARBRON. | 18/11/16 | | | 29/11/18 |
| 2/Lt. B. W. SPROWELL. | 2/10/18 | | | 13/12/18 |

### 4th Battalion.

| Name. | Missing. | Interned. | Repatriated. |
|---|---|---|---|
| 2/Lt. G. A. HALSTEAD. | 25/3/18 | | 26/12/18 |

*Attached from Wiltshire Yeomanry.
†Attached T.M.B.

## MANCHESTER REGIMENT—continued.

### 5th Battalion.

| Name. | Missing. | Interned. | Repatriated. |
|---|---|---|---|
| Capt. R. P. PORTER. | 21/3/18 | | 29/11/18 |
| Capt. G. TWEEDALE. | 21/3/18 | | 10/12/18 |
| Lieut. W. A. E. URIE. | 21/3/18 | | 8/12/18 |
| *Lieut. W. H. E. N. GRIFFITH. | 21/3/18 | | 29/11/18 |
| Lieut. S. R. ELLIS. | 21/3/18 | | 2/12/18 |
| Lieut. H. D. ATKIN. | 21/3/18 | | 2/12/18 |
| Lieut. R. A. THORNTON. | 21/3/18 | | 14/12/18 |
| 2/Lt. A. B. C. DYER. | 21/3/18 | | 29/11/18 |
| 2/Lt. J. H. WELLARD. | 21/3/18 | | 2/12/18 |
| 2/Lt. J. R. GRIFFITH. | 21/3/18 | | 25/12/18 |
| 2/Lt. S. KEYS. | 21/3/18 | | -/12/18 |
| 2/Lt. J. CHANDLER. | 21/3/18 | | 14/12/18 |
| 2/Lt. H. ELLISON. | 21/3/18 | | -/12/18 |
| 2/Lt. F. C. G. BENSON. | 21/3/18 | | 29/11/18 |
| 2/Lt. J. F. SCHOFIELD. | 21/3/18 | | 2/12/18 |
| 2/Lt. L. PULPHER. | 21/3/18 | | 14/12/18 |
| Major E. L. FISHER. | 22/3/18 | | 18/12/18 |
| Lieut. T. NICHOLSON. | 22/3/18 | | 28/11/18 |
| 2/Lt. W. A. CHURCH. | 22/3/18 | | 14/12/18 |
| Capt. K. G. MAXWELL. | 23/3/18 | | -/12/18 |
| 2/Lt. W. J. McBEATH. | 24/3/18 | | 25/12/18 |

### 6th Battalion.

| Name. | Missing. | Interned. | Repatriated. |
|---|---|---|---|
| Lieut. J. H. B. SEWELL. | 21/3/18 | | 29/11/18 |
| Lieut. H. MAKINSON. | 21/3/18 | | -/11/19 |
| 2/Lt. H. BAGGS. | 21/3/18 | | 29/11/18 |
| 2/Lt. H. W. H. ORAM. | 21/3/18 | | 18/12/18 |
| 2/Lt. E. WILKINSON. | 21/3/18 | | 25/12/18 |
| 2/Lt. F. BRADLEY. | 22/3/18 | | 29/11/18 |
| Capt. S. L. BRIDGFORD. | 23/3/18 | (*Died* 6/4/18 at Ghent). | |
| 2/Lt. R. P. HOLLAND. | 24/3/18 | | 29/11/18 |
| 2/Lt. B. K. WHITTAKER. | 25/3/18 | | 28/11/18 |
| 2/Lt. F. L. C. SIMONS. | 25/3/18 | | 2/12/18 |

### 7th Battalion.

| Name. | Missing. | Interned. | Repatriated. |
|---|---|---|---|
| *Major N. A. B. BAILLIE-HAMILTON. | 21/3/18 | | 18/12/18 |
| Capt. J. A. SCHOLFIELD. | 21/3/18 | | -/12/18 |
| Lieut. A. G. ALDRED. | 21/3/18 | | 11/12/18 |
| Lieut. E. H. SHAW. | 21/3/18 | | 29/11/18 |
| Lieut. R. W. FOX. | 21/3/18 | | 25/12/18 |
| 2/Lt. J. N. HODGKINSON. | 21/3/18 | | 18/12/18 |
| 2/Lt. F. P. FREEMAN. | 21/3/18 | | 29/11/18 |
| 2/Lt. J. M. HAYES. | 21/3/18 | | 5/12/18 |
| 2/Lt. F. ANDREW. | 25/3/18 | (*Died* 31/3/18 at Bohain). | |

### 8th Battalion.

| Name. | Missing. | Interned. | Repatriated. |
|---|---|---|---|
| Capt. K. V. BAILEY. | 21/3/18 | | 14/12/18 |
| Lieut. W. GIBBONS. | 21/3/18 | | -/11/18 |
| 2/Lt. F. ROBSON. | 21/3/18 | | 12/10/18 |
| 2/Lt. A. N. TONGUE. | 21/3/18 | | 6/12/18 |
| 2/Lt. G. PARSONS. | 21/3/18 | | 29/11/18 |
| 2/Lt. C. HASLAM. | 25/3/18 | | -/12/18 |
| Lieut. A. S. WOMERSLEY. | 12/4/18 | | 1/12/18 |

*Attached T.M.B.     *Attached from Black Watch.

## MANCHESTER REGIMENT—continued.

### 9th Battalion.

| Name. | Missing. | Interned. | Repatriated. |
|---|---|---|---|
| Capt. H. E. BUTTERWORTH. | 21/3/18 | | 25/12/18 |
| *Capt. F. WOOD. | 21/3/18 | | 29/11/18 |
| 2/Lt. G. HUNT. | 21/3/18 | | 18/12/18 |
| 2/Lt. W. WITTY. | 4/4/18 | | 2/12/18 |

### 10th Battalion.

| | | | |
|---|---|---|---|
| *Major E. G. SOTHAM. | 21/3/18 | | 6/12/18 |
| 2/Lt. F. J. DURRANT. | 21/3/18 | | 8/12/18 |

### 12th Battalion.

| | | | |
|---|---|---|---|
| Capt. J. T. BROMLEY. | 8/9/17 | | 6/12/18 |
| Lieut. R. B. HAMER. | 21/3/18 | | 18/12/18 |
| 2/Lt. M. LIGGETT. | 24/3/18 | | 18/12/18 |
| 2/Lt. F. F. TAYLOR. | 24/3/18 | | 17/12/18 |
| 2/Lt. A. H. JACOBS. | 24/3/18 | | 18/12/18 |
| 2/Lt. G. S. BAILEY. | 8/9/18 | | 28/11/18 |
| 2/Lt. E. WINDER. | 12/10/18 | | 8/12/18 |
| †2/Lt. J. BRADLEY. | 12/10/18 | | 16/12/18 |

### 14th Battalion.

| | | | |
|---|---|---|---|
| 2/Lt. J. S. PARTINGTON. | 1/7/16 | Holland 15/6/18 | 22/11/18 |
| 2/Lt. F. S. SHAW. | 26/4/18 | | 2/12/18 |

### 16th Battalion.

| | | | |
|---|---|---|---|
| Major R. N. R. GIBBON. | 21/3/18 | | 13/12/18 |
| Capt. J. GUEST. | 21/3/18 | | 2/1/19 |
| Capt. O. T. PRICHARD. | 21/3/18 | | 14/12/18 |
| Capt. P. H. HEYWOOD. | 21/3/18 | | 14/12/18 |
| Lieut. E. T. HOLLINS. | 21/31/8 | | 18/12/18 |
| Lieut. M. D. PLEASANCE. | 21/3/18 | | 14/12/18 |
| Lieut. J. CLARKE. | 21/3/18 | (*Died* at Cologne). | |
| 2/Lt. F. HAYES. | 21/3/18 | | –/12/18 |
| 2/Lt. J. A. BIRCHENOUGH. | 21/3/18 | | 11/12/18 |
| 2/Lt. W. DEAN. | 21/3/18 | | 14/12/18 |
| 2/Lt. J. A. BENTLEY. | 21/3/18 | | 27/11/18 |
| 2/Lt. W. McQUINN. | 21/3/18 | (*Died* 6/8/18 at Wittenberg). | |
| 2/Lt. F. W. KEELING. | 22/3/18 | | 14/12/18 |
| 2/Lt. A. WOODACRE. | 26/4/18 | | 2/12/18 |
| 2/Lt. H. T. RINGHAM. | 26/4/18 | | 3/12/18 |
| 2/Lt. E. JONES. | 26/4/18 | | 6/12/18 |
| 2/Lt. E. BRADWELL. | 26/4/18 | | 2/12/18 |

### 17th Battalion.

| | | | |
|---|---|---|---|
| 2/Lt. C. W. ROBERTSON. | 10–11/7/16 | (*Died* 22/8/16 at Le Cateau). | |
| Lieut. L. B. HUMPHREYS. | 11/7/16 | | 22/1/19 |
| Lieut. W. F. SWIFT. | 23/4/17 | | 4/1/19 |
| 2/Lt. A. T. S. HOLT. | 23/4/17 | | 4/12/18 |
| Capt. W. G. WOODWARD. | 22/3/18 | | 2/12/18 |
| Capt. J. L. CLAYTON. | 22/3/18 | | 1/12/18 |
| Lieut. G. DUNSCOMBE. | 22/3/18 | (*Died* at Graudenz). | |
| 2/Lt. F. V. HARRISON. | 22/3/18 | | 18/12/18 |
| 2/Lt. C. S. MILES. | 22/3/18 | | 12/12/18 |

*Attached from Lancashire Fusiliers.
†Attached from South Lancs.

## MANCHESTER REGIMENT—continued.

### 17th Battalion—continued.

| Name. | Missing. | Interned. | | Repatriated. |
|---|---|---|---|---|
| 2/Lt. T. LONGWORTH. | 22/3/18 | | | 18/12/18 |
| 2/Lt. S. A. JACKSON. | 22/3/18 | | | 18/12/18 |
| 2/Lt. W. H. SMITH. | 26/4/18 | | | 2/12/18 |
| 2/Lt. L. RATHBONE. | 26/4/18 | | | 3/12/18 |
| 2/Lt. S. W. CANNON. | 26/4/18 | | | –/12/18 |
| 2/Lt. J. HILLIAN. | 26/4/18 | | | 2/12/18 |
| 2/Lt. C. T. M. MARSHALL. | 26/4/18 | | | 2/12/18 |

### 18th Battalion.

| Name. | Missing. | Interned. | | Repatriated. |
|---|---|---|---|---|
| 2/Lt. D. BLENKIRON. | 29/1/16 | Holland | 19/4/18 | 23/10/18 |
| Capt. F. WOLFENDEN. | 1/8/16 | | | 29/11/18 |
| Capt. W. F. ROUTLEY. | 1/8/16 | Switzerland | 9/12/17 | 24/3/18 |
| Capt. J. O. McELROY. | 14/12/17 | | | 3/12/18 |
| 2/Lt. H. WHINCUP. | 14/12/17 | | | 27/11/18 |
| *Capt. H. A. HENDRIE. | 21/3/18 | | | 10/12/18 |
| *Lieut. W. EVANS. | 21/3/18 | | | 25/12/18 |

### 19th Battalion.

| Name. | Missing. | Interned. | | Repatriated. |
|---|---|---|---|---|
| Capt. W. M. CLARKE. | 24/7/16 | Switzerland | 19/12/16 | 14/6/18 |
| Lieut. J. A. CALDWELL. | 24/7/16 | Holland | 15/6/18 | 1/2/19 |
| Lieut. G. LERESCHE. | 24/7/16 | | | 22/11/18 |
| 2/Lt. N. H. CRASTON. | 24/7/16 | Holland | 15/6/18 | 22/11/18 |

### 20th Battalion.

| Name. | Missing. | Interned. | Repatriated. |
|---|---|---|---|
| Lieut. R. K. MATHESON. | 3/9/16 | (*Died* 8/9/16). | |
| Lieut. F. H. BISHOP. | 18/4/18 | | 14/12/18 |

### 21st Battalion.

| Name. | Missing. | Interned. | Repatriated. |
|---|---|---|---|
| 2/Lt. S. R. SMITH. | 15/5/17 | | 23/12/18 |
| 2/Lt. W. B. PURVIS. | 26/10/17 | | 2/12/18 |

### 22nd Battalion.

| Name. | Missing. | Interned. | Repatriated. |
|---|---|---|---|
| Lieut. H. GRIMWOOD. | 14/3/17 | | –/11/18 |
| 2/Lt. H. WILLIAMS. | 6/10/17 | | 13/12/18 |

## NORTH STAFFORDSHIRE REGIMENT.

### 1st and 2nd Battalions.

| Name. | Missing. | Interned. | | Repatriated. |
|---|---|---|---|---|
| Lieut. L. J. JONES. | 28/10/14 | Holland | 24/2/18 | 28/1/19 |
| Lieut. J. ADAMS. | | Holland | 24/2/18 | 22/11/18 |
| Lieut. J. R. WHYTE. | | Switzerland | 27/12/17 | 14/6/18 |
| Capt. C. B. STARTIN. | 21/3/18 | | | 10/12/18 |
| Capt. D. M. SMYTH. | 21/3/18 | | | 10/12/18 |
| *2/Lt. R. MANSELL. | 21/3/18 | | | 11/1/19 |
| 2/Lt. H. V. TATTERSALL. | 21/3/18 | (*Died* 22/4/18 at Halle). | | |
| 2/Lt. L. REDFERN. | 21/3/18 | | | 11/12/18 |
| 2/Lt. F. J. SHUTT. | 21/3/18 | | | 11/12/18 |

### 4th Battalion.

| Name. | Missing. | Interned. | Repatriated. |
|---|---|---|---|
| †2/Lt. F. M. W. SIEMS. | 3/11/17 | | 3/12/18 |

*Attached T.M.B.  †Attached from 7th Londons.

## NORTH STAFFORDSHIRE REGIMENT—continued.

### 5th Battalion.

| Name. | Missing. | Interned. | Repatriated. |
|---|---|---|---|
| 2/Lt. G. E. E. WILLIAMS. | 14/3/17 | | 7/1/18 |
| 2/Lt. P. B. ROSS. | 1/7/17 | | 6/12/18 |
| 2/Lt. R. F. JOHNSON. | 1–5/7/17 | | 6/12/18 |
| Colonel H. JOHNSON. | 21/3/18 | | 8/12/18 |
| Capt. T. E. TILDESLEY. | 21/3/18 | | 29/11/18 |
| Capt. L. C. GRICE. | 21/3/18 | | 52/12/18 |
| Capt. V. B. SHELLEY. | 21/3/18 | | 29/11/18 |
| Capt. M. SETTLE. | 21/3/18 | (Died 23/12/18). | |
| 2/Lt. G. L. KING. | 21/3/18 | | 3/12/18 |
| 2/Lt. A. M. JONES. | 21/3/18 | | –/11/18 |
| 2/Lt. W. A. BERESFORD. | 21/3/18 | | 29/11/18 |
| 2/Lt. H. ST. J. B. WATSON. | 21/3/18 | | 11/12/18 |
| 2/Lt. F. R. TUNNICLIFFE. | 21/3/18 | | 29/11/18 |
| 2/Lt. L. M. McKNIGHT. | 17/4/18 | | 25/12/18 |

### 6th Battalion.

| Name. | Missing. | Interned. | | Repatriated. |
|---|---|---|---|---|
| 2/Lt. G. D. COLLIS. | 2/7/16 | Holland | 16/5/18 | 21/1/19 |
| 2/Lt. C. W. WHITEHURST. | 2/7/16 | Holland | 16/5/18 | 22/11/18 |
| Major O. J. F. KEATING. | 21/3/18 | | | 29/11/18 |
| *Capt. N. ST. C. PALMER. | 21/3/18 | | | 13/12/18 |
| Capt. C. W. SMITH. | 21/3/18 | | | 10/12/18 |
| Capt. G. ADAMS. | 21/3/18 | | | 2/1/19 |
| Lieut. G. P. RATHBONE. | 21/3/18 | | | 5/12/18 |
| †2/Lt. J. PAXTON. | 21/3/18 | | | 13/12/18 |
| †2/Lt. W. N. PRICE. | 21/3/18 | | | –/12/18 |
| †2/Lt. J. S. COLBOURNE. | 21/3/18 | | | 11/12/18 |
| †2/Lt. S. P. HUDSON. | 21/3/18 | | | 18/12/18 |
| 2/Lt. S. G. HOWE. | 21/3/18 | | | 11/12/18 |
| 2/Lt. R. HEATON. | 21/1/18 | | | 2/12/18 |
| 2/Lt. O. L. PAGET. | 21/3/18 | | | 29/11/18 |
| 2/Lt. E. M. COPE. | 21/3/18 | | | 25/12/18 |
| ‡2/Lt. J. C. V. JENNINGS. | 21/3/18 | | | 6/12/18 |
| 2/Lt. P. H. BATCHELOR. | 21/3/18 | (Died). | | |
| §2/Lt. A. C. IRVINE. | 21/3/18 | | | 25/12/18 |
| Capt. A. G. PAXTON. | 15/4/18 | | | 25/12/18 |
| Lieut. W. P. SHORT. | 15/4/18 | | | 25/12/18 |
| 2/Lt. E. BENTLEY. | 15/4/18 | | | –/12/18 |
| 2/Lt. J. STANSBY. | –/–/16 | Holland | 16/5/18 | 22/12/18 |

### 8th Battalion.

| Name. | Missing. | Interned. | | Repatriated. |
|---|---|---|---|---|
| 2/Lt. T. MAUGHFLING. | 17–20/11/16 | Switzerland | 27/12/17 | 24/3/18 |
| Lt. Col. C. L. ANDERSSON. | 18/11/16 | Switzerland | 27/12/17 | –/2/19 |
| Capt. G. C. JAMES. | 18/11/16 | | | 17/12/18 |
| 2/Lt. G. S. CARVER. | 24/3/18 | | | 3/12/18 |

## YORK AND LANCASTER REGIMENT.

### 1st Battalion.

| Name. | Missing. | Interned. | | Repatriated. |
|---|---|---|---|---|
| Lieut. G. C. R. MARTIN. | 20/10/14 | Holland (Died 12/9/18). | 6/2/18 | |
| Lieut. S. H. TAYLOR. | 20/10/14 | Holland | 6/2/18 | 18/11/18 |

\*Attached from Hertfordshire Regiment. †Attached from Warwickshire Regiment.
‡Attached from K.O.R.L. §Attached from Border Regiment.

## YORK AND LANCASTER REGIMENT—continued.

### 2nd Battalion.

| Name. | Missing. | Interned. | | Repatriated. |
|---|---|---|---|---|
| Capt. W. E. SHEPHERD. | 21/3/18 | | | –/12/18 |
| 2/Lt. H. CAMERON. | 21/3/18 | | | 13/12/18 |
| 2/Lt. F. J. W. LYONS. | 21/3/18 | | | 18/12/18 |
| 2/Lt. E. MERRALL. | 21/3/18 | | | 17/12/18 |
| 2/Lt. W. R. MUFF. | 21/3/18 | | | 2/12/18 |
| 2/Lt. A. L. NORMAN. | 21/3/18 | | | 3/12/18 |
| *2/Lt. A. RACE. | 21/3/18 | | | 3/12/18 |
| †2/Lt. H. SINGLETON. | 21/3/18 | | | 23/10/18 |
| 2/Lt. M. J. WHITEHEAD. | 21/3/18 | | | 2/12/18 |

### 4th Battalion.

| | | | | |
|---|---|---|---|---|
| Lieut. C. UTLEY. | 12/4/18 | | | 1/12/18 |
| Lieut. E. A. HOLMES. | 14/4/18 | | | 2/12/18 |
| Lieut. R. H. WALKER. | 14/4/18 | | | 2/12/18 |
| Lieut. J. D. M. MORTON. | 13/10/18 | | | 24/11/18 |
| 2/Lt. S. E. WARBURTON. | 13/10/18 | | | 27/11/18 |

### 5th Battalion.

| | | | | |
|---|---|---|---|---|
| Lieut. J. HAIGH. | 2/7/16 | Holland | 16/5/18 | 22/11/18 |
| 2/Lt. H. M. GREENHOW. | 7/7/16 | Holland | 16/5/18 | 18/11/18 |
| Capt. A. S. FURNISS. | 22/2/17 | Holland | 7/5/18 | 23/10/18 |
| Lieut. A. H. HICKS. | 22/2/17 | | | 31/12/18 |
| *2/Lt. L. M. C. COLLINS. | 9/1/18 | | | 27/11/18 |
| 2/Lt. E. COOKE. | 26/3/18 | | | 14/12/18 |
| 2/Lt. J. W. KIRKBY. | 11/4/18 | | | 3/12/18 |
| Capt. J. W. BEAUMONT. | 13/10/18 | | | 3/12/18 |

### 6th Battalion.

| | | | | |
|---|---|---|---|---|
| Lieut. A. S. C. BARNARD. | 9/10/17 | | | 6/12/18 |

### 9th Battalion.

| | | | | |
|---|---|---|---|---|
| 2/Lt. F. KEMPTON. | 15/6/18 | | | 20/11/18 |

### 10th Battalion.

| | | | | |
|---|---|---|---|---|
| Lieut. G. J. WHITAKER. | 26/9/15 | Holland | 19/4/18 | 18/11/18 |
| 2/Lt. H. D. HUGHES. | 21/3/18 | | | 18/12/18 |

### 13th Battalion.

| | | | | |
|---|---|---|---|---|
| Lieut. F. H. WESTBY. | 26/3/18 | | | 10/12/18 |
| 2/Lt. C. S. SMITH. | 12/4/18 | | | –/12/18 |

## DURHAM LIGHT INFANTRY.

### 2nd Battalion.

| Name. | Missing. | Interned. | Repatriated. |
|---|---|---|---|
| Major G. SOPWITH. | 21/3/18 | | 14/12/18 |
| Capt. E. FAWCETT. | 21/3/18 | | 29/11/18 |
| Capt. M. P. GRIFFITH-JONES. | 21/3/18 | | 3/12/18 |
| Capt. H. A. PICKERING. | 21/3/18 | | 29/11/18 |
| Lieut. MILES HUTCHINSON. | 21/3/18 | | 25/12/18 |
| Lieut. R. M. HOGG. | 21/3/18 | (Died 1/4/18 at Cologne). | |
| Lieut. E. W. TUFFS. | 21/3/18 | | 18/12/18 |

* Attached from West Riding Regiment.      † Attached from East Lancashire Regiment.

## DURHAM LIGHT INFANTRY—continued.

### 2nd Battalion—continued.

| Name. | Missing. | Interned. | Repatriated. |
|---|---|---|---|
| Lieut. L. A. HARTSHORN. | 21/3/18 | (Died 26/3/18 at Zancourt). | |
| Lieut. W. HENDERSON. | 21/3/18 | | |
| 2/Lt. K. E. ALEXANDER. | 21/3/18 | | —/1/19 |
| 2/Lt. N. BROWN. | 21/3/18 | | 29/11/18 |
| 2/Lt. J. J. LUNN. | 21/3/18 | | |
| 2/Lt. H. H. CARMICHAEL. | 21/3/18 | | 29/11/18 |
| 2/Lt. J. E. ECCLES. | 22/3/18 | | 17/12/18 |
| 2/Lt. M. R. PINKNEY. | 28/3/18 | | 6/12/18 |
| *Lieut. L. SILBURN. | 24/9/18 | | 8/12/18 |

### 5th Battalion.

| Name. | Missing. | Interned. | Repatriated. |
|---|---|---|---|
| 2/Lt. A. E. W. PEREIRA | 23/4/17 | | 25/12/18 |
| 2/Lt. H. J. W. SCOTT | 23/3/18 | | 12/10/18 |
| Capt. L. W. TAYLOR. | 27/3/18 | | 25/12/18 |
| Lieut. J. N. SLACK. | 27/3/18 | | 10/12/18 |
| Lieut. G. F. ROWE. | 11/4/18 | | 25/12/18 |
| 2/Lt. C. L. HADDON. | 11/4/18 | | 18/12/18 |
| Capt. F. W. B. JOHNSON. | 27/5/18 | | —/12/18 |
| Capt. A. B. HILL. | 27/5/18 | | —/12/18 |
| Lieut. R. W. B. ROBINSON. | 27/5/18 | | 30/12/18 |
| Lieut. O. J. WILLIAMS. | 27/5/18 | | 13/12/18 |
| Lieut. A. L. B. CHILDE. | 27/5/18 | | 31/12/18 |
| †Lieut. J. LEIGH. | 27/5/18 | | 2/1/19 |
| †2/Lt. K. McN. PHILLIPS. | 27/5/18 | | 2/1/19 |
| †2/Lt. W. S. WRAY. | 27/5/18 | | —/12/18 |
| 2/Lt. R. J. HADDON. | 27/5/18 | | 30/12/18 |
| 2/Lt. E. J. LOWES. | 27/5/18 | (Died 2/6/18 at Liesse). | |
| ‡2/Lt. P. GODDING. | 27/5/18 | | 6/12/18 |
| §p2/Lt. W. S. KIRKUP. | 27/5/18 | | 30/12/18 |
| Lieut. W. A. CAMPBELL. | 21/7/18 | | 30/12/18 |

### 6th Battalion.

| Name. | Missing. | Interned. | Repatriated. |
|---|---|---|---|
| 2/Lt. A. DOBSON. | 31/3/18 | | 18/12/18 |
| 2/Lt. R. RAILTON. | 9/4/18 | | 11/12/18 |
| Capt. P. H. Bowes LYON. | 27/5/18 | | 18/12/18 |
| ‡Lieut. L. W. WILSON. | 27/5/18 | | —/12/18 |
| ‡2/Lt. T. F. GRAVES. | 27/5/18 | | —/12/18 |
| Lieut. G. P. RUDGE. | 27/5/18 | | 30/12/18 |
| Lieut. G. D. ROBERTS. | 27/5/18 | | 13/12/18 |
| Lieut. R. GREEN. | 27/5/18 | | 25/12/18 |
| 2/Lt. A. B. GILES. | 27/5/18 | | 13/12/18 |
| 2/Lt. J. L. GOTT. | 27/5/18 | | 25/12/18 |
| 2/Lt. G. A. GRAY. | 27/5/18 | | —/12/18 |
| §2/Lt. H. C. HOWELL. | 27/5/18 | | 31/12/18 |
| §2/Lt. B. HOWARTH. | 27/5/18 | | 17/12/18 |
| 2/Lt. W. E. G. PRIEST. | 27/5/18 | | —/12/18 |
| 2/Lt. N. B. THOMPSON. | 27/5/18 | | 17/12/18 |
| 2/Lt. C. BROWN. | 27/5/18 | | —/12/18 |
| 2/Lt. A. S. BOSTOCK. | 27/5/18 | | 17/12/18 |
| **Lieut. C. H. SYMES. | 28/5/18 | | 31/12/18 |

\* Attached from A.S.C.  
† Attached from Northumberland Fusiliers.  
‡ Attached from Royal Irish Rifles.  
§ Attached from Border Regiment.  
** Attached from Gloucesters.

## DURHAM LIGHT INFANTRY—continued.

### 7th Battalion.

| Name. | Missing. | Interned. | Repatriated. |
|---|---|---|---|
| Lieut. A. V. GRAYSTON. | | | 29/11/18 |
| 2/Lt. G. NIXON. | 29/3/18 | | 18/12/18 |
| Lieut. F. W. R. NESBITT. | 11/4/18 | (*Died* 19/4/18 at Lille). | |
| Capt. L. BENNETT. | 27/5/18 | | 17/12/18 |
| Capt. W. F. LAING. | 27/5/18 | | -/12/18 |
| Capt. H. H. JOSEPH. | 27/5/18 | | 6/12/18 |
| *pCapt. R. W. W. PARKER. | 27/5/18 | | 14/12/18 |
| Lieut. R. V. ILES. | 27/5/18 | | 31/12/18 |
| Lieut. G. W. BOSUSTOW. | 25/7/18 | | -/12/18 |
| Lieut. P. WALKER. | 27/5/18 | | -/12/18 |
| Lieut. F. GRAHAM. | 27/5/18 | | -/12/18 |
| Lieut. J. P. B. GREY. | 27/5/18 | | 25/12/18 |
| Lieut. L. J. FOSTER. | 27/5/18 | | -/12/18 |
| 2/Lt. P. GIBSON. | 27/5/18 | | -/12/18 |
| 2/Lt. F. C. MAJOR. | 27/5/18 | | -/12/18 |
| 2/Lt. E. B. F. ARTHY. | 27/5/18 | | 13/12/18 |

### 8th Battalion.

| Name. | Missing. | Interned. | | Repatriated. |
|---|---|---|---|---|
| Major J. R. RITSON. | 27/4/15 | Holland | 23/3/18 | 1/11/18 |
| Capt. W. H. COULSON. | 27/4/15 | Holland | 17/8/18 | 23/10/18 |
| Lieut. G. E. BLACKETT. | 27/4/15 | Holland | 23/3/18 | 1/11/18 |
| Lieut. E. A. LEYBOURNE. | 27/4/15 | | | 3/12/17 |
| Lieut. C. SAYER. | 27/4/15 | (*Died* 7/6/15). | | |
| Lieut. J. L. WOOD. | 27/4/15 | Holland | 19/3/18 | 18/11/18 |
| 2/Lt. J. O. WILSON. | 27/4/15 | Holland | 19/3/18 | 4/10/18 |
| 2/Lt. D. H. RICHARDSON. | 27/4/15 | (*Died* 31/5/15). | | |
| 2/Lt. A. W. NESBITT. | 27/4/15 | Holland | 23/3/18 | 18/11/18 |
| 2/Lt. J. N. ROGERS. | 27/4/15 | Holland | 19/3/18 | 22/11/18 |
| Capt. R. BURDON. | 21/3/18 | | | 2/12/18 |
| Capt. H. J. MOWLAM. | 28/3/18 | | | 12/10/18 |
| 2/Lt. W. J. RICHARDSON. | 28/3/18 | | | -/1/19 |
| Lieut. A. RANSON. | 10/4/18 | | | 29/11/18 |
| 2/Lt. H. I'ANSON. | 10/4/18 | | | 8/12/18 |
| Lieut. A. G. N. GREEN. | 11/4/18 | | | 2/12/18 |
| Capt. H. WILKINSON. | 27/5/18 | | | -/12/18 |
| Capt. J. HUTCHINSON. | 27/5/18 | | | 14/12/18 |
| Capt. J. H. BURRELL. | 27/5/18 | | | -/12/18 |
| Capt. J. W. E. TURNBULL. | 27/5/18 | | | -/12/18 |
| Capt. R. H. WHARRIER. | 27/5/18 | | | 14/12/18 |
| Lieut. A. L. WILSON. | 27/5/18 | | | -/12/18 |
| Lieut. F. ARKLESS. | 27/5/18 | | | -/12/18 |
| Lieut. E. A. ARMBRISTER | 27/5/18 | | | 25/12/18 |
| Lieut. W. R. HILL. | 27/5/18 | (*Died* 6/11/18 at Stralsund). | | |
| Lieut. M. HOPPER. | 27/5/18 | | | 25/12/18 |
| Lieut. E. A. PIKE. | 27/5/18 | | | -/12/18 |
| †Lieut. A. N. MONTGOMERY. | 27/5/18 | | | 31/12/18 |
| †2/Lt. D. SLOANE. | 27/5/18 | | | 31/12/18 |
| †2/Lt. T. E. McQUISTON. | 27/5/18 | | | 31/12/18 |
| 2/Lt. F. C. S. HARRISON | 27/5/18 | | | 30/12/18 |
| 2/Lt. C. A. MACE. | 27/5/18 | | | 15/12/18 |

\* Attached from Army Cyclist Corps.    † Attached from Royal Irish Rifles.

## DURHAM LIGHT INFANTRY—continued.

### 9th Battalion.

| Name. | Missing. | Interned. | Repatriated. |
|---|---|---|---|
| 2/Lt. E. W. MANNERS. | 5/11/16 | | 21/12/18 |
| 2/Lt. L. A. HOWE. | 5/11/16 | | 18/12/18 |
| 2/Lt. T. E. COULSON. | 5/11/16 | | 18/12/18 |

### 11th Battalion.

| Name. | Missing. | Interned. | Repatriated. |
|---|---|---|---|
| 2/Lt. H. RUTHERFORD. | 22/3/18 | | 1/12/18 |
| 2/Lt. W. T. ALEXANDER. | 22/3/18 | | 18/12/18 |
| *2/Lt. C. A. MORRIS. | 22/3/18 | | 18/12/18 |
| 2/Lt. W. G. CRAIG. | 22/3/18 | (*Died* at Graudenz). | |
| 2/Lt. F. NAYLOR. | 23/3/18 | | 17/12/18 |
| Lieut. R. BUSHELL. | 29/3/18 | | 1/12/18 |
| 2/Lt. D. E. ELLWOOD. | 29/3/18 | | 14/12/18 |
| 2/Lt. T. W. APPLEGARTH. | 29/3/18 | (*Died*). | |

### 13th Battalion.

| Name. | Missing. | Interned. | Repatriated. |
|---|---|---|---|
| 2/Lt. E. A. CROSLAND. | 6/4/16 | Holland 30/4/18 | 18/11/18 |
| 2/Lt. F. AUDAS. | 5/10/18 | | 29/11/18 |

### 14th Battalion.

| Name. | Missing. | Interned. | Repatriated. |
|---|---|---|---|
| 2/Lt. C. E. BROGDEN. | | | 25/12/18 |
| *2/Lt. R. M. MALCOLM. | 3/12/17 | | 3/12/18 |
| 2/Lt. H. FORBES. | 3/12/17 | | 27/11/18 |

### 15th Battalion.

| Name. | Missing. | Interned. | Repatriated. |
|---|---|---|---|
| 2/Lt. A. SHEARER. | 22/12/17 | | 7/11/18 |
| Capt. T. A. L. WELCH. | 24/3/18 | | –/12/18 |
| 2/Lt. V. G. DAVIES. | 27/5/18 | | 30/12/18 |
| 2/Lt. F. BURGESS. | 27/5/18 | | 13/12/18 |
| †2/Lt. E. JOICEY. | 27/5/18 | | 5/1/19 |
| †2/Lt. A. E. FOSTER. | 28/5/18 | | –/12/18 |
| Capt. J. B. CUNNINGHAM. | 24/8/18 | | 29/11/18 |

### 20th Battalion.

| Name. | Missing. | Interned. | Repatriated. |
|---|---|---|---|
| 2/Lt. G. OLIVER. | | | 3/12/18 |

### 22nd Battalion.

| Name. | Missing. | Interned. | Repatriated. |
|---|---|---|---|
| Lieut. H. E. RAINE. | | | 18/12/18 |
| 2/Lt. J. AITCHISON. | 22/3/18 | | 18/12/18 |
| Lieut. J. H. PATTISON. | 24/3/18 | | –/12/18 |
| 2/Lt. C. B. PICKARD. | 25/3/18 | | –/1/19 |
| 2/Lt. W. H. O'DELL. | 25/3/18 | | 18/12/18 |
| 2/Lt. J. W. JAMIESON. | 25/3/18 | | 18/12/18 |
| 2/Lt. R. WHITE. | 27/3/18 | | 18/12/18 |
| Capt. J. ATKINSON. | 27/5/18 | | 19/1/19 |
| 2/Lt. W. H. DAVIES. | 27/5/18 | | 25/12/18 |
| 2/Lt. C. H. LISTER. | 27/5/18 | | –/12/18 |

### 29th Battalion.

| Name. | Missing. | Interned. | Repatriated. |
|---|---|---|---|
| 2/Lt. H. M. RIDLEY. | 19/4/18 | (*Died* 23/5/18 at Iseghem). | |

\* Attached from Border Regiment.
† Attached from Northumberland Fusiliers.

## HIGHLAND LIGHT INFANTRY.

### 1st and 2nd Battalions.

| Name. | Missing. | | Interned. | Repatriated. |
|---|---|---|---|---|
| Lieut. D. D. BARRY. | 21/12/14 | Holland | 1/3/18 | 18/11/18 |
| 2/Lt. T. A. GRAY. | 27/1/15 | Holland | 1/3/18 | 14/12/18 |
| Lieut. W. ROLLO. | 26/9/15 | Holland | 6/2/18 | 28/11/18 |
| 2/Lt. J. F. HOLMS. | 25/2/17 | | | 29/11/18 |
| Capt M. A. KINCAID-SMITH. | 24/3/18 | | | 13/12/18 |
| Capt. W. NEILSON. | 24/3/18 | | | 25/12/18 |
| Lieut. W. J. DONELLY. | 24/3/18 | | | –/12/18 |
| *Capt. J. GILLIES. | | | | 29/11/18 |

### 5th Battalion.

| Name. | Missing. | Repatriated. |
|---|---|---|
| 2/Lt. P. F. LEITH. | –/3/18 | 18/12/18 |
| Capt. R. M. MILLER. | 24/8/18 | 13/12/18 |
| Lieut. J. W. PARR. | 24/8/18 | 13/12/18 |
| 2/Lt. J. McKIE. | 24/8/18 | 13/12/18 |

### 9th Battalion.

| Name. | Missing. | Repatriated. |
|---|---|---|
| 2/Lt. W. M. ANDREW. | 20/5/17 | 8/12/18 |
| 2/Lt. A. G. M. WATT. | 12/4/18 | 11/12/18 |
| Lieut. T. H. DICKIE. | 29/9/18 | 28/11/18 |
| 2/Lt. R. MENZIES. | 29/9/18 | 28/11/18 |
| Lieut. J. R. PATERSON. | 26/10/18 | 8/12/18 |

### 10th Battalion.

| Name. | Missing. | Repatriated. |
|---|---|---|
| 2/Lt. M. G. HOOD. | 21/3/18 | 29/11/18 |
| 2/Lt. M. G. CAMPBELL. | 22/3/18 | 18/12/18 |
| Lieut. A. McKAY. | 31/8/18 | 29/11/18 |

### 10/11th Battalions.

| Name. | Missing. | Repatriated. |
|---|---|---|
| 2/Lt. C. D. THOMSON. | 1/8/17 | 14/12/18 |
| 2/Lt. A. W. GILL. | 1/8/17 | 14/12/18 |
| 2/Lt. K. D. McNEILL. | 1/8/17 | 17/12/18 |
| 2/Lt. J. C. WHYTE. | 1/8/17 | 13/12/18 |
| Capt. H. T. KINLOCH. | 22/3/18 | 1/12/18 |
| Lieut. J. B. BLACK. | 22/3/18 | 3/12/18 |
| 2/Lt. W. D. WHITE. | 22/3/18 | 6/12/18 |
| 2/Lt. L. A. SHUTTE. | 22/3/18 | 21/12/18 |
| †2/Lt. R. F. FRANCIS. | 22/3/18 | 21/12/18 |
| 2/Lt. I. D. MacNEILL. | 25/3/18 | 14/1/19 |
| Capt. T. CHRISTIE. | 9/4/18 | 3/12/18 |
| Lieut. R. A. CUTHBERTSON. | 9/4/18 | 29/11/19 |
| Lieut. A. A. BOWMAN. | 9/4/18 | 29/11/18 |
| Lieut. D. STALKER. | 9/4/18 | 8/12/18 |
| 2/Lt. P. HUGHES. | 9/4/18 | 3/12/18 |
| ‡2/Lt. J. ELLIS. | 9/4/18 | 29/11/18 |

### 12th Battalion.

| Name. | Missing. | Repatriated. |
|---|---|---|
| Lieut. J. HUNTER. | 25/3/18 | 10/12/18 |

\* Attached T.M.B.
† Attached from Suffolks.     ‡ Attached from Lovat's Scouts.

## HIGHLAND LIGHT INFANTRY—continued.

### 14th Battalion.

| Name. | Missing. | Interned. | Repatriated. |
|---|---|---|---|
| 2/Lt. J. BEVERIDGE. | 24/11/17 | | 3/12/18 |
| Capt. G. C. SMITH. | 26/11/17 | | 22/12/18 |
| Lieut. R. HADDOCK. | 26/11/17 | | 3/6/18 |
| 2/Lt. W. B. McGEORGE. | 26/11/17 | | 2/1/19 |
| 2/Lt. A. R. SCLANDERS. | 26/11/17 | | 3/12/18 |
| 2/Lt. A. WATT. | 26/11/17 | | 3/12/18 |
| 2/Lt. H. W. M. THOMAS. | 26/11/17 | | 3/12/18 |
| 2/Lt. G. E. B. McINDOE. | 26/11/17 | | 31/10/18 |
| 2/Lt. F. G. McLEOD. | 26/11/17 | | 3/12/18 |
| 2/Lt. S. SOUDEN. | 26/11/17 | | 3/12/18 |
| Capt. J. G. B. WALKER. | 25/3/18 | | 10/12/18 |
| 2/Lt. KENNETH REID. | 3/4/18 | | 4/12/18 |
| Capt. R. D. BLACKLEDGE. | 9/4/18 | | 8/12/18 |
| Capt. H. N. S. MUMMERY. | 9/4/18 | (*Died* 6/8/18 at Pforzheim). | |
| Capt. H. Y. G. HENDERSON. | 9/4/18 | | 10/12/18 |
| Lieut. G. W. WOTHERSPOON. | 9/4/18 | | 29/11/18 |
| Lieut. G. L. DICKSON. | 9/4/18 | | 18/12/18 |
| Lieut. A. C. CURLE. | 9/4/18 | | 8/12/18 |
| 2/Lt. J. S. ROBERTSON. | 9/4/18 | | 3/12/18 |
| 2/Lt. J. C. PICKEN. | 9/4/18 | | 3/12/18 |
| 2/Lt. C. C. JENNINGS. | 9/4/18 | | 10/12/18 |
| 2/Lt. J. D. EDWARD. | 9/4/18 | (*Died* 26/4/18). | |

### 15th Battalion.

| Name. | Missing. | Interned. | Repatriated. |
|---|---|---|---|
| Capt. W. T. MITCHELL. | 3/7/16 | Holland 16/5/18 | 22/11/18 |
| 2/Lt. H. A. ADAMSON. | 4/3/17 | | |

### 16th Battalion.

| Name. | Missing. | Interned. | Repatriated. |
|---|---|---|---|
| Lieut. A. SKENE. | 18/11/16 | | 4/12/18 |
| 2/Lt. J. STEWART. | 18/11/16 | | 17/12/18 |
| 2/Lt. F. SCOTT. | 18/11/16 | | 17/12/18 |
| 2/Lt. M. M. LYON. | | | 29/11/18 |

## SEAFORTH HIGHLANDERS.

### 2nd Battalion.

| Name. | Missing. | Interned. | Repatriated. |
|---|---|---|---|
| 2/Lt. J. TOOTHILL. | 23/10/18 | | 27/11/18 |

### 4th Battalion.

| Name. | Missing. | Interned. | Repatriated. |
|---|---|---|---|
| Capt. T. H. PEVERELL. | 21/11/17 | | 19/5/18 |
| 2/Lt. G. M. COOPER. | 22/3/18 | | 18/12/18 |
| Capt. F. W. BROWN. | 23/3/18 | | 1/12/18 |
| Capt. P. C. KNIGHT. | 23/3/18 | | 10/12/18 |
| Lieut. A. MACRAE. | 23/3/18 | | 25/12/18 |
| 2/Lt. J. DAVIDSON. | 23/3/18 | | 9/1/19 |
| 2/Lt. W. WEIR. | 11/4/18 | | 11/12/18 |
| *Major M. JOBSON. | 12/4/18 | (*Died* at Tourcoing 3/5/18). | |
| Lieut. J. A. HERMON. | 28/10/18 | | 30/12/18 |
| 2/Lt. C. T. BOYD. | 28/10/18 | | 27/11/18 |

\* Attached from King's Own Scottish Borderers.

## SEAFORTH HIGHLANDERS—continued.
### 5th Battalion.

| Name. | Missing. | Interned. | Repatriated. |
|---|---|---|---|
| Capt. J. R. BLACK. | 21/3/18 | | 28/11/18 |
| Capt. R. F. SINCLAIR. | 21/3/18 | | -/1/19 |
| Lieut. L. A. MEREDITH. | 21/3/18 | | 13/12/18 |
| 2/Lt. A. MOWAT. | 23/3/18 | | 11/12/18 |
| 2/Lt. W. NOBLE. | 10/4/18 | | 18/12/18 |
| 2/Lt. I. G. MACDONALD. | 11/4/18 | | -/12/18 |
| Lieut. J. B. SIMPSON. | 12/4/18 | | 2/12/18 |

### 2/5th Battalions.

| Name. | Missing. | Interned. | Repatriated. |
|---|---|---|---|
| Lieut. G. CUMMING. | 12/4/18 | | 29/11/18 |

### 6th Battalion.

| Name. | Missing. | Interned. | Repatriated. |
|---|---|---|---|
| 2/Lt. J. W. BLAIR. | 12/12/16 | | 17/12/18 |
| Capt. W. LEGGE. | 23–25/4/17 | | 31/12/18 |
| Capt. W. R. PETRIE. | 23–25/4/17 | | 14/12/18 |
| Lieut. D. M. FORSYTH. | 23–25/4/17 | | 31/12/18 |
| 2/Lt. P. MOTTRAM. | 15/5/17 | | 6/12/18 |
| Major W. H. DOIG. | 25/3/18 | | 18/12/18 |
| Capt. L. FRASER. | 25/3/18 | | -/12/18 |
| Capt. W. STEWART. | 25/3/18 | (*Died* at Beaulencourt) | |
| 2/Lt. A. A. GUNN. | 25/3/18 | | 29/12/18 |
| Lieut. S. C. M. DOUGLAS. | 11/4/18 | | -/12/18 |
| Lieut. H. OLIVER. | 11/4/18 | | 11/12/18 |
| 2/Lt. R. F. CUMMING. | 11/4/18 | | 25/12/18 |
| 2/Lt. R. A. L. FRASER-MACKENZIE. | 11/4/18 | | 13/12/18 |
| 2/Lt. A. F. HEDLEY. | 11/4/18 | | 2/12/18 |
| Lieut. W. M. ASHER. | 12/4/18 | | 12/12/18 |
| 2/Lt. J. MACDONALD. | 12/4/18 | | 18/12/18 |
| 2/Lt. C. W. STEWART. | 12/4/18 | | 18/12/18 |

### 7th Battalion.

| Name. | Missing. | Interned. | Repatriated. |
|---|---|---|---|
| Lieut. R. A. BEGG. | 21/3/18 | | 10/12/18 |
| Lieut. J. W. M. MACKAY. | 23/3/18 | | 18/12/18 |
| 2/Lt. M. MOWAT. | 24/3/18 | | 18/12/18 |

### 8th Battalion.

| Name. | Missing. | Interned. | Repatriated. |
|---|---|---|---|
| 2/Lt. A. McKENZIE. | 8/7/17 | | 27/11/18 |
| Lieut. R. F. W. PATRICK. | 28/7/18 | | 13/12/18 |

### 9th Battalion.

| Name. | Missing. | Interned. | Repatriated. |
|---|---|---|---|
| Lieut. J. H. ANDERSON. | 24/3/18 | | -/12/18 |

## GORDON HIGHLANDERS.
### 1st and 2nd Battalions.

| Name. | Missing. | Interned. | | Repatriated. |
|---|---|---|---|---|
| Colonel F. H. NEISH. | 10/9/14 | Switzerland | 12/8/16 | 11/9/17 |
| Colonel W. E. GORDON. | 10/9/14 | | Exchanged | 25/1/16 |
| Major C. J. SIMPSON. | 10/9/14 | Switzerland | 19/1/17 | 13/9/17 |
| Capt. W. NEISH. | 10/9/14 | Holland | 6/2/18 | 22/11/18 |
| Capt. Hon. A. A. FRASER. | 10/9/14 | Holland | 22/1/18 | 22/11/18 |
| Capt. H. L. PELHAM BURN. | 10/9/14 | Holland | 22/1/18 | -/12/18 |

## GORDON HIGHLANDERS—continued.
### 1st and 2nd Battalions.—continued.

| Name. | Missing. | Interned. | | Repatriated. |
|---|---|---|---|---|
| Capt. I. PICTON-WARLOW. | 10/9/14 | Holland | 22/1/18 | 22/11/18 |
| Capt. F. BELL. | 10/9/14 | Switzerland | –/12/17 | 23/12/18 |
| Lieut. A. D. L. STEWART. | 10/9/14 | Holland | 22/1/18 | 23/10/18 |
| Lieut. D. W. HUNTER-BLAIR. | 10/9/14 | Holland | 6/2/18 | 23/11/18 |
| Lieut. J. F. H. HOULDSWORTH. | 10/9/14 | Holland | 6/2/18 | 23/10/18 |
| Lieut. I. B. M. HAMILTON. | 10/9/14 | Holland | 6/2/18 | 16/11/18 |
| 2/Lt. R. D. GILLESPIE. | 10/9/14 | Holland | 1/3/18 | 9/1/19 |
| 2/Lt. A. W. M. ROBERTSON. | | Holland | 6/2/18 | 22/11/18 |
| Lieut. C. M. USHER. | 16/9/14 | Holland | 22/1/18 | 18/11/18 |
| Capt. M. H. O. FORBES. | 24/10/14 | Holland | 24/2/18 | 18/11/18 |
| Capt. G. H. G. FOWKE. | 24/10/14 | Holland | 24/2/18 | 18/11/18 |
| Lieut. H. S. KEVILLE-DAVIES. | 24/10/14 | Holland | 24/2/18 | 23/9/18 |
| Lieut. A. E. S. MILLER-STERLING. | 24/10/14 | Holland | 24/2/18 | 18/11/18 |
| Lieut. J. F. J. WATSON. | 24/10/14 | Holland | 24/2/18 | 18/11/18 |
| 2/Lt. G. W. NELSON. | 18/7/16 | Switzerland | 13/12/16 | 13/9/17 |
| Capt. I. CUMMING. | 21/3/18 | | | 18/12/18 |
| 2/Lt. A. THOMPSON. | 28/3/18 | | | 30/12/18 |
| 2/Lt. G. N. McLEAN. | 31/10/14 | | | 14/1/19 |

### 4th Battalion.

| Name. | Missing. | Interned. | Repatriated. |
|---|---|---|---|
| 2/Lt. W. ADDISON. | 26/9/15 | Holland | 18/11/18 |
| 2/Lt. J. CAMPBELL. | 21/3/18 | | 19/12/18 |
| 2/Lt. W. A. N. ROSS. | 22/3/18 | | 1/12/18 |
| 2/Lt. J. T. STEPHEN. | 22/3/18 | | 11/12/18 |
| 2/Lt. W. PRING. | 22/3/18 | | 11/12/18 |
| 2/Lt. A. MILNE. | 22/3/18 | | 28/11/18 |
| Lieut. G. L. ALLARDYCE. | 20/10/18 | | 1/12/18 |
| Lieut. R. T. L. MITCHELL. | 27/10/18 | (*Died* 30/11/18 at Louvain). | |
| 2/Lt. A. CLARK. | 27/10/18 | | 3/12/18 |

### 5th Battalion.

| Name. | Missing. | Interned. | Repatriated. |
|---|---|---|---|
| *Lt. Col. M. F. McTAGGART. | 20–21/3/18 | | –/12/18 |
| Major C. T. A. ROBERTSON. | 21/3/18 | (*Died* 23/3/18). | |
| Capt. A. KELLY. | 21/3/18 | | 29/11/18 |
| 2/Lt. W. ENDSON. | 21/3/18 | | 29/11/18 |
| 2/Lt. A. CRUDEN. | 21/3/18 | | 13/12/18 |
| 2/Lt. J. J. CHALMERS. | 21/3/18 | | 20/11/18 |
| 2/Lt. W. GORDON. | 21/3/18 | | 18/12/18 |
| †2/Lt. A. G. McPHAIL. | 21/3/18 | | –/12/18 |
| 2/Lt. A. R. MURRAY. | 21/3/18 | | 2/12/18 |
| 2/Lt. J. MORT. | 21/3/18 | | 19/12/18 |
| 2/Lt. C. W. HODGINS. | 21/3/18 | | 18/12/18 |
| 2/Lt. G. HENDERSON. | 21/3/18 | | 13/12/18 |

### 6th Battalion.

| Name. | Missing. | Interned. | | Repatriated. |
|---|---|---|---|---|
| Lieut. J. B. TURNBULL. | 26/9/15 | Holland | –/4/18 | 22/11/18 |
| Lieut. A. G. McLEAN. | | | | 2/12/18 |
| 2/Lt. T. B. TURNER. | 21/3/18 | | | 2/12/18 |
| 2/Lt. B. CARRE. | 21/3/18 | | | 5/1/19 |
| Major C. E. CORNWALL. | 25/3/18 | | | 21/12/18 |
| 2/Lt. G. RUTHERFORD. | 25/3/18 | | | 11/12/18 |
| Capt. J. R. CHRISTIE. | 10/4/18 | | | 17/12/18 |
| Lieut. P. W. LYON. | 10/4/18 | | | 3/12/18 |
| 2/Lt. A. D. MILLER. | 10/4/18 | | | 5/12/18 |

\* Attached from 5th Lancers.  † Attached from Black Watch.

## GORDON HIGHLANDERS—continued.

### 7th Battalion.

| Name. | Missing. | Interned. | Repatriated. |
|---|---|---|---|
| *Lieut. W. H. BURGESS. | 21/3/18 | | 13/12/18 |
| *Lieut. W. N. BUYERS. | 21/3/18 | | 12/12/18 |
| *2/Lt. N. K. ROBSON. | 21/3/18 | | –/12/18 |
| Capt. B. M. HENDERSON. | 22/3/18 | | |
| Lieut. G. H. E. HAZLEWOOD. | 22/3/18 | | 10/12/18 |
| 2/Lt. J. C. E. MURRAY. | 22/3/18 | | 11/12/18 |
| 2/Lt. G. J. ROBERTSON. | 22/3/18 | | 11/12/18 |
| 2/Lt. H. G. FRYER. | 22/3/18 | | 2/12/18 |
| 2/Lt. R. I. MAPLETON. | 22/3/18 | | 11/12/18 |
| Lieut. J. J. FERGUSON. | 25/3/18 | | 18/12/18 |
| †2/Lt. B. A. MORRIS. | 25/3/18 | | 18/12/18 |
| 2/Lt. D. W. MILNE. | 25/3/18 | | 18/12/18 |
| 2/Lt. A. S. CLARK. | 25/3/18 | | 18/12/18 |
| 2/Lt. W. J. M. BROWN. | 25/5/18 | | –/1/19 |

### 8th Battalion.

| | | | |
|---|---|---|---|
| Lieut. W. C. L. SMITH. | 9/11/15 | (*Died* 10/11/15). | |

### 10th Battalion.

| | | | |
|---|---|---|---|
| †Lieut. R. S. KNOX. | 28/3/18 | | 10/12/18 |
| 2/Lt. A. CANTLAY. | 24/5/18 | | –/12/18 |

## CAMERON HIGHLANDERS.

### 1st and 2nd Battalions.

| | | | |
|---|---|---|---|
| Major G. SOREL-CAMERON. | Holland | 24/2/18 | 23/10/18 |
| Capt. Lord J. T. STEWART-MURRAY. | | Holland  1/3/18 | 21/1/19 |
| Lieut. J. R. CUMMING. | | Holland  24/2/18 | 3/1/19 |
| Major D. A. NICHOLSON. | | (*Died* 25/9/15 at Crefeld). | |
| Capt. L. NAPIER. | 22/7/16 | (*Died*). | |

### 4th Battalion.

| | | | |
|---|---|---|---|
| *Lieut. W. FALCONER. | 28/3/18 | | 18/12/18 |

### 5th Battalion.

| | | | |
|---|---|---|---|
| Lieut. D. H. SOUTAR. | 22/3/18 | | 10/12/18 |
| Capt. W. H. RIACH. | 23/3/18 | (*Died* 5/5/18). | |
| Lieut. W. ELLIOT. | 25/4/18 | | 13/12/18 |
| Lieut. H. H. T. DAVIES. | 25/4/18 | | 14/12/18 |
| Lieut. J. McINNES. | 29/4/18 | | 4/12/18 |

### 6th Battalion.

| | | | |
|---|---|---|---|
| Capt. H. S. WALKER. | 27/2/16 | Holland  16/5/18 | |
| 2/Lt. G. HAMILTON. | 31/7/17 | | 13/5/18 |
| 2/Lt. F. S. SANDEMAN. | 1/8/17 | | 1/12/18 |
| 2/Lt. A. G. McGRUER. | 1/8/17 | | 17/12/18 |
| 2/Lt. J. R. MacKAY. | 1/8/17 | | 1/12/18 |
| 2/Lt. J. G. GIBSON. | 1/8/17 | (*Died* 12/9/17 at Langensalza). | |
| ‡2/Lt. T. P. PHILLIPS. | 26/3/18 | | 8/12/18 |
| Lieut. A. D. MILLIGAN. | 28/3/18 | | –/12/18 |
| 2/Lt. J. W. DOGHERTY. | 28/3/18 | | 2/12/18 |
| ‡2/Lt. G. R. JOHNSTONE. | 28/3/18 | | 13/12/18 |

\* Attached T.M.B.  
† Attached from Royal Scots.  
‡ Attached from 14th Londons (London Scottish).

## CAMERON HIGHLANDERS—continued.
### 7th Battalion.

| Name. | Missing. | Interned. | | Repatriated. |
|---|---|---|---|---|
| Capt. E. K. CAMERON. | 26/9/15 | Holland | 7/10/18 | 8/12/18 |
| 2/Lt. D. TAYLOR. | 18/7/16 | Holland | −/6/18 | 22/11/18 |
| 2/Lt. A. C. McCUISH. | 23/12/16 | | | 17/12/18 |
| 2/Lt. Lacplan McLEOD. | 23/3/18 | | | 1/12/18 |
| *2/Lt. H. R. RENNIE. | 28/3/18 | (*Died* 10/7/18 at Posen). | | |
| *2/Lt. P. DRUMMOND. | 28/3/18 | | | −/1/19 |
| 2/Lt. J. S. McNAB. | 28/3/18 | | | 1/12/18 |
| 2/Lt. J. A. DONALD. | 28/3/18 | | | 25/12/18 |
| 2/Lt. T. S. DENHOLM. | 28/3/18 | (*Died* 5/4/18 at Douai). | | |
| 2/Lt. W. F. GRIEVE. | 28/3/18 | | | 1/12/18 |

### 11th Battalion.

| | | | | |
|---|---|---|---|---|
| 2/Lt. I. CAMPBELL. | 17/9/18 | | | 8/12/18 |

## ROYAL IRISH RIFLES.
### 1st and 2nd Battalions.

| Name. | Missing. | Interned. | | Repatriated. |
|---|---|---|---|---|
| Lieut. Qmr. W. CLARKE. | 10/9/14 | Holland | 5/1/18 | 28/10/18 |
| Capt. A. T. JONSSON. | 27/10/14 | Holland | 6/2/18 | 18/11/18 |
| Lieut. F. L. FINLAY. | 27/10/14 | Holland | 24/2/18 | 19/12/18 |
| Major H. R. CHARLEY. | 21/3/15 | | | 11/9/17 |
| 2/Lt. A. DAVISON. | 23/10/17 | | | 3/12/18 |
| Lieut. S. H. WALKER. | 21/3/18 | | | 6/12/18 |
| Capt. J. C. BRYANS. | 24/3/18 | | | 29/11/18 |
| Lieut. J. K. BOYLE. | 24/3/18 | (*Died* −/−/18 at Cologne). | | |
| 2/Lt. E. C. STROHM. | 24/3/18 | | | 11/12/18 |
| 2/Lt. A. W. WALKER. | 2/10/18 | | | 8/12/18 |
| 2/Lt. A. A. L. MacMANUS. | 2/10/18 | | | 13/12/18 |
| 2/Lt. J. T. GARDINER. | 21/10/18 | | | |

### 6th Battalion.

| | | | | |
|---|---|---|---|---|
| 2/Lt. L. J. ROSS. | 27/5/18 | | | 31/12/18 |

### 8th Battalion.

| | | | | |
|---|---|---|---|---|
| Lieut. S. HUNTER. | 29/11/15 | Holland | 19/4/18 | 18/11/18 |
| 2/Lt. S. W. MAXWELL. | 1/7/16 | (*Died*). | | |

### 9th Battalion.

| | | | | |
|---|---|---|---|---|
| Capt. J. H. BERRY. | 1/7/16 | | | 11/9/17 |
| Lieut. L. N. RICHARDSON. | 1/7/16 | Switzerland | 9/12/17 | 9/12/18 |
| 2/Lt. K. W. GOULD. | 1/7/16 | Switzerland | 27/12/17 | 14/6/18 |
| Lieut. R. H. MORTON. | 2/7/16 | Holland | 16/5/18 | 22/11/18 |
| 2/Lt. A. W. HENRY. | 27/3/18 | | | 25/12/18 |

### 10th Battalion.

| | | | | |
|---|---|---|---|---|
| 2/Lt. F. A. J. DAVIDSON. | 9/10/16 | | | 7/1/18 |
| Lieut.-Qmr. C. H. T. DAWSON. | 24/3/18 | (*Died*). | | |

### 11th Battalion.

| | | | | |
|---|---|---|---|---|
| Major Adam JENKINS. | 1/7/16 | | | 11/9/17 |
| Capt. C. C. CRAIG. | 1/7/16 | Holland | 15/6/18 | 4/10/18 |
| Lieut. E. VANCE. | 1/7/16 | (*Died* 15/7/16). | | |
| 2/Lt. J. W. SALTER. | 1/7/16 | Holland | 16/5/18 | 22/11/18 |

* Attached from 14th London (London Scottish).

## ROYAL IRISH RIFLES—continued.

### 11/13th Battalions.

| Name. | Missing. | Interned. | Repatriated. |
|---|---|---|---|
| 2/Lt. W. T. W. ELLIOT. | 28/3/18 | | 19/12/18 |
| 2/Lt. J. S. ADAIR. | 28/3/18 | | 25/12/18 |

### 12th Battalion.

| Name. | Missing. | Interned. | Repatriated. |
|---|---|---|---|
| 2/Lt. W. A. HAYDEN. | 16/8/17 | | 17/12/18 |
| Major A. H. HALL. | 21/3/18 | | 28/11/18 |
| Capt. L. J. JOHNSTON. | 21/3/18 | | 8/12/18 |
| Capt. H. ST. J. MORRISON. | 21/3/18 | | 18/12/18 |
| Capt. T. S. ADAMSON. | 21/3/18 | | –/11/18 |
| Lieut. T. A. BLACKWOOD. | 21/3/18 | | 29/11/18 |
| Lieut. T. H. WILSON. | 21/3/18 | | 10/12/18 |
| 2/Lt. A. SMITH. | 21/3/18 | | 11/12/18 |
| 2/Lt. H. D. SWAYNE. | 21/3/18 | | 28/11/18 |
| 2/Lt. J. BURNSIDE. | 21/3/18 | | 25/12/18 |
| 2/Lt. R. J. RAGGETT. | 21/3/18 | | 25/12/18 |
| 2/Lt. A. T. BELL. | 21/3/18 | | 28/11/18 |
| 2/Lt. J. ROBINSON. | 21/3/18 | | 11/12/18 |
| 2/Lt. H. F. WALDEN. | 21/3/18 | | 11/12/18 |
| 2/Lt. A. H. OSBOROUGH. | 21/3/18 | | 11/12/18 |
| *2/Lt. W. F. IRVINE. | 21/3/18 | | 11/12/18 |
| 2/Lt. J. A. C. KENNEDY. | 21/3/18 | | 6/12/18 |
| †2/Lt. E. W. JOHNSTON. | 21/3/18 | | 25/12/18 |
| 2/Lt. T. SHEARER. | 21/3/18 | | 11/12/18 |
| 2/Lt. J. G. MALONE. | 21/3/18 | | 8/12/18 |
| 2/Lt. J. MORTON. | 21/3/18 | | 29/11/18 |
| 2/Lt. H. L. WEIR. | 21/3/18 | (*Died* / /18 at Cologne). | |
| 2/Lt. R. MONTEITH. | 22/3/18 | | 28/11/18 |
| 2/Lt. H. L. KEMPSON. | 23/3/18 | | 17/12/18 |
| 2/Lt. W. FERGUSON. | 23/3/18 | | 29/11/18 |
| 2/Lt. H. YOUNG. | 15/4/18 | | 5/12/18 |

### 13th Battalion.

| Name. | Missing. | Interned. | Repatriated. |
|---|---|---|---|
| 2/Lt. R. C. KINNIBURGH. | 1/7/16 | Holland 16/5/18 | 1/2/19 |
| 2/Lt. D. J. McGILTON. | 21/3/18 | | 6/12/18 |
| Capt. R. M. PRYDE. | 24/3/18 | | 6/12/18 |

### 14th Battalion.

| Name. | Missing. | Interned. | Repatriated. |
|---|---|---|---|
| 2/Lt. R. V. GRACEY. | 1/7/16 | | 13/9/17 |
| Lieut. A. J. E. GIBSON. | 23/3/18 | | 13/12/18 |
| Lieut. D. B. TAYLOR. | 24/3/18 | | 18/12/18 |

### 15th Battalion.

| Name. | Missing. | Interned. | Repatriated. |
|---|---|---|---|
| 2/Lt. J. BARRY BROWN. | 5/7/16 | Switzerland 19/12/16 | 23/12/18 |
| 2/Lt. H. G. BUCHANAN. | 22/11/17 | | 3/12/18 |
| Colonel C. G. COLE-HAMILTON. | 21/3/18 | | 14/12/18 |
| Capt. J. H. STEWART. | 21/3/18 | | 6/12/18 |
| Capt. J. E. S. CONDON. | 21/3/18 | | 6/12/18 |
| Lieut. W. WILSON. | 21/3/18 | | 6/12/18 |
| Lieut. S. A. LYNCH. | 21/3/18 | | 6/12/18 |
| Lieut. W. CLARKE. | 21/3/18 | | 25/12/18 |
| 2/Lt. S. C. HUGHES. | 21/3/18 | | 6/12/18 |
| 2/Lt. P. HILDER. | 21/3/18 | | 4/12/18 |
| 2/Lt. L. K. REID. | 21/3/18 | | 6/12/18 |

\* Attached from Royal Irish Fusiliers.   † Attached T.M.B.

## ROYAL IRISH RIFLES—continued.
### 15th Battalion—continued.

| Name. | Missing. | Interned. | Repatriated. |
|---|---|---|---|
| 2/Lt. H. G. CARDOZO. | 21/3/18 | | 6/12/18 |
| 2/Lt. J. ARMSTRONG. | 21/3/18 | | 14/12/18 |
| 2/Lt. A. SCOTT. | 21/3/18 | | 6/12/18 |
| 2/Lt. C. P. SEATH. | 21/3/18 | | 11/12/18 |
| 2/Lt. R. SPROTT. | 21/3/18 | | 6/12/18 |
| 2/Lt. J. K. WYLIE. | 21/3/18 | | 14/12/18 |
| 2/Lt. C. HIND. | 23–25/3/18 | | –/12/18 |
| 2/Lt. A. E. TODD. | 31/3/18 | | 6/12/18 |

### 16th Battalion.

| Name. | Missing. | Interned. | Repatriated. |
|---|---|---|---|
| 2/Lt. J. W. FURBISHER. | 21/3/18 | | 28/11/18 |
| 2/Lt. J. H. K. FREELAND. | 21/3/18 | | 28/11/18 |
| 2/Lt. E. CROKER. | 21/3/18 | | 28/11/18 |
| 2/Lt. G. A. DAY. | 21/3/18 | | 10/12/18 |
| 2/Lt. W. O. REA. | 21/3/18 | | 17/12/18 |
| 2/Lt. W. H. K. GIBSON. | 21/3/18 | | 28/11/18 |
| 2/Lt. N. F. IRWIN. | 21/3/18 | | 14/12/18 |
| 2/Lt. C. HALLINAN. | 21/3/18 | | 14/12/18 |

### 17th Battalion.

| Name. | Missing. | Interned. | Repatriated. |
|---|---|---|---|
| 2/Lt. W. C. HATHERALL. | 27/5/18 | | 31/12/18 |

## ROYAL IRISH FUSILIERS.
### 1st Battalion.

| Name. | Missing. | Interned. | Repatriated. |
|---|---|---|---|
| Major R. A. GRAY. | 17/9/14 | Holland  6/2/18 | 18/11/18 |
| Lieut. H. A. H. WARNOCK. | 13/8/15 | (*Died* 16/8/15 at Bapaume). | |
| Lieut. A. V. OLPHERT. | | Holland  24/2/18 | 21/1/19 |
| Lieut. J. POLLACK. | 11/4/17 | | 8/1/18 |
| 2/Lt. E. E. HARRIS. | 11/4/17 | (*Died* 21/4/17 at Julich). | |
| 2/Lt. C. M. HARRIS. | 3/5/17 | | 6/12/18 |
| Capt. W. W. NEVILLE. | 21/3/18 | | 25/12/18 |
| Capt. G. A. DEANE. | 21/3/18 | (*Died* 11/4/18). | |
| Lieut. W. D. BRADLEY. | 21/3/18 | | 1/12/18 |
| 2/Lt. G. H. LEMON. | 21/3/18 | | 25/12/18 |
| 2/Lt. T. F. HALL. | 21/3/18 | | 28/11/18 |
| Colonel M. FURNELL. | 26/3/18 | | 2/12/18 |
| Major S. U. L. CLEMENTS. | 27/3/18 | | 29/11/18 |
| Capt. B. ST. J. GALVIN. | 27/3/18 | | 25/12/18 |
| Lieut. B. J. EYRE. | 27/3/18 | | 25/12/18 |
| Lieut. T. HOUSTON. | 27/3/18 | | 18/12/18 |
| Lieut. H. GRAY. | 27/3/18 | | –/12/18 |
| 2/Lt. T. S. HASWELL. | 27/3/18 | | 25/12/18 |
| 2/Lt. C. N. McKENNY. | 27/3/18 | | 25/12/18 |
| 2/Lt. R. M. MOORE. | 27/3/18 | | –/12/18 |
| 2/Lt. R. E. GLOVER. | 28/3/18 | | 25/12/18 |
| 2/Lt. T. R. COGHLAN. | 23/10/18 | | |

### 2nd Battalion.

| Name. | Missing. | Interned. | Repatriated. |
|---|---|---|---|
| 2/Lt. L. J. HARRISON. | 21/3/18 | (*Died* –/4/18 at Germersheim). | |

### 4th Battalion.

| Name. | Missing. | Interned. | Repatriated. |
|---|---|---|---|
| 2/Lt. J. F. CALDWELL. | | | 18/12/18 |
| 2/Lt. O. B. McMANUS. | 24/3/18 | | 18/12/18 |

## ROYAL IRISH FUSILIERS—continued.

| Name. | Missing. | Interned. | Repatriated. |
|---|---|---|---|
| **6th Battalion.** | | | |
| 2/Lt. R. L. V. WINTER. | 21/3/18 | | 25/12/18 |
| Lieut. A. JOULE. | 27/3/18 | | 11/12/18 |
| **7th Battalion.** | | | |
| Lieut. H. H. E. Q. COLES. | 27/3/18 | | 25/12/18 |
| **8th Battalion.** | | | |
| 2/Lt. J. H. DICKSON. | 16/8/17 | | 14/12/18 |
| **9th Battalion.** | | | |
| 2/Lt. D. H. WRIGHT. | 16/8/17 | | 14/12/18 |
| 2/Lt. C. J. T. PERKINS. | 21/3/18 | | 11/12/18 |
| 2/Lt. J. H. CONNOR. | 22/3/18 | | 25/12/18 |
| Capt. T. SLATTER. | 24/3/18 | | 1/12/18 |
| Capt. M. HENEHAN. | 24/3/18 | | 18/12/18 |
| 2/Lt. E. H. GILMER. | 26/3/18 | | 25/12/18 |
| Lieut. G. I. O'F. JOHNSTON. | 27/3/18 | | 10/12/18 |
| Lieut. J. J. McE. POLLOCK. | 27/3/18 | | 4/12/18 |
| 2/Lt. T. BREMNER. | 27/3/18 | | 18/12/18 |
| 2/Lt. N. CLARKE. | 27/3/18 | | 18/12/18 |
| 2/Lt. F. L. H. DONALDSON. | 27/3/18 | | 25/12/18 |
| 2/Lt. R. L. SMITH. | 27/3/18 | | –/12/18 |
| 2/Lt. J. SCOTT. | 27/3/18 | | 25/12/18 |
| 2/Lt. G. HARDY. | 12/4/18 | (*Died* 31/4/18 at Kortryk). | |
| Capt. J. BENSON. | 11/8/18 | | 13/12/18 |
| 2/Lt. R. A. RICHEY. | 30/9/18 | | 13/12/18 |
| **12th Battalion.** | | | |
| 2/Lt. G. FOY. | 23/3/18 | | 17/12/18 |

## CONNAUGHT RANGERS.

### 1st and 2nd Battalions.

| Name. | Missing. | Interned. | Repatriated. |
|---|---|---|---|
| Lieut. C. A. TURNER. | –/8/14 | | 13/9/17 |
| Lt.-Col. A. W. ABERCROMBIE. | 10/9/14 | (*Died* 25/11/15 at Magdeburg). | |
| Capt. W. G. S. BARKER. | 10/9/14 | | Exchanged 29/6/15 (*Died*). 2/6/16 |
| Capt. W. W. ROCHE. | 10/9/14 | Holland 6/2/18 | 10/1/19 |
| Lieut. J. L. HARDY. | 10/9/14 | | 14/3/18 |
| Lieut. W. H. REES. | 20/10/14 | Holland 6/2/18 | 28/11/18 |
| 2/Lt. H. S. KIRKWOOD. | 21/3/18 | | 31/12/18 |
| **5th Battalion.** | | | |
| Lieut. H. J. SHANLEY. | 10/10/18 | | 8/12/18 |
| 2/Lt. H. MATTISON. | 10/10/18 | | 1/1/19 |
| **6th Battalion.** | | | |
| 2/Lt. P. L. N. GORDON-RALPH. | 19/2/17 | | 7/12/18 |
| Capt. B. J. START. | 21/3/18 | | 17/12/18 |
| Capt. R. ROUSSEL. | 21/3/18 | | 29/11/18 |
| Lieut. J. A. V. KENT, M.C. | 21/3/18 | | 13/12/18 |
| Lieut. A. RIBBONS. | 21/3/18 | | 14/12/18 |
| 2/Lt. H. E. HALL. | 21/3/18 | | 13/12/18 |
| 2/Lt. H. E. TAGGERT. | 21/3/18 | | 14/12/18 |

## ARGYLL AND SUTHERLAND HIGHLANDERS.
### 1st and 2nd Battalions.

| Name. | Missing. | Interned. | | Repatriated. |
|---|---|---|---|---|
| Capt. A. J. H. MacLEAN. | 6/9/14 | Holland | 24/1/18 | 1/11/18 |
| Lieut. G. F. CONNAL ROWAN. | 11/9/14 | Holland | 1/5/18 | 22/1/19 |
| Capt. A. STIRLING. | 11/9/14 | Holland | 1/5/18 | 1/2/19 |
| Capt. M. G. SANDEMAN. | 21/10/14 | Holland | 24/2/18 | 18/11/18 |
| Lieut. C. L. CAMPBELL. | 21/10/14 | Holland | 6/2/18 | 7/9/18 |
| Capt. J. D. TYSON. | 11/12/17 | | | 6/12/18 |
| 2/Lt. W. H. DUNCAN. | 24/9/18 | | | 10/12/18 |
| 2/Lt. O. L. DUNLEY. | 12/12/17 | | | 3/12/18 |

### 6th Battalion.

| | | | |
|---|---|---|---|
| Capt. T. GREENLEES. | 18/10/18 | | 27/11/18 |

### 7th Battalion.

| | | | |
|---|---|---|---|
| Capt. E. R. ORR. | 22/11/17 | | 25/12/18 |
| Lieut. James McLAREN. | 21/3/18 | | 18/12/18 |
| Capt. J. CUNNINGHAM. | 23/3/18 | | 3/12/18 |
| 2/Lt. T. GEMMELL. | 23/3/18 | (*Died* 7/5/18 at Valenciennes). | |
| 2/Lt. F. CAMERON. | 23/3/18 | | 25/12/18 |
| Lieut. Wm. SCOTT. | 25/3/18 | | 11/12/18 |
| Lieut. W. S. JOHNSTON. | 21/3/18 | (*Died* 23/3/18 at Inchy). | |
| Major W. McCRACKEN. | 27/5/18 | | 13/12/18 |

### 8th Battalion.

| | | | |
|---|---|---|---|
| 2/Lt. A. D. HUMBLE. | 15/5/17 | | 2/1/19 |
| 2/Lt. T. P. JOHNSTON. | 15/5/17 | | 2/1/19 |
| Lieut. W. McN. SNADDEN. | 15/5/17 | | 14/12/18 |
| 2/Lt. G. C. HALDANE. | 6/9/17 | | 30/12/18 |
| *2/Lt. D. McCHLEARY. | 21/3/18 | | 14/12/18 |
| 2/Lt. A. S. MURRAY. | 22/3/18 | | –/1/19 |
| Capt. James ROSS. | 22/3/18 | | 8/12/18 |
| Lieut. G. C. CAMPBELL. | 1/4/18 | | 18/12/18 |

### 9th Battalion.

| | | | |
|---|---|---|---|
| Lieut. O. A. OWEN. | 21/7/15 | | 22/11/18 |

### 10th Battalion.

| | | | |
|---|---|---|---|
| 2/Lt. James BLAIR. | 30/9/18 | | 8/12/18 |

### 11th Battalion.

| | | | |
|---|---|---|---|
| Lieut. A. H. D. RICHMOND. | 22/8/17 | | 14/12/18 |

### 14th Battalion.

| | | | |
|---|---|---|---|
| Capt. H. Boswell SANDEMAN. | 21/3/18 | | 10/12/18 |
| Capt. A. McMILLAN. | 25/3/18 | | 10/12/18 |

## LEINSTER REGIMENT.
### 1st and 2nd Battalions.

| Name. | Missing. | Interned. | | Repatriated. |
|---|---|---|---|---|
| Lieut. A. W. BARTON. | 21/10/14 | Holland | 6/2/18 | 18/11/18 |
| Lieut. G. S. HAMILTON. | 21/10/14 | Holland | 6/2/18 | 18/11/18 |
| Lieu. R. D. O'CONNOR. | 21/10/14 | Holland | 19/3/18 | 18/11/18 |
| Capt. B. DEANE. | 15/2/15 | Holland | 19/3/18 | 29/11/18 |
| Lieut. H. C. BERNE. | 2/12/16 | | | 17/12/18 |
| 2/Lt. G. C. PARKS. | 22/3/18 | | | 2/12/18 |
| 2/Lt. E. C. SMYTH. | 22/3/18 | | | 3/1/19 |
| 2/Lt. W. M. SURTEES. | 22/3/18 | | | 17/12/18 |
| Lieut. R. G. HOLMES. | 25/3/18 | | | 18/12/18 |
| 2/Lt. E. DANIEL. | 28/3/18 | | | 25/12/18 |

* Attached T.M.B.

## LEINSTER REGIMENT—continued.
### 11th Battalion.

| Name. | Missing. | Interned. | Repatriated. |
|---|---|---|---|
| 2/Lt. C. H. SPENCER. | 21/3/18 | | 18/12/18 |

## ROYAL MUNSTER FUSILIERS.
### 1st Battalion.

| | | | |
|---|---|---|---|
| Capt. C. D. DRAKE. | | Holland 22/1/18 | 18/11/18 |
| Capt. C. R. RAWLINSON. | 29/8/14 | Holland 22/1/18 | 20/7/18 |
| Capt. H. S. JERVIS. | 29/8/14 | Holland 6/2/18 | 31/8/18 |
| Capt. C. R. HALL. | 29/8/14 | Switzerland 27/12/17 | 24/3/18 |
| Lieut. J. F. O'MALLEY. | 29/8/14 | Holland 6/2/18 | 22/11/18 |
| Lieut. H. A. NEWSON. | 16/9/14 | Holland 6/2/18 | 18/11/18 |
| Lieut. R. A. D. MOSELEY. | 16/9/14 | Holland 6/2/18 | 18/11/18 |
| Capt. D. WISE. | 29/9/14 | Holland 6/2/18 | 18/11/18 |
| Lieut. E. W. GOWER. | 29/9/14 | Holland 6/2/18 | |
| Lieut. H. G. WHELAN. | 21/3/18 | (*Died* 11/4/18 at Rastatt). | |
| 2/Lt. T. F. O'DONNELL. | 22/3/18 | | 8/12/18 |
| 2/Lt. O. J. O'HARE. | 22/3/18 | | 2/12/18 |
| 2/Lt. L. W. R. MURPHY. | 22/3/18 | | 28/11/18 |
| 2/Lt. C. BOURCHIER. | 22/3/18 | | 2/12/18 |
| 2/Lt. T. G. CAHILL. | 22/3/18 | | -/12/18 |

### 2nd Battalion.

| | | | |
|---|---|---|---|
| 2/Lt. T. T. PRICE. | 9/5/15 | Holland 10/4/18 | 1/2/19 |
| Capt. A. H. BATTEN-POOLL. | 10/11/17 | Switzerland 27/12/17 | 24/3/18 |
| Capt. J. C. R. DELMEGE. | 10/11/17 | | 3/12/18 |
| Lieut. H. B. FISHER. | 10/11/17 | (*Died* 23/11/17). | |
| 2/Lt. H. J. McELNEA. | 21/3/18 | | 1/12/18 |
| 2/Lt. P. A. DENAHY. | 21/3/18 | | 6/12/18 |
| *2/Lt. L. A. CARTER. | 21/3/18 | | 18/12/18 |
| Lieut. C. E. O'CALLAGHAN. | 27/3/18 | | 18/12/18 |
| *2/Lt. A. H. STRACHAN. | 27/3/18 | | 18/12/18 |
| *2/Lt. J. F. NASH. | 27/3/18 | | 1/12/18 |
| †2/Lt. P. M. J. ARDAGH. | 27/3/18 | | 1/12/18 |
| 2/Lt. J. DOORLEY. | 27/3/18 | | 18/12/18 |
| ‡Major M. M. HARTIGAN. | 31/3/18 | | -/12/18 |

### 3rd Battalion.

| | | | |
|---|---|---|---|
| Capt. R. W. THOMAS. | 16/9/14 | | 13/9/17 |

## ROYAL DUBLIN FUSILIERS.
### 1st Battalion.

| | | | |
|---|---|---|---|
| Major H. M. SHEWIN. | 4/9/14 | | 25/11/18 |
| Lieut. J. E. VERNON. | 4/9/14 | Exchanged | 26/8/15 |
| Lieut. F. DOBBS. | 4/9/14 | | 17/11/18 |
| Lieut. F. E. S. MACKY. | 4/9/14 | Holland 6/2/18 | 8/2/19 |
| Lieut. C. H. L'E. WEST. | 4/9/14 | Holland 6/2/18 | 22/1/19 |
| Major G. S. HIGINSON. | 13/9/14 | Switzerland 9/12/17 | 24/3/18 |
| Capt. R. L. H. CONLAN. | 13/9/14 | Switzerland 9/12/17 | 24/3/18 |
| 2/Lt. A. L. KENT. | 28/2/17 | | 4/12/18 |
| 2/Lt. A. J. McCANN. | 5/10/17 | Switzerland 21/10/18 | 8/12/18 |
| Capt. G. E. COWLEY. | 21/3/18 | (*Died* 18/6/18 at Le Cateau). | |
| Capt. H. M. LETCHWORTH. | 21/3/18 | | 29/11/18 |
| Lieut. G. H. CHANDLER. | 21/3/18 | | -/1/19 |

\* Attached from Royal Dublin Fusiliers.     † Attached from Jersey Militia.
‡ Attached from South African Force.

## ROYAL DUBLIN FUSILIERS—continued.

### 1st Battalion—continued.

| Name. | Missing. | Interned. | Repatriated. |
|---|---|---|---|
| Lieut. R. PEACEY. | 21/3/18 | | —/12/18 |
| 2/Lt. W. N. GOURLAY. | 21/3/18 | | 29/11/18 |
| 2/Lt. P. McCARTHY. | 21/3/18 | | 21/12/18 |
| 2/Lt. R. G. HUNTER. | 21/3/18 | (*Died* 25/4/18 at Stettin). | |
| 2/Lt. G. A. CLARKE. | 21/3/18 | (*Died* 22/3/18 at Cambrai). | |
| 2/Lt. W. R. W. BRISCOE. | 27/3/18 | | 25/12/18 |
| 2/Lt. G. P. G. CRAWFORD. | 27/3/18 | | |
| 2/Lt. F. M. LAIRD. | 27/3/18 | | 25/12/18 |
| 2/Lt. C. K. KIRWAN. | 3/6/18 | | —/1/19 |
| 2/Lt. JAMES OWENS. | 4/9/18 | | 29/11/18 |

### 2nd Battalion.

| Name | Missing | Interned | | Repatriated |
|---|---|---|---|---|
| 2/Lt. W. Y. SHANKS. | 25/5/15 | Holland | 10/4/18 | 26/12/18 |
| Lieut. W. BRADDELL. | 6/7/15 | Holland | 6/2/18 | 23/9/18 |
| *2/Lt. V. M. MacKEAG. | 14/7/15 | Holland | 10/4/18 | 18/11/18 |
| Lieut. J. P. SCOTT. | 27/5/17 | | | 7/1/18 |
| 2/Lt. A. HOLMES. | 27/5/17 | | | 14/12/18 |
| 2/Lt. M. W. O'CONNELL. | 21/3/18 | | | 17/12/18 |
| 2/Lt. W. J. GREENE. | 21/3/18 | | | 8/12/18 |
| 2/Lt. G. PETIT | 21/3/18 | | | |
| 2/Lt. F. E. KENNEDY. | 21/3/18 | | | 3/12/18 |
| 2/Lt. M. AHERN. | 21/3/18 | | | 25/12/18 |
| 2/Lt. F. G. W. WILKIN. | 21/3/18 | | | 2/12/18 |
| 2/Lt. D. F. WARREN. | 21/3/18 | | | 2/12/18 |
| 2/Lt. H. FIELDING. | 21/3/18 | | | 2/12/18 |
| Capt. S. DUFF-TAYLOR. | 27/3/18 | | | 25/12/18 |
| Capt. A. S. TRIGONNA. | 11/4/18 | | | 10/12/18 |

### 9th Battalion.

| Name | Missing | Repatriated |
|---|---|---|
| 2/Lt. N. V. FORREST. | 27/4/17 | 1/1/19 |

### 10th Battalion.

| Name | Missing | Interned | | Repatriated |
|---|---|---|---|---|
| Lieut. W. J. MOUNT. | 14/10/16 | Holland | 7/9/18 | 18/12/18 |
| 2/Lt. C. ADAMS. | 1/2/17 | | | 14/12/18 |
| Capt. R. BOYD. | 27/3/18 | | | 8/12/18 |

### 11th Battalion.

| Name | Missing | Repatriated |
|---|---|---|
| 2/Lt. A. F. McCANN. | 21/3/18 | 2/12/18 |

## RIFLE BRIGADE.

### 1st and 2nd Battalions.

| Name | Missing | Interned | | Repatriated |
|---|---|---|---|---|
| Capt. G. E. W. LANE. | 26/8/14 | Switzerland | 27/12/17 | 9/12/18 |
| Lieut. E. W. S. FOLJAMBE. | 13/9/14 | | | 13/9/17 |
| Capt. W. W. YOUNG. | 24/8/16 | Holland | 12/10/18 | 21/1/19 |
| 2/Lt. B. W. DENNIS. | 20/1/17 | | | 2/1/19 |
| 2/Lt. H. BARKER. | 16/8/17 | | | 17/12/18 |
| 2/Lt. T. C. LEWIS. | 24/3/18 | | | 13/12/18 |
| Capt. R. C. S. STEVENSON. | 24/4/18 | | | 3/12/18 |
| 2/Lt. R. K. GARNER. | 24/4/18 | | | 29/11/18 |
| 2/Lt. D'A. F. THUILLIER. | 24/4/18 | | | 3/12/18 |

* Attached from Leinsters.

## RIFLE BRIGADE—continued.
### 1st and 2nd Battalions—continued.

| Name. | Missing. | Interned. | Repatriated. |
|---|---|---|---|
| *2/Lt. W. LOFTUS. | 24/4/18 | | 3/12/18 |
| †2/Lt. E. A. H. ODDY. | 24/4/18 | | 3/12/18 |
| 2/Lt. W. MacKECHNIE. | 24/4/18 | | 29/11/18 |
| 2/Lt. A. H. BURMAN. | 24/4/18 | | 3/12/18 |
| 2/Lt. H. YOUNG. | 24/4/18 | | 29/11/18 |
| Major A. A. TOD. | 27/5/18 | | 25/12/18 |
| Capt. E. W. CREMER. | 27/5/18 | | 25/12/18 |
| Capt. G. H. G. ANDERSON. | 27/5/18 | | 23/12/18 |
| Lieut. A. N. WARREN. | 27/5/18 | | 30/12/18 |
| Lieut. G. PURVES. | 27/5/18 | | 31/12/18 |
| †2/Lt. J. FARRELL. | 27/5/18 | | –/12/18 |
| 2/Lt. H. N. ABERCROMBIE. | 27/5/18 | | 25/12/18 |
| 2/Lt. R. BEATTIE. | 27/5/18 | | 25/12/18 |
| 2/Lt. O. BRUCE. | 27/5/18 | (Died 21/6/18). | |
| 2/Lt. E. P. HORGAN. | 27/5/18 | | 31/12/18 |
| ‡2/Lt. W. H. HARRIS. | 27/5/18 | | –/12/18 |
| 2/Lt. R. T. CALDWELL. | 27/5/18 | | –/12/18 |
| Capt. A. W. M. RISSIK. | 2/9/18 | | 8/12/18 |

### 3rd Battalion.

| Name. | Missing. | Interned. | Repatriated. |
|---|---|---|---|
| 2/Lt. J. MUNDAY. | 20/1/18 | | 14/12/18 |
| 2/Lt. G. G. F. GREIG. | 21/3/18 | | 18/12/18 |
| 2/Lt. A. E. WARD. | 21/3/18 | | 25/12/18 |

### 7th Battalion.

| Name. | Missing. | Interned. | Repatriated. |
|---|---|---|---|
| Lt.-Col. A. J. H. SLOGGETT. | 21/3/18 | | 19/1/19 |
| Capt. F. A. HAWKINS. | 21/3/18 | | 28/11/18 |
| Capt. J. A. SAUNDERS. | 21/3/18 | | 29/11/18 |
| Lieut. M. D. CHILD. | 21/3/18 | | 29/11/18 |
| Lieut. J. A. SOWERBUTTS. | 21/3/18 | | 29/11/18 |
| 2/Lt. H. P. GRAHAM. | 21/3/18 | | 28/11/18 |
| 2/Lt. W. BAKEL. | 21/3/18 | | 18/12/18 |
| §2/Lt. W. A. ROBBINS. | 21/3/18 | | 29/11/18 |
| 2/Lt. W. P. McCAFFREY. | 21/3/18 | | 18/12/18 |
| 2/Lt. F. ATTERTON. | 21/3/18 | | 28/11/18 |
| 2/Lt. S. ARNOLD. | 21/3/18 | | 18/12/18 |
| 2/Lt. M. J. MONAGHAN. | 21/3/18 | | –/11/18 |
| 2/Lt. W. G. MILLS. | 21/3/18 | | 28/11/18 |
| 2/Lt. D. B. McPHERSON. | 21/3/18 | | 29/11/18 |
| 2/Lt. C. HOLBROOK. | 21/3/18 | | 18/12/18 |
| 2/Lt. A. McALLISTER. | 21/3/18 | | 18/12/18 |
| 2/Lt. G. H. KING. | 21/3/18 | | 18/12/18 |
| 2/Lt. H. W. LETHBRIDGE. | 21/3/18 | | 29/11/18 |
| 2/Lt. W. D. ORCHARD. | 21/3/18 | | 28/11/18 |
| 2/Lt. W. WOODHEAD. | 23/3/18 | | 18/12/18 |

### 8th Battalion.

| Name. | Missing. | Interned. | Repatriated. |
|---|---|---|---|
| 2/Lt. D. H. MILLER. | 24/3/16 | Holland 30/4/18 | 18/11/18 |
| 2/Lt. J. F. SMITH. | 23/3/18 | | –/12/18 |
| **2/Lt. E. P. BLUNDELL. | 23/3/18 | | 29/11/18 |
| 2/Lt. A. W. McCRORIE. | 24/3/18 | | 29/11/18 |
| ††2/Lt. A. GRAY. | 4/4/18 | | 25/12/18 |
| 2/Lt. F. W. RICHARDS. | 4/4/18 | | –/12/18 |

\* Attached from King's Own Yorkshire Light Infantry.  
† Attached King's Royal Rifles.  
‡ Attached T.M.B.  
§ Attached from Liverpools.  
∥ Attached Signals, R.E.  
** Attached from Liverpool Regiment.  
†† Attached from Yorkshire Regiment.

## RIFLE BRIGADE—continued.

### 9th Battalion.

| Name. | Missing. | Interned. | Repatriated. |
|---|---|---|---|
| Capt. Ralph WILSON. | 20/3/18 | | —/12/18 |
| 2/Lt. W McGEOCH. | 21/3/18 | | 2/12/18 |
| *Major J. H. BOARDMAN. | 23/3/18 | (*Died* 25/4/18 at Heilbronn). | |
| 2/Lt. W. L. McKECHNIE. | 23/3/18 | | —/12/18 |
| 2/Lt. H. CHANDLER. | 23/3/18 | | 18/12/18 |
| 2/Lt. Robert WILSON. | 23/3/18 | | 17/12/18 |

### 10th Battalion.

| Name. | Missing. | Interned. | Repatriated. |
|---|---|---|---|
| 2/Lt. R. T. URRY. | 20/2/17 | | 17/12/18 |
| 2/Lt. A. W. B. FINCH. | 20/2/17 | | 29/11/18 |
| Lt.-Col. L. H. W. TROUGHTON. | 30/11/17 | | 30/12/18 |
| 2/Lt. M. A. YOUNG. | 30/11/17 | | 21/1/19 |
| 2/Lt. W. H. RODGER. | 30/11/17 | | 27/11/18 |
| 2/Lt. S. EIDMANS. | 30/11/17 | | 23/3/18 |

### 11th Battalion.

| Name. | Missing. | Interned. | Repatriated. |
|---|---|---|---|
| Lieut. G. DAVIDSON. | 24/3/18 | | 18/12/18 |
| †2/Lt. H. A. HOGG. | 24/3/18 | | 6/12/18 |

### 12th Battalion.

| Name. | Missing. | Interned. | Repatriated. |
|---|---|---|---|
| 2/Lt. B. R. C. READ. | 14/2/16 | Holland 9/4/18 | 18/11/18 |
| 2/Lt. F. W. BLOORE. | 22/3/18 | | 18/12/18 |
| 2/Lt. D. H. DE PASS. | 22/3/18 | | 2/12/18 |
| 2/Lt. G. L. RUMBLE. | 22/3/18 | | 11/12/18 |
| 2/Lt. W. I. HENDERSON. | 30/3/18 | | 29/11/18 |

### 16th Battalion.

| Name. | Missing. | Interned. | Repatriated. |
|---|---|---|---|
| Capt. E. F. H. SMITH. | 22/3/18 | | 6/1/19 |
| Capt. G. C. COOPER. | 22/3/18 | | 18/12/18 |
| 2/Lt. H. BARNABY. | 22/3/18 | | 2/12/18 |
| 2/Lt. H. A. SYKES. | 22/3/18 | | 2/12/18 |
| 2/Lt. J. H. SUMMERSKILL. | 26/3/18 | | 25/12/18 |
| 2/Lt. C. A. BENNETT. | 27/3/18 | | 1/12/18 |

## ARMY CYCLISTS CORPS.

| Name. | Missing. | Interned. | Repatriated. |
|---|---|---|---|
| Major D. P. DAVIES. | 9/4/18 | | 25/12/18 |
| Capt. A. S. LUCAS. | 9/4/18 | | 25/12/18 |
| Capt. D. E. WIGGANS. | 9/4/18 | | 29/11/18 |
| Lieut. F. E. STARKEY. | 9/4/18 | | 18/12/18 |
| ‡Lieut. C. H. SCOTT. | 9/4/18 | | 25/12/18 |
| §Lieut. G. F. LOWSON. | 9/4/18 | | 18/12/18 |
| Lieut. E. R. BEWLEY. | 9/4/18 | | 18/12/18 |

## MACHINE GUN CORPS.

| Name. | Missing. | Interned. | Repatriated. |
|---|---|---|---|
| 2/Lt. T. C. NICHOLAS. | | Holland —/6/18 | 21/1/19 |
| 2/Lt. A. L. HYSLOP. | 2/4/17 | | 1/1/19 |
| Lieut. C. S. HADDEN. | 23/4/17 | | 31/12/18 |
| 2/Lt. A. S. DRABBLE. | 29/4/17 | | 1/1/19 |
| 2/Lt. A. YOUNG. | 16/5/17 | | 6/12/18 |

\* Attached from Oxford and Bucks Light Infantry.  † Attached from Border Regiment.
‡ Attached from Liverpools.  § Attached from East Yorks.

## MACHINE GUN CORPS—continued.

| Name. | Missing. | Interned. | Repatriated. |
|---|---|---|---|
| 2/Lt. H. BAKER. | 10/7/17 | | 17/12/18 |
| Lieut. E. PEARCE. | 31/7/17 | Switzerland 27/10/17 | 9/12/18 |
| 2/Lt. A. McLEOD. | 1/8/17 | | 6/1/19 |
| Capt. R. L. HARTLEY. | 1/8/17 | | 14/12/18 |
| 2/Lt. L. R. FORSTER. | 5/8/17 | | 14/12/18 |
| 2/Lt. J. S. ANDERSON. | 25/9/17 | | 3/12/18 |
| 2/Lt. W. B. PARKER. | 26/9/17 | | 6/12/18 |
| 2/Lt. T. BOWKER. | 22/10/17 | | 28/11/18 |
| Lieut. M. M. HOLDEN. | 30/11/17 | | 14/12/18 |
| Lieut. J. E. McERVEL. | 30/11/17 | | 3/12/18 |
| Lieut. H. WILSON. | 30/11/17 | | 6/1/19 |
| Lieut. H. J. DAVEY. | 30/11/17 | | 1/1/19 |
| 2/Lt. W. BAILEY. | 30/11/17 | | 25/12/18 |
| 2/Lt. S. S. IRWIN. | 30/11/17 | | 6/12/18 |
| 2/Lt. J. H. KINAHAN. | 30/11/17 | | 17/12/18 |
| 2/Lt. J. B. HILL. | 30/11/17 | | 17/12/18 |
| 2/Lt. G. GAY. | 30/11/17 | | 27/11/18 |
| 2/Lt. F. W. SHEBBEARE. | 1/12/17 | | 23/2/18 |
| 2/Lt. J. H. WALMSLEY. | 1/12/17 | | 27/11/18 |
| Lieut. P. P. PERRY. | 2/12/17 | | 14/12/18 |
| 2/Lt. E. D. KIPPEN. | 3/12/17 | | 14/12/18 |
| 2/Lt. A. S. PAYNE. | 3/12/17 | | 6/1/19 |
| 2/Lt. G. CHAMBERS. | 6/12/17 | | 14/12/18 |
| Capt. G. R. GOLDINGHAM. | 30/12/17 | | 27/11/18 |
| 2/Lt. A. W. DACOMBE. | 31/1/18 | | 1/1/19 |
| Lieut. J. A. ROBOTHAM. | 21/3/18 | | 11/12/18 |
| 2/Lt. H. I. KAY. | 21/3/18 | | 2/12/18 |
| Capt. A. WOODS. | 23/3/18 | | 6/12/18 |
| 2/Lt. T. GUYATT. | 24/3/18 | | 25/12/18 |
| 2/Lt. F. G. H. SMALL. | 24/3/18 | (*Died* 9/6/18 at Cassel). | |
| 2/Lt. N. ROBERTS. | 24/3/18 | | 28/11/18 |
| 2/Lt. R. METCALF. | 26/3/18 | | 13/12/18 |
| Lieut. L. S. WINN. | 28/3/18 | | 1/12/18 |
| 2/Lt. H. J. C. ALBRECHT. | 9/4/18 | | 28/11/18 |
| 2/Lt. R. MORRISON. | 10/4/18 | (*Died* 14/4/18 at Vignies). | |
| 2/Lt. H. A. WHARTON. | 27/5/18 | | 13/12/18 |
| Lieut. A. M. DUNAND. | 24/8/18 | | 13/12/18 |
| Lt. Col. Sir W. R. CODRINGTON. | 31/10/18 | | —/12/18 |
| Lieut. C. W. F. WOOLNOUGH. | | | |
| 2/Lt. G. WARBURTON. | | | 17/12/18 |
| 2/Lt. N. D. DALTON. | | | 11/12/18 |

### 1st Battalion.

| | | | |
|---|---|---|---|
| Capt. L. MARSH. | 31/10/18 | | |

### 2nd Battalion.

| | | | |
|---|---|---|---|
| Lieut. A. WAUGH. | 28/3/18 | | 4/12/18 |
| Lieut. T. SIME. | 28/3/18 | | 17/12/18 |

### 5th Battalion.

| | | | |
|---|---|---|---|
| 2/Lt. A. MacFARLANE. | 21/3/18 | | 18/12/18 |

## MACHINE GUN CORPS—continued.

### 6th Battalion.

| Name. | Missing. | Interned. | Repatriated. |
|---|---|---|---|
| Lieut. J. J. ANDERSON. | 21/3/18 | | 3/1/19 |
| 2/Lt. T. F. NEWBERY. | 21/3/18 | | 15/12/18 |
| 2/Lt. A. A. DODD. | 21/3/18 | | –/12/18 |
| 2/Lt. S. G. BALL. | 21/3/18 | | 11/12/18 |
| 2/Lt. F. W. HOCKADAY. | 21/3/18 | | 17/12/18 |
| Lieut. W. T. REDGRAVE. | 22/3/18 | | 18/12/18 |
| Lieut. H. McCORMICK. | 26/4/17 | (Died 8/5/17). | |

### 8th Battalion.

| Name. | Missing. | Interned. | Repatriated. |
|---|---|---|---|
| 2/Lt. J. M. EMERSON. | 23/3/18 | (Died 2/4/18 at Rosiers). | |
| 2/Lt. W. H. SKINNER. | 25/3/18 | (Died 27/3/18). | |
| Lieut. W. HARDY. | 24/4/18 | | –/12/18 |
| Lieut. D. E. S. BROWNE. | 24/4/18 | | 3/12/18 |
| 2/Lt. J. M. HOOD. | 24/4/18 | | 3/12/18 |
| 2/Lt. C. H. REEVES. | 24/4/18 | | 3/12/18 |
| Capt. W. TONKS. | 27/5/18 | | –/12/18 |
| Lieut. G. E. CROWDER. | 27/5/18 | | 8/12/18 |
| Lieut. F. W. ARTHURTON. | 27/5/18 | | 25/12/18 |
| Lieut. F. R. LOCKHART. | 27/5/18 | | –/12/18 |
| Lieut. A. C. CRONE. | 27/5/18 | | 25/12/18 |
| Lieut. H. E. WALKER. | 27/5/18 | | –/12/18 |
| 2/Lt. A. A. TARVER. | 27/5/18 | | –/12/18 |
| 2/Lt. S. TELFER. | 27/5/18 | | –/12/18 |
| 2/Lt. R. W. BROWN. | 27/5/18 | | –/12/18 |
| 2/Lt. S. ROBEY. | 27/5/18 | | –/12/18 |
| 2/Lt. W. B MILLS | 27/5/18 | | –/12/18 |
| 2/Lt. E. J. JOBERNS. | 27/5/18 | | –/12/18 |
| 2/Lt. S. H. KEEN. | 27/5/18 | | –/12/18 |
| 2/Lt. L. L CLARKE. | 27/5/18 | | 25/12/18 |
| 2/Lt. L. F. DOWDEN. | 27/5/18 | | 31/12/18 |

### 9th Battalion.

| Name. | Missing. | Interned. | Repatriated. |
|---|---|---|---|
| Lieut. F. J. BRIDGES. | 21/3/18 | | 4/12/18 |
| 2/Lt. P. A. KENNEDY. | 21/3/18 | | 18/12/18 |
| Lieut. G. A. HISKENS. | 16/4/18 | | 1/12/18 |
| Lieut. R. B. ROBB. | 16/4/18 | | 3/12/18 |
| Lieut. W. L. W. LEACH. | 25/4/18 | | 3/12/18 |

### 10th Battalion.

| Name. | Missing. | Interned. | Repatriated. |
|---|---|---|---|
| Lieut. E. F. HARDMAN. | 28/3/18 | | 1/12/18 |

### 12th Battalion.

| Name. | Missing. | Interned. | Repatriated. |
|---|---|---|---|
| Lieut. J. S. PHILLIPS. | 30/10/18 | | 8/11/18 |

### 14th Battalion.

| Name. | Missing. | Interned. | Repatriated. |
|---|---|---|---|
| Lieut. R. E. DAVENHILL. | 21/3/18 | | 14/12/18 |
| Lieut. W. F. PORTEOUS. | | | 14/12/18 |
| Lieut. J. ROLPH. | 21/3/18 | | 26/12/18 |
| Lieut. T. C. SKINNER. | 21/3/18 | | 14/12/18 |
| Lieut. G. N. MASKELL. | 21/3/18 | | 10/12/18 |
| 2/Lt. G. ROBBINS. | 21/3/18 | | 2/12/18 |
| 2/Lt. E. G. BELL. | 21/3/18 | | |
| 2/Lt. S. C. WOOD. | 21/3/18 | | 11/12/18 |
| 2/Lt. H. D. GREEN. | 21/3/18 | | 14/12/18 |
| 2/Lt. H. LATHAM. | 22/11/16 | | 2/1/19 |

## MACHINE GUN CORPS—continued.

### 15th Battalion.

| Name. | Missing. | Interned. | Rapatriated. |
|---|---|---|---|
| 2/Lt. J. C. ASHBURNER. | 28/3/18 | | 17/12/18 |
| 2/Lt. W. J. TAYLOR. | 28/3/18 | | 2/12/18 |

### 16th Battalion.

| | | | |
|---|---|---|---|
| Lieut. F. A. KIRKLAND. | 21/3/18 | | –/12/18 |
| Lieut. E. S. F. TURNER. | 21/3/18 | | 2/12/18 |
| 2/Lt. J. DONALDSON. | 29/3/18 | | 8/12/18 |

### 18th Battalion.

| | | | |
|---|---|---|---|
| Lieut. A. B. JONES. | 21/3/18 | | 2/12/18 |
| 2/Lt. F. C. CHEESEMAN. | 21/3/18 | | 2/12/18 |
| 2/Lt. R. F. GALBRAITH. | 21/3/18 | | 18/12/18 |

### 19th Battalion.

| | | | |
|---|---|---|---|
| Lieut. G. W. HARGRAVES. | 22/3/18 | | 18/12/18 |
| 2/Lt. S. BOWKER. | 24/3/18 | | 25/12/18 |
| 2/Lt. W. G. BARUGH. | 24/3/18 | | 18/12/18 |
| 2/Lt. H. E. BAGGS. | 24/3/18 | (*Died* 30/6/18 at Cassel). | |
| Capt. L. E. JONES. | 25/3/18 | | 2/11/18 |
| Lieut. B. B. GASCOYNE. | 25/3/18 | | 11/12/18 |
| Lieut. J. ANDERSON. | 10/4/18 | | 29/11/18 |
| 2/Lt. M. C. GREGORY. | 10/4/18 | | 18/12/18 |
| 2/Lt. J. S. SPEAR. | 10/4/18 | | 29/11/18 |
| Capt. F. P. DAVIS. | 11/4/18 | | 18/12/18 |
| 2/Lt. E. D. JONES. | 11/4/18 | | 25/11/18 |
| 2/Lt. A. M. HODGSON. | 12/4/18 | | 18/12/18 |

### 20th Battalion.

| | | | |
|---|---|---|---|
| 2/Lt. W. HILL. | 20/3/18 | | 18/12/18 |
| 2/Lt. R. DELL. | 22/3/18 | (*Died* 8/5/18 Avesnes). | |
| Lieut. J. T. CUFFLEY. | 24/3/18 | (*Died* 31/3/18 at Dury). | |

### 21st Battalion.

| | | | |
|---|---|---|---|
| 2/Lt. F. O. LANE. | 21/3/18 | | 22/12/18 |
| Lieut. F. A. R. WADSWORTH. | 22/3/18 | | 29/11/18 |
| 2/Lt. W. G. ATTER. | 22/3/18 | | 23/1/19 |
| 2/Lt. S. EDMUNDSON. | 22/3/18 | | 17/12/18 |
| 2/Lt. G. W. JACK. | 22/3/18 | | 18/12/18 |
| 2/Lt. G. LESLIE. | 23/3/18 | | –/12/18 |
| Capt. S. J. CHITTENDEN. | 24/3/18 | | 1/12/18 |
| Lieut. J. E. ENRIGHT. | 24/3/18 | | –/2/19 |
| Lieut. J. P. AINSCOUGH. | 24/3/18 | | –/12/18 |
| 2/Lt. A. W. H. BLACK. | 24/3/18 | | 2/12/18 |
| Lieut. W. E. BARCLAY. | 24/3/18 | | 12/12/18 |
| 2/Lt. L. J. DILLIWAY. | 24/3/18 | | 18/12/18 |
| 2/Lt. C. E. SANDERS. | 24/3/18 | | 11/12/18 |
| Lieut. J. CAMPBELL. | 28/4/18 | | 18/12/18 |
| 2/Lt. E. MYERS. | 27/5/18 | | 17/12/18 |
| 2/Lt. H. W. KNOTT. | 27/5/18 | | 17/12/18 |
| 2/Lt. S. E. SINCLAIR. | 27/5/18 | | –/12/18 |

### 22nd Battalion.

| | | | |
|---|---|---|---|
| Capt. T. C. B. UDALL. | 27/5/18 | | 17/12/18 |

## MACHINE GUN CORPS—continued.

### 24th Battalion.

| Name. | Missing. | Interned. | Repatriated. |
|---|---|---|---|
| Capt. R. DARBY. | 21/3/18 | | 4/12/18 |
| Lieut. C. D. ARMSTRONG. | 21/3/18 | | 18/12/18 |
| 2/Lt. S. M. WILLIAMS. | 21/3/18 | | 12/12/18 |
| 2/Lt. J. G. HOLT. | 21/3/18 | | 23/9/18 |
| Capt. R. G. DUMARESQ. | 11/4/18 | | 3/12/18 |

### 25th Battalion.

| Name. | Missing. | Interned. | Repatriated. |
|---|---|---|---|
| 2/Lt. F. BENTLEY. | 21/3/18 | | 1/12/18 |
| Major L. E. FABER. | 23/3/18 | | 28/11/18 |
| Lieut. F. O. RHODES. | 23/3/18 | | 11/12/18 |
| Lieut. W. D. LAWSON. | 23/3/18 | | 10/12/18 |
| Lieut. F. P. SPOONER. | 25/3/18 | | 1/12/18 |
| Lieut. F. W. JACOB. | 10/4/18 | | 29/11/18 |
| Lieut. E. J. C. MADDISON. | 10/4/18 | | 29/11/18 |
| Lieut. F. H. C. REDINGTON. | 14/4/18 | | 2/12/18 |
| Lieut. S. MORRISON. | 17/4/18 | | 2/12/18 |
| 2/Lt. H. M. PERRYMAN. | 18/4/18 | | 3/12/18 |
| 2/Lt. H. F. HAYES. | 25/4/18 | | 2/12/18 |
| Lieut. A. S. CALVERT. | 27/5/18 | | 25/12/18 |
| Lieut. G. H. COATON. | 27/5/18 | | –/12/18 |
| Lieut. D. J. COLEMAN. | 27/5/18 | | 10/1/19 |
| Lieut. R. H. COCKSEDGE. | 27/4/18 | | 14/12/18 |
| Lieut. W. K. RENNIE. | 27/5/18 | | –/12/18 |

### 29th Battalion.

| Name. | Missing. | Interned. | Repatriated. |
|---|---|---|---|
| 2/Lt. A. H. SUTCLIFFE. | 12/4/18 | | 25/12/18 |
| 2/Lt. P. JAMIESON. | 11/4/18 | | –/1/19 |

### 30th Battalion.

| Name. | Missing. | Interned. | Repatriated. |
|---|---|---|---|
| Lieut. T. W. ASHLEY. | 21/3/18 | | –/1/19 |
| 2/Lt. R. B. MORISON. | 21/3/18 | | 1/12/18 |
| 2/Lt. H. FIELD. | 21/3/18 | | 16/1/19 |
| 2/Lt. H. T. MORGAN. | 21/3/18 | | 7/12/18 |
| 2/Lt. W. T. HOWARTH. | 21/3/18 | | 11/1/19 |
| 2/Lt. A. McCOLL. | 23/3/18 | | 18/12/18 |

### 31st Battalion.

| Name. | Missing. | Interned. | Repatriated. |
|---|---|---|---|
| Capt. D. M. CULE. | 12/4/18 | | 18/12/18 |
| 2/Lt. J. W. E. PALMER. | 12/4/18 | (*Died* at Lille). | |
| 2/Lt. A. F. ADAMS. | 12/4/18 | | 1/12/18 |

### 33rd Battalion.

| Name. | Missing. | Interned. | Repatriated. |
|---|---|---|---|
| 2/Lt. A. S. HUNT. | 2/10/18 | | 28/11/18 |

### 34th Battalion.

| Name. | Missing. | Interned. | Repatriated. |
|---|---|---|---|
| 2/Lt. J. R. LLOYD-ATKINS. | 21/3/18 | | 1/12/18 |
| 2/Lt. F. C. BENSON. | 21/3/18 | | 25/12/18 |
| 2/Lt. G. R. W. LAWSON. | 21/3/18 | | 25/12/18 |
| 2/Lt. W. STENSON. | 21/3/18 | | 1/12/18 |
| 2/Lt. J. H. PATON. | 21/3/18 | | 11/12/18 |
| 2/Lt. W. H. HANCOCK. | 10/4/18 | | 25/12/18 |
| 2/Lt. E. N. MATHIESON. | 13/4/18 | | 1/12/18 |
| 2/Lt. J. S. PEGG. | 13/4/18 | | 18/12/18 |
| Lieut. A. JACKSON. | 29/7/18 | | 14/12/18 |

## MACHINE GUN CORPS—continued.

### 36th Battalion.

| Name. | Missing. | Interned. | Repatriated. |
|---|---|---|---|
| Lieut. V. E. OSBORNE. | 21/3/18 | (*Killed* while trying to escape). | |
| Lieut. T. B. REYNOLDS. | 21/3/18 | | 14/12/18 |
| Lieut. A. J. LAMPORT. | 21/3/18 | | –/12/18 |
| Lieut. J. BARKER. | 21/3/18 | | 14/12/18 |
| Lieut. H. W. ROOT. | 21/3/18 | (*Died* 22/3/18 Labancourt). | |
| Lieut. J. T. SAUNDERS. | 21/3/18 | | 29/11/18 |
| 2/Lt. J. W. J. SLOAN. | 21/3/18 | | 10/12/18 |
| 2/Lt. T. G. WEALL. | 21/3/18 | | 17/12/18 |

### 38th Battalion.

| Name. | Missing. | Interned. | Repatriated. |
|---|---|---|---|
| 2/Lt. E. P. MARTIN. | 24/3/18 | | 2/12/18 |

### 39th Battalion.

| Name. | Missing. | Interned. | Repatriated. |
|---|---|---|---|
| 2/Lt. R. J. PRITCHARD. | 23/3/18 | | 2/12/18 |
| 2/Lt. W. A. NEWMAN. | 30/3/18 | | 7/9/18 |

### 40th Battalion.

| Name. | Missing. | Interned. | Repatriated. |
|---|---|---|---|
| 2/Lt. J. GORDON. | 22/3/18 | | 18/12/18 |
| 2/Lt. B. HOWARD. | 24/3/18 | | 11/12/18 |
| Lieut. J. G. ELMITT. | 9/4/18 | | 10/12/18 |
| 2/Lt. W. G. FINCH. | 9/4/18 | | 11/12/18 |
| 2/Lt. W. C. WICKHAM. | 9/4/18 | | 8/12/18 |
| 2/Lt. E. L. WILLIAMS. | 9/4/18 | | 8/12/18 |
| 2/Lt. C. P. DUNN. | 9/4/18 | | 11/12/18 |

### 41st Battalion.

| Name. | Missing. | Interned. | Repatriated. |
|---|---|---|---|
| 2/Lt. L. S. P. H. RAYNER. | 21/3/18 | | 8/12/18 |
| Capt. A. McK. REID. | 24/3/18 | | 14/12/18 |

### 47th Battalion.

| Name. | Missing. | Interned. | Repatriated. |
|---|---|---|---|
| 2/Lt. S. F. PETERS. | 21/3/18 | | 11/12/18 |
| Lieut. E. H. TAYLOR. | 24/3/18 | | 4/12/18 |
| Lieut. V. R. L. HUTCHINGS. | 24/3/18 | | 8/12/18 |
| Lieut. N. H. L. BARNI. | 24/3/18 | (*Died* 29/3/18 at Lesdain). | |
| 2/Lt. A. C. BLACK. | | | 22/11/18 |

### 48th Battalion.

| Name. | Missing. | Interned. | Repatriated. |
|---|---|---|---|
| 2/Lt. P. OSWIN. | 21/3/18 | | 14/12/18 |
| 2/Lt. F. S. S. DAWKINS. | 25/4/18 | | –/12/18 |

### 49th Battalion.

| Name. | Missing. | Interned. | Repatriated. |
|---|---|---|---|
| 2/Lt. F. P. HARRISON. | 21/3/18 | | 28/11/18 |
| 2/Lt. H. CLARKE. | 14/4/18 | | 18/12/18 |
| 2/Lt. J. C. LAMONT. | 16/4/18 | | 2/12/18 |
| Major W. MILNE. | 25/4/18 | (*Died* at Munster 25/7/18). | |
| Capt. M. FitzG. KINDER. | 25/4/18 | | 1/12/18 |
| Lieut. J. B. BROWN. | 25/4/18 | | 13/12/18 |
| Lieut. A. K. STEEL. | 26/4/18 | | 18/12/18 |
| 2/Lt. A. H. CLARK. | 26/4/18 | (*Died*). | |

## MACHINE GUN CORPS—continued.

### 50th Battalion.

| Name. | Missing. | Interned. | Repatriated. |
|---|---|---|---|
| Lieut. P. H. HIGHT. | 22/3/18 | | 18/12/18 |
| 2/Lt. T. WAINWRIGHT. | 22/3/18 | | 28/11/18 |
| Capt. W. R. THOMSON. | 11/4/18 | | –/12/18 |
| Lieut. E. HAZELEY. | 11/4/18 | | 13/12/18 |
| 2/Lt. B. M. BALBI. | 11/4/18 | | 18/12/18 |
| Major J. S. DAWBARN. | 27/5/18 | | –/12/18 |
| Major R. C. MOON. | 27/5/18 | | –/12/18 |
| Major M. B. DOUGLAS. | 27/5/18 | | –/12/18 |
| Capt. G. R. McPHAIL. | 27/5/18 | | 25/12/18 |
| Capt. A. O. COOPER. | 27/5/18 | | 31/12/18 |
| Capt. T. H. NEEDHAM. | 27/5/18 | | –/12/18 |
| Lieut. I. A. LAUDER. | 27/5/18 | | 30/12/18 |
| Lieut. F. F. MUNRO. | 27/5/18 | | 26/12/18 |
| Lieut. A. SPENCER. | 27/5/18 | | 11/1/19 |
| Lieut. J. R. GRAHAM. | 27/5/18 | | 25/12/18 |
| Lieut. B. BURDETT. | 27/5/18 | | 2/1/19 |
| Lieut. G. C. J. BURTON. | 27/5/18 | | 30/12/18 |
| Lieut. G. C. ODOM. | 27/5/18 | | –/12/18 |
| Lieut. T. W. WALDING. | 27/5/18 | | 14/12/18 |
| 2/Lt. R. ROPNER. | 27/5/18 | | –/12/18 |
| 2/Lt. R. S. ROBERTSON. | 27/5/18 | | –/12/18 |
| 2/Lt. W. J. S. RANKEN. | 27/5/18 | | –/12/18 |
| 2/Lt. H. J. P. TEAGUE. | 27/5/18 | | 25/12/18 |
| 2/Lt. F. BETHELL. | 27/5/18 | | –/12/18 |
| 2/Lt. J. S. McVEY. | 27/5/18 | | 8/12/18 |
| 2/Lt. W. T. HUNTER. | 27/5/18 | | –/12/18 |

### 51st Battalion.

| Name. | Missing. | Interned. | Repatriated. |
|---|---|---|---|
| Lieut. J. EDGAR. | 21/3/18 | | 25/12/18 |
| 2/Lt. W. SIMPSON. | 21/3/18 | | 11/12/18 |
| 2/Lt. G. E. MOSS. | 21/3/18 | | 11/12/18 |
| 2/Lt. T. G. MANNERS. | 21/3/18 | | 11/12/18 |
| 2/Lt. J. R. McC. MITCHELL. | –/3/18 | | 29/11/18 |
| 2/Lt. R. A. BARKER. | 21/3/18 | | 28/11/18 |
| Lieut. J. N. HENDRY. | 22/3/18 | | 29/11/18 |
| Lieut. D. MENZIES. | 22/3/18 | | 19/12/18 |
| 2/Lt. H. BIRCHWOOD. | 22/3/18 | | 1/12/18 |
| Lieut. S. E. CHARLTON. | 23/3/18 | | 18/12/18 |
| Lieut. L. V. CULY. | 24/3/18 | | |
| 2/Lt. C. M. APPERLEY. | 24/3/18 | (*Died* 28/3/18). | |
| Lieut. R. S. MORPETH. | 11/4/18 | | 29/11/18 |
| 2/Lt. E. H. SINCLAIR. | | | 18/12/18 |
| 2/Lt. E. F. HARTLEY. | 12/4/18 | | 2/12/18 |
| 2/Lt. F. J. FRENCH. | 12/4/18 | | 18/12/18 |

### 55th Battalion.

| Name. | Missing. | Interned. | Repatriated. |
|---|---|---|---|
| 2/Lt. W. ADDISON. | 9/4/18 | | 25/12/18 |

### 56th Battalion.

| Name. | Missing. | Interned. | Repatriated. |
|---|---|---|---|
| 2/Lt. W. J. BATTING. | 28/3/18 | | 18/12/18 |

### 57th Battalion.

| Name. | Missing. | Interned. | Repatriated. |
|---|---|---|---|
| Lieut. E. C. JONES. | 4/10/18 | | 25/12/18 |

## MACHINE GUN CORPS—continued.

### 58th Battalion.

| Name. | Missing. | Interned. | Repatriated. |
|---|---|---|---|
| 2/Lt. T. OWEN. | 22/3/18 | | 2/12/18 |
| 2/Lt. J. ROBERTSON. | 22/3/18 | | 2/12/18 |
| 2/Lt. J. D. HAMPTON. | 24/8/18 | | 13/12/18 |

### 59th Battalion.

| | | | |
|---|---|---|---|
| 2/Lt. E. D. LANE. | 30/11/17 | (*Died* 8/12/17 at Candry). | |
| Capt. E. NEEDHAM. | 21/3/18 | | 25/12/18 |
| Lieut. D. YATES. | 21/3/18 | | 11/12/18 |
| Lieut. F. C. WILSON. | 21/3/18 | | 29/12/18 |
| 2/Lt. E. J. FRIEND. | 21/3/18 | | 18/12/18 |
| 2/Lt. R. A. EDKINS. | 21/3/18 | | 14/12/18 |
| 2/Lt. G. H. BANDEY. | 21/3/18 | (*Died* at Graudenz). | |
| 2/Lt. J. G. TOWNSEND. | 21/3/18 | | 29/11/18 |
| 2/Lt. T. A. MAY. | 21/3/18 | | 1/12/18 |

### 61st Battalion.

| | | | |
|---|---|---|---|
| Lieut. F. W. CASWELL. | 21/3/18 | | –/12/18 |
| Lieut. E. C. DOUGLASS. | 21/3/18 | | 2/12/18 |
| Lieut. A. E. KER. | 21/3/18 | | 16/12/18 |
| Lieut. W. O. JONES. | 21/3/18 | | 2/12/18 |
| Lieut. H. KAY. | 21/3/18 | | 28/11/18 |
| Lieut. S. C. GOODE. | 21/3/18 | | 6/12/18 |
| 2/Lt. S. P. GREER. | 21/3/18 | | 13/12/18 |
| 2/Lt. E. R. FORWARD. | 21/3/18 | | 8/12/16 |
| 2/Lt. L. N. FENN. | 21/3/18 | | 29/11/18 |
| 2/Lt. G. H. FARROW. | 21/3/18 | | 6/12/18 |
| 2/Lt. P. ORGILL. | 21/3/18 | (*Died* 31/3/18 at Bohain). | |
| 2/Lt. G. EARL. | 21/3/18 | | 6/12/18 |
| 2/Lt. W. E. WICKS. | 21/3/18 | | 6/12/18 |
| 2/Lt. H. G. JONES. | 12/4/18 | | 18/12/18 |

### 63rd Battalion.

| | | | |
|---|---|---|---|
| 2/Lieut. R. E. W. SANDISON. | 22/3/18 | | 17/12/18 |

### 66th Battalion.

| | | | |
|---|---|---|---|
| Lieut. E. S. HAY. | 21/3/18 | | 5/12/18 |
| Lieut. T. S. BICKERSTAFFE. | 21/3/18 | | 2/12/18 |
| 2/Lt. W. B. HOLWILL. | 21/3/18 | (*Died* 16/5/18). | |
| 2/Lt. S. S. MARSH. | 21/3/18 | | 3/12/18 |
| 2/Lt. H. B. JONES. | 22/3/18 | | 25/12/18 |
| Lieut. H. B. BEAUMONT. | 27/3/18 | | 18/12/18 |

### 103rd Battalion.

| | | | |
|---|---|---|---|
| Lieut. H. H. LESLIE. | 21/3/18 | | 13/12/18 |

### 109th Battalion.

| | | | |
|---|---|---|---|
| 2/Lt. G. R. ROLSTON. | 21/3/18 | | –/12/18 |

### 117th Battalion.

| | | | |
|---|---|---|---|
| Lieut. R. WILSON. | 21/3/18 | | 25/12/18 |

### 197th Battalion.

| | | | |
|---|---|---|---|
| Capt. R. W. H. MOLINE. | 22/3/18 | | 28/11/18 |

## MACHINE GUN CORPS—continued.

### 200th Battalion.

| Name. | Missing. | Interned. | Repatriated. |
|---|---|---|---|
| 2/Lt. A. R. ANDREW. | 21/3/18 | | 18/12/18 |

### TANK CORPS.

#### "A" Battalion.

| | | | |
|---|---|---|---|
| Lieut. J. K. LIPSCOMB. | 20/11/17 | | 18/12/18 |

#### "B" Battalion.

| | | | |
|---|---|---|---|
| Capt. F. VANS-AGNEW. | 23/11/17 | | 31/1/19 |
| Lieut. A. A. DALBY. | 23/11/17 | | 2/1/19 |

#### "C" Battalion.

| | | | |
|---|---|---|---|
| 2/Lt. D. F. BRUNDRITT. | 20/11/17 | | 25/12/18 |
| 2/Lt. H. W. ASHWORTH. | 20/11/17 | | 27/11/18 |

#### "D" Battalion.

| | | | |
|---|---|---|---|
| 2/Lt. D. R. LEWIS. | 22/8/17 | | 2/1/19 |
| Major E. N. MARRIS. | 20/11/17 | | –/1/19 |
| 2/Lt. J. de B. SHAW. | 20/11/17 | | 3/12/18 |

#### "E" Battalion.

| | | | |
|---|---|---|---|
| Capt. A. H. TATNELL. | 23/11/17 | | 3/12/18 |

#### "F" Battalion.

| | | | |
|---|---|---|---|
| Capt. A. E. ARNOLD. | 22/8/17 | | 6/12/18 |
| Lieut. C. W. CARLES. | 21/11/17 | | 2/12/18 |
| Lieut. A. E. SMITH. | 27/11/17 | | 27/11/18 |
| 2/Lt. H. D. CURRY. | 27/11/17 | | 14/12/18 |
| 2/Lt. K. ASHCROFT. | 27/11/17 | | 2/12/18 |
| 2/Lt. C. I. H. TOLLEY. | 27/11/17 | | 23/12/18 |
| 2/Lt. J. P. WETENHALL. | 27/11/17 | | 3/12/18 |
| Capt. V. DUPREE. | 1/12/17 | | 3/12/18 |

#### "H" Battalion.

| | | | |
|---|---|---|---|
| 2/Lt. E. L. BOSTOCK. | 25/10/17 | | 17/12/18 |

#### "I" Battalion.

| | | | |
|---|---|---|---|
| 2/Lt. G. E. WILLIAMS | 23/11/17 | | 13/12/18 |

#### 1st Battalion.

| | | | |
|---|---|---|---|
| 2/Lt. A. J. HUME. | 3/5/18 | (*Died* 21/5/18 at Le Quesnoy). | |
| Capt. S. HOULTON. | 8/8/18 | | 13/12/18 |
| 2/Lt. T. RHODES. | 8/8/18 | | –/1/19 |
| 2/Lt. E. R. FRISBY. | 8/8/18 | | 31/12/18 |
| 2/Lt. A. AYERS. | 8/8/18 | | 13/12/18 |

#### 2nd Battalion.

| | | | |
|---|---|---|---|
| 2/Lt. F. G. SINKINSON. | 22/3/18 | (*Died* 26/3/18 at Ghent). | |
| 2/Lt. J. TURNER. | 22/3/18 | (*Died* 13/4/18 at Cassel). | |
| *Capt. F. A. HAMLET | 18/9/18 | | 10/12/18 |

* Attached from Royal Dublin Fusiliers.

## TANK CORPS—continued.

### 3rd Battalion.

| Name. | Missing. | Interned. | Repatriated. |
|---|---|---|---|
| 2/Lt. F. L. A. FIELD. | 9/8/18 | | 13/12/18 |
| 2/Lt. P. RIDLEY. | 9/8/18 | | 28/11/18 |
| Lieut. L. B. HORE. | 21/8/18 | | 28/11/18 |

### 4th Battalion.

| | | | |
|---|---|---|---|
| Lieut. R. F. NALDER. | 22/3/18 | | 17/12/18 |
| 2/Lt. J. C. ELLIS. | 22/3/18 | (*Died* 21/4/18 at Villers Faucon). | |
| 2/Lt. R. G. VERGETTE. | 12/4/18 | | 18/12/18 |
| 2/Lt. W. J. BEALE. | 9/8/18 | | 13/12/18 |
| 2/Lt. F. CARTMELL. | 10/8/18 | | 13/12/18 |

### 5th Battalion.

| | | | |
|---|---|---|---|
| 2/Lt. E. C. REES. | 22/3/18 | | 14/12/18 |
| 2/Lt. J. LANDERS. | 22/3/18 | | 29/11/18 |
| 2/Lt. C. B. BROWN. | 16/4/18 | | 25/12/18 |
| 2/Lt. G. BRIDGE. | 16/4/18 | | —/1/19 |
| 2/Lt. C. W. MIDGLEY. | 16/4/18 | | 25/12/18 |
| 2/Lt. A. E. BAKER. | 16/4/18 | | 25/12/18 |
| 2/Lt. V. E. JONES. | 17/4/18 | | 30/12/18 |

### 6th Battalion.

| | | | |
|---|---|---|---|
| Lieut. C. B. ARNOLD. | 9/8/18 | | 6/12/18 |
| 2/Lt. N. O. BENNETT. | 9/8/18 | | 14/12/18 |
| Lieut. C. B. PLANT. | 6/11/18 | | 18/12/18 |
| 2/Lt. H. F. JONES. | 6/11/18 | | 20/12/18 |

### 7th Battalion.

| | | | |
|---|---|---|---|
| 2/Lt. G. G. KING. | 15/4/18 | | 18/12/18 |
| *2/Lt. R. B. YENDELL. | 29/9/18 | | 28/11/18 |

### 8th Battalion.

| | | | |
|---|---|---|---|
| 2/Lt. J. G. W. FERGUSON. | 21/3/18 | | 25/12/18 |
| 2/Lt. M. WILSON. | 24/3/18 | | 17/12/18 |

### 9th Battalion.

| | | | |
|---|---|---|---|
| 2/Lt. R. H. HARROP. | 23/8/18 | | 28/11/18 |

### 10th Battalion.

| | | | |
|---|---|---|---|
| 2/Lt. J. P. CHAMPNEY. | 9/8/18 | | 13/12/18 |
| 2/Lt. G. T. L. BAYLIFF. | 21/8/18 | | 13/12/18 |
| 2/Lt. J. R. HAMILTON. | 21/8/18 | | 28/11/18 |
| 2/Lt. C. WEBB. | 21/8/18 | | 13/12/18 |

### 11th Battalion.

| | | | |
|---|---|---|---|
| Lieut. F. A. BURTON. | 25/8/18 | | 29/11/18 |
| 2/Lt. B. BOLGER. | 29/9/18 | | 11/12/18 |

### 12th Battalion.

| | | | |
|---|---|---|---|
| Lieut. R. ACKROYD. | 31/8/18 | | 8/12/18 |
| Lieut. S. GANLEY. | 2/9/18 | | 8/12/18 |
| 2/Lt. G. C. SOUTAR. | 2/9/18 | | 13/12/18 |

* Attached from Monmouthshire Regiment.

## TANK CORPS—continued.

### 13th Battalion.

| Name. | Missing. | Interned. | Repatriated. |
|---|---|---|---|
| Capt. H. P. WHITE. | 25/4/18 | | 12/10/18 |
| *2/Lt. G. SMITH. | 25/4/18 | | 3/12/18 |
| 2/Lt. T. DOWER. | 8/8/18 | | -/12/18 |
| 2/Lt. H. BENSON. | 24/9/18 | | 13/12/18 |

### 14th Battalion.

| | | | |
|---|---|---|---|
| Lieut. T. F. MURPHY. | 9/8/18 | | 13/12/18 |
| 2/Lt. A. F. C. LUMLEY. | 9/8/18 | | 13/12/18 |
| 2/Lt. H. S. GINGER. | 9/8/18 | | 13/12/18 |

### 16th Battalion.

| | | | |
|---|---|---|---|
| 2/Lt. H. E. DUPRE. | 20/9/18 | | 27/11/18 |

### 17th Battalion.

| | | | |
|---|---|---|---|
| 2/Lt. J. H. DAVIES. | 27/9/18 | | 29/11/18 |
| 2/Lt. F. H. PHIPPARD. | 29/9/18 | | 29/11/18 |

### LABOUR CORPS.

| | | | |
|---|---|---|---|
| 2/Lt. D. E. A. HORNE | 30/11/17 | | 14/12/18 |

## MONMOUTHSHIRE REGIMENT.
### 1st and Second Battalions.

| Name | Missing | Interned | | Repatriated |
|---|---|---|---|---|
| Lieut. R. E. LONES. | 26/4/15 | Holland | 23/3/18 | 23/10/18 |
| Lieut. J. COTTRELL. | 26/4/15 | Holland | 23/3/18 | 23/11/18 |
| Lieut. E. T. STEALEY. | 8/5/15 | Holland | 23/3/18 | 25/11/18 |
| Capt. F. G. DAWSON. | 11/5/15 | Holland | 10/4/18 | 23/10/18 |
| Capt. M. C. LLEWELLIN. | 11/5/15 | Holland | 23/3/18 | 22/11/18 |
| Lieut. D. G. C. MURPHY. | 11/5/15 | Holland | 23/3/18 | 18/11/18 |
| Lieut. L. LLEWELLIN. | 11/5/15 | | | 26/8/15 |
| 2/Lt. N. C. NEWLAND. | 11/5/15 | (Died 31/5/15/. | | |
| 2/Lt. T. G. LOWE. | 11/5/15 | Holland | 23/3/18 | 18/11/18 |
| Lieut. J. F. C. RAIKES. | 13/10/15 | | | 11/9/17 |
| Capt. G. E. FOSTER. | 12/4/18 | | | 18/12/18 |
| Lieut. F. C. STRONG. | 12/4/18 | | | -/12/18 |
| 2/Lt. R. S. DAVIES. | 12/4/18 | | | 13/12/18 |

## CAMBRIDGE REGIMENT.
### 1st and 2nd Battalions.

| | | | |
|---|---|---|---|
| Lieut. G. E. RAWLINSON. | 20/7/16 | (*Died* at Seclin). | |
| Lieut. W. SHAW. | 16/9/16 | (*Died* 27/9/16 at Cambrai). | |
| 2/Lt. W. C. BROWN. | 24/3/18 | | 18/12/18 |
| 2/Lt. C. L. SHAW. | 26/3/18 | | 1/12/18 |
| 2/Lt. R. W. T. ROLFE. | 26/4/18 | | 13/12/18 |
| 2/Lt. J. N. McNISH. | 8/10/18 | | 8/12/18 |
| †2/Lt. J. V. MEYER. | 12/10/18 | | 24/11/18 |

## LONDON REGIMENT.
### 1st Battalion.

| | | | |
|---|---|---|---|
| 2/Lt. G. B. HOOPER. | 16/8/17 | | 17/12/18 |
| *Lieut. F. S. WARREN. | 21/3/18 | | 2/12/18 |

\* Attached from York and Lancaster Regiment.   ‡ Attached T.M.B.
† Attached from Suffolks.

## LONDON REGIMENT—continued.

### 2nd Battalion.

| Name. | Missing. | Interned. | Repatriated. |
|---|---|---|---|
| 2/Lt. C. A. FIELD. | 14/1/17 | | 30/12/18 |
| 2/Lt. A. N. B. CLARK. | 3/5/17 | | 1/1/19 |
| 2/Lt. R. Y. ROSS. | 16/8/17 | | 16/12/18 |
| 2/Lt. A. PHILLIPS. | 16/8/17 | | 14/12/18 |
| 2/Lt. L. H. NEWTON. | 26/10/17 | | 21/12/18 |
| Lt.-Col. A. R. RICHARDSON. | 21/3/18 | | 29/11/18 |
| Capt. B. J. BARTON. | 21/3/18 | | 6/12/18 |
| Capt. J. HOWIE. | 21/3/18 | | 1/12/18 |
| Lieut. L. W. BINDON. | 21/3/18 | | 18/12/18 |
| 2/Lt. P. M. WITH. | 21/3/18 | | 18/12/18 |
| 2/Lt. L. MOUTRIE. | 21/3/18 | | 1/12/18 |
| 2/Lt. W. G. PHILPOTT. | 21/3/18 | | –/12/18 |
| 2/Lt. G. T. ROBERTS. | 21/3/18 | | 2/12/18 |
| 2/Lt. L. W. DIXON. | 21/3/18 | | 28/11/18 |
| 2/Lt. S. W. B. CLAPHAM. | 21/3/18 | | 25/12/18 |
| 2/Lt. R. J. H. BROWN. | 21/3/18 | | –/11/18 |
| 2/Lt. H. F. BOON. | 21/3/18 | | 18/12/18 |
| 2/Lt. T. H. GLADSTONE. | 21/3/18 | | 12/12/18 |
| 2/Lt. D. de F. GILLINGS. | 21/3/18 | | 20/12/18 |
| 2/Lt. P. D. GIBSON. | 21/3/18 | | 28/11/18 |
| 2/Lt. M. L. HARPER. | 21/3/18 | | 18/12/18 |
| *2/Lt. J. E. MUNDY. | 24/4/18 | (Died). | |
| *2/Lt. W. E. MAY. | 24/4/18 | | 18/12/18 |
| *2/Lt. F. G. HAYES. | 24/4/18 | | 18/12/18 |
| 2/Lt. G. G. SHADBOLT. | 24/4/18 | | 11/12/18 |
| Lieut. N. GARDINER. | 25/4/18 | | 18/12/18 |
| 2/Lt. A. H. STREETS. | 25/4/18 | | 31/12/18 |
| 2/Lt. P. R. TAYLOR. | 25/4/18 | | 18/12/18 |
| 2/Lt. H. G. MITCHINER. | 25/4/18 | | 18/12/18 |
| 2/Lt. A. H. EDGE. | 10/9/18 | | 11/12/18 |
| 2/Lt. A. R. FOX. | 10/9/18 | | 28/11/18 |
| 2/Lt. J. H. J. DEWEY. | 10/9/18 | | 8/12/18 |
| 2/Lt. H. A. GRAHAM. | 10/9/18 | | 5/1/19 |
| 2/Lt. T. W. N. WATSON. | 13/10/18 | | 29/12/18 |
| 2/Lt. J. M. STOTESBURY. | 6/11/18 | | 10/12/18 |

### 3rd Battalion.

| Name. | Missing. | Interned. | Repatriated. |
|---|---|---|---|
| Capt. E. N. WILCOX. | 4/5/17 | Switzerland 27/12/17 | 3/2/19 |
| 2/Lt. E. W. CUNNINGHAM. | 4/5/17 | | 1/1/19 |
| Capt. H. Seppings LIDIARD | 26/10/17 | | 17/12/18 |
| †2/Lt. W. N. HARRIS. | 21/3/18 | | 25/12/18 |
| Capt. P. W. HERAPATH. | 21/3–4/4/18 | | 18/12/18 |
| Lieut. S. JOHNSON. | 21/3–4/4/18 | | 2/12/18 |
| 2/Lt. A. J. CORRIE. | 21/3–4/4/18 | | 18/12/18 |
| 2/Lt. F. BUCKLE. | 23/3/18 | | 25/12/18 |
| 2/Lt. C. E. CARR. | 26/3/18 | | 2/12/18 |
| 2/Lt. F. de C. CALLENDER. | 24/4/18 | | 17/12/18 |
| 2/Lt. S. N. CLEMOW. | 24/4/18 | | 18/12/18 |
| 2/Lt. G. D. HAIGH. | 8/8/18 | | 13/12/18 |

### 4th Battalion.

| Name. | Missing. | Interned. | Repatriated. |
|---|---|---|---|
| Lieut. A. G. BLUNN. | 1/7/16 | | 14/12/18 |
| 2/Lt. R. McDOWELL | 15/6/17 | | 23/12/18 |
| 2/Lt. E. MONKMAN. | 15/6/17 | | 6/1/19 |
| 2/Lt. E. A. STEVENSON. | 16/6/17 | Holland 7/3/18 | 18/8/18 |
| Lieut. H. W. DURLACHER. | 21/3/18 | | 2/12/18 |

* Attached from Middlesex Regiment. † Attached T.M.B.

## LONDON REGIMENT—continued.
### 4th Battalion—continued.

| Name. | Missing. | Interned. | | Repatriated. |
|---|---|---|---|---|
| 2/Lt. L. F. WARDLE. | 21/3/18 | | | 2/12/18 |
| 2/Lt. S. H. E. CRANE. | 21/3–4/4/18 | | | 2/12/18 |
| 2/Lt. G. E. LESTER. | 21/3–4/4/18 | | | 2/12/18 |
| Lieut. C. W. FRY. | 24/3/18 | | | 1/12/18 |
| 2/Lt. H. O. MORRIS. | 28/3/18 | | | 28/11/18 |
| *2/Lt. C. W. DENNING. | 28/3/18 | | | 29/11/18 |
| 2/Lt. D. F. CRAWFORD. | 30/3–4/4/18 | | | 25/12/18 |

### 5th Battalion.

| Name. | Missing. | Interned. | | Repatriated. |
|---|---|---|---|---|
| 2/Lt. A. R. L. GOODSON. | 3/6/16 | Holland | 30/4/18 | 18/11/18 |
| Capt. A. T. B. DE COLAGAN. | 1/7/16 | Holland | 16/5/18 | 12/1/19 |
| Capt. W. J. GRACE | 28/3/18 | | | 3/12/18 |
| 2/Lt. R. C. THOMPSON. | 28/3/18 | | | 4/12/18 |
| †2/Lt. C. S. TRESILIAN. | 28/3/18 | | | 13/12/18 |
| 2/Lt. F. C. SILLS. | 28/3/18 | | | 11/12/18 |
| 2/Lt. W. R. B. KETTLE. | 28/3/18 | | | 27/12/18 |
| 2/Lt. R. F. L. HEWLETT. | 28/3/18 | | | 11/12/18 |
| 2/Lt. H. G. HIGHAM. | 28/3/18 | | | 11/12/18 |
| 2/Lt. P. ADAMS. | 28/3/18 | | | 18/12/18 |
| 2/Lt. T. C. K. POWELL. | 28/3/18 | | | 10/12/18 |
| 2/Lt. J. A. T. DERHAM. | 5/5/18 | | | 18/12/18 |
| 2/Lt. C. M. KING. | 5/11/18 | | | 17/12/18 |
| 2/Lt. S. GOULD. | 28/3/17 | | | 18/12/18 |

### 6th Battalion.

| Name. | Missing. | Interned. | | Repatriated. |
|---|---|---|---|---|
| Capt. H. G. NOBBS. | 9/9/16 | | | 9/12/16 |
| 2/Lt. E. O. COZENS. | 21/5/17 | | | 23/9/18 |
| Capt. A. T. CANNON. | 29/11/17 | | | 25/12/18 |
| 2/Lt. H. K. FORSTER. | 29/11/17 | (*Died* at Bouchain). | | |
| 2/Lt. C. H. FARRINGTON. | 29/11/17 | | | –/12/18 |
| 2/Lt. C. H. RAVEN. | 28/3/18 | | | 11/12/18 |

### 7th Battalion.

| Name. | Missing. | Interned. | | Repatriated. |
|---|---|---|---|---|
| Capt. F. M. DAVIS. | 21/5/16 | Holland | 30/4/18 | 4/10/18 |
| 2/Lt. W. V. BROOKS. | 21–22/5/16 | Holland | 16/5/18 | 15/11/18 |
| 2/Lt. M. JURISS. | 21–22/5/16 | Holland | 27/6/18 | 23/10/18 |
| 2/Lt. G. B. SLATER. | 7/10/16 | | | 18/12/18 |
| 2/Lt. A. C. ROBINSON. | 23/3/18 | | | 1/1/19 |
| 2/Lt. C. J. A. COULSHAW. | 18/4/18 | | | 14/12/18 |
| Lieut. F. E. MOYLAN. | 26/8/18 | | | 13/12/18 |
| 2/Lt. H. COCKROFT. | 26/8/18 | | | 13/12/18 |
| 2/Lt. C. D. MENZIES. | 16/8/17 | | | 14/12/18 |

### 8th Battalion.

| Name. | Missing. | Interned. | | Repatriated. |
|---|---|---|---|---|
| 2/Lt. C. L'E. WALLACE. | 21/5/16 | Holland | 30/4/18 | 21/1/19 |
| Capt. G. M. B. PORTMAN. | 21–22/5/16 | Holland | 30/4/18 | 21/12/18 |
| Capt. G. N. CLARK. | 21–22/5/16 | Holland | 30/4/18 | 19/12/18 |
| 2/Lt. J. GURNEY. | 21–22/5/16 | Holland | 30/4/18 | 22/11/18 |
| 2/Lt. N. L. AMES. | 21–22/5/16 | Holland | 30/4/18 | 13/12/18 |
| 2/Lt. E. A. HOWELL. | 21–22/5/16 | Holland | 30/4/18 | 23/11/18 |
| 2/Lt. V. WHEELER. | 22/3/18 | | | 8/12/18 |
| 2/Lt. D. F. WILKINSON. | 22/3/18 | | | 1/12/18 |
| 2/Lt. W. G. HEWETT. | 22/3/18 | | | 2/12/18 |
| 2/Lt. A. H. MILLER. | 23/3/18 | | | 29/11/18 |
| 2/Lt. A. ODDLAFSON. | 23/3/18 | | | 1/12/18 |
| 2/Lt. H. R. STONE. | 23/3/18 | (*Died* 17/4/18 at Valenciennes). | | |
| 2/Lt. S. R. POWL. | 14/10/18 | | | 13/12/18 |
| 2/Lt. E. M. ROBINSON. | 14/10/18 | | | 13/12/18 |

\* Attached T.M.B.    † Attached from Middlesex Regiment.

## LONDON REGIMENT—continued.

### 9th Battalion.

| Name. | Missing. | Interned. | | Repatriated. |
|---|---|---|---|---|
| 2/Lt. C. P. FLEETWOOD. | 1/7/16 | (*Died* 12/7/16 at Le Cateau). | | |
| 2/Lt. R. BENNETT. | 1/7/16 | Holland | 16/5/18 | –/1/19 |

### 10th Battalion.

| | | | | |
|---|---|---|---|---|
| 2/Lt. J. C. HEROLD. | | | | 8/12/18 |

### 12th Battalion.

| | | | | |
|---|---|---|---|---|
| Lieut. G. F. RICKETT. | 8/5/15 | Holland | 23/3/18 | 18/11/18 |
| 2/Lt. W. G. PARKER. | 1/7/16 | Holland | 7/10/18 | 19/11/18 |
| 2/Lt. T. W. S. GARNHAM. | 24/8/18 | | | 14/12/18 |
| Capt. K. H. J. ANDERSON. | 12/9/18 | | | 28/11/18 |
| Lieut. K. H. S. CLARKE. | 12/9/18 | | | 29/11/18 |
| Lieut. A. A. BAKER. | 12/9/18 | | | 29/11/18 |

### 13th Battalion.

| | | | | |
|---|---|---|---|---|
| 2/Lt. R. C. MALBY. | | Holland | 10/4/18 | 18/11/18 |
| 2/Lt. P. R. PIKE. | 1/7/16 | Holland | 16/5/18 | 22/11/18 |

### 14th Battalion.

| | | | | |
|---|---|---|---|---|
| Capt. IAN HENDERSON. | 1/11/14 | Switzerland | 30/5/16 | 9/12/18 |
| Lieut. T. H. K. ALLSOP. | 1/11/14 | Switzerland | 9/12/18 | 6/12/18 |
| Capt. F. C. WALKER. | 24/11/17 | | | 17/12/18 |
| Capt. H. L. LAMB. | 24/11/17 | | | 19/1/19 |
| 2/Lt. A. L. WISDON. | 28/3/18 | | | 18/12/18 |

### 15th Battalion.

| | | | | |
|---|---|---|---|---|
| Major H. F. M. WARNE. | 6/12/17 | | | 6/1/19 |
| Capt. L. L. BURTT. | 6/12/17 | | | 2/1/19 |
| Lieut. W. A. S. HOUSLOP. | 6/12/17 | | | 3/12/18 |
| 2/Lt. J. P. POTTS. | 6/12/17 | Holland | 6/2/18 | 23/10/18 |
| 2/Lt. A. E. KING. | 6/12/17 | | | 17/12/18 |
| Capt. R. MIDDLETON. | 22/3/18 | (Doubtful) | | |
| 2/Lt. F. A. BRIGHT. | 22/3/18 | | | 11/12/18 |
| 2/Lt. J. A. SCHOFIELD. | 25/4/18 | | | 18/12/18 |
| 2/Lt. F. GRAY. | 2/9/18 | | | 8/12/18 |

### 16th Battalion.

| | | | | |
|---|---|---|---|---|
| Lieut. P. SPENCER SMITH. | | Holland | 16/5/18 | 19/12/18 |
| Capt. G. E. COCKERILL. | 1/7/16 | (*Died* 3/7/16 at Vrancourt). | | |
| Lieut. D. F. UPTON. | 1/7/16 | Switzerland | 9/12/17 | 24/3/18 |

### 17th Battalion.

| | | | | |
|---|---|---|---|---|
| Lieut. G. B. LOVELL. | –/3/18 | | | 11/12/18 |
| 2/Lt. C. S. RICHARDS. | 28/3/18 | | | 11/12/18 |
| 2/Lt. G. A. MARCHANT. | 10/9/18 | | | –/12/18 |
| 2/Lt. S. A. STROUD. | 10/9/18 | | | 6/12/18 |

### 18th Battalion.

| | | | | |
|---|---|---|---|---|
| 2/Lt. P. R. PARKES. | 21–26/3/18 | (*Died* 4/4/18 at Le Cateau). | | |
| *Lieut. G. B. NEWTON. | 22/3/18 | | | 11/12/18 |
| †2/Lt. A. ELTRINGHAM. | 22/3/18 | | | 25/12/18 |
| Lieut. R. W. MONYPENY. | 23/3/18 | | | 29/11/18 |
| 2/Lt. A. M. PILCHER. | 23/3/18 | (*Died* 6/6/18 at Valenciennes). | | |
| 2/Lt. C. E. HENNING. | 23/3/18 | | | 29/11/18 |
| 2/Lt. J. W. CARRINGTON. | 24/3/18 | | | 11/12/18 |
| Capt. R. MACDONALD. | 3/10/18 | | | 29/11/18 |

*Attached T.M.B.     † Attached from 3rd London Yeomanry.

## LONDON REGIMENT—continued.
### 19th Battalion.

| Name. | Missing. | Interned. | Repatriated. |
|---|---|---|---|
| Capt. H. FOX. | 24/3/18 | | 10/12/18 |
| Capt. J. B. MORRISON. | 24/3/18 | | 10/12/18 |
| *Capt. C. H. SMITH. | 24/3/18 | | 29/11/18 |
| *Lieut. A. D. BATES. | 24/3/18 | | 6/12/18 |
| Lieut. J. A. McFIE. | 24/3/18 | | 29/11/18 |
| 2/Lt. I. C. SMITH. | 24/3/18 | | 11/12/18 |
| 2/Lt. A. C. BALL. | 24/3/18 | | 11/12/18 |
| 2/Lt. L. L. KIRBY. | 24/3/18 | | 11/12/18 |
| 2/Lt. H. F. McELROY. | 24/3/18 | | 11/12/18 |
| †2/Lt. W. E. S. JOTCHAM. | 28/3/18 | | 11/12/18 |

### 20th Battalion.

| Name. | Missing. | Interned. | Repatriated. |
|---|---|---|---|
| Lt.-Col. F. R. GRIMWOOD. | 24/3/18 | | 14/1/19 |
| Capt. R. E. PERRETT. | 24/3/18 | | 20/1/19 |
| Capt. W. R. WOOD. | 24/3/18 | | 25/12/18 |
| Capt. W. T. C. CAVE. | 24/3/18 | | 25/12/18 |
| Lieut. W. R. CRESSWELL. | 24/3/18 | | 25/12/18 |
| Lieut. C. J. ADAMS. | 24/3/18 | | 25/12/18 |
| 2/Lt. S. J. CONSTABLE. | 24/3/18 | | 25/12/18 |
| 2/Lt. R. MATTHEWS. | 24/3/18 | | 28/11/18 |
| 2/Lt. O. L. FULLER. | 25/3/18 | (*Died* 18/10/18 at Cologne). | |

### 22nd Battalion.

| Name. | Missing. | Interned. | Repatriated. |
|---|---|---|---|
| Lieut. E. J. PORTER. | 16/9/16 | (*Died* 22/9/16 at Cambrai). | |
| Major L. A. BOOSEY. | 25/3/18 | | 25/12/18 |

### 23rd Battalion.

| Name. | Missing. | Interned. | Repatriated. |
|---|---|---|---|
| Capt. G. BRETT. | 21/3/18 | | 6/12/18 |
| Lieut. R. K. LANGLEY. | 21/3/18 | | 11/12/18 |
| 2/Lt. P. B. BRAMBROUGH. | 21/3/18 | | 2/1/19 |
| 2/Lt. W. G. PARISH. | 23/3/18 | | 11/12/18 |
| 2/Lt. F. J. C. SPURGE. | 23/3/18 | | 11/12/18 |
| 2/Lt. A. H. AMEY. | 24/3/18 | | 11/12/18 |
| 2/Lt. W. J. KEMP. | 5/4/18 | | 25/12/18 |
| 2/Lt. G. CRISP. | 5/4/18 | | 8/12/18 |
| Capt. A. J. HARMAN. | 22/8/18 | | 10/12/18 |
| Capt. G. C. PHILLIPS. | 22/8/18 | | 8/12/18 |
| 2/Lt. R. P. GOLDSMITH. | 22/8/18 | | 13/12/18 |
| 2/Lt. J. H. HORNBY. | 22/8/18 | | 29/11/18 |
| 2/Lt. H. T. CLEMENTS. | 22/8/18 | | 13/12/18 |

### 24th Battalion.

| Name. | Missing. | Interned. | Repatriated. |
|---|---|---|---|
| Capt. L. C. GAMAGE. | 23/3/18 | | 10/12/18 |
| Capt. G. N. C. DALZIEL. | 23/3/18 | | 25/12/18 |
| Capt. R. F. SIEVERS. | 22/8/18 | | 29/11/18 |
| 2/Lt. C. C. B. MARSHALL. | 5/11/18 | | 6/1/19 |

### 28th Battalion.

| Name. | Missing. | Interned. | Repatriated. |
|---|---|---|---|
| 2/Lt. E. HARVEY. | 2/7/16 | Holland 16/5/18 | 22/11/18 |
| *2/Lt. C. A. R. PARK. | 30/12/17 | | 27/11/18 |
| Capt. G. C. KITCHING. | 24/3/18 | | 25/12/18 |
| Lieut. R. E. PETLEY. | 24/3/18 | | 25/12/18 |
| 2/Lt F. H. SILCOCK. | 24/3/18 | | –/1/19 |

* Attached from 3rd London Yeomanry. † Attached T.M.B.

## LONDON REGIMENT—continued.
### 34th Battalion.

| Name. | Missing. | Interned. | Repatriated. |
|---|---|---|---|
| 2/Lt. W. H. BOND. | 2/9/18 | | 13/12/18 |

## HERTFORDSHIRE REGIMENT.
### 1st Battalion.

| Name | Missing | Interned | Repatriated |
|---|---|---|---|
| Lieut. W. F. FRANCIS. | 31/7/17 | | 14/12/18 |
| Lieut. R. L. HARDY. | 31/7/17 | | 6/1/19 |
| 2/Lt. W. THOMPSON. | 31/7/17 | | 14/12/18 |
| 2/Lt. F. S. WALTHEW. | 31/7/17 | | 6/1/19 |
| Lieut. G. F. C. GUDGEON. | 22/3/18 | | 14/12/18 |
| 2/Lt. R. F. B. BORRODALE. | 22/3/18 | | 14/12/18 |
| 2/Lt. E. FREEDMAN. | 22/3/18 | | 14/12/18 |
| Lt.-Col. E. C. M. PHILLIPS. | 23/3/18 | | 25/12/18 |
| 2/Lt. F. E. ALLEN. | 23/3/18 | | 17/12/18 |

## HEREFORDSHIRE REGIMENT.
### 1st Battalion.

| Name | Missing | Interned | Repatriated |
|---|---|---|---|
| 2/Lt. A. C. EDWARDS. | 4/9/18 | | 13/12/18 |

## ARMY SERVICE CORPS.

| Name | Missing | Interned | Repatriated |
|---|---|---|---|
| Lt.-Col. C. D. CHRISTOPHER. | | Switzerland 30/5/18 | 13/9/17 |
| Lieut. D. POTTS. | | Holland 6/2/18 | 23/10/18 |
| Lieut. L. G. HUMPHREYS. | | Holland 6/2/18 | 15/12/18 |
| Capt. J. A. D. BELL. | | Holland 6/2/18 | 23/10/18 |
| 2/Lt. C. V. EVITT. | 15/5/18 | | 18/12/18 |
| 2/Lt. W. L. MALLABAR. | 27/5/18 | | 18/12/18 |

## ROYAL ARMY MEDICAL CORPS.

*(See also page 131A).*

| Name | Notes | Interned | Repatriated |
|---|---|---|---|
| Major W. FRY. | (*Died* 17/3/15 at Wittenberg) | 31/8/14 | |
| Capt. A. SUTCLIFF. | (*Died* 26/4/15 at Wittenberg) | 31/8/14 | |
| Capt. H. E. PRIESTLY. | | 12/9/14 | 282//16 |
| Capt. A. C. VIDAL. | | 13/9/14 | 28/2/16 |
| Lieut. J. LAUDER. | | 8/10/14 | 29/1/16 |
| Capt. B. JOHNSON. | Att. 16th Lancers. | 10/10/14 | 15/12/15 |
| Capt. C. EDMUNDS. | | -/-/14 | 13/1/16 |
| Lieut. J. M. GILLESPIE. | Att. 2/Northumberland Fus. | 26/5/15 | 1/7/15 |
| Capt. D. A. LAIRD. | Att. 2/Yorkshire Regt. | 25/9/15 | 29/1/16 |
| Lieut. J. R. SPENSLEY. | Att. 8/East Kent Regt. (*Died* 10/11/15 at Mainz) | 26/9/15 | |
| Capt. V. D. O. LOGAN. | Att. 7/Suffolk Regt. | 3/7/16 | 23/2/18 |
| Capt. E. D. F. HAYES. | Att. 1/Northants Regt. | 10/7/17 | 23/2/18 |
| Capt. H. K. WARD. | Att. 2/K.R.R.C. | 10/7/17 | 23/2/18 |
| Lieut. J. RICKARDS. | | 1/8/17 | |
| Lt.-Col. G. S. WILLIAMSON. | | 29/8/17 | 23/2/18 |
| Lieut. K. ATKIN. | Att. 2/6th South Staffs. | 22/9/17 | 23/2/18 |
| Capt. R. T. BRUCE. | | 22/11/17 | 23/2/18 |
| Lt.-Col. C. D. RANKIN. | | 30/11/17 | 23/2/18 |
| Capt. H. D. CLEMENTI-SMITH. | | 30/11/17 | 23/2/18 |
| Capt. F. W. FAWSETT. | Att. 5/Loyal North Lancs. | 30/11/17 | 23/2/18 |
| Capt. C. F. DILLON-KELLY. | Att. 7/East Surrey Regt. | 30/11/17 | 23/2/18 |

## ROYAL ARMY MEDICAL CORPS.—continued.

| Name. | Missing. | Exchanged. |
|---|---|---|
| Capt. W. BEAMAN. | 31/8/14 | 29/6/15 |
| Lieut. A. BROWN. | 12/9/14 | 29/6/15 |
| Major J. BRUNSKILL. | 12/9/14 | 29/6/15 |
| Lieut. P. BUTLER. | 21/8/14 | 29/6/15 |
| Lieut. W. CRYMBLE. | -/-/14 | 1/7/15 |
| Capt. R. J. CAHILL. | 11/9/14 | 29/6/15 |
| Major P. H. COLLINGWOOD. | -/-/14 | 1/7/15 |
| Capt. D. M. CORBETT. | 17/10/14 | 29/6/15 |
| Capt. W. CROKER. | -/-/14 | 1/7/15 |
| Capt. A. E. G. FRAZER. | 27/10/14 | 29/6/15 |
| Capt. F. G. GARLAND. | 22/9/14 | 29/6/15 |
| Major J. FURNESS. | 12/9/14 | 29/6/15 |
| Capt. J. GRAHAM. | -/-/14 | 26/8/15 |
| Lieut. Y. R. HAYMAN. | 23/10/14 | 29/6/15 |
| Lieut. T. E. HEPPER. | 26/10/14 | 29/6/15 |
| Lieut. H. HILLS. | -/-/14 | 1/7/15 |
| Lieut. J. L. JACKSON. | -/-/14 | 1/7/15 |
| Major H. LONG. | 10/9/14 | 29/6/15 |
| Capt. J. P. LYNCH. | -/-/14 | 1/7/15 |
| Surg. M. B. LEARY. | 11/9/14 | 1/7/15 |
| Major H. Kelly. | 13/8/14 | 29/6/15 |
| Capt. A. A. MEADON. | 3/11/14 | 29/6/15 |
| Capt. E. MIDDLETON. | 13/9/14 | 29/6/15 |
| Capt. W. MITCHELL | 6/9/14 | 29/6/15 |
| Lieut. A. PRESTON. | -/-/14 | 1/7/15 |
| Capt. A. M. POLLARD. | 30/10/14 | 29/6/15 |
| Capt. H. PERRY. | 10/9/14 | 29/6/15 |
| Capt. A. D. O'CARROLL. | -/-/14 | 29/6/15 |
| Lieut. G. STEVENSON. | 26/8/14 | 29/6/15 |
| Lieut. J. A. STENHOUSE. | 27/4/15 | 29/6/15 |
| Capt. W. T. THOMPSON. | 26/8/14 | 29/6/15 |
| Major A. M. THOMPSON. | 12/9/14 | 29/6/15 |
| Lieut. — WINTER. | 1/11/14 | 29/6/15 |
| Lieut. E. DAVIES. | -/-/14 | 1/7/15 |
| Capt. P. DAVY. | 16/9/14 | 1/7/15 |
| Lieut. R. DOLBEY. | -/-/14 | 1/7/15 |
| Capt. W. EGAN. | -/-/14 | 1/7/15 |
| Lieut. L. ROUTH. | 12/9/14 | 29/6/15 |
| Capt. A. M. ROSE. | 3/11/14 | 29/6/15 |

**ROYAL ARMY MEDICAL CORPS**—continued.

| Name. | Missing. | Interned. | Repatriated. |
|---|---|---|---|
| Capt. F. M. WALKER. | *Att. R.H.A.* | 30/11/17 | 22/3/18 |
| Capt. G. A. D. McARTHUR. | *Att. 11/K.R.R.C.* | 30/11/17 | 22/3/18 |
| Capt. E. L. F. NASH. | | 30/11/17 | 23/2/18 |
| Capt. C. R. WILLS. | *Att. 10/Rifle Brigade.* | 30/11/17 | 23/2/18 |
| Capt. F. B. RYAN. | *Att. R.E.* | 30/11/17 | 23/2/18 |
| Capt. A. G. BRYCE. | *Att. 7/Suffolk Regt.* | 30/11/17 | 22/3/18 |
| Lieut. T. F. RYAN. | | 30/11/17 | 23/2/18 |
| Capt. H. H. FAIRFAX. | *Att 2/5th Warwick Regt.* | 3/12/17 | 22/3/18 |
| Capt. H. J. DAVIDSON. | *Att. 7/Royal Fusiliers* | 30/12/17 | 22/3/18 |
| *Lieut. F. K. MILLER. | *Att. 9/Royal Welsh Fus.* | 20/3/18 | 11/1/19 |
| Major A. C. HEPBURN. | *Att. 97/Field Ambulance.* | 21/3/18 | 1/11/18 |
| Major J. KENNEDY. | | 21/3/18 | 1/11/18 |
| Major J. S. McCONNACHIE. | | 21/3/18 | 1/11/18 |
| Capt. F. T. H. DAVIES. | *Att. 7/Sherwood Foresters.* | 21/3/18 | 13/12/18 |
| Capt. D. McNAIR. | *Att. 6/Sherwood Foresters.* | 21/3/18 | 1/11/18 |
| Capt. Colin MEARNE. | *Att. 5/Sherwood Foresters.* | 21/3/18 | 1/11/18 |
| Capt. W. WARBURTON. | *Att. 2/Royal Dublin Fus.* | 21/3/18 | 1/11/18 |
| Capt. J. C. MUIR. | *Att. 2/Durham L.I.* | 21/3/18 | 1/11/18 |
| Capt. S. SMITH. | *Att. 1/West Yorkshire Regt.* | 21/3/18 | 26/12/18 |
| Capt. H. A. SANDIFORD. | *Att. 8/Lancashire Fus.* | 21/3/18 | 6/12/18 |
| Capt. D. C. HANSON. | *Att. 9/K.R.R.C.* | 21/3/18 | 30/12/18 |
| Capt. G. B. BUCKLEY. | *Att. 8/K.R.R.C.* | 21/3/18 | –/1/19 |
| Capt. J. ANDERSON. | *Att. 6/Black Watch* | 21/3/18 | –/1/19 |
| Capt. C. E. P. HUSBAND. | *Att. 22/Northumberland Fus.* | 21/3/18 | 1/11/18 |
| Capt. E. H. GRIFFIN. | *Att. 13/15 Northumberland Fus.* | 21/3/18 | 1/11/18 |
| Capt. P. B. CORBETT. | *Att. 25/Northumberland Fus.* | 21/3/18 | –/1/19 |
| Capt. H. S. MOORE. | *Att. 7/Royal West Kents.* | 21/3/18 | 10/1/19 |
| Capt. G. R. LIPP. | *Att. 5/North Staffs Regt.* | 21/3/18 | 18/1/19 |
| Capt. W. M. CHRISTIE. | *Att. 6/South Staffs Regt.* | 21/3/18 | 8/12/18 |
| Capt. D. M. SPRING. | *Att. 5/East Lancs. Regt.* | 21/3/18 | 5/1/19 |
| Capt. R. HODGSON JONES. | *Att. 1/R. Inniskilling Fus.* | 21/3/18 | 1/11/18 |
| Capt. L. S. H. GLANVILLE. | *Att. 13/Royal Irish Rifles.* | 21/3/18 | 1/11/18 |
| *Capt. F. J. CAHILL. | *Att. 2/4 Ox. & Bucks. L.I.* | 21/3/18 | |
| Capt. D. A. WILSON. | *Att. 2/1 North Midland Field Ambulance* | 21/3/18 | 1/11/18 |
| Capt. F. P. SMITH. | *Att. 2/1 East Lancs. Field Ambulance* | 21/3/18 | 1/11/18 |
| *Capt. R. M. DEMING. | *Att. 1/2 Highland Field Ambulance, with 5/Seaforths* | 21/3/18 | |
| Capt. M. T. ASCOUGH. | *Att. 2/1 Field Ambulance* | 21/3/18 | 1/11/18 |
| Capt. A. T. C. MacDONALD. | *Att. 2/1 Field Ambulance* | 21/3/18 | 30/12/18 |
| Capt. G. TORRANCE. | *Att. 2/1 Field Ambulance* | 21/3/18 | 1/11/18 |
| Capt. J. G. ELDER. | *Att. 2/1 Field Ambulance* | 21/3/18 | 1/11/18 |
| Capt. D. F. DOBSON. | *Att. 2/2 Field Ambulance* | 21/3/18 | 30/12/18 |
| Capt. E. A. WALKER. | *Att. 98/Field Ambulance* | 21/3/18 | –/12/18 |
| Capt. J. A. GILFILLAN. | *Att. 98/Field Ambulance* | 21/3/18 | 17/12/18 |
| Capt. E. UNDERHILL. | *Att. 109/Field Ambulance* | 21/3/18 | 13/12/18 |
| Capt. D. R. E. ROBERTS. | | 21/3/18 | 5/1/19 |
| Capt. C. E. REDMAN. | | 21/3/18 | 28/11/18 |
| Capt. W. A. ARNOTT. | | 21/3/18 | 1/11/18 |
| Capt. C. H. C. BRYNE. | | 21/3/18 | 28/11/18 |
| Capt. James TATE. | | 21/3/18 | 1/11/18 |
| Capt. F. R. TICKLE. | (*Died* 5/11/18 in London) | 21/3/18 | 1/11/18 |
| Capt. T. E. A. CARR. | | 21/3/18 | 27/12/18 |
| Capt. R. R. DUNCAN. | | 21/3/18 | 6/12/18 |

* U.S.A.

## ROYAL ARMY MEDICAL CORPS—continued.

| Name. | Regiment. | Missing. | Repatriated. |
|---|---|---|---|
| Capt. W. O'BRIAN. | | 21/3/18 | 1/11/18 |
| Capt. C. C. G. GIBSON. | | 21/3/18 | 10/12/18 |
| Capt. T. W. LEIGHTON. | | 21/3/18 | 29/12/18 |
| Lieut. H. M. GILBERTSON. | Att. 6/Somerset L.I. | 21/3/18 | |
| *Lieut. J. E. QUIGLEY. | Att. 6/Black Watch. | 21/3/18 | |
| *Lieut. A. STRAUSS. | Att. /Connaught Rangers | 21/3/18 | |
| Lieut. O. L. F. MILBURN. | Att. 1/R. Dublin Fusiliers | 21/3/18 | 1/11/18 |
| Lieut. J. F. POWER. | Att. 2/R. Inniskilling Fus. | 21/3/18 | 1/11/18 |
| Lieut. W. H. ROWDEN. | | 21/3/18 | 1/11/18 |
| Lieut. H. CRASSWELLER. | Att. 11/Royal Sussex Regt. | 21/3/18 | 1/11/18 |
| Capt. W. H. McCARTER. | Att. 5/Leinster Regt. | 22/3/18 | 30/12/18 |
| Capt. H. B. JONES. | Att. 2/Bedfordshire Regt. | 22/3/18 | 13/12/18 |
| Capt. J. P. THIERENS. | Att 6/Leicester Regt. | 22/3/18 | 6/12/18 |
| Capt. A. G. BISSET. | Att. 1/R. Munster Fus. | 22/3/18 | 1/11/18 |
| Capt. D. F. TORRENS. | Att. 6/North Staffs. Regt. | 22/3/18 | 10/12/18 |
| *Lieut. S. MILLER. | Att. 8/Worcestershire Regt. | 22/3/18 | |
| Lieut. E. S. PHILLIPS. | | 22/3/18 | 1/11/18 |
| Capt. A. J. CHILLINGWORTH. | Att. 10/Royal West Kents | 23/3/18 | 11/12/18 |
| Capt. S. J. DARKE. | Att. Royal West Surrey Regt. | 23/3/18 | 1/11/18 |
| Capt. I. C. MacLEAN. | Att. 2/Rifle Brigade (Died 4/4/18 at Bohain). | 24/3/18 | |
| Capt. G. L. JONES. | Att. Scottish Rifles | 24/3/18 | 1/11/18 |
| *Lieut. H. A. GOODRICH. | At. 6/Wiltshire Regt. | 24/3/18 | 30/12/18 |
| Capt. F. DALLIMORE. | Att. 22/London Regt. | 25/3/18 | 24/1/19 |
| *Lieut. J. A. GORDON. | Att. 63/Royal Naval Division | 25/3/18 | |
| Capt. W. J. HIRST. | | 26/3/18 | 30/12/18 |
| Capt. P. H. GREEN. | Att. 21/South Midland Field Ambulance | 26/3/18 | 1/11/18 |
| Capt. J. B. BALL. | Att. 15/West Yorkshire Regt. | 27/3/18 | 17/12/18 |
| Capt. R. M. SOAMES. | Att. 7/Norfolk Regt. | 27/3/18 | 1/11/18 |
| Lieut. J. A. LOUGHBRIDGE. | | 27/3/18 | 13/12/18 |
| Capt. R. A. LEEMBRUGGEN. | Att. 2/Suffolk Regt. | 28/3/18 | 1/1/19 |
| Capt. E. E. MATHER. | Att. 8/Durham L.I. | | 5/12/18 |
| Capt. J. G. MOLONY. | Att. 4/London Regt. | 28/3/18 | 5/1/19 |
| Lieut. E. N. P. MARTLAND. | Att. 5/London Regt. | 28/3/18 | 8/12/18 |
| *Lieut. R. B. RHETT. | Att. 16/London Regt. | 28/3/18 | |
| *Lieut. B. J. GALLAGHER. | Att. Gloucestershire Regt. | 29/3/18 | |
| Capt. S. A. FORBES. | | 4/4/18 | 25/12/18 |
| Capt. C. A. MEADEN. | Att. Middlesex.Regt. | 9/4/18 | 1/11/18 |
| Capt. C. K. O'MALLEY. | Att. 21/Middlesex Regt. | 9/4/18 | 18/1/19 |
| Capt. A. H. LITTLE. | Att. 11/Loyal North Lancs. | 9/4/18 | –/12/18 |
| Capt. J. SULLIVAN. | Att. 5/Manchester Regt. | 9/4/18 | 1/11/18 |
| *Lieut. F. B. PEDRICK. | Att. 13/East Surrey Regt. | 9/4/18 | |
| Capt. F. C. NICHOLS. | Att. 4/South Staffs. Regt. | 10/4/18 | 1/11/18 |
| *Lieut. P. W. HUNTER. | Att. 10/Worcesters | 10/4/18 | |
| Capt. W. J. ISBISTER. | Att. 8/Border Regt. | 11/4/18 | 1/11/18 |
| Capt. F. J. NATTRASS. | Att. 2/South Wales Bordrs. | 11/4/18 | 30/12/18 |
| *Lieut. L. M. EDENS. | Att. 1/Wiltshire Regt. | 11/4/18 | |
| Capt. J. R. H. ROSS. | Att. 8/Royal Scots | | 1/11/18 |
| Capt. S. S. MEIGHAM. | Att. 2/Highland Field Ambulance | 12/4/18 | 10/1/19 |
| *Lieut. M. S. REDMOND. | Att. 10/Cheshire Regt. | 12/4/18 | |

* U.S.A.

## ROYAL ARMY MEDICAL CORPS—continued.

| Name. | Regiment. | Missing. | Repatriated. |
|---|---|---|---|
| Capt. S. V. P. PILL. | Att. 1/Wiltshire Regt. | 13/4/18 | 1/11/18 |
| Capt. A. G. CLARK. | Att. 2/South Lancs. Regt. | 13/4/18 | 18/12/18 |
| Capt. A. B. CLUCKIE. | Att. 19/Lancashire Fus. | 25/4/18 | 30/12/18 |
| Lieut. D. ROBERTSON. | Att. 12/Royal Scots | 25/4/18 | 1/11/18 |
| Col. A. MILNE-THOMSON. | | —/5/18 | 1/11/18 |
| Lt.-Col. H. B. KELLY. | Att. 77/Field Ambulance | 27/5/18 | 1/11/18 |
| Major A. M. WOOD. | | 27/5/18 | 27/12/18 |
| Major F. G. LESCHER. | Att. 77/Field Ambulance | 27/5/18 | 14/12/18 |
| Major N. A. A. HUGHES. | Att. 25/Field Ambulance | 27/5/18 | —/12/18 |
| Major R. M. HANDFIELD-JONES. | | 27/5/18 | 1/11/18 |
| Capt. R. M. COALBANK. | Att. 11/Lancashire Fus. | 27/5/18 | 24/1/19 |
| *Capt. H. F. KANE. | Att. 2/Devonshire Regt. | 27/5/18 | |
| Capt. R. W. PEARSON. | Att. 22/Durham L.I. | 27/5/18 | 1/11/18 |
| Capt. D. Munro SMITH. | Att. 2/Northants Regt. | 27/5/18 | 8/12/18 |
| Capt. W. A. REES. | Att. 250/Bde. R.F.A. | 27/5/18 | 1/11/18 |
| Capt. T. BLACKWOOD. | Att. 33/Bde. R.F.A. | 27/5/18 | 1/11/18 |
| Capt. M. S. ESLER. | Att. 2/Middlesex Regt. | 27/5/18 | 1/11/18 |
| Capt. C. R. CROWTHER. | Att. 25/Field Ambulance | 27/5/18 | 1/11/18 |
| Capt. A. B. SIMPSON. | Att. 25/Field Ambulance | 27/5/18 | 1/11/18 |
| Capt. W. T. P. MEADE-KING. | Att. 25/Field Ambulance | 27/5/18 | 1/11/18 |
| Capt. M. DONALDSON. | Att. 37/Casualty Clearing Station | 27/5/18 | 13/12/18 |
| Capt. J. D. GENESE. | Att. 37/Casualty Clearing | 27/5/18 | 13/12/18 |
| Capt. F. C. H. BENNETT. | | 27/5/18 | 13/12/18 |
| Capt. F. H. McCAUGHEY. | | 27/5/18 | 30/12/18 |
| Capt. J. M. MacKENZIE. | | 27/5/18 | |
| Capt. W. G. HARNETT. | | 27/5/18 | 1/11/18 |
| Capt. D. GILLESPIE. | | 27/5/18 | 1/11/18 |
| Capt. C. W. FOWLER. | Att. 2/Royal Berks Regt. | 27/5/18 | 1/11/18 |
| Capt. W. F. DUNLOP. | Att. 12/13 Northumberland Fus. | 27/5/18 | 1/11/18 |
| Lieut. A. M. McCORMICK. | Att. 12/13 Northumberland Fus. | 27/5/18 | 1/11/18 |
| *Lieut. G. D. TIBBETTS. | Att. 4/East Yorks Regt. | 27/5/18 | |
| Lieut. J. W. JONES. | Att. Rifle Brigade | 27/5/18 | 1/11/18 |
| Lieut. J. FINDLAY. | Att. Worcestershire Regt. | 27/5/18 | —/1/19 |
| Lieut A S. FINDLAY. | Att. 77/Field Ambulance | 27/5/18 | —/12/18 |
| Lieut. F. W. D. CARTER. | Att. 24/Field Ambulance | 27/5/18 | 1/11/18 |
| Lieut. A. BOYLE. | Att. 24/Field Ambulance | 27/5/18 | 1/11/18 |
| Lieut. F. W. M. LAMB. | Att. 26/Field Ambulance | 27/5/18 | 18/1/19 |
| Lieut. F. B. O'DOWD. | | 27/5/18 | 1/11/18 |
| Lieut. G. V. W. ANDERSON. | | 27/5/18 | —/12/18 |
| Lt.-Col. A. C. H. GRAY. | Att. 37/Casualty Clearing Station | 28/5/18 | 1/11/18 |
| Major E. J. TILBURY. | Att. 37/Casualty Clearing Station | 28/5/18 | 8/12/18 |
| Capt. F. G. P. HEATHCOTE. | Att. 2/East Lancs. Regt. | 28/5/18 | 1/11/18 |
| Lieut. A. M. CLARE. | Att. 6/Durham L.I. | 27/6/18 | 13/12/18 |
| Capt. C. WITTS. | | 19/7/18 | 1/11/18 |
| Capt. E. H. JONES. | Att. 37/Casualty Clearing Station | 25/7/18 | 13/12/18 |
| Capt. C. Crawford JONES. | | | 6/1/19 |

*U.S.A.

## M.O.R.C., U.S.A.
### (With British Army.)

| Name. | Regiment. | Missing. | Repatriated. |
|---|---|---|---|
| Capt. B. BURPEE. | | | |
| Lieut. C. W. MAXSON. | Att. 26/Field Ambulance | | |
| Capt. A. S. ROBINSON. | | | |
| Lieut. C. P. NASH. | | | |
| Lieut. Julian N. DOW. | | | |

## ARMY CHAPLAINS' DEPARTMENT.

| Name | Regiment | Missing | Repatriated |
|---|---|---|---|
| Rev. A. GRANT. | Att. Highland Field Ambulance | 22/11/17 | 23/2/18 |
| Rev. C. B. PIKE. | Att. 5/Loyal North Lancs. | 30/11/17 | 22/3/18 |
| Rev. P. SINCLAIR. | Att. Highland Field Ambulance | 21/3/18 | 1/11/18 |
| Rev. P. CASEY. | | 21/3/18 | 14/12/18 |
| Rev. R. BIRD. | | 21/3/18 | -/12/18 |
| Rev. J. K. MITCHELSON. | Att. 25/Northumberland Fus. | 21/3/18 | 10/12/18 |
| Rev. A. B. L. KARNEY. | Att. 22/Northumberland Fus. | 21/3/18 | 1/11/18 |
| Rev. A. F. PENTNEY. | | 21/3/18 | 28/11/18 |
| Rev. W. AMCOATS. | | 21/3/18 | 1/11/18 |
| Rev. H. A. SMITH-MASTERS. | Att. 178/L.T.M.B. | 21/3/18 | 25/12/18 |
| Rev. W. P. YOUNG. | Att. 1/5 Seaforths | 21/3/18 | 1/11/18 |
| Rev. J. C. DAVIES. | Att. 1/North Staffs. | 21/3/18 | 1/11/18 |
| Rev. G. C. R. COOKE. | Att. 7/Royal West Kents | 21/3/18 | 6/12/18 |
| Rev. W. FITZMAURICE. | Att. 2/Royal Irish Regt. | 21/3/18 | 1/11/18 |
| Rev. W. F. MORRIS. | Att. 15/Royal Irish Rifles | 21/3/18 | 1/11/18 |
| Rev. W. A. SCANLEN. | Att. Royal Field Arty. | 21/3/18 | 9/1/19 |
| Rev. E. DALY. | Att. 18/Field Ambulance | 21/3/18 | 28/11/18 |
| Rev. J. G. LANE-DAVIES. | Att. 2/Durham L.I. | 21/3/18 | 13/12/18 |
| Rev. T. F. DUGGAN. | | 22/3/18 | 1/11/18 |
| Rev. N. L. LYCETT. | | 22/3/18 | 27/11/18 |
| Rev. W. R. A. BROWN. | | 24/3/18 | 1/11/18 |
| Rev. H. DAVIES. | Att. 20/Middlesex Regt. | 9/4/18 | -/1/19 |
| Rev. L. N. FORSE. | Att. King's Liverpools | 9/4/18 | 1/11/18 |
| Rev. J. L. A. EDWARDS. | Att. 4/East Yorks | 27/5/18 | 1/11/18 |
| Rev. E. HERBERT. | Att. 23/Durham L.I. | 27/5/18 | 1/11/18 |
| Rev. C. G. BROWN. | Att. 22/Durham L.I. | 27/5/18 | 1/11/18 |
| Rev. J. NOLAN. | | 27/5/18 | 1/11/18 |
| Rev. C. STEER, M.C. | Att. Royal Field Arty. | 27-31/5/18 | 1/11/18 |
| Rev. G. A. WESTON. | | | 4/10/18 |
| Rev. H. J. CHAPMAN. | | | 6/12/18 |
| Rev. C. S. ROSE. | | | 6/12/18 |
| Rev. J. G. SMITH. | | | 7/12/18 |
| Rev. E. H. BEATTIE. | | | 9/12/18 |
| Rev. T. E. GRIFFITHS. | | | 9/12/18 |
| Rev. J. TODD. | | | 23/12/18 |
| Rev. J. HILL-WILLIAMS. | | | 31/1/19 |
| Rev. O. RORKE. | 4/Field Ambulance | -/-/14 | 1/7/15 |

## ROYAL GUERNSEY LIGHT INFANTRY.
### 1st Battalion.

| Name. | Missing. | Interned. | Repatriated. |
|---|---|---|---|
| Lieut J C. O. BEUTTLER. | 30/11/17 | | 14/12/18 |
| Lieut. G. K. F. BORRETT. | 30/11/17 | | 14/12/18 |
| *Lieut. A. V. ANDREWS. | 30/11/17 | | 3/12/18 |
| Lieut. F. A. HOVIL. | 12/4/18 | | 18/12/18 |
| Lieut. I. F. MacALPINE. | 12/4/18 | | 14/1/19 |
| 2/Lt. P. STRANGER. | 12/4/18 | | 18/12/18 |

*Attached from Buffs.

## AUSTRALIANS.

### Infantry.

| Name. | Missing. | Interned. | | Repatriated. |
|---|---|---|---|---|
| Lieut. N. G. BLANCHARD. | 6/5/16 | Holland | 16/5/18 | |
| 2/Lt. M. B. DOBIE. | 28/5/16 | (Died). | | |
| Capt. A. G. FOX. | | Switzerland | 9/12/17 | 9/12/18 |
| Lieut. A. W. M. BOWMAN. | 19/7/16 | Holland | 7/10/18 | 21/1/19 |
| Capt. C. ARBLASTER. | 19/7/16 | (Died 24/7/16 at Douai). | | |
| Capt. F. R. RANSON. | 19/7/16 | Holland | 30/8/18 | |
| Capt. R. A. KEAY. | 20/7/16 | Holland | –/6/18 | |
| Major J. J. HUGHES. | 20/7/16 | | | 21/1/19 |
| Capt. C. MILLS. | 20/7/16 | Switzerland | 9/12/17 | 12/1/19 |
| Lieut. J. H. MATTHEWS. | 20/7/16 | Switzerland | 27/12/17 | 7/12/18 |
| Lieut. V. D. BERNARD. | 20/7/16 | Switzerland | 27/12/17 | 7/12/18 |
| Lieut. H. R. LOVEJOY. | 20/7/16 | Holland | –/6/18 | 21/1/19 |
| 2/Lt. G. D'A. FOLKARD. | 20/7/16 | Holland | –/6/18 | |
| 2/Lt. G. CUMMINS. | 20/7/16 | Holland | –/6/18 | 25/11/18 |
| Capt. A. S. ROBERTSON. | | | | 18/12/18 |
| 2/Lt. T. BRINE. | 24/7/16 | Holland | –/6/18 | 4/10/18 |
| Capt. A. K. KENNEDY. | 28/7/16 | (Died 26/8/16 at Gottingen). | | |
| 2/Lt. A. McGOWN. | 12/8/16 | Holland | 12/10/18 | 19/11/18 |
| Capt. F. J. S. HOAD. | 18/8/16 | Switzerland | 9/12/17 | 7/12/18 |
| 2/Lt. R. H. DABB. | 18/8/16 | (Died 22-28/9/16 at Munster). | | |
| 2/Lt. L. C. O'KELLY. | 18/8/16 | | | 6/1/19 |
| Lieut. H. C. ANTHONY. | 19/8/16 | Holland | 12/10/18 | |
| Lieut. E. H. CHINNER. | | (Died). | | |
| Lieut. C. B. MEYER. | | Switzerland | –/12/16 | 14/9/17 |
| Lieut. W. A. HALVORSEN. | | | | 31/12/18 |
| Capt. W. H. GURTRELL. | 14/11/16 | (Died at Morchies). | | |
| Lieut. A. E. DENT. | 14/11/16 | Switzerland | 27/12/17 | 14/6/18 |
| 2/Lt. L. GRIEVE. | 21/11/16 | | | 14/12/18 |
| 2/Lt. W. MURDOCH. | 2/2/17 | | | 31/12/18 |
| Capt. W. A. CULL. | 26/2/17 | Switzerland | 29/12/17 | 24/3/18 |
| 2/Lt. V. W. CHARKER. | 27/3/17 | | | 31/12/18 |
| Capt. D. L. TODD. | 3/4/17 | | | 14/12/18 |
| Lieut. M. GORE. | 3/4/17 | | | 14/12/18 |
| Lieut. J. E. EDWARDS. | 3/4/17 | | | 17/12/18 |
| Major V. J. WAINE. | 11/4/17 | | | 25/12/18 |
| Capt. H. S. HUMMERSTON. | 11/4/17 | | | 31/12/18 |
| Capt. A. LANAGAN. | 11/4/17 | | | 31/12/18 |
| Capt. G. G. GARDINER. | 11/4/17 | | | 14/12/18 |
| Capt. D. DUNSWORTH. | 11/4/17 | Holland | –/4/18 | 18/8/18 |
| Capt. D. P. WELLS. | 11/4/17 | Switzerland | 27/12/17 | 14/6/18 |
| Capt. J. E. MOTT. | 11/4/17 | | | 11/10/17 |
| Lieut. O. C. D. GOWER. | 11/4/17 | | | 2/1/19 |
| Lieut. R. H. O. CUMMING. | 11/4/17 | | | 31/12/18 |
| Lieut. P. McCALLUM. | 11/4/17 | | | 30/12/18 |
| Lieut. W. STONES. | 11/4/17 | Switzerland | 29/12/17 | 10/2/19 |
| Lieut. R. MORRIS. | 11/4/17 | | | 25/12/18 |
| Lieut. R. E. SANDERS. | 11/4/17 | | | –/12/18 |
| Lieut. J. H. HONEYSETT. | 11/4/17 | | | 17/12/18 |
| Lieut. A. J. McQUIGGAN. | 11/4/17 | | | 7/1/18 |
| Lieut. O. S. GLUYAS. | 11/4/17 | | | 3/12/18 |
| Lieut. J. M. COONEY. | 11/4/17 | | | 31/12/18 |
| Lieut. M. F. BURKE. | | | | 4/12/18 |
| 2/Lt. G. D. McLEAN. | 11/4/17 | | | 26/12/18 |

## AUSTRALIANS—Infantry—continued.

| Name. | Missing. | Interned. | Repatriated. |
|---|---|---|---|
| 2/Lt. K. L. JOHNSON. | 11/4/17 | | 1/1/19 |
| 2/Lt. J. P. M. COURTNEY. | 11/4/17 | | 10/1/19 |
| 2/Lt. J. R. GALLAGHER. | 11/4/17 | | 4/12/18 |
| 2/Lt. G. C. SMITH. | 11/4/17 | | 31/12/18 |
| 2/Lt. E. J. L. EDMONDS. | 11/4/17 | | 29/11/18 |
| 2/Lt. W. J. LYON. | 11/4/17 | | |
| 2/Lt. E. BINNINGTON. | 11/4/17 | | 2/1/19 |
| 2/Lt. A. M. MARSHALL. | 11/4/17 | | 14/12/18 |
| 2/Lt. M. J. D'ARCY. | 11/4/17 | | 31/12/18 |
| 2/Lt. J. INGRAM. | 11/4/17 | | 6/12/18 |
| 2/Lt. F. N. CULVERWELL. | 11/4/17 | | 1/1/19 |
| 2/Lt. J. H. WATSON. | 11/4/17 | | 31/12/18 |
| 2/Lt. M. J. WALTON. | 11/4/17 | | 1/1/19 |
| 2/Lt. L. P. RIDGWELL. | 11/4/17 | | 14/12/18 |
| 2/Lt. F. BROOMFIELD. | 11/4/17 | | 14/12/18 |
| 2/Lt. A. V. WATKINSON. | 11/4/17 | | 4/12/18 |
| Lieut. R. BEATTIE. | 15/4/17 | | 31/12/18 |
| Lieut. C. W. HOOPER. | 15/4/17 | | 31/12/18 |
| Lieut. P. W. LYON. | 15/4/17 | | 26/12/18 |
| 2/Lt. J. E. A. STUART. | 15/4/17 | | 10/2/19 |
| Lieut. A. W. B. PETTIT. | 16/4/17 | | 1/1/19 |
| 2/Lt. S. B. SMITH. | | *(Died)*. | |
| 2/Lt. K. AHNALL. | | *(Died)*. | |
| Lieut. H. S. RAMSAY. | 3/5/17 | | 16/8/18 |
| 2/Lt. H. C. FITZGERALD | 3/5/17 | | 25/12/18 |
| 2/Lt. W. L. THOMASON. | 16/5/17 | Switzerland 27/12/17 | 14/6/18 |
| 2/Lt. N. J. HILL. | 26/9/17 | | 6/12/18 |
| Lieut. H. F. B. CASTLE. | 26/9/17 | | 3/12/18 |
| Lieut. L. A. WHITINGTON. | | | 17/12/18 |
| Lieut. L. E. THOMPSON. | | | |
| Capt. D. LESLIE. | | | |
| 2/Lt. J. D. A. COLLIER. | 13/10/17 | | 15/12/18 |
| 2/Lt. A. C. H. GIBBS. | 13/10/17 | | 19/7/18 |
| Lieut. L. C. BOASE. | 4/4/18 | | 25/12/18 |
| 2/Lt. H. T. LEWIS. | 4/4/18 | | 11/12/18 |
| Capt. A. H. FRASER. | 5/4/18 | | 2/12/18 |
| Lieut. W. GOODSALL. | 5/4/18 | | 1/12/18 |
| Lieut. H. W. MARSON. | 5/4/18 | | 31/12/18 |
| Lieut. J. E. SMITH. | 5/4/18 | | 1/12/18 |
| Lieut. E. ROBINSON. | 5/4/18 | | 1/12/18 |
| 2/Lt. J. H. ALLEN. | 5/4/18 | | 1/12/18 |
| Lieut. W. J. KILPATRICK. | 7/4/18 | | 1/12/18 |
| Capt. P. H. AULD. | 25/4/18 | | 1/12/18 |
| Capt. H. H. McMINN. | 8/5/18 | | 1/12/18 |
| Lieut. L. S. McMAHON. | 8/5/18 | | 1/12/18 |
| Lieut. A. J. FELL. | 8/5/18 | | 1/12/18 |
| Lieut. G. C. W. REID. | 14/5/18 | | |
| Lieut. L. N. JENNINGS. | 14/5/18 | | 1/12/18 |
| Lieut. A. T. DOIG. | 23/5/18 | (*Died* 27/6/18 at Le Quesnoy). | |
| Lieut. H. C. MORRISON. | 10/8/18 | | 4/12/18 |
| Lieut. F. FEARNSIDE. | 12/8/18 | | 12/12/18 |
| 2/Lt. W. S. MISSINGHAM. | 11/4/17 | | 30/12/18 |
| 2/Lt. H. L. KILLINGSWORTH. | 28/5/17 | (*Died*). | |
| Lieut. J. H. B. ARMSTRONG. | 18/8/18 | | 29/11/18 |
| Lieut. R. MALLINSON. | 18/8/18 | | 29/11/18 |

## AUSTRALIANS—Infantry—continued.

| Name. | Missing. | Interned. | Repatriated. |
|---|---|---|---|
| Lieut. H. A. RIGBY. | 18/8/18 | | 29/11/18 |
| Lieut. E. J. COX. | 30/8/18 | | 8/12/18 |
| 2/Lt. J. W. PEACOCK. | 5/10/18 | | 13/1/19 |
| Lieut. N. CUMMING. | -/-/16 | | 2/7/18 |

### Engineers.

| Name. | Missing. | Interned. | Repatriated. |
|---|---|---|---|
| 2/Lt. W. M. MORTENSEN. | | | 2/1/19 |

### Machine Gun Corps.

| Name. | Missing. | Interned. | Repatriated. |
|---|---|---|---|
| Lieut. G. C. DODD. | 11/4/17 | | 1/1/19 |
| Lieut. G. KIRKLAND. | 11/4/17 | (Died 13/4/17 at Hem-Lenglet). | |
| 2/Lt. V. G. VENESS. | 11/4/17 | | 1/1/19 |
| 2/Lt. W. J. COX. | 11/4/17 | | 31/12/18 |
| 2/Lt. H. JOHNSON. | 15/4/17 | | 30/11/17 |
| 2/Lt. H. A. FERGUSON. | 20/9/17 | | 14/12/18 |
| Lieut. C. C. DIGHT. | | | 1/12/18 |
| Lieut. J. S. COOLAHAN. | -/4/18 | (Died 3/5/18). | |
| Lieut. F. C. A. MYERS. | 5/4/18 | | -/12/18 |
| 2/Lt. W. A. CARNE. | 31/8/18 | | 11/12/18 |
| Major T. R. MARSDEN. | 17/9/18 | | 28/11/18 |

### Flying Corps.

| Name. | Missing. | Interned. | Repatriated. |
|---|---|---|---|
| 2/Lt. A. WEARNE. | 26/7/17 | | 14/12/18 |
| 2/Lt. I. C. F. AGNEW. | 2/10/17 | | 29/11/18 |
| 2/Lt. V. J. PARKINSON. | -/3/18 | | |
| 2/Lt. W. H. NICHOLLS. | 16/3/18 | | 14/12/18 |
| Lieut. O. T. FLIGHT. | 28/3/18 | | 13/12/18 |
| Lieut. C. M. FEEZ. | | | 13/12/18 |
| Lieut. H. K. LOVE. | 10/4/18 | | 1/12/18 |
| Lieut. A. R. RACKETT. | 1/6/18 | | 30/12/18 |
| 2/Lt. A. RINTOUL. | 1/6/18 | | 13/12/18 |
| Lieut. R. C. NELSON. | 14/7/18 | | 26/12/18 |
| 2/Lt. A. F. G. McCULLOCH. | 28/7/18 | | 13/12/18 |
| Lieut. L. TAPLIN. | 5/9/18 | | 28/12/18 |
| Lieut. George COX. | 21/9/18 | | 23/12/18 |
| Lieut. M. J. KILSBY. | 30/10/18 | | 24/12/18 |
| Lieut. E. J. GOODSON. | 5/11/18 | | 27/11/18 |
| Lieut. C. W. RHODES. | 5/11/18 | | 26/11/18 |

## CANADIANS.

### Infantry.

| Name. | Missing. | Interned. | | Repatriated. |
|---|---|---|---|---|
| Lieut. V. A. McLEAN | 24/4/15 | Holland | 19/3/18 | 18/11/18 |
| Capt. E. C. CULLING. | 26/4/15 | | | |
| Capt. W. H. V. HOOPER. | 26/4/15 | Switzerland | 19/12/17 | 24/3/18 |
| Lieut. J. E. McLURG. | 26/4/15 | | | 22/12/17 |
| Lieut. C. R. SCOTT. | 26/4/15 | | | 11/9/17 |
| Major A. E. KIRKPATRICK | 27/4/15 | | | 3/12/18 |
| Major D. R. McCUAIG. | 27/4/15 | Holland | 23/3/18 | 12/10/18 |
| Capt. L. S. MORRISON. | 27/4/15 | Switzerland | 9/12/17 | |
| Capt. P. J. LOCKE. | 27/4/15 | Holland | 19/3/18 | 18/11/18 |
| Capt. J. E. L. STREIGHT. | 27/4/15 | Switzerland | 9/12/17 | 24/3/18 |
| Lieut. C. G. PITBLADO. | 27/4/15 | Holland | 23/3/18 | 18/11/18 |
| Lieut. B. L. JOHNSTON. | 27/4/15 | Holland | 19/3/18 | |

**CANADIANS—Infantry—continued.**

| Name. | Missing. | Interned. | | Repatriated. |
|---|---|---|---|---|
| Lieut. G. E. D. GREENE. | 27/4/15 | Holland | 10/4/18 | 18/11/18 |
| Lieut. D. G. ALLAN. | 27/4/15 | Holland | 19/3/18 | 18/11/18 |
| Capt. T. V. S. SCUDAMORE. | 28/4/15 | Switzerland | 19/12/16 | 24/3/18 |
| Capt. C. FRYER. | 28/4/15 | Switzerland | 9/12/17 | 2/6/18 |
| Capt. G. M. ALEXANDER. | 28/4/15 | Holland | 19/3/18 | 18/11/18 |
| Capt. R. S. CORY. | 28/4/15 | Holland | 19/3/18 | 18/11/18 |
| Capt. J. E. OSBORNE. | 28/4/15 | Holland | 19/3/18 | 18/11/18 |
| Capt. G. ANDREWS. | 28/4/15 | Holland | 19/3/18 | 18/11/18 |
| Capt. G. W. NORTHWOOD | 28/4/15 | Holland | 19/3/18 | |
| Capt. R. HARVEY. | 28/4/15 | (*Died* 8/5/15). | | |
| Lieut. E. C. BATH. | 28/4/15 | Holland | 19/3/18 | 1/11/18 |
| Lieut. R. P. STEEVES. | 28/4/15 | Holland | 19/3/18 | |
| Lieut. V. A. G. MacDOWELL. | 28/4/15 | Holland | 19/3/18 | |
| Lieut. E. D. BELLEW. | 28/4/15 | Switzerland | 27/12/17 | 9/12/18 |
| Lieut. G. A. COLDWELL. | 28/4/15 | Holland | 1/3/18 | |
| Lieut. H. A. BARWICK. | 28/4/15 | Holland | 19/3/18 | 18/11/18 |
| Lieut. J. K. BELL. | 28/4/15 | Switzerland | 27/12/17 | 9/12/18 |
| Lieut. H. E. L. OWEN. | 28/4/15 | Holland | 19/3/18 | |
| Lieut. F. G. SMITH. | 28/4/15 | Holland | 19/3/18 | 29/1/19 |
| Lieut. R. R. McKESSOCK. | 28/4/15 | Holland | 4/3/18 | 12/10/18 |
| Lieut. F. H. C. MacDONALD. | 28/4/15 | Holland | 19/3/18 | 20/12/18 |
| Lieut. F. V. JONES. | 28/4/15 | Holland | 19/3/18 | |
| Lieut. C. V. FESSENDEN. | 28/4/15 | Holland | 23/3/18 | 18/11/18 |
| Lieut. J. C. THORN. | 28/4/15 | Holland | 23/3/18 | 31/8/18 |
| Lieut. W. de C. O'GRADY. | 28/4/15 | | | 11/9/17 |
| Lieut. G. N. GORDON. | 14/8/15 | Holland | 10/4/18 | 18/11/18 |
| Lieut. D. W. ELLIOTT. | 8/4/16 | Switzerland | 7/5/18 | 7/12/18 |
| Lieut. H. St. J. BIGGS. | 20/4/16 | Holland | 30/4/18 | 16/11/18 |
| Major-General V. WILLIAMS. | 3/6/16 | Switzerland | 27/12/17 | 24/3/18 |
| Major S. L. JONES. | 3/6/16 | (*Died* 8/6/16). | | |
| Major P. BYNG HALL. | | Holland | 19/3/18 | 18/11/18 |
| Lieut. A. W. SIME. | 3/6/16 | Holland | 30/4/18 | 31/8/18 |
| Lieut. W. G. COLQUHOUN. | | Holland | 1/3/18 | |
| Lieut. H. W. MacDONNELL. | 5/6/16 | Switzerland | 13/12/16 | 29/6/18 |
| Lieut. C. J. LAWRENCE. | 6/6/16 | Holland | 30/4/18 | 23/9/18 |
| Lieut. K. JARVIS. | 7/6/16 | Holland | 30/4/18 | 18/11/18 |
| Lieut. R. W. NEIL. | 7/6/16 | Holland | 30/4/18 | |
| Lieut. G. G. D. MURPHY. | 7/6/16 | Holland | 30/4/18 | 18/11/18 |
| Lieut. F. C. R. ANSTEY. | 9/7/16 | Holland | 16/5/18 | |
| Lieut. J. G. MURRAY. | 8/9/16 | | | –/11/18 |
| Lieut. F. C. HOWARD. | 9/9/16 | (*Died* 9/9/16). | | |
| Lieut. W. CLARK. | 25/9/16 | Holland | 5/1/18 | 23/10/18 |
| Lieut. E. W. MINGO. | | | | 18/12/18 |
| Lieut. E. H. SIMPSON. | 8/10/16 | | | 18/12/18 |
| Lieut. J. W. H. ELLIS. | 8/10/16 | | | 18/12/18 |
| Lieut. H. E. BALFOUR. | 8–10/10/16 | | | 31/1/19 |
| Lieut. G. C. HAMILTON. | 9/10/16 | | | 18/12/18 |
| Lieut. J. D. GUNN. | 9/10/16 | Switzerland | 27/12/17 | 14/6/18 |
| Lieut. R. S. W. FORDHAM. | 9/10/16 | Switzerland | 27/12/17 | 24/3/18 |
| Capt. R. SNOWDEN. | | Switzerland | –/2/17 | |
| Capt. Russell TAYLOR. | | Switzerland | –/2/17 | |
| Lieut. W. L. BACK. | 23/12/16 | | | 7/1/19 |
| Lieut. A. C. LUMSDEN. | 1/3/17 | | | 31/12/18 |
| Lieut. C. G. ROBERTSON. | 9–12/4/17 | | | 7/1/19 |
| Lieut. H. S. LEWIS. | 9–12/4/17 | (*Died*). | | |
| Lieut. J. LADLER. | 25/4/17 | (*Died* 2/5/17). | | |

## CANADIANS—Infantry—continued.

| Name. | Missing. | Interned. | | Repatriated. |
|---|---|---|---|---|
| Lieut. F. G. LAWSON. | 8/5/17 | | | 6/12/18 |
| Lieut. W. D. HARDING. | 9/4/17 | | | 30/12/18 |
| Lieut. H. E. BRIDGE. | 8/5/17 | Holland | 15/4/18 | 31/8/18 |
| Capt. R. A. BRODIE. | 15/8/17 | | | 6/12/18 |
| Lieut. J. B. ROSE. | 19/8/17 | | | 3/12/18 |
| Lieut. K. R. M. MORRISON. | 23/8/17 | | | 14/12/18 |
| Lieut. C. L. HEATHER, M.C. | 11/11/17 | | | 1/1/19 |
| Lieut. A. W. BANNARD. | 11/12/17 | | | 27/11/18 |
| Lieut. B. E. MOBERLY, M.C. | 25/3/18 | | | –/11/18 |
| Lieut. D. CLELLAND. | 12/4/18 | | | 29/11/18 |
| Lieut. G. A. CLOUTIER. | 24/5/18 | | | 26/12/18 |
| Lieut. A. B. PIKE. | 21/6/18 | | | 26/12/18 |
| Lieut. R. CARLETON. | 14/8/18 | | | 13/12/18 |
| Lieut. J. STEWART. | 6/9/18 | | | 30/12/18 |
| Lieut. A. E. P. PALMER. | 29/9/18 | | | 30/12/18 |
| Capt. W. W. JOHNSON. | 1/10/18 | | | 30/12/18 |
| Lieut. H. CAMPBELL. | 1/10/18 | | | 28/11/18 |
| Lieut. J. C. LITTLE. | 10/10/18 | | | –/12/18 |
| Lieut. J. A. ROSS. | 10/10/18 | | | –/12/18 |
| Lieut. J. H. MOLSON. | 10/10/18 | | | –/12/18 |
| Lieut. D. G. L. CUNNINGTON. | | | | 26/12/18 |
| Lieut. B. STEVENS. | 8/11/18 | | | 25/11/18 |
| Lieut. G. S. LENNOX. | 27/7/17 | (*Died* at Henin-Lietard). | | |

### Army Medical Corps.

| Name. | Missing. | Interned. | | Repatriated. |
|---|---|---|---|---|
| Capt. W. M. HART. | 27/4/15 | Exchanged | | 29/6/15 |
| Capt. W. R. W. HAIGHT. | | | | 23/2/18 |

### Engineers.

| Name. | Missing. | Interned. | | Repatriated. |
|---|---|---|---|---|
| Lieut. R. G. BARNES | 3/6/16 | | | 13/9/17 |
| Lieut. A. GAUL. | 3/6/16 | Holland | 30/4/18 | |
| Lieut. J. D. WILSON. | 3/7/16 | Holland | 30/4/18 | |
| Lieut. W. E. MASSEY-COOKE. | 3/6/16 | Holland | 30/4/18 | 14/1/19 |
| Capt. G. B. FIELD. | 30/9/18 | | | 29/11/18 |

### Machine Gun Corps.

| Name. | Missing. | Interned. | | Repatriated. |
|---|---|---|---|---|
| Lieut. R. BABB. | 24/3/18 | | | 18/12/18 |
| Lieut. J. A. S. GARDINER. | 8/8/18 | | | 13/12/18 |
| Lieut. W. W. BENNY. | 1/10/18 | | | |

### Chaplains' Department.

| Name. | Missing. | Interned. | | Repatriated. |
|---|---|---|---|---|
| Capt. Rev. A. G. WILKEN. | 3/6/16 | | | 23/2/18 |

### Mounted Rifles.

| Name. | Missing. | Interned. | | Repatriated. |
|---|---|---|---|---|
| Lt.-Col. J. F. H. USSHER. | 3/6/16 | Switzerland | 9/12/17 | 9/12/18 |
| Capt. H. N. FRASER. | 3/6/16 | Holland | 30/4/18 | 18/11/18 |
| Capt. A. F. CROSSMAN. | 3/6/16 | Holland | 8/10/18 | |
| Capt. M. A. SCOVIL. | 3/6/16 | Holland | 30/4/18 | |
| Capt. F. S. PARK. | 3/6/16 | | | 23/2/18 |
| Capt. A. H. LIGHTBOURNE. | 3/6/16 | Holland | 30/4/18 | 19/12/18 |
| Capt. J. E. LATTIMER. | 3/6/16 | Switzerland | 9/12/17 | 24/3/18 |
| Lieut. J. R. MARTIN. | 3/6/16 | Switzerland | 9/12/18 | 24/3/18 |
| Lieut. H. G. ROGERS. | | | | 17/12/18 |
| Lieut. J. H. DOUGLAS. | 3/6/16 | | | 11/9/17 |
| Lieut. N. L. WELLS. | 3/6/16 | Holland | 30/4/18 | |

## CANADIANS—Mounted Rifles—continued.

| Name. | Missing. | Interned. | | Repatriated. |
|---|---|---|---|---|
| Lieut. F. S. HUBBS. | 3/6/16 | Switzerland | 13/12/16 | 14/6/18 |
| Lieut. S. E. GOODERHAM. | 3/6/16 | Holland | 30/4/18 | 18/11/18 |
| Lieut. H. E. SMITH. | 3/6/16 | Holland | 30/4/18 | |
| Lieut. F. H. WOOD. | 3/6/16 | Holland | 30/4/18 | |
| Lieut. C. B. GADD. | 3/6/17 | Holland | 30/4/18 | 1/11/18 |
| Lieut. E. SMITH. | 3/6/16 | | | 11/9/17 |
| Major F. PALMER. | 5/6/16 | Holland | 30/4/18 | 12/10/18 |
| Capt. G. A. B. BUCHANAN. | 5/6/16 | | | 18/11/18 |
| Cpat. H. R. RICHARDSON. | 5/6/16 | Holland | 30/4/18 | 25/11/18 |
| Lieut. J. WALKER. | 5/6/16 | Holland | 30/4/18 | 1/11/18 |
| Lieut. F. H. WILSON. | 5/6/16 | | | 31/12/18 |
| Lieut. E. S. SKEAD. | 5/6/16 | Switzerland | 27/12/17 | 23/12/18 |
| Lieut. E. H. HALL. | 11/5/17 | | | 6/1/18 |

### NEWFOUNDLAND REGIMENT.

| | | | | |
|---|---|---|---|---|
| 2/Lt. A. M. CLOUSTON. | 14/4/17 | | | 14/12/18 |
| 2/Lt. A. B. BAIRD. | 14/4/17 | Switzerland | 27/12/17 | 6/12/18 |
| 2/Lt. W. A. GRACE. | 14/4/17 | | | 14/12/18 |
| 2/Lt. L. MOORE. | 12/4/18 | | | 8/12/18 |

### NEW ZEALAND FORCE.
#### Rifle Brigade.

| | | | |
|---|---|---|---|
| Capt. G. A. AVEY. | 26/6/17 | | 14/12/18 |
| Lieut. W. A. GRAY. | 8/8/17 | | 12/10/18 |
| Lieut. R. J. RICHARDS. | 26/10/18 | | 8/12/18 |

#### Auckland Battalion.

| | | |
|---|---|---|
| Lieut. D. MILLAR. | 1/10/18 | 29/11/18 |

#### Engineers.

| | | |
|---|---|---|
| Lieut. W. M. DURANT. | 14/9/16 | (*Died* 14/9/16 near Arras) |

#### Canterbury Battalion.

| | | |
|---|---|---|
| 2/Lt. A. L. OWEN. | 29/9/18 | 28/11/18 |

#### Wellington Battalion.

| | | |
|---|---|---|
| 2/Lt. J. T. THOMAS. | 26/4/18 | 18/12/18 |

### SOUTH AFRICAN FORCE.

| | | |
|---|---|---|
| Brig.-General F. S. DAWSON. | 24/3/18 | 30/12/18 |

#### 1st Infantry.

| | | | | |
|---|---|---|---|---|
| Lieut. C. J. BATE. | 20/7/16 | | | 17/11/18 |
| Lieut. W. D. HENRY. | 20/7/16 | Holland | 15/6/18 | 14/1/19 |
| 2/Lt. E. C. K. O'KEEFE. | 19/10/16 | | | 18/12/18 |
| 2/Lt. E. A. BUDGEON. | 19/10/16 | | | 18/12/18 |
| Major T. ORMISTON. | 23/3/18 | | | —/1/19 |
| Capt. E. A. DAVIES. | 23/3/18 | | | 29/11/18 |
| Capt. A. W. LIEFELDT. | 23/3/18 | | | 28/11/18 |
| Lieut. A. FRIELINGHAUS. | 23/3/18 | | | 1/12/18 |
| Lieut. P. W. FURMIDGE. | 23/3/18 | | | 29/11/18 |
| Lieut. F. P. MacKENZIE. | 23/3/18 | | | 2/12/18 |
| Lieut. M. A. GRAHAM. | 23/3/18 | | | 1/12/18 |

## SOUTH AFRICAN FORCE—1st Infantry—continued.

| Name. | Missing. | Interned. | | Repatriated. |
|---|---|---|---|---|
| Lieut. W. C. ROBERTSON. | 23/3/18 | | | 25/12/18 |
| Lieut. W. SCALLEN. | 23/3/18 | | | 2/12/18 |
| 2/Lt. T. VUCOVITCH. | 23/3/18 | | | 1/12/18 |
| 2/Lt. C. STRADLING. | 23/3/18 | | | 28/11/18 |
| 2/Lt. W. F. FAULDS. | 23/3/18 | | | 28/11/18 |
| 2/Lt. H. F. ROFFE. | 23/3/18 | | | 28/11/18 |
| 2/Lt. J. D. GIBBS. | 23/3/18 | | | 1/12/18 |
| 2/Lt. G. CURTIS. | 23/3/18 | | | 1/12/18 |
| 2/Lt. E. CARTER. | 23/3/18 | | | 1/12/18 |

### 2nd Infantry.

| Name. | Missing. | Interned. | | Repatriated. |
|---|---|---|---|---|
| Capt. S. E. ROGERS. | 22/3/18 | | | 18/8/18 |
| Lt.-Col. E. CHRISTIAN. | 23/3/18 | | | 25/12/18 |
| Major I. McDOUGALL. | 23/3/18 | | | 17/12/18 |
| Capt. J. ADDISON. | 23/3/18 | | | 3/12/18 |
| Capt. C. J. STEIN. | 23/3/18 | | | 10/12/18 |
| Lieut. T. GARSTANG. | 23/3/18 | | | 2/12/18 |
| Lieut. D. F. BELL. | 23/3/18 | | | 30/11/18 |
| 2/Lt. G. E. MARSHALL. | 23/3/18 | | | 29/11/18 |
| 2/Lt. G. V. MERRIMAN. | 23/3/18 | | | 2/12/18 |
| 2/Lt. J. C. CRAGG. | 23/3/18 | | | 5/12/18 |
| 2/Lt. W. HADLOW. | 23/3/18 | | | 14/12/18 |
| 2/Lt. J. A. GOODING. | 23/3/18 | | | 18/12/18 |

### 3rd Infantry.

| Name. | Missing. | Interned. | | Repatriated. |
|---|---|---|---|---|
| Capt. R. F. C. MEDLICOTT. | | Holland | 15/6/18 | –/11/18 |
| Capt. D. A. PIRIE. | | Holland | 15/6/18 | |
| Lieut. H. HIRTZEL. | | Holland | 15/6/18 | –/10/18 |
| 2/Lt. F. K. St. M. RITCHIE. | | Holland | 30/4/18 | 23/9/18 |
| 2/Lt. S. G. GUARD. | 20/7/16 | Holland | 15/6/18 | –/2/19 |
| Lieut. G. H. de B. THOMAS. | | Holland | 15/6/18 | |

### 4th Infantry.

| Name. | Missing. | Interned. | | Repatriated. |
|---|---|---|---|---|
| Lieut. H. M. NEWSON. | | Holland | 15/6/18 | 19/11/18 |
| 2/Lt. K. S. EARP. | 22/3/18 | | | 3/12/18 |
| 2/Lt. D. R. McINTOSH. | 22/3/18 | | | 29/11/18 |
| 2/Lt. E. H. de M. McINTOSH. | 22/3/18 | | | 25/12/18 |
| 2/Lt. J. KIRKPATRICK. | 22/3/18 | | | 3/12/18 |
| Capt. H. BUNCE. | 23/3/18 | | | 1/12/18 |
| *2/Lt. R. K. ANDERSON. | 23/3/18 | | | 1/12/18 |
| 2/Lt. A. D. MITCHELL. | 23/3/18 | | | 29/11/18 |
| Capt. B. H. L. DOUGHERTY. | 24/3/18 | | | –/12/18 |
| Lieut. G. LEIGHTON. | 24/3/18 | | | –/12/18 |
| 2/Lt. R. B. CORNOCK. | 24/3/18 | | | –/12/18 |
| 2/Lt. W. A. COOK. | 24/3/18 | | | –/11/18 |
| 2/Lt. H. E. SULSTON. | 24/3/18 | | | 2/12/18 |
| 2/Lt. R. C. COOK. | 24/3/18 | | | –/11/18 |
| 2/Lt. W. L. BELL. | 24/3/18 | | | 1/12/18 |
| 2/Lt. S. S. SLATEM. | 24/3/18 | | | 3/12/18 |
| 2/Lt. V. MOGRIDGE. | 24/3/18 | | | 29/11/18 |
| 2/Lt. C. R. ROBINSON. | 24/3/18 | | | –/12/18 |
| 2/Lt. H. M. RETHMAN. | 24/3/18 | | | 3/12/18 |
| 2/Lt. R. J. READ. | 24/3/18 | | | 5/12/18 |
| 2/Lt. F. PEACOCK. | 24/3/18 | | | 5/12/18 |
| 2/Lt. C. G. MASON. | 24/3/18 | | | 28/11/18 |
| Lieut. W. H. THOMPSON. | 11/4/18 | | | –/12/18 |

* Attached T.B.M.

## SOUTH AFRICAN FORCE—continued.
### Chaplains' Department.

| Name. | Missing. | Interned. | Repatriated. |
|---|---|---|---|
| Capt. E. St. C. HILL. | –/3/18 | | –/12/18 |

### Medical Corps.

| | | | |
|---|---|---|---|
| Capt. P. J. MONAGHAN. | 27/3/18 | | –/11/18 |

## INDIAN ARMY.
### 129th Baluchis.

| | | | | |
|---|---|---|---|---|
| Capt. R. D. DAVIES. | 20/12/14 | Holland | 1/3/18 | |

### 9th Bhopal Infantry.

| Capt. R. W. GASKELL. | 24/11/14 | Holland | 24/2/18 | |
| Lieut. J. C. D. MULLALY. | 24/11/14 | Holland | 24/2/18 | 14/1/19 |

### 97th Deccan Infantry.

| Capt. W. T. FLETCHER. | 24/11/14 | Holland | 24/2/18 | 1/11/18 |

### Gurkha Rifles.

| Capt. MacL. WYLIE. | | Holland | 1/3/18 | 15/12/18 |
| Capt. R. D. ALEXANDER. | | Switzerland | 30/5/16 | 13/9/17 |

### Punjabis.

| Capt. C. B. HARCOURT. | 25/9/15 | Holland | 10/4/18 | 23/9/18 |
| Capt. H. J. DANIELL. | | (*Died*) | | |
| Lieut. J. P. GULLAND. | | Holland | 10/4/18 | 18/11/18 |

### 24th Sikh Pioneers.

| Capt. G. E. H. WILSON. | | Holland | 24/2/18 | 28/2/19 |

### Indian Medical Service.

| *Lieut. A. S. GAREWAL. | 30/11/17 | Holland | 19/3/18 | 22/3/18 |

### Nigerian Regiment.

| Capt. G. SECCOMBE. | Taken on S.S. "Appam" | | | 6/12/18 |
| Capt. W. T. McG. BATE. | Taken on S.S. "Appam" | | | 17/11/18 |

## ROYAL NAVAL DIVISION.

| Capt. F. C. GROVER. | | Holland | 6/2/18 | 18/11/18 |
| Commodore W. HENDERSON. | | | | |
| Lieut. R. PRICE. | | Holland | 6/2/18 | |
| Major R. CROSSMAN. | | | | 24/3/18 |

### 188th T.M.B.

| Sub-Lt. E. H. C. McNAUGHTON. | 24/3/18 | | | 6/1/19 |

### 190th T.M.B.

| Lieut. R. E. HOLROYDE. | 25/3/18 | | | 25/12/18 |

### 63rd Div. M.G. Battalion.

| Lieut. D. A. DAVIDSON. | 5/4/18 | | | |

* Attached 2nd Lancers.

## ROYAL NAVAL DIVISION—continued.

### R.M.L.I.

| Name. | Missing. | Interned. | Repatriated. |
|---|---|---|---|
| 2/Lt. W. E. LLEWELYN. | 28/4/17 | | 31/12/18 |
| 2/Lt. A. FARMER. | 28/4/17 | | 17/12/18 |
| 2/Lt. R. R. BLACKBURN. | 28/4/17 | | 6/12/18 |
| 2/Lt. E. G. VAGG. | 28/4/17 | | 28/11/18 |
| Lieut. W. C. GWYNNE. | 23/3/18 | | |
| Capt. R. J. WILLIAMS. | 24/3/18 | | 17/12/18 |
| Lieut. P. WATTS. | 24/3/18 | | 17/12/18 |
| 2/Lt. F. DEATON. | 24/3/18 | | 17/12/18 |
| Surgeon H. C. BROADHURST. | 24–28/3/18 | | 18/12/18 |
| Sub-Lt. C. V. ENGLISH. | 24–28/3/18 | | 25/12/18 |
| Sub-Lt. R. G. GRAY. | 24–28/3/18 | | 25/12/18 |
| 2/Lt. M. E. TAYLOR. | 24–28/3/18 | | 17/12/18 |
| 2/Lt. H. J. IRWIN. | 24–28/3/18 | | 29/12/18 |
| 2/Lt. S. S. CAILES. | 24–28/3/18 | | 17/12/18 |
| 2/Lt. W. G. STUART. | 28/3/18 | | 5/12/18 |
| Capt. J. M. PALMER. | 22–23/4/18 | | |
| Lieut. J. HAMMOND. | –/–/15 | Switzerland 9/12/17 | 24/3/18 |

### "Anson" Battalion.

| | | | |
|---|---|---|---|
| Sub-Lt. F. BLAKE. | 26/10/17 | | 3/12/18 |
| Sub-Lt. W. JOHNSTON. | 26/3/18 | (*Died* at Graudenz) | |
| *Capt. C. A. SCOTTT. | 25/8/18 | | 13/12/18 |
| Sub-Lt. D. A. INGLIS. | 25/8/18 | | 28/11/18 |
| Sub-Lt. S. V. WILD. | 30/9/18 | | 28/11/18 |

### "Collingwood" Battalion.

| | | | |
|---|---|---|---|
| Lieut. M. A. M. DILLON. | | | 1/12/18 |

### "Drake" Battalion.

| | | | |
|---|---|---|---|
| Sub-Lt. H. K. LUNN. | 5/2/17 | | 29/11/18 |
| Sub-Lt. G. M. LOVE. | 30/12/17 | | 27/11/18 |
| Sub-Lt. W. M. HUME. | 30/12/17 | | |
| Sub-Lt. T. H. BENNETT. | 30/12/17 | | 27/11/18 |
| Capt. E. E. CONSTABLE. | 24/3/18 | | 31/12/18 |
| Surgeon W. A. McKERROW. | 24/28/3/18 | | 6/12/18 |
| Lieut. W. C. JOHNSON. | 24–28/3/18 | | 14/1/19 |
| Lieut. J. BARCLAY. | 25/3/18 | | 29/11/18 |
| Sub-Lt. H. J. COLLINGS. | 25/3/18 | | 13/12/18 |
| Lt.-Com. J. W. TURRELL. | 28/3/18 | | 14/1/19 |
| Sub-Lt. R. DONALDSON. | 3/9/18 | | 8/12/18 |

### "Hawke" Battalion.

| | | | |
|---|---|---|---|
| Lieut. J. L. BROMFIELD. | | | 1/12/18 |
| Sub-Lt. A. M. PERRY. | 21/3/18 | | 18/12/18 |
| Sub-Lt. L. STEPHENSON. | 25/8/18 | | 13/12/18 |
| Sub-Lt. A. A. LEIGHTON. | 25/8/18 | | |

### "Hood" Battalion.

| | | | |
|---|---|---|---|
| Sub-Lt. A. FULLERTON. | 22/1/17 | | 14/12/18 |
| Sub-Lt. A. W. M. HILLAM. | 4/2/17 | | 6/1/19 |
| Sub-Lt. H. BEARDSMORE. | 31/12/17 | | 27/11/18 |
| Sub-Lt. S. W. GIBBONS. | 31/12/17 | | 27/11/18 |
| Lieut. T. M. FOX. | 24/3/18 | | 29/11/18 |
| Lieut. H. GRANT-DALTON. | 24/3/18 | (*Died* 28/4/18 at Ohrdruf). | |

* Attached from South Staffs Regiment.

## ROYAL NAVAL DIVISION—continued.
### "Hood" Battalion—continued.

| Name. | Missing. | Interned. | Repatriated. |
|---|---|---|---|
| Sub-Lt. H. HAWKER. | 24/3/18 | | 25/12/18 |
| Sub-Lt. H. W. BISHOP. | 24/3/18 | | 3/12/18 |
| Sub-Lt. J. H. COWAN. | 24/3/18 | | 25/12/18 |
| Sub-Lt. A. WALPOLE. | 24/3/18 | | 4/12/18 |
| Sub-Lt. W. S. PARRY. | 24/3/18 | | 2/12/18 |
| Sub-Lt. H. RAWSON. | 24/3/18 | | 2/12/18 |
| Sub-Lt. R. STRONG. | 24/3/18 | | 2/12/18 |
| Sub-Lt. J. W. STOTT. | 24/3/18 | | 14/12/18 |
| Sub-Lt. J. RAMWELL. | 24/3/18 | | 18/12/18 |
| 2/Lt. T. H. DICKSON. | 24/3/18 | | 18/12/18 |

### "Howe" Battalion.

| Name. | Missing. | Interned. | Repatriated. |
|---|---|---|---|
| Sub-Lt. W. R. McCHLERY. | 30/12/17 | | 27/11/18 |
| Sub-Lt. E. R. CRUMMER. | 30/12/17 | | 27/11/18 |
| Sub-Lt. W. S. DAIN. | 30/12/17 | | 27/11/18 |
| Sub-Lt. J. M. CALDWELL. | 24/3/18 | | 29/11/18 |

## ROYAL NAVAL RESERVE.

| Name. | Missing. | Interned. | | Repatriated. |
|---|---|---|---|---|
| Sub-Lt. W. H. D. GARDNER. | | | | 14/12/18 |
| Lieut. J. W. JOHNSON. | | | | 14/12/18 |
| Sub-Lt. B. W. DURRANT. | | | | 9/12/18 |
| Lieut. G. N. S. JOHNSTON. | | | | |
| Capt. W. OLPHERT. | | Holland | 24/2/18 | |
| Lieut. A. B. LAMBLE. | | Holland | 19/4/18 | |
| Lieut. H. HARRIS. | 24/6/17 | | | 17/12/18 |
| Lieut. W. S. LANE. | | | | |
| Lieut. J. COODE-BATE. | | | | |
| Lieut. W. M. M. HUTCHINGS. | 26/7/17 | | | 14/12/18 |

### R.N.V.R.

Sub-Lt. G. MARCUS.

## ROYAL AIR FORCE.

| Name. | Missing. | Interned. | | Repatriated. |
|---|---|---|---|---|
| Capt. D. S. CROSBIE | —/—/14 | | | 18/11/18 |
| Lieut. H. T. MAYNE. | | | | |
| Lieut. V. S. E. LINDOP. | 9/9/14 | Holland | 6/2/18 | 22/11/18 |
| Capt. R. GREY. | 5/10/14 | Holland | 6/2/18 | 4/10/18 |
| Capt. R. A. BOGER. | 5/10/14 | Holland | 6/2/18 | 30/1/19 |
| Lieut. K. RAWSON-SHAW. | 27/10/14 | Holland | 24/2/18 | 21/1/19 |
| Lieut. H. G. L. MAYNE. | 27/10/14 | Holland | 24/2/18 | 22/11/18 |
| Lt. Joubert de la FERTE. | | | | —/2/18 |
| 2/Lt. M. R. CHIDSON. | 28/2/15 | Holland | 1/3/18 | 17/12/18 |
| 2/Lt. D. C. W. SANDERS. | 28/2/15 | Switzerland | 30/5/16 | —/8/17 |
| Lieut. E. H. EASTWOOD. | 10/3/15 | Escaped | | 2/8/15 |
| Lieut. O. MANSEL MOULLIN. | 12/3/15 | | | 15/11/18 |
| Lieut. G. N. HUMPHREYS. | 20/3/15 | Holland | 1/3/18 | 14/1/19 |
| Lieut. D. M. VETCH. | 21/3/15 | Escaped | | 12/10/15 |
| 2/Lt. T. E. H. DAVIES. | 22/3/15 | Holland | 23/8/18 | 21/1/19 |
| Lieut. C. A. GLADSTONE. | 30/4/15 | Holland | 23/3/18 | 18/11/18 |
| Lieut. S. A. SANFORD. | 9/5/15 | Holland | 10/4/18 | —/11/18 |
| Lieut. E. E. HODGSON. | 5/6/15 | (19/11/18—R.A.F., rep. escaped). | | |
| Capt. A. D. GAYE. | 5/6/15 | Holland (interned) | | 31/10/18 |
| 2/Lt. F. B. ADAMS. | 3/7/15 | Holland (interned) | | 11/11/18 |
| 2/Lt. G. E. R. MEAKIN. | 3/7/15 | Holland (interned) | | 5/10/18 |
| Capt. J. C. LEECH. | 4/7/15 | Holland | 23/1/18 | —/11/18 |
| Lieut. E. WALKER. | 4/7/15 | | | 7/12/18 |
| Sub-Lieut. J. O. GROVES. | 5/7/15 | Switzerland | 22/5/18 | |
| 2/Lt. W. M. CRABBE. | 14/7/15 | Holland | 10/4/18 | 17/11/18 |
| 2/Lt. H. M. GOODE. | 14/7/15 | | | 11/9/17 |
| Capt. R. E. B. HUNT. | 21/7/15 | Holland (interned) | | 21/11/18 |
| Lieut. F. H. JACKSON. | 21/7/15 | Holland (interned) | | |
| Lieut. H. F. HANKIN. | 26/7/15 | Holland | 10/4/18 | 21/1/19 |
| Lieut. A. G. WEIR. | 26/7/15 | Holland | 10/4/18 | 22/11/18 |
| Lieut. P. A. BRODER. | 29/7/15 | Holland | 10/4/18 | 22/11/18 |
| 2/Lt. R. C. MacPHERSON. | 29/7/15 | Holland | 10/4/18 | 29/1/19 |
| 2/Lt. W. REID. | 1/8/15 | Switzerland | 30/5/16 | 11/3/18 |
| Lieut. W. DALZELL. | 6/8/15 | Holland | 10/4/18 | 23/10/18 |
| 2/Lt. C. DOLLINGSMITH. | 6/8/15 | Holland | 10/4/18 | 18/11/18 |
| 2/Lt. D. D. DRURY. | 16/8/15 | Switzerland | 27/12/17 | 24/3/18 |
| 2/Lt. W. A. MacLEAN. | 16/8/15 | | | 10/11/18 |
| Capt. F. J. C. WILSON. | 1/9/15 | Switzerland | 12/8/16 | 11/7/17 |
| Lieut. E. R. C. SCHOLEFIELD. | 1/9/15 | Holland | 10/4/18 | 18/11/18 |
| Capt. T. W. M. MORGAN. | 13/9/15 | Escaped | | —/4/17 |
| Capt. J. N. S. STOTT. | 19/9/15 | Holland | 10/4/18 | 25/11/18 |
| Lieut. W. SUGDEN-WILSON. | 21/9/15 | Holland | 10/4/18 | 25/11/18 |
| 2/Lt. M. W. GREENHOW. | 25/9/15 | Holland | 10/4/18 | 18/11/18 |
| 2/Lt. J. N. C. WASHINGTON. | 25/9/15 | (*Died* at Bapaume 2/10/15) | | |
| Capt. F. B. BINNEY. | 26/9/15 | | | 14/6/18 |
| Lieut. N. C. SPRATT. | 28/9/15 | Holland | 10/4/18 | 17/11/18 |
| 2/Lt. H. B. STUBBS. | 28/9/15 | Holland | 10/4/15 | 18/11/18 |
| Lieut. D. LEESON. | 10/10/15 | Holland | 19/4/18 | 18/11/18 |
| Lieut. R. POTTER. | 10/10/15 | Holland | 10/4/18 | 22/11/18 |
| 2/Lt. B. WILKIN. | 11/10/15 | Holland | 19/4/18 | 18/11/18 |
| 2/Lt. A. J. BURNIE. | 11/10/15 | Holland | 19/4/18 | 18/11/18 |
| 2/Lt. A. C. COLLIER. | 22/10/15 | Holland | 19/4/18 | 26/11/18 |
| Capt. G. C. DARLEY. | 26/10/15 | Switzerland | 30/5/16 | 14/6/17 |
| 2/Lt. R. J. SLADE. | 26/10/15 | Holland | 19/4/18 | 18/11/18 |
| Lieut. F. H. EBERLI. | 9/5/15 | Holland | 10/4/18 | 18/11/18 |

## ROYAL AIR FORCE—continued.

| Name. | Missing. | Interned. | Repatriated. |
|---|---|---|---|
| 2/Lt. J. B. ROBINSON. | 2/11/15 | | –/5/18 |
| Lieut. A. W. BROWN. | 9/11/15 | Switzerland 19/1/17 | 11/9/17 |
| 2/Lt. H. W. MEDLICOTT. | 10/11/15 | (–/6/18 shot in trying to escape) | |
| 2/Lt. J. E. P. HOWEY. | 11/11/15 | Switzerland 13/2/17 | 19/7/17 |
| 2/Lt. V. M. GRANTHAM. | 11/11/15 | Holland 19/4/18 | 22/11/18 |
| Lieut. W. A. HARVEY. | 11/11/15 | (Died in Switzerland 7/11/17) | |
| Lieut. T. C. SHILLINGTON. | 19/11/15 | Switzerland 12/8/16 | 11/9/17 |
| 2/Lt. H. S. WARD. | 30/11/15 | Escaped | –/4/16 |
| Lieut. S. E. BUCKLEY. | 30/11/15 | Escaped | –/6/17 |
| Lieut. D. W. GRINNELL-MILNE. | 1/12/15 | Escaped | –/4/18 |
| Capt. C. C. STRONG. | 1/12/15 | Holland 19/4/18 | 18/11/18 |
| 2/Lt. G. S. M. INSALL. | 14/12/15 | Escaped | –/9/17 |
| Lieut. G. T. PORTER. | 27/12/15 | Holland 19/4/18 | 18/11/18 |
| Lieut. E. J. STROVER. | 28/12/15 | Holland 19/4/18 | 18/11/18 |
| 2/Lt. A. L. RUSSELL. | –/1/16 | Holland 19/4/18 | 22/11/18 |
| Lieut. G. C. FORMILLI. | 5/1/16 | Holland 18/4/18 | 18/11/18 |
| 2/Lt. W. E. SOMERVELL. | 5/1/16 | Holland 19/4/18 | 18/11/18 |
| 2/Lt. F. ADAMS. | 10/1/16 | Holland 19/4/18 | 2/7/18 |
| 2/Lt. J. G. McEWAN. | 10/1/16 | Holland 19/4/18 | 22/11/18 |
| 2/Lt. H. T. KEMP. | 12/1/16 | Holland 19/4/18 | 18/11/18 |
| Lieut. K. W. GRAY. | 12/1/16 | Holland 19/4/18 | –/11/18 |
| Lieut. C. B. WILSON. | 19/1/16 | Holland 19/4/18 | 10/7/18 |
| 2/Lt. L. J. PEARSON. | 5/2/16 | Holland 7/10/18 | 22/11/18 |
| Lieut. E. ALEXANDER. | 5/2/16 | Holland 19/4/18 | |
| 2/Lt. L. A. NEWBOLD. | 29/2/16 | Holland 30/4/18 | Ret. for duty |
| 2/Lt. H. F. CHAMPION. | 29/2/16 | | –/3/16 |
| 2/Lt. C. W. PALMER. | 2/3/16 | (Died 29/3/16) | |
| 2/Lt. L. R. HEYWOOD. | 9/3/16 | Holland 7/10/18 | 19/11/18 |
| 2/Lt. D. B. GAYFORD. | 9/3/16 | Switzerland 24/4/18 | 8/12/18 |
| 2/Lt. M. A. H. ORDE. | 13/3/16 | Switzerland 27/12/17 | 14/6/18 |
| 2/Lt. O. LERWILL. | 25/3/16 | Holland 30/4/18 | 22/11/18 |
| 2/Lt. A. E. HALFORD. | 29/3/16 | Holland 7/10/18 | 22/11/18 |
| 2/Lt. F. G. PINDER. | 29/3/16 | Switzerland 9/12/17 | 24/3/18 |
| 2/Lt. T. C. WILSON. | 30/3/16 | | 14/8/18 |
| 2/Lt. W. JOYCE. | 31/3/16 | Holland 30/4/18 | 29/1/19 |
| 2/Lt. G. S. CASTLE. | 31/3/16 | Holland 30/4/18 | 18/11/18 |
| 2/Lt. F. N. GRIMWADE. | 1/4/16 | Switzerland 6/6/17 | 11/9/17 |
| 2/Lt. H. G. FROST. | 1/4/16 | Switzerland | 13/9/17 |
| 2/Lt. C. W. P. SELBY. | 16/4/16 | Switzerland 24/12/16 | 11/9/17 |
| 2/Lt. N. A. G. SCOTT-BROWN. | 23/4/16 | | |
| 2/Lt. MORTIMER-PHELAN. | 23/4/16 | Holland 30/4/18 | 18/11/18 |
| Capt. D. GRINNELL-MILNE. | 16/5/16 | Holland 30/4/18 | 20/11/18 |
| 2/Lt. H. L. C. AKED. | 21/5/16 | Holland 30/4/18 | 18/11/18 |
| Lieut. A. CAIRNDUFF. | 31/5/16 | Holland 30/4/18 | 18/11/18 |
| 2/Lt. G. E. MAXWELL. | 31/5/16 | Holland 30/4/18 | 18/11/18 |
| Lieut. S. C. T. LITTLEWOOD. | 1/6/16 | Holland 30/4/18 | 1/1/19 |
| Capt. D. L. GRANT. | 1/6/16 | Holland 30/4/18 | 17/11/18 |
| 2/Lt. A. R. L. GOODSON. | 3/6/16 | Holland 30/4/18 | 18/11/18 |
| Lieut. H. B. RUSSELL. | 26/6/16 | Switzerland 9/12/17 | 24/3/18 |
| Lieut. J. R. DENNISTOUN. | 26/6/16 | (Died 9/8/16). | |
| Lieut. W. TUDOR-HART. | 1/7/16 | | 22/11/18 |
| Capt. T. W. P. L. CHALONER. | 1/7/16 | Holland 16/5/18 | 21/1/19 |
| 2/Lt. L. A. WINGFIELD. | 1/7/16 | Escaped | 21/10/17 |
| 2/Lt. C. T. Van NOSTRAND. | 1/7/16 | Holland 16/5/18 | 11/12/18 |
| 2/Lt. J. H. FIRSTBROOK. | 1/7/16 | Switzerland 13/12/16 | 11/9/17 |
| 2/Lt. J. W. TOONE. | 2/7/16 | Holland 16/5/18 | 11/12/18 |

## ROYAL AIR FORCE—continued.

| Name. | Missing. | Interned. | | Repatriated. |
|---|---|---|---|---|
| 2/Lt. S. H. ELLIS. | 3/7/16 | | | 7/1/18 |
| Lieut. W. CASTLE. | 3/7/16 | Holland | 16/5/18 | 26/11/18 |
| 2/Lt. W. B. ELLIS. | 3/7/16 | Holland | 16/5/16 | 16/11/18 |
| 2/Lt. R. W. NICHOL. | 9/7/16 | Holland | 16/5/18 | —/11/18 |
| 2/Lt. D. H. MACINTYRE. | 9/7/16 | Holland | 16/5/18 | Ret. for duty |
| 2/Lt. H. FLOYD. | 9/7/16 | (*Died* at Fabreuil 11/7/16) | | |
| Capt. W. W. JEFFERD. | 10/7/16 | Holland | 16/5/18 | 22/11/18 |
| Lieut. W. J. M. TOMSON. | 10/7/16 | Holland | 16/5/18 | 11/12/18 |
| 2/Lt. C. KERR. | 11/7/16 | Holland | 16/5/18 | 19/12/18 |
| 2/Lt. H. O. LONG. | 16/7/16 | Holland | 15/6/18 | 22/11/18 |
| Lieut. H. C. FINNERTY. | 19/7/16 | Holland | 15/6/18 | 22/11/18 |
| Capt. A. J. EVANS. | | Escaped | | —/6/17 |
| Lieut. NORMAN ROBINSON. | | | | |
| Lieut. D. S. C. MacASKIE. | 20/7/16 | Switzerland | 24/12/16 | 14/9/17 |
| 2/Lt. C. J. SANDYS-THOMAS. | 20/7/16 | Holland | 15/6/18 | 15/11/18 |
| Lieut. R. M. WILSON-BROWNE. | 21/7/16 | (*Died*) | | |
| 2/Lt. J. G. ROBERTSON. | 25/7/16 | Holland | 15/6/18 | —/11/18 |
| 2/Lt. L. N. GRAHAM. | 30/7/16 | Holland | 15/6/18 | 21/1/19 |
| Lieut. E. R. FARMER. | 30/7/16 | Holland | 15/6/18 | 15/1/19 |
| Capt. C. W. SNOOK. | 2/8/16 | Holland | 15/4/18 | 7/9/18 |
| 2/Lt. J. A. N. ORMSBY. | 2/8/16 | (*Died 5/8/16*). | | |
| Lieut. J. C. TURNER. | 3/8/16 | (*Died* at Namur 3/8/16) | | |
| 2/Lt. C. W. BLAIN. | 7/8/16 | Escaped | | —/8/18 |
| 2/Lt. C. D. GRIFFITHS. | 7/8/16 | Holland | 12/10/18 | 22/11/18 |
| Capt. E. W. LEGGATT. | 9/8/16 | Escaped | | —/8/18 |
| 2/Lt. C. GEEN. | 13/8/16 | Holland | 12/10/18 | 22/11/18 |
| Lieut. H. H. WHITEHEAD. | 20/8/16 | (*Died* at Remy 21/8/16) | | |
| 2/Lt. R. T. GRIFFIN. | 20/8/16 | Holland | 12/10/18 | 22/11/18 |
| 2/Lt. K. K. TURNER. | 25/8/16 | | | 21/1/19 |
| 2/Lt. C. SMITH. | 25/8/16 | | | 18/12/18 |
| Lieut. R. D. WALKER. | 25/8/16 | | | 18/12/18 |
| 2/Lt. A. W. REYNELL. | 27/8/16 | | | 18/12/18 |
| Lieut. H. M. CORBOLD. | —/8/16 | (*Died* at Roisel 26/8/16) | | |
| 2/Lt. S. P. BRIGGS. | 27/8/16 | | | 18/12/18 |
| 2/Lt. B. M. WAINWRIGHT. | 28/8/16 | | | 1/1/19 |
| Lieut. H. F. MASE. | 28/8/16 | | | 18/12/18 |
| Lieut. G. V. ODLING. | 28/8/16 | Holland | 12/10/18 | 22/11/18 |
| 2/Lt. D. S. CAIRNS. | 29/8/16 | | | 18/12/18 |
| 2/Lt. K. E. TULLOCH. | 29/8/16 | Switzerland | 10/7/18 | 6/12/18 |
| Capt. O. L. WHITTLE. | 31/8/16 | | | 18/12/18 |
| 2/Lt. H. M. STRANGE. | 31/8/16 | | | 18/12/18 |
| 2/Lt. A. J. O. O'BYRNE. | 31/8/16 | Switzerland | 27/12/17 | 24/3/18 |
| 2/Lt. F. G. MACINTOSH. | 31/8/16 | Switzerland | 9/12/17 | 24/3/18 |
| 2/Lt. J. D. A. MACFIE. | 31/8/16 | Switzerland | 13/12/16 | 14/9/17 |
| Lieut. D. STEWART. | 2/9/16 | Escaped | | —/4/17 |
| 2/Lieut. F. W. GRIFFITHS. | 2/9/16 | (2/1/19—R.A.F. rep. escaped) | | |
| 2/Lt. E. BURTON. | 2/9/16 | | | 18/12/18 |
| Capt. R. E. WILSON. | 2/9/16 | | | 18/12/18 |
| Capt. H. G. SALMOND. | 2/9/16 | | | 18/12/18 |
| 2/Lt. A. F. ORGAN. | | | | 18/12/18 |
| 2/Lt. F. D. H. SAMS. | 3/9/16 | | | 18/12/18 |
| 2/Lt. J. C. TAYLOR. | 6/9/16 | Switzerland | 27/12/17 | 9/12/18 |
| 2/Lt. J. N. TULLIS. | 6/9/16 | Escaped | | —/8/18 |
| Lieut. L. R. BRIGGS. | 11/9/16 | Switzerland | 9/12/17 | 9/12/18 |
| 2/Lt. J. V. BOWRING. | 14/9/16 | | | 16/12/18 |
| 2/Lt. C. J. KENNEDY. | 15/9/16 | | | 18/12/18 |
| Capt. J. D. F. McEWAN. | 16/7/16 | Holland | 15/6/18 | 4/1/19 |
| 2/Lt. C. A. RIDLEY. | 3/8/16 | Escaped | | 16/8/18 |

## ROYAL AIR FORCE—continued.

| Name. | Missing. | Interned. | Repatriated. |
|---|---|---|---|
| 2/Lt. F. H. BOWYER. | 15/9/16 | | 7/1/18 |
| 2/Lt. C. ELPHINSTON. | 15/9/16 | | 18/12/18 |
| 2/Lt. D. CUSHING. | 16/9/16 | | 18/12/18 |
| Lieut. G. KLINGENSTEIN. | 16/9/16 | | 7/1/18 |
| Lieut. J. W. SANDERS. | 16/9/16 | | 18/12/18 |
| 2/Lt. A. L. PINKERTON. | 16/9/16 | | 18/12/18 |
| 2/Lt. L. F. B. MORRIS. | 17/9/16 | (Died at Cambrai) | |
| Lieut. R. R. N. MONEY. | 17/9/16 | | 18/12/18 |
| Lieut. L. B. HELDER. | 17/9/16 | | 18/12/18 |
| Capt. D. B. GRAY. | 17/9/16 | Escaped | -/8/18 |
| 2/Lt. R. WOOD. | 17/9/16 | Holland 9/4/18 | 2/7/18 |
| Lieut. W. H. S. CHANCE. | 17/9/16 | | 18/12/18 |
| 2/Lt. A. F. A. PATTERSON. | 17/9/16 | (Died at Cambrai 25/9/16) | |
| 2/Lt. T. P. L. MOLLOY. | 17/9/16 | | 18/12/18 |
| 2/Lt. R. N. CARTER. | 21/9/16 | | 18/12/18 |
| 2/Lt. W. J. GRAY. | 21/9/16 | | 21/1/19 |
| 2/Lt. F. A. A. HEWSON. | 22/9/16 | | 18/12/18 |
| 2/Lt. R. D. HERMAN. | 22/9/16 | (Died at Epehy) | |
| 2/Lt. J. L. TIBBETTS. | 23/9/16 | | 30/12/18 |
| 2/Lt. E. N. WINGFIELD. | 24/9/16 | Holland 12/10/18 | 29/1/19 |
| 2/Lt. S. DENDRINO. | 27/9/16 | (Died 27/9/16) | |
| Leiut. J. H. LOWSON. | 27/9/16 | | 18/12/18 |
| 2/Lt. M. S. FARADAY. | 27/9/16 | | 18/12/18 |
| 2/Lt. A. T. EASON. | 28/9/16 | | 18/12/18 |
| 2/Lt. W. R. C. CARMICHAEL. | 2/10/16 | Switzerland 17/12/17 | 24/3/18 |
| 2/Lt. C. KENNARD. | 9/10/16 | Escaped | -/8/18 |
| Lieut. G. WADDEN. | 10/10/16 | | 18/12/18 |
| Lieut. J. B. LAWTON. | 10/10/16 | | 18/12/18 |
| Lieut. A. H. M. COPELAND. | 10/10/16 | | 14/12/18 |
| 2/Lt. N. MIDDLEBROOK. | 11/10/16 | | 18/12/18 |
| 2/Lt. A. R. CRISP. | 16/10/16 | | 18/12/18 |
| 2/Lt. C. MOORE KELLY. | 16/10/16 | | 20/1/18 |
| 2/Lt. C. L. ROBERTS. | 17/10/16 | | -/12/18 |
| 2/Lt. J. K. PARKER. | 17/10/16 | | -/1/19 |
| Lieut. W. H. N. WHITEHEAD. | 19/10/16 | | 27/1/19 |
| 2/Lt. R. L. DINGLEY. | 19/10/16 | | 17/12/18 |
| 2/Lt. W. BLACK. | 20/10/16 | Switzerland 27/12/17 | 14/6/18 |
| Lieut. A. B. RAYMOND-BARKER. | 21/10/16 | | 18/12/18 |
| 2/Lt. A. L. M. SHEPHERD. | 22/10/16 | (Died at Vitry 3/11/16) | |
| 2/Lt. W. T. WILLCOX. | 22/10/16 | | 18/12/18 |
| 2/Lt. R. WATTS. | 22/10/16 | | 27/1/19 |
| 2/Lt. P. F. HEPPEL. | 27/10/16 | Holland 9/4/18 | 18/8/18 |
| 2/Lt. H. B. O. MITCHELL. | 27/10/16 | Holland 9/4/18 | 16/8/18 |
| Lieut. T. M. JOHNS. | 31/10/16 | | 18/12/18 |
| Lieut. G. H. NICHOLSON. | 31/10/16 | | 18/12/18 |
| 2/Lt. W. E. KNOWLDEN. | 3/11/16 | | 18/12/18 |
| Lieut. A. ANDERSON. | 3/11/16 | | -/12/18 |
| 2/Lt. L. C. L. COOK. | 3/11/16 | Holland 9/4/18 | 4/10/18 |
| 2/Lt. H. A. HALLAM. | 9/11/16 | | 18/12/18 |
| 2/Lt. B. W. A. ORDISH. | 9/11/16 | Holland 9/4/18 | 7/9/18 |
| Lieut. G. F. KNIGHT. | 9/11/16 | Escaped | 13/9/17 |
| Capt. T. MAPPLEBECK. | 9/11/16 | | 29/1/19 |
| 2/Lt. T. CURLEWIS. | 9/11/16 | | 7/1/18 |
| Capt. A. C. BOLTON. | 9/11/16 | | 7/1/18 |
| Lieut. T. H. CLARKE. | 20/11/16 | | 17/12/18 |
| 2/Lt. J. C. LEES. | 20/11/16 | | 1/1/19 |
| 2/Lt. K. F. HUNT. | 22/9/16 | | 18/12/18 |
| 2/Lt. H. F. EVANS. | 9/11/16 | | 2/6/18 |

**ROYAL AIR FORCE**—continued.

| Name. | Missing. | Interned. | Rapatriated. |
|---|---|---|---|
| Lieut. R. CORBETT. | 22/11/16 | Switzerland 27/12/17 | 24/3/18 |
| 2/Lt. B. W. BLAYNEY. | 24/11/16 | | 30/12/18 |
| 2/Lt. W. B. CLARK. | 26/11/16 | | -/12/18 |
| 2/Lt. G. S. DEANE. | 26/11/16 | | 17/12/18 |
| Lieut. B. P. G. HUNT. | 11/12/16 | Holland 9/4/18 | 18/11/18 |
| Lieut. C. H. WINDRUM. | 20/12/16 | | -/12/18 |
| Lieut. J. A. HOLLIS. | 20/12/16 | | 17/12/18 |
| 2/Lt. D. W. DAVIS. | 21/12/16 | Holland 7/5/18 | 27/11/18 |
| 2/Lt. F. N. INSOLL. | 26/12/16 | | -/12/18 |
| 2/Lt. F. A. MANN. | 7/1/17 | | 18/12/18 |
| 2/Lt. J. E. McLENNAN. | 24/1/17 | | 2/1/19 |
| Capt. O. GREIG. | 24/1/17 | | 22/12/18 |
| 2/Lt. S. ALDER. | 25/1/17 | | -/12/18 |
| Lieut. R. W. WHITE. | 25/1/17 | | 28/11/18 |
| 2/Lt. F. H. BRONSKILL. | 28/1/17 | | 2/1/19 |
| Lieut. C. B. BIRD. | 28/1/17 | | -/12/18 |
| 2/Lt. W. A. REEVES. | 1/2/17 | Retained in Germany for duty | |
| Lieut. T. G. HOLLEY. | 2/2/17 | | 14/12/18 |
| 2/Lt. R. T. WHITNEY. | 2/2/17 | | -/1/19 |
| Capt. A. P. V. DALY. | -/2/17 | Holland 7/5/18 | 31/8/18 |
| 2/Lt. H. BLYTHE. | 2/2/17 | (*Died* at Croissiles 10/2/17) | |
| Flight Sub-Lt. G. BOWLES. | | (Interned in Holland) | |
| Flight Sub-Lt. BRANTFORD. | | (Interned in Holland) | |
| 2/Lt. M. E. WOODS. | 6/2/17 | | 30/12/18 |
| 2/Lt. J. V. FAIRBAIRN. | 14/2/17 | Holland 15/4/18 | 18/8/18 |
| Lieut. C. H. MARCH. | 15/2/17 | | 2/1/19 |
| Capt. A. LEES. | 4/3/17 | | 14/12/18 |
| 2/Lt. M.J.J.G. MARE-MONTEMBAULT. | 5/3/17 | | -/1/19 |
| 2/Lt. A. G. RYALL. | 6/3/17 | | 14/12/18 |
| Lieut. F. E. HILLS. | 6/3/17 | | 17/12/18 |
| 2/Lt. V. O. LONSDALE. | 6/3/17 | | 28/11/18 |
| Capt. W. S. R. BLOOMFIELD. | 6/3/17 | | 2/1/19 |
| Lieut. H. G. SOUTHON. | 6/3/17 | Switzerland 29/12/17 | -/5/18 |
| 2/Lt. T. SHEPARD. | 9/3/17 | | 1/1/19 |
| 2/Lt. W. B. HILLS. | 9/3/17 | | 17/12/18 |
| 2/Lt. G. F. HASELER | 9/3/17 | | 17/12/18 |
| Lieut. A. D. WHITEHEAD. | 11/3/17 | | 20/1/18 |
| 2/Lt. A. HOLDEN. | 11/3/17 | | 1/1/19 |
| 2/Lt. C. A. R. SHUM. | 11/3/17 | | 15/12/18 |
| 2/Lt. R. W. CROSS. | 17/3/17 | | 22/12/18 |
| Lieut. W. ANDERSON. | 17/3/17 | | -/1/19 |
| Lieut. C. F. LODGE. | 17/3/17 | | 31/12/18 |
| Lieut. D. B. WOOLLEY. | 17/3/17 | | -/1/19 |
| 2/Lt. P. E. H. VanBAERLE. | 18/3/17 | | 17/12/18 |
| Lieut. S. HARRYMAN. | 18/3/17 | (*Died* at Hambaline) | |
| 2/Lt. C. R. DOUGALL. | 18/3/17 | | 2/1/19 |
| Lieut. F. H. WILSON. | 19/3/17 | | 31/12/18 |
| 2/Lt. T. W. JAY. | 19/3/17 | | 18/12/18 |
| 2/Lt. S. S. B. PURVES. | 19/3/17 | Escaped | -/8/18 |
| Lieut. J. R. MIDDLETON. | 24/3/17 | (*Died* at Mulheim 21/6/17) | |
| Lieut. H. S. WHITESIDE. | 24/3/17 | | 11/1/19 |
| Capt. W. H. COSTELLO. | 24/3/17 | | 2/1/19 |
| Lieut. C. G. GILBERT. | 25/3/17 | | 2/12/18 |
| Lieut. R. P. BAKER. | 25/3/17 | | 22/12/18 |
| Lieut. C. S. VANE TEMPEST. | 25/3/17 | (*Died* at Ligny 27/3/17) | |
| Lieut. F. ALLINSON. | 25/3/17 | (*Died* at Ligny 27/3/17) | |
| 2/Lt. C. D. BENNETT. | 14/2/17 | | 6/12/18 |
| 2/Lt. F. C. COOPS. | 11/3/17 | | 18/12/18 |

**ROYAL AIR FORCE**—continued.

| Name. | Missing. | Interned. | Repatriated. |
|---|---|---|---|
| Sub-Lieut. H. W. OWEN. | 28/3/17 | | 14/1/19 |
| 2/Lt. N. L. KNIGHT. | 28/3/17 | | 14/12/18 |
| 2/Lt. L. A. T. STRANGE. | 31/3/17 | | 31/12/18 |
| 2/Lt. A. P. WARREN. | 2/4/17 | | 17/12/18 |
| 2/Lt. N. C. DENISON. | 2/4/17 | | 3/1/19 |
| Capt. H. TOMLINSON. | 2/4/17 | (*Died* at Oignies) | |
| Lt.-Col. C. E. H. RATHBONE. | —//417 | Escaped | —/8/18 |
| Lieut. G. P. HARDING. | —/4/17 | Escaped | —/10/17 |
| Lieut. L. DODSON. | 3/4/17 | | 22/12/18 |
| 2/Lt. S. A. SHARPE. | 3/4/17 | | 3/1/19 |
| 2/Lt. D. P. MacDONALD. | 3/4/17 | | —/12/18 |
| 2/Lt. E. L. HEYWORTH. | 3/4/17 | | 18/8/18 |
| 2/Lt. C. P. THORNTON. | 5/4/17 | | 25/12/18 |
| 2/Lt. E. D. WARBURTON. | 5/4/17 | | 14/12/18 |
| Capt. W. L. ROBINSON. | 5/4/17 | (*Died* 31/12/18) | 14/12/18 |
| Lieut. A. T. ADAMS. | 5/4/17 | | 14/12/18 |
| Lieut. D. J. STEWART. | 5/4/17 | | 31/12/18 |
| 2/Lt. W. T. B. TASKER. | 5/4/17 | | 17/12/18 |
| Lieut. H. A. COOPER. | 5/4/17 | | 20/1/18 |
| Lieut. H. D. K. GEORGE. | 5/4/17 | (*Died*) | |
| 2/Lt. A. BOLDISON. | 5/4/17 | | 2/1/19 |
| Lieut. N. A. BIRKS. | 5/4/17 | | 14/12/18 |
| 2/Lt. V. C. MORRIS. | 6/4/17 | | 2/1/19 |
| 2/Lt. H. D. HAMILTON. | 6/4/17 | | 1/1/19 |
| 2/Lt. A. R. M. RICKARDS. | 6/4/17 | | 14/12/18 |
| Lieut. E. J. D. TOWNESEND. | 6/4/17 | | 20/1/18 |
| 2/Lt. M. LEWIS. | 6/4/17 | | 17/12/18 |
| Lieut. R. T. B. SCHREIBER. | 6/4/17 | | —/12/18 |
| Lieut. T. F. BURRILL. | 6/4/17 | | 14/12/18 |
| Lieut. J. K. BOUSFIELD. | 6/4/17 | Holland | 4/8/18 Escaped |
| 2/Lt. A. C. PEPPER. | 6/4/17 | | 17/12/18 |
| Capt. M. B. KNOWLES. | 7/4/17 | | 17/12/18 |
| Lieut. R. J. BEVINGTON. | 7/4/17 | | 17/11/18 |
| 2/Lt. D. C. BIRCH. | 8/4/17 | | 18/12/18 |
| 2/Lt. L. BUTLER. | 8/4/17 | | 31/12/18 |
| 2/Lt. R. A. LOGAN. | 8/4/17 | | 2/1/19 |
| Lieut. F. R. HENRY. | 8/4/17 | | 14/12/18 |
| 2/Lt. E. A. V. BELL. | 8/4/17 | | 11/12/18 |
| 2/Lt. J. S. HEAGERTY. | 8/4/17 | | 17/12/18 |
| Lieut. A. H. K. McCALLUM. | 8/4/17 | | 16/12/18 |
| 2/Lt. H. E. HERVEY. | 8/4/17 | | 17/12/18 |
| 2/Lt. F. B. GOODISON. | 8/4/17 | (*Died* at Mainz 26/5/17) | |
| 2/Lt. S. ROCHE. | 11/4/17 | | 17/12/18 |
| 2/Lt. F. MATTHEWS. | 11/4/17 | | 2/1/19 |
| 2/Lt. G. N. BROCKHURST. | 11/4/17 | | 31/12/18 |
| 2/Lt. C. B. BOUGHTON. | 11/4/17 | | 31/12/18 |
| Capt. D. W. TIDMARSH. | 11/4/17 | | —/12/18 |
| 2/Lt. C. B. HOLLAND. | 11/4/17 | | 30/12/18 |
| 2/Lt. R. E. ADENEY. | 11/4/17 | (*Died* at Douai) | |
| 2/Lt. E. T. DUNFORD. | 11/4/17 | (*Died* at Douai) | |
| Lieut. A. TODD. | 12/4/17 | (*Died*) | |
| Lieut. O. D. MAXTED. | 12/4/17 | | 2/1/19 |
| 2/Lt. H. D. DAVIES. | 13/4/17 | | 17/12/18 |
| 2/Lt. R. S. L. WORSLEY. | 13/4/17 | | 1/1/19 |
| Lieut. W. H. GREEN. | 13/4/17 | Switzerland 21/10/18 | 8/12/18 |
| 2/Lt. C. W. D. HOLMES. | 14/4/17 | | 14/12/18 |
| 2/Lt. A. N. LECKLER. | 5/4/17 | Holland 9/4/18 | 7/9/18 |

## ROYAL AIR FORCE—continued.

| Name. | Missing. | Interned. | Repatriated. |
|---|---|---|---|
| Lieut. H. R. DAVIES. | 14/4/17 | | 18/12/18 |
| Lieut. W. O. RUSSELL. | 14/4/17 | | 2/1/19 |
| Lieut. J. R. SAMUEL. | 14/4/17 | | 2/1/19 |
| 2/Lt. E. R. LAW. | 14/4/17 | | 31/12/18 |
| Capt. A. BINNIE. | 14/4/17 | | 7/1/18 |
| Lieut. W. HARLE. | 14/4/17 | Switzerland 27/12/17 | 14/6/18 |
| 2/Lt. A. WATSON. | 14/4/17 | | 19/5/18 |
| 2/Lt. A. E. CRISP. | 20/4/17 | | -/12/18 |
| 2/Lt. G. A. NEWENHAM. | 20/4/17 | | -/12/18 |
| 2/Lt. F. C. CRAIG. | 22/4/17 | | 14/12/18 |
| 2/Lt. K. R. FURNISS. | 22/4/17 | (*Died* at Cambrai 31/4/17) | |
| Lieut. A. W. WOOD. | 22/4/17 | | 7/12/18 |
| 2/Lt. J. G. H. FREW. | -/4/17 | | 23/2/18 |
| 2/Lt. R. S. CAPON. | 24/4/17 | | 31/12/18 |
| Lieut. G. E. HICKS. | 24/4/17 | | 17/12/18 |
| Lieut. E. J. DILLNUTT. | 25/4/17 | | 14/12/18 |
| 2/Lt. J. D. M. STEWART. | 25/4/17 | | 17/12/18 |
| 2/Lt. G. O. McENTEE. | 26/4/17 | | -/12/18 |
| Lieut. G. M. HOPKINS. | 26/4/17 | | 17/12/18 |
| 2/Lt. J. H. PRICE. | 26/4/17 | | 30/12/18 |
| Capt. H. R. HAWKINS. | 26/4/17 | | 14/12/18 |
| Lieut. A. V. BURBURY. | 26/4/17 | | 14/12/18 |
| 2/Lt. F. STEDMAN. | 27/4/17 | | 1/1/19 |
| 2/Lt. J. A. CAIRNS. | 27/4/17 | | 3/1/19 |
| 2/Lt. F. J. KIRKHAM. | 28/4/17 | | 31/12/18 |
| 2/Lt. A. A. BAERLEIN. | 28/4/17 | | 25/12/18 |
| 2/Lt. J. V. WISCHER. | 28/4/17 | | 6/1/19 |
| Lieut. D. K. PARIS. | 28/4/17 | | 1/1/19 |
| 2/Lt. C. REECE. | 28/4/17 | | 16/1/19 |
| 2/Lt. V. L. A. BURNS. | 29/4/17 | | 25/12/18 |
| 2/Lt. E. PERCIVAL. | 29/4/17 | | 14/12/18 |
| 2/Lt. F. A. W. HANDLEY. | 29/4/17 | | 31/12/18 |
| Lieut. H. B. MILLING. | 29/4/17 | | 31/12/18 |
| 2/Lt. D. L. HOUGHTON. | 29/4/17 | | 28/11/18 |
| Lieut. W. N. HAMILTON. | 29/4/17 | | 1/1/19 |
| 2/Lt. J. E. DAVIES. | 29/4/17 | | -/12/18 |
| 2/Lt. R. H. UPSON. | 30/4/17 | | 31/12/18 |
| Lieut. J. R. LINGARD. | 30/4/17 | | 31/12/18 |
| 2/Lt. S. T. WILLS. | 30/4/17 | | 17/12/18 |
| 2/Lt. A. E. FEREMAN. | 30/4/17 | | 2/1/19 |
| Lieut. P. T. BOWERS. | 30/4/17 | | 14/12/18 |
| 2/Lt. E. D. JENNINGS. | 30/4/17 | | 30/12/18 |
| 2/Lt. D. McTAVISH. | 30/4/17 | | 1/1/19 |
| 2/Lt. H. KIRBY. | | | -/1/19 |
| Lieut. C. R. O'BRIEN. | 1/5/17 | | -/12/18 |
| 2/Lt. E. L. EDWARDS. | 1/5/17 | | 18/12/18 |
| Lieut. G. S. FRENCH. | 1/5/17 | | 14/12/18 |
| 2/Lt. A. FRASER. | 3/5/17 | | 22/12/18 |
| 2/Lt. V. H. ADAMS. | 4/5/17 | (*Died* 5/5/17) | |
| 2/Lt. L. G. BACON. | 5/5/17 | | 7/1/18 |
| 2/Lt. G. D. HUNTER. | 6/5/17 | | 20/1/18 |
| 2/Lt. C. W. McKISSOCK. | 6/5/17 | | 17/12/18 |
| 2/Lt. A. W. MARTIN. | 7/5/17 | | 30/12/18 |
| 2/Lt. M. M. KAIZER. | 7/5/17 | | 25/12/18 |
| Lieut. J. B. B. de M. **HARVEY.** | 9/5/17 | | 17/12/18 |
| 2/Lt. F. D. WOOLLIAMS. | 9/5/17 | | 17/12/18 |

## ROYAL AIR FORCE—continued.

| Name. | Missing. | Interned. | Repatriated. |
|---|---|---|---|
| 2/Lt. C. W. LANE. | 9/5/17 | | 2/1/19 |
| 2/Lt. C. A. FURLONGER. | 9/5/17 | | 3/1/19 |
| 2/Lt. G. C. T. HADRILL. | 9/5/17 | | 1/1/19 |
| Lieut. T. H. WICKETT. | 10/5/17 | | 3/6/18 |
| 2/Lt. W. O. B. WINKLER. | 11/5/17 | | 30/12/18 |
| 2/Lt. J. DANIEL. | 11/5/17 | | 2/1/19 |
| 2/Lt. E. S. MOORE. | 11/5/17 | | 1/1/19 |
| Lieut. A. B. RAYMOND. | 13/5/17 | | -/1/19 |
| 2/Lt. A. M. SUTHERLAND. | 13/5/17 | | 1/1/19 |
| Sub-Lieut. E. J. GROUT. | 15/5/17 | | 12/12/18 |
| 2/Lt. J. D. V. HOLMES. | 18/5/17 | | 2/1/19 |
| 2/Lt. T. H. LINES. | 18/5/17 | | 14/12/18 |
| 2/Lt. S. T. ALLABARTON. | 19/5/17 | | 3/1/19 |
| Lieut. C. E. FRENCH. | 20/5/17 | | 14/12/18 |
| Lieut. A. C. LEE. | 20/5/17 | | 1/1/19 |
| Lieut. J. H. BLACKALL. | 21/5/17 | | 17/12/18 |
| 2/Lt. B. C. MOODY. | 21/5/17 | | 17/12/18 |
| Lieut. R. A. P. JOHNS. | 23/5/17 | | -/1/19 |
| Capt. L. A. SMITH. | 24/5/17 | Switzerland 27/12/17 | 14/6/18 |
| Lieut. C. C. F. OSBORN. | 24/5/17 | | 17/12/18 |
| Lieut. J. H. H. GOODALL. | 24/5/17 | | 1/1/19 |
| 2/Lt. L. HOLMAN. | 24/5/17 | | 17/12/18 |
| 2/Lt. W. GILCHRIST. | 25/5/17 | | 17/11/18 |
| 2/Lt. T. S. MILLAR. | 25/5/17 | | -/12/18 |
| 2/Lt. J. JOHNSTONE. | 25/5/17 | | 2/1/19 |
| 2/Lt. R. R. MacINTOSH. | 26/5/17 | | -/12/18 |
| 2/Lt. Y. TOOGOOD. | 26/5/17 | Switzerland 27/12/17 | 24/3/18 |
| Lieut. C. F. SMITH. | 26/5/17 | | 14/12/18 |
| 2/Lt. G. M. ROBERTSON. | 26/5/17 | Switzerland 27/12/17 | 7/12/18 |
| Lieut. S. S. HUME. | 27/5/17 | | 28/8/18 |
| 2/Lt. E. A. L. LLOYD. | 27/5/17 | | 2/1/19 |
| Lieut. T. N. SOUTNORN. | 27/5/17 | | 17/12/18 |
| Lieut. V. SMITH. | 28/5/17 | | -/12/18 |
| 2/Lt. E. H. STEVENS. | 28/5/17 | (*Died* at Tournai 16/6/17) | |
| Capt. A. DE SELINCOURT. | 28/5/17 | | 17/12/18 |
| Lieut. H. COTTON. | 28/5/17 | | 14/12/18 |
| Lieut. R. M. ROBERTS. | 28/5/17 | | 17/12/18 |
| Lieut. F. W. KANTEL. | 30/5/17 | | 14/12/18 |
| 2/Lt. B. S. LISTER. | 1/6/17 | | 14/12/18 |
| Lieut. E. A. STEWARDSON. | 1/6/17 | | 30/12/18 |
| 2/Lt. F. BARRIE. | 2/6/17 | | 31/12/18 |
| 2/Lt. H. E. WATERS. | 2/6/17 | | 14/12/18 |
| Lieut. D. R. CAMERON. | 3/6/17 | | 14/12/18 |
| Lieut. A. S. BOURINOT. | 3/6/17 | | 14/12/18 |
| 2/Lt. D. T. STEEVES. | 4/6/17 | | 17/12/18 |
| 2/Lt. C. D. GRIERSON. | 5/6/17 | | 17/12/18 |
| Lieut. B. SMITH. | 5/6/17 | | 17/12/18 |
| 2/Lt. B. G. CHALMERS. | 5/6/17 | | 26/12/18 |
| Capt. F. P. DON. | 5/6/17 | | -/1/18 |
| 2/Lt. H. HARRIS. | 5/6/17 | | 17/12/18 |
| Lieut. T. M. DICKINSON. | 6/6/17 | | 19/1/19 |
| 2/Lt. F. DURKIN. | 7/6/17 | | 18/12/18 |
| Lieut. A. P. MITCHELL. | 7/6/17 | | 2/1/19 |
| 2/Lt. COUNT L. T. B. DI BALME. | 7/6/17 | | 14/12/18 |
| 2/Lt. N. B. HAIR. | 7/6/17 | | 17/12/18 |
| 2/Lt. F. W. ILLINGWORTH. | 7/6/17 | | -/12/18 |

**ROYAL AIR FORCE**—continued.

| Name. | Missing. | Interned. | Repatriated. |
|---|---|---|---|
| Lieut. J. W. SHAW. | 7/6/17 | | 17/12/18 |
| 2/Lt. R. M. MARSH. | 7/6/17 | | 17/12/18 |
| 2/Lt. G. C. STEAD. | 7/6/17 | | —/1/19 |
| 2/Lt. R. S. L. BOOTE. | 8/6/17 | | 18/12/18 |
| 2/Lt. F. D. SLEE. | 8/6/17 | | 5/12/18 |
| Lieut. F. SHARPE. | 9/6/17 | | 2/1/19 |
| 2/Lt. W. J. MUSSARED. | 9/6/17 | | 15/12/18 |
| Lieut. H. ROGERSON. | 14/6/17 | | 31/12/18 |
| Lieut. W. T. COLES. | 17/6/17 | | 31/12/18 |
| Lieut. H. D. SPEARPOINT. | 17/6/17 | | 17/12/18 |
| Capt. T. DAVIDSON. | 19/6/17 | | 14/12/18 |
| 2/Lt. G. C. ATKINS. | 19/6/17 | | 5/12/18 |
| 2/Lt. G. T. HARKER. | 23/6/17 | | 28/12/18 |
| 2/Lt. T. M. STURGESS. | 24/6/17 | | 17/12/18 |
| 2/Lt. F. E. VIPOND. | 26/6/17 | | 17/12/18 |
| Lieut. D. C. G. MURRAY. | 27/6/17 | Switzerland 27/12/17 | 9/12/18 |
| Lieut. G. P. SIMON. | 27/6/17 | | 2/1/19 |
| Lieut. V. A. NORVILL. | 29/6/17 | | 8/1/18 |
| Lieut. J. C. MacGOWN. | 7/7/17 | | 17/12/18 |
| 2/Lt. A. J. SAVORY. | 11/7/17 | | 2/1/19 |
| 2/Lt. R. TRATTLES. | 11/7/17 | | 31/12/18 |
| 2/Lt. W. A. STRICKLAND. | 12/7/17 | | 31/12/18 |
| 2/Lt. H. M. LEWIS. | 12/7/17 | | 17/12/18 |
| Lieut. D. S. WELD. | 12/7/17 | | 14/12/18 |
| 2/Lt. J. C. GRIFFITH. | 12/7/17 | | 25/12/18 |
| 2/Lt. W. C. SMITH. | 13/7/17 | | 7/1/18 |
| Lieut. C. G. MATHEW. | 13/7/17 | | 17/12/18 |
| Lieut. F. W. WINTERBOTHAM. | 13/7/17 | | 6/1/19 |
| Capt. F. N. HUDSON. | 13/7/17 | | 19/12/18 |
| Lieut. E. D. SLITER. | 13/7/17 | | 19/5/18 |
| 2/Lt. D. H. PALMER. | 14/7/17 | | 17/12/18 |
| 2/Lt. N. H. MARSHALL. | 14/7/17 | | 14/1/19 |
| 2/Lt. G. DAVIS. | 14/7/17 | | 18/12/18 |
| 2/Lt. V. C. COOMBS. | 15/7/17 | | 14/12/18 |
| 2/Lt. H. M. TAYLER. | 15/7/17 | | 20/1/18 |
| 2/Lt. G. A. H. PARKES. | 15/7/17 | | 23/12/18 |
| 2/Lt. C. T. FELTON. | 17/7/17 | | 20/1/18 |
| Lieut. O. J. PARTINGTON. | 17/7/17 | | 2/1/19 |
| Lieut. W. E. GROSSERT. | 17/7/17 | | 23/12/18 |
| 2/Lt. J. C. TRULOCK. | 22/7/17 | | 25/8/18 |
| Lieut. C. C. KNIGHT. | 22/7/17 | Holland 30/4/18 | 18/11/18 |
| Lieut. M. MOORE. | 22/7/17 | | 1/1/19 |
| Capt. G. H. COCK. | 23/7/17 | | —/12/18 |
| Lieut. W. D. CULLEN. | | | 14/12/18 |
| 2/Lt. A. B. HILL. | 24/7/17 | | 14/12/18 |
| Lieut. W. B. MACKAY. | 27/7/17 | | 14/12/18 |
| 2/Lt. J. CHAPMAN. | 27/7/17 | | —/1/19 |
| 2/Lt. T. W. WHITE. | 27/7/17 | | 25/12/18 |
| 2/Lt. A. S. SHEPHERD. | 27/7/17 | (*Died* at Fandvoorde) | |
| 2/Lt. J. B. HINE. | 28/7/17 | | 2/1/19 |
| 2/Lt. R. C. HUME. | 28/7/17 | | 2/1/19 |
| Capt. H. O. D. WILKINS. | 28/7/17 | | 14/12/18 |
| Lieut. A. C. MALLOCH. | 28/7/17 | | 14/12/18 |
| Lieut. H. O. MACDONALD. | 29/7/17 | | 16/1/19 |
| Lieut. C. H. BELDAM. | 31/7/17 | | 28/12/18 |
| 2/Lt. W. B. KELLOG. | 31/7/17 | | 13/12/18 |

## ROYAL AIR FORCE—continued.

| Name. | Missing. | Interned. | Repatriated. |
|---|---|---|---|
| Lt. M. T. WRIGHT. | 16/8/17 | | 8/12/18 |
| Lt. C. B. WATERS. | 16/8/17 | | 19/12/18 |
| 2/Lt. W. H. WATT. | 31/7/17 | | –/1/19 |
| Lieut. H. J. ELLAM. | 5/8/17 | | 29/11/18 |
| Lieut. C. A. S. BEAN. | 9/8/17 | | –/1/19 |
| Lieut. W. H. HOWES. | 9/8/17 | | 17/12/18 |
| 2/Lt. W. R. K. SKINNER. | 9/8/17 | | 17/12/18 |
| 2/Lt. J. F. HENDERSON. | 10/8/17 | | 2/1/19 |
| Lieut. E. P. FULTON. | 10/8/17 | | 14/12/18 |
| 2/Lt. A. N. BARLOW. | 10/8/17 | | 2/1/19 |
| 2/Lt. C. G. MALLOUS. | 10/8/17 | | 25/12/18 |
| Lieut. C. D. HUTCHINSON. | 10/8/17 | (*Died* at Menlebeke 12/8/17) | |
| 2/Lt. R. N. W. JEFF. | 11/8/17 | | –/12/18 |
| 2/Lt. H. G. TINNEY. | 11/8/17 | | 6/1/19 |
| 2/Lt. G. COLLEDGE. | 11/8/17 | | 18/12/18 |
| 2/Lt. C. G. GUY. | 11/8/17 | (*Died* Wynendaele 12/8/17) | |
| 2/Lt. L. READ. | 12/8/17 | | 17/12/18 |
| 2/Lt. J. G. YOUNG. | 14/8/17 | | 2/1/19 |
| Capt. A. R. HUDSON. | 16/8/17 | | 29/11/18 |
| 2/Lt. A. T. SHIPWRIGHT. | 16/8/17 | | 25/12/18 |
| Lieut. C. D. THOMPSON. | 16/8/17 | | 25/12/18 |
| Lieut. A. E. S. BARTON. | 16/8/17 | | 27/12/18 |
| 2/Lt. G. M. SMITH. | 16/8/17 | | 5/1/19 |
| 2/Lt. P. A. O'BRIEN. | 17/8/17 | Escaped | –/11/17 |
| 2/Lt. R. S. PHELAN. | 17/8/17 | | 17/12/18 |
| Lieut. D. S. WILKINSON. | 17/8/17 | (*Died* Kortryk 26/8/17) | |
| Lieut. R. T. LEIGHTON. | 17/8/17 | | –/1/19 |
| 2/Lt. G. A. ROSE. | 18/8/17 | | 2/1/19 |
| 2/Lt. W. B. STYLES. | 18/8/17 | | 17/12/18 |
| Capt. H. N. RUSHWORTH. | 18/8/17 | | 12/10/18 |
| Lieut. H. R. HART-DAVIES. | 19/8/17 | | 28/11/18 |
| 2/Lt. S. F. THOMPSON. | 19/8/17 | | 6/1/19 |
| 2/Lt. C. R. RICHARDS. | 19/8/17 | | 2/1/19 |
| 2/Lt. H. E. A. WARING. | 19/8/17 | | –/1/19 |
| 2/Lt. C. P. ADAMSON. | 20/8/17 | | 18/12/18 |
| 2/Lt. Sidney THOMPSON. | 21/8/17 | | 17/12/18 |
| 2/Lt. C. W. DAVIES. | 21/8/17 | | 17/12/18 |
| Lieut. W. B. HUTCHESON. | 21/8/17 | | 14/12/18 |
| Lieut. J. A. MANNERS SMITH. | 21/8/17 | | –/12/18 |
| 2/Lt. E. H. GARLAND. | 22/8/17 | | –/11/18 |
| 2/Lt. L. WIGLEY. | 23/8/17 | | 19/12/18 |
| 2/Lt. H. G. TAMBLING. | 23/8/17 | | 14/12/1-8 |
| Lieut. J. B. C. MADGE. | 1/9/17 | | 17/12/18 |
| 2/Lt. W. A. L. SPENCER. | 2/9/17 | | 30/11/18 |
| Lieut. S. W. WILLIAMS. | 3/9/17 | | 17/12/18 |
| Lieut. A. F. BIRD. | 3/9/17 | | 14/12/18 |
| Lieut. K. W. MACDONALD. | 3/9/17 | (*Died* at Menin) | |
| 2/Lt. A. C. PICKETT. | 3/9/17 | | 2/1/19 |
| 2/Lt. F. SCARBOROUGH. | 3/9/17 | | 17/12/18 |
| Capt. C. C. SHARP. | 4/9/17 | | 2/1/19 |
| Lieut. S. A. HARPER. | 4/9/17 | | 2/1/19 |
| 2/Lt. T. M. WEBSTER. | 5/9/17 | | 14/12/18 |
| Lieut. J. W. F. NEILL. | 5/9/17 | Holland  9/4/18 | 31/8/18 |
| 2/Lt. J. C. HUGGARD. | 5/9/17 | | 14/12/18 |
| 2/Lt. E. G. C. QUILTER. | 6/9/17 | | 18/12/18 |
| 2/Lt. W. E. DE B. DIAMOND. | 9/9/17 | | 18/12/18 |
| Lieut. N. C. SAWARD. | 9/9/17 | | 6/1/19 |
| 2/Lt. G. P. ROBERTSON. | 10/9/17 | | 25/12/18 |
| 2/Lt. D. P. COLLIS. | 10/8/17 | | 4/1/19 |
| 2/Lt. J. W. GILLESPIE. | 19/8/17 | | 2/1/19 |

**ROYAL AIR FORCE**—continued.

| Name. | Missing. | Interned. | | Repatriated. |
|---|---|---|---|---|
| 2/Lt. A. F. ORR-EWING | 20/9/17 | | | 3/1/19 |
| 2/Lt. H. T. HAMMOND. | 14/9/17 | | | 31/12/18 |
| 2/Lt. E. B. DENISON. | 11/9/17 | | | 3/1/19 |
| Sub-Lt. E. D. ABBOTT. | 13/9/17 | | | 17/12/18 |
| 2/Lt. S. H. TAYLOR. | 14/9/17 | | | 6/1/19 |
| Lieut. E. G. C. SEN. | 14/9/17 | | | 17/12/18 |
| 2/Lt. J. B. H. WYMAN. | 15/9/17 | Holland | 7/5/18 | –/1/19 |
| 2/Lt. H. IBBOTSON. | 15/9/17 | | | 29/11/18 |
| 2/Lt. E. E. F. LOYD. | 15/9/17 | | | 17/12/18 |
| Lieut. T. G. DEASON. | 15/9/17 | | | 17/12/18 |
| 2/Lt. A. H. SKINNER. | 16/9/17 | | | 17/12/18 |
| 2/Lt. L. F. WHEELER. | 16/9/17 | | | 17/12/18 |
| Lieut. G. B. McMICHAEL. | 16/9/17 | | | –/1/19 |
| 2/Lt. L. M. SHADWELL. | 16/9/17 | | | 17/12/18 |
| 2/Lt. C. A. SUTCLIFFE. | 19/9/17 | | | 17/12/18 |
| Lieut. G. W. MUMFORD. | 19/9/17 | | | 14/12/18 |
| 2/Lt. N. J. TAYLOR. | 19/9/17 | | | 14/12/18 |
| 2/Lt. C. G. D. GRAY. | 20/9/17 | | | 14/12/18 |
| 2/Lt. C. H. F. NOBBS. | 20/9/17 | | | 2/1/19 |
| 2/Lt. T. HUMBLE. | 20/9/17 | | | 2/1/19 |
| Capt. A. C. HATFIELD. | 20/9/17 | | | 13/12/18 |
| 2/Lt. R. R. MACGREGOR. | 20/9/17 | | | –/12/18 |
| 2/Lt. D. P. FitzG. UNIACKE. | 21/9/17 | | | –/12/18 |
| 2/Lt. E. A. COOKE. | 21/9/17 | | | 19/12/18 |
| 2/Lt. G. R. BAYNTON. | 23/9/17 | | | 25/12/18 |
| 2/Lt. H. ROTHERY. | 23/9/17 | | | –/12/18 |
| 2/Lt. W. ENGLISH. | 24/9/17 | | | 14/12/18 |
| 2/Lt. M. E. HALL. | 24/9/17 | | | 14/12/18 |
| 2/Lt. P. J. CASEY. | 24/9/17 | | | 18/12/18 |
| 2/Lt. F. C. ANDREWS. | 26/9/17 | | | 5/12/18 |
| 2/Lt. C. N. L. LOMAX. | 26/9/17 | | | –/12/18 |
| 2/Lt. A. L. SUTCLIFFE. | 26/9/17 | | | 23/2/18 |
| 2/Lt. C. E. STUART. | 26/9/17 | | | 6/1/19 |
| 2/Lt. T. B. FENWICK. | 26/9/17 | | | 7/12/18 |
| 2/Lt. A. TAYLOR. | 26/9/17 | | | –/12/18 |
| 2/Lt. J. L. HAIGHT. | 28/9/17 | | | 17/12/18, |
| 2/Lt. J. W. FROST. | 29/9/17 | | | 15/11/18 |
| 2/Lt. F. L. SMITH. | 29/9/17 | | | 15/11/18 |
| Lieut. G. F. WESTCOTT. | 29/9/17 | | | –/12/18 |
| 2/Lt. E. A. V. ELLERBECK. | 29/9/17 | | | 14/12/18 |
| Lieut. J. W. BOUMPHREY. | 30/9/17 | | | 14/12/18 |
| 2/Lt. J. F. BUSHE. | 1/10/17 | | | 2/1/19 |
| 2/Lt. L. A. COLBERT. | 1/10/17 | | | 17/12/18 |
| Lieut. F. H. BERRY. | 2/10/17 | | | 14/12/18 |
| 2/Lt. C. G. CRANE. | 2/10/17 | | | 17/12/18 |
| 2/Lt. F. M. NASH. | 3/10/17 | | | 2/1/19 |
| Lieut. C. H. JEFFS. | 5/10/17 | | | 17/12/18 |
| 2/Lt. J. G. STEVENSON. | 5/10/17 | | | –/1/19 |
| 2/Lt. J. J. FITZGERALD. | 5/10/17 | | | 17/12/18 |
| Capt. D. D. WALROND-SKINNER. | 5/10/17 | | | 10/1/19 |
| Lieut. G. R. LONG. | 6/10/17 | | | 14/12/19 |
| 2/Lt. R. H. RICHARDSON. | 6/10/17 | | | 2/1/19 |
| Lieut. E. Cola CARROLL. | 6/10/17 | | | 14/12/18 |
| Lieut. W. D. CHAMBERS. | 8/10/17 | | | –/1/19 |
| 2/Lt. M. A. PEACOCK. | 9/10/17 | | | –/1/19 |
| Lieut. D. G. POWELL. | 10/10/17 | | | –/12/18 |
| Lieut. R. F. HILL. | 10/10/17 | | | –/1/19 |
| Lieut. R. I. V. HILL. | 11/10/17 | | | 14/12/18 |
| 2/Lt. K. G. CRUIKSHANK. | 11/9/17 | (Died 29/9/17). | | |
| 2/Lt. S. W. DRONSFIELD. | 12/9/17 | | | 2/1/19 |

## ROYAL AIR FORCE—continued.

| Name. | Missing. | Interned. | Repatriated. |
|---|---|---|---|
| 2/Lt. S. L. WHITEHOUSE. | 27/10/17 | | 27/11/18 |
| 2/Lt. R. S. GILBERT. | 11/10/17 | | 24/1/19 |
| 2/Lt. A. E. TURVEY. | 11/10/17 | | 6/1/19 |
| 2/Lt. W. H. WINTER. | 11/10/17 | | 13/12/18 |
| 2/Lt. W. G. MORGAN. | 12/10/17 | (Died 23/10/17) | |
| 2/Lt. W. NEWCOMB. | 12/10/17 | | 2/1/19 |
| 2/Lt. H. PUGHE-EVANS. | 12/10/17 | | 13/12/18 |
| 2/Lt. F. W. TALBOT. | 12/10/17 | Holland 9/4/18 | -/11/18 |
| 2/Lt. G. W. ARMSTRONG. | 12/10/17 | | 17/12/18 |
| 2/Lt. R. W. B. MATTHEWSON. | 12/10/17 | | 2/1/19 |
| 2/Lt. J. M. ATKINSON. | 12/10/17 | Holland 30/4/18 | 18/8/18 |
| 2/Lt. P. C. NORTON. | 13/10/17 | | 13/12/18 |
| 2/Lt. W. W. VICK. | 13/10/17 | | 13/12/18 |
| 2/Lt. J. C. GARRETT. | 14/10/17 | | 17/12/18 |
| 2/Lt. B. F. BRAITHWAITE. | 14/10/17 | | 18/12/18 |
| Lieut. C. SMYTHE. | 14/10/17 | | 25/12/18 |
| 2/Lt. A. A. WARD. | 14/10/17 | | 14/12/18 |
| 2/Lt. T. Vernon LORD. | 14/10/17 | | 2/1/19 |
| 2/Lt. H. S. WELLBY. | 15/10/17 | | -/12/18 |
| 2/Lt. F. J. ORTWEILER. | 16/10/17 | Escaped | -/10/18 |
| Fl. Sub.-Lt. M. T. WATSON. | | | 19/12/18 |
| 2/Lt. E. SCHOLTZ. | 17/10/17 | | 16/12/18 |
| 2/Lt. E. L. FOSSE. | 17/10/17 | | 19/5/18 |
| 2/Lt. H. C. WOOKEY. | 17/10/17 | | 16/12/18 |
| Lieut. S. M. PARK. | 18/10/17 | | 17/12/18 |
| 2/Lt. G. W. FORBES. | 18/10/17 | | |
| Lieut. B. B. PERRY. | 18/10/17 | | 2/1/19 |
| Capt. H. PATCH. | 18/10/17 | (Died at Bevereu 19/10/17) | |
| Lieut. C. H. BARTLETT. | 18/10/17 | | 17/12/18 |
| 2/Lt. W. E. WATTS. | 20/10/17 | | -/1/19 |
| 2/Lt. F. B. FARQUHARSON. | 20/10/17 | | 2/1/19 |
| 2/Lt. G. R. EDWARDS. | 21/10/17 | | 14/1/19 |
| 2/Lt. O. M. HILLS. | 21/10/17 | | 2/1/19 |
| 2/Lt. D. McLAURIN. | 21/10/17 | | 2/1/19 |
| 2/Lt. F. L. YEOMANS. | 21/10/17 | | 17/12/18 |
| Capt. D. OWEN. | 21/10/17 | Holland 30/4/18 | 16/8/18 |
| 2/Lt. A. E. HEMPEL. | 21/10/17 | | 17/12/18 |
| 2/Lt. B. HARKER. | 21/10/17 | | 3/6/18 |
| 2/Lt. P. GOODBEHERE. | 22/10/17 | | 17/12/18 |
| Fl. Sub.-Lt. H. G. B. LINNELL. | | | 14/12/18 |
| Lieut. J. S. GODDARD. | 24/10/17 | | 17/12/18 |
| 2/Lt. K. L. GOLDING. | 24/10/17 | | 18/8/18 |
| Lieut. R. L. GREENSLADE. | 24/10/17 | | 14/12/18 |
| 2/Lt. L. N. ARCHIBALD. | 24/10/17 | | 17/12/18 |
| 2/Lt. E. C. S. RINGER. | 25/10/17 | | 17/12/18 |
| 2/Lt. J. A. M. FLEMING. | 25/10/17 | | 5/12/18 |
| 2/Lt. E. A. L. F. SMITH. | 26/10/17 | | 17/12/18 |
| Lieut. R. J. E. P. GOODE. | 27/10/17 | | 17/12/18 |
| 2/Lt. R. A. CARTLEDGE. | 27/10/17 | | 14/12/18 |
| 2/Lt. A. W. RUSH. | 28/10/17 | | 14/12/18 |
| 2/Lt. W. H. JONES. | 29/10/17 | | 17/12/18 |
| 2/Lt. F. S. CLARK. | 29/10/17 | | 18/12/18 |
| 2/Lt. N. H. KEMP. | 31/10/17 | | 17/12/18 |
| 2/Lt. R. M. SMITH. | 31/10/17 | | 17/12/18 |
| 2/Lt. H. G. ROBINSON. | 3/11/17 | | -/12/18 |
| Lieut. T. B. BRUCE. | 6/11/17 | Escaped. | -/1/18 |
| 2/Lt. E. H. CUTBILL. | 6/11/17 | | 14/12/18 |
| 2/Lt. R. G. FRITH. | 5/11/17 | | 2/12/18 |
| 2/Lt. J. D. LAING. | 24/10/17 | (Died 28/1/18). | |

**ROYAL AIR FORCE**—continued.

| Name. | Missing. | Interned. | Repatriated. |
|---|---|---|---|
| 2/Lt. A. G. CRIBB. | 6/11/17 | | 17/12/18 |
| 2/Lt. E. P. WILMOT. | 6/11/17 | | 17/12/18 |
| 2/Lt. E. G. S. GORDON. | 6/11/17 | | 14/12/18 |
| Lieut. R. C. TAYLOR. | 6/11/17 | | 17/12/18 |
| 2/Lt. F. G. BAKER. | 6/11/17 | | 17/12/18 |
| Lieut. W. L. HARRISON. | 6/11/17 | | 27/11/18 |
| 2/Lt. W. C. PRUDEN. | 8/11/17 | | 1/12/18 |
| 2/Lt. W. R. KINGSLAND. | 8/11/17 | | –/12/18 |
| Lieut. F. R. C. COBBOLD. | 8/11/17 | | 12/12/18 |
| 2/Lt. F. J. B. HAMMERSLEY. | 8/11/17 | | 6/1/19 |
| Lieut. W. G. MEGGITT. | 8/11/17 | | 2/6/18 |
| 2/Lt. A. THOMPSON. | 9/11/17 | | 17/12/18 |
| Lieut. K. S. MORRISON. | 12/11/17 | Holland 14/4/18 | 18/8/18 |
| 2/Lt. T. P. MORGAN. | 15/11/17 | | 27/11/18 |
| 2/Lt. S. S. HENRY. | 15/11/17 | | 27/11/18 |
| Lieut. J. M. LEACH. | 15/11/17 | | 13/12/18 |
| 2/Lt. T. J. KENT. | 20/11/17 | | 14/12/18 |
| 2/Lt. M. B. W. STEAD. | 20/11/17 | | 14/12/18 |
| Lieut. T. MORSE. | 20/11/17 | | |
| Lieut. J. MacRAE. | 20/11/17 | | 14/12/18 |
| Lieut. L. N. WARD. | 20/11/17 | | 13/12/18 |
| 2/Lt. T. L. ATKINSON. | 22/11/17 | | 17/12/18 |
| Capt. G. B. CROLE. | 22/11/17 | | 18/12/18 |
| 2/Lt. E. F. MARCHAND. | 22/11/17 | | 2/1/19 |
| Lieut. C. F. KELLER. | 23/11/17 | | 17/12/18 |
| 2/Lt. R. MAIN. | 23/11/17 | | 29/12/18 |
| 2/Lt. A. MUIR. | 24/11/17 | | 17/12/18 |
| Lieut. L. KERT. | 27/11/17 | | 14/12/18 |
| 2/Lt. C. H. BROWN. | 28/11/17 | | 22/11/18 |
| Lieut. A. DODDS. | 29/11/17 | | 18/12/18 |
| 2/Lt. L. W. TIMMIS. | 30/11/17 | | 14/12/18 |
| Lieut. R. E. DUSGATE. | 30/11/17 | (Died) | |
| Capt. D. B. KING. | 30/11/17 | | 14/1/19 |
| Lieut. H. WHITWORTH. | 30/11/17 | | 17/12/18 |
| 2/Lt. G. G. W. PETERSON. | 2/12/17 | | 14/12/18 |
| 2/Lt. S. G. SPIRO. | 2/12/17 | | 17/12/18 |
| Capt. J. E. JOHNSTON. | 2/12/17 | | –/12/18 |
| 2/Lt. D. MILLER. | 2/12/17 | | 17/12/18 |
| 2/Lt. A. F. GOODCHAP. | 3/12/17 | | 14/12/18 |
| 2/Lt A. H. MIDDLETON. | 3/12/17 | | 14/12/18 |
| 2/Lt. C. E. OGDEN. | 5/12/17 | | 17/12/18 |
| 2/Lt. L. G. NIXON. | 5/12/17 | | 17/12/18 |
| 2/Lt. S. KENDALL. | 5/12/17 | | 17/12/18 |
| 2/Lt. H. A. YEO. | 7/12/17 | | 17/12/18 |
| 2/Lt. A. W. PALMER. | 7/12/17 | | 17/12/18 |
| 2/Lt. T. W. CALVERT. | 7/12/17 | | 28/12/18 |
| 2/Lt. J. A. M. ROBERTSON. | 8/12/17 | | 4/12/18 |
| Lieut. H. V. CAUNT. | 15/12/17 | | 14/12/18 |
| 2/Lt. I. D. CAMERON. | 18/12/17 | | 18/12/18 |
| 2/Lt. R. H. COWAN. | 18/12/17 | | 14/12/18 |
| Lieut. James BRENT. | | Holland. | |
| Lieut. L. B. MAY. | 19/12/17 | | 29/11/18 |
| 2/Lt. G. F. TURNER. | 24/12/17 | | 17/12/18 |
| 2/Lt. A. F. CASTLE | 24/12/17 | | 18/12/18 |
| 2/Lt A. L. CLARK. | –/12/17 | | 11/1/19 |
| 2/Lt. J. BRYDONE. | 28/12/17 | | 18/12/18 |

## ROYAL AIR FORCE—continued.

| Name. | Missing. | Interned. | Repatriated. |
|---|---|---|---|
| 2/Lt. H. E. GALER. | 29/12/17 | | 17/12/18 |
| 2/Lt. A. L. KIDD. | 1/1/18 | | 17/12/18 |
| 2/Lt. R. J. G. STEWART. | 3/1/18 | | 22/12/18 |
| 2/Lt. A. F. WYNNE. | 4/1/18 | | 17/12/18 |
| Capt. E. E. E. POPE. | 4/1/18 | | 17/12/18 |
| 2/Lt. O. THAMER. | 6/1/18 | Holland | 22/11/18 |
| Lieut. C. W. LEGGATT. | 10/1/18 | | 17/12/18 |
| 2/Lt. J. H. YOUNG. | 12/1/18 | (*Died* at Seboncourt) | |
| Lieut. J. D. BARNES. | 12/1/18 | | 20/11/18 |
| Lieut. G. N. GOLDIE. | 12/1/18 | | 21/11/18 |
| Lieut. J. BOYD. | 12/1/18 | | 18/12/18 |
| 2/Lt. T. B. URWIN. | 12/1/18 | (*Died* at Bohain) | |
| 2/Lt. F. B. WILLMOTT. | 13/1/18 | | 14/12/18 |
| 2/Lt. H. V. BIDDINGTON. | 13/1/18 | | 14/12/18 |
| 2/Lt. H. E. DAVIES. | 13/1/18 | | 14/12/18 |
| 2/Lt. A. M. OHRT. | 19/1/18 | | 17/12/18 |
| Lieut. C. W. REID. | 21/1/18 | | 17/12/18 |
| 2/Lt. F. W. DOGHERTY. | 22/1/18 | | 18/12/18 |
| 2/Lt. L. G. TAYLOR. | 21/1/18 | | 17/12/18 |
| 2/Lt. F. E. Le FEVRE. | 24/1/18 | | 17/12/18 |
| 2/Lt. H. S. CLEMONS. | 25/1/18 | | 1/12/18 |
| 2/Lt. L. J. WILLIAMS. | 28/1/18 | | 17/12/18 |
| Lieut. K. M. RODGER. | 29/1/18 | | 13/12/18 |
| 2/Lt. A. H. PEILE. | 31/1/18 | | 14/12/18 |
| Major J. F. POWELL. | 2/2/18 | | –/12/18 |
| 2/Lt. F. D. C. GORE. | 2/2/18 | | 29/12/18 |
| 2/Lt. P. C. C. MARTIN. | 3/2/18 | Escaped. | –/8/18 |
| Lieut. E. G. GREEN. | 3/2/18 | | 2/12/18 |
| 2/Lt. A. C. BALL. | 5/2/18 | | 14/12/18 |
| 2/Lt. E. O. CUDMORE. | 5/2/18 | | 18/12/18 |
| 2/Lt. A. G. D. ALDERSON. | 6/2/18 | | 17/12/18 |
| 2/Lt. A. FIELDING-CLARKE. | 9/2/18 | | 18/12/18 |
| 2/Lt. O. B. SWART. | 9/2/18 | | 17/12/18 |
| 2/Lt. G. A. C. MANLEY. | 9/2/18 | | 14/12/18 |
| Capt. S. J. SIBLEY. | 14/2/18 | | 14/12/18 |
| 2/Lt. F. C. GILBERT. | 16/2/18 | | 14/12/18 |
| 2/Lt. R. MACDONALD. | 16/2/18 | | 29/11/18 |
| 2/Lt. O. G. S. CRAWFORD. | 17/2/18 | | 17/12/18 |
| 2/Lt. C. J. W. McKEOWN. | 18/2/18 | | 17/12/18 |
| 2/Lt. G. G. JACKSON. | 18/2/18 | | 14/12/18 |
| 2/Lt. H. A. HEWITT. | 19/2/18 | | 17/12/18 |
| Lieut. W. ROSS. | 19/2/18 | | 17/12/18 |
| 2/Lt. G. C. LOGAN. | 21/2/18 | | 11/12/18 |
| 2/Lt. S. G. WILLIAMS. | 21/2/18 | Escaped. | 1/5/18 |
| 2/Lt. A. COUSTON. | 21/2/18 | | 19/12/18 |
| 2/Lt. B. C. WINDLE. | 21/2/18 | | 17/12/18 |
| 2/Lt. W. B. RANDELL. | 24/2/18 | | 14/12/18 |
| Capt. K. B. MONTGOMERY. | 22/2/18 | | 20/11/18 |
| 2/Lt. G. R. T. MARSH. | 24/2/18 | | 13/12/18 |
| 2/Lt. C. H. S. ACKERS. | 26/2/18 | | 14/12/18 |
| 2/Lt. H. F. DOUGALL. | 26/2/18 | | –/12/18 |
| Lieut. J. R. LAW. | 26/2/18 | | 14/12/18 |
| 2/Lt. J. M. ALLEN. | 26/2/18 | | 13/12/18 |
| 2/Lt. C. H. CROSBIE. | 26/2/18 | | 18/12/18 |
| 2/Lt. D. C. DOYLE. | 26/2/18 | | 14/12/18 |
| Lieut. G. M. SHAW. | 26/2/18 | | 18/12/18 |
| Capt. BIHELLER. | 19/1/18 | | 23/9/18 |
| Lt. D. C. WRIGHT. | 20/2/18 | (*Died* at Vienna 22/2/18). | |

## ROYAL AIR FORCE—continued.

| Name. | Missing. | Interned. | Repatriated. |
|---|---|---|---|
| 2/Lt. R. A. MAYNE. | 16/3/18 | | 19/12/18 |
| Flt.Sub.-Lt. K. D. CAMPBELL. | | | 14/12/18 |
| Lieut. W. F. POULTER. | 5/3/18 | (*Died* at Outreaux 6/3/18) | |
| Lieut. R. E. DUKE. | 6/3/18 | | 17/12/18 |
| 2/Lt. A. P. C. WIGAN. | 6/3/18 | | 14/12/18 |
| Lieut. R. H. TOPLISS. | 8/3/18 | | 17/12/18 |
| Lieut. H. R. CASGRAIN. | 8/3/18 | | 7/12/18 |
| 2/Lt. P. La T. FOSTER. | 9/3/18 | | 14/12/18 |
| 2/Lt. R. CALDECOTT. | 10/3/18 | | 17/12/18 |
| Lieut. C. H. FLERE. | 10/3/18 | | 14/12/18 |
| 2/Lt. E. P. P. EDMONDS. | 10/3/18 | (*Died* at Denain 18/3/18) | |
| Lieut. G. P. F. THOMAS. | 10/3/18 | | 14/12/18 |
| Lieut. H. B. P. BOYCE. | 12/3/18 | | 14/12/18 |
| 2/Lt. C. B. FENTON. | 12/3/18 | | 17/12/18 |
| 2/Lt. J. A. A. FERGUSON. | 12/3/18 | | 18/12/18 |
| 2/Lt. H. J. SPARKS. | 12/3/18 | | 13/12/18 |
| 2/Lt. L. C. F. CLUTTERBUCK. | 12/3/18 | | 17/12/18 |
| Lieut. G. R. CRAMMOND. | 13/3/18 | | 14/12/18 |
| Lieut. E. E. HEATH. | 13/3/18 | | 25/12/18 |
| 2/Lt. T. S. WILSON. | 13/3/18 | | 17/12/18 |
| 2/Lt. N. B. WELLS. | 13/3/18 | | 17/12/18 |
| 2/Lt. N. T. WATSON. | 13/3/18 | | 25/12/18 |
| 2/Lt. W. H. TAYLOR. | 16/3/18 | | 14/12/18 |
| 2/Lt. C. V. SHAKESBY. | 16/3/18 | | 17/12/18 |
| 2/Lt. A. L. T. TAYLOR. | 16/3/18 | | 14/12/18 |
| Flt. Commdr. R. P. MINIFIE. | 17/3/18 | | 14/12/18 |
| 2/Lt. W. J. IVAMY. | 18/3/18 | | 14/12/18 |
| Capt. F. L. LUXMOORE. | 18/3/18 | | 17/12/18 |
| Lieut. E. B. LEE. | 18/3/18 | | 17/12/18 |
| Capt. A. P. MacLEAN. | 18/3/18 | (*Died*) | |
| 2/Lt. A. W. MATSON. | 18/3/18 | | 14/12/18 |
| Lieut. G. T. STEEVES. | 18/3/18 | | 17/12/18 |
| Lieut. J. H. WENSLEY. | 18/3/18 | | 14/12/18 |
| 2/Lt. A. T. ISBELL. | 21/3/18 | | 18/12/18 |
| 2/Lt. F. K. KNELLER. | 21/3/18 | (*Died*) | |
| 2/Lt. R. B. SMITH. | 21/3/18 | | 17/12/18 |
| 2/Lt. T. E H. BIRLEY. | 22/3/18 | | 13/12/18 |
| 2/Lt. H. K. CASSELS. | 22/3/18 | | 17/12/18 |
| Lieut. R. W. COUTTS. | 22/3/18 | | 17/12/18 |
| 2/Lt. C. H. CLARKE. | 23/3/18 | | 13/12/18 |
| 2/Lt. H. P. BLAKE. | 23/3/18 | | 17/12/18 |
| 2/Lt. A. F. G. CLARKE. | 23/3/18 | | 14/12/18 |
| Lieut. R. H. EDELSTON. | 23/3/18 | | 23/12/18 |
| Lieut. D. W. KENT-JONES. | 23/3/18 | | 26/12/18 |
| Lieut. W. G. FLUKE. | 24/3/18 | | 17/12/18 |
| Lieut. C. W. COOK. | 24/3/18 | | 25/12/18 |
| 2/Lt. R. M. WYNNE-EYTON. | 24/3/18 | | 15/11/18 |
| 2/Lt. J. O. BUTLER. | 24/3/18 | (*Died* at Mons 11/4/18) | |
| Lieut. J. D. CURRIE. | 24/3/18 | | 14/12/18 |
| 2/Lt. N. H. THACKRAH. | 24/3/18 | | 14/12/18 |
| 2/Lt. A. A. MILES. | 24/3/18 | | 14/12/18 |
| 2/Lt. C. F. WESTING. | 24/3/18 | | 1/12/18 |
| Lieut. E. M. CHANT. | 25/3/18 | (*Died* at Cambrai 4/4/18) | |
| 2/Lt. G. G. NEWBURY. | 25/3/18 | | 13/12/18 |
| 2/Lt. W. M. R. GRAY. | 26/3/18 | | 14/12/18 |
| Lieut. A. HOLLIS. | 26/3/18 | | 1/12/18 |
| 2/Lt. A. T. W. LINDSAY. | 26/3/18 | | 1/12/18 |
| Lieut. G. D. FALKENBERG. | 12/3/18 | | 18/12/18 |

**ROYAL AIR FORCE**—continued.

| Name. | Missing. | Interned. | Repatriated. |
|---|---|---|---|
| 2/Lt. G. R. NORMAN. | 26/3/18 | | 14/12/18 |
| 2/Lt. R. C. D. OLIVER. | 26/3/18 | | 17/12/18 |
| Lieut. F. J. WESTFIELD. | 26/3/18 | | 17/12/18 |
| 2/Lt. F. C. B. WEDGWOOD. | 27/3/18 | | –/1/19 |
| 2/Lt. D. VAUGHAN. | 27/3/18 | | 17/12/18 |
| Lieut. J. C. THOMPSON. | 27/3/18 | | 17/12/18 |
| 2/Lt. E. W. PICKFORD. | 27/3/18 | | 1/12/18 |
| Capt. J. H. HEDLEY. | 27/3/18 | | 17/12/18 |
| Capt. R. K. KIRKMAN. | 27/3/18 | | 17/12/18 |
| Capt. E. B. CAHUSAC. | 27/3/18 | | 14/12/18 |
| Capt. T. S. SHARPE. | 27/3/18 | | –/12/18 |
| Lieut. H. S. REDPATH. | 28/3/18 | | 18/12/18 |
| 2/Lt. A. D. POPE. | 28/3/18 | | 1/12/18 |
| 2/Lt. R. J. OWEN. | 28/3/18 | | 1/12/18 |
| Lieut. D. D. RICHARDSON. | 28/3/18 | | 2/12/18 |
| 2/Lt. F. D. SHREEVE. | 29/3/18 | | 18/12/18 |
| Lieut. A. JERRARD. | 30/3/18 | | –/11/18 |
| 2/Lt. H. W. BROWNE. | 30/3/18 | | 1/12/18 |
| 2/Lt. A. S. HANNA. | 31/3/18 | | 18/12/18 |
| 2/Lt. C. B. COLEMAN. | 31/3/18 | | 18/12/18 |
| 2/Lt. R. A. BURNARD. | 31/3/18 | | 18/12/18 |
| Lieut. F. BEAUMONT. | 1/4/18 | | 17/12/18 |
| 2/Lt. B. MACPHERSON. | 1/4/18 | | 25/12/18 |
| 2/Lt. J. J. MEREDITH. | 1/4/18 | | 1/12/18 |
| Capt. J. L. TROLLOPE. | | | 12/10/18 |
| 2/Lt. A. K. LOMAX. | 2/4/18 | | 1/12/18 |
| 2/Lt. H. DEAN. | 3/4/18 | | 18/12/18 |
| 2/Lt. L. L. F. TOWNE. | 3/4/18 | | –/12/18 |
| 2/Lt. S. R. WELLS. | 5/4/18 | | 17/12/18 |
| Lieut. P. H. O'LIEFF. | 5/4/18 | | 17/12/18 |
| Lieut. D. G. GOLD. | 6/4/18 | | 17/12/18 |
| Lieut. H. G. DUGAN. | 6/4/18 | | –/12/18 |
| 2/Lt. M. F. PEILER. | 6/4/18 | | 1/12/18 |
| 2/Lt. F. D. HUDSON. | 6/4/18 | (*Died* at Paderborn) | |
| 2/Lt. T. R. V. HILL. | 6/4/18 | | 17/12/18 |
| 2/Lt. E. SMITHERS. | 6/4/18 | | 1/12/18 |
| Lt. A. G. WINGATE GRAY. | 6/4/18 | Switzerland –/10/18 | 25/12/18 |
| Lieut. R. G. H. ADAMS. | 7/4/18 | | 17/12/18 |
| Flt. Lieut. K. R. COLE. | 7/4/18 | | 18/12/18 |
| Lieut. D. C. HOPEWELL. | 7/4/18 | | 17/12/18 |
| Lieut. G. A. MERCER. | 9/4/18 | | 1/12/18 |
| 2/Lt. F. J. HOPGOOD. | 10/4/18 | | 18/12/18 |
| Lieut. G. G. McPHEE. | 10/4/18 | | 1/12/18 |
| Capt. W. D. PATRICK. | 10/4/18 | | 14/12/18 |
| Lieut. H. INMAN. | 11/4/18 | | 18/12/18 |
| 2/Lt. L. M. GERSON. | 11/4/18 | | 18/12/18 |
| 2/Lt. R. G. LAWSON. | 11/4/18 | | –/1/19 |
| Lieut. A. C. DEAN. | 12/4/18 | | 14/12/18 |
| 2/Lt. A. L. PEMBERTON. | 12/4/18 | | 13/12/18 |
| Lieut. C. McCANN. | 12/4/18 | | 1/12/18 |
| Lieut. A. W. MILLER. | 12/4/18 | | 18/12/18 |
| Lieut. F. R. KNAPP. | 16/4/18 | | –/12/18 |
| 2/Lt. D. G. LEWIS. | 20/4/18 | | 1/12/18 |
| 2/Lt. B. W. ROBINSON. | 20/4/18 | | 6/12/18 |
| Lieut. S. C. H. BEGBIE. | 21/4/18 | (*Died* at Lille 22/4/18) | |
| 2/Lt. C. J. FITZGIBBON. | 21/4/18 | | 17/12/18 |

**ROYAL AIR FORCE**—continued.

| Name. | Missing. | Interned. | Repatriated. |
|---|---|---|---|
| Lieut. W. RUDMAN. | 21/4/18 | | 18/12/18 |
| 2/Lt. C. St. C. PARSONS. | 22/4/18 | | –/12/18 |
| Capt. C. J. THOMSEN. | 23/4/18 | | 27/11/18 |
| Lieut. H. V. N. BANKES. | 24/4/18 | | 25/11/18 |
| 2/Lt. P. G. RATLIFF. | 24/4/18 | | 4/12/18 |
| Lieut. H. B. D. HARRINGTON. | 24/4/18 | | 1/12/18 |
| Capt. T. COLVILL-JONES. | 25/4/18 | (*Died* at Frankfurt 14/5/18) | |
| Lieut. C. J. GILLAN. | 25/4/18 | | 1/12/18 |
| Lieut. W. DUCE. | 25/4/18 | | 1/12/18 |
| Lieut. C. G. TYSOE. | 29/4/18 | | 25/12/18 |
| 2/Lt. C. V. CARR. | 29/4/18 | | 30/12/18 |
| Capt. E. G. S. WALKER. | | | 7/12/18 |
| Lieut. M. T. McKELVEY. | 11/4/18 | | 13/12/18 |
| Flt. Sub.-Lt. J. H. T. CARRE. | | R.N.A.S. | 14/12/18 |
| Sub.-Lt. N. J. ATTWOOD. | | | |
| 2/Lt. W. J. PRIER. | | | 17/12/18 |
| 2/Lt. W. H. TAYLOR. | | | –/12/18 |
| Lieut. G. HAMILTON. | 2/5/18 | | 19/12/18 |
| 2/Lt. A. C. G. BROWN. | 3/5/18 | (*Died* at Herleville 7/5/18) | |
| Capt. G. CHADWICK. | 3/5/18 | | 2/1/19 |
| 2/Lt. A. F. DAWES. | 3/5/18 | | 18/12/18 |
| Lieut. P. R. HAMPTON. | 3/5/18 | | 13/12/18 |
| Lieut. L. C. LANE. | 3/5/18 | | –/12/18 |
| 2/Lt. R. L. G. SKINNER. | 3/5/18 | (*Died*) | |
| 2/Lt. R. A. SLIPPER. | 4/5/18 | | 30/12/18 |
| Lieut. S. A. HUSTWITT. | 6/5/18 | | 1/12/18 |
| Lieut. N. A. SMITH. | 6/5/18 | | 18/12/18 |
| 2/Lt. J. C. WOOD. | 8/5/18 | | 13/12/18 |
| Capt. C. C. CLARK. | 8/5/18 | | 14/12/18 |
| Lieut. S. BIRCH. | 9/5/18 | | 1/1/19 |
| Lieut. T. RATCLIFFE. | 9/5/18 | | 1/1/19 |
| 2/Lt. A. V. JONES. | 10/5/18 | | 13/12/18 |
| Lieut. Geraint THOMAS. | 10/4/18 | | 14/12/18 |
| Lieut. E. G. FORDER. | 11/5/18 | | 28/11/18 |
| Lieut. A. P. BOLLINS. | 12/5/18 | | 30/12/18 |
| Lieut. C. E. TYLOR. | 12/5/18 | | 30/12/18 |
| Lieut. J. B. BIRKHEAD. | 12/5/18 | | –/12/18 |
| Lieut. J. HANDLEY. | 12/5/18 | | 25/12/18 |
| 2/Lt. L. R. SINCLAIR. | 14/5/18 | | 29/11/18 |
| Capt. EDWARDS. | | (*Died* at Mossel 14/5/18) | |
| 2/Lt. D. S. ANDERSON. | 15/5/18 | | 18/12/18 |
| Lieut. W. L. ANDREW. | 15/5/18 | | –/12/18 |
| 2/Lt. W. LAMONT. | 15/5/18 | | 25/12/18 |
| Lieut. C. C. ROBSON. | 15/5/18 | | –/12/18 |
| Lieut. H. B. B. WILSON. | 15/5/18 | | |
| 2/Lt. F. E. BOULTON. | 16/5/18 | | –/12/18 |
| Capt. P. R. WHITE. | 16/5/18 | | 25/12/18 |
| Lieut. W. E. COWAN. | 16/5/18 | | –/12/18 |
| 2/Lt. H. G. HOLMAN. | 16/5/18 | | 6/12/18 |
| Lieut. W. A. LESLIE. | 16/5/18 | | 30/12/18 |
| 2/Lt. J. C. WILLIAMSON. | 17/5/18 | | 30/12/18 |
| Lieut. N. F. PENRUDDOCKE. | 17/5/18 | | 31/12/18 |
| 2/Lieut. M. F. SUTTON. | 17/5/18 | | –/12/18 |
| 2/Lt. A. S. CROSS. | 17/5/18 | | 30/12/18 |
| Lieut. H. J. LEAVITT. | 17/5/18 | | –/12/18 |
| 2/Lt. V. W. HILLYARD. | 17/5/18 | | 13/12/18 |

**ROYAL AIR FORCE**—continued.

| Name. | Missing. | Interned. | Repatriated. |
|---|---|---|---|
| 2/Lt. D. J. RUSSELL. | 17/5/18 | | –/12/18 |
| 2/Lt. K. HUNT. | 17/5/18 | | 8/12/18 |
| Lieut. W. F. SCOTT-KERR. | 18/5/18 | | 26/12/18 |
| 2/Lt. C. B. LAW. | 18/5/18 | | –/12/18 |
| Major A. D. CARTER. | 18/5/18 | | 13/12/18 |
| 2/Lt. F. J. BULL. | 18/5/18 | | –/12/18 |
| Lieut. F. ATKINSON. | 19/5/18 | (*Died*) | |
| 2/Lt. H. A. CLARKE. | 19/5/18 | | –/12/18 |
| Capt. H. CLAYE. | 19/5/18 | | 30/12/18 |
| 2/Lt. H. MITCHELL. | 19/5/18 | | 30/12/18 |
| 2/Lt. A. J. PATENAUDE. | 19/5/18 | | 1/1/19 |
| Lieut. H. C. HUNTER. | 19/5/18 | | 8/12/18 |
| Lieut. L. SEYMOUR. | 19/5/18 | | 9/1/18 |
| 2/Lt. S. B. REECE. | 21/5/18 | | 1/1/19 |
| Lieut. R. W. PEAT. | 21/5/18 | | –/12/18 |
| 2/Lt. T. G. DREW-BROOK. | 21/5/18 | | 17/12/18 |
| 2/Lt. N. B. HARRIS. | 21/5/18 | | 13/12/18 |
| 2/Lt. H. E. TANSLEY. | 21/5/18 | | 30/12/18 |
| Lieut. H. E. TOWNSEND. | 21/5/18 | | 14/12/18 |
| 2/Lt. G. A. RAINIER. | 22/5/18 | | 13/12/18 |
| 2/Lt. W. I. CRAWFORD. | 23/5/18 | | 4/1/19 |
| Lieut. H. L. Le ROY. | 23/5/18 | | –/12/18 |
| 2/Lt. F. H. BLAXILL. | 27/5/18 | | –/12/18 |
| Lieut. D. A. MacDONALD. | 27/5/18 | | 30/12/18 |
| Lt.-Col. P. F. M. FELLOWES. | 27/5/18 | | 28/11/18 |
| Capt. D. J. BELL. | 27/5/18 | (*Died*) | |
| 2/Lt. V. R. BROWN. | 28/5/18 | | 14/1/19 |
| 2/Lt. R. S. MILANI. | 28/5/18 | | 17/12/18 |
| Lieut. W. A. SCOTT. | 30/5/18 | | 30/12/18 |
| Lieut. J. A. EATON. | 30/5/18 | *Holland* | |
| Flt. Lieut. E. F. BENSLEY. | | | 13/12/18 |
| Lieut. H. C. E. BOCKETT-PUGH. | | | 29/11/18 |
| 2/Lt. J. L. H. ANDERSON. | 31/5/18 | (*Died* at Karlsruhe) | |
| Lieut. E. McN. HAND. | 1/6/18 | | 14/11/18 |
| Lieut. I. A. PEERS. | 1/6/18 | | 31/12/18 |
| Lieut. J. R. ZIEMAN. | 2/6/18 | | 30/12/18 |
| 2/Lt. A. R. COWAN. | 3/6/18 | | 14/12/18 |
| Lieut. B. A. BIRD. | 3/6/18 | | 6/12/18 |
| Capt. R. F. L. DICKEY. | 4/6/18 | | –/8/18 |
| Capt. R. F. PAUL. | 4/6/18 | *Holland* | |
| Lieut. A. G. HODGSON. | 4/6/18 | *Holland* | 21/7/18 |
| 2/Lt. A. JOHNSON. | | | |
| 2/Lt. R. J. GREGORY. | 5/6/18 | | 13/12/18 |
| 2/Lt. E. A. MAGEE. | 5/6/18 | | –/12/18 |
| 2/Lt. J. E. W. SUGDEN. | 5/6/18 | | 13/12/18 |
| Lieut. C. H. DUNSTER. | 5/6/18 | | 18/12/18 |
| Lieut. F. CLARKE. | | | |
| Lieut. A. F. BARTLETT. | 6/6/18 | | 6/12/18 |
| Lieut. L. A. HACKLETT. | 7/6/18 | | 13/12/18 |
| Lieut. G. D. McLEOD. | 8/6/18 | | 21/11/18 |
| 2/Lt. E. M. BROWN. | 9/6/18 | | 12/12/18 |
| Lieut. C. A. GORDON. | 9/6/18 | | 20/11/18 |
| Lieut. C. MARSDEN. | 9/6/18 | | 13/12/18 |
| 2/Lt. W. BRECKENRIDGE. | 9/6/18 | | –/1/19 |
| Lieut. J. H. JOHNSON. | 9/6/18 | | |
| Lieut. J. F. PATTINSON. | | *Holland* | |
| 2/Lt. H. TANNENBAUM. | 2/6/18 | | 1/1/19 |

**ROYAL AIR FORCE**—continued.

| Name. | Missing. | Interned. | Repatriated. |
|---|---|---|---|
| Lieut. R. J. R. D. FYFE. | | Holland. | 15/11/18 |
| Lieut. B. W. DE LEYSON. | 10/6/18 | | |
| 2/Lt. J. L. BROWN. | 12/6/18 | | 18/12/18 |
| Capt. J. WEAVER. | 12/6/18 | | 17/12/18 |
| Lieut. G. F. THOMSON. | 12/6/18 | | 13/12/18 |
| Lieut. H. H. GILE. | 13/6/18 | U.S.A. | |
| Lieut. C. R. HALL. | 13/6/18 | | 13/12/18 |
| 2/Lt. R. G. LEWIS. | 13/6/18 | | 13/12/18 |
| 2/Lt. E. M. NICHOLAS. | 13/6/18 | | 13/12/18 |
| 2/Lt. W. H. A. RICKETT. | 16/6/18 | | 13/12/18 |
| Capt. R. O. PURRY. | 16/6/18 | | 14/1/19 |
| 2/Lt. C. E. WHARTON. | 16/6/18 | | 13/12/18 |
| Lieut. J. W. PRYOR. | 16/6/18 | | 13/12/18 |
| Lieut. H. VICK. | 16/6/18 | | 30/12/18 |
| Lieut. H. E. THOMSON. | 16/6/18 | | 13/12/18 |
| 2/Lt. G. H. GLASSPOOLE. | 16/6/18 | | 14/12/18 |
| 2/Lt. V. MERCER-SMITH. | 16/6/18 | | 13/12/18 |
| 2/Lt. P. KEMP. | 16/6/18 | | 13/12/18 |
| 2/Lt. J. R. JACKMAN. | 17/6/18 | (*Died*) | |
| Lieut. G. D. COWARD. | 17/6/18 | | 21/11/18 |
| Lieut. J. F. REID. | 17/6/18 | | 15/11/18 |
| 2/Lt. W. J. T. ATKINS. | 17/6/18 | | 13/12/18 |
| 2/Lt. S. M. CONNOLLY. | 18/6/18 | | 23/12/18 |
| Lieut. S. M. ROBINS. | 19/6/18 | | 20/11/18 |
| Lieut. H. MASON. | 20/6/18 | | 13/12/18 |
| Lieut. H. S. COLLETT. | 21/6/18 | | 12/12/18 |
| Lieut. H. B. EVANS. | 21/6/18 | | 13/12/18 |
| 2/Lt. R. G. CARR. | 21/6/18 | Escaped | 18/7/18 |
| Lieut. K. W. J. HALL. | 21/6/18 | | 13/12/18 |
| Lieut. W. K. WILSON. | 21/6/18 | | 30/12/18 |
| 2/Lt. A. J. COBBIN. | 23/6/18 | (*Died* at Le Quesnoy 14/7/18) | |
| Lieut. A. D. R. JONES. | 23/6/18 | | 13/12/18 |
| Lieut. J. W. THOMSON. | 23/6/18 | | 13/12/18 |
| Lieut. L. J. W. INGRAM. | 23/6/18 | | 13/12/18 |
| Lieut. C. W. PECKHAM. | 23/6/18 | | 4/12/18 |
| Flt. Lieut. MURTON. | | | 17/12/18 |
| 2/Lt. W. C. TEMPEST. | 24/6/18 | | 31/12/18 |
| 2/Lt. W. TURNER. | 24/6/18 | | 13/12/18 |
| 2/Lt. E. ROBERTS. | 25/6/18 | | 13/12/18 |
| Lieut. N. H. MUIRDEN. | 25/6/18 | | |
| Lieut. F. DALTREY. | 25/6/18 | | 1/1/19 |
| 2/Lt. J. ARNOLD. | 25/6/18 | | 13/12/18 |
| Lieut. S. C. M. PONTIN. | 25/6/18 | | 13/12/18 |
| Lt. O. J. F. JONES-LLOYD. | 25/6/18 | | 13/12/18 |
| Lieut. W. H. STUBBS. | 25/6/18 | (*Died*) | |
| 2/Lt. A. J. ELVIN. | 26/6/18 | | 13/12/18 |
| Lieut. J. E. DOE. | 26/6/18 | | 13/12/18 |
| Lieut. C. BOOTHMAN. | 26/6/18 | (*Died*) | |
| Lieut. F. F. H. BRYAN. | 26/6/18 | | 14/12/18 |
| Lieut. C. G. JENYNS. | 26/6/18 | | 13/12/18 |
| Lieut. J. WEBSTER. | 27/6/18 | | 30/12/18 |
| Lieut. G. M. GRAY. | 27/5/18 | | 17/12/18 |
| Lieut. J. C. ROBINSON. | 27/6/18 | | 13/12/18 |
| 2/Lt. L. G. COCKING. | 27/6/18 | | 13/12/18 |
| Capt. J. A. GRAY. | 27/6/18 | Holland | 12/11/18 |
| Lieut. S. C. WELINKER. | 27/6/18 | (*Died* 30/6/18) | |

**ROYAL AIR FORCE**—continued.

| Name. | Missing. | Interned. | Repatriated. |
|---|---|---|---|
| 2/Lt. J. J. COMERFORD. | 27/6/18 | Holland | 12/11/18 |
| Capt. W. A. FORSYTH. | 27/6/18 | *(Died)* | |
| 2/Lt. J. FULTON. | 27/6/18 | | 13/12/18 |
| Lieut. A. L. GARRETT. | 28/6/18 | | 13/12/18 |
| Lieut. H. AUSTIN. | 28/6/18 | | 13/12/18 |
| Lieut. A. E. BINGHAM. | 28/6/18 | | 13/12/18 |
| 2/Lt. J. L. SMITH. | 28/6/18 | | –/12/18 |
| Lieut. P. C. MICHELL. | 28/6/18 | | 13/12/18 |
| Lieut. C. EATON. | 29/6/18 | | 14/12/18 |
| Lieut. G. BALLANCE. | 29/6/18 | | –/12/18 |
| Lieut. R. P. WHYTE. | 29/6/18 | | 13/12/18 |
| 2/Lt. D. BOE. | 29/6/18 | | 13/12/18 |
| Lieut. E. G. TURNER. | 29/6/18 | | 13/12/18 |
| Lieut. E. W. TATNALL. | 29/6/18 | | 13/12/18 |
| Lieut. J. D. VANCE. | 30/6/18 | | 15/11/18 |
| Lieut. J. E. SYDIE. | 30/6/18 | | 16/1/19 |
| 2/Lt. K. C. B. WOODMAN. | 1/7/18 | | 13/12/18 |
| Lieut. W. G. NORDEN. | 1/7/18 | | 13/12/18 |
| Lieut. G. C. BODY. | 1/7/18 | | 13/12/18 |
| Lieut. G. L. CASTLE. | 1/7/18 | | 18/12/18 |
| Lieut. A. H. HARRISON. | 1/7/18 | | 13/12/18 |
| Lieut. J. D. MANCE. | 1/7/18 | Holland | |
| 2/Lt. S. B. PORTER. | 1/7/18 | Holland | 15/11/18 |
| Capt. H. V. PUCKRIDGE. | 1/7/18 | | 13/12/18 |
| Lieut. T. L. MacCONCHIE. | 1/7/18 | | 5/12/18 |
| Lieut. A. J. FRICKER. | 4/7/18 | | 17/12/18 |
| 2/Lt. W. J. SAUNDERS. | 6/7/18 | | 13/12/18 |
| Lieut. M. J. DUCRAY. | 7/7/18 | | 26/11/18 |
| Lieut. A. MOORE. | 7/7/18 | | 13/12/18 |
| 2/Lt. H. W. BURRY. | 8/7/18 | | 14/12/18 |
| Lieut. J. A. CHUBB. | 8/7/18 | | 14/12/18 |
| 2/Lt. H. K. SCRIVENER. | 8/7/18 | | 13/12/18 |
| 2/Lt. R. H. DUNN. | 9/7/18 | | 17/12/18 |
| 2/Lt. H. E. HINCHLIFFE. | 9/7/18 | | 11/1/19 |
| Lieut. M. H. K. KANE. | 10/7/18 | | 14/12/18 |
| Lieut. J. LOUPINSKI. | 10/7/18 | | 13/12/18 |
| Lieut. C. B. RIDLEY. | 10/7/18 | | 13/12/18 |
| Lieut. T. F. BLIGHT. | 11/7/18 | | 23/1/19 |
| 2/Lt. A. T. SIMONS. | 11/7/18 | | 26/12/18 |
| 2/Lt. H. R. WHITEHEAD. | 11/7/18 | | 18/1/19 |
| 2/Lt. R. ARNOTT. | 11/7/18 | | 23/9/18 |
| 2/Lt. D. MALLETT. | 14/7/18 | | 13/12/18 |
| 2/Lt. J. S. BURN. | 14/7/18 | | 13/12/18 |
| 2/Lt. B. N. GARRETT. | 14/7/18 | | 16/12/18 |
| Lieut. R. A. YATES. | 14/7/18 | | 13/12/18 |
| 2/Lt. N. H. MARSHALL. | 14/7/18 | | 14/1/19 |
| Lieut. R. H. GRAY. | 15/7/18 | | 13/12/18 |
| Lieut. E. B. CRICKMORE. | 16/7/18 | | 13/12/18 |
| Lieut. J. A. PUGH. | 16/7/18 | | 13/12/18 |
| 2/Lt. R. E. WHITE. | 17/7/18 | | 5/12/18 |
| Lieut. R. A. STRANG. | 17/7/18 | | 27/11/18 |
| Lieut. G. ROSE. | 18/7/18 | | 13/12/18 |
| Lieut. F. KEMP. | 18/7/18 | | 17/12/18 |
| Lieut. W. M. F. BAYLISS. | 18/7/18 | | 13/12/18 |
| Lieut. A. SMITH. | 18/7/18 | | 13/12/18 |
| Lieut. R. A. VOSPER. | 18/7/18 | | 13/12/18 |

## ROYAL AIR FORCE—continued.

| Name. | Missing. | Interned. | Repatriated. |
|---|---|---|---|
| Lieut. H. BOSHER. | 18/7/18 | | 14/12/18 |
| Lieut. L. W. D. T. TRATMAN. | 18/7/18 | | 23/12/18 |
| Lieut. J. A. Van TILBURG. | 19/7/18 | | 14/12/18 |
| 2/Lt. H. L. CROSS. | 19/7/18 | | 13/12/18 |
| Lieut. A. M. ROBERTS. | 19/7/18 | U.S.A.S. | |
| Lieut. E. SCADDING. | 19/7/18 | | 17/12/18 |
| Lieut. A. R. JONES. | 19/7/18 | | 14/12/18 |
| Lieut. F. G. THOMPSON. | 20/7/18 | | 28/12/18 |
| 2/Lt. K. R. ANGUS. | 20/7/18 | | 13/12/18 |
| 2/Lt. S. C. THORNLEY. | 20/7/18 | | 13/12/18 |
| Lieut. A. J. CYR. | 20/7/18 | | 13/12/18 |
| Lieut. T. CONLAN. | 20/7/18 | | 8/12/18 |
| 2/Lt. E. J. RILEY. | 20/7/18 | | 23/12/18 |
| Lieut. A. SOMMERFELT. | 21/7/18 | | 13/12/18 |
| Lieut. A. LEWIS. | 21/7/18 | | 14/12/18 |
| 2/Lt. J. GONDRE. | 21/7/18 | | 13/12/18 |
| 2/Lt. B. M. BATTEY. | 21/7/18 | | 12/12/18 |
| Lieut. WILLIAMS. | 21/7/18 | Holland | |
| Lieut. JACKSON. | 21/7/18 | Holland | |
| 2/Lt. E. DAWSON. | 21/7/18 | Holland | 26/12/18 |
| Lieut. W. E. COULSON. | 22/7/18 | | 13/12/18 |
| 2/Lt. W. H. E. LABATT. | 22/7/18 | | 13/12/18 |
| Lieut. E. BULLEN. | 22/7/18 | | 13/12/18 |
| Lieut. W. S. G. KIDDER. | 22/7/18 | | 5/12/18 |
| Lieut. H. C. TUSSAUD. | 22/7/18 | | 29/11/18 |
| Lieut. W. R. HENDERSON. | 22/7/18 | | 13/12/18 |
| Lieut. C. F. BROWN. | 25/7/18 | (Died 3/8/18) | |
| 2/Lt. A. G. S. BLAKE. | 25/7/18 | | 13/12/18 |
| Lieut. F. S. COGHILL. | 25/7/18 | | 13/12/18 |
| 2/Lt. K. S. LAURIE. | 25/7/18 | | 13/12/18 |
| Lieut. H. M. STRUBEN. | 25/7/18 | | 13/12/18 |
| 2/Lt. N. WILSON. | 25/7/18 | (*Died* at Munster 18/10/18) | |
| Lieut. W. A. CARVETH. | 26/7/18 | | 13/12/18 |
| 2/Lt. G. TRAVERS. | 26/7/18 | | 13/12/18 |
| Lieut. W. S. STEPHENSON. | 28/7/18 | | 30/12/18 |
| Lieut. R. V. IRWIN. | 28/7/18 | (*Died* at Cologne 2/10/18) | |
| Lieut. L. C. GILMOUR. | 31/7/18 | | 13/12/18 |
| Lieut. W. H. SHELL. | 31/7/18 | | 13/12/18 |
| Lieut. R. L. HOLLINGSWORTH. | 31/7/18 | | 5/12/18 |
| Lieut. J. FARQUHAR. | 31/7/18 | (*Died* near Rooselaure 1/8/18) | |
| Lieut. D. C. TOWNLEY. | 31/7/18 | | 13/12/18 |
| Lieut. J. E. GOW. | 31/7/18 | (*Died* 10/8/18) | |
| Lieut. W. J. HUTCHINSON. | 31/7/18 | | 23/12/18 |
| Lieut. L. W. C. PEARCE. | 31/7/18 | Holland | 12/11/18 |
| 2/Lt. F. H. BUGGE. | 31/7/18 | Holland | 12/11/18 |
| Lieut. G. H. STEPHENSON. | 31/7/18 | | 13/12/18 |
| 2/Lt. F. SMITH. | 31/7/18 | | 13/12/18 |
| 2/Lt. E. SINGLETON. | 31/7/18 | | 13/12/18 |
| 2/Lt. T. M. RITCHIE. | 31/7/18 | | 13/12/18 |
| Lieut. M. T. S. PAPENFUS. | 31/7/18 | | 13/12/18 |
| Lieut. W. J. GARRITY. | 31/7/18 | | -/12/18 |
| 2/Lt. K. H. ASHTON. | 31/7/18 | | 13/12/18 |
| Lieut. A. L. BENJAMIN. | 31/7/18 | | 29/11/18 |
| Lieut. S. McB. BLACK. | 31/7/18 | | -/12/18 |
| Lieut. D. W. WILSON. | 2/8/18 | Holland | |
| Lieut. L. C. BOWER. | 2/8/18 | Holland | |

## ROYAL AIR FORCE.—continued.

| Name. | Missing. | Interned. | Repatriated. |
|---|---|---|---|
| Capt. E. P. HARDMAN. | 2/8/18 | | 20/11/18 |
| 2/Lt. E. S. COOMBES. | 3/8/18 | | 13/12/18 |
| Lieut. A. F. FORSYTH. | 3/8/18 | | 13/12/18 |
| Lieut. ALBERTSON. | 4/8/18 | U.S.A.S. | |
| Lieut. J. D. ANDERSON. | 7/8/18 | | 17/12/18 |
| 2/Lt. C. E. A. LOVELL. | 7/8/18 | | 13/12/18 |
| 2/Lt. B. C. PEARSON. | 8/8/18 | | 13/12/18 |
| Lieut. J. C. NUTTALL. | 8/8/18 | | 23/12/18 |
| Lieut. L. H. RIDDELL. | 8/8/18 | | 3/1/19 |
| Lieut. R. H. HEMMENS. | 8/8/18 | | 14/12/18 |
| 2/Lt. L. K. DAVIDSON. | 8/8/18 | Holland | 12/11/18 |
| 2/Lt. W. L. BING. | 8/8/18 | Holland | 12/11/18 |
| Lieut. R. E. TAYLOR. | 8/8/18 | | 23/12/18 |
| Capt. G. H. P. WHITFIELD. | 8/8/18 | | 13/12/18 |
| 2/Lt. G. WIGNALL. | 8/8/18 | | 13/12/18 |
| Capt. F. G. POWELL. | 8/8/18 | | 25/12/18 |
| Lieut. W. GOFFE. | 8/8/18 | | 5/1/19 |
| 2/Lt. D. E. CHASE. | 8/8/18 | | 29/12/18 |
| Lieut. G. W. GORMAN. | 8/8/18 | | 5/12/18 |
| 2/Lt. G. L. CARTER. | 8/8/18 | | 23/12/18 |
| Capt. M. E. GONNE. | 8/8/18 | (*Died* at Villers-Carbonnel) | |
| 2/Lt. C. F. W. ILLINGWORTH. | 8/8/18 | | 30/12/18 |
| Lieut. F. C. RUSSELL. | 8/8/18 | | 13/12/18 |
| 2/Lt. M. TISON. | 8/8/18 | | 23/12/18 |
| Lieut. G. R. TOUCHSTONE. | 8/8/18 | | 8/12/18 |
| Capt. R. MANZER. | 8/8/18 | | 13/12/18 |
| Capt. H. RAMPLING. | 8/8/18 | Holland. | |
| Lieut. J. A. YATES. | 8/8/18 | | 23/12/18 |
| 2/Lt. G. R. SCHOOLING. | 8/8/18 | | 13/12/18 |
| Lieut. H. P. MALLETT. | 8/8/18 | | 13/12/18 |
| 2/Lt. R. KELLY. | 8/8/18 | | –/12/18 |
| Lieut. F. E. BEAUCHAMP. | 8/8/18 | | 14/12/18 |
| Lieut. F. I. ROGERS. | 8/8/18 | | 17/12/18 |
| 2/Lt. H. ELLIOTT | 8/8/18 | | 13/12/18 |
| Lieut. I. L. BROWN. | 8/8/18 | | 13/12/18 |
| 2/Lt. A. E. DONCASTER. | 8/8/18 | | 13/12/18 |
| Lieut. N. O. N. FOGGO. | 8/8/18 | | 5/1/19 |
| 2/Lt. W. COX. | 8/8/18 | | 13/12/18 |
| Lieut. H. M. BROWN. | 8/8/18 | | 24/12/18 |
| Lieut. L. H. FORREST. | 8/8/18 | | 12/12/18 |
| Lieut. S. W. P. FOSTER-SUTTON. | 8/8/18 | | 25/11/18 |
| Lieut. A. McCONNELL-WOOD. | 8/8/18 | | 17/12/18 |
| Lieut. C. B. H. LEFROY. | 8/8/18 | | 4/2/19 |
| Lieut. F. CARPENTER. | 9/8/18 | | 13/12/18 |
| 2/Lt. H. S. MUSGROVE. | 9/8/18 | | |
| 2/Lt. A. S. SINCLAIR. | 9/8/18 | | 23/12/18 |
| Lieut. W. E. JACKSON. | 9/8/18 | | 13/12/18 |
| 2/Lt. P. T. A. REVELEY. | 9/8/18 | | 30/12/18 |
| Lieut. L. H. BUTTON. | 9/8/18 | | 29/1/19 |
| Lieut. B. HALL. | 9/8/18 | | 5/12/18 |
| Lieut. L. A. CLACK. | 9/8/18 | | 13/12/18 |
| Lieut. J. E. T. SUTCLIFFE. | 9/8/18 | | 1/1/19 |
| Lieut. S. R. COWARD. | 9/8/18 | | 10/1/19 |
| 2/Lt. S. J. HILL. | 9/8/18 | | 13/12/18 |
| 2/Lt. H. HARTLEY. | 10/8/18 | | 11/12/18 |
| Lieut. H. T. FLINTOPP. | 10/8/18 | | 12/12/18 |

## ROYAL AIR FORCE—continued.

| Name. | Missing. | Interned. | Repatriated. |
|---|---|---|---|
| Lieut. G. S. HARVEY. | 10/8/18 | | 5/12/18 |
| Lieut. T. T. SHIPMAN. | 10/8/18 | | 1/1/19 |
| Lieut. C. L. WOOD. | 10/8/18 | (*Died* at Tournai 17/8/18) | |
| 2/Lt. E. H. CLAYTON. | 11/8/18 | (*Died*) | |
| Lieut. S. D. CONNOLLY. | 11/8/18 | | –/12/18 |
| Lieut. W. W. BRADFORD. | 11/8/18 | | 26/11/18 |
| 2/Lt. J. E. PARKE. | 11/8/18 | | 26/11/18 |
| 2/Lt. J. M. McPHERSON. | 11/8/18 | | 10/12/18 |
| 2/Lt. J. V. RISK. | 11/8/18 | | 13/12/18 |
| 2/Lt. G. F. METSON. | 11/8/18 | | 14/12/18 |
| 2/Lt. C. A. ATKINS. | 12/8/18 | | 13/12/18 |
| 2/Lt. J. IVENS. | 12/8/18 | | 18/1/19 |
| Lieut. O. F. MEYER. | 12/8/18 | | 13/12/18 |
| Lieut. G. H. PATMAN. | 12/8/18 | | 13/12/18 |
| Lieut. S. C. J. ASKIN. | 12/8/18 | | 23/12/18 |
| Lieut. A. R. STEDMAN. | 12/8/18 | | |
| Capt. I. K. SUMMERS. | 12/8/18 | | 23/12/18 |
| Lieut. H. H. WOOD. | 12/8/18 | | 17/12/18 |
| Lieut. J. L. C. SUTHERLAND. | 13/8/18 | (*Died* at Metz 19/8/18) | |
| Lieut. E. J. C. McCRACKEN. | 13/8/18 | | 14/12/18 |
| 2/Lt. G. R. HOWARD. | 14/8/18 | | 16/12/18 |
| 2/Lt. J. HILLS. | 14/8/18 | | 23/12/18 |
| 2/Lt. H. A. O'SHEA. | 14/8/18 | | |
| 2/Lt. C. E. THORPE. | 14/8/18 | | 23/12/18 |
| 2/Lt. G. A. R. HILL. | 14/8/18 | | 18/12/18 |
| Lieut. A. G. LAWE. | 15/8/18 | | 13/12/18 |
| Lieut. T. J. ARTHUR. | 15/8/18 | | 14/12/18 |
| Lieut. D. E. CULVER. | 15/8/18 | | |
| 2/Lt. J. MUNRO. | 16/8/18 | Holland | |
| Lieut. A. C. LLOYD. | 16/8/18 | Holland | 15/11/18 |
| 2/Lt. M. G. WILSON. | 16/8/18 | Holland | 15/11/18 |
| 2/Lt. T. B. DODWELL. | 16/8/18 | Holland | 15/11/18 |
| Lieut. C. H. DENNY | 16/8/18 | | 13/12/18 |
| Lieut. E. H. KILBOURNE. | 16/8/18 | | 13/12/18 |
| 2/Lt. D. E. STEPHENS. | 16/8/18 | (*Died* at Karlsruhe) | |
| Lieut. A. T. PARTRIDGE. | | | 25/12/18 |
| Lieut. W. H. POLLARD. | 16/8/18 | | 18/1/19 |
| 2/Lt. B. P. JENKINS. | 16/8/18 | (*Died* at Aachen) | |
| 2/Lt. F. J. KEBLE. | 16/8/18 | | 8/12/18 |
| Lieut. H. BURTON. | 16/8/18 | | |
| 2/Lt. J. R. FOX. | 16/8/18 | (*Died*) | |
| Lieut. D. R. HARRIS. | 16/8/18 | Holland | |
| Lieut. W. G. CLAXTON. | 17/8/18 | | 1/12/18 |
| Capt. R. S. S. INGRAM. | 18/8/18 | | 10/12/18 |
| 2/Lt. A. W. WYNCOLL. | 18/8/18 | | 11/12/18 |
| Capt. C. J. VENTER. | 18/8/18 | | 13/12/18 |
| 2/Lt. J. M. DUNLOP. | 19/8/18 | | 11/12/18 |
| 2/Lt. F. F. SCHORN. | 19/8/18 | | 11/12/18 |
| Lieut. N. E. WILLIAMS. | 19/8/18 | | 10/11/18 |
| 2/Lt. A. C. PORTER. | 19/8/18 | | 30/12/18 |
| 2/Lt. J. WOODING. | 21/8/18 | | 13/12/18 |
| Lieut. R. H. ELLIS. | 21/8/18 | U.S.A.S. | |
| Lieut. R. A. C. BRIE. | 22/8/18 | | 13/12/18 |
| Lieut. N. E. GWYER. | 22/8/18 | | 19/11/18 |
| 2/Lt. T. R. HILTON. | 22/8/18 | | 20/11/18 |
| Capt. D. LATIMER. | 22/8/18 | | 31/12/18 |

## ROYAL AIR FORCE—continued.

| Name. | Missing. | Interned. | Repatriated. |
|---|---|---|---|
| Lieut. J. S. ANDREWS. | 22/8/18 | | 13/12/18 |
| Lieut. M. E. BURNHAM. | 22/8/18 | | 13/12/18 |
| Lieut. D. F. BURTON. | 22/8/18 | | 13/12/18 |
| 2/Lt. C. K. DAVID. | 22/8/18 | | 13/12/18 |
| 2/Lt. G. ROCHESTER. | 22/8/18 | | 13/12/18 |
| Lieut. H. P. WELLS. | 22/8/18 | U.S.A.S. | |
| Lieut. J. VALENTINE. | 22/8/18 | | 17/12/18 |
| Lieut. G. H. B. SMITH. | 22/8/18 | | 8/12/18 |
| 2/Lt. R. J. SEARLE. | 22/8/18 | | 15/12/18 |
| 2/Lt. J. H. RADFIELD. | 22/8/18 | | |
| Capt. E. A. MACKAY. | 22/8/18 | | 8/12/18 |
| Capt. J. B. H. HAY. | 22/8/18 | | 13/12/18 |
| 2/Lt. C. G. HITCHCOCK. | 22/8/18 | | 13/12/18 |
| 2/Lt. R. F. GLAZEBROOK. | 23/8/18 | | 13/12/18 |
| Lieut. C. E. G. GILL. | 23/8/18 | | 18/11/18 |
| Lieut. M. K. CURTIS. | 24/8/18 | U.S.A.S. | |
| Lieut. J. A. DEAR. | 24/8/18 | Holland | 15/11/18 |
| 2/Lt. J. F. J. PETERS. | 24/8/18 | Holland | 15/11/18 |
| Lieut. H. J. W. ROBERTS. | 24/8/18 | | 23/12/18 |
| Lieut. C. H. STEPHENS. | 25/8/18 | | 23/12/18 |
| 2/Lt. L. G. TAYLOR. | 25/8/18 | | 23/12/18 |
| Lieut. F. M. SELLARS. | 27/8/18 | | 4/12/18 |
| 2/Lt. A. R. HEAVER. | 27/8/18 | | 23/12/18 |
| Lieut. A. H. BELLIVEAU. | 27/8/18 | | 1/1/19 |
| Capt. S. G. GILMOUR. | 28/8/18 | | 13/12/18 |
| Lieut. P. H. GOODHUGH. | 28/8/18 | | |
| Lieut. W. K. MacFARLANE. | 29/8/18 | | 11/12/18 |
| Capt. L. G. LOUDOUN. | 29/8/18 | | 23/12/18 |
| 2/Lt. S. E. CROOKELL. | 29/8/18 | | 8/12/18 |
| 2/Lt. W. T. S. LEWIS. | 29/8/18 | | 9/12/18 |
| 2/Lt. W. R. JACKSON. | 30/8/18 | | 8/12/18 |
| Lieut. K. A. W. LEIGHTON. | 30/8/18 | | 23/12/18 |
| 2/Lt. A. S. PAPWORTH. | 30/8/18 | | 23/12/18 |
| Lieut. H. H. DOEHLER. | 30/8/18 | U.S.A.S. | |
| 2/Lt. A. J. C. GORMLEY. | 30/8/18 | | 23/12/18 |
| Lieut. J. MACDONALD. | 30/8/18 | | –/11/18 |
| Lieut. R. B. LUARD. | 30/8/18 | | 8/12/18 |
| 2/Lt. G. E. HERRING. | 31/8/18 | | 6/12/18 |
| Capt. W. G. SHEDEL. | 31/8/18 | | 23/12/18 |
| Capt. J. MACKERETH. | 31/8/18 | | 17/12/18 |
| 2/Lt. G. PURYEAR. | | U.S.A.S. | |
| Capt. R. MARSHALL. | | | |
| 2/Lt. C. H. A. BRIDGE. | 31/8/18 | | |
| 2/Lt. Z. MILLER. | | | |
| Lieut. W. S. MARS. | –/9/18 | Holland | 15/11/18 |
| Lieut. G. L. BARRITT. | 1/9/18 | | 28/11/18 |
| 2/Lt. R. BOYS. | 1/9/18 | | 23/12/18 |
| 2/Lt. M. E. CHALLIS. | 1/9/18 | | 23/12/18 |
| 2/Lt. R. D. HUGHES. | 1/9/18 | | 23/12/18 |
| 2/Lt. J. G. DUGDALE. | 1/9/18 | | 13/12/18 |
| Lieut. H. V. FELLOWES. | 1/9/18 | | 8/12/18 |
| Lieut. D. A. MARTIN. | 1/9/18 | | 22/12/18 |
| 2/Lt. R. L. SCARFF. | 1/9/18 | | 30/12/18 |
| 2/Lt. H. V. PEELING. | 1/9/18 | | 8/12/18 |
| 2/Lt. L. B. RAYMOND. | 1/9/18 | | 2/12/18 |
| 2/Lt. F. B. ROBINSON. | 1/9/18 | | 8/12/18 |

**ROYAL AIR FORCE**—continued.

| Name. | Missing. | Interned. | Repatriated. |
|---|---|---|---|
| Lieut. O. O'CONNOR. | 2/9/18 | | 8/12/18 |
| 2/Lt. I. M. McCULLOCH. | 2/9/18 | | 11/12/18 |
| Lieut. J. J. AMBLER. | 2/9/18 | | 8/12/18 |
| 2/Lt. D. ROSE. | 2/9/18 | | 24/12/18 |
| 2/Lt. J. B. COCKIN. | 2/9/18 | | 18/1/19 |
| Lieut. W. A. HALL. | 2/9/18 | | 11/12/18 |
| 2/Lt. C. H. LIVING. | 2/9/18 | | 8/12/18 |
| 2/Lt. O. MANDEL. | 2/9/18 | | |
| 2/Lt. J. S. STRINGER. | 2/9/18 | | 11/12/18 |
| Lieut. R. A. B. POPE. | 2/9/18 | | 8/12/18 |
| 2/Lt. H. A. SCRIVENER. | 2/9/18 | | 2/1/19 |
| 2/Lt. D. B. SINCLAIR. | 2/9/18 | | 8/12/18 |
| Lieut. W. M. STRATHEARNE. | 2/9/18 | | 8/12/18 |
| 2/Lt. J. C. BOYLE. | 4/9/18 | | 30/12/18 |
| 2/Lt. G. T. COLES. | 4/9/18 | | 8/12/18 |
| Lieut. J. LEVESON-GOWER. | 4/9/18 | | 10/12/18 |
| Lieut. R. McPHEE. | 4/9/18 | | –/12/18 |
| Lieut. S. W. ROCHFORD. | 4/9/18 | | 11/12/18 |
| Lieut. W. M. HERRIOT. | 4/9/18 | | 11/12/18 |
| Capt. J. H. FORMAN. | 4/9/18 | | 10/12/18 |
| Lieut. W. K. SWAYZE. | 4/9/18 | | 4/1/19 |
| Lieut. W. E. HALL. | 4/9/18 | | 24/12/18 |
| 2/Lt. C. H. P. KILLICK. | 4/9/18 | | 23/12/18 |
| Lieut. E. R. SPROULE. | 4/9/18 | | 5/1/19 |
| 2/Lt. A. M. MILLER. | 5/9/18 | | 23/12/18 |
| 2/Lt. R. BEESLEY. | 5/9/18 | | 8/12/18 |
| 2/Lt. V. HARLEY. | 5/9/18 | | 23/12/18 |
| Lieut. W. A. F. COWGILL. | 5/9/18 | | 13/12/18 |
| 2/Lt. C. E. FRANCIS. | 5/9/18 | | 8/12/18 |
| Lieut. E. V. HOLLAND. | 5/9/18 | | 11/12/18 |
| Capt. H. A. PATEY. | 5/9/18 | | 22/12/18 |
| 2/Lt. A. PRESTON. | 5/9/18 | | –/1/19 |
| 2/Lt. A. R. THATCHER. | 5/9/18 | | 23/12/18 |
| Capt. G. A. WELLS. | 5/9/18 | | 8/12/18 |
| Lieut. L. YEREX. | 5/9/18 | | –/12/18 |
| 2/Lt. T. W. BRODIE. | 6/9/18 | Holland | –/11/18 |
| Lieut. J. G. MUNRO. | 6/9/18 | Holland | –/11/18 |
| Lieut. M. A. DUNN. | 7/9/18 | | 5/12/18 |
| Lieut. G. BROADBENT. | 7/9/18 | | 10/12/18 |
| 2/Lt. W. E. L. COURTNEY. | 7/9/18 | | 29/11/18 |
| 2/Lt. J. E. KEMP. | 7/9/18 | | 23/12/18 |
| 2/Lt. A. R. SABEY. | 7/9/18 | (*Died* 10/9/18) | |
| 2/Lt. E. B. SMAILES. | 7/9/18 | (*Died* 13/9/18) | |
| Lieut. J. C. WALKER. | 7/9/18 | | 13/1/19 |
| Capt. J. E. DOYLE. | 8/9/18 | | 19/12/18 |
| Lieut. R. A. HENRY. | 8/9/18 | | 8/12/18 |
| Lieut. J. P. LLOYD. | 10/9/18 | | 1/1/19 |
| Lieut. H. A. COLE. | 12/9/18 | | 8/12/18 |
| 2/Lt. C. R. GAGE. | 12/9/18 | | 13/12/18 |
| 2/Lt. W. A. JOHNSTON. | 14/9/18 | | 28/11/18 |
| Lieut. J. E. REID. | 14/9/18 | | 13/12/18 |
| 2/Lt. G. A. SHIPTON. | 14/9/18 | | 26/11/18 |
| Lieut. W. F. OGILVY. | 14/9/18 | | –/11/18 |
| Lieut. E. F. WRIGHT. | 15/9/18 | | 13/12/18 |
| Lieut. J. H. M. YEOMANS. | 15/9/18 | | 11/12/18 |
| Capt. O. C. HOLLERAN. | 15/9/18 | | 5/12/18 |

## ROYAL AIR FORCE—continued.

| Name. | Missing. | Interned. | Repatriated. |
|---|---|---|---|
| 2/Lt. J. A. MATTHEWS. | 15/9/18 | | 8/12/18 |
| Lieut. E. J. STOCKMAN. | 15/9/18 | | 8/12/18 |
| 2/Lt. P. PAYNE. | 15/9/18 | | 8/12/18 |
| 2/Lt. E. A. MARCHANT. | 15/9/18 | | –/12/18 |
| Lieut. R. W. HEINE. | 15/9/18 | | 13/12/18 |
| Lieut. F. F. JEWETT. | 15/9/18 | U.S.A.S. | |
| 2/Lt. H. MERCER. | 15/9/18 | | 13/12/18 |
| Lieut. C. B. NAYLOR. | 15/9/18 | | 8/12/18 |
| 2/Lt. G. C. RUSSELL. | 15/9/18 | | 13/12/18 |
| 2/Lt. F. E. FINCH. | 15/9/18 | | 13/12/18 |
| Lieut. G. F. ANDERSON. | 15/9/18 | | 13/12/18 |
| 2/Lt. C. THOMAS. | 15/9/18 | Holland | 15/11/18 |
| Lieut. J. J. MacDONALD. | 15/9/18 | Holland | 15/11/18 |
| 2/Lt. F. B. COX. | 15/9/18 | Holland | 15/11/18 |
| 2/Lt. G. E. McMANUS. | 15/9/18 | Holland | 15/11/18 |
| 2/Lt. J. B. RICHARDSON. | 15/9/18 | | 1/1/19 |
| 2/Lt. A. TAPPING. | 15/9/18 | | 23/12/18 |
| 2/Lt. C. GUILD. | 15/9/18 | | 23/12/18 |
| 2/Lt. H. DAVIES. | 15/9/18 | | 1/1/19 |
| 2/Lt. W. J. N. CHALKLIN. | 15/9/18 | | 23/12/18 |
| 2/Lt. A. G. HARRISON. | 15/9/18 | | 23/12/18 |
| 2/Lt. L. G. HALL. | 15/9/18 | U.S.A.S. | |
| 2/Lt. W. D. EVANS. | 15/9/18 | | 23/12/18 |
| 2/Lt. E. L. BADDELY. | 15/9/18 | | 23/12/18 |
| 2/Lt. R. H. ROSE. | 15/9/18 | | 24/12/18 |
| 2/Lt. H. T. HEMPSALL. | 15/9/18 | | –/12/18 |
| Capt. W. R. E. HARRISON. | 15/9/18 | Holland | 15/11/18 |
| Sub-Lieut. A. B. D. CAMPBELL. | 15/9/18 | | 13/12/18 |
| 2/Lt. C. H. SENECAL. | 16/9/18 | | 13/12/18 |
| 2/Lt. E. J. NORRIS. | 16/9/18 | | 29/12/18 |
| 2/Lt. A. HINDER. | 16/9/18 | (Died) | |
| 2/Lt. P. J. A. FLEMING. | 16/9/18 | | 8/12/18 |
| 2/Lt. W. E. JOHNS. | 16/9/18 | | 25/12/18 |
| 2/Lt. R. H. STONE. | 16/9/18 | | 8/12/18 |
| Lieut. N. F. ADAMS. | 16/9/18 | | 9/12/18 |
| 2/Lt. F. F. ANSLOW. | 16/9/18 | | 1/1/19 |
| Capt. AYRTON (F. A.) | 16/9/18 | | 18/12/18 |
| 2/Lt. R. S. LIPSETT. | 16/9/18 | | 23/12/18 |
| Lieut. H. V. BRISBIN. | 16/9/18 | | 11/12/18 |
| Lieut. R. C. PITMAN. | 17/9/18 | | 24/12/18 |
| 2/Lt. F. H. CHAINEY. | 17/9/18 | | 23/12/18 |
| Lieut. F. R. JOHNSON. | 17/9/18 | | 24/12/18 |
| 2/Lt. H. H. SENIOR. | 17/9/18 | | 6/12/18 |
| 2/Lt. W. A. WILSON. | 17/9/18 | | 29/11/18 |
| 2/Lt. C. E. USHER-SOMERS. | 17/9/18 | | 12/12/18 |
| Lieut. W. W. CHREIMAN. | 17/9/18 | | 5/12/18 |
| 2/Lt. F. W. KING. | 17/9/18 | | 13/12/18 |
| Lieut. B. NORCROSS. | 17/9/18 | | 28/12/18 |
| 2/Lt. R. H. COLE. | 17/9/18 | (Died 30/9/19) | |
| Lieut. E. G. GALLAGHER. | 17/9/18 | Luxemburg | 28/11/18 |
| Lieut. R. S. COBHAM. | 17/9/18 | Luxemburg | 28/11/18 |
| Lieut. E. E. TAYLOR. | 17/9/18 | Luxemburg | 28/11/18 |
| 2/Lt. C. C. FISHER. | 17/9/18 | Holland | 15/11/18 |
| 2/Lt. R. S. OAKLEY. | 17/9/18 | Holland | 15/11/18 |
| Lieut. J. B. LACY. | 17/9/18 | | –/12/18 |
| Lieut. G. H. LOCKE. | 17/9/18 | Holland | |

## ROYAL AIR FORCE—continued.

| Name. | Missing. | Interned. | Repatriated. |
|---|---|---|---|
| Lieut. H. B. MONAGHAN. | 17/9/18 | | 13/12/18 |
| 2/Lt. A. FAIRHURST. | 17/9/18 | | 8/12/18 |
| 2/Lt. E. C. JEFFKINS. | 17/9/18 | | 26/11/18 |
| Lieut. H. E. HYDE. | 17/9/18 | | 8/12/18 |
| 2/Lt. R. T. DOWN. | 17/9/18 | | 1/1/19 |
| 2/Lt. C. N. YELVERTON. | 17/9/18 | | 23/12/18 |
| Lieut. G. W. MITCHEL. | 17/9/18 | | –/12/18 |
| Lieut. C. M. HOLBROOK. | 18/9/18 | | 8/12/18 |
| Lieut. E. G. ROLPH. | 20/9/18 | | 13/12/18 |
| 2/Lt. T. NEWEY. | 20/9/18 | | 22/11/18 |
| 2/Lt. C. G. MILNE. | 20/9/18 | | 23/12/18 |
| Lieut. E. P. LARRABEE. | 20/9/18 | | 5/12/18 |
| 2/Lt. J. N. KIER. | 20/9/18 | | 23/12/18 |
| Lieut. G. F. C. CASWELL. | 20/9/18 | | 8/12/18 |
| Capt. S. CARLIN. | 21/9/18 | | 13/12/18 |
| Lieut. D. A. NEVILLE. | 22/9/18 | | 13/12/18 |
| 2/Lt. J. C. GUNN. | 22/9/18 | | 28/11/18 |
| 2/Lt. T. WARBURTON. | 24/9/18 | | 13/12/18 |
| 2/Lt. J. M. DANDY. | 24/9/18 | | 5/12/18 |
| Lieut. H. S. MANTLE. | 24/9/18 | | 13/12/18 |
| Lieut. N. N. COOPE. | 24/9/18 | | 29/11/18 |
| Lieut. H. J. BENNETT. | 24/9/18 | | |
| 2/Lt. R. H. ARMSTRONG. | 24/9/18 | | 13/12/18 |
| 2/Lt. H. J. PRETTY. | 24/9/18 | | 14/12/18 |
| Lieut. C. C. CONOVER. | 24/9/18 | | 10/12/18 |
| 2/Lt. J. OLERENSHAW. | 24/9/18 | Holland | 15/11/18 |
| 2/Lt. R. L. KINGHAM. | 24/9/18 | Holland | 15/11/18 |
| 2/Lt. H. J. C. ELWIG. | 25/9/18 | | 13/12/18 |
| Lieut. C. R. GROSS. | 25/9/18 | | 28/11/18 |
| Capt. A. LINDLEY. | 25/9/18 | | 29/11/18 |
| 2/Lt. J. W. BROWN. | 25/9/18 | | 13/12/18 |
| Lieut. B. H. KEWLEY. | 25/9/18 | | 29/11/18 |
| 2/Lt. A. B. HENDERSON. | 25/9/18 | | 30/12/18 |
| Lieut. N. W. HELWIG. | 25/9/18 | | 29/11/18 |
| Lieut. C. B. E. LLOYD. | 25/9/18 | | 13/12/18 |
| Capt. C. CRAWFORD. | 25/9/18 | | 29/11/18 |
| Lieut. C. P. SPARKES. | 25/9/18 | | 16/12/18 |
| 2/Lt. C. B. SANDERSON. | 25/9/18 | (*Died* at Hautmont 17/10/18) | |
| 2/Lt. R. C. PRETTY. | 25/9/18 | | 13/12/18 |
| 2/Lt. A. C. HEYES. | 25/9/18 | | 13/12/18 |
| Lieut. G. B. DUNLOP. | 25/9/18 | | 13/12/18 |
| 2/Lt. G. R. BARTLETT. | 25/9/18 | | 13/12/18 |
| Lieut. E. FULFORD. | 26/9/18 | | 28/11/18 |
| 2/Lt. W. H. COGHILL. | 26/9/18 | | 13/12/18 |
| Lieut. H. CROSSLEY. | 26/9/18 | | –/11/18 |
| 2/Lt. W. H. G. GILLET. | 26/9/18 | | 13/12/18 |
| Lieut. T. H. SWANN. | 26/9/18 | | 26/11/18 |
| Capt. P. E. WELCHMAN. | 26/9/18 | | 28/11/18 |
| Lieut. W. R. THORNTON. | 26/9/18 | | 13/12/18 |
| 2/Lt. L. G. SMITH. | 26/9/18 | (*Died*) | |
| Lieut. J. A. PARKINSON. | 26/9/18 | | 13/12/18 |
| 2/Lt. O. R. HIBBERT. | 26/9/18 | | 19/12/18 |
| Capt. J. F. CHISHOLM. | 26/9/18 | Holland | 15/11/18 |
| Lieut. F. H. STRINGER. | | | 13/12/18 |
| 2/Lt. J. O. WOOD. | 27/9/18 | | 13/12/18 |
| Lieut. N. D. WILLIS. | 27/9/18 | | 14/12/18 |

## ROYAL AIR FORCE—continued.

| Name. | Missing. | Interned. | Repatriated. |
|---|---|---|---|
| 2/Lt. N. F. MOXON. | 29/9/18 | | 31/1/19 |
| 2/Lt. C. H. WILCOX. | 27/9/18 | | 25/12/18 |
| Lieut. P. M. WALLACE. | 27/9/18 | | 13/12/18 |
| Lieut. P. S. MANLEY. | 27/9/18 | | –/12/18 |
| 2/Lt. C. A. HARRISON. | 27/9/18 | | 13/12/18 |
| 2/Lt. C. F. CAWLEY. | 27/9/18 | | 27/11/18 |
| Lieut. R. C. BENNETT. | 27/9/18 | | 29/12/18 |
| Capt. R. J. MORGAN. | 28/9/18 | | 5/12/18 |
| Lieut. G. J. SMITH. | 28/9/18 | | 29/11/18 |
| Lieut. T. M. STEELE. | 28/9/18 | | 16/12/18 |
| Lieut. D. L. MELVIN. | 28/9/18 | | 13/12/18 |
| Lieut. W. A. RANKIN. | 28/9/18 | | 13/12/18 |
| Lieut. P. C. JENNER. | 28/9/18 | | 28/11/18 |
| 2/Lt. A. FLETCHER. | 28/9/18 | | 13/12/18 |
| Lieut. R. C. MITTEN. | 28/9/18 | | 17/12/18 |
| 2/Lt. J. C. MALCOLMSON. | 28/9/18 | | 13/12/18 |
| Lieut. J. M. McLENNAN. | 28/9/18 | | 13/12/18 |
| Lieut. F. EDSTEAD. | 28/9/18 | | 5/12/18 |
| Lieut. D. A. O'LEARY. | 28/9/18 | | 10/12/18 |
| Lieut. B. R. ROLFE. | 28/9/18 | | 8/12/18 |
| Capt. E. C. HOY. | 28/9/18 | | 28/11/18 |
| Lieut. W. L. DOUGAN. | 28/9/18 | | 26/12/18 |
| 2/Lt. W. MITCHELL. | 28/9/18 | (*Died* at Lenze) | |
| 2/Lt. H. B. HEWAT. | 28/9/18 | | 13/1/19 |
| Lieut. P. B. COOKE. | 28/9/18 | | 29/11/18 |
| 2/Lt. G. GEDGE. | 28/9/18 | | 13/12/18 |
| Lieut. H. P. BRUMMELL. | 28/9/18 | | 29/12/18 |
| Capt. A. V. BOWATER. | 28/9/18 | | 8/12/18 |
| 2/Lt. E. DARBY. | 28/9/18 | | 13/12/18 |
| Lieut. C. R. MOORE. | 28/9/18 | | 8/12/18 |
| Lieut. A. F. SMITH. | 28/9/18 | | 13/12/18 |
| 2/Lt. H. C. TELFER. | 28/9/18 | | 13/12/18 |
| 2/Lt. D. A. THOMSON. | 28/9/18 | | 29/11/18 |
| 2/Lt. O. V. JUDKINS. | 28/9/18 | | 2/1/19 |
| 2/Lt. W. J. JOHNSON. | 28/9/18 | | |
| 2/Lt. D. M. JOHN. | 28/9/18 | Holland | 15/11/18 |
| Lieut. F. G. PYM. | –/9/18 | | 30/12/18 |
| 2/Lt. A. C. J. PAYNE. | 29/9/18 | | 13/12/18 |
| Lieut. M. R. MAHONY. | –/9/18 | | 23/12/18 |
| Lieut. R. M. MacDONALD. | 29/9/18 | | 29/11/18 |
| Lieut. C. W. M. THOMPSON. | 29/9/18 | | 30/12/18 |
| Lieut. L. R. JAMES. | 29/9/18 | | 28/11/18 |
| Lieut. W. HENLEY-MOONEY. | 29/9/18 | U.S.A.S. | |
| Lieut. L. ELWORTHY. | 29/9/18 | | 13/12/18 |
| 2/Lt. A. M. ALLAN. | 29/9/18 | | –/12/18 |
| 2/Lt. J. M. KELLY. | | | 12/11/18 |
| Lieut. T. BECK. | 1/10/18 | (*Died*) | |
| Capt. W. BUCKINGHAM. | 1/10/18 | | 13/12/18 |
| 2/Lt. F. R. EVELEIGH. | 1/10/18 | | 13/12/18 |
| Lieut. A. M. MATHESON. | 1/10/18 | | 29/12/18 |
| 2/Lt. R. J. HAGENBUSH. | 1/10/18 | U.S.A.S. | |
| Lieut. F. L. STRANGWARD. | 2/10/18 | | 13/12/18 |
| Lieut. R. HALL. | 2/10/18 | | 13/12/18 |
| 2/Lt. J. E. JENNINGS. | 2/10/18 | | 13/12/18 |
| Lieut. J. K. SHOOK. | 2/10/18 | | 13/12/18 |
| Lieut. I. W. AWDE. | 5/10/18 | | 25/12/18 |
| 2/Lt. H. M. D. SPEAGELL. | 5/10/18 | | 13/12/18 |
| Lieut. E. C. LANSDALE. | 30/9/16 | (*Died* as Prisoner 1/12/16) | |

## ROYAL AIR FORCE—continued.

| Name. | Missing. | Interned. | Repatriated. |
|---|---|---|---|
| Capt. A. G. INGLIS. | 5/10/18 | | 13/12/18 |
| Lieut. W. G. L. BODLEY. | 5/10/18 | | 29/1/19 |
| 2/Lt. A. BRANDRICK. | 5/10/18 | | 21/12/18 |
| Lieut. F. E. BOND. | 5/10/18 | | 13/12/18 |
| 2/Lt. C. V. A. BUCKNALL. | 5/10/18 | | 13/12/18 |
| 2/Lt. D. P. DAVIES. | 5/10/18 | | 13/12/18 |
| Lieut. C. KNIGHT. | 5/10/18 | | 26/12/18 |
| Lieut. C. HANCOCK. | 5/10/18 | | 14/12/18 |
| 2/Lt. H. L. PRIME. | 5/10/18 | | |
| 2/Lt. J. H. PERRING. | 5/10/18 | | 13/12/18 |
| Lieut. R. CALROW. | 6/10/18 | | -/11/18 |
| 2/Lt. W. T. S. CAIRNS. | 6/10/18 | | 13/12/18 |
| 2/Lt. W. PENDLETON. | | Holland | 15/11/18 |
| 2/Lt. B. LOCKEY. | 7/10/18 | Holland | 15/11/18 |
| 2/Lt. H. E. POWER. | | Holland | 15/11/18 |
| 2/Lt. F. CORNWALL. | 8/10/18 | | 1/1/19 |
| 2/Lt. R. W. HOPPER. | 8/10/18 | | 13/12/18 |
| Lieut. J. P. MURPHY. | 8/10/18 | | -/12/18 |
| Lieut. W. E. BARDGETT. | 9/10/18 | | 2/12/18 |
| Lieut. C. F. PINEAU. | 9/10/18 | | -/12/18 |
| Lieut. J. E. SITCH. | 9/10/18 | | 27/11/18 |
| Lieut. D. S. FOX. | 9/10/18 | | 14/11/18 |
| Lieut. C. HOULGRAVE. | 9/10/18 | | 30/12/18 |
| 2/Lt. H. H. WHITLOCK. | 14/10/18 | | 30/12/18 |
| Capt. E. W. CORNISH. | 14/10/18 | | 11/12/18 |
| Lieut. R. J. FARQUHARSON. | 14/10/18 | | 8/12/18 |
| 2/Lt. P. C. S. McCREA. | 14/10/18 | | 13/12/18 |
| 2/Lt. P. L. PHILLIPS. | 14/10/18 | | -/12/18 |
| 2/Lt. J. C. J. McDONALD. | 14/10/18 | | 15/12/18 |
| 2/Lt. L. TIMMINS. | 18/10/18 | | 13/12/18 |
| 2/Lt. R. COULTHARD. | 18/10/18 | | 13/12/18 |
| 2/Lt. G. E. HUGHES. | 21/10/18 | | -/11/18 |
| 2/Lt. A. L. MAWER. | 21/10/18 | | 18/11/18 |
| Lieut. M. H. WINKLER. | 21/10/18 | | 5/12/18 |
| Capt. W. E. WINDOVER. | 21/10/18 | | 8/12/18 |
| Lieut. R. W. L. THOMSON. | 21/10/18 | | 8/12/18 |
| 2/Lt. J. A. SIMSON. | 21/10/18 | | 8/12/18 |
| Major L. G. S. REYNOLDS. | 21/10/18 | | 13/12/18 |
| 2/Lt. R. RIFFKIN. | 21/10/18 | | 8/12/18 |
| Lieut. J. M. PEARSON. | 21/10/18 | | 25/11/18 |
| Lieut. S. L. MUCKLOW. | 21/10/18 | | 8/12/18 |
| 2/Lt. P. KING. | 21/10/18 | | 26/11/18 |
| 2/Lt. A. W. R. EVANS. | 21/10/18 | | 8/12/18 |
| 2/Lt. M. W. DUNN. | 21/10/18 | | -/12/18 |
| Lieut. R. W. SILK. | 23/10/18 | | 11/1/19 |
| 2/Lt. F. H. REED. | 23/10/18 | | |
| Lieut. J. T. SORLEY. | 23/10/18 | | 8/12/18 |
| 2/Lt. A. P. C. BRUCE. | 23/10/18 | | 8/12/18 |
| 2/Lt. H. H. ROFE. | 23/10/18 | | 8/12/18 |
| 2/Lt. B. S. CASE. | 23/10/18 | (*Died* 31/10/18) | |
| 2/Lt. H. BRIDGER. | 23/10/18 | | 26/11/18 |
| 2/Lt. J. C. COLLINS. | 23/10/18 | | 8/12/18 |
| Lieut. L. H. SMITH. | 25/10/18 | | 8/12/18 |
| Lieut. H. E. HASTIE. | 25/10/18 | | -/11/18 |
| 2/Lt. F. H. V. COOMBER. | 26/10/18 | | 7/12/18 |
| 2/Lt. H. THOMAS. | 26/10/18 | | 7/12/18 |

## ROYAL AIR FORCE—continued.

| Name. | Missing. | Interned. | Repatriated. |
|---|---|---|---|
| 2/Lt. M. McLEAN. | 26/10/18 | | 8/12/18 |
| 2/Lt. K. O. BRACKEN. | 27/10/18 | | 30/11/18 |
| Lieut. E. W. O. HALL. | 27/10/18 | | 27/11/18 |
| Capt. C. L. KING. | 27/10/18 | | 30/11/18 |
| 2/Lt. N. SMITH. | 27/10/18 | | -/11 '18 |
| 2/Lt. W. SANDERS. | 27/10/18 | | 13/12/18 |
| Lieut. H. G. LEWIS. | 27/10/18 | | -/12/18 |
| 2/Lt. A. R. PRATT. | 27/10/18 | | 11/12/18 |
| 2/Lt. C. A. CRICHTON. | 27/10/18 | | 19/11/18 |
| Lieut. I. O. GAZE. | 28/10/18 | | 27/11/18 |
| Lieut. N. T. TREMBATH. | 28/10/18 | | 22/1/19 |
| 2/Lt. L. G. STOCKWELL. | 28/10/18 | | 8/12/18 |
| 2/Lt. J. P. COLEMAN. | 28/19/18 | | 8/12/18 |
| 2/Lt. C. M. ALLAN. | 28/10/18 | | 10/12/18 |
| Lieut. J. E. HALLENQUIST. | 29/10/18 | | 25/11/18 |
| 2/Lt. L. H. EYRES. | 29/10/18 | | 8/12/18 |
| Lieut. H. F. MULHALL. | 30/10/18 | | 5/1/19 |
| 2/Lt. T. W. SLEIGHT. | 30/10/18 | | 19/11/18 |
| 2/Lt. W. AMORY. | 30/10/18 | | 18/12/18 |
| Lieut. F. LYNN. | 30/10/18 | | 13/12/18 |
| 2/Lt. R. V. MURRAY. | 30/10/18 | | 13/12/18 |
| 2/Lt. C. N. BOYD. | 30/10/18 | | 27/11/18 |
| Lieut. R. W. DUFF. | 30/10/18 | | 22/11/18 |
| Lieut. A. BUCHANAN. | 30/10/18 | | 19/12/18 |
| 2/Lt. J. B. VICKERS. | 30/10/18 | | 26/11/18 |
| 2/Lt. S. J. GOODFELLOW. | 30/10/18 | | 8/12/18 |
| 2/Lt. J. B. ISAACS. | 30/10/18 | | 5/12/18 |
| 2/Lt. H. LANSDALE. | 31/10/18 | | 23/1/19 |
| 2/Lt. H. J. GEMMEL. | 31/10/18 | | 4/12/18 |
| Lieut. R. G. DOBESON. | 1/11/18 | | -/12/18 |
| 2/Lt. F. G. MILLS. | 1/11/18 | | 29/12/18 |
| 2/Lt. W. G. GADD. | 1/11/18 | | 8/12/18 |
| 2/Lt. J. M. PAYNE. | 1/11/18 | | 8/12/18 |
| 2/Lt. P. S. TENNANT. | 2/11/18 | | 31/12/18 |
| 2/Lt. G. L. P. DRUMMOND. | 2/11/18 | | 10/12/18 |
| 2/Lt. H. R. ABEY. | 2/11/18 | | -/12/18 |
| Lieut. F. S. BOWLES. | 3/11/18 | | 9/12/18 |
| Lieut. P. G. GREENWOOD. | 3/11/18 | | 27/11/18 |
| Lieut. W. SHACKLETON. | 4/11/18 | | 8/12/18 |
| Lieut. J. E. RADLEY. | 4/11/18 | | 8/12/18 |
| 2/Lt. D. M. DEE. | 4/11/18 | | 27/11/18 |
| 2/Lt. J. PUGH. | 4/11/18 | | 29/11/18 |
| 2/Lt. J. F. McNAMARA. | 4/11/18 | | 27/11/18 |
| Capt. A. A. HARCOURT-VERNON. | 4/11/18 | | 27/11/18 |
| 2/Lt. W. J. POTTS. | 4/11/18 | | 17/12/18 |
| Lieut. C. W. NEWSTEAD. | 4/11/18 | | 28/11/18 |
| Lieut. A. C. MacAULAY | 4/11/18 | | 25/11/18 |
| 2/Lt. H. G. LUTHER. | 4/11/18 | | 29/11/18 |
| 2/Lt. D. C. MacDONALD. | 4/11/18 | | 27/11/18 |
| Lieut. J. G. CAREY. | 4/11/18 | | 27/11/18 |
| Lieut. H. J. BERRY. | 5/11/18 | | 29/11/18 |
| 2/Lt. H. A. HAMLET. | 5/11/18 | | 27/11/18 |
| 2/Lt. E. W. THRESHER. | 6/11/18 | | 1/12/18 |
| Lt. G. T. RICHARDSON. | 6/11/18 | | 29/1/19 |
| 2/Lt. W. H. TRESHAM. | 6/11/18 | | 1/12/18 |
| Lieut. H. L. WREN. | 6/11/18 | | 28/12/18 |

## ROYAL AIR FORCE—continued.

| Name. | Missing. | Interned. | Repatriated. |
|---|---|---|---|
| Lieut. H. W. RUSSELL. | 8/11/18 | | 28/11/18 |
| Lieut. E. O. AMM. | 9/11/18 | | 28/11/18 |
| 2/Lt. F. B. CANDY. | 9/11/18 | Holland | |
| 2/Lt. O. E. COLEMAN. | 9/11/18 | Holland | |
| 2/Lt. J. FREEMAN. | 9/11/18 | Holland | |
| 2/Lt. C. H. THOMAS. | 10/11/18 | — | 28/2/19 |
| Lieut. A. M. ROSENBLEET. | 10/11/18 | | 25/11/18 |
| 2/Lt. H. T. C. GOMPERTZ. | 10/11/18 | | –/11/18 |
| 2/Lt. S. COATES. | 10/11/18 | | 23/11/18 |
| Lieut. A. B. AGNEW. | 10/11/18 | | 23/11/18 |
| 2/Lt. E. A. C. BRITTON. | 10/11/18 | | 25/11/18 |
| Lieut. J. MARTIN. | | Holland | –/12/18 |
| Lieut. J. LISTER. | | Holland | 15/11/18 |
| Lieut. C. J. LOCKE. | | Holland | 15/11/18 |
| Lieut. F. N. HUDSON. | | Holland | 15/11/18 |
| 2/Lt. T. N. ENRIGHT. | | Holland | 14/11/18 |
| Capt. F. E. FRYER. | | Holland | 15/11/18 |
| Lieut. E. S. FARRAND. | | | 14/12/18 |
| Capt. W. E. FOSTER. | | | 27/11/18 |
| Lieut. J. B. HULME. | | | 27/11/18 |
| Capt. T. E. LANDER. | | | 27/11/18 |
| Capt. C. B. WILSON. | | | 19/11/18 |
| Lt. E. J. COOPER. | | | 7/2/19 |
| Lt. A. COPLEY. | | | 9/2/19 |
| Lt. G. WALLACE SIMPSON. | | | 9/2/19 |
| Capt. G. C. F. OWEN. | | | 4/2/19 |

## ROYAL NAVAL AIR SERVICE.

| Name. | Missing. | Interned. | | Repatriated. |
|---|---|---|---|---|
| Lieut. R. INGE. | | Holland | 30/4/18 | 26/11/18 |
| Lieut. A. T. COWLEY. | | Holland | 30/4/18 | 18/11/18 |
| Lieut. H. G. REID. | | Holland | 27/6/18 | 31/8/18 |
| Midshipman J. M. D'ARCY LEVY. | | Holland | 9/4/18 | 18/11/18 |
| Lieut. D. C. TOOKE. | | Holland | 12/10/18 | 21/2/19 |
| Lieut. F. W. MARDOCK. | | | | 19/12/18 |
| Lieut. J. F. BAILEY. | | Holland | 15/6/18 | 21/1/19 |
| Lieut. C. BUTTERWORTH. | | Holland | 6/2/18 | 18/11/18 |
| Lieut. C. NEWMAN. | | | | 18/12/18 |
| Lieut. J. ROCKEY. | | | | 18/12/18 |
| Flt. Sub.-Lieut. C. G. KNIGHT. | | Holland | 30/4/18 | |
| Flt. Lieut. G. G. G. HODGE. | | | | 12/12/18 |
| Lieut. G. LLEWELLYN-DAVIES. | | | | 6/1/19 |
| Lieut. W. WALKER. | | | | 19/12/18 |
| Lieut. G. L. ELLIOTT. | | | | 14/12/18 |
| Flt. Sub.-Lieut. L. P. PAINE. | | | | 14/1/19 |
| Lieut. S. R. HIBBARD. | | | | 13/12/18 |
| Capt. G. FLEMING. | | (*Died* 17/4/17) | | |
| Lieut. H. C. VEREKER. | | | | 3/1/19 |
| 2/Lt. H. EDWARDS. | | | | 14/1/19 |
| Lieut. J. C. CROFT. | | | | 6/1/19 |
| Flt. Sub.-Lieut. H. M. BURTON. | | | | |
| Lieut. N. M. HEWITT. | | | | 20/12/18 |
| Sub.-Lieut. A. J. BEATTIE. | 3/1/18 | | | 16/12/18 |
| Lieut. A. C. STEVENS. | 28/11/16 | | | 17/12/18 |

**ROYAL NAVAL AIR SERVICE**—continued.

| Name. | Missing. | Interned. | Repatriated. |
|---|---|---|---|
| Lieut. C. RATTBORNE. | | | 5/8/18 |
| Lieut. K. SLATER. | | | 6/1/19 |
| Sub.-Lieut. A. MATHER. | | | 31/12/18 |
| Flt. Sub.-Lt. W. R. WING. | | | |
| Flt. Sub.-Lt. C. LAURENCE. | | | 14/12/18 |
| Sub.-Lt. L. J. BENNETT. | Holland | 4/8/18 | 16/8/18 |
| Flt. Lieut. G. E. NASH. | | | 1/1/19 |
| Sub.-Lt. R. L. KENT. | | | 1/1/19 |
| Flt. Sub.-Lt. A. B. HOLCROFT. | | | 19/12/18 |
| Flt. Sub.-Lt. V. G. AUSTEN. | | | 25/12/18 |
| Sub.-Lt. A. D. M. LEWIS. | | | 25/12/18 |
| Flt. Sub.-Lt. N. D. HALL. | | | 2/1/19 |
| Flt. Sub.-Lt. H. H. BOOTH. | | | 14/12/18 |
| Flt. Sub.-Lt. E. W. DESBARATS. | | | 6/1/19 |
| Capt. R. MACK. | | | 20/1/18 |
| Flt. Sub.-Lt. J. R. WILFORD. | | | 14/12/18 |
| Flt. Sub.-Lt. H. S. BROUGHALL. | | | 25/12/18 |
| Flt. Sub.-Lt. R. E. MacMILLAN. | | | 14/12/18 |
| Lieut. D. F. LEWIS. | | | |
| Flt. Sub.-Lt. W. INGLESON. | | | 17/12/18 |
| Flt. Sub.-Lt. A. W. PHILLIPS. | | | 26/12/18 |
| Flt. Sub.-Lt. E. FOSTER. | | | 2/1/19 |
| Flt. Lieut. W. PERHAM. | Holland | 26/10/17 | |
| Sub.-Lt. H. C. GOOCH. | | | 15/11/18 |
| Flt. Sub.-Lt. J. C. AKESTER. | | | 18/12/18 |
| Flt. Sub.-Lt. W. E. B. OAKLEY. | | | 14/12/18 |
| Flt. Sub.-Lt. G. ANDREWS. | | | 17/12/18 |
| Flt. Sub.-Lt. A. MacDONALD. | | | 17/12/18 |
| Flt. Sub.-Lt. J. S. SERCOMBE SMITH. | | | 18/12/18 |
| Flt. Lieut. L. G. SIEVEKING. | | | 17/12/18 |
| Lieut. S. E. HOBLYN. | Holland | 30/4/18 | 26/11/18 |
| Flt. Lieut. W. S. MAGRATH. | Holland | 6/5/18 | 14/12/18 |
| Lieut. A. A. D. GREY. | | | 1/1/19 |
| Lieut. J. HAY. | Holland | 19/4/18 | 4/10/18 |
| Flt. Sub.-Lt. J. G. CLARK. | | | 18/12/18 |
| Sub.-Lt. H. WHITE. | | | 19/12/18 |
| Sub.-Lt. H. P. SALTER. | | | 31/12/18 |
| Flt. Sub.-Lt. H. St. J. E. YOUENS. | | | 14/12/18 |
| Flt. Sub.-Lt. J. H. T. CARR. | 25/1/18 | | 18/12/18 |

# EAST THEATRE OF WAR.

## TURKISH PRISONERS.
### DARDANELLES.

| Name. | Regiment. | Missing. | Repatriated. |
|---|---|---|---|
| Lieut. Sir R. J. PAUL. | R.E. att. French Flying Corps | | 17/12/18 |
| Capt. B. S. ATKINS. | 11/Rajputs att. R.A.F. | 16/9/15 | 7/12/18 |
| Lieut. Douglas BRANSON. | R.N.A.S. | –/2/16 | 16/12/18 |
| Lieut. R. T. A. MacDONALD. | 16/Australian Inf. | 30/4/15 | 9/1/19 |
| Lieut. W. E. ELSTON. | 16/Australian Inf. | 30/4/15 | –/11/18 |
| Lieut. S. L. STORMOUTH. | 15/Australian Inf. | 7/6/15 | 16/12/18 |
| 2/Lt. L. H. LUSCOMBE. | 14/Australian Inf. | | 16/12/18 |
| Lieut. S. R. JORDAN. | 9/Australian Inf. | | 8/12/18 |
| Capt. W. H. TRELOAR. | Australian Flying Corps | 16/9/15 | –/11/18 |
| Lieut. S. T. W. GOODWIN. | 6/Australian Inf. | 20/12/15 | 16/12/18 |
| Lieut. John L. STONE. | 4/Worcestershire Regt. | 6/8/15 | –/12/18 |
| Capt. J. M. B. ENTWHISTLE. | 4/Worcestershire Regt. (Died 2/12/18 at Alexandria) | 6/8/15 | |
| Capt. H. A. BRETT. | 9/Lincolnshire Regt. | 6/8/15 | 7/12/18 |
| Capt. R. D. ELLIOT. | 5/East Yorks Regt. | 7–11/8/15 | 16/12/18 |
| Lieut. R. A. RAWSTORNE. | 6/East Yorks Regt. | 7–11/8/15 | 13/12/18 |
| Lieut. J. STILL. | 6/East Yorks Regt. | 7–11/8/15 | 7/12/18 |
| Capt. H. DYSON. | 8/West Riding Regt. | 7–11/8/15 | 7/12/18 |
| 2/Lt. H. DAVENPORT. | 9/West Yorks Regt. | 11/8/15 | 16/12/18 |
| Capt. A. C. M. COXON. | 5/Norfolk Regt. | 12/8/15 | 16/12/18 |
| 2/Lt. W. G. S. FAWKES. | 5/Norfolk Regt. | 12/8/15 | 16/12/18 |
| Lieut. S. WHITE. | Egyptian Police | | 24/11/18 |
| Capt. A. J. DAWES. | 9/Somerset L.I. att. Gurkhas (Died 22/6/17 at Constantinople) | 14/8/15 | |
| Lieut. A. D. PASS. | 1/Dorset Yeomanry | 21/9/15 | 16/12/18 |

### PALESTINE.

| Name. | Regiment. | Missing. | Repatriated. |
|---|---|---|---|
| Lieut. A. W. M. BUDGETT. | Berkshire Yeomanry | 28/11/17 | 16/12/18 |
| Capt. S. R. E. SNOW. | Devon Yeomanry | 1/12/17 | 7/12/18 |
| Lieut. S. E. ARMITAGE. | Dorset Yeomanry att. from Dragoon Guards | 12/11/17 | 7/12/18 |
| Lieut. A. W. STRICKLAND. | Gloucestershire Yeomanry | 23/4/16 | 16/12/18 |
| 2/Lt. C. C. HERBERT. | Gloucestershire Yeomanry | 23/4/16 | 7/12/18 |
| Lt.-Col. Hon. C. J. COVENTRY. | Worcestershire Yeomanry | 23/4/16 | 7/12/18 |
| Major F. S. WILLIAMS THOMAS. | Worcestershire Yeomanry | 23/4/16 | –/12/18 |
| Capt. W. R. O'FARRELL. | R.A.M.C. att. Worcestershire Yeomanry | 23/4/16 | 29/12/18 |
| Capt. E. S. WARD. | Worcestershire Yeomanry | 23/4/16 | 7/12/18 |
| Lieut. W. BELL. | Worcestershire Yeomanry | 23/4/16 | 7/12/18 |
| Lieut. J. H. T. DAWSON. | Worcestershire Yeomanry | 23/4/16 | 1/1/19 |
| Lieut. A. V. HOLYOAKE. | Worcestershire Yeomanry | 23/4/16 | 1/1/19 |
| 2/Lt. W. B. CHAMBERLAIN. | Worcestershire Yeomanry | 23/4/16 | 1/1/19 |
| 2/Lt. A. HICKMAN. | Worcestershire Yeomanry | 23/4/16 | 1/1/19 |
| 2/Lt. B. A. JERVIS. | Worcestershire Yeomanry | 23/4/16 | 23/12/18 |
| 2/Lt. J. MARSH. | Worcestershire Yeomanry (Died at Yozgad 23/10/18) | 23/4/16 | |
| 2/Lt. F. W. OSBORNE. | Worcestershire Yeomanry att. from Dragoon Guards | 23/4/16 | 7/12/18 |
| 2/Lt. G. B. WRIGHT. | Worcestershire Yeomanry | 23/4/16 | 7/12/18 |
| 2/Lt. J. A. TWINBERROW. | Worcestershire Yeomanry | 23/4/16 | 11/12/18 |

**PALESTINE**—continued.

| Name. | Regiment. | Missing. | Repatriated. |
|---|---|---|---|
| Lieut. C. W. HILL. | Royal Air Force | 23/4/16 | 11/12/18 |
| Capt. R. J. TIPTON. | Royal Air Force | 18/6/16 | 24/10/17 |
| 2/Lt. A. LAZARUS-BARLOW. | Royal Air Force | 15/2/17 | 9/12/18 |
| Lieut. E. A. FLOYER. | Royal Air Force | 5/3/17 | 7/12/18 |
| 2/Lt. C. B. PALMER. | Royal Air Force | 5/3/17 | 8/12/18 |
| Lieut. L. W. HEATHCOTE. | Royal Air Force | | 8/12/18 |
| 2/Lt. E. A. NEWTON. | Royal Naval Air Service | 11/10/17 | 18/12/18 |
| Lieut. P. PARKINSON. | Royal Air Force | 10/1/18 | |
| Lieut. C. G. BRONSON. | Royal Naval Air Service | | 16/12/18 |
| Lieut. F. W. HANCOCK. | Royal Air Force | | 16/12/18 |
| 2/Lt. A. A. POOLE. | Royal Air Force | | 16/12/18 |
| Lt. L. H. PAKENHAM-WALSH. | Royal Air Force | 28/1/18 | 16/12/18 |
| Capt. A. J. BOTT. | Royal Air Force | 22/4/18 | 16/12/18 |
| Major M. R. McG. TURNBULL. | Royal Air Force | 25/4/18 | –/1/19 |
| 2/Lt. R. T. CHALLONOR. | Australian Flying Corps | 1/5/18 | 24/11/18 |
| 2/Lt. J. McELLIGOTT. | Australian Flying Corps | 1/5/18 | 24/11/18 |
| Lieut. F. W. HAIG. | Australian Flying Corps | | 16/12/18 |
| Lieut. J. N. GARNETT. | Royal Air Force | 15/7/18 | |
| Lieut. J. S. WESSON. | Royal Air Force | 29/9/18 | 4/1/19 |
| Lieut. W. STEELE. | Royal Air Force | 29/9/18 | 9/1/19 |
| Capt. F. N. G. TAYLOR. | Royal Engineers | 23/4/16 | 20/12/18 |
| Lieut. O. H. LITTLE. | Royal Engineers | 23/4/16 | 1/1/19 |
| Lieut. D. S. McGHIE. | Royal Engineers | 23/4/16 | 16/12/18 |
| 2/Lt. J. KILLIN. | Royal Engineers | 23/4/16 | 16/12/18 |
| Lt.-Col. S. F. NEWCOMBE. | Royal Engineers | 1/11/17 | 4/11/18 |
| 2/Lt. F. C. CARR. | Machine Gun Corps (Died of wounds 24/4/17) | 19/4/17 | |
| Lieut. W. STUART. | Machine Gun Corps | 27/10/17 | 16/12/18 |
| 2/Lt. C. D. McMILLAN. | Machine Gun Corps | 1/11/17 | 16/12/18 |
| 2/Lt. H. J. BRADSHAW. | 4/Norfolk Regt. (Died at Nazareth) | 19/4/17 | |
| Capt. W. C. GARDINER. | 5/Norfolk Regt. | 2/11/17 | 16/12/18 |
| 2/Lt. G. H. L. TALLENT. | 5/Norfolk Regt. att. from Northants. | 29/11/17 | 16/12/18 |
| 2/Lt. J. WINDSOR. | 16/Devonshire Regt. | 3/12/17 | 16/12/18 |
| 2/Lt. H. G. WITHERS. | 16/Devonshire Regt. att. Devon Yeomanry | 3/12/17 | 27/11/18 |
| 2/Lt. K. M. WATT. | 5/Bedfordshire Regt. (Died of wounds) | 1/10/17 | |
| 2/Lt. E. E. DENNIS. | 5/Bedfordshire Regt. att. from R. Berks. | 1/10/17 | 9/1/19 |
| Capt. J. F. FERGUSON. | 2/Leicestershire Regt. att. from Durham L.I. | 17/4/18 | –/1/19 |
| 2/Lt. F. M. PRYCE. | 25/R. Welsh Fusiliers att. from S. Wales Borderers | 30/11/17 | 16/12/18 |
| 2/Lt. G. B. JOHNSTON. | 4/Royal Sussex Regt. (Died at Yozgad 23/10/18) | 27/3/17 | |
| 2/Lt. A. T. C. ASKIN. | 8/Hampshire Regt. | 19/4/17 | 16/12/18 |
| 2/Lt. R. A. BLOFIELD. | Hampshire Regt. (Died of wounds 20/4/17) | 19/4/17 | |
| 2/Lt. H. A. COX. | 8/Hampshire Regt. | 19/4/17 | 7/12/18 |
| 2/Lt. W. S. ROBERTS. | 8/Hampshire Regt. | 19/4/17 | 16/12/18 |
| 2/Lt. V. C. SCLATER. | 2/4 Dorsetshire Regt. | 9/4/18 | –/12/18 |
| Major D. H. PEARSON. | 7/Essex Regt. | 27/3/17 | 7/12/18 |
| 2/Lt. S. C. RIDGEWELL. | 7/Essex Regt. (Died) | 27/11/17 | |

## PALESTINE—continued.

| Name. | Regiment. | Missing. | Repatriated. |
|---|---|---|---|
| Capt. P. G. THOMPSON. | 2/4 Royal West Kent Regt. | 28/3/17 | 27/11/18 |
| 2/Lt. B. K. CATTELL. | 2/10 Middlesex Regt. | 1/11/17 | 13/12/18 |
| 2/Lt. W. DICK. | 6/Highland Light Infantry att. from A. & S. Hldrs. | 10/8/17 | 8/12/18 |
| 2/Lt. F. G. CHALLIS. | 1/Herefordshire Regt. | 26/3/17 | 16/12/18 |
| 2/Lt. R. E. M. Du CANE. | 10th London Regt. | 19/4/17 | 8/12/18 |
| 2/Lt. D. R. WARE. | 2/14 London Regt. | 8/3/18 | 7/12/18 |
| Lt. W. S. L. M. PEARSON. | 17/London Regt. | 2/5/18 | 16/12/18 |
| Lieut. H. M. JUSTICE. | 2/21 London Regt. | 28/3/18 | 16/12/18 |
| Lieut. J. BROWN. | Royal Army Medical Corps | | –/1/19 |
| Capt. A. J. WILCOX. | Army Chaplains Department | 23/4/16 | 9/1/19 |
| 2/Lt. F. ALLSUPP. | Auckland Mtd. Rifles N.Z. | 3/8/16 | –/11/18 |
| 2/Lt. F. S. SHERIDAN. | Indian Army Reserve of Officers | 25/3/17 | 8/12/18 |
| Lieut. P. M. G. BALDWIN. | Indian Lancers att. Mysore Cavalry | 14/7/17 | 3/1/19 |
| Lieut. W. F. PATTON. | 3/Gurkha Rifles | 19/4/18 | 16/12/18 |
| Capt. D. St. P. BUNBURY. | Camel Corps | | 7/12/18 |
| Lieut. W. MILLER. | Camel Corps att. from Rifle Bde. | 1/11/17 | 24/11/18 |

## PERSIAN GULF.

| Name. | Regiment. | Missing. | Repatriated. |
|---|---|---|---|
| Major H. L. REILLY. | R.A.F. att. from 82/Punjabis | –/11/15 | 16/12/18 |
| 2/Lt. E. J. FULTON. | R.A.F. att. from 1/Lancers | 23/11/15 | –/11/18 |
| Lieut. C. R. GOAD. | Royal Indian Marines | –/11/15 | 16/12/18 |
| Capt. H. G. BRODIE. | 103/Mahratta L.I. (Died 26/4/17 at Constantinople) | –/12/15 | |
| Lieut J. G. STILWELL. | 1/4th Hampshire Regt. | 23/1/16 | 27/11/18 |

## MESOPOTAMIA.

| Name. | Regiment. | Missing. | Repatriated. |
|---|---|---|---|
| Commander G. B. DACRE. | R.A.F. | 1/16 | 16/12/18 |
| Lieut. A. J. BARLOW. | R.A.F. | 15/2/17 | 9/1/19 |
| Sub.-Lt. G. T. BYSSHE. | R.A.F. | | 16/12/18 |
| Lieut. B. A. TREACHMAN. | R.A.F. | | 16/12/18 |
| Lieut. T. E. LANDER. | R.A.F. | | 27/11/18 |
| 2/Lt. M. L. MAGUIRE. | R.A.F. (Died –/5/17) | 28/4/17 | |
| Capt. J. R. PHILPOTT. | R.A.F. (Died 15/1/18 at Afion) | 25/9/17 | |
| Lieut. M. G. BEGG. | R.A.F. | 25/9/17 | 16/12/18 |
| Lieut. E. M. BAILLON. | R.A.F. | 25/9/17 | 16/12/18 |
| 2/Lt. J. W. BLAKE. | R.A.F. | | 24/11/18 |
| Lieut. J. D. G. McRAE. | R.A.F. | 5/10/17 | 16/12/18 |
| 2/Lt. P. PRICE. | R.A.F. | 19/10/17 | |
| 2/Lt. J. B. WELMAN. | R.A.F. | 31/10/17 | 7/12/18 |
| Lieut. A. S. MILLS. | R.A.F. | 17/1/18 | 16/12/18 |
| 2/Lt. W. TAYLOR. | R.A.F. | 17/1/18 | 16/12/18 |
| Lieut. E. ROBINSON. | R.A.F. | /18 | |
| Lieut. J. C. JENKS. | R.A.F. | /18 | |
| Capt. A. J. EVERARD. | R.A.F. | | |
| Capt. W. L. HAIGHT. | R.A.F. | 12/3/18 | 16/12/18 |
| Capt. D. W. RUTHERFORD. | R.A.F. | | –/11/18 |
| Lieut. H. L. N. HANCOCK. | R.A.F. | | 16/12/18 |
| Lieut. EDWARDS. | R.A.F. (Died 14/5/18 at Mosul) | 2/5/18 | |
| Lieut. A. WARD. | R.A.F. | | 7/12/18 |
| Lieut. G. J. WILLIAMS. | R.A.F. | | 16/12/18 |

## MESOPOTAMIA—continued.

| Name. | Regiment. | Missing. | Repatriated. |
|---|---|---|---|
| Lt. A. A. CULLEN. | R.A.F. | 31/8/18 | –/1/19 |
| Major A. J. EVANS. | R.A.F. | | 7/12/18 |
| Lieut. E. P. OSMOND. | R.A.F. | | –/11/18 |
| 2/Lt. H. G. PENWARDEN. | R.A.F. | | –/11/18 |
| Capt. S. L. PETTIT. | R.A.F. | 29/7/18 | 16/12/18 |
| Capt. T. W. WHITE. | Australian Flying Corps | 12/11/15 | –/12/18 |
| Capt. F. C. YEATS-BROWN. | Australian Flying Corps | 12/11/15 | 6/12/18 |
| 2/Lt. N. L. STEELE. | Australian Flying Corps | | (Died) |
| 2/Lt. C. H. VAUTIN. | Australian Flying Corps | 8/7/17 | 16/12/18 |
| Commander A. W. CLEMSON. | Australian Flying Corps | 11/10/17 | 16/12/18 |
| Capt. R. A. AUSTIN. | Australian Flying Corps | 19/3/18 | 24/11/18 |
| Lieut. M. C. LEE. | Australian Flying Corps | 19/3/18 | 24/11/18 |
| Lieut. V. J. PARKINSON. | Australian Flying Corps | | –/10/18 |
| Lieut. L. H. SMITH. | Australian Flying Corps | | –/10/18 |
| 2/Lt. C. B. GASSON. | R.N.A.S. | | |
| Lieut. A. MAITLAND-HERIOT. | R.N.A.S. | | 6/12/18 |
| Lieut. W. C. JAMESON. | R.N.A.S. | | |
| Lieut. P. WOODLAND. | R.N.A.S. | | 30/12/18 |
| Lieut. A. J. NIGHTINGALE. | R.N.A.S. | | 30/12/18 |
| Sub.-Lt. W. E. FOSTER. | R.N.A.S. | | 27/11/18 |
| Sub.-Lt. H. BURNS. | R.N.A.S. | | 16/12/18 |
| Lieut. J. W. ALCOCK. | R.N.A.S. | | 16/12/18 |
| Commander T. HACKMAN. | R.N.A.S. | 22/2/18 | 7/12/18 |
| Lieut. T. H. PIPER. | R.N.A.S. | 22/2/18 | 16/12/18 |
| Capt. L. MURPHY. | R.A.M.C. | | 1/1/19 |
| Capt. W. L. E. FRETZ. | R.A.M.C. | (Exchanged | –/–/16) |
| Capt. A. S. CANE. | R.A.M.C. | (Exchanged | –/–/16) |
| Capt. J. BUCHANAN. | R.A.M.C. att. 9/Warwicks | 2/9/18 | 30/12/18 |
| Father P. J. MULLAN. | Army Chaplains' Department | | 7/12/18 |
| 2/Lt. E. A. PINNINGTON. | 13/Hussars | 5/3/17 | 18/2/18 |
| Lieut. T. WILLIAMS-TAYLOR. | 13/Hussars | 5/11/17 | –/12/18 |
| 2/Lt. E. H. JONES. | R.F.A. | | 18/11/18 |
| Lieut. P. S. LEWIS. | R.F.A. 10/Brigade | (Exchanged | –/–/16) |
| Lieut. H. S. D. McNEAL. | R.F.A. 10/Brigade | (Exchanged | –/–/16) |
| Major H. G. THOMSON. | R.F.A. | (Exchanged | –/–/16) |
| Lieut. C. K. WOOLLEY. | R.F.A. | | 16/12/18 |
| 2/Lt. T. W. ABBOTT. | Royal Engineers | (Exchanged | –/–/16) |
| Major G. A. BEAZELEY. | Royal Engineers | 2/5/18 | 16/12/18 |
| 2/Lt. F. W. WOODFIELD. | 2/Leicestershire Regt. | 11/3/16 | 16/12/18 |
| 2/Lt. F. H. E. WATSON. | 10/Norfolk (Exchanged –/–/16) | 15–16/3/16 | |
| 2/Lt. H. BIRCH. | 8/Royal Welsh Fus. | 9/4/16 | (Died) |
| 2/Lt. T. H. R. DANIELS. | 6/K.O. Royal Lancaster Regt. | 9·4·16 | |
| Lieut. W. B. H. PARKER. | 8/Cheshire Regt. (Died 26/4/16) | –/4/16 | |
| 2/Lt. A. B. JONES. | 8/Cheshire Regt. | 30/4/17 | 16/12/18 |
| Lieut. J. H. T. BRABAZON. | 4/Connaught Rangers | 17–18/4/16 | 9/12/18 |
| 2/Lt. J. A. SHANNON. | Highland Light Infantry | 17–18/4/16 | 16/12/18 |
| 2/Lt. T. McK. COWIE. | 2/Black Watch | 17/2/17 | 1/3/17 |
| 2/Lt. A. H. QUINE. | 2/Black Watch | 21/4/17 | 16/12/18 |
| Capt. T. M. JENKINS. | 4/South Wales Borderers | 30/4/17 | 1/1/19 |
| Capt. E. G. STAPLES. | 4/South Wales Borderers | 30/4/17 | 16/12/18 |
| 2/Lt. Sir J. W. L. NAPIER. | 4/South Wales Borderers | 30/4/17 | 16/12/18 |
| 2/Lt. A. W. BROCKS. | 16/Devonshire Regt. att. from 3/Cheshires) (Died 10/3/18 at Afion-kara-Hissar) | 3/12/17 | |

## MESOPOTAMIA—continued.

| Name. | Regiment. | Missing. | Repatriated. |
|---|---|---|---|
| Lieut. C. W. ROGERS. | 9/Royal Warwickshire Regt. | 1/9/18 | 28/11/18 |
| Lieut. H. L. COLLINS. | South African Field Arty. | 16/2/18 | 16/12/18 |
| Major S. BOSE. | Indian Medical Service | | (Exchanged -/-/16) |
| Asst. Surg. A. DE SOUZA. | Indian Medical Service | | |
| Asst. Surg. A. J. HIXON. | Indian Medical Service | | |
| Asst. Surg. R. P. LEWIS. | Indian Medical Service | | |
| Asst. Surg. D. MACKAY. | Indian Medical Service | | |
| Capt. P. O. WESTON. | Indian Medical Service | | |
| Capt. J. S. S. MARTIN. | Indian Medical Service | | 7/12/18 |
| Capt. M. L. PURI. | Indian Medical Service | | 6/10/18 |
| Lieut. A. PAEO. | Indian Medical Service | | 1/1/19 |
| Asst. Surg. H. W. STEWART. | Indian Medical Service | | 17/12/18 |
| Asst. Surg. H. A. T. WELLS. | Indian Medical Service | | 17/12/18 |
| Asst. Surg. E. DUCKWORTH. | Indian Medical Service | | 17/12/18 |
| Lieut. J. M. BALLIN. | Supply & Transport Corps I.A. | | 17/12/18 |
| 2/Lt. G. E. C. FLYNN. | 103/Mahratta L.I., I.A. | 1-2/12/15 | 7/12/18 |
| Capt. P. WOOD. | 89/Punjabis, I.A. | 11/3/16 | (Died) |
| Capt. R. CLIFFORD. | 24/Punjabis, I.A. | | |
| Lieut. H. G. TRANCHELL. | 2/Rajputs, I.A. | (Exchanged | -/-/16) |
| 2/Lt. H. SOUTHERN. | 47/Sikhs, I.A. | 17-18/4/16 | |
| Capt. W. K. COOK. | Indian Army | | 16/12/18 |
| Lieut. E. P. LARKIN. | 20/Deccan Horse I.A. | 10/7/18 | 16/12/18 |
| Lieut. W. R. BOYCE. | I.A.R.O. | | 28/12/18 |

### KUT GARRISON.

| Name. | Regiment. | Missing. | Repatriated. |
|---|---|---|---|
| General C. V. F. TOWNSHEND. | | | 9/11/18 |
| Brig.-General N. W. EVANS. | | | 11/11/18 |
| Brig.-General HAMILTON-HAMILTON. | | | 27/11/18 |
| Major-General DELAMAIN. | | | 27/11/18 |
| Major-General C. G. MELLIS. | | | 11/11/18 |
| Major E. G. DUNN. | General Staff | | 7/12/18 |
| Major B. G. PEEL. | General Staff | | 30/12/18 |
| Capt. E. S. HALFORD. | Staff | | 7/12/18 |
| Lt. F. T. DRAKE-BROCKMAN. | 7/Lancers | | 24/11/18 |
| Lieut. C. A. FORBES. | 7/Lancers | | 7/12/18 |
| Capt. C. H. KIRKWOOD. | 23/Daly's Horse | | 16/12/18 |
| Lieut. R. BRIERLEY. | 23/Daly's Horse | | 7/12/18 |
| Lieut. C. H. C. MONROE. | 33/Indian Cavalry | | 16/12/18 |
| Lt.-Col. J. DAVIE. | 34/Poona Horse | | 7/12/18 |
| Lt.-Col. McV. CRICHTON. | Indian Army Reserve | | 7/12/18 |
| Major H. J. COTTON. | Indian Army Reserve | (Died) | |
| Major C. W. NEUMANN. | Indian Army Reserve | | 24/11/18 |
| Capt. E. W. BURDETT. | Indian Army Reserve | | 16/12/18 |
| Capt. L. V. HOYNE-FOX. | Indian Army Reserve | | |
| Capt. H. G. MORRELL. | Indian Army att. Div. Signal Coy. | | 16/12/18 |
| Capt. H. M. SPINK. | Indian Army Reserve | | 30/12/18 |
| Lieut. J. L. BATEY. | Indian Army Reserve | | 1/1/19 |
| Lieut. H. S. CHESHIRE. | Indian Army Reserve att. Sappers and Miners | | 16/12/18 |
| Lieut. E. S. FAIRBROTHER. | Indian Army Reserve | | 8/12/18 |
| Lieut. LABOTHER. | Indian Army Reserve. | | |
| Lieut. LECKYARD. | Indian Army Reserve | | |
| 2/Lt. DUXBURY. | Indian Army Reserve | | 8/12/18 |
| Lieut. H. A. CLIFTON. | Staff | | 19/12/18 |

## KUT GARRISON—continued.

| Name. | Regiment. | Missing. | Repatriated. |
|---|---|---|---|
| 2/Lt. O. G. KIERNANDER | Indian Army Reserve | | 11/11/18 |
| 2/Lt. G. R. LEIGH-BENNETT. | Indian Army Reserve | | 7/12/18 |
| 2/Lt. C. LESMOND. | Indian Army Reserve | | 6/1/19 |
| 2/Lt. G. N. ROGERS. | Indian Army Reserve | | 24/11/18 |
| 2/Lt. M. L. C. SMITH. | Indian Army Reserve | | —/11/18 |
| Lt.-Col. H. O. PARR. | 7/Rajputs | | 7/12/18 |
| Major F. C. TREGEAR. | 7/Rajputs | | 29/12/18 |
| Capt. A. R. THOMSON. | 7/Rajputs | | 24/11/18 |
| Lieut. M. CORBEY-SMITH. | 7/Rajputs | | 30/12/18 |
| Lieut. W. S. HALLILEY. | 7/Rajputs. | | 9/1/19 |
| 2/Lt. T. E. FURNEAUX. | 7/Rajputs | | 28/11/18 |
| Capt. G. R. RAE. | 9/Rajputs | | 7/12/18 |
| Major J. C. McKENNA. | 16/Rajputs | | |
| Capt. H. J. DANIELL. | 20/Punjabis | (Died at Mossul 19/8/16) | |
| Major A. SUTHERLAND. | 22/Punjabis | | 6/12/18 |
| Capt. W. WALLACE. | 22/Punjabis | | 7/12/18 |
| Capt. C. T. WARNER. | 22/Punjabis | | 16/12/18 |
| Lieut. G. R. HUDDLESTON. | 22/Punjabis | | 16/12/18 |
| Lieut. H. MEARS. | 22/Punjabis | | 16/12/18 |
| Lieut. L. R. POTTER. | 22/Punjabis | | 24/11/18 |
| Lt.-Col. H. A. V. CUMMINS. | 24/Punjabis | | 27/11/18 |
| Capt. A. B. HAIG. | 24/Punjabis | | 18/9/18 |
| Capt. A. C. H. TREVOR. | 24/Punjabis | | 16/12/18 |
| Lieut. W. A. PHILLIPS. | 24/Punjabis | | 1/1/19 |
| 2/Lt. H. BROWNE. | 24/Punjabis | | |
| Lieut. H. E. STAPLETON. | 25/Punjabis | | 16/12/18 |
| Capt. H. CARDEW. | 29/Rifles | | 29/12/18 |
| Capt. A. GATHERER. | 46/Punjabis | | 30/12/18 |
| Colonel A. J. N. HARVARD. | 48/Pioneers | | 27/11/18 |
| Major M. E. S. JOHNSON. | 48/Pioneers | | 7/12/18 |
| Capt. BIGNELL. | 48/Pioneers | | |
| Capt. R. D. CORBETT. | 48/Pioneers | (Died at Krangri 25/12/17) | |
| Capt. C. A. RAYNOR. | 48/Pioneers | | 7/12/18 |
| 2/Lt. S. W. BIDEN. | 48/Pioneers | | 16/12/18 |
| 2/Lt. L. F. SOUTER. | 48/Pioneers | | 13/12/18 |
| Major W. F. G. GILCHRIST. | 52/Sikhs | | 29/12/18 |
| Lt.-Col. A. MOORE. | 66/Punjabis | | 10/1/19 |
| Capt. C. H. STOCKLEY. | 66/Punjabis | | 9/1/19 |
| 2/Lt. H. W. BISHOP. | 66/Punjabis | | 24/10/17 |
| 2/Lt. A. R. UBSDELL. | 66/Punjabis | | 16/12/18 |
| Major C. E. S. COX. | 67/Punjabis | | 16/12/18 |
| Capt. R. F. ATKINS. | 67/Punjabis | | 16/12/18 |
| Capt. R. A. P. GRANT. | 67/Punjabis | | 16/10/18 |
| Lt. F. N. C. ARMSTRONG. | 67/Punjabis | | 7/12/18 |
| Major E. MILFORD. | 76/Punjabis | | 11/11/18 |
| Major N. V. I. RYBOT. | 76/Punjabis | | 7/12/18 |
| Capt. S. Van B. LAING. | 76/Punjabis | | 16/12/18 |
| Capt. G. R. REYNE. | 76/Punjabis | | 16/12/18 |
| Capt. J. HOOD. | 83/Punjabis | (Died at Bagdad 6/4/16) | |
| Colonel W. H. BROWN. | 103/Mahratta Light Infantry | | 28/11/18 |
| Major A. C. THORNE. | 103/Mahratta Light Infantry | | 29/12/18 |
| Capt. H. W. GOLDFRAP. | 103/Mahratta Light Infantry | | 7/12/18 |
| Lieut. B. W. REYNOLDS. | 103/Mahratta Light Infantry (Died at Castamouni 20/7/16) | | |
| Capt. C. M. S. MANNERS. | 104/Wellesley Rifles | | 16/12/18 |
| Lieut. B. AYER. | 104/Wellesley Rifles | | |

## KUT GARRISON—continued.

| Name. | Regiment. | Missing. | Repatriated. |
|---|---|---|---|
| 2/Lt. L. BELL-SYER. | 104/Wellesley Rifles | | 16/12/18 |
| 2/Lt. A. C. LOCH. | 104/Wellesley Rifles (Died at Castamouni 1/8/16) | | |
| 2/Lt. F. N. PUNCHARD. | 104/Wellesley Rifles | | 9/1/19 |
| Major C. H. HILL. | 110/Mahratta Light Infantry | | 7/12/18 |
| Capt. A. D. GUNN. | 110/Mahratta Light Infantry | | 10/1/19 |
| Lieut. R. O. CHAMIER. | 110/Mahratta Light Infantry | | 9/1/19 |
| Lt. C. V. HERON-JONES. | 110/Mahratta Light Infantry | | 1/1/19 |
| 2/Lt. A. MacFADYEN. | 110/Mahratta Light Infantry | | 7/12/18 |
| 2/Lt. J. H. O'DONOGHUE. | 110/Mahratta Light Infantry (Died at Nisiebin 27/6/16) | | |
| Capt. S. A. HUNGERFORD. | 117/Mahratta Light Infantry | | –/1/19 |
| Lieut. A. TAYLOR. | 117/Mahratta Light Infantry | | 24/11/18 |
| 2/Lt. H. D. STEARNS. | 117/Mahratta Light Infantry | | 9/1/19 |
| Brev.-Col. W. W. CHITTY. | 119/Mooltan Regt. | | 27/11/18 |
| Capt. F. I. BRICKMANN. | 119/Mooltan Regt. | | 16/12/18 |
| Lieut. E. Le PATOUREL. | 119/Mooltan Regt. | | 6/1/19 |
| 2/Lt. E. H. KEELING. | 119/Mooltan Regt. | | 6/10/17 |
| Major P. F. POCOCK. | 120/Rajput Infantry | | 16/12/18 |
| Capt. W. L. MISKIN. | 120/Rajput Infantry | | 16/12/18 |
| Lieut. W. GALLOWAY. | 120/Rajput Infantry | | 16/12/18 |
| Lieut. R. LECKY. | 120/Rajput Infantry | | 1/1/19 |
| Lieut. H. H. RICH. | 120/Rajput Infantry | | 20/1/19 |
| Major J. BARRARD. | 128/Pioneers (Died at Bagdad 7/5/16) | | |
| Lieut. L. MATHIAS. | 128/Pioneers | | 29/12/18 |
| Lt.-Col. A. N. TAYLOR. | 7/Gurkha Rifles | | 7/12/18 |
| Capt. G. R. CHANNER. | 7/Gurkha Rifles | | 28/11/18 |
| Capt. N. M. WILSON. | 7/Gurkha Rifles | | 28/11/18 |
| Lt.-Col. W. B. POWELL. | 2/7 Gurkha Rifles | | 24/11/18 |
| Major W. JOHNSTON. | 2/7 Gurkha Rifles | | 7/12/18 |
| Lieut. R. BAMPTON. | 2/7 Gurkha Rifles | | 16/12/18 |
| Lieut. R. SWEET. | 2/7 Gurkha Rifles (Died at Yozgad) | | |
| 2/Lt. A. M. CLARK. | 2/7 Gurkha Rifles | | 17/12/18 |
| Brig.-General H. D. GRIER. | Indian Mounted Artillery Brigade | | 26/11/18 |
| Lieut. R. D. MERRIMAN. | Royal Indian Marines | | 29/12/18 |
| Colonel P. HEHIR. | Indian Medical Service. | | 25/9/16 |
| Major McM. PEARSON. | Indian Medical Service. | | 27/11/18 |
| Major E. A. WALKER. | Indian Medical Service. | | 7/12/18 |
| Capt. L. A. P. ANDERSON. | Indian Medical Service. | | 7/12/18 |
| Capt. F. AQUINO. | Indian Medical Service. | | 17/12/18 |
| Capt. D. ARTHUR. | Indian Medical Service. (Died at Entelli 31/7/17). | | |
| Capt. L. H. FOX. | Indian Medical Service. (Died at Yozgad). | | |
| Capt. S. HAUGHTON. | Indian Medical Service. | | 7/12/18 |
| Capt. H. KING. | Indian Medical Service. | | 25/9/16 |
| Capt. C. NEWCOMB. | Indian Medical Service. | | 7/12/18 |
| Capt. J. S. STARTIN. | Indian Medical Service. | | 17/12/18 |
| Lieut. P. E. DONOGHUE. | Indian Medical Service. | | 1/1/19 |
| Lieut. R. V. MARTIN. | Indian Medical Service. | | 9/1/19 |
| Lieut. W. O. SPACKMAN. | Indian Medical Service. | | 16/12/18 |
| Brig.-Gen. G. B. SMITH. | 6/Division Royal Artillery. | | 2/12/18 |
| Lt.-Col. H. S. MAULE. | Royal Field Artillery. | | 7/12/18 |
| Lt.-Col. H. B. SMITH. | Royal Field Artillery. | | –/12/18 |
| Major A. J. ANDERSON. | Royal Field Artillery. | | 7/12/18 |

## KUT GARRISON—continued.

| Name. | Regiment. | Missing. | Repatriated. |
|---|---|---|---|
| Major E. CORBOULD-WARREN. | Royal Field Artillery. | | 6/11/18 |
| Major W. C. R. FARMAR. | Royal Field Artillery. | | 11/12/18 |
| Major A. F. B. HARVEY. | Royal Field Artillery | | 16/12/18 |
| Major O. S. LLOYD. | Royal Field Artillery. | | 16/12/18 |
| Capt. E. L. J. BAYLEY. | Royal Field Artillery | | 7/12/18 |
| Capt. T. R. M. CARLISLE. | Royal Field Artillery | | 29/12/18 |
| Capt. L. H. G. DORLING. | Royal Field Artillery | | –/12/18 |
| Capt. K. F. FREELAND. | Royal Field Artillery | | 29/12/18 |
| Capt. V. R. GUISE. | Royal Field Artillery | | 16/12/18 |
| Capt. E. T. MARTIN. | Royal Field Artillery. | | 16/11/16 |
| Capt. V. R. REEKS. | Royal Field Artillery | | |
| Lieut. F. DAVERN. | Royal Field Artillery | | 8/12/18 |
| Lieut. W. DEVEREUX. | Royal Field Artillery | | 16/12/18 |
| Lieut. P. EDMONDS. | Royal Field Artillery | | 11/11/18 |
| Lieut. H. C. GALLUP. | Royal Field Artillery | | 8/12/18 |
| Lieut. M. A. B. JOHNSTON. | Royal Field Artillery. | | 16/10/18 |
| Lieut. H. E. JONES. | Royal Field Artillery. | | |
| Lieut. E. O. MOUSLEY. | Royal Field Artillery | | –/12/18 |
| Lieut. R. SPENCE. | Royal Field Artillery | | 1/1/19 |
| Lieut. W. TOZER. | Royal Field Artillery. | *(Died).* | |
| Lieut. F. W. B. WILSON. | Royal Field Artillery. | | 16/12/18 |
| 2/Lt. W. E. TRAFFORD. | Royal Field Artillery. | | 16/12/18 |
| Major R. C. ALEXANDER. | Royal Garrison Artillery | | 7/12/18 |
| Capt. R. C. LOWNDES. | Royal Garrison Artillery | | 1/1/19 |
| Lieut. R. L. FLUX. | Royal Garrison Artillery | | 7/12/18 |
| Lieut. R. G. PARSONS. | Royal Garrison Artillery | | 24/11/18 |
| Lieut. E. J. WILLIAMS. | Royal Garrison Artillery | | 16/12/18 |
| Lieut. F. P. G. WILLIAMS. | Royal Garrison Artillery | | 7/12/18 |
| Lt.-Col. F. A. WILSON. | Royal Engineers | | 27/11/18 |
| Major J. S. BARKER. | Royal Engineers | | 7/12/18 |
| Major F. BOOTH. | Royal Engineers (Signal Service) att. from K.O.R. Lancs. | | 6/12/18 |
| Major H. E. WINSLOE. | Royal Engineers. | | 16/11/16 |
| Capt. C. E. COLBECK. | Royal Engineers. | | 7/12/18 |
| Capt. E. W. C. SANDES. | Royal Engineers. | | –/12/18 |
| Capt. R. E. STACE. | Royal Engineers. | | 7/12/18 |
| Capt. H. W. TOMLINSON. | Royal Engineers. | | 7/12/18 |
| Capt. K. D. YEARSLEY. | Royal Engineers. | | 16/10/18 |
| Lieut. W. BOYES. | Royal Engineers. | | 10/12/18 |
| Lieut. K. B. S. CRAWFORD. | Royal Engineers. | | 16/12/18 |
| Lieut. C. L. E. GREENWOOD. | Royal Engineers. | | 7/12/18 |
| Lieut. A. B. MATTHEWS. | Royal Engineers. | | 6/1/19 |
| Lieut. J. A. POCOCK. | Royal Engineers. | | 8/12/18 |
| 2/Lt. J. McCONVILLE. | Sappers and Miners att. from King's Liverpool Regt. | | 17/12/18 |
| Lieut. F. MAYO. | Sappers and Miners | | 7/12/18 |
| Col. A. S. R. ANNESLEY. | Supply and Transport Corps. | | 27/11/18 |
| Major T. L. BALL. | Supply and Transport Corps. | | 16/12/18 |
| Major H. W. DAVIES. | Supply and Transport Corps. | | 17/12/18 |
| Major E. E. FORBES. | Supply and Transport Corps. | | 20/1/19 |
| Mjaor T. LEESON-BALL. | Supply and Transport Corps. | | |
| Major R. W. H. MIDDLEMASS. | Supply and Transport Corps. | | 16/12/18 |
| Major H. W. PRICE. | Supply and Transport Corps. | | 24/11/18 |
| Major P. C. SAUNDERS. | Supply and Transport Corps. | | 16/12/18 |
| Major A. F. STEWART. | Supply and Transport Corps. | | 16/12/18 |
| Major H. H. SYER. | Supply and Transport Corps. | | 16/12/18 |

## KUT GARRISON—continued.

| Name. | Regiment. | Missing. | Repatriated. |
|---|---|---|---|
| Capt. G. H. BURROUGHS. | *Supply and Transport Corps.* | | 7/12/18 |
| Capt. C. B. HEREPATH. | *Supply and Transport Corps.* | | 24/11/18 |
| Capt. J. W. PHILIPS. | *Supply and Transport Corps.* | | 29/12/18 |
| Capt. G. WHITE. | *Supply and Transport Corps.* | | 7/12/18 |
| Lieut. R. BAIRD. | *Supply and Transport Corps.* | | 16/12/18 |
| Lieut. S. FOWLES. | *Supply and Transport Corps.* | | 17/12/18 |
| Lieut. J. H. C. GAYER. | *Supply and Transport Corps.* | | 24/11/18 |
| Lieut. A. LANG. | *Supply and Transport Corps.* | | 17/12/18 |
| Lieut. F. C. SLY. | *Supply and Transport Corps.* | | 8/12/18 |
| 2/Lt. C. H. McDERMOTT. | *Supply and Transport Corps.* | | 8/12/18 |
| Lieut. J. C. HORWOOD. | *Mechanical Transport Corps.* | | 16/12/18 |
| 2/Lt. J. A. DOOLEY. | *Mechanical Transport Corps.* | | 9/1/19 |
| Capt. C. B. MUNDEY. | *Royal Flying Corps.* | | –/11/18 |
| Capt. T. A. WELLS. | *Royal Flying Corps.* | | 7/12/18 |
| Capt. S. C. WINFIELD-SMITH. | *Royal Flying Corps.* | | 7/12/18 |
| Lieut. H. STEPHENSON. | *Army Veterinary Corps.* | | 16/12/18 |
| Lieut. W. B. K. ANDEESN. | *Postal Department.* | | 17/12/18 |
| Lieut. W. APPLEBY. | *Postal Department* | | |
| Capt. H. SPOONER. | *Army Chaplains Department* | | 1/1/19 |
| Capt. A. Y. WRIGHT. | *Army Chaplains Department* | | 16/12/18 |
| Colonel H. O. B. BROWNE-MASON. | *Royal Army Medical Corps* | | 16/11/16 |
| Lt.-Col. E. F. BAINES. | *Royal Army Medical Corps.* | | 7/12/18 |
| Lt.-Col. J. HENNESSY. | *Royal Army Medical Corps.* | | 16/11/16 |
| Major E. V. AYLEN. | *Royal Army Medical Corps.* | | 16/11/16 |
| Major C. H. BARBER. | *Royal Army Medical Corps.* | | 25/9/16 |
| Major E. BENNETT. | *Royal Army Medical Corps.* | | 11/11/18 |
| Major T. JENKINSON. | *Royal Army Medical Corps'* (Died at Mosul 8/7/16). | | |
| Capt. L. ANDERSON. | *Royal Army Medical Corps.* | | |
| Capt. E. G. S. CANE. | *Royal Army Medical Corps.* | | 16/12/18 |
| Capt. R. C. CLIFFORD. | *Royal Army Medical Corps.* | | 14/12/18 |
| Capt. C. E. JONES. | *Royal Army Medical Corps.* | | 9/1/19 |
| Capt. A. T. S. McCREARY. | *Royal Army Medical Corps.* | | 16/11/16 |
| Capt. J. D. MARTIN. | *Royal Army Medical Corps.* | | |
| Capt. T. E. OSMOND. | *Royal Army Medical Corps.* | | 7/12/18 |
| Capt. P. E. O'DONOGHUE. | *Royal Army Medical Corps.* | | 10/12/18 |
| Lieut. J. W. NEWBOLD. | *Royal Army Medical Corps.* | | |
| Lieut. J. S. TWINBERROW. | *Worcestershire Yeomanry.* | | 1/1/19 |
| Major W. THOMAS. | *Worcestershire Yeomanry.* | | |
| Lieut. E. B. BURNS. | *2/East Kent Regt.* | | 7/12/18 |
| Lt.-Col. F. C. LODGE. | *2/Norfolk Regt.* | | 7/12/18 |
| Major W. E. CRAMER-ROBERTS. | *2/Norfolk Regt.* | | 7/12/18 |
| Capt. G. de GREY. | *2/Norfolk Regt.* | | |
| Capt. A. B. FLOYD. | *2/Norfolk Regt.* | | 30/12/18 |
| Capt. A. J. SHAKESHAFT. | *2/Norfolks.* | | 1/1/19 |
| Lieut. T. CAMPBELL. | *2/Norfolk Regt.* | | 30/12/18 |
| Lieut. H. L. PEACOCK. | *2/Norfolk Regt.* | | 1/12/18 |
| Lieut. J. F. W. READ. | *2/Norfolk Regt.* | | 1/1/19 |
| Lieut. J. P. RICHARDSON. | *2/Norfolk Regt.* | | 16/11/16 |
| Lieut. S. B. GREGORY. | *4/Devonshire Regt.* (Died at Mosul 3/6/16). | | |
| Lieut. W. SNELL. | *4/Devonshire Regt.* | | 8/12/18 |
| Capt. F. R. ELLIS. | *4/Duke of Cornwall's L.I.* | | 16/10/18 |
| 2/Lt. P. W. KEARNEY. | *4/Duke of Cornwall's L.I.* | | 9/1/19 |
| Major S. JULIUS. | *1/Royal Sussex Regt.* | | 13/1/19 |

**KUT GARRISON**—continued.

| Name. | Regiment. | Missing. | Repatriated. |
|---|---|---|---|
| Major F. L. FOOTNER. | 4/Hampshire Regt. | | 9/1/19 |
| Capt. N. REEKS. | 4/Hampshire Regt. | | 16/12/18 |
| Lieut. G. ELTON. | 4/Hampshire Regt. | | 16/12/18 |
| Lieut. A. G. FORBES. | 4/Hampshire Regt. | | 27/11/18 |
| Lieut. J. H. HARRIS. | 4/Hampshire Regt. | | 16/10/18 |
| Lieut. R. S. LACY. | 4/Hampshire Regt. | | 6/12/18 |
| Lieut. F. J. PATMORE. | 4/Hampshire Regt. | | 6/12/18 |
| 2/Lt. C. CHITTY. | 4/Hampshire Regt. | | 16/12/18 |
| Major G. M. HERBERT. | 2/Dorsetshire Regt. | | 7/12/18 |
| Major J. McKENNA. | 2/Dorsetshire Regt. | | |
| Capt. G. W. R. BISHOP. | 2/Dorsetshire Regt., att. from Somerset L.I. | | 10/12/18 |
| Capt. A. BROWN. | 2/Dorsetshire Regt. | | 29/12/18 |
| Capt. C. T. HIGHETT. | 2/Dorsetshire Regt. | | 1/1/19 |
| Capt. W. H. MILES. | 2/Dorsetshire Regt. | | 7/12/18 |
| Lieut. S. MILLER. | 2/Dorsetshire Regt. | | 30/12/18 |
| Lieut. D. A. SIMMONS. | 2/Dorsetshire Regt. | | 30/12/18 |
| Lieut. H. G. WALDRAM. | 2/Dorsetshire Regt., att. from Devonshire Regt. | | 30/12/18 |
| 2/Lt. W. BARTON. | 2/Dorsetshire Regt. | | 5/1/19 |
| 2/Lt. C. P. CRAWLEY. | 2/Dorsetshire Regt. | | 8/1/19 |
| Lt.-Col. E. LETHBRIDGE. | 1/Oxford & Bucks L.I. | | 7/12/18 |
| Major C. F. HENLEY. | 1/Oxford & Bucks L.I. | | 7/12/18 |
| Capt. T. IVEY. | 1/Oxford & Bucks L.I. | | 7/12/18 |
| Capt. W. MORLAND. | 1/Oxford & Bucks L.I. | | 21/11/18 |
| Lieut. G. L. HEAWOOD. | 1/Oxford & Bucks L.I., att. from Wilshire Regt. | | 20/11/16 |
| Lieut. A. E. MASON. | 1/Oxford & Bucks L.I. | | 8/12/18 |
| Lieut. J. S. P. MELLOR. | 1/Oxford & Bucks L.I., att. from Somerset L.I. | | 16/12/18 |
| Lieut. G. NAYLOR. | 1/Oxford & Bucks L.I. | | 16/12/18 |
| Major J. W. NELSON. | 2/Royal West Kent Regt. | | 16/12/18 |
| Capt. V. S. CLARKE. | 2/Royal West Kent Regt. | | –/9/18 |
| Capt. M. J. DINWIDDY. | 2/Royal West Kent Regt. | | 16/12/18 |
| Capt. O. Y. HIBBERT. | 2/Royal West Kent Regt. | | 7/12/18 |
| 2/Lt. J. MILLS. | 2/Royal West Kent Regt. | | 16/12/18 |
| Lieut. T. E. GRANGER. | 7/Manchester Regt. | | 16/12/18 |
| Lieut. J. M. McCOMBIE. | Gordon Highlanders | | 16/12/18 |
| Lieut. W. REED. | Royal Navy | | 16/12/18 |
| Lieut. L. TUDWAY. | Royal Navy | | 7/12/18 |
| Lieut. S. NICHOLSON. | H.M.S. "Zaida" | | 16/12/18 |
| Lieut. H. DUNLOP. | H.M.S. "Zaida" | | 16/12/18 |

**AEGEAN GROUP.**

| Name. | Regiment. | Missing. | Repatriated. |
|---|---|---|---|
| Lieut. C. G. CLARK. | R.A.F. | 29/7/18 | 16/12/18 |
| Major J. P. B. FERRAND. | R.A.F. | –/9/18 | 9/1/19 |
| Lieut. S. P. O. HAUGHTON. | R.A.F. | 21/9/18 | 9/1/19 |
| Lieut. Kenneth WITHERS. | R.A.F. | 17/10/18 | –/12/18 |
| Lieut. W. BAMBER. | R.A.F. | 17/10/18 | –/12/18 |

**BALKANS.**

| Name. | Regiment. | Missing. | Repatriated. |
|---|---|---|---|
| Sub.-Lt. B. A. MILLARD. | R.A.F. (late R.N.A.S.) | | 3/1/19 |
| 2/Lt. A. N. D. POCOCK. | R.A.F. | 5/1/17 | 19/10/18 |
| 2/Lt. S. SMITH. | R.A.F. | 21/7/17 | –/11/18 |
| 2/Lt. A. C. STOPHER | R.A.F. | 12/2/17 | 28/11/18 |

**BALKANS**—continued.

| Name. | Regiment. | Missing. | Repatriated. |
|---|---|---|---|
| Lieut. J. C. F. OWEN. | R.A.F. | 18/2/17 | 16/10/18 |
| 2/Lt. A. LESLIE-MOORE. | R.A.F. | 18/6/17 | 19/1/18 |
| Capt. J. E. A. O'DWYER. | R.A.F. | 8/7/17 | 28/11/17 |
| Lieut. S. WISE. | R.A.F. | 1/10/17 | 8/12/18 |
| 2/Lt. J. R. F. GUBBINS. | R.A.F. (Died 20/11/17) | 29/10/17 | |
| Lieut. A. ROWAN. | R.A.F. | 3/1/18 | 29/11/18 |
| 2/Lt. H. A. TRACEY. | R.A.F. | 3/1/18 | 29/11/18 |
| 2/Lt. H. F. GAYNOR. | R.A.F. | 15/3/18 | 28/11/18 |
| 2/Lt. G. HANNAN. | R.A.F. | 14/4/18 | 28/11/18 |
| Sub.-Lt. G. BLANDY. | R.N.A.S. | | –/10/18 |
| Lieut. E. J. COOPER. | R.N.A.S. | | 22/10/18 |
| Sub.-Lt. R. W. FRAZIER. | R.N.A.S. | –/12/16 | 28/11/18 |
| 2/Lt. C. W. GREIG. | R.N.A.S. (Died 12/9/18) | | |
| Sub.-Lt. S. G. BEARE. | R.N.A.S. | | 28/11/18 |
| 2/Lt. E. P. HYDE. | R.N.A.S. | | 21/9/18 |
| Viscount TORRINGTON. | R.N.A.S. | | 25/10/18 |
| Lieut. B. J. BRADY. | R.N.A.S. | | 21/9/18 |
| Sub.-Lt. L. MARSH. | R.N.A.S. | | –/10/18 |
| Capt. G. B. BAKER. | R.N.A.S. | | |
| Lieut. Hugh AIRD. | R.N.A.S. | 30/9/17 | 16/12/18 |
| 2/Lt. M. MALONEY. | 6/Royal Dublin Fus. | 6–11/12/15 | –/10/18 |
| 2/Lt. R. G. HOWE. | 6/Royal Dublin Fus. | 6–11/12/15 | –/10/18 |
| Capt. S. SPIRA. | 9/K.O. Royal Lancaster Regt. | 12/12/15 | –/10/18 |
| Capt. L. W. HARRIES. | 9/K.O. Royal Lancaster Regt. | 12/12/15 | –/10/18 |
| 2/Lt. G. H. COLE. | 2/K.O. Royal Lancaster Regt. | 27/10/17 | 28/11/18 |
| Lieut. G. T. BENNETT. | 10/Hampshire Regt. | 31/5/16 | –/11/18 |
| 2/Lt. S. C. BARBER. | 11/Northumberland Fus. | 10/9/16 | –/10/18 |
| 2/Lt. H. G. TAYLOR. | 2/Northumberland Fus. | 10/9/16 | 21/9/18 |
| Capt. H. U. SCRUTTON. | 2/Northumberland Fus. | 10/9/17 | (Died) |
| Capt. R. E. WALKER. | 1/York & Lancaster Regt. | 12/10/16 | –/10/18 |
| 2/Lt. G. C. TUNBRIDGE. | 1/York & Lancaster Regt. (Died 27/4/18 ) | 18/4/18 | |
| Lieut. J. L. W. CRAIG. | 11/Royal Welsh Fus. | 21/2/17 | 20/1/18 |
| Lieut. R. A. W. P. RICHARDES. | 11/Royal Welsh Fus. | 22/9/18 | 6/1/19 |
| 2/Lt. R. B. LLOYD. | 11/Worcestershire Regt. | 25/4/17 | 11/1/19 |
| 2/Lt. C. DE. LEMOS. | 11/Worcestershire Regt. | –/18 | 21/9/18 |
| Lieut. A. A. TOWNSEND. | 7/Royal Munster Fus. | 6–11/12/15 | –/10/18 |
| Lieut. D. J. COWAN. | 5/Connaught Rangers | 6–11/12/15 | –/10/18 |
| Lieut. W. E. GILLILAND. | 10/Norfolk Regt. | 6–11/12/15 | –/11/18 |
| 2/Lt. G. ALEXANDER. | 3/Royal Irish Rifles | 24/10/16 | 29/11/18 |
| 2/Lt. E. L. FOOKS. | R.F.A. | 31/10/16 | (Died) |
| 2/Lt. L. G. H. DEAN. | 3/Middlesex Regt. | 8/4/17 | –/10/18 |
| 2/Lt. T. W. GREENSTREET. | 2/Royal Irish Fus. att. from 3/Northants | 20/4/17 | 21/9/18 |
| Lieut. J. A. TAYLOR. | 7/Wiltshire Regt. | 24–25/4/17 | 21/9/18 |
| 2/Lt. J. D. WALLIS. | 12/Argyll & Sutherland Highlanders att. from Scottish Horse | 8–9/5/17 | –/10/18 |
| 2/Lt. W. S. EBDEN. | 8/K. Shropshire L.I. att. from 11/Gloucesters | 16/5/17 | 28/11/18 |
| Lieut. A. B. RIDDLE. | 2/5th Durham L.I. | 7/6/17 | 28/11/18 |
| Capt. H. S. STEWART. | 1/Lothian & Border Horse | 19/9/17 | 24/12/18 |
| 2/Lt. P. STEWART. | 9/South Lancs. Regt. | 15/10/18 | 29/11/18 |
| Lieut. J. N. HERAPATH. | 10/Devonshire Regt. | 26/1/18 | –/11/18 |
| 2/Lt. A. J. JONES. | 2/Cheshire Regt. att. from Royal Berks. | 14/4/18 | 29/12/18 |

## BALKANS—continued.

| Name. | Regiment. | Missing. | Repatriated. |
|---|---|---|---|
| Lieut. J. A. READ. | 4/Rifle Brigade | 15/4/18 | 29/11/18 |
| Capt. J. E. STONES. | 8/Royal Scots. Fus. att. from 11/Middlesex | 19/9/18 | 25/12/18 |
| Lieut. F. H. MITCHELL. | R.N.V.R. | 2/12/16 | (Died) |
| Lieut. R. G. BLAKESLEY. | R.N.V.R. |  | 22/10/18 |

## WEST AFRICA.

| Name. | Regiment. | Missing. | Repatriated. |
|---|---|---|---|
| Capt. A. L. DE C. STRETTON. | South Lancs. att. W.A.F.F. | 6/9/14 | 8/1/16 |
| Capt. M. J. PARKER. | South Staffs. att. W.A.F.F. | 6/9/14 | 8/1/16 |
| Lieut. O. G. BODY. | R.A. att. W.A.F.F. | 6/9/14 | 8/1/16 |
| Lieut. R. R. TAYLOR. | K.O.S.B. att. W.A.F.F. | 6/9/14 | 8/1/16 |

## EAST AFRICA.

| Name. | Regiment. | Missing. | Repatriated. |
|---|---|---|---|
| Lieut. G. S. FRAME. | R.A.F. | -/-/17 | 10/10/17 |
| 2/Lt. C. F. STRANGHAM. | R.A.F. | -/-/17 | 18/11/17 |
| Lieut. G. G. R. WILLIAMS. | 2/Loyal North Lancs. Regt. | -/-/15 | 18/11/17 |
| Capt. H. STOKES. | R.A.M.C. | -/-/17 | -/-/17 |
| Lieut. J. R. McGREGOR. | R.A.M.C. | 3/7/18 | 27/8/18 |
| Capt. G. PERKINS. | R.A.M.C. | 22/7/18 | 9/9/18 |
| Lieut. C. MURRAY. | R.A.M.C. | 24/8/18 | -/10/18 |
| Lieut. G. HOARE. | A.S.C. | -/12/16 | (Released) |
| Capt. H. G. SEALY. | 130/Baluchis I.A. | -/16 | 18/11/17 |
| Major J. H. G. BULLER. | 57/Wilde's Rifles, I.A. | 10/8/16 |  |
| Lieut. D. POWELL. | 30/Punjabis, I.A. | 3/8/17 | 1/10/17 |
| Lieut. G. W. PALIN. | 129/Baluchis, I.A. | 5/8/17 | 18/11/17 |
| Lieut. T. WILSON. | South African Engineers | -/12/16 | (Released) |
| Capt. H. WALLIS. | 8/South African Inf. | 19/7/17 | 18/11/17 |
| Lieut. H. E. W. BARRETT. | 1/South African Horse | 10/3/16 | 18/11/17 |
| Lieut. A. H. G. BARR. | 9/South African Horse | 1/1/17 | 18/11/17 |
| Lieut. S. G. INGLESBY. | 9/South African Horse | 1/1/17 | 18/11/17 |
| Lieut. S. G. CHAMPION. | 2/King's African Rifles | -/2/17 | (Died) |
| Lieut. C. V. GRAY. | 2/King's African Rifles | 25/4/17 | 18/11/18 |
| Lieut. F. H. BLACKIE. | 1/King's African Rifles. | 16/5/17 |  |
| Lieut. P. NOTTIDGE. | 3/King's African Rifles | 19/7/17 | 18/11/17 |
| Capt. V. H. SMITH. | 1/King's African Rifles | 11/4/18 | 21/5/18 |
| Lt.-Col. H. C. DICKINSON. | 3/King's African Rifles | 22/7/18 | -/11/18 |
| Capt. J. E. G. RANSOME. | 3/King's African Rifles | 22/7/18 | -/11/18 |
| Lieut. S. H. JARDINE. | 3/King's African Rifles | 22/7/18 | -/11/18 |
| Lieut. H. M. SHAW. | 3/King's African Rifles | 22/7/18 | -/11/18 |
| Lieut. W. JOHNSON. | 4/King's African Rifles | 22/7/18 | 3/11/18 |
| Capt. F. H. BUSTARD. | 3/King's African Rifles | 23/7/18 | -/9/18 |
| Lieut. C. H. McELROY. | 3/King's African Rifles | 23/7/18 | -/11/18 |
| Lieut. J. M. BRINK. | 3/King's African Rifles | 23/7/18 | 18/10/18 |
| Lieut. H. N. TITTERTON. | 3/King's African Rifles | 23/7/18 | -/11/18 |
| Major P. GARRARD. | 4/King's African Rifles (Died 18/9/18) | 24/8/18 |  |
| Lieut. K. E. ISAACS. | Gold Coast Regt. | 12/10/16 | 18/11/17 |
| Lieut. E. STRINGER. | Nyasaland Field Force | -/12/16 | (Released) |
| Major R. D. GARDNER. | 3/Nigerian Regt. | 29/1/17 | 18/11/17 |
| Lieut. M. D. E. JEFFREYS. | 3/Nigerian Regt. | 29/1/17 | 18/11/17 |
| Lieut. E. B. B. SHAW. | 4/Nigerian Carrier Corps | 16/10/17 | 18/11/17 |
| Agent G. PERKS. | Intelligence Dept. | -/16 | 15/11/17 |
| Agent R. S. HALL. | Intelligence Dept. | -/16 | 18/11/17 |

# INDEX.

Abbott, E. D., Sub-Lt. 156
——— T. W., 2/Lt. ...181
——— W. J. G., 2/Lt. 62
——— W. N., 2/Lt. 48
——— W. S., Lieut. 36
Abel, J. E., 2/Lt. ... 83
Abell, A. R., 2/Lt. ... 36
Abercrombie, H. N., 2/Lt. ... ... 115
——— A. W., Lt.-Col. 111
Abey, H. R., 2/Lt. ... 175
——— H. W., 2/Lt. ... 14
Abrahall, A. S., Lieut. 62
Abraham, Michael, Lieut. 10
Acheson, J. E., Lieut. ... 33
——— G. J., Lieut. ... 42
Ackerley, J. R., Capt. 65
Ackroyd, C. H., Capt.... 85
——— Reginald, Lieut. ... ... 125
Ackers, C. H. S., 2/Lt. 159
Acocks, A. W., 2/Lt. ... 46
Adair, J. Sinclair, 2/Lt. 109
Adam, W. A., Capt. ... 71
Adams, A. F., 2/Lt. ... 120
——— A. T., Lieut. ... 151
——— C., 2/Lt. ... 114
——— C. Boys, Capt. ... 70
——— C. J., Lieut. ... 130
——— F., 2/Lt. ... 147
——— F. B., Lieut. ... 91
——— F. B., 2/Lt. ... 146
——— Godfrey, Capt. ... 98
——— J., 2/Lt. ... 97
——— N. F., Lieut. ... 171
——— P., 2/Lt. ... 128
——— P. E., Lieut. ... 40
——— R. G. H., Lieut. 161
——— R. H., 2/Lt. ... 29
——— V. H., 2/Lt.... 152
Adamson, C. P., 2/Lt. ... 155
——— H. A., 2/Lt. ... 104
——— J., 2/Lt. ... 52
——— T. S., Capt. ... 109
Addington, E. G., Lieut. 41
Addison, Julian, Capt. 142
——— W., 2/Lt. ... 106
——— Wm., 2/Lt. ... 122
Adeney, R. E., 2/Lt. ... 151
Agerskow, O. Randall, 2/Lt. ... ... 50
Agnew, A. B., Lieut. ... 176
——— I. C. F., 2/Lt. 138
Ahnall, K., 2/Lt. ... 137
Ahern, M., 2/Lt. ... 114
Ainger, Frank S., Capt. 66
Ainscough, J. P., Lieut. 119
Ainscow, H. M., 2/Lt. ... 50
Ainsley, C., Capt. ... 37
Ainsworth, R. W., Capt. 79
Aird, Hugh, Fl. Lt. ... 188
Airth, E. C., 2/Lt. ... 81
Aitchison, J., 2/Lt. ... 102
——— S. W., Lieut. ... 59
Aitken, Frank Douglas, 2/Lt. ... ... 88
——— J. D., 2/Lt. ... 86
——— J. S., 2/Lt. ... 20
Aked, H. L. C., 2/Lt. ... 147
Akester, Gordon, 2/Lt. 44
——— J. C., Fl.Sub-Lt.177
Albert, C. H., 2/Lt. ... 63
Albertson, Lieut. ... 167

Albrecht, Henry J. C. 2/Lt. ... ... ... 117
Alcock, J. H., 2/Lt. ... 36
——— J. W., Fl. Lt. 181
Alder, S., 2/Lt. ... 150
Alderson, A. G. w., 2/Lt 159
Aldred, A. G., Lieut. ... 95
Alexander, A. H., 2/Lt. 32
——— E., Lieut. ... 147
——— G., 2/Lt. ... 188
——— G. M., Capt. ... 139
——— J., 2/Lt. ... 24
——— K. E., 2/Lt. ... 100
——— P. S., Capt. ... 9
——— R. C., Major ... 185
——— R. D., Capt. ... 143
——— W. T., 2/Lt ... 102
Allabarton, S. T., 2/Lt. 153
Alison, J. S., 2/Lt. ... 18
Allan, A. M., 2/Lt. ... 173
——— C. Maitland, 2/Lt. ... ... 175
——— D. G., Lieut. 139
——— P. J., 2/Lt. ... 23
Allardyce, G. L., Lieut. 106
Allason, H. W., Lieut. 66
Allbon-Bennett, K. R. A., 2/Lt. ... ... 32
Allen, C., 2/Lt. ... ... 90
——— E. N., 2/Lt. ... 83
——— F. E., 2/Lt. 131
——— H. F., 2/Lt. ... 44
——— John, 2/Lt. ... 50
——— J. H., 2/Lt. ... 137
——— J. M., 2/Lt. 159
——— L. T. M., 2/Lt. 22
——— L. W., 2/Lt. ... 78
——— R., Capt. ... 25
——— T., 2/Lt. ... 78
——— W. G., 2/Lt. ... 35
——— Wm. R., Capt. ... 24
Alleyne, W. H. Capt. ... 21
Allinson, F., Lieut. ... 150
Allis, W. Henry ... 49
Allison, C. J., 2/Lt ... 33
Allistone, A. B. W. Lieut. 88
Allsop, H., 2/Lt. ... 15
——— T. H. K., Lieut.129
Allsupp, F., 2/Lt. ... 180
Allworth, C. R. H., Capt. 84
Almond, H. B., Lieut. ... 53
Alston, R. W., 2/Lt. ... 35
Ambler, E., Capt. ... 40
——— J. J., Lieut. ... 170
Ambrose-Smith, J., Major 53
Amcoats, W., Capt, the Rev. ... ... 135
Ames, N. L., 2/Lt. ... 128
Amey, A. H., 2/Lt. ... 130
Amis, H. G., Capt. ... 49
Amm, E. O., Lieut. ... 176
Amory, W., 2/Lt. ... 175
Amps, J. P., Lieut. ... 76
Andeesn, W. B. K., Lieut.186
Anderson, A., Lieut. ... 149
——— Alex., 2/Lt.... 59
——— A. E. B., Capt. 47
——— A. J., Major 184
——— A. P., 2/Lt. ... 26
——— D. S., 2/Lt. 162
——— G. A., 2/Lt. ... 74
——— G. F., Lieut. ... 171
——— G. H. G., Capt. 115

Anderson, G. V. W., Lieut.134
——— H. S., Lieut. 11
——— J., Lieut. ... 119
——— James, Capt. 132
——— J. D., Lieut. 167
——— J. G., 2/Lt. ... 51
——— J. H., Lieut. ... 105
——— J. J., Lieut. ... 118
——— J. L. H., 2/Lt. 163
——— J. S., 2/Lt. ... 117
——— K. H. J., Capt. 129
——— L., Capt. ... 186
——— L. A. P., Capt. 184
Anderson, Robert ... 39
——— R. B., 2/Lt.... 74
——— R. K., 2/Lt. ... 142
——— W., Lieut. ... 150
Andersson, C. L., Lt.-Col 98
Anderton, N. H., 2/Lt. 52
Andrew, A. R., 2/Lt. ... 124
——— Frank, 2/Lt. 95
——— G. S. B., 2/Lt. 31
——— R., 2/Lt. ... 20
——— W. Leslie, Lieut. ... 162
——— W. M., 2/Lt. 103
Andrews, A. A., Capt.... 39
——— A. V., Lieut. 135
——— F. C., 2/Lt. ... 156
——— F. E., 2/Lt., A/Capt. ... 77
——— Geoffrey, Fl. Sub.-Lt. 177
——— G. M., Capt. ... 139
——— J. S., Lieut. 169
Angus, K. R., 2/Lt. ... 166
Annandale, J. R., 2/Lt. 10
Annesley, A. S. R., Col. 185
Anns, K., Capt., Adj., M.C. ... ... 65
Ansell, A. C., Lieut. ... 45
Anslow, F. F., Lieut. ... 171
Ansted, D. A., Lieut. ... 93
Anstee, G. A., Capt. ... 45
Anstey, F. C. R., Lieut. 139
Anthony, H. C., Lieut. 136
Antill, H. B., Lieut. ... 83
Apperley, Charles M., 2/Lt. ... ... 122
Appleby, A. W., 2/Lt. ... 49
——— W., Lieut. ... 186
Appleford, H. N., Lieut. 51
Applegarth, Thomas W., 2/Lt. ... ... 102
Appleton, Richard, 2/Lt. 85
Apps, E. W., 2/Lt. ... 94
Aquino, F., Med. Officer 184
Arblaster, C., Capt. ... 136
Arbuthnott, R. K., Capt., M.C. ... ... 73
Archer, Ben, 2/Lt. ... 41
——— F. J., 2/Lt. ... 79
Archibald, A. D., 2/Lt. 58
——— L. N., 2/Lt. 157
Ardagh, P. M. J., Lieut. 113
Ardill, J. R., 2/Lt. ... 69
Arkless, Frank, Lieut. 101
Armbrister, E. A., Lieut. 101
Armitage, E. L., Lieut. 10
——— J. A., 2/Lt. ... 85
——— S. E., Lieut.... 178
Armstrong, A., Capt. ... 59
——— C. D., Lieut. 120

Armstrong, C. J., Lieut. 60
——— F. N. C., Lieut. 183
——— G. W., 2/Lt. ... 157
——— J., 2/Lt. ... 110
——— J. H. B., Lieut. 137
——— R. H., 2/Lt.... 172
Arnold, A. E., Capt., M.C. ... ... 124
——— C. B., Lieut. 125
——— G. B., 2/Lt. ... 76
——— J., 2/Lt. ... 164
——— S., 2/Lt. ... 115
Arnott, J. F., Capt., M.C. 93
——— R., 2/Lt. ... 165
——— T. H., 2/Lt. ... 68
——— W. A., Capt. ... 132
Arthur, D., Capt. ... 184
——— T. J., Lieut.... 168
Arthurton, F. W., Lieut. 118
Arthy, E. B. F., 2/Lt. ... 101
Ashburner, J. C., 2/Lt. 119
Ascough, M. T., Capt.... 132
Ashby, J., 2/Lt. ... 18
Ashcroft, E. S., Lieut.... 34
——— K., 2/Lt. ... 124
Asher, W. J., Capt. ... 79
——— W. M., Lieut. 105
Ashforth, H. W., 2/Lt. 124
Ashley, T. W., 2/Lt. ... 130
Ashton, H. C. S., Capt. 9
——— K. H., 2/Lt.... 166
Ashworth, L., 2/Lt. ... 42
Askin, A. T. C., 2/Lt. ... 179
——— S. C. J., Lieut. 168
Asquith, B. I., 2/Lt. ... 46
Astbury, B. E., 2/Lt. ... 26
Aston, R., Lieut. ... 29
Atkin, H. D., Lieut. ... 95
——— K., Lieut. ... 131
Atkins, C. A., 2/Lt. ... 168
——— B. S., Capt. ... 178
——— G. C., 2/Lt. ... 154
——— R. F., Capt. ... 183
——— W. J. T., 2/Lt. 164
Atkinson, Alan, 2/Lt. ... 17
——— F., Lieut. ... 163
——— J., Capt. (? 2/Lt.) ... 102
——— J. M., 2/Lt. ... 49
——— J. M., 2/Lt. ... 157
——— T. C., 2/Lt. ... 65
——— T. L., 2/Lt. ... 158
Attenborough, E. G., Lieut. ... ... 14
Atter, W. G., 2/Lt. ... 119
Atterton, F., 2/Lt. ... 115
Attwell, R. H., 2/Lt. ... 29
Attwood, N. J., Sub.-Lt. 162
Auchinleck, W. J. A. H., Lieut. ... ... 60
Audas, Francis, 2/Lt. ... 102
Auld, R. T. K., Capt. ... 24
——— P. H., Capt. ... 137
Austen, V. G., Fl.Sub-Lt. 177
Austin, A. G., 2/Lt. ... 94
——— R. A., Capt. ... 181
——— H., Lieut. ... 165
——— W. M., Capt. ... 94
——— W. S., 2/Lt. ... 66
Auty, D. R., 2/Lt. ... 52
Avey, G. A., Capt. ... 141
Awde, I. W., Lieut. ... 173
Axe, F., 2/Lt. ... ... 41

| | PAGE | | PAGE | | PAGE | | PAGE |
|---|---|---|---|---|---|---|---|
| Ayer, B., Lieut. | 183 | Bambrough, P. B., 2/Lt. | 130 | Bastard, R., Lt.-Col. | 35 | Bell, A. J., Lieut. | 91 |
| Ayers, Austin, 2/Lt. | 124 | Bampton, R., Lt. | 184 | Bastow, S. F., 2/Lt. | 44 | ——— A. T., 2/Lt. | 109 |
| Aylen, E. V., Major | 186 | Bandey, G. H., 2/Lt. | 123 | Batchelor, P. H., 2/Lt. | 96 | ——— D. F., Lieut. | 142 |
| Aylett, E. R. C., Capt., M.C. | 81 | Banks, D. J., Capt. | 75 | Bate, C. I., Lieut. | 141 | ——— D. J., Capt. | 163 |
| | | ——— R. H., Capt., M.C. | 87 | ——— W. T. McGuire, Capt. | 143 | ——— E. A. V., 2/Lt. | 151 |
| Ayre, F., Capt. | 29 | Bankes, H. V. N., Lieut. | 162 | Bateman, K. S. B., 2/Lt. | 71 | ——— E. G., 2/Lt. | 118 |
| Ayrton, F. A., Capt. | 171 | Bann, E. H., Lieut. | 56 | ——— W., Lieut. | 85 | ——— F., Capt. | 106 |
| | | Bannard, A. W., Lieut. | 140 | Bates, A. D., Lieut. | 130 | ——— G., 2/Lt. | 52 |
| **Babb**, R., Lieut. | 140 | Bantock, E. G., 2/Lt. | 42 | Batey, J. L., Lieut. | 182 | ——— J., 2/Lt. | 33 |
| Baber, W. H., 2/Lt. | 66 | Barber, C. H., Major | 186 | Bath, E. O., Lieut. | 139 | ——— J. A. D., Major | 131 |
| Back, W. L., Lieut. | 139 | ——— N. E., Major | 90 | Batten, E. V., 2/Lt. | 21 | ——— J. K., Lieut. | 139 |
| Backhouse, E. H. W., Lieut. | 37 | ——— S. C., 2/Lt. | 188 | Batten-Pooll, A. H., Capt., V.C., M.C. | 113 | ——— R. P. M., Capt. | 58 |
| Bacon, L. G., 2/Lt. | 152 | Barchard, D. M., Lieut. | 56 | Battersby-Harford, J. V., Lieut. | 40 | ——— T. C., Capt. | 74 |
| Badcock, H. V., Lieut. | 69 | Barclay, James, Lieut. | 144 | | | ——— W., Lieut. | 178 |
| Baddely, E. L., 2/Lt. | 171 | ——— W. E., Lieut. | 119 | Battey, B. M., 2/Lt. | 166 | ——— W. L., 2/Lt. | 142 |
| Baerlein, A. A., 2/Lt. | 152 | Bardgett, W. E., Lieut. | 174 | Batting, W. J., 2/Lt. | 122 | Bell-Syer, L., 2/Lt. | 184 |
| Baggs, H., 2/Lt. | 95 | Bardsley, R. J., Lieut. | 14 | Battle, T. H. N., Lieut. | 15 | Bellerby, H. R. B., 2/Lt. | 26 |
| ——— H. E., 2/Lt. | 119 | Barham, H. C., 2/Lt. | 78 | Batty, E. A. F., 2/Lt. | 7 | Bellew, E. D., Lieut. | 139 |
| Bagley, C. G., 2/Lt. | 29 | Barker, C. A., 2/Lt. | 48 | Batty-Smith, S. H., Lieut. | 79 | Bellingham, E. H. C. P., Brig.-Gen. | 7 |
| Bagshaw, A. N., 2/Lt. | 45 | ——— H., 2/Lt. | 114 | Baxter, N. E., Capt. | 69 | Bellis, A. W., Lieut. | 80 |
| Baguley, W. A., 2/Lt. | 46 | ——— H. E., 2/Lt. | 77 | ——— R., 2/Lt. | 71 | Belliveau, A. H., Lieut. | 169 |
| Bailey, C. J., 2/Lt. | 48 | ——— J., Lieut. | 121 | Bayles, J. H. G., Capt. | 50 | Bellville, G. E., Capt. | 9 |
| ——— F. J., Lieut. | 176 | ——— J. S., Major | 185 | Bayley, E. L. J., Capt. | 185 | Belshaw, S. A., 2/Lt. | 67 |
| ——— G. S., 2/Lt. | 29 | ——— R. A., 2/Lt. | 122 | Bayliff, G. T. L., 2/Lt. | 125 | Benedictus, J. H., 2/Lt. | 15 |
| ——— H. R. B., Lieut. | 49 | ——— W., 2/Lt. | 83 | Baylis, H. G., Capt. | 89 | Benjamin, A. L., Lieut. | 166 |
| ——— J., 2/Lt. | 48 | ——— W. G. S., Lieut. | 111 | ——— H. J., 2/Lt. | 37 | Bennett, C. A., 2/Lt. | 116 |
| ——— K. V., Capt. | 95 | Barlow, A. E., 2/Lt. | 34 | Bayliss, J. E., Lieut. | 88 | ——— C. D., 2/Lt. | 150 |
| ——— P. J., Major, D.S.O. | 9 | ——— A. J., Lieut. | 180 | ——— W. Murray F., Lieut. | 165 | ——— E., Major | 186 |
| ——— V. T., Brig.-Gen. | 7 | ——— A. N., 2/Lt. | 155 | Bayly, A. R., Major | 10 | ——— F. C. H., Capt. | 134 |
| ——— W., 2/Lt. | 117 | ——— C. N., Capt. | 92 | Baynton, G. R., Lieut. | 156 | ——— F. W., 2/Lt. | 38 |
| Baillie-Hamilton, Major A/Col. | 95 | ——— John, 2/Lt. | 52 | Beach, B. A., Capt. | 85 | ——— G. T., Lieut. | 188 |
| Baillon, E. M., Lieut. | 180 | ——— N. W., Major | 69 | Beale, W. J., 2/Lt. | 125 | ——— H. J., Major | 75 |
| Baines, E. F., Lt.-Col. | 186 | Barnaby, H., 2/Lt. | 116 | Bealey, F. A. H., Capt. | 51 | ——— H. J., Lieut. | 172 |
| Baird, A. B., 2/Lt. | 141 | Barnard, A. S. C., Lieut. | 99 | Beaman, W., Capt. | 131 | ——— J., Lieut. | 67 |
| ——— J. A., Capt. | 55 | Barnardiston, S., Major | 37 | Bean, C. A. S., Lieut. | 155 | ——— J. B., 2/Lt. | 12 |
| ——— R. Lt. | 186 | Barnes, A. F., Lieut. | 61 | Beard, C. A., Lieut. | 55 | ——— J. M., 2/Lt. | 82 |
| Baird-Smith, A. G., Lieut.-Col. | 54 | ——— A. W., 2/Lt. | 28 | Beardsmore, H., Sub-Lt. | 144 | ——— L., Capt. | 101 |
| Bairstow, T., 2/Lt. | 41 | ——— C. H. R., Lieut. | 93 | Beare, S. G., Fl.-Sub-Lt. | 188 | ——— L. J., Sub-Lt. | 177 |
| Bakel, W., 2/Lt. | 115 | ——— D. T., Capt. | 75 | Bearn, J. A. | 93 | ——— N. O., 2/Lt. | 125 |
| Baker, A. A., Lieut. | 129 | ——— J. D., Lieut. | 159 | Beattie, A. J., Sub.-Lt. | 176 | ——— R., 2/Lt. | 129 |
| ——— A. C., Lieut. | 62 | ——— R. G., Lieut. | 140 | ——— E. H., Rev. | 135 | ——— R. C., Lieut. | 173 |
| ——— A. E., 2/Lt. | 125 | Barnet, H. F. W., 2/Lt. | 81 | ——— H. W., 2/Lt. | 84 | ——— T. H., Sub-Lt. | 144 |
| ——— A. H., Lieut. | 45 | Barnett, H. M., 2/Lt. | 90 | ——— R., 2/Lt. | 115 | Benny, W. W., Lieut. | 140 |
| ——— C. D., 2/Lt. | 94 | ——— C. E., Capt. | 65 | ——— R., Lt. | 137 | Bensley, E. F., Fl.-Lt. | 163 |
| ——— C. G., 2/Lt. | 91 | ——— V. G., Capt. | 56 | Beauchamp, F. E., 2/Lt. | 87 | Benson, F. C., 2/Lt. | 120 |
| ——— F. G., 2/Lt. | 158 | Barni, N. H. L., Lieut. | 121 | ——— F. E., Lieut. | 167 | ——— John, Capt. | 111 |
| ——— G. B., Capt. | 188 | Barr, A. H. G., Lieut. | 189 | Beaumont, F., Lieut. | 161 | ——— F. C. G., 2/Lt. | 95 |
| ——— H., 2/Lt. | 53 | ——— R. J., 2/Lt. | 64 | ——— H. B., Capt. | 123 | ——— H., 2/Lt. | 126 |
| ——— H., 2/Lt. | 117 | Barrard, James, Major | 184 | ——— J. W., Capt. | 99 | Bentley, A. C., Lieut. | 48 |
| ——— L., Capt. | 37 | Barrell, K. C., Lt. | 16 | ——— W. S., 2/Lt. | 16 | ——— Ernest, 2/Lt. | 98 |
| ——— R. P., Lieut. | 150 | Barrett, C. F. M., 2/Lt. | 55 | Beavan, W. F., Lieut. | 22 | ——— F., 2/Lt. | 120 |
| ——— W. G., Lieut. | 59 | ——— F. R. C., Lieut. | 79 | ——— R. M. P., Lieut. | 94 | ——— J. A., 2/Lt. | 96 |
| Balbi, B. M., 2/Lt. | 122 | ——— H. E. W. C., Lt. | 189 | Beazley, E. B., Capt. | 34 | ——— J. H., 2/Lt. | 84 |
| Balden, C. A., Lieut. | 25 | ——— W. S., Lieut. | 48 | Beazeley, G. A., Major | 181 | ——— N. E., 2/Lt. | 67 |
| Baldwin, P. M. G., Lieut. | 180 | ——— W. L., Lieut. | 36 | Beck, T., Lieut. | 173 | Beresford, C. V., Capt. | 62 |
| ——— R. H., Lt.-Col. | 65 | Barrie, Frank, 2/Lt. | 153 | Beckett, J. S., 2/Lt. | 79 | ——— M. de la P., 2/Lt. | 13 |
| Balfour, O., Lieut. | 16 | Barritt, G. L., Lieut. | 169 | Beddow, W. E., 2/Lt. | 56 | ——— W. A., 2/Lt. | 98 |
| ——— H. E., Lieut. | 139 | Barrow, A. J., Capt. | 52 | Bedell-Sivwright, T., Capt. | 48 | Berger-Wheeler, F. E. Allister, Capt. | 62 |
| Ball, A. C., 2/Lt. | 130 | ——— E. E., Capt. | 66 | Bedford, A. E., Lieut. | 49 | Bernard, A. B., Capt. | 92 |
| ——— A. C., 2/Lt. | 159 | Barrowcliff, F., 2/Lt. | 49 | ——— F. H., Lieut. | 25 | ——— C. E. B., 2/Lt. | 41 |
| ——— F. L., Capt. | 43 | Barry, D. D., Lieut. | 103 | Bee, J. R., Lieut. | 40 | ——— V. D., Lieut. | 136 |
| ——— F. S., Capt. | 21 | ——— W. A., Capt. | 55 | ——— Percy, Capt. | 80 | Berne, H. C., Lieut. | 112 |
| ——— John, 2/Lt. | 53 | Barter, T. A., Capt. | 80 | Beedham, N. H., Capt. | 77 | Berney-Ficklin, H. P. M., Capt. | 7 |
| ——— J. B., Capt. | 133 | ——— W. H., 2/Lt. | 34 | Bees, F. H., 2/Lt. | 57 | Berrill, F. C., Lieut. | 37 |
| ——— S. G., 2/Lt. | 118 | Bartlett, A. F., Lieut. | 163 | Beesley, R., 2/Lt. | 170 | Berry, A. E., 2/Lt. | 82 |
| ——— S. W., 2/Lt. | 11 | ——— C. H., Lieut. | 157 | Begbie, S. C. H., Lieut. | 161 | ——— F., Lieut. | 71 |
| ——— T. L., Major | 185 | ——— G. R., 2/Lt. | 172 | Begg, M. G., Lieut. | 180 | ——— F. H., Lieut. | 156 |
| Ballance, G., Lieut. | 165 | Barton, A. E. S., Lieut. | 155 | ——— R. A., Lieut. | 105 | ——— H. J., Lieut. | 175 |
| Ballin, J., Lieut. | 182 | ——— A. W., Lieut. | 112 | Beighton, J. D. K., 2/Lt. | 91 | ——— J. H., Capt. | 108 |
| Bamber, Walter, Lieut. | 187 | ——— B. J., Capt. | 127 | Belcher, S., 2/Lt. | 53 | ——— R. B., Lieut. | 62 |
| | | ——— Basil K., Capt. | 14 | Beldam, C. H., Lieut. | 154 | ——— T. W., Lieut. | 74 |
| | | ——— E. de L., Capt. | 21 | Beldon, Eric, Lieut. | 41 | Bertioli, W. S., 2/Lt. | 87 |
| | | ——— W., 2/Lt. | 187 | | | | |
| | | Barugh, W. G., 2/Lt. | 119 | | | | |
| | | Barwick, H. A., Lieut. | 139 | | | | |

| Name | Page |
|---|---|
| Besant, P. E., Capt. | 28 |
| Besley, E. M., Capt. | 16 |
| Bester, P. M., 2/Lt. | 89 |
| Beswick, J. C., 2/Lt. | 24 |
| Bethell, F., 2/Lt. | 122 |
| Betts, E. L., Lieut. | 93 |
| ——— T. W., 2/Lt. | 76 |
| Beuttler, J. C. O., Lieut. | 135 |
| Bevan, F. H. | 7 |
| ——— J. A., Lieut. | 23 |
| Beveridge, H., Capt. | 71 |
| ——— J., 2/Lt. | 104 |
| Beverland, C. F., Lieut. | 60 |
| Beverley, R., Capt., M.C. | 7 |
| Bevington, R. J., Lieut. | 151 |
| Bewley, E. R., Lieut. | 116 |
| Beyfus, G. H., 2/Lt. | 67 |
| Bibby, J. D., Capt. | 9 |
| Bickerstaffe, T. S., Lieut. | 123 |
| Biddington, H. V., 2/Lt. | 159 |
| Biddolph, N., Capt. | 20 |
| ——— T. J., Major | 51 |
| Biden, S. W., 2/Lt. | 183 |
| Biggs, Henry, Lieut. | 37 |
| ——— H. St. J., Lt. | 139 |
| Bigland, E. W., Capt. | 56 |
| Bignell, Capt. | 183 |
| Biheller, W., Capt. | 159 |
| Bindon, L. W., Lieut. | 127 |
| Biner, B. C., 2/Lt. | 44 |
| Bing, W. L., 2/Lt. | 167 |
| Bingham, A. E., Lieut. | 165 |
| ——— Hon. R., Lieut. | 56 |
| Binney, F. B., Capt. | 146 |
| Binnie, Alan, Capt. | 152 |
| Binnington, E., 2/Lt. | 137 |
| Binns, John | 50 |
| ——— W. A. F., 2/Lt. | 93 |
| Birch, D. C., 2/Lt. | 151 |
| ——— H., 2/Lt. | 181 |
| ——— J. G., Lt.-Col. | 90 |
| ——— S., Lieut. | 162 |
| Birchenough, J. A., 2/Lt. | 96 |
| Birchwood, H., 2/Lt. | 122 |
| Bird, A. F., Lieut. | 155 |
| ——— B. A., Lieut. | 163 |
| ——— C. B., Lieut. | 150 |
| ——— C. R., 2/Lt. | 88 |
| ——— E., Capt. | 86 |
| ——— H. D., 2/Lt. | 31 |
| ——— R., Rev. | 135 |
| ——— R. G., 2/Lt. | 68 |
| ——— T. H., Lieut. | 60 |
| ——— W. H. F., Lieut. | 11 |
| Birkhead, J. B., Lieut. | 162 |
| Birkinshaw, J. H., 2/Lt. | 42 |
| Birkumshaw, S. E., 2/Lt. | 32 |
| Birks, N. A., Lieut. | 151 |
| Birley, R. A., Major | 10 |
| ——— T. E. H., Lieut. | 160 |
| Birt, W. B., Capt. | 65 |
| Bishop, B., 2/Lt. | 65 |
| ——— E. W., Capt. | 57 |
| ——— F. H., Lieut. | 97 |
| ——— G. W. R., Capt. | 187 |
| ——— H. C. W., 2/Lt. | 183 |
| ——— H. W., Sub.-Lt. | 145 |
| ——— J. F., 2/Lt. | 78 |
| Bisset, A. G., Capt. | 133 |
| Bittleston, N. A., Lieut. | 37 |
| Binsted, H. M., 2/Lt. | 65 |
| Black, A. C., 2/Lt. | 121 |
| ——— A. W. H., 2/Lt. | 119 |
| ——— J. B., Lieut. | 103 |
| Black, J. R., Capt. | 105 |
| ——— K. E., Lieut. | 43 |
| ——— S. McBrayne, Lieut. | 166 |
| ——— W., 2/Lt. | 149 |
| Blackall, J. H., 2/Lt. | 153 |
| Blackburn, R. R., 2]Lt. | 144 |
| ——— T., Capt. | 58 |
| Blacker, R., 2/Lt. | 40 |
| Blackett, G. E., Capt. | 101 |
| Blackledge, R. D., Capt., M.C. | 104 |
| Blackie, F. H., Lieut. | 189 |
| Blacklock, H. A., 2/Lt. | 66 |
| Blackwell, K. R., 2/Lt. | 13 |
| Blackwood, T., Capt. | 134 |
| ——— T. A., Lieut. | 109 |
| Blain, C. W., 2/Lt. | 148 |
| Blair, James, 2/Lt. | 112 |
| ——— J. W., 2/Lt. | 105 |
| Blake, A. G. S., 2/Lt. | 166 |
| ——— C. H., 2/Lt. | 93 |
| ——— F., Sub.-Lt. | 144 |
| ——— H. P., 2/Lt. | 160 |
| ——— J. W., 2/Lt. | 180 |
| ——— N. G., 2/Lt. | 22 |
| ——— O. P. T. N., Lieut. | 56 |
| Blakesley, R. G., Lieut. | 189 |
| Blamires, Charles, 2/Lt. | 35 |
| Blanch, J. A., 2/Lt. | 38 |
| Blanchard, F. W., Capt. | 28 |
| ——— N. G., Lieut. | 136 |
| Bland, C. F. R., Lieut. | 83 |
| Blandford, T. C., Lieut. | 81 |
| Blandy, G., Sub.-Lt. | 188 |
| Blatch, H. E., 2/Lt. | 66 |
| Blaxill, F. H., 2/Lt. | 163 |
| Blayney, B. W., 2/Lt. | 150 |
| Bleckly, A. K., Lieut. | 93 |
| Blenkiron, D., 2/Lt. | 97 |
| Blight, B. W., 2/Lt. | 37 |
| ——— T. F., Lieut. | 165 |
| Blofield, R. A., 2/Lt. | 179 |
| Bloomfield, C. W., 2/Lt. | 70 |
| ——— V. E., 2/Lt. | 76 |
| ——— W. S. R., Capt. | 150 |
| Bloore, F. W., 2/Lt. | 116 |
| Blount, G. A., 2/Lt. | 80 |
| Blower, M. S., Lieut. | 65 |
| Blundell, E. P., 2/Lt. | 115 |
| ——— H. A., 2/Lt. | 12 |
| Blunn, A. G., Lieut. | 127 |
| Blunt, P. K., Capt. | 46 |
| Blythe, H., 2/Lt. | 150 |
| Blythe Lamble, A. E., Lieut. | 145 |
| Boardman, A. J., 2/Lt. | 43 |
| ——— J. H., Major | 116 |
| Boase, L. C., Lt. | 137 |
| Bockett-Pugh, H. C. E., Lieut. | 163 |
| Bodley, W. G. L., 2/Lt. | 174 |
| Body, G. C., Lieut. | 165 |
| ——— G. T., Capt. | 79 |
| ——— O. G., Lieut. | 189 |
| Bodycombe, J., 2/Lt. | 73 |
| Boe, D., 2/Lt. | 165 |
| Boger, D. C., Lt.-Col. | 54 |
| ——— R. A., Capt. | 146 |
| Boldison, A., 2/Lt. | 151 |
| Bolger, B., 2/Lt. | 125 |
| Bollam, A. D., Capt. | 11 |
| Bollins, A. P., Lieut. | 162 |
| Bolton, A. C., Capt. | 149 |
| ——— R. G. I., Lt.-Col. | 18 |
| Bolton, R. H., Lieut. | 54 |
| ——— W. E., 2/Lt. | 12 |
| ——— W. O., 2/Lt. | 50 |
| Bond, F. E., Lieut. | 174 |
| ——— R. C., Lt.-Col. | 85 |
| ——— U. A., 2/Lt. | 58 |
| ——— W. H., 2/Lt. | 131 |
| Bone, Ernest H., 2/Lt. | 46 |
| Bonshor, John, 2/Lt. | 71 |
| ——— J. H., 2/Lt. | 46 |
| Boon, H. F., 2/Lt. | 127 |
| Boosey, L. A., Major | 130 |
| Boot, W. A., 2/Lt. | 50 |
| Boote, R. S. L., 2/Lt. | 154 |
| Booth, F., Major | 185 |
| ——— H. H., F. Sub.-Lt. | 177 |
| ——— P. J., Capt. | 59 |
| ——— W. R., Lieut. | 13 |
| Boothman, C., Lieut. | 164 |
| Boothroyd, E., 2/Lt. | 77 |
| Boraston, C. A., Lieut. | 17 |
| Borrett, G. K. F., Lieut. | 135 |
| Borrodale, R. F. B., 2/Lt. | 131 |
| Borrow, C. E., 2/Lt. | 81 |
| Borthwick, W., Capt., Hon. | 90 |
| Boscawen, G.; Maj. The Hon. | 13 |
| Bose, S., Major | 182 |
| Bosher, H., Lieut. | 166 |
| Bostock, A., Lieut. | 14 |
| ——— A. S., 2/Lt. | 100 |
| ——— E. L., 2/Lt. | 124 |
| Boston, C. A. N., 2/Lt. | 82 |
| ——— J., 2/Lt. | 81 |
| Bosustow, G. W., Lieut. | 101 |
| Boswell, K. C., 2/Lt. | 15 |
| Bott, A. J., Capt. | 179 |
| Bottomley, J. W., 2/Lt. | 52 |
| Botton, O. V., 2/Lt. | 21 |
| Boughton, C. B., 2/Lt. | 151 |
| Boulton, F. E., 2/Lt. | 162 |
| Boumphrey, J. W., Lieut. | 156 |
| Bourchier, C., 2/Lt. | 113 |
| Bourdillon, T. E., 2/Lt. | 81 |
| Bourinot, A. S., Lieut. | 153 |
| Bousfield, Hugh D., Lt.-Col. | 41 |
| ——— J. K., Lieut. | 151 |
| Bowater, A. V., Capt. | 173 |
| Bowen, E. E. W., 2/Lt. | 65 |
| ——— J. L., Lieut. | 53 |
| ——— L. A. G., Capt., M.C. | 38 |
| ——— R. L., Major | 90 |
| ——— T. O., 2/Lt. | 52 |
| Bower, L. C., Lieut. | 166 |
| Bowers, P. T., Lieut. | 152 |
| ——— V. R., Lieut. | 32 |
| Bowker, S., 2/Lt. | 119 |
| ——— T., 2/Lt. | 117 |
| Bowles, F. H., Capt. | 61 |
| ——— F. S., Lieut. | 175 |
| ——— G. P., Fl. Sub.-Lt. | 150 |
| Bowman, A. A., Lieut. | 103 |
| ——— A. W. M., Lieut. | 136 |
| ——— W. L., 2/Lt. | 27 |
| Bowring, F. A., Capt. | 65 |
| ——— J. V., 2/Lt. | 148 |
| Bowskill, J., 2/Lt. | 84 |
| Bowyer, F. H., 2/Lt. | 149 |
| Box, T., 2/Lt. | 32 |
| Boyall, A. M., Lt.-Col. | 40 |
| Boyce, H. B. P., Lieut. | 160 |
| ——— W. R., Lieut. | 182 |
| ——— H. F., Lieut. | 39 |
| Boycott, R. G., Lieut. | 71 |
| Boyd, C. N., 2/Lt. | 175 |
| ——— C. T., 2/Lt. | 104 |
| ——— J., Lieut. | 159 |
| ——— R., Capt. | 114 |
| ——— W., 2/Lt. | 27 |
| Boyes, W., Lieut. | 185 |
| Boyle, A., Lieut. | 134 |
| ——— E. P. O., Lieut. | 53 |
| ——— J. C., 2/Lt. | 170 |
| ——— J. K., Lieut., M.C. | 108 |
| ——— R. M., Capt. | 60 |
| Boys, Randolph, 2/Lt. | 169 |
| Brabazon, J. H. T., Lieut. | 181 |
| Brace, R. B., 2/Lt. | 78 |
| Bracken, K. O., 2/Lt. | 175 |
| Bradbury, A., 2/Lt. | 34 |
| Braddell, W., Capt. | 114 |
| Braddy, A. R., 2/Lt. | 35 |
| Bradford, W., Lieut. | 168 |
| Bradley, Arthur, 2/Lt. | 55 |
| ——— C. E., Brig.-Gen. | 7 |
| ——— F., 2/Lt. | 95 |
| ——— James, 2/Lt. | 96 |
| ——— W. D., Lieut. | 110 |
| Bradshaw, H. J., 2/Lt. | 179 |
| Bradwell, E., 2/Lt. | 96 |
| Brady, D. W., 2/Lt. | 68 |
| ——— B. J., Fl.-Lt. | 188 |
| Brailsford, J., 2/Lt. | 13 |
| Brain, E. R., Lieut. | 26 |
| Braithwaite, B. F., 2/Lt. | 157 |
| Brakell, J. F., 2/Lt. | 9 |
| Branch, H. G. S., Capt. | 42 |
| Brander, G. L., Lieut. | 19 |
| Brandon, G., Lieut. | 16 |
| Brandrick, Arthur, 2/Lt. | 174 |
| Branfoot, G., Capt. | 25 |
| Branson, D., Lieut. | 178 |
| Brantford, Fl. Sub.-Lt. | 150 |
| Brattle, C. C., 2/Lt. | 22 |
| Breach, G. A., 2/Lt. | 78 |
| Breckenridge, W., 2/Lt. | 163 |
| Bredin, W. E., 2/Lt. | 47 |
| Breedon, F. J., Capt., M.C. | 29 |
| Breen, T. | 7 |
| Bremner, T., 2/Lt. | 111 |
| ——— T. P., Lieut. | 31 |
| Brent, James, Lieut. | 158 |
| Breton, B. W. F., 2/Lt. | 15 |
| Brett, G., Capt. | 130 |
| ——— H. A., Capt. | 178 |
| Brettell, F. A., Lieut. | 29 |
| Brewer, B. D. M., Lieut. | 11 |
| Brewster, J. A., Lieut. | 30 |
| Brickmann, F. I., Capt. | 184 |
| Bridge, C. H. A., 2/Lt. | 169 |
| ——— Gordon, 2/Lt. | 125 |
| ——— H. E., Lieut. | 140 |
| Bridger, H., 2/Lt. | 174 |
| Bridges, F. J., Lieut, M.C. | 118 |
| Bridgford, S. L., Capt. | 95 |
| Brie, R. A. C., Lieut. | 168 |
| Brien, H. S. A., 2/Lt. | 80 |
| Brierley, R., Lt. | 182 |
| Brigham, W., 2/Lt. | 26 |
| Briggs, L. P., Lieut. | 148 |

| | PAGE | | PAGE | | PAGE | | PAGE |
|---|---|---|---|---|---|---|---|
| Briggs. S. P., 2/Lt. | 148 | Brown, I. L., Lieut. | 167 | Burdett, Basil, Lieut. | 122 | Bye, H. T., 2/Lt. | 88 |
| Bright, A. S., Capt. | 78 | ———— K. E., Capt. | 75 | ———— E. W., Capt. | 182 | Byng Hall, P., Major, D.S.O. | 139 |
| ———— F. A., 2/Lt. | 129 | ———— N., 2/Lt. | 100 | Burdon, Rowland, Capt. | 101 | Byrne, C. H. C., Capt. | 132 |
| ———— F. C., Lieut. | 62 | ———— R. P. M., 2/Lt. | 15 | Burges-Short, H. G. R., Lt.-Col. | 67 | ———— J. O., Capt., M.C. | 26 |
| Brindley, E. G., 2/Lt. | 45 | ———— R. S., 2/Lt. | 22 | Burgess, E. H. V., 2/Lt. | 91 | Byron, E. F., 2/Lt. | 55 |
| Brine, T., 2/Lt. | 136 | ———— R. J. H., 2/Lt. | 127 | ———— F., 2/Lt. | 102 | Bysshe, G. T., Sub.-Lt. | 180 |
| Brink, J. M., Lieut. | 189 | ———— R. W., 2/Lt. | 118 | ———— F. G., 2/Lt. | 39 | Bytheway, A. W., 2/Lt. | 55 |
| Brisbin, H. V., Lieut. | 171 | ———— S. J., Capt. | 20 | ———— P. G., 2/Lt. | 21 | | |
| Briscoe, W. R. W., 2/Lt. | 114 | ———— V. L. W., 2/Lt. | 64 | ———— W. H., Lieut. | 107 | Cable, D., Capt., Adj. | 74 |
| Brislee, F. R., 2/Lt. | 35 | ———— V. R., 2/Lt. | 163 | Burgoyne, J. S., 2/Lt. | 55 | Cade, C. E., 2/Lt. | 88 |
| Britton, E. A. C., 2/Lt. | 176 | ———— W. C., 2/Lt. | 126 | ———— R. M., Capt. | 53 | Cahill, F. J., Capt. | 132 |
| Broackes, E. W., Major | 73 | ———— W. D., 2/Lt. | 68 | Burke, G. M., 2/Lt. | 60 | ———— T. G., 2/Lt. | 113 |
| Broadbent, G., Lieut. | 170 | ———— W. E., 2/Lt. | 77 | ———— J. W., 2/Lt. | 60 | ———— R. J., Capt. | 131 |
| ———— G. A., 2/Lt. | 52 | ———— W. H., Col. | 183 | ———— M. F., Lieut. | 136 | Cahusac, E. B., Capt., M.C. | 161 |
| Broadhurst, H. C., Surg. | 144 | ———— W. J., 2/Lt. | 107 | ———— U. B., Capt. | 36 | | |
| Broadwood, J., Capt. | 7 | ———— W. R. A., Capt., Rev. | 135 | Burlton, G. P., Lieut. | 34 | Cailes, S. S., 2/Lt. | 144 |
| Brockhurst, G. N., 2/Lt. | 151 | Browne, D. E. S., Lt. | 118 | Burman, A. H., 2/Lt. | 115 | Cairnduff, A., Lieut. | 147 |
| Brocklebank, H. A., Capt. | 23 | ———— H., 2/Lt. | 183 | Burn, H. L. P., Capt. | 105 | Cairnes, D. S., 2/Lt. | 148 |
| Brocks, A. W., 2/Lt. | 181 | ———— M. G., Capt. | 63 | ———— J. S., 2/Lt. | 165 | Cairns, Fred., 2/Lt. | 45 |
| Brockwell, S. G., Lieut. | 9 | ———— H. W., 2/Lt. | 161 | Burnand, G. A., Lieut. | 71 | ———— J. A., 2/Lt. | 152 |
| Broder, P. A., Lieut. | 146 | Browne-Mason, H. O. B., Col. | 186 | Burnard, R. A., 2/Lt. | 161 | ———— W. T. S., 2/Lt. | 174 |
| Broderip, J. Y. M., Capt. | 38 | Browning, L. W., 2/Lt. | 83 | Burnham, M. E., Lieut. | 169 | Caldecott, R., 2/Lt. | 160 |
| Brodhurst-Hill, R., Capt. | 21 | Bruce, A. P. C., 2/Lt. | 174 | Burnie, A. J., 2/Lt. | 146 | Calder, G., 2/Lt. | 92 |
| Brodie, H. G., Capt. | 180 | ———— C. D., Brig.-Gen. | 7 | Burnley, C. P., 2/Lt. | 21 | ———— H. G., Lieut. | 35 |
| ———— R. A., Capt. | 140 | ———— O., 2/Lt. | 115 | Burns, E. B., Lt. | 186 | Caldwell, D. C., 2/Lt. | 59 |
| ———— T. W., 2/Lt. | 170 | ———— R. T., Capt. | 131 | ———— H., Fl. Sub-Lt. | 181 | ———— J., 2/Lt. | 81 |
| Brogden, C. E., 2/Lt. | 102 | ———— T. B., Lieut. | 157 | ———— V. I. A., 2/Lt. | 152 | ———— J. A., Lieut. | 97 |
| Bromfield, J. L., Lieut. | 144 | ———— W. F., Major | 16 | Burnside, J., 2/Lt. | 109 | ———— J. F., 2/Lt. | 110 |
| Bromley, J. T., Capt. | 96 | Brumell, H. P., Lieut. | 173 | Burpee, B., Capt. | 135 | ———— J. M., Sub.-Lt. | 145 |
| Bronskill, F. H., 2/Lt. | 150 | Brundritt, D. F., 2/Lt. | 124 | Burr, E. H., 2/Lt. | 64 | ———— J. C., 2/Lt. | 92 |
| Bronson, C. G., Lieut. | 179 | Brunskill, J., Major | 131 | Burr, P., Lieut. | 17 | ———— R. T., 2/Lt. | 115 |
| Brooker, H. H., 2/Lt. | 30 | Bryan, C. A., 2/Lt. | 80 | Burrell, J. H., Capt. and Adjt. | 101 | Caley, R., 2/Lt. | 64 |
| Brookes, A. A., 2/Lt. | 21 | ———— E. F., 2/Lt. | 13 | Burrill, T. F., Lieut. | 151 | Call, Felix, Major | 48 |
| Brookfield, C. W., 2/Lt. | 12 | ———— F. F. H., Lieut. | 164 | Burrington, H. S., Capt. | 39 | Callender, F. de C., 2/Lt. | 127 |
| Brooking, H. W., Capt. | 31 | Bryans, J. C., Capt. | 108 | Burroughs, G. H., Capt. | 186 | Calrow, Richard, Lieut. | 174 |
| Brooks, Edgar, 2/Lt. | 40 | Bryant, H. G., Capt. | 86 | Burrow, R., 2/Lt. | 33 | Calvert, A. S., Lieut. | 120 |
| ———— W. J., Capt. | 13 | ———— J. W., Lieut. | 23 | Burrows, M. B., Lieut. | 8 | ———— J. H., 2/Lt. | 64 |
| ———— W. V., 2/Lt. | 128 | Bryce, A. G., Capt. | 132 | ———— R. F. G., Lieut. | 94 | ———— T. W., 2/Lt. | 158 |
| Broomfield, F., 2/Lt. | 137 | ———— M. S., 2/Lt. | 27 | Burry, H. W., 2/Lt. | 165 | Cameron, D. R., Lieut. | 153 |
| Brough, Harry, Lieut. | 88 | Brydone, James, 2/Lt. | 158 | Burt, G. C., Lieut. | 17 | ———— E. K., Capt. | 108 |
| Broughall, H. S., F. Sub-Lt. | 177 | Buchanan, A., Lieut. | 175 | Burton, D. F., Lieut. | 169 | ———— F., 2/Lt. | 112 |
| Brown, A., Lieut. | 131 | ———— G. A. B., Capt. | 141 | ———— E., 2/Lt. | 148 | ———— G. W., Lieut. | 23 |
| ———— A., Capt. | 187 | ———— H. G., 2/Lt. | 109 | ———— F. A., Lieut. | 125 | ———— H., 2/Lt. | 99 |
| ———— A. A. C., 2/Lt. | 28 | ———— John, Capt. | 181 | ———— F. T., 2/Lt. | 35 | ———— I. D., 2/Lt. | 158 |
| ———— A. C. G., 2/Lt. | 162 | Buck, Harry, 2/Lt. | 65 | ———— G. C. J., Lieut. | 122 | Campbell, A. B. D., Sub-Lt. | 171 |
| ———— A. E., 2/Lt. | 25 | Buckingham, W., Capt., M.C. | 173 | ———— H. M., Fl. Sub.-Lt. | 176 | ———— A. J., Lieut. | 8 |
| ———— A. G., 2/Lt. | 23 | Buckland, G. F., 2/Lt. | 44 | ———— R. J., 2/Lt. | 63 | ———— A. M., Capt. | 83 |
| ———— A. L., Capt. | 59 | Buckle, F., 2/Lt. | 127 | Burtt, L. L., Capt. | 129 | ———— C. L., Lieut. | 112 |
| ———— A. W., Lieut. | 147 | Buckley, F., 2/Lt. | 24 | Bury, H., Capt. | 69 | ———— D. B., 2/Lt. | 94 |
| ———— C., 2/Lt. | 100 | ———— G. B., Capt. | 132 | Busby, R. I., Capt. | 51 | ———— G. C., Lieut. | 112 |
| ———— C. B., 2/Lt. | 125 | ———— S. E., Lieut. | 147 | Bush, H. K., 2/Lt. | 34 | ———— H., Lieut. | 140 |
| ———— C. D., Lieut. | 46 | ———— S. J., 2/Lt. | 70 | Bushe, J. F., 2/Lt. | 156 | ———— Ivan, 2/Lt. | 108 |
| ———— C. F., Lieut. | 166 | Bucknall, C. V. A., /Lt. | 174 | Bushell, R., Lieut. | 102 | ———— J., 2/Lt. | 106 |
| ———— C. G., 2/Lt. | 21 | Budd, F. W., Lieut. | 33 | Bustard, C. R. D., 2/Lt. | 31 | ———— James, Lt. | 119 |
| ———— C. G., Capt., Rev. | 135 | Budden, E. B., Lieut. | 88 | ———— F. H., Capt. | 189 | ———— J. W., 2/Lt. | 44 |
| ———— C. H., 2/Lt. | 158 | Budge, A. E. V., 2/Lt. | 30 | Buston, S. J., 2/Lt. | 35 | ———— K. D., Fl. Sub.-Lt. | 160 |
| ———— E. A., 2/Lt. | 63 | Budgeon, E. A., 2/Lt. | 141 | Buswell, H. B., 2/Lt. | 79 | ———— M. G., 2/Lt. | 103 |
| ———— E. C., 2/Lt. | 44 | Budgett, A. W. M., Lieut. | 178 | Butler, A. T., Capt. | 63 | ———— Robert, Capt. | 65 |
| ———— E. M., 2/Lt. | 163 | Bugge, F. H., 2/Lt. | 166 | ———— J. O., Lieut. | 160 | ———— T., Lieut. | 186 |
| ———— F. A., 2/Lt. | 51 | Bull, F. J., 2/Lt. | 163 | ———— L., 2/Lt. | 151 | ———— W. A., Lieut. | 100 |
| ———— F. W., Capt. | 104 | Bullen, Edward, Lieut. | 166 | ———— L. C., 2/Lt. | 91 | ———— W. M., Capt. | 37 |
| ———— F. W., 2/Lt. | 64 | ———— R. V., 2/Lt. | 76 | ———— P., Lieut. | 131 | Candler, W., 2/Lt. | 36 |
| ———— G. A., Capt. | 27 | Buller, J. H. G., Major | 189 | ———— W., 2/Lt. | 94 | Candy, F. B., 2/Lt. | 176 |
| ———— H. C., 2/Lt. | 24 | Bulling, H., 2/Lt. | 14 | ———— W. T., Lieut. | 71 | Cane, A. S., Capt. | 181 |
| ———— H. M., Lieut. | 167 | Bullock, A. D., 2/Lt. | 69 | Butt, L. M., 2/Lt. | 44 | ———— E. G. S., Capt. | 186 |
| ———— I. A., Capt. | 28 | ———— W., 2/Lt. | 87 | ———— Thomas, Lieut. | 85 | Cannon, A. T., Capt. | 128 |
| ———— J., 2/Lt. | 68 | Bunbury, D. St. P., Capt. | 180 | Butterworth, C., Lieut. | 176 | ———— S. W., 2/Lt. | 97 |
| ———— J., Lieut. | 180 | Bunce, H., Capt. | 142 | ———— H. E., Capt. | 96 | Cant, J. A. V., 2/Lt. | 66 |
| ———— J. A., 2/Lt. | 15 | ———— J. P., 2/Lt. | 92 | ———— S., Capt. | 54 | Cantlay, A., 2/Lt. | 107 |
| ———— J. A., 2/Lt. | 12 | Bunn, H. P., 2/Lt. | 71 | Buttifant, E., 2/Lt. | 91 | Capes, G., 2/Lt. | 83 |
| ———— J. B., 2/Lt. | 109 | Burbidge, G. E. D., 2/Lt. | 25 | Button, G. T., Lieut. | 75 | Capon, R. S., 2/Lt. | 152 |
| ———— J. B., Lieut. | 121 | Burbury, A. V., Lieut. | 152 | ———— L. H., Lieut. | 167 | Capper, E. R., Capt., M.C. | 76 |
| ———— J. L., 2/Lt. | 164 | | | Buyers, W. N., Lieut. | 107 | | |
| ———— J. W., 2/Lt. | 172 | | | | | | |

| Name | Page | Name | Page | Name | Page | Name | Page |
|---|---|---|---|---|---|---|---|
| Cardall, H., 2/Lt. | 47 | Caunt, A. E., 2/Lt. | 70 | Childe, A. L. B., Lieut. | 100 | Clarke, J., Lieut. | 96 |
| Cardew, H., Capt. | 183 | ——— H. V., Lieut. | 158 | Chillingworth, A. J., Capt. | 133 | ——— J. B., 2/Lt. | 86 |
| ——— F. B. A., 2/Lt. | 24 | Caunter, J. A., Capt. | 61 | ——— Major | 84 | ——— K. H. S., Lieut. | 129 |
| Cardozo, H. G., 2/Lt. | 110 | Causton, L. P., Capt. | 22 | Chinner, E. H., Lieut. | 136 | ——— L. L., 2/Lt. | 118 |
| Carey, J. G., Lieut. | 175 | Cavanagh, T. J., 2/Lt. | 49 | Chisholm, D. C., Lieut. | 81 | ——— N., 2/Lt. | 111 |
| ——— R. O'D., Lieut. | 67 | Cave, W. T. C., Capt. | 130 | ——— J. F., Capt. | 172 | ——— S. E., 2/Lt. | 38 |
| Carles, C. W., Lieut. | 124 | Cawdron, Harold, 2/Lt. | 87 | Chittenden, S. J., Capt. | 119 | ——— T. C. A., 2/Lt. | 45 |
| Carless, R. J., 2/Lt. | 86 | Cawley, C. F., 2/Lt. | 173 | Chitty, A. A. E., Lt. | 83 | ——— T. H., Lieut. | 149 |
| Carleton, R., Lieut. | 140 | Cawthra, A., 2/Lt. | 67 | ——— C., 2/Lt. | 187 | ——— V. S., Capt. | 187 |
| Carlisle, T. R. M., Capt. | 185 | Cayley, A., Lieut. | 15 | ——— W. W., Brevet-Col. | 184 | ——— Wm., Lieut. | 109 |
| Carlin, S., Capt. | 172 | ——— K. H. E., 2/Lt. | 37 | Chown, J. S., 2/Lt. | 91 | ——— W. E., 2/Lt. | 14 |
| Carlyon, E. T. R., Capt. | 79 | Cayzer, C. W., Lt., Sir | 9 | Chreiman, W. W., Lieut. | 171 | ——— W. M., Capt. | 97 |
| Carlyle, Geo., 2/Lt. | 57 | Chadwick, C. R., 2/Lt. | 15 | Christian, Ewan, Lt.-Col. D.S.O. | 142 | Clarkson, R. W., 2/Lt. | 42 |
| Carmichael, H. H., 2/Lt. | 100 | ——— Geo., Capt. | 162 | Christie, J. R., Capt. | 106 | ——— W., 2/Lt. | 44 |
| ——— W., Lieut. | 30 | Chainey, F. H., 2/Lt. | 171 | ——— T., Capt. | 103 | Claxton, W. G., Lieut. | 168 |
| ——— W. R. C., 2/Lt. | 149 | Chalklin, W. J. N., 2/Lt. | 171 | ——— W. M., Capt. | 132 | Claydon, M. S., 2/Lt. | 76 |
| Carmody, C., Capt., M.C. | 50 | Challenor, B. H., Capt. | 35 | Christie-Miller, E., Capt. | 18 | Claye, H., Capt. | 163 |
| Carne, W. A., 2/Lt. | 138 | Challinor, R. T., 2/Lt. | 179 | Christopher, C. D., Lt.-Col. | 131 | Clayton, F. H., 2/Lt. | 168 |
| Carpenter, C. E., 2/Lt. | 36 | Challis, A., 2/Lt. | 33 | Chubb, J. A., Lieut. | 165 | ——— J. L., Capt. | 96 |
| ——— F., Lt. | 167 | ——— F. G., 2/Lt. | 180 | ——— J. E. V., 2/Lt. | 20 | Cleall, P. W., Lieut. | 76 |
| Carr, A. M., 2/Lt. | 18 | ——— M. E., 2/Lt. | 169 | Chuck, Arthur, 2/Lt. | 56 | Clean, R. L. J., Lieut. | 69 |
| ——— A. R., 2/Lt. | 54 | Chalmers, B. G., 2/Lt. | 153 | Church, W. A., 2/Lt. | 95 | Clegg, J. H., 2/Lt. | 42 |
| ——— C. E., 2/Lt. | 127 | ——— J. J., 2/Lt. | 106 | Churchill, W. F. N., Capt. | 12 | ——— W. L., Capt. | 36 |
| ——— E. de G., Capt. | 36 | Chaloner, T. W. P. L., Capt., Hon. | 147 | Churchouse, H. P., Capt. | 28 | Cleland, A. L. H., 2/Lt. | 41 |
| ——— F. C., 2/Lt. | 179 | Chamberlain, W. B., 2/Lt. | 178 | Cinnamond, F., 2/Lt. | 60 | Clelland, David, 2/Lt. | 140 |
| ——— G. W., 2/Lt. | 12 | Chambers, A. H., 2/Lt. | 77 | Clack, L. A., Lieut. | 167 | Clementi-Smith, H. D., Capt. | 131 |
| ——— C. V., 2/Lt. | 162 | ——— G., 2/Lt. | 117 | Clancy, J., 2/Lt. | 59 | Clements, H. T., 2/Lt. | 130 |
| ——— R., 2/Lt. | 72 | ——— James, 2/Lt. | 80 | Clapham, S. W. B., 2/Lt. | 127 | ——— S. U. L., Major | 110 |
| ——— R. G., 2/Lt. | 164 | ——— W. D., Lieut. | 156 | Clare, A. D. | 82 | Clemons, H. S., 2/Lt. | 159 |
| ——— T. E. A., Capt. | 132 | Chamier, R. O., Lieut. | 184 | ——— A. E., 2/Lt. | 65 | Clemow, S. N., 2/Lt. | 127 |
| Carre, B., 2/Lt. | 106 | Champion, H. T., Capt. | 147 | ——— A. M., Lieut. | 134 | Clemson, E. G., 2/Lt. | 14 |
| ——— J. H. T., Fl. Sub.-Lt. | 162 | ——— S. G., Lieut. | 189 | Claret, A. E., Lieut. | 22 | ——— A. W., Fl. Com. | 181 |
| Carrington, J. W., 2/Lt. | 129 | Champney, H. D'A., 2/Lt. | 50 | Claridge, C. G., 2/Lt. | 79 | ——— T. H., Capt. | 85 |
| Carroll, E. Cola, Lieut. | 156 | ——— J. P., 2/Lt. | 125 | Clark, Alex., 2/Lt. | 106 | Clenshaw, W. F., Lieut. | 21 |
| Carrow, R. B., 2/Lt. | 23 | Chance, W. H. S., Lieut. | 149 | ——— A. F., 2/Lt. | 46 | Clerihew, Clive, 2/Lt. | 69 |
| Carruthers, P. G., 2/Lt. | 89 | Chandler, A., 2/Lt. | 41 | ——— A. G., Capt. | 134 | Clibborn, R., Capt. | 86 |
| Carson, H. R., Lieut. | 55 | ——— A. H., 2/Lt. | 45 | ——— A. H., 2/Lt. | 121 | Clidero, H. A., 2/Lt. | 49 |
| ——— S. B., 2/Lt. | 34 | ——— G. H., Lieut. | 113 | ——— A. L., 2/Lt. | 158 | Cliffe, F. V., 2/Lt. | 72 |
| Carter, A. D., Major | 163 | ——— H., 2/Lt. | 116 | ——— A. M., 2/Lt. | 184 | Clifford, G. C., 2/Lt. | 31 |
| ——— A. E., Lieut. | 27 | ——— J., 2/Lt. | 95 | ——— A. N. B., 2/Lt. | 127 | ——— R., Capt. | 182 |
| ——— C. W., 2/Lt. | 14 | ——— R. H., 2/Lt. | 84 | ——— A. S., 2/Lt. | 107 | ——— R. C., Capt. | 186 |
| ——— E., 2/Lt. | 142 | Channer, G. R., Capt. | 184 | ——— C. A., Major, M.C. | 66 | Clifton, H. A., Lieut. | 182 |
| ——— E. P. Q., Capt. | 28 | Chant, W. E., Capt. | 22 | ——— C. C., Capt. | 162 | ——— H. N., 2/Lt. | 18 |
| ——— F. W. B., Lt. and Qtmr. | 134 | ——— E. M., Lieut. | 160 | ——— C. G., Lieut. | 187 | Clinton, W. L., Capt. | 90 |
| ——— G. L., 2/Lt. | 167 | Chantrill, A. I., Capt. | 14 | ——— D. R., 2/Lt. | 60 | Clough, A. C., 2/Lt. | 56 |
| ——— H. S., 2/Lt. | 50 | Chapman, A. F., Capt. | 61 | ——— E., 2/Lt. | 32 | Clouston, A. M., 2/Lt. | 141 |
| ——— L. A., 2/Lt. | 113 | ——— E. F. G., Lieut. | 64 | ——— E. G. U., 2/Lt. | 34 | Cloutier, G. A., Lieut. | 140 |
| ——— R. N., 2/Lt. | 149 | ——— G., Major | 13 | ——— E. H. B., 2/Lt. | 14 | Clubb, A. D., Lieut. | 40 |
| Carthew, P. R., Lieut. | 37 | ——— H. J., Capt. | 135 | ——— F. H., Lieut. | 78 | Cluckie, A. B., Capt. | 134 |
| Cartledge, R. A., 2/Lt. | 157 | ——— J., 2/Lt. | 154 | ——— F. S., 2/Lt. | 157 | Clutterbuck, A., Capt. | 71 |
| Cartmell, F., 2/Lt. | 125 | ——— J. R. S., 2/Lt. | 87 | ——— G. N., Capt. | 128 | ——— L. C. F., 2/Lt. | 160 |
| Cartwright, H. A., Capt. | 87 | ——— T., 2/Lt. | 41 | ——— J. A., 2/Lt. | 52 | Coalbank, R. M., Capt. | 134 |
| ——— H. B., Lieut. | 53 | Charker, V. W., 2/Lt. | 136 | ——— J. G., Fl. Sub.-Lt. | 177 | Coates, S., 2/Lt. | 176 |
| Carver, G. S., 2/Lt. | 98 | Charlesworth, J. L., 2/Lt. | 60 | ——— S. A., 2/Lt. | 76 | Coaton, G. H., Lieut. | 120 |
| Carveth, W. A., Lt. | 166 | Charley, H. R., Major | 108 | ——— W., Lieut. | 139 | Cobbin, A. J., 2/Lt. | 164 |
| Case, B. S., 2/Lt. | 174 | Charlton, G., Lt.-Col. | 27 | ——— W., Lieut. and Qtmr. | 108 | Cobbold, F. R. C., Lieut. | 158 |
| ——— R. J., Capt. | 77 | ——— G. S., 2/Lt. | 53 | ——— W. B., 2/Lt. | 150 | Cobden, H., Capt. | 58 |
| Casey, O. P., 2/Lt. | 33 | ——— S. E., Lieut. | 122 | ——— W. G., 2/Lt. | 72 | Cobham, R. S., Lieut. | 171 |
| ——— Pat, Rev. | 135 | Charters, R. J., 2/Lt. | 49 | Clarke, A. C., Major | 78 | Cochrane, D. C., 2/Lt. | 19 |
| ——— P. J., 2/Lt. | 156 | Chase, D. E., 2/Lt. | 167 | ——— A. E., 2/Lt. | 29 | ——— W. A., 2/Lt. | 15 |
| Casgrain, H. R., Lt. | 160 | Cheeseman, F. C., 2/Lt. | 119 | ——— A. F. G., 2/Lt. | 160 | Cock, G. H., Capt., M.C. | 154 |
| Cassels, H. K., 2/Lt. | 160 | Cheesman, P., Lieut. | 40 | ——— B. H., 2/Lt. | 26 | Cockburn, J. S., Lieut., M.C. | 9 |
| Castle, G. D., 2/Lt. | 11 | Cheetham, F. L., Lieut. | 32 | ——— C. H., 2/Lt. | 160 | Cockburn-Mercer, T. H., Capt. | 59 |
| Castle, A. F., 2/Lt. | 158 | Chellingworth, H. G., 2/Lt. | 29 | ——— E. B., 2/Lt. | 61 | Cockerill, G. E., Capt. | 129 |
| ——— G. Lloyd, Lieut. | 165 | Cherry, John, 2/Lt. | 68 | ——— F., Lieut. | 163 | Cockin, John B., 2/Lt. | 170 |
| ——— G. S., 2/Lt. | 147 | Cheshire, H. S., Lt. | 182 | ——— F. W. H., 2/Lt. | 46 | Cocking, J. C. O., 2/Lt. | 72 |
| ——— H. F. B., Lieut. | 137 | Chetwynd-Stapleton, B., Major | 54 | ——— G. A., 2/Lt. | 114 | ——— L. G., 2/Lt. | 164 |
| ——— W., Lieut. | 148 | Chevis, H., 2/Lt. | 90 | ——— Harold, 2/Lt. | 121 | Cockram, F. S., Capt. | 89 |
| Caswell, C. W., 2/Lt. | 82 | Cheyne, C. L., 2/Lt. | 19 | ——— H. A., 2/Lt. | 163 | Cockroft, H., 2/Lt. | 128 |
| ——— F. W., Lieut. | 123 | Chichester-Constable, C. H. J., Lieut. | 28 | | | Cocksedge, R. H., Lieut. | 120 |
| ——— G. F. C., Lieut. | 172 | Chidson, M. R., 2/Lt | 146 | | | Coddington, H. F., Capt. | 93 |
| Cater, J. W., Capt. | 88 | Child, M. D., Lieut. | 115 | | | Codrington, W. R., Lt.-Col. Sir | 117 |
| Cattell, B. K., 2/Lt | 180 | | | | | | |
| Cattley, L. A., Major | 44 | | | | | | |

|   |   |   |   |
|---|---|---|---|
| Coe, W., 2/Lt. ... 68 | Connor, J. H., 2/Lt. ... 111 | Costello, W. H., Capt. 150 | Crane, S. H. E., 2/Lt. ... 128 |
| Coghill, F. S., Lieut. 166 | ———— R., Major ... 61 | Cottis, P. E., Lieut. ... 35 | Cranswick, A. N., Capt. 92 |
| ———— W. H., 2/Lt. 172 | Conover, C. C., Lieut. ... 172 | Cotton, F. J., 2/Lt. ... 64 | Crassweller, H., Capt. ... 133 |
| Coghlan, T. R., 2/Lt. ... 110 | Considine, H. W. H., 2/Lt. 92 | ———— H., Lieut. ... 153 | Craston, N. H., 2/Lt. ... 97 |
| Cogill, N. H. V., 2/Lt. ... 81 | Constable, D. C. J., 2/Lt. 39 | ———— H. J., Major... 182 | Craven, J. L. A., Lieut. 66 |
| Cohen, W. R., Lieut. ... 21 | ———— E. E., Capt. ... 144 | ———— W. A., 2/Lt. ... 78 | Crawford, Ch., Capt. ... 172 |
| Coke, J., Capt. The Hon. 18 | ———— S. J., 2/Lt. ... 130 | Cottrell, A. E., Lieut. ... 39 | ———— D. F., 2/Lt. ... 128 |
| Colbeck, C. E., Capt. ... 185 | Conway, C. H., 2/Lt. ... 69 | ———— J., Lieut. ... 126 | ———— G. P. G., 2/Lt. ... 114 |
| Colbert, L. A., 2/Lt. ... 156 | ———— R., 2/Lt. ... 48 | Couchman, M., 2/Lt. ... 41 | ———— J. N., Lt.-Col., |
| Colbourne, J. S., 2/Lt. ... 98 | Conyngham, E. J., 2/Lt. 89 | Coulshaw, C. J. A., 2/Lt. 128 | D.S.O. ... 59 |
| Coldicott, A. C., Capt., | Coode-Bate, J., Lieut. ... 145 | Coulson, A., Lieut. ... 10 | ———— K. B. S., Lieut. 185 |
| M.C. ... ... 29 | Cook, C. W., Lieut. ... 160 | ———— T. E., 2/Lt. ... 102 | ———— O. G. S., 2/Lt. ... 159 |
| Coldwell, G. A., Lieut.... 139 | ———— E. C., Lieut. ... 75 | ———— W. H., Capt. ... 101 | ———— W. I., 2/Lt. ... 163 |
| Cole, C. F., 2/Lt. ... 32 | ———— H. M., 2/Lt. ... 90 | ———— W. E., Lieut. ... 166 | Crawley, E. P., 2/Lt. ... 187 |
| ———— F. G., 2/Lt. ... 35 | ———— L. C. L., 2/Lt. ... 149 | Coulston, J. H. C., Lieut. ... 23 | Cremer, E. W., Capt. ... 115 |
| ———— H. A., Lieut. ... 170 | ———— R. C., 2/Lt. ... 142 | Coulthard, Robert, 2/Lt. 174 | Cresswell, H. J., 2/Lt.... 46 |
| ———— G. H., 2/Lt. ... 188 | ———— W. A., 2/Lt.... 142 | Couper, C. M., Capt. ... 74 | ———— W. R., Lieut. ... 130 |
| ———— J. M., Lieut. ... 161 | Cooke, E., 2/Lt. ... 99 | ———— J. M., Lieut. ... 11 | Cressy, H. R., Lieut. ... 30 |
| ———— K. R., Fl.Lieut. 161 | ———— E. A., 2/Lt. ... 156 | Courage, H., Lieut. ... 56 | Creswell, R. G., 2/Lt. ... 75 |
| ———— M., Capt. ... 30 | ———— G. C. R., Rev., | Courteir, R F., 2/Lt. ... 70 | Cribb, A. G., 2/Lt. ... 158 |
| ———— O. J. B., 2/Lt. ... 15 | M.C. ... 135 | Courtney, J. P. M., 2/Lt. 137 | Crichton, C. A., 2/Lt. ... 175 |
| ———— R. H., 2/Lt.... 171 | ———— P. B., Lieut. ... 173 | ———— W. E. L., 2/Lt. ... 170 | Crichton, McV., Lt.-Col. 182 |
| ———— W. R. T., 2/Lt. ... 27 | ———— W. K., Capt. ... 182 | Couston, A., 2/Lt. ... 159 | Crickmore, E. B., Lieut. 165 |
| Cole-Hamilton, G. C., | Cookson, F., 2/Lt. ... 40 | Coutts, R. W., Lieut. ... 160 | Crighton, J. S., 2/Lt. ... 84 |
| Col., C.M.G., D.S.O. 109 | ———— P., 2/Lt. ... 55 | Coventry, the Hon. C. J., | Crisp, A. E., 2/Lt. ... 152 |
| ———— H. A. W., Major 40 | Coolahan, J. S., Lieut.... 138 | Lt.-Col. ... ... 178 | ———— A. R., 2/Lt. ... 149 |
| Coleman, C. B., 2/Lt. ... 161 | Coole, R. S., 2/Lt. ... 55 | Coverdale, S., 2/Lt. ... 43 | ———— G., 2/Lt. ... 130 |
| ———— D. J., Lieut. ... 120 | Coombes, E. S., 2/Lt. ... 167 | Cowan, A. R., 2/Lt. ... 163 | Crittall, H. P., Lieut. ... 89 |
| ———— J. P., 2/Lt. ... 175 | Coomber, F. H. V., 2/Lt. 174 | ———— D. J., Lieut.... 188 | Croal, B. V., 2/Lt. ... 14 |
| ———— O. E., 2/Lt. ... 176 | Coombs, V. C., 2/Lt. ... 154 | ———— J. H., Sub.-Lt. 145 | Crockett, G. P., 2/Lt. ... 54 |
| Coles, G. T., 2/Lt. ... 170 | Cooney, J. M., Lieut. ... 136 | ———— J. M., Capt. ... 53 | Crockford, F. R., 2/Lt. ... 52 |
| ———— H. H. E. Q., | Coope, N. N., Lieut. ... 172 | ———— R. H., 2/Lt. ... 158 | Croft, C.E., 2/Lt. ... 41 |
| Lieut. ... 111 | Cooper, A. O., Capt. ... 122 | ———— S. W., 2/Lt. ... 69 | ———— J. C., Lieut.... 176 |
| ———— W. T., Lieut. ... 154 | ———— E. J., Lieut. ... 176 | ———— W. E., Lieut. ... 162 | ———— J. W., 2/Lt. ... 29 |
| Colledge, G., 2/Lt. ... 155 | ———— E. J., Lieut. ... 188 | Coward, G. B., Lieut. ... 164 | ———— W. A., 2/Lt. ... 35 |
| Colles, T. O., 2/Lt. ... 78 | ———— E. P., 2/Lt. ... 44 | ———— S. R., Lieut. ... 167 | Crofts, E. C. J., 2/Lt. ... 58 |
| Collett, H. S., Lieut. ... 164 | ———— G. C., Capt. ... 116 | Cowell, R. G., 2/Lt. ... 45 | ———— T. A., 2/Lt., ... 25 |
| Colley, A., Capt. ... 79 | ———— G. M., 2/Lt. ... 104 | Cowgill, W. A. F., Lieut. 170 | Croker, E., 2/Lt. ... 110 |
| Collier, A. C., 2/Lt. ... 146 | ———— G. W., Lieut. ... 49 | Cowie, T. McK., 2/Lt. ... 181 | Croker, W., Capt. ... 131 |
| ———— J. D. A., 2/Lt. ... 137 | ———— H., 2/Lt. ... 61 | Cowley, A. T., Fl.-Lt. ... 176 | Crole, G. B., Capt. ... 158 |
| Collinge, F. J., 2/Lt. ... 75 | ———— H. A., Lieut. ... 151 | ———— G. E., Capt. ... 113 | Croll, A. G., 2/Lt. ... 68 |
| ———— J. C., 2/Lt. ... 51 | Coops, F. C., 2/Lt. ... 150 | ———— R. L., 2/Lt. ... 81 | Crompton, W., 2/Lt. ... 24 |
| Collings, H. J., Sub-Lieut. 144 | Coote, C. M., Lieut. ... 61 | Cownley, J. J., 2/Lt. ... 48 | Crone, A. C., Lieut. ... 118 |
| ———— L., 2/Lt. ... 32 | Cope, E. M., 2/Lt. ... 98 | Cox, A. G., 2/Lt. ... 34 | Crookell, S. E., 2/Lt. ... 169 |
| Collingwood, P. H., Major 131 | ———— H. A., 2/Lt. ... 39 | ———— C. E. S., Major 183 | Crook, H. W., 2/Lt. ... 38 |
| ———— T. F., 2/Lt. ... 88 | ———— H. S., Lieut. ... 76 | ———— D., 2/Lt. ... 37 | ———— W., 2/Lt. ... 29 |
| Collins, C., Capt. ... 76 | Copeland, A. H. M., | ———— E. J., Lieut. ... 138 | Crosbie, C. H., 2/Lt. ... 159 |
| ———— E. R., Major ... 63 | Lieut. ... ... 149 | ———— F. B., 2/Lt. ... 171 | ———— D. S., Capt. ... 146 |
| ———— H. L., Lieut. ... 182 | ———— George, 2/Lt. ... 26 | ———— George, Lieut. ... 138 | ———— J., 2/Lt. ... 53 |
| ———— I. T. M., 2/Lt. ... 45 | Copestake, T. A. B., | ———— H. A., 2/Lt.... 179 | Cross, A. S., 2/Lt. ... 162 |
| ———— J. C., 2/Lt. ... 174 | Lieut. ... ... 11 | ———— P. H., Lieut. ... 17 | ———— H. L., 2/Lt. ... 166 |
| ———— L. G., Lieut.... 50 | Copley, A., Lieut. ... 176 | ———— S. H., Capt. ... 36 | ———— J. G., Lieut. ... 49 |
| ———— L. M. C., 2/Lt. ... 99 | Corbett, Chas. H., 2/Lt. 68 | ———— W., 2/Lt. ... 167 | ———— R. W., Lieut. ... 150 |
| ———— N. B. F., Capt. ... 28 | ———— D. M., Capt.... 131 | ———— W. C. C., 2/Lt. ... 35 | ———— W. T., 2/Lt. ... 36 |
| ———— W. G., Lieut. ... 34 | ———— P. B., Capt. ... 132 | ———— W. J., 2/Lt. ... 138 | Crossland, E. A., 2/Lt. 102 |
| Collis, D. P., 2/Lt. ... 155 | ———— R., Lieut. ... 150 | ———— W. R., 2/Lt. ... 58 | Crossley, F. S., Lieut., |
| ———— G. D., 2/Lt. ... 98 | ———— R. D., Capt. ... 183 | Coxon, A. C. M., Capt. ... 178 | The Hon. ... 9 |
| Collison, A. J., 2/Lt. ... 33 | Corbett-Winder, F., | Cozens, E. O., 2/Lt. ... 128 | ———— H., Lieut. ... 172 |
| Colquhoun, H. G., 2/Lt. 19 | Lieut. ... ... 50 | Crabb, R. B., 2/Lt. ... 65 | Crossman, A. F., Capt. 140 |
| ———— W. G., Lieut. ... 139 | Corbey-Smith, M., Lt.... 183 | Crabbie, W. M., 2/Lt. ... 146 | ———— R., Major ... 143 |
| Colville, F. M., Capt. ... 72 | Corbould-Warren, E., | Crabtree, C. P., 2/Lt. ... 56 | Crosthwaite, J. D., |
| Colvill-Jones, T., Capt. 162 | Major ... ... 185 | Craddock, D. V. L., Lieut. 17 | Lt.-Col. ... ... 84 |
| Comerford, J. J., 2/Lt. 165 | Corcoran, J. P., 2/Lt. ... 47 | ———— P. E., 2/Lt. ... 75 | Crow, Alex, 2/Lt. ... 19 |
| Comley, R. H., 2/Lt. ... 26 | Corfe, A. C., Lt.-Col. ... 84 | Cragg, J. C., 2/Lt. ... 142 | Crowder, G. E., Lieut., |
| Compton, F., 2/Lt. ... 82 | Cork, C. H., Capt., M.C. 92 | Craig, C. C. Capt. ... 108 | M.C. ... ... 118 |
| Condon, D., 2/Lt. ... 24 | Corlett, R. F., 2/Lt. ... 85 | ———— F. C., 2/Lt. ... 152 | ———— W. H., Lieut. ... 11 |
| ———— J. E. S., Capt., | Cornish, E. W., Capt. ... 174 | ———— J. L., 2/Lt. ... 15 | Crowson, A. H. T., 2/Lt. 47 |
| M.C. ... ... 109 | ———— P. A., Lieut.... 70 | ———— J. L. W., Lieut. 188 | Crowther, C. R., Capt.... 134 |
| Conheeny, G., 2/Lt. ... 24 | Cornock, R. B., 2/Lt. ... 142 | ———— J. W. H., 2/Lt. 64 | ———— E., Lieut. ... 42 |
| Conlan, R. L. H., Capt. 113 | Cornwall, C. E., Major... 106 | ———— W. G., 2/Lt. ... 102 | Cruden, A., 2/Lt. ... 106 |
| ———— Tom, Lieut.:... 166 | Cornwell, S. F., 2/Lt. ... 88 | Craigie, B. E., Lieut. ... 86 | Cruikshank, J. P., 2/Lt. 31 |
| Connal Rowan, G. F., | ———— F., 2/Lt. ... 174 | Crake, J. W., Lieut. ... 25 | ———— K. G., 2/Lt. ... 156 |
| Lieut. ... ... 112 | Corps, E. L., 2/Lt. ... 76 | Cramer Roberts, W. E., | Crummer, E. R., Sub-Lt. 145 |
| Connolly, S. D., Lieut. 168 | Corrie, J. B., 2/Lt. ... 127 | Major ... ... 186 | Crump, A. G., 2/Lt. ... 51 |
| ———— S. M., 2/Lt. ... 164 | Cory, R. S., Capt. ... 139 | Crammond, G. R., Lieut. 160 | Crutchley, G. E. V., 2/Lt. 18 |
| Conolly, T. P., 2/Lt. ... 27 | Costar, D. H., 2/Lt. ... 14 | Crane, C. G., 2/Lt. ... 156 | Cruttenden, C., 2/Lt. ... 17 |
| Connon, F. G. W., 2/Lt. 91 | | | |

|  |  |  |  |
|---|---|---|---|
| Crymble, William ... 131 | Dalziel, G. N. C., Capt. 130 | Davies, T. H., 2/Lt. ... 12 | Deming, R. M., Capt., M.O. ... ... 132 |
| Cudmore, E. O., 2/Lt. 159 | Dams, F. D., Lieut. ... 41 | ———— T. E. H., 2/Lt. 146 | Denahy, P. A., 2/Lt. ... 113 |
| Cuffley, J. T., Lieut. ... 119 | Dana, H. F., 2/Lt. ... 23 | ———— V. G., 2/Lt. ... 102 | Dendrino, S., 2/Lt. ... 149 |
| Cule, D. M., Capt. ... 120 | Dandy, J. M., 2/Lt. ... 172 | ———— W. H., 2/Lt. ... 102 | Denham-Smith, H. F., 2/Lt. ... ... 10 |
| Cull, W. A., Capt. ... 136 | Daniel, E., 2/Lt. ... 112 | ———— W. W., 2/Lt. ... 55 | Denholm, T. S., 2/Lt. ... 108 |
| Cullen, A. A., Lt. ... 181 | Daniell, H. J., Capt. ... 143 | Davis, A. J., Lieut. ... 42 | Denison, E. B., 2/Lt. ... 156 |
| ———— H. W., 2/Lt... 51 | ———— H. J., Capt. ... 183 | ———— D. W., 2/Lt. ... 150 | ———— N. C., 2/Lt. ... 151 |
| ———— W. D., Lieut. 154 | ———— J. B., 2/Lt. ... 153 | ———— E. B., Lieut.... 67 | Denning, C. W., 2/Lt. ... 128 |
| Cullings, E. C., Capt. 138 | Daniels, T. H. R., 2/Lt. 181 | ———— F. M., Capt. ... 128 | Dennis, B. W., 2/Lt. ... 114 |
| Culver, D. E., Lieut. ... 168 | Dann, D. G., 2/Lt. ... 44 | ———— F. P., Capt. ... 119 | ———— E. E., 2/Lt. ... 179 |
| ———— J. G., M.C., 2/Lt. ... 76 | Danson, F. A., 2/Lt. ... 24 | ———— F. T., 2/Lt. ... 27 | ———— R. T., 2/Lt. ... 25 |
| ———— R., Capt. 93 | Darby, E., 2/Lt. ... 173 | ———— G., 2/Lt. ... 154 | Dennistoun, J. R., Lieut. 147 |
| Culverwell, F. N., 2/Lt. 137 | ———— R., Capt. ... 120 | ———— L. D. McN., Capt. ... 36 | Denny, C. H., Lieut. ... 168 |
| Culy, L. V., Lieut. ... 122 | Darbyshire, J. F. R., 2/Lt. ... ... 60 | ———— R. A., 2/Lt. ... 33 | Dennys, K. G. G., 2/Lt. 38 |
| Cumming, G., Lieut. ... 105 | D'Arcy, M. J., 2/Lt. ... 137 | ———— R. H. L., 2/Lt. 86 | Dee, D. M., 2/Lt. ... 175 |
| ———— I., Capt. ... 106 | Darke, S. J., Capt. ... 133 | Davison, Alex., 2/Lt. ... 108 | Dent, A. E., Lieut. ... 136 |
| ———— J. R., Lieut. ... 107 | Darley, C. B., 2/Lt. ... 10 | ———— C., Capt. ... 48 | Denton, J. S., Lieut. ... 81 |
| ———— N., Lieut. ... 138 | ———— C. C., Capt. ... 146 | ———— D. J., 2/Lt. ... 22 | ———— W. H., Lieut. ... 81 |
| ———— R. H. O., Lieut.136 | Darling, E., M.C., Capt. 14 | ———— R. M. R., Capt. 47 | De Paravicini, C. P. E., Lieut. ... ... 92 |
| ———— R. F., 2/Lt. ... 105 | Darnell, W. G., 2/Lt. ... 12 | Davy, G. M. O., 2/Lt. ... 13 | De Pass, D. H., 2/Lt. ... 116 |
| ———— S. C., 2/Lt. ... 20 | Darvell, S., Capt. ... 56 | ———— P., Capt. ... 131 | De Pennington, D., 2/Lt. 72 |
| Cummins, G., 2/Lt. ... 136 | Darwent, G. T., 2/Lt. ... 67 | ———— W. H. C., Major ... 87 | De Quetteville, R. G., Capt., M.C. ... 50 |
| ———— H. A. V., Lt.-Col. ... 183 | Davenhill, R. E., Lieut. 118 | ———— W. K., 2/Lt. ... 32 | Derbyshire, H., 2/Lt. ... 34 |
| Cunliffe, W. R., Major... 11 | Davenport, H., 2/Lt. ... 178 | Dawbarn, J. S., Major... 122 | Derham, J. A. T., 2/Lt. 128 |
| Cunningham, E. W., 2/Lt. ... ... 127 | ———— J. A., Capt. ... 50 | Dawes, A. J., Capt. ... 178 | Derrett, J. H., 2/Lt. ... 49 |
| ———— G. J., 2/Lt. ... 52 | Davern, F., Lt.... ... 185 | ———— A. F., 2/Lt. ... 162 | Desbarats, E. W., Fl. Sub-Lt. ... 177 |
| ———— J., Capt. ... 112 | Davey, B. E., 2/Lt. ... 81 | Dawkins, F. S. S., 2/Lt. 121 | De Selincourt, A., Capt. 153 |
| ———— J. B., Capt. ... 102 | ———— H. J., Lieut.... 117 | Dawney, C. S., 2/Lt. ... 12 | De Souza, S. A., Asst. Surg. ... ... 182 |
| ———— J. C., 2/Lt. ... 75 | ———— T. E., Lieut. ... 77 | Dawson, C. H. T., Lieut. Qtmr. ... 108 | De St. Legier, G. W., 2/Lt., M.C. ... 82 |
| ———— K. E., Capt. 67 | David, C. K., 2/Lt. ... 169 | ———— E., 2/Lt. ... 166 | De Trafford, O., Capt. 70 |
| Cunnington, D. G. L., Lieut. ... ... 140 | Davidson, C., Lieut. ... 57 | ———— F. G., Capt. ... 126 | Devereux, W., Lieut. ... 185 |
| Curle, A. C., Lieut. ... 104 | ———— D. A., Lieut. 143 | ———— F. S., Brig.-Gen., C.M.G. 141 | Devlin, A. C., Lt., A/Capt. 72 |
| Curlewis, T., 2/Lt. ... 149 | ———— F. A. J., 2/Lt. 108 | ———— J. H. T., Lieut. 178 | De Voil, W. H., 2/Lt. ... 40 |
| Curphey, E. J., 2/Lt. ... 14 | ———— F. W., Lieut. 60 | ———— L., Lieut. ... 66 | Dewey, J. H. J., 2/Lt. 127 |
| Currie, J. D., Lieut. ... 160 | ———— G., Lieut. ... 116 | ———— W. R., Capt. ... 19 | Diamond, W. E. de B., 2/Lt. ... ... 155 |
| Curry, H. D., 2/Lt. ... 124 | ———— H. J., Capt. ... 132 | ———— W. V., Capt. ... 11 | Di Balme, L. T. B., Count ... ... 153 |
| Curtis, A. E., 2/Lt. ... 15 | ———— J., 2/Lt. ... 104 | Day, A. F., Lieut. ... 16 | Dicey, G., 2/Lt. ... 54 |
| ———— C. R., 2/Lt. ... 51 | ———— L. K., 2/Lt. ... 167 | ———— D. A. L., Major 28 | Dick, W., 2/Lt.... ... 180 |
| ———— G., 2/Lt. ... 142 | ———— M. R., Lieut. ... 94 | ———— G. A., 2/Lt. ... 110 | Dick-Cunyngham, J. K., Brig.-Gen. ... 7 |
| ———— H. A., Capt. ... 82 | ———— N., 2/Lt. ... 27 | ———— G. W., Lieut. ... 55 | Dickey, R. F. L., Capt. 163 |
| ———— M. K., Lieut. 169 | ———— T., Capt. ... 154 | ———— H. M., 2/Lt. ... 90 | Dickie, T. H., Lieut. ... 103 |
| Cushing, D., 2/Lt. ... 149 | Davie, J., Lt.-Col. ... 182 | ———— J. F., 2/Lt. ... 21 | Dickins, W. A., Lieut.... 70 |
| Cust, L. G. A., Lieut. ... 13 | Davies, A. V., Lieut. ... 50 | ———— O., 2/Lt. ... 42 | Dickinson, A. M., Capt. 63 |
| Cuthbert, J. P., Staff Capt. ... ... 7 | ———— C. W., 2/Lt. ... 155 | Deacon, C. H., 2/Lt. ... 31 | ———— C. F., Capt. ... 44 |
| Cutbill, A., Capt. ... 37 | ———— D. H., 2/Lt.... 93 | Dean, A. C., Lieut. ... 161 | ———— H. C., Lt.-Col. 189 |
| ———— E. H., 2/Lt.... 157 | ———— D. M., 2/Lt. ... 73 | ———— H., 2/Lt. ... 161 | ———— H. W., 2/Lt.... 26 |
| Cuthbertson, R. A., Lieut. ... ... 103 | ———— D. P., 2/Lt. ... 174 | ———— L. G. H., 2/Lt. 188 | ———— J., 2/Lt. ... 32 |
| Cyr, A. J., Lieut. ... 166 | ———— D. P., Major... 116 | ———— W., 2/Lt. ... 96 | ———— T. M., Lieut. 153 |
|  | ———— E., Lieut. ... 131 | Deane, B., Capt. ... 112 | ———— W., 2/Lt. ... 72 |
| **Dabb**, R. H., 2/Lt. ... 136 | ———— E. A., Capt.... 141 | ———— G. A., Capt. ... 110 | ———— W. C., 2/Lt. ... 26 |
| Dabbs, J. C., 2/Lt. ... 38 | ———— E. H., Capt. ... 52 | ———— G. S., 2/Lt. ... 150 | Dickson, G. I., Lieut. ... 104 |
| Dacombe, A. W., 2/Lt. 117 | ———— E. O., 2/Lt. ... 58 | Dear, J. A., Lieut. ... 169 | ———— G. L., 2/Lt. ... 33 |
| Dacre, G. D., Flt. Com. 180 | ———— F. T. H., Capt. 132 | Dearman, C. S., 2/Lt. ... 47 | ———— H. E. B., 2/Lt. 37 |
| Dagg, L. S., 2/Lt. ... 91 | ———— H., 2/Lt. ... 171 | Deason, T. G., Lieut. ... 156 | ———— J. H., 2/Lt. ... 111 |
| Dain, W. S., Sub.-Lt. ... 145 | ———— H., Lieut. ... 57 | Deaton, F., 2/Lt. ... 144 | ———— T. H., 2/Lt. ... 145 |
| Dakin, E. L. V., Major... 16 | ———— H., Rev. ... 135 | De Carteret, H. J. T., Capt. ... ... 23 | Digby, T. K., 2/Lt. ... 43 |
| Dalby, A. A., Lieut. ... 124 | ———— H. D., 2/Lt. ... 151 | De Colagan, A. T. B., Capt. ... ... 128 | Dight, C. C., Lieut. ... 138 |
| Dale, G., Lieut. ... 75 | ———— H. E., 2/Lt. ... 159 | Deedes, J., Capt. ... 86 | Dilliway, L. J., 2/Lt. ... 119 |
| ———— P. E., Lieut.... 76 | ———— H. G., Capt. ... 24 | de Grey, Capt. & Adj. ... 186 | Dillon, M. A. M., Capt. 144 |
| ———— W., 2/Lt. ... 52 | ———— H. H., 2/Lt. ... 27 | Dehn, H. G., 2/Lt. ... 93 | Dillon-Kelly, C. F., Capt. 131 |
| Dalgarno, J. H., Capt.... 89 | ———— H. H. T., Lieut.107 | Dekin, G., Major ... 30 | Dillnutt, E. J., Lieut. ... 152 |
| Dalgety, G. H., 2/Lt. ... 20 | ———— H. R., Lieut. 152 | Delamain, Major Gen.... 182 | Dimmock, W., 2/Lt. ... 30 |
| Dallimore, F., Capt. ... 133 | ———— H. V., 2/Lt. ... 29 | Delaney, V., 2/Lt. ... 51 | Dingley, K. M., 2/Lt. ... 37 |
| D'Alton, A. J., Lieut. ... 91 | ———— H. W., Major 185 | Del Court, S. Fitz-W., Capt. ... ... 88 | ———— R. L., 2/Lt. ... 149 |
| Dalton, N. D., 2/Lt. ... 117 | ———— H. W., Major 63 | De Lemo:, C., 2/Lt. ... 188 | Dinwiddy, M. J., Capt. 187 |
| Daltrey, H., Lieut. ... 164 | ———— J. C., Capt., The Rev. ... 135 | Dell, R., 2/Lt. ... 119 | Diplock, P. B., 2/Lt. ... 91 |
| Daly, A. P. V., Capt. ... 150 | ———— J. E., 2/Lt. ... 152 | Delmege, J. C. R., Capt. 113 |  |
| ———— E., Capt., Rev. 135 | ———— J. H., 2/Lt. ... 126 | De Lozey, L., 2/Lt. ... 52 |  |
| ———— McC., 2/Lt. ... 33 | ———— J. H., 2/Lt. ... 12 | De Mauny, L., 2/Lt. ... 77 |  |
| Dalzell, W., Lieut. ... 146 | ———— J. L., Major ... 76 |  |  |
|  | ———— L. A., Lieut. ... 39 |  |  |
|  | ———— R. D., Capt. ... 143 |  |  |
|  | ———— R. S., 2/Lt. ... 126 |  |  |
|  | ———— T., Lieut. ... 17 |  |  |

| | PAGE | | PAGE | | PAGE | | PAGE |
|---|---|---|---|---|---|---|---|
| Dixon, E. C., Lieut. | 55 | Dowson, S. T., 2/Lt. | 93 | Durlacher, H. W., 2/Lt., | | Ellenberger, G. F., Capt. | 86 |
| ——— L. W., 2/Lt. | 127 | ——— W. B., Capt. | 33 | M.C. | 127 | Ellerbeck, E. A. V., 2/Lt. | 156 |
| Dobeson, R. G., Lieut. | 175 | Dowty, G. D., Lieut. | 88 | Durnford, H. G. E., 2/Lt. | 10 | Ellinger, C., 2/Lt. | 16 |
| Dobbie, E. T., Major | 11 | Doyle, A. J., Lt. | 40 | Durrant, B. W., Sub.-Lt. | 145 | Elliot, G. A., Capt. | 47 |
| ——— G. N., Lieut. | 20 | ——— D. C., 2/Lt. | 159 | ——— F. J., 2/Lt. | 96 | ——— W., Lieut. | 107 |
| Dobbs, F., Lieut. | 113 | ——— J. E., Capt. | 170 | Dusgate, R. E., Lieut. | 158 | ——— W. T. W., 2/Lt. | 109 |
| Dobie, M. B., 2/Lt. | 136 | Drabble, A. S., 2/Lt. | 116 | Dutton, A. H. D., 2/Lt. | 55 | Elliott, A. H., 2/Lt. | 30 |
| ——— P., 2/Lt. | 53 | Draffen, F. G. W., Lt.-Col. | 59 | Duxbury, 2/Lt. | 182 | ——— C., Lieut. | 21 |
| Dobson, Alan, 2/Lt. | 100 | Drain, W. F., 2/Lt. | 84 | Dyer, A. B. C., 2/Lt. | 95 | ——— D. W., Lt. | 139 |
| ——— D. F., Capt. | 132 | Drake, C. D., Capt. | 113 | ——— A. J. L., Major | 54 | ——— G. L., Lieut. | 176 |
| Dodd, G. C., Lieut. | 138 | ——— R. G. C., Lieut., | | Dyson, H., Capt. | 178 | ——— J. E., 2/Lt. | 14 |
| ——— A. A., 2/Lt. | 118 | M.C. | 39 | ——— M. J. S., 2/Lt. | 46 | ——— H., 2/Lt. | 167 |
| ——— H. F., 2/Lt. | 26 | ——— W., Lieut. | 16 | ——— W. E., 2/Lt. | 36 | ——— H. E. D., Lieut. | 76 |
| ——— W. R., 2/Lt. | 25 | Drake-Brockman, F. T., Lieut. | 182 | Dyte, S. T., 2/Lt. | 39 | ——— R. D., Capt. | 178 |
| Dodds, A., Lieut. | 158 | | | | | ——— W. G. R., Capt. | 54 |
| ——— J., 2/Lt. | 12 | Drew, G. A., 2/Lt. | 37 | Eadie, W. E., 2/Lt. | 64 | Elliott-Cooper, N. B., | |
| ——— H. G., Capt. | 25 | ——— G. M., Lieut. | 59 | Eagar, E. F., Major | 60 | Col., V.C., D.S.O., M.C. | 30 |
| ——— W. M., Capt. | 27 | Drew-Brook, T. G., 2/Lt. | 163 | Earl, G., 2/Lt. | 123 | Ellis, A. H., 2/Lt. | 34 |
| Dodridge, B. J. S., 2/Lt. | 46 | Driver, H. S., 2/Lt. | 19 | Earle, M., Lt.-Col. | 17 | ——— C., 2/Lt. | 86 |
| Dodson, I., Lieut. | 151 | Dronsfield, S. W., 2/Lt. | 156 | Earp, K. S., 2/Lt. | 142 | ——— F. G., 2/Lt. | 78 |
| Dodwell, C. G. S., 2/Lt. | 63 | Druce, G. C., Lieut. | 87 | Eason, A. A., Lieut. | 84 | ——— F. H., Lieut. | 23 |
| ——— T. B., 2/Lt. | 168 | Druitt, H. H. W., Lt. | 45 | ——— A. T., 2/Lt. | 149 | ——— F. R., Capt. | 186 |
| Doe, J. E., Lieut. | 164 | Drummond, G. L. P., 2/Lt. | 175 | Eastman, A. J., Lieut. | 82 | ——— G., 2/Lt. | 61 |
| Doehler, H. H., 2/Lt. | 169 | | | ——— T. J. G., 2/Lt. | 92 | ——— J., 2/Lt. | 103 |
| Dogherty, F. W., 2/Lt. | 159 | ——— P., 2/Lt. | 108 | Easton, J., 2/Lt. | 31 | ——— J. C., 2/Lt. | 125 |
| ——— J. W., 2/Lt. | 107 | ——— W., Capt. | 7 | Eastwood, E. H., Lieut. | 146 | ——— J. L., 2/Lt. | 12 |
| Doig, A. T., Lieut. | 137 | Drury, D. D., 2/Lt. | 146 | Eaton, C., Lieut. | 165 | ——— J. W. H., Lieut. | 139 |
| ——— W. H., Major | 105 | Drury-Lowe, W., Capt. | 77 | ——— J. A., Lieut. | 163 | ——— R. H., Lieut. | 168 |
| Doke, T. W., 2/Lt. | 70 | Du Cane, R. E. M., 2/Lt. | 180 | Ebden, W. S., 2/Lt. | 188 | ——— S. A., 2/Lt. | 55 |
| Dolbey, R., Lieut. | 131 | Duce, William | 162 | Eberli, F. H., Lieut. | 146 | ——— S. H., 2/Lt. | 148 |
| Dollingsmith, C., 2/Lt. | 146 | Ducksbury, O. H., 2/Lt. | 80 | Eccles, C. E. S. S., Lieut. | 90 | ——— S. R., Lieut. | 95 |
| Doman, G. H. R., 2/Lt. | 26 | Duckworth, E., Asst. Surg. | 182 | ——— J. E., 2/Lt. | 100 | ——— T. W. R., 2/Lt. | 39 |
| Domville, C. L., Capt., M.C. | 90 | | | Edbrooke, F., Capt. | 39 | ——— W. B., 2/Lt. | 148 |
| Don, F. P., Major | 153 | ——— G. R. J., 2/Lt. | 30 | Edelston, R. H., Lieut. | 160 | ——— W. O. H., Lieut. | 56 |
| Donald, J. A., 2/Lt. | 108 | Ducray, M. J., Lieut. | 165 | Edgar, A. P., 2/Lt. | 62 | Ellison, H., 2/Lt. | 95 |
| Donaldson, E. J., Major | 62 | Duff, F. M., 2/Lt. | 20 | ——— J., Lieut. | 122 | ——— J. H. E., 2/Lt. | 31 |
| ——— F. L. H., 2/Lt. | 111 | ——— R. W., Lieut. | 175 | ——— J., Capt. | 51 | Ellmann, J., Capt. | 17 |
| ——— J., 2/Lt. | 119 | Duff-Taylor, S., Capt. | 114 | Edge, A. H., 2/Lt. | 127 | Ellwood, A. G. F., Lieut. | 78 |
| ——— M., Capt. | 134 | Dugan, H. G., Lieut. | 161 | Edkins, R. A., 2/Lt. | 123 | ——— D. E., 2/Lt. | 102 |
| ——— R., Sub.-Lt. | 144 | Dugdale, J. G., 2/Lt. | 169 | Edmonds, E. J. L., 2/Lt. | 137 | ——— E. S., Lieut. | 51 |
| Doncaster, A. E., 2/Lt. | 167 | Duggan, T. F., Capt. Rev. | 135 | ——— E. P., 2/Lt. | 160 | Elmitt, J. G., Lieut. | 121 |
| Donell, F., 2/Lt. | 35 | | | ——— G. M., Lieut. | 81 | Elphinston, C., 2/Lt. | 149 |
| Donnelly, J. A., Lieut. | 10 | Duggins, C. J., 2/Lt. | 21 | ——— P., 2/Lt. | 185 | Elston, A. J., 2/Lt. | 35 |
| ——— W. J., Lieut. | 103 | Duggleby, R., 2/Lt. | 43 | Edmunds, C., Capt. | 131 | ——— W. E., Lieut. | 178 |
| Donoghue, P. E., Lieut. | 184 | Dugmore, W. L. E., Capt. | 54 | Edmundson, S., 2/Lt. | 119 | Eltham, G., 2/Lt. | 29 |
| Donovan, J. J., Lieut. | 47 | | | Edsted, F., Lieut. | 173 | Elton, G., Lieut. | 187 |
| Dooley, J. A., 2/Lt. | 186 | Duke, L. G., Lieut. | 21 | Edward, E. J., Lieut. | 15 | Eltringham, A., 2/Lt. | 129 |
| Doorley, J., 2/Lt. | 113 | ——— R. E., Lieut. | 160 | ——— J. D., 2/Lt. | 104 | Elvin, A. J., 2/Lt. | 164 |
| Dore, J. W., 2/Lt. | 86 | Dumaresq, R. G., Capt. | 120 | Edwards, Capt. | 162 | Elwes, R. P., Capt. | 18 |
| Dorling, L. H. G., Capt. | 185 | Dunand, A. M., Lieut. | 117 | ——— | 180 | Elwig, H. J. C., 2/Lt. | 172 |
| Dougall, A. R., 2/Lt. | 54 | Duncan, H. J., 2/Lt. | 39 | ——— A. G., 2/Lt. | 131 | Elworthy, L., Lieut. | 173 |
| ——— C. R., 2/Lt. | 150 | ——— R. R., Capt. | 132 | ——— A. V., 2/Lt. | 30 | Ely, E. J. W., 2/Lt. | 83 |
| ——— H. F., 2/Lt. | 159 | ——— W., Lieut. | 33 | ——— E. H., 2/Lt. | 52 | Emberson, A. E., 2/Lt. | 72 |
| Dougan, W. I., Lieut. | 173 | ——— W. H., 2/Lt. | 112 | ——— E. L., 2/Lt. | 152 | Emblem, E., Lieut. | 73 |
| Dougherty, B. H. L., Capt. | 142 | Dunford, E. T., 2/Lt. | 151 | ——— G., Lieut. | 77 | Emerson, J. M., 2/Lt. | 118 |
| Doughty, E. C., Major | 37 | Dunley, O. I., 2/Lt. | 112 | ——— G. B., Capt. | 32 | Emmett, R. B., Lieut. | 78 |
| Douglas, A. B., Capt. | 60 | Dunlop, G. B., Lieut. | 172 | ——— G. H., 2/Lt. | 32 | Emslie, A., 2/Lt. | 68 |
| ——— A. S. D., Baird, Lieut. | 23 | ——— H., Lieut. | 187 | ——— G. R., 2/Lt. | 157 | Enderby, S. H., Lt.-Col. | 24 |
| | | ——— J. M., 2/Lt. | 168 | ——— H., 2/Lt. | 176 | Endsor, W., 2/Lt. | 106 |
| ——— Ed. M., Lieut. | 72 | ——— W. F., Capt. | 134 | ——— H. J., 2/Lt. | 57 | England, R., Capt., M.C. | 38 |
| ——— J. H., Lieut. | 140 | Dunn, E. G., Major | 182 | ——— J. E., Lieut. | 136 | English, C. V., Sub.-Lt. | 144 |
| ——— M. B., Major | 122 | ——— E. J., 2/Lt. | 52 | ——— J. L. A., Capt., Rev. | 135 | ——— J. W., 2/Lt. | 16 |
| ——— S. C. M., Lieut. | 105 | ——— C. P., 2/Lt. | 121 | | | ——— T. H., 2/Lt. | 42 |
| ——— W. L., 2/Lt. | 19 | ——— M. A., Lieut. | 170 | ——— J. R., 2/Lt. | 12 | ——— W., 2/Lt. | 156 |
| Douglass, E. C., Lieut. | 123 | ——— M. W., 2/Lt. | 174 | ——— L. D., Lieut. | 36 | Enright, J. E., Lieut. | 119 |
| Dow, J. N., Lieut. | 135 | ——— R. H., 2/Lt. | 165 | ——— R. H., 2/Lt. | 94 | ——— T. N., 2/Lt. | 176 |
| Dowden, L. F., 2/Lt. | 118 | Dunnington, J. W., 2/Lt. | 40 | ——— R. O., 2/Lt. | 35 | Entwisle, N., 2/Lt. | 80 |
| Dower, T., 2/Lt. | 126 | Dunscombe, G., Lieut. | 96 | ——— R. W., 2/Lt. | 92 | Entwhistle, J. M. B., Capt. | 178 |
| Dowie, A. B. B., 2/Lt. | 20 | Dunster, C. H., Lieut. | 163 | ——— W. E., 2/Lt. | 71 | Erskine, B. L., Capt. | 94 |
| Down, R. T., 2/Lt. | 172 | Dunsworth, D., Capt. | 136 | Egan, S. F., 2/Lt. | 27 | Esler, M. S., Capt. | 134 |
| Downes, A., 2/Lt. | 71 | Dunthorne, S. W., 2/Lt. | 30 | ——— W., Capt. | 131 | Estcourt, T. E. S., Capt. | 8 |
| Downing, A., Lieut. | 66 | Dupre, H. E., 2/Lt. | 126 | Eidmans, S., 2/Lt. | 116 | Estridge, I. A., Lieut. | 39 |
| ——— H. G. O., Lieut. | 47 | Dupree, V., Capt. | 124 | Elcock, R. R. E., 2/Lt. | 61 | Etherton, H., 2/Lt. | 69 |
| Downman, T. F. C., 2/Lt. | 77 | Durant, W. M., Lieut. | 141 | Elder, J. G., Capt. | 132 | Evans, A. J., Major | 181 |
| | | Durkin, F. V., 2/Lt. | 153 | Ell, N. S., 2/Lt. | 84 | ——— A. J., Capt. | 148 |
| | | | | Ellam, H. J., Lieut. | 155 | | |

| | PAGE | | PAGE | | PAGE | | PAGE |
|---|---|---|---|---|---|---|---|
| Evans, A. M. G., Lieut. | 56 | Farrow, G. H., 2/Lt. | 123 | Fisher, H. B., Lieut. | 113 | Forman, H., Lieut. | 54 |
| ——— A. W. R., 2/Lt. | 174 | Faulder, J. H., Lieut. | 27 | ——— H. G., Major, A/Lt.-Col., D.S.O. | | ——— J. H., Capt. | 170 |
| ——— D. | 86 | Faulds, W. F., V.C., 2/Lt. | 142 | | | Formilli, G. C., Lieut. | 147 |
| ——— D. C., 2/Lt. | 21 | Faulkner, B. B., Lieut. | 9 | | 13 | Forrest, L. H., Lieut. | 167 |
| ——— E. V., Lieut. | 73 | Fawcett, E., Capt., M.C. | 99 | ——— H. I. H., 2/Lt. | 15 | ——— N. V., 2/Lt. | 114 |
| ——— F. M. St. H., Lieut. | 73 | Fawkes, W. G. S., 2/Lt. | 178 | ——— J., 2/Lt. | 60 | ——— W. A., 2/Lt. | 74 |
| | | Fawsett, F. W., Capt. | 131 | ——— J. E., 2/Lt. | 24 | Forrester, G. R., 2/Lt. | 19 |
| ——— H. B., Lieut. | 164 | Fearnside, F., Lieut. | 137 | ——— J. R., 2/Lt. | 20 | Forsdike, L., Lieut. | 86 |
| ——— H. F., 2/Lt. | 149 | Featherstone, I. W., 2/Lt. | 26 | ——— R. E., 2/Lt. | 26 | Forse, L. N., Rev. | 135 |
| ——— H. G., 2/Lt. | 55 | Feetham, O. J., Capt. | 68 | Fison, F. G., Capt. | 91 | Forshaw, J., Lieut. | 80 |
| ——— H. W. D., 2/Lt. | 86 | Feez, C. M., Lieut. | 138 | Fitch, W. R., 2/Lt. | 76 | Forster, E. S., Capt. | 32 |
| ——— J., 2/Lt. | 73 | Fehr, A. H., 2/Lt. | 85 | Fitzgerald, H. C., 2/Lt. | 137 | ——— H. K., 2/Lt. | 128 |
| ——— N. W., Brig.-Gen. | 182 | Fell, A. J., Lieut. | 137 | ——— J., Capt. | 47 | ——— L. A., Capt. | 54 |
| | | ——— C. A., Lieut. | 11 | ——— J. J., 2/Lt. | 156 | ——— L. P., 2/Lt. | 117 |
| ——— R. B., Capt. | 20 | Fellowes, H. V., Lieut. | 169 | ——— M. R., Lieut. | 18 | Forsyth, A. F., Lieut. | 167 |
| ——— R. D., 2/Lt. | 91 | ——— P. F. M., Lt.-Col. | 163 | ——— R. J., Lieut., M.C. | 62 | ——— D. M., Lieut. | 105 |
| ——— R. du Boulay, 2/Lt. | 86 | Felton, C. T., 2/Lt. | 154 | Fitzgibbon, C. J., 2/Lt. | 161 | ——— D. S., 2/Lt. | 91 |
| ——— R. J., Lieut. | 31 | Fenn, L. N., 2/Lt. | 123 | Fitzmaurice, W., Rev. | 135 | ——— W. A., Capt. | 165 |
| ——— W., Lieut. | 97 | Fennell, A. H., 2/Lt. | 17 | Fitzpatrick, H. A. C., Capt. | 44 | Forward, E. R., 2/Lt. | 123 |
| ——— W. A., Capt. | 46 | Fenner, H. R., Capt. | 83 | | | Foss, B. T., Capt. and Adjt. | 90 |
| ——— W. D., 2/Lt. | 171 | Fenton, C. B., 2/Lt. | 160 | ——— R. D., 2/Lt. | 42 | | |
| ——— W. G., 2/Lt. | 37 | ——— W. G., Lieut. | 35 | Fitzroy, R., Lieut. | 18 | Fosse, E. L., 2/Lt. | 157 |
| Eveleigh, F. R., 2/Lt. | 173 | Fenwick, B., Capt. | 65 | Fitzwygram, F. L. F., Capt., Sir | 18 | Foster, A. E., 2/Lt. | 102 |
| Everard, A. J., Capt. | 180 | ——— C., 2/Lt. | 44 | | | ——— E., Fl. Sub.-Lt. | 177 |
| Everitt, J. W., 2/Lt. | 92 | ——— T. B., 2/Lt. | 156 | Flanagan, J. T., 2/Lt. | 60 | ——— F. P., Lieut. | 78 |
| Evershed, A. P., Major, M.C. | 13 | ——— W., 2/Lt. | 22 | Fleetwood, C. P., 2/Lt. | 129 | ——— G. E., Lieut. | 126 |
| | | Fereman, A. E., 2/Lt. | 152 | ——— G., Capt. | 53 | ——— J. W., 2/Lt. | 55 |
| Evitt, C. V., 2/Lt. | 131 | Ferguson, H. A., 2/Lt. | 138 | Fleming, A., Lieut. | 59 | ——— L. J., Lieut. | 101 |
| Ewart, G. D., Major | 71 | ——— J. A., 2/Lt. | 160 | ——— E. L., Lieut. | 68 | ——— P. J., Major | 28 |
| Ewen, L. McK. | 59 | ——— J. D., Lieut. | 20 | ——— F., Lt.-Col. | 13 | ——— P. La T., 2/Lt. | 160 |
| Exley, J., 2/Lt. | 39 | ——— J. F., Capt. | 179 | ——— I., 2/Lt. | 15 | ——— R. C. G., Capt. | 21 |
| Eyden, M. V., 2/Lt. | 81 | ——— J. G. W., 2/Lt. | 125 | ——— J. A. M., 2/Lt. | 157 | ——— W., Lieut. | 70 |
| Eyre, B. J., Lieut. | 110 | ——— J. J., Lieut. | 107 | ——— P. J. A., 2/Lt. | 171 | ——— W. E., Capt. | 176 |
| ——— F., Lieut. | 52 | ——— R. G., Capt. | 53 | Flere, C. H., 2/Lt. | 160 | ——— W. E., Fl. Sub.-Lt. | 181 |
| Eyres, L. H., 2/Lt. | 175 | ——— W., 2/Lt. | 109 | Fletcher, A., 2/Lt. | 173 | | |
| | | ——— W. G., 2/Lt. | 34 | ——— A. D. S. A., Capt. | 64 | Foster-Sutton, S. W. P., Lieut. | 167 |
| Faber, L. E., Major | 120 | Fergusson, J. A., Capt. | 36 | ——— G., 2/Lt. | 64 | Fothergill, R. A., 2/Lt. | 61 |
| Facer, G. S., 2/Lt. | 65 | Fernie, W. Y., 2/Lt. | 68 | ——— W. T., Lieut. | 143 | Foulds, C. L., Capt. | 41 |
| Fairall, T. W. R., 2/Lt. | 89 | Ferrand, J. P. B., Major | 187 | Flight, H. E., 2/Lt. | 82 | ——— D. T., 2/Lt. | 87 |
| Fairbank, F. E., 2/Lt. | 41 | Ferte, J. de la, Lieut. | 146 | ——— O. T., Lieut. | 138 | Foulkes, K., Lieut. | 47 |
| Fairbairn, J. V., 2/Lt. | 150 | Fessenden, C. V., Lieut. | 139 | Flint, A. H., Lieut. | 15 | ——— R. W., 2/Lt. | 32 |
| Fairclough, P. H. E., 2/Lt. | 87 | Ffrench, C. F. T. O'B., Lieut. | 47 | ——— C., 2/Lt. | 89 | Foulkes—Roberts, P. R., Capt. | 56 |
| Fairfax, H. H., Capt. | 132 | Field, C. A., 2/Lt. | 127 | Flintoft, H. T., Lieut. | 167 | | |
| Fairhurst, A., 2/Lt. | 172 | ——— F. L. A., 2/Lt. | 125 | Florance, J. B., Capt. | 28 | Fowke, G. H. G., Capt. | 106 |
| Fairweather, I., Lieut. | 54 | ——— G., 2/Lt. | 23 | Flower, N. L., Capt. | 94 | Fowler, C. W., Capt. | 134 |
| Falconer, W., Lieut. | 107 | ——— G. B., Capt. | 140 | Floyd, A. B., Capt. | 186 | Fowles, S., Lieut. | 186 |
| Falkenberg, G. D., Lieut. | 160 | ——— G. C., Capt. | 29 | ——— H., 2/Lt. | 148 | Fox, A. G., Capt. | 136 |
| Fane, H. W. N., 2/Lt. | 12 | ——— H., 2/Lt. | 120 | Floyer, E. A., 2/Lt. | 179 | ——— A. R., 2/Lt. | 127 |
| Faraday, M. S., 2/Lt. | 149 | Fielder, T. L., Lieut. | 40 | Fluke, W. G., Lieut. | 160 | ——— C. V., Capt. | 18 |
| Farbon, S. E., 2/Lt., M.C. | 81 | Fielding, H., 2/Lt. | 114 | Flux, R. L., Lieut. | 185 | ——— D. S., Lieut. | 174 |
| Farbrother, E. S., Lieut. | 182 | Fielding-Clarke, A., 2/Lt. | 159 | Flynn, G. E. C., 2/Lt. | 182 | ——— H., Capt. | 130 |
| Farmar, W. C. R., Major | 185 | Fife, N. B., 2/Lt. | 54 | ——— J. A. A., 2/Lt. | 49 | ——— J. R., 2/Lt. | 168 |
| Farmer, A., 2/Lt. | 144 | Filby, T. C., Capt. | 21 | Foggo, N. O. N., Lieut. | 167 | ——— L. H., Capt. | 184 |
| ——— A. E., 2/Lt. | 82 | Fillery, T. C., 2/Lt. | 22 | Foley, H. A., Capt. | 39 | ——— R. W., Lieut. | 95 |
| ——— E. R., Lieut. | 148 | Finch, A. W. B., 2/Lt. | 116 | Foljambe, E. W. S., Lieut. | 114 | ——— T. M., Lieut. | 144 |
| ——— G. M. G., Lieut. | 15 | ——— F. E., 2/Lt. | 171 | | | Foy, G., 2/Lt. | 111 |
| ——— N. J. C., Capt. | 16 | ——— L. H., Capt. | 77 | Folkard, G. D'A., 2/Lt. | 136 | Frame, G. S., Lieut. | 189 |
| ——— S. A., 2/Lt. | 43 | ——— L. H. K., Lt.-Col. | 70 | Fooks, E. L., 2/Lt. | 188 | Frampton, H. L., 2/Lt. | 38 |
| Farnham, A. K., Lt.-Col. Lord | 60 | ——— W. G., 2/Lt. | 121 | Footman, D. J., Capt. | 83 | Francis, C. E., 2/Lt. | 170 |
| Farquhar, J., Lieut. | 166 | Findlay, A. S., Lieut. | 134 | Footner, F. L., Major | 187 | ——— F. H., 2/Lt. | 72 |
| Farquharson, A. A., Lieut. | 20 | ——— J., Lieut. | 134 | Forbes, A. G., Lieut. | 187 | ——— F. W., Lieut. | 54 |
| ——— A. G., 2/Lt. | 58 | Findley, H. E., 2/Lt. | 25 | ——— C. A., Lieut. | 182 | ——— L. E., Capt. | 92 |
| ——— F. B., 2/Lt. | 157 | Fine, H., Capt. | 22 | ——— E. E., Major | 185 | ——— R. F., 2/Lt. | 103 |
| ——— R. J., Lieut. | 174 | Finlay, F. L., Lieut. | 108 | ——— G. W., 2/Lt. | 157 | ——— R. H., 2/Lt. | 87 |
| Farquharson-Hicks, V., Lieut. | 48 | Finlayson, A., 2/Lt. | 15 | ——— H., 2/Lt. | 102 | ——— W. F., Lieut. | 131 |
| Farr, L. C., 2/Lt. | 62 | Finnerty, H. C., Lieut. | 148 | ——— J. N., Lt.-Col. | 93 | ——— W. J., Lieut. | 87 |
| Farrand, E. S., Lieut. | 176 | Firminger, F. W., 2/Lt. | 32 | ——— M. H. O., Capt. | 106 | Frank, C. C., 2/Lt. | 41 |
| Farrar, G. R., 2/Lt. | 74 | Firstbrook, J. H., 2/Lt. | 147 | ——— S. Alex., Capt. | 133 | ——— C. O., Lieut. | 14 |
| Farrell, J., 2/Lt. | 115 | Firth, C. R., 2/Lt. | 40 | Ford, E. L., Lieut. | 64 | ——— J. N., Capt. | 68 |
| ——— J. T., 2/Lt. | 48 | ——— G., Lieut. | 9 | ——— H. S., 2/Lt. | 68 | Franklin, J. S., 2/Lt. | 58 |
| ——— P., 2/Lt. | 53 | ——— H. W., Lieut. | 35 | Forder, E. G., Lieut. | 162 | Fraser, A., 2/Lt. | 152 |
| Farren, R. H., Major | 11 | Fisher, C. C., 2/Lt. | 171 | Fordham, R. S. W., Lieut. | 139 | ——— Hon. A. A. | 105 |
| Farrington, C. H., 2/Lt. | 128 | ——— E. L., Major | 95 | Foreshew, C. E. P., Capt. | 75 | ——— A. H., Capt. | 137 |
| | | | | | | ——— A. S., Capt. | 71 |

| Name | Page |
|---|---|
| Fraser, H. N., Capt. | 140 |
| Fraser-Lyn, Capt., M.C. | 105 |
| Fraser-MacKenzie, 2/Lt | 105 |
| Frayne, E., Lieut. | 87 |
| Frazer, A., Lieut. | 47 |
| ——— A. E. G., Capt. | 131 |
| Frazier, R. W., Sub.-Lt. | 188 |
| Free, J. A., 2/Lt., M.C. | 33 |
| Freedman, E., 2/Lt. | 131 |
| ——— P. A., Lieut. | 28 |
| Freeland, K. F., Capt. | 185 |
| ——— J. H. K., 2/Lt. | 110 |
| Freeman, F. P., 2/Lt. | 95 |
| ——— J., 2/Lt. | 176 |
| ——— L. W., 2/Lt. | 89 |
| ——— W., 2/Lt. | 76 |
| French, A. W., 2/Lt. | 40 |
| ——— C. E., Lieut. | 153 |
| ——— E. F., 2/Lt. | 12 |
| ——— F. J., 2/Lt. | 122 |
| ——— G. S., Lieut. | 152 |
| ——— H. R., Capt. | 15 |
| Fretz, W. L. E., Capt. | 181 |
| Frew, J. G. H., 2/Lt. | 152 |
| Fricker, A. J., Lieut. | 165 |
| Frielinghaus, A., Lieut. | 141 |
| Friend, E. J., 2/Lt. | 123 |
| Frisby, E. R., 2/Lt. | 124 |
| Frith, R. G., 2/Lt. | 157 |
| Frost, H. G., 2/Lt. | 147 |
| ——— J. W., 2/Lt. | 156 |
| Fry, C. W., Lieut. | 128 |
| ——— D. A. B., 2/Lt. | 30 |
| ——— H. E., 2/Lt. | 83 |
| ——— H. W., Lieut. | 82 |
| ——— R. H., 2/Lt. | 39 |
| ——— W., Major | 131 |
| Fryar, M.S., Capt. | 77 |
| Fryer, A. E., 2/Lt. | 62 |
| ——— C., Capt. | 139 |
| ——— F. E., Capt. | 176 |
| ——— F. E., Capt. | 15 |
| ——— H. G., 2/Lt. | 107 |
| ——— K. G., 2/Lt. | 84 |
| ——— P. S., Capt. | 39 |
| Fulford, E., Lieut. | 172 |
| Fuller, O. L., 2/Lt. | 130 |
| Fullerton, A., Sub.-Lt. | 144 |
| Fulton, E. J., 2/Lt. | 180 |
| ——— E. P., Lieut. | 155 |
| ——— J., 2/Lt. | 165 |
| Furbisher, J. W., 2/Lt. | 110 |
| Furlonger, C. A., 2/Lt. | 153 |
| Furmidge, P. W., Lieut | 141 |
| Furneaux, T. E., 2/Lt. | 183 |
| Furnell, G. O. E., Capt. | 47 |
| ——— M., Col. | 110 |
| Furness J., Major | 131 |
| Furniss, A. S., Capt. | 99 |
| ——— K. R., 2/Lt. | 152 |
| Furrell, S., 2/Lt. | 51 |
| Furze, E. K. B., Lt.-Col. | 93 |
| Fyfe, R. J. R. Duff, Lieut | 164 |
| **Gadd**, C. B., Lieut. | 141 |
| ——— H. R., Lt.-Col. M.C. | 77 |
| ——— W. G., 2/Lt. | 175 |
| Gade, F. W., Capt. | 30 |
| Gage, C. R., 2-Lt. | 170 |
| Gage-Brown, C. J., Lieut | 8 |
| Galbraith, R. F., 2/Lt., M.C. | 119 |
| Galer, H. E., 2/Lt. | 159 |
| Gall, W. S., Lieut. | 14 |
| Gallagher, B. J., Lieut. | 133 |
| ——— E. G., Lieut. | 171 |
| Gallagher, J. R., 2/Lt. | 137 |
| Gallie, A. H., Lieut. | 76 |
| Galloway, W., Lieut. | 184 |
| Gallup, H. C., Lieut. | 185 |
| Galvin, B. St. J., Capt., M.C. | 110 |
| Gamage, L. C., Capt. | 130 |
| Gamble, H., 2/Lt. | 72 |
| Ganley S., Lieut. | 125 |
| Garbett, L. C., 2/Lt. | 72 |
| Garbutt, D. G., 2/Lt. | 40 |
| Garden, Douglas, Lieut. | 79 |
| Gardiner, G. G., Capt. | 136 |
| ——— Noel, Lieut. | 127 |
| ——— J. T., 2/Lt. | 108 |
| ——— W. C., Capt. | 179 |
| Gardner, J.A.S., Lieut. | 140 |
| ——— J. W., 2/Lt. | 40 |
| ——— R. D., Major | 189 |
| ——— W. F., 2/Lt. | 17 |
| ——— W.H.D., Sub-Lieut. | 145 |
| Garewal, A. S., Lieut. | 143 |
| Garland, E. H., 2/Lt. | 155 |
| ——— F. G., Capt. | 131 |
| ——— F. J. R., 2/Lt. | 61 |
| Garlies, Lord, 2/Lt. | 18 |
| Garner, Robert K., 2/Lt | 114 |
| ——— W. P., 2/Lt. | 73 |
| Garnett, F., 2/Lt. | 15 |
| ——— J. N., Lieut. | 179 |
| Garnham, T. W. Scott 2/Lt. | 129 |
| Garrard, J.G., Capt., M.C. | 25 |
| ——— P., Major | 189 |
| Garrett, A. L., Lieut. | 165 |
| ——— B. N., 2/Lt. | 165 |
| ——— J. C., 2/Lt. | 157 |
| Garrity, Wm. J., Lieut. | 166 |
| Garrow, W., 2/Lt. | 33 |
| Garstang, T., Lieut. | 142 |
| Gascoyne, B. B., Lieut. | 119 |
| ——— C., Capt. | 78 |
| Gaskell, R. W., Capt. | 143 |
| Gasson, C. B., 2/Lt. | 181 |
| ——— C. G., Capt. | 25 |
| ——— N. E., 2/Lt. | 43 |
| Gatacre, W. E., Capt. | 85 |
| Gates, C. E., 2/Lt. | 15 |
| ——— Richard, Lieut | 49 |
| Gateshill, H. V., 2/Lt. | 26 |
| Gatherer, A., Capt. | 183 |
| Gatheral, G. M., 2/Lt. | 33 |
| ——— T. M., Lieut. | 14 |
| Gaul, A., Lieut. | 140 |
| Gay, G., 2/Lt. | 117 |
| Gaye, A. D., Capt. | 146 |
| Gayer, J. H. C., Lieut. | 186 |
| Gayford, D. B., 2/Lt. | 147 |
| Gaynor, H. F., 2/Lt. | 188 |
| Gaze, I. O., Lieut. | 175 |
| Gedge, G., 2/Lt. | 173 |
| Gee, F. W., 2/Lt. | 65 |
| Geen, C., 2/Lt. | 148 |
| Geggie, D., 2/Lt. | 26 |
| Gell, E. A. S., Lt.-Col. | 51 |
| Gemmel, H. J., 2/Lt. | 175 |
| Gemmell, T., 2/Lt. | 112 |
| Genese, J. D., Hon., Capt. and Qmr. | 134 |
| Gentry-Birch, C., Capt. | 83 |
| George, H. D. K., Lieut. | 151 |
| ——— J. B., Capt. | 47 |
| ——— P. A. R., 2/Lt. | 33 |
| ——— T. E., 2/Lt. | 34 |
| George, T. L., Lieut. | 37 |
| Gerrity, W. B., 2/Lt. | 40 |
| Gerson, Louis M., 2/Lt. | 161 |
| Gerstenberg, R.A., 2/Lt. | 53 |
| Geyton, John A., 2/Lt. | 71 |
| Gibbon, R.N.R., Major | 96 |
| Gibbons, F. R., 2/Lt. | 35 |
| ——— P. H., Lieut. | 11 |
| ——— S. W., Sub-Lt. | 144 |
| ——— Wm., Lieut. | 95 |
| Gibbs, A. C. H., 2/Lt. | 137 |
| ——— G. M., 2/Lt. | 31 |
| ——— J. A., Lt.-Col. | 67 |
| ——— J. D., 2/Lt. | 142 |
| ——— J. E., Capt. | 18 |
| ——— J. W., 2/Lt. | 69 |
| Gibson, A., 2/Lt. | 27 |
| ——— A. J. E., Lieut. | 109 |
| ——— C. C. G., Capt. | 133 |
| ——— E. G., 2/Lt. | 72 |
| ——— E. M., 2/Lt. | 55 |
| ——— Geo. M., 2/Lt. | 27 |
| ——— J., 2/Lt. | 20 |
| ——— J. A., 2/Lt. | 60 |
| ——— J. E., Lieut. | 91 |
| ——— J. G., 2/Lt. | 107 |
| ——— J. H. S., 2/Lt. | 32 |
| ——— Norman, Lieut | 44 |
| ——— P., 2/Lt. | 101 |
| ——— P. D., 2/Lt. | 127 |
| ——— P. J., Lieut. | 48 |
| ——— W.H.K., 2/Lt. | 110 |
| Gilbert, C. G., Lieut. | 150 |
| ——— F. C., 2/Lt. | 159 |
| ——— L., Lt.-Col. | 79 |
| ——— R. S., 2/Lt. | 157 |
| Gilbertson, H. Marshall Lieut. | 133 |
| Gilchrist, W., 2/Lt. | 153 |
| ——— W.F.G., Major | 183 |
| Gile, H. H., 1st Lieut. | 164 |
| ——— A. B., 2/Lt. | 100 |
| Gilfillan, J. A., Capt. | 132 |
| Gill, A. W., 2/Lt. | 103 |
| ——— C.E.G., Lieut. | 169 |
| Gillan, Chas. J., Lieut. | 162 |
| Gillespie, D., Capt. | 134 |
| ——— J. M., Lieut. | 131 |
| ——— J. W., 2/Lt. | 155 |
| ——— R. D., 2/Lt. | 106 |
| Gillet, W. H. G., 2/Lt. | 172 |
| Gilliat, R. S., Lieut. | 82 |
| Gillies, W. L., Lieut. | 74 |
| ——— J., Capt. | 103 |
| Gilliland, L. G., 2/Lt. | 79 |
| ——— W. E., Lieut. | 188 |
| Gillings, V. De F., 2/Lt. | 127 |
| Gillitt, W., Lieut. | 81 |
| Gillmore, N. J., 2/Lt. | 52 |
| Gilmer, E. H., 2/Lt. | 111 |
| Gilmour, L. C., Lieut. | 166 |
| ——— S. G., Capt. | 169 |
| Ginger, H. S., 2/Lt. | 126 |
| Girling, F. A., Lieut. | 45 |
| Gladstone, C. A., Lieut. | 146 |
| ——— T. H., 2/Lt. | 127 |
| Glanville, A. E., 2/Lt. | 25 |
| ——— L. S. H., Capt. | 132 |
| Glass, H. E. L., Capt. | 87 |
| Glasspoole, G. H., 2/Lt. | 164 |
| Gladding E., Lieut. | 79 |
| Glazebrook, R. F., 2/Lt. | 169 |
| Gleave, P. N., 2/Lt. | 15 |
| Glenn, G. F., 2/Lt. | 15 |
| Glover, C., 2/Lt. | 45 |
| ——— G. E., Capt. | 67 |
| Glover, R. E., 2/Lt. | 110 |
| Gluyas, O. S., Lieut. | 136 |
| Glynn, T. W., Lieut. | 94 |
| Goodhugh, P. H., Lieut. | 169 |
| Goad, C. R., Lieut. | 180 |
| ——— J.F.E., Lieut. | 90 |
| Goddard, J. S., Lieut. | 157 |
| ——— Samuel George, 2/Lt. | 24 |
| Goddin, P., 2/Lt. | 100 |
| Godfrey, A. D., 2/Lt. | 46 |
| ——— E. N., Lieut. | 11 |
| ——— F., Capt. | 21 |
| Godly, A., Capt. | 84 |
| Godman, F. T., Capt. | 69 |
| ——— J., Capt. | 9 |
| Godsal, P., Capt. | 75 |
| Godsall, S. A., Capt. | 63 |
| Godson, R. G., Lieut. | 17 |
| Goetz, C. E. G., Major | 10 |
| Goffe, W., Lieut. | 167 |
| Going, A. J., 2/Lt. | 13 |
| Gold, D. G., Lieut. | 161 |
| Goldfrap, H. W., Capt. | 183 |
| Goldie, G. N., Lieut. | 159 |
| Golding, C. B., Capt., M.C. | 13 |
| ——— K. L., 2/Lt. | 157 |
| ——— W., Major | 13 |
| Goldingham, G.R., Capt | 117 |
| Goldsack, L. J., 2/Lt. | 92 |
| Goldsmith, R. L., Lieut. | 16 |
| ——— R. P., 2/Lt. | 130 |
| Goldstein, L., Lieut. | 10 |
| Gompertz, H. T. C., 2/Lt | 176 |
| Gondre, Jean, 2/Lt. | 166 |
| Gonne, M. E., Capt. | 167 |
| Gooch, H. C., Sub-Lt. | 177 |
| Goodall, J. H., Lieut. | 153 |
| Goodbehere, P., 2/Lt. | 157 |
| Goodchap, A. F., 2/Lt. | 158 |
| Goode, H. M., Lieut. | 146 |
| ——— R. J. E. P. Lieut. | 157 |
| ——— S. C., Lieut. | 123 |
| Goodenough, K.M. 2/Lt. | 14 |
| Gooderham, S.E., Lieut. | 141 |
| Goodfellow, S. J., 2/Lt. | 175 |
| Gooding, Jack A., 2/Lt. | 142 |
| Goodison, F. B., 2/Lt. | 181 |
| Goodman, E. V., Lieut. | 11 |
| Goodrich, H. A., Lieut | 133 |
| Goodridge, T.W.W., 2/Lt | 11 |
| Goodsall, W., Lieut. | 137 |
| Goodship, G. R., Lieut. | 83 |
| Goodson, A. R. L., 2/Lt. | 147 |
| ——— E. J., Lieut. | 138 |
| Goodwin, F. W., Lieut. | 50 |
| ——— S.T.W., Lieut. | 178 |
| Goolden, R. O., 2/Lt. | 62 |
| Gopsill, E., 2/Lt. | 29 |
| Gordon, Chas. A., Lieut. | 163 |
| ——— E. G. S., Lieut | 158 |
| ——— G. N., Lieut. | 139 |
| ——— John, 2/Lt. | 121 |
| ——— J. A., Lieut. | 133 |
| ——— J. R., Lieut. | 74 |
| ——— Jas. S., Capt. | 40 |
| ——— Pat., 2/Lt. | 11 |
| ——— W., 2/Lt. | 106 |
| ——— W. E., Col., V.C | 105 |
| Gordon-Ralph, P. L. N. 2/Lt. | 111 |
| Gore, F. D. C., 2/Lt. | 159 |
| ——— M., Lieut. | 136 |
| Gore-Brown, R. F., 2/Lt. | 10 |

| | PAGE | | PAGE | | PAGE | | PAGE |
|---|---|---|---|---|---|---|---|
| Goring, A. L., 2/Lt. A/Capt. | 49 | Gray, Frank, 2/Lt. | 129 | Grice, L. C., Capt., M.C. | 98 | Hacklett, L. A., Lieut. | 163 |
| Gorman, G. W., Lieut. | 167 | ———— G., Capt. | 50 | Grier, H. D., Brig.-Gen. | 184 | Hackman, T., Fl.-Com. | 181 |
| Gormley, A. J. C., 2/Lt. | 169 | ———— G. A., 2/Lt. | 100 | Grierson, C. D., 2/Lt. | 153 | Hackney, J. S. G., Lieut. | 73 |
| Goschen, C. G., Lieut. | 17 | ———— G. Morgan, Lt. | 164 | Grieve, L., 2/Lt. | 136 | Hadden, A. Barnes, 2/Lt. | 48 |
| Gosden, A. C., Lieut. | 72 | ———— H., Lieut. | 110 | ———— M. D., 2/Lt. | 35 | ———— C. S., Lieut. | 116 |
| Gosling, H. M., Lt.-Col. | 90 | ———— H. M., 2/Lt. | 75 | ———— W. F., 2/Lt. | 108 | ———— F. K., 2/Lt. | 31 |
| Gosmore, E., 2/Lt. | 11 | ———— J., 2/Lt. | 25 | Griffin, E. H., Capt. | 132 | Haddock, R., Lieut. | 104 |
| Gotch, D. I., Lieut. | 81 | ———— J. A., Capt. | 164 | ———— G. B., 2/Lt. | 94 | Haddon, C. L., 2/Lt. | 100 |
| Gott, J. I., 2/Lt. | 100 | ———— J. B., Capt. | 92 | ———— H., 2/Lt. | 81 | ———— J. B., Capt. | 28 |
| ———— W. H. E., Lieut. | 90 | ———— J. H., 2/Lt. | 12 | ———— J.A.A.,Lt.-Col | 82 | ———— R. J., 2/Lt. | 100 |
| Gough, C., Lieut. | 44 | ———— K. W., Lieut. | 147 | ———— J. W., Capt. | 29 | Haddow, Robert B., 2/Lt. | 82 |
| ———— G.V.H., Lieut. | 90 | ———— R. A., Major | 110 | ———— R. T., 2/Lt. | 148 | Hadley, G. H., Lieut. | 29 |
| ———— R.G.H., 2/Lt. | 75 | ———— R. H., Lieut. | 165 | Griffith, H. M., Capt. | 91 | Hadlow, Wm., 2/Lt. | 142 |
| ———— T. A., 2/Lt. | 71 | ———— R. G., Sub.-Lt. | 144 | ———— J. C., 2/Lt. | 154 | Hadrill, G. C. T., 2/Lt. | 153 |
| Gould, K. W., 2/Lt. | 108 | ———— T. A., 2/Lt. | 103 | ———— J.F.U., Capt. | 51 | Hadwick, W., 2/Lt. | 50 |
| ———— S., 2/Lt. | 128 | ———— V. C., 2/Lt. | 75 | ———— J. W., 2/Lt. | 95 | Haffield, C. C., 2/Lt. | 63 |
| ———— W. T., 2/Lt. | 30 | ———— William, Lieut. | 48 | ———— T. C., Lieut. | 79 | Hagen, E. C., Capt. | 10 |
| Goulding, H. R., Capt. | 61 | ———— Wm. A., Lieut. | 141 | ———— W. H. E. N. Lieut. | 95 | Hagenbush, R. J., 2/Lt. | 173 |
| Gourlay, Wm. N., 2/Lt. | 114 | ———— W. J., 2/Lt. | 149 | Griffith-Jones, Melville | | Hague, W., 2/Lt. | 77 |
| Govan, H. F. C., 2/Lt. | 74 | ———— W.M.R., 2/Lt. | 160 | P., Capt. | 99 | Haig, A. B., Capt. | 183 |
| Gow, J. E., Lieut. | 166 | Grayston, A. V., Lieut. | 101 | Griffiths, C. D., 2/Lt. | 148 | ———— A. E., Major | 58 |
| ———— W.S.P., 2/Lt. | 91 | ———— S. E., 2/Lt. | 77 | ———— E. C., 2/Lt. | 92 | ———— A L., Lieut. | 21 |
| Gower, O. C. D., Lieut. | 136 | Greaves, H. P., Capt. | 78 | ———— F. W., 2/Lt. | 148 | ———— F. W., Lieut. | 179 |
| ———— E. W., Lieut. | 113 | ———— J. A., 2/Lt. | 63 | ———— H. E., 2/Lt. | 57 | Haigh, G. D., 2/Lt. | 127 |
| Grace, H. C., Capt. | 81 | Green, A. G. N., Lieut. | 101 | ———— T. E., Rev. | 135 | ———— J., Lieut. | 99 |
| ———— W. A., 2/Lt. | 141 | ———— E. G., Lieut. | 159 | Grigg, Raymond, Lieut. | 85 | Haight, J. L., 2/Lt. | 156 |
| ———— W. J., Capt. | 128 | ———— E. M. L., 2/Lt. | 45 | Griggs, B. L., Lieut. | 59 | ———— W. L., Capt. | 180 |
| Gracey, R. V., 2/Lt. | 109 | ———— G. A., 2/Lt. | 49 | Grimwade, F. N., 2/Lt. | 147 | ———— W.R.W., Capt. | 140 |
| Gracie, J. McA. C., 2/Lt. | 54 | ———— G. W., 2/Lt. | 82 | Grimwood, F. R., Major | | Haighton, E. S., Lieut. | 82 |
| Graham, F., Lieut. | 101 | ———— H. D., 2/Lt. | 118 | A/Lt.-Col. | 130 | Haile, W. L., 2/Lt. | 83 |
| ———— F. H. H., 2/Lt. | 52 | ———— J. H., 2/Lt. | 47 | ———— H., Lieut. | 97 | Hair, N. B., 2/Lt. | 153 |
| ———— G. L., Capt. | 29 | ———— P. H., Capt. | 133 | Grinling, F. W., Capt. | 25 | Haldane, G. C., Lieut. | 112 |
| ———— Henry, Capt. | 25 | ———— R., Lieut., M.C. | 100 | Grinnell-Milne, D. D. | | Hale, L. E., Lieut. | 84 |
| ———— H. A., 2/Lt. | 127 | ———— R. R., 2/Lt. | 12 | Capt. | 147 | Haley, H., 2/Lt. | 33 |
| ———— H. P., Lieut. | 115 | ———— W., Capt. | 21 | ———— D. W., Lieut. | 147 | Halford, A. E., 2/Lt. | 147 |
| ———— J., Capt. | 131 | ———— W. H., Lieut. | 151 | Groner, R. E. A., Lieut. | 77 | ———— E. S., Capt. | 182 |
| ———— J. R., Lieut. | 122 | ———— W. E., 2/Lt. | 13 | Gross, C. R., Lieut. | 172 | Halkyard, A., Lieut. | 47 |
| ———— L. N., Capt. | 148 | Greenaway, G. K., 2/Lt. | 58 | Grosset, W. E., Lieut. | 154 | Hall, A. H., Major | 109 |
| ———— M. A., Lieut. | 141 | Greene, G. E. D., Lieut. | 139 | Grosvenor, Lord G., Lieut. | 18 | ———— B., Lieut. | 167 |
| ———— N., Lieut. | 68 | ———— Wm. A., 2/Lt. | 114 | Grout, E. J., Sub.-Lt. | 153 | ———— C. C., 2/Lt. | 75 |
| ———— Peter, Lieut. | 25 | Greenfield, C. R. M., 2/Lt. | 26 | Grover, C. W., Capt. | 23 | ———— C. F., Capt. | 84 |
| ———— R. P., Capt. | 91 | ———— W. T., 2/Lt. | 77 | ———— F. C., Capt. | 143 | ———— C. R., Capt. | 113 |
| ———— W., 2/Lt. | 14 | Greenhill, B. M., 2/Lt. | 8 | Groves, J. O., Sub.-Lt. | 146 | ———— C. R., Lieut. | 164 |
| Graham-Toler, L. J., Capt. | 87 | Greenhow, H. M., 2/Lt. | 99 | Grundy, Percy, 2/Lt. | 32 | ———— C. T. M., 2/Lt. | 88 |
| Graham-Watson, A. F., | | ———— M. W., 2/Lt. | 146 | Guard, S. G., 2/Lt. | 142 | ———— E. H., Lieut. | 141 |
| Capt. | 19 | Greenless, T., Capt. | 112 | Gubbins, J. R. F., 2/Lt. | 188 | ———— E. W., Capt. | 89 |
| Granger, A. G., 2/Lt. | 63 | Greenslade, D. A., Capt. | 61 | Gudgeon, G.F.C., Lieut. | 131 | ———— E.W.O., Lieut. | 175 |
| ———— T. E., Lt. | 187 | ———— R. L., Lieut. | 157 | ———— R.E., Capt., M.C. | 11 | ———— G. W., Lieut. | 40 |
| Grant, A., Rev., C. F. | 135 | Greensmith, E. B., Capt. | 77 | Guest, J., Capt. | 96 | ———— H. E., 2/Lt. | 111 |
| ———— A. E., Lieut. | 22 | ———— W., 2/Lt. | 77 | ———— J.E.C., 2/Lt. | 28 | ———— J. G., 2/Lt. | 72 |
| ———— A. I., 2/Lt. | 20 | Greenstreet, T. W., 2/Lt. | 188 | Guild C., 2/Lt. | 171 | ———— J. N., Lieut. | 26 |
| ———— A. V. S., 2/Lt. | 93 | Greenwood, C. L. E., Lieut. | 185 | Guildford, T.W.F., 2/Lt. | 75 | ———— J. R., Lieut. | 13 |
| ———— D., Capt. | 22 | ———— C. J. R., Capt. | 16 | Guise, V. R., Capt. | 185 | ———— K.W.J., Lieut. | 164 |
| ———— D. L., Capt. | 147 | ———— G., 2/Lt. | 11 | Gulich, J. D., 2/Lt. | 33 | ———— L. C., Capt. | 16 |
| ———— H. D., 2/Lt. | 59 | ———— O., Lieut. | 43 | Gulland, J. P., Lieut. | 143 | ———— L. G., 2/Lt. | 171 |
| ———— J. H., 2/Lt. | 27 | ———— P. G., Lieut. | 175 | Gummer, H. L., 2/Lt. | 15 | ———— M. A., Lieut. | 36 |
| ———— Jack R., Capt. (A/Major), M.C. | 17 | Greer, S. P., 2/Lt. | 123 | Gunn, A. A., 2/Lt. | 105 | ———— M. E., 2/Lt. | 156 |
| ———— R. A. P., Capt. | 183 | Gregg, C., 2/Lt. | 59 | ———— A. D., Capt. | 184 | ———— N. D., F.-Sub-Lt. | 177 |
| Grant-Dalton, E. F., | | Gregory, B. W., 2/Lt. | 36 | ———— J. C., 2/Lt. | 172 | ———— R., Lieut. | 173 |
| Capt. | 39 | ———— H. P., Lieut. | 49 | ———— J. D., Lieut. | 139 | ———— Robert, 2/Lt. | 11 |
| ———— H., Lieut. | 144 | ———— H. W., 2/Lt. | 71 | Gunner, F. H., Bde.-Maj | 7 | ———— R.S., Agent. | 189 |
| ———— L., Lieut. | 71 | ———— J. L., 2/Lt. | 36 | Gunston, F. J. D., 2/Lt. | 62 | ———— T. F., Lieut. | 110 |
| Grantham, V. M., 2/Lt. | 147 | ———— M. C., 2/Lt. | 119 | Gurney, Henry, Capt. | 8 | ———— W. A., Lieut. | 170 |
| ———— W., Capt. | 67 | ———— R. J., 2/Lt. | 163 | ———— J., 2/Lt. | 128 | ———— W. E., Lieut. | 170 |
| Graves, Cecil, Lieut. | 53 | ———— S. B., Lieut. | 186 | ———— K. G., 2/Lt. | 61 | Hallam, H. A., 2/Lt. | 149 |
| ———— T. F., 2/Lt. | 100 | Greig, C. W., 2/Lt. | 188 | ———— P. S., 2/Lt. | 15 | Hallenquist, J. E., Lieut. | 175 |
| Gray, Archibald, 2/Lt. | 115 | ———— D. S., Capt. | 74 | Gurtrell, W. H., Capt. | 136 | Halley, G. S., 2/Lt. | 82 |
| ———— A. C. H., Lt.-Col. | 134 | ———— G. G. F., 2/Lt. | 115 | Guthrie, H. S., 2/Lt. | 74 | Halliley, W. S., Lieut. | 183 |
| ———— B. W., Lieut. | 33 | ———— O., Capt. | 150 | ———— L. W., 2/Lt. | 20 | Hallinan, C., 2/Lt. | 110 |
| ———— Cyril, Lieut. | 51 | ———— R., Lieut. | 88 | Guy, C. G., 2/Lt. | 155 | Halls, S., Lieut. | 69 |
| ———— C. G. D., 2/Lt. | 156 | Grey, A. A. D., Lieut. | 177 | Guyatt, T., 2/Lt. | 117 | Hallsmith, G., 2/Lt. | 38 |
| ———— C. V., Lieut. | 189 | ———— J.P.B., Lieut. | 101 | Gwyer, N. E., Lieut. | 168 | Halstead, G. A., Lieut. | 94 |
| ———— D. B., Capt. | 149 | ———— R., Capt. | 146 | Gwynne, W. C., Lieut. | 144 | Halvorsen, W. A., Lieut. | 136 |
| | | Gribble, J. R., Capt., V.C. | 29 | Hacking, E. J., 2/Lt. | 93 | Hambling, T. C., 2/Lt. | 62 |
| | | ———— R. H., 2/Lt. | 10 | | | | |

| Name | Page | Name | Page | Name | Page | Name | Page |
|---|---|---|---|---|---|---|---|
| Hamer, R. B., Lieut. | 96 | Harman, A. J., Capt., M.C. | 130 | Harvey, Robt., Capt. | 139 | Heaton, R., 2/Lt. | 98 |
| Hamilton, G. S., Lieut. | 112 | ——— C. E., Lieut. | 89 | ——— R. G., Lieut. | 37 | Heaver, A. R., 2/Lt. | 169 |
| ——— G., 2/Lt. | 107 | Harmer, J. M., 2/Lt. | 38 | ——— S. A., 2/Lt. | 23 | Heawood, G. L., Lieut. | 187 |
| ——— Gail, Lieut. | 162 | Harness, F. G., Lieut. | 16 | ——— W. A., Lieut. | 147 | Hedges, A., 2/Lt. | 30 |
| ——— G. C., Lieut. | 139 | Harnett, W. G., Capt. | 134 | Harvey-Samuel, G. D., Lieut. | 88 | Hedley, A. F., 2/Lt. | 105 |
| ——— H. D., 2/Lt. | 151 | Harper, F., 2/Lt. | 47 | Haseler, G. F., 2/Lt. | 150 | ——— J. H., Capt. | 161 |
| ——— H. F. T., 2/Lt. | 38 | ——— M. L., 2/Lt. | 127 | Haslam, Cyril, 2/Lt. | 95 | Heelis, H. L., Lieut. | 52 |
| ——— I. B. M., Lieut. | 106 | ——— C. G., 2/Lt. | 78 | ——— S. A., Lieut. | 155 | Heggie, A. D., 2/Lt. | 15 |
| ——— J. R., 2/Lt. | 125 | Harries, L. W., Capt. | 188 | Haslett, H. R., Major | 43 | Heine, R. W., Lieut. | 171 |
| ——— W. N., Lieut. | 152 | Harrington, H., Capt. | 39 | Hastie, H. E., Lieut. | 174 | Hehir, P., Col. | 184 |
| Hamilton-Hamilton, Brig.-General | 182 | ——— H.B.D., Lieut. | 162 | Hastings, E. W., Lieut. | 45 | Helder, L. B., Lieut. | 149 |
| Hamlet, F. A., Capt. | 124 | ——— H. N., Lieut. | 54 | Hastings, H., Lieut. | 51 | Hele, G. Melvin, Capt. | 62 |
| ——— H. A., 2/Lt. | 175 | ——— T. F., 2/Ly. | 22 | Haswell, T. S., 2/Lt. | 110 | Hellier, Maurice J., Capt | 87 |
| Hammersley, F. J. B., 2/Lt. | 158 | Harris, A. C., 2/Lt. | 77 | Hatfield, A. C., Capt. | 156 | Helwig, N. W., Lieut. | 172 |
| Hammond, F., 2/Lt. | 55 | ——— C. M., 2/Lt. | 110 | ——— R. E., 2/Lt. | 43 | Hemmens, R. H., Lieut. | 167 |
| ——— H. T., 2/Lt. | 156 | ——— D. R., Lieut. | 168 | Hatherall, W. C., 2/Lt. | 110 | Hempel, A. E., 2/Lt. | 157 |
| ——— John, Lieut. | 144 | ——— E. E., 2/Lt. | 110 | Hatton, G. A. L., Capt. | 83 | Hemphill, H. H., Capt. | 46 |
| ——— R. M., Lieut. | 11 | ——— F. E., Lieut. | 36 | ——— J., 2/Lt. | 40 | Hempsall, H. T., 2/Lt. | 171 |
| Hammonds, E. H., 2/Lt. | 37 | ——— H., 2/Lt. | 153 | Haughton, J. W., Capt. | 38 | Hemstock, F., 2/Lt. | 79 |
| Hampton, J. D., 2/Lt. | 123 | ——— H., Lieut. | 145 | ——— S. Capt. | 184 | Henderson, A. B., 2/Lt. | 172 |
| ——— P. R., Lieut. | 162 | ——— H. R. Dale, Lieut. | 11 | ——— S. P. O., Lieut | 187 | ——— B. M., Capt. | 107 |
| Hancock, C., Lieut. | 174 | ——— J. A., 2/Lt. | 92 | Havill, F., 2/Lt. | 76 | ——— E. E. J., 2/Lt. | 94 |
| ——— F. W., Lieut. | 179 | ——— N. B., 2/Lt. | 163 | Haward, C. P., Capt. | 21 | ——— G., 2/Lt. | 89 |
| ——— H.L.N., Lieut. | 180 | ——— J. H., Lieut. | 187 | Hawker, H., Sub-Lt. | 145 | ——— G., 2/Lt. | 106 |
| ——— W. H., 2/Lt. | 120 | ——— R. T., 2/Lt. | 28 | Hawkins, F. A., Capt. and Adjt. | 115 | ——— G. D., Capt. D.S.O., M.C. | 22 |
| Hand, E. McN., Lieut. | 163 | ——— W., 2/Lt. | 46 | Hawkins, H. R., Capt. | 152 | ——— G. H., 2/Lt. | 20 |
| Handfield-Jones, R. M., Major | 134 | ——— W. N., 2/Lt. | 115 | ——— T., 2/Lt. | 38 | ——— G. R. B., 2/Lt. | 74 |
| Handford, W., 2/Lt. | 47 | ——— W. N., 2/Lt. | 127 | Haworth, C., 2/Lt. | 71 | ——— H. G., 2/Lt. | 67 |
| Handley, F. A. W., 2/Lt. | 152 | Harrison, Aidan, Capt., D.S.O. | 79 | ——— T. T., 2/Lt. | 29 | ——— H. Y. G., Capt. | 104 |
| ——— J., Capt. | 81 | ——— A. G., 2/Lt. | 171 | Hay, A. F. A., 2/Lt. | 21 | ——— J., Capt. | 19 |
| ——— J., Lieut. | 162 | ——— A. H., Lieut. | 165 | ——— E. S., Lieut. | 123 | ——— Ian, Capt. | 129 |
| Hankin, H. M., Capt. | 146 | ——— C. A., 2/Lt. | 173 | ——— Hon. Ivan | 9 | ——— J. E., 2/Lt. | 27 |
| Hanley, E. D., Capt. | 47 | ——— C., Capt. | 77 | ——— J., Lieut. | 177 | ——— J. F., 2/Lt. | 155 |
| Hanna, A. S., 2/Lt. | 161 | ——— F. A., 2/Lt. | 28 | ——— J. B., Home Capt. | 169 | ——— K.S.S., Capt. | 39 |
| Hannam, W. J., 2/Lt. | 36 | ——— F. C. S., 2/Lt. | 101 | Hayden, W. A., 2/Lt. | 109 | ——— M. J., 2/Lt. | 53 |
| Hannan, G., 2/Lt. | 188 | ——— F. P., 2/Lt. | 121 | Haydon, J. S., 2/Lt. | 70 | ——— R.W.M., 2/Lt. | 48 |
| ——— L., Lieut. | 11 | ——— F. V., 2/Lt. | 96 | Hayer, J., 2/Lt. | 88 | ——— W., Lieut. | 100 |
| Hannay, J., 2/Lt., M.C. | 92 | ——— H. H., Lieut. | 25 | Hayes, E. D. F., Capt. | 131 | ——— Wilfred, Commodore | 143 |
| Hanney, W. C. A., 2/Lt. | 83 | ——— L. J., 2/Lt. | 110 | ——— Frank, Lieut. | 80 | ——— W. I., 2/Lt. | 116 |
| Hanson, D. C., Capt. | 132 | ——— M. C. C., Capt. | 47 | ——— F., 2/Lt. | 96 | ——— W. R., Lieut. | 166 |
| Harbord, E. R., Capt. | 54 | ——— W., 2/Lt. | 24 | ——— Fredk. Graham 2/Lt. | 127 | Hendry, S. J., Lieut. | 32 |
| Harbour, E. R., Lieut. | 48 | ——— W. L., Lieut. | 158 | ——— H. F., 2/Lt. | 120 | Hendrie, H. A., Capt. | 97 |
| Harbron, Frank, 2/Lt. | 94 | ——— W.R.E., Capt. | 171 | ——— J. Milton, 2/Lt | 95 | Hendry, John N., Lieut. | 122 |
| Harcourt, C. B., Capt. | 143 | Harrop, R. H., Lieut. | 125 | ——— W. E., 2/Lt. | 39 | Henehan, M., Capt. | 111 |
| Harcourt-Vernon, A. A., Capt. | 175 | Harrower, A. P., Lieut. | 26 | Hayes-Newington, B. V. Lieut. | 54 | Henley, A. E., 2/Lt. | 82 |
| Harding, G. P., Lieut. | 151 | Harryman, S., Lieut. | 150 | Hayford, A. R., 2/Lt. | 89 | ——— C. F., Major | 187 |
| Harding, W. D., Lieut. | 140 | Hart, A. L., 2/Lt. | 84 | Haygarth, C.H.S., Lieut | 16 | Henley-Mooney, W. Lieut. | 173 |
| Hardman, E. F., Lieut. | 118 | ——— J. W., 2/Lt. | 13 | Hayley, J. P., Lieut. | 64 | Hennessy, J., Lt.-Col. | 186 |
| ——— E. P., Capt. | 167 | ——— N. N., 2/Lt. | 23 | Haylock, F. A., 2/Lt. | 34 | ——— P., 2/Lt. | 60 |
| Hardy, E. H., 2/Lt. | 43 | ——— Percy G., 2/Lt | 94 | Hayman, E.W.P., 2/Lt. | 22 | Henning, C. E., 2/Lt. | 129 |
| ——— F., 2/Lt. | 29 | ——— W. M., Capt. | 140 | ——— Y. R., Lieut. | 131 | Henry, A. W., 2/Lt. | 108 |
| ——— George, Lieut. | 28 | Hart-Davies, H. R., 2/Lt. | 155 | Haywood, C., Lieut. | 45 | ——— F. R., Lieut. | 151 |
| ——— G., 2/Lt. | 111 | Hartley, E. F., 2/Lt. | 122 | ——— R., 2/Lt. | 83 | ——— N. C., 2/Lt. | 27 |
| ——— J. L., Lieut. | 111 | ——— R. L., Capt. | 117 | Hazard, C. J., Major | 70 | ——— R. Alex., Lieut | 170 |
| ——— R. L., Lieut. | 131 | ——— H., 2/Lt. | 167 | Hazeley, E., Lieut. | 122 | ——— S. S., 2/Lt. | 158 |
| ——— V. C., 2/Lt. | 24 | ——— R. W., 2/Lt. | 35 | Hazell, A. N., 2/Lt. | 72 | ——— W. D., Lieut. | 141 |
| ——— W., Lieut. | 118 | Hartshorn, J. E., Lieut. | 78 | Hazlewood, Geo. H. E., Lieut. | 107 | Henshaw, J. E., Lieut. | 16 |
| Hargreaves, G. W., Lieut. | 119 | ——— L. A., Lieut. | 100 | Heagerty, J. S., Lieut. | 151 | Henslow, E. I., Capt. | 93 |
| ——— A., Capt. | 38 | Hartigan, M. M., Major | 113 | Heale, W. V., Lieut. | 83 | Hepburn, A. C., Major | 132 |
| ——— B. F., Capt. | 72 | Harvard, A. J. N., Col. | 183 | Heanley, R. E. M., Capt. | 25 | Heppel, Philip F., 2/Lt. | 149 |
| ——— C. F., Capt. | 63 | Harvey, A., Major | 185 | Heaphy, G. M., 2/Lt. | 84 | Hepper, T. E., Lieut. | 131 |
| Harker, B., 2/Lt. | 157 | ——— A. M., 2/Lt. | 36 | Heard, A. P., Capt. | 89 | Heptinstall, P. M., 2/Lt. | 16 |
| ——— G. T., 2/Lt. | 154 | ——— A. W., Capt. | 92 | ——— F. S., Lieut. | 88 | Hepton, A., Lieut. | 49 |
| ——— M. J., 2/Lt. | 12 | ——— C. M., Lieut. | 14 | Hearder, Stanley F. 2/Lt. | 57 | Hepworth, L., Capt. | 37 |
| ——— R. H., Lieut. | 66 | ——— E., 2/Lt. | 130 | Hearn, G. S., 2/Lt. | 65 | Herapath, C. B., Capt. | 186 |
| Harkin, F. W., 2/Lt. | 32 | ——— F. W., 2/Lt. | 61 | Heath, H. E., Lieut. | 160 | ——— J. N., Lieut. | 188 |
| Harland, Robert, 2/Lt. | 16 | ——— F. W., Lieut. | 55 | Heathcote, F.G.P., Capt | 134 | ——— P. W., Capt. | 127 |
| Harle, W., Lieut. | 152 | ——— G. S., Lieut. | 168 | ——— L. W., Lieut. | 179 | Herbage, P. F. W., 2/Lt. | 28 |
| Harley, N. F., 2/Lt. | 94 | ——— H. C., Lieut. | 69 | Heather, C. L., Lieut. | 140 | Herbert, C. C., 2/Lt. | 178 |
| ——— Vivian, 2/Lt. | 170 | ——— J. B. B. de M. Lieut. | 152 | | | ——— E., Rev. | 135 |
| | | ——— J. H. F., Lieut. | 87 | | | ——— G. M., Major | 187 |
| | | | | | | Herman, R. D., 2/Lt. | 149 |
| | | | | | | Hermon, J. A., Lieut | 104 |

| Name | Page | Name | Page | Name | Page | Name | Page |
|---|---|---|---|---|---|---|---|
| Herold, J. C., 2/Lt. | 129 | Hillman, E. C., Major, M.C. | 17 | Hollis, G. T., Lieut. | 43 | Houslop, W.A.S., Lieut. | 129 |
| Heron-Jones,C. V., Lieut. | 184 | Hills, F. E., Lieut. | 150 | ——— H. R., 2/Lt. | 44 | Houston, T., Lieut. | 110 |
| Herring, A. C., 2/Lt. | 81 | ——— H., Lieut. | 131 | ——— J. A., Lieut. | 150 | Hovil, F. A., Lieut. | 135 |
| ——— David, D., 2/Lt. | 62 | ——— J., 2/Lt. | 168 | Holloway, C. P., 2/Lt. | 83 | Howard, B., 2/Lt. | 121 |
| ——— Gordon, E., 2/Lt. | 160 | ——— O.M.,2/Lt.,M.C. | 157 | ——— G. W., Lieut. | 41 | ——— C. E., Lieut. | 92 |
| Herriot, W. M., Lieut. | 170 | ——— W. B. B., 2lLt. | 150 | Holman, H. G., 2/Lt. | 162 | ——— De W., 2/Lt. | 87 |
| Hervey, H. E. 2/Lt. | 151 | Hillyard, Victor W., 2/Lt. | 162 | ——— L., 2/Lt. | 153 | ——— Douglas W., 2/Lt. | 51 |
| Hett, E. J. R., Capt. | 35 | Hilpern, W. H. T., 2/Lt. | 63 | ——— S. A., Capt. | 27 | ——— F. C., Lieut. | 139 |
| Hewat, H. B., 2/Lt. | 173 | Hilton, T. R., 2/Lt. | 168 | Holme, J. J., Lieut. | 25 | ——— G. R., 2/Lt. | 168 |
| ——— W. E., Lieut. | 43 | Hinchcliffe, G., Capt. | 82 | Holme-Barnett, K., 2/Lt. | 13 | ——— P. L., 2/Lt. | 83 |
| Hewetson, R. J. P., Capt. | 80 | ——— H. Edgar, 2/Lt. | 165 | Holmes, A., 2/Lt. | 114 | Howard-Bury, C. K., Lt.-Col. | 91 |
| Hewett, W. G., 2/Lt. | 128 | Hind, C., 2/Lt. | 110 | ——— C. W. D., 2/Lt. | 151 | Howarth, A., Lieut. | 42 |
| Hewitt, F. B., 2/Lt. | 80 | Hinder, A., 2/Lt. | 171 | ——— E. A., Lieut. | 99 | ——— B., 2/Lt. | 100 |
| ——— Harold, 2/Lt. | 51 | Hindson, R. E., Lieut. | 56 | ——— E. G., 2/Lt. | 15 | ——— G. H., 2/Lt. | 64 |
| ——— H. A., 2/Lt. | 159 | Hine, J. B., 2/Lt. | 154 | ——— J. D. V., 2/Lt. | 153 | ——— H., 2/Lt. | 87 |
| ——— N. M., Lieut. | 176 | Hinwood, H. C., 2/Lt. | 10 | ——— R. G., Lieut. | 112 | ——— J., 2/Lt. | 52 |
| Hewlett, R. F. L., 2/Lt. | 128 | Hirst, J., Capt., M.C. | 44 | ——— W., 2/Lt. | 23 | ——— Wm. T., 2/Lt. | 120 |
| Hewson, F. A. A., 2/Lt. | 149 | ——— W. S., Capt. | 133 | ——— W. R., 2/Lt. | 49 | Howat, W. D., 2/Lt. | 20 |
| Heyes, A. C., 2/Lt. | 172 | Hirtzel, H., Lieut. | 142 | Holms, J. F., 2/Lt. | 103 | Howe, G. R., Lieut. | 22 |
| Heywood, L. R., 2/Lt. | 147 | Hiskens, G. A., Lieut. | 118 | Holroyde, R. E., Lieut. | 143 | ——— L. A., 2/Lt. | 102 |
| ——— P. H., A/Capt. | 96 | Hislop, J., 2/Lt. | 74 | Holt, A. T. S., 2/Lt. | 96 | ——— R. G., 2/Lt. | 188 |
| Heyworth, E. L., Lieut. | 151 | Hitchcock, C. G., 2/Lt. | 169 | ——— G., 2/Lt. | 80 | ——— S. G., 2/Lt. | 98 |
| Hibbard, S. R., Lieut. | 176 | ——— C. H., 2/Lt. | 38 | ——— J., 2/Lt. | 120 | Howell, E. A., 2/Lt. | 128 |
| Hibbert, H. B., Capt. | 85 | Hixon, A. J. Asst. Surg. | 182 | Holwill, W. B., 2/Lt. | 123 | ——— H. C., 2/Lt. | 100 |
| ——— J. E., 2/Lt. | 48 | Hoad, F. J. S., Capt. | 136 | Holyoake, A. V., Lieut. | 178 | ——— Reg., Lieut. | 61 |
| ——— O. R., 2/Lt. | 172 | Hoare, George, Lieut. | 189 | Hommert, L. A. E. E., Lieut. | 36 | Howes, R. M., Capt. | 49 |
| ——— O. Y., Capt. | 187 | Hobbs, J., 2/Lt. | 20 | Honeyman, W. M., 2/Lt. | 58 | ——— W. H., Lieut. | 155 |
| Hibbett, H., 2/Lt. | 83 | Hoblyn, S. E., Lieut. | 177 | Honeysett, J. H., Lieut. | 136 | Howey, J. E. P., 2/Lt. | 147 |
| Hickman Sir A. | 8 | Hobson, E. C., 2/Lt. | 29 | Hood, John, Capt. | 183 | Howie, J., Capt., M.C. | 127 |
| ——— A., 2/Lt. | 178 | ——— H. N., 2/Lt. | 80 | ——— J. M., 2/Lt. | 118 | Howitt, N. J., 2/Lt. | 64 |
| ——— H., 2/Lt. | 78 | ——— S., 2/Lt. | 46 | ——— M. G., 2/Lt. | 103 | ——— W., 2/Lt. | 46 |
| ——— J. H., 2/Lt. | 71 | Hodgins, C. W., 2/Lt. | 106 | Hooper, A. S., Capt. | 93 | Howl, R., 2/Lt. | 11 |
| Hicks, A. H., Lieut. | 99 | Hockaday, F. W., 2/Lt. | 118 | ——— C. W., Lieut. | 137 | Howlett, J. W., Capt. | 35 |
| ——— A. L., Lieut. | 47 | Hodder, F. J., 2/Lt. | 14 | ——— E. T., 2/Lt. | 89 | Hoy, E. C., Capt. | 173 |
| ——— C. M. H., 2/Lt. | 12 | Hodge, G. G. G., Fl. Lt. | 176 | ——— G. B., 2/Lt. | 126 | Hoyne-Fox, L. V., Capt. | 182 |
| ——— G. E., Lieut. | 152 | Hodges, F., 2/Lt. | 40 | ——— Kenneth, Lieut. | 63 | Hubbs, F. S., Lieut. | 141 |
| ——— V. W. F., Lieut. | 47 | ——— F. A., 2/Lt. | 11 | ——— W.H.V., Capt. | 138 | Huddleston, G., Lieut. | 183 |
| ——— W. B., Capt. | 25 | Hodgkin, H. S., Col. | 78 | Hope, J. B. A., 2/Lt. | 68 | Hudson, A. R., Capt. | 155 |
| Hield, V., 2/Lt. | 70 | Hodgkinson, J. N., 2/Lt. | 95 | ——— M. B., 2/Lt. | 90 | ——— F. D., 2/Lt. | 161 |
| Higgins, J., 2/Lt. | 35 | Hodgson, A. G., Lieut. | 163 | ——— Sydney, 2/Lt. | 34 | ——— F. N., Lieut. | 176 |
| Higham, H. G., 2/Lt. | 128 | ——— A. M., 2/Lt. | 119 | Hopegood, C. J. T. F., Lt. (A/Capt.) | 76 | ——— F. N., Capt. M.C. | 154 |
| Highett, C. T., Capt. | 187 | ——— E. E., Lieut. | 146 | Hopewell, D. C., Lieut. | 161 | ——— G. L., Capt. | 85 |
| Hight, P. H., Lieut. | 122 | Hodgson-Jones, R., Capt. | 132 | Hopgood, F. J., 2/Lt. | 161 | ——— G. L., Capt. | 85 |
| Highton, R. D. C., Capt. | 21 | Hodgson-Smith, W. B., Capt. | 83 | Hopkins, G., Lieut. | 38 | ——— J. H., Capt. | 13 |
| Higinson, G. S., Major | 113 | Hogan, G. S., 2/Lt. | 92 | ——— G. M., 2/Lt. | 152 | ——— S. P., 2/Lt. | 98 |
| Higson, J. T., 2/Lt. | 81 | Hogg, H. A., 2/Lt. | 116 | ——— G. W. S., Capt. | 28 | ——— T., Lieut. | 77 |
| Hilder, P., 2/Lt. | 109 | ——— H. J., Lieut. | 17 | ——— J. A. S., Capt. | 60 | Huggard, J. C., 2/Lt. | 155 |
| Hildyard, B. V., 2/Lt. | 43 | ——— R. M., Lieut. | 99 | Hopper, M., Lieut. | 101 | Hughes, G. E., 2/Lt. | 174 |
| Hill, A. S., 2/Lt. | 154 | Hoggarth, N. S., 2/Lt. | 46 | ——— R. W., 2/Lt. | 174 | ——— G. R., 2/Lt. | 33 |
| ——— A. B., Capt. | 100 | Holbrook, C., 2/Lt. | 115 | Hopton, H. P., 2/Lt. | 34 | ——— H. D., 2/Lt. | 99 |
| ——— A. C. L., 2/Lt. | 34 | ——— C. M., Lieut. | 172 | Hopwood, W., 2/Lt. | 76 | ——— H. L., Lieut. | 76 |
| ——— C. H., Major | 184 | Holcroft, A. B., Fl.-Sub.-Lt. | 177 | Hore, L. B., Lieut., M.C. | 125 | ——— J. B. W., 2/Lt. | 61 |
| ——— C. W., Lieut. | 179 | Holden, A., 2/Lt. | 150 | Horgan, E. P., 2/Lt. | 115 | ——— John P., 2/Lt. | 27 |
| ——— D., Lieut. | 10 | ——— H. S., 2/Lt. | 80 | Horn, A. K., 2/Lt. | 64 | ——— J. J., Major | 136 |
| ——— E. St. C., Capt. | 143 | ——— J. F., 2/Lt. | 80 | Hornby, J. H., 2/Lt. | 130 | ——— N.A.A., Major | 134 |
| ——— F. C. R., 2/Lt. | 83 | ——— M. M., Lieut. | 117 | ——— R. D., Lieut. | 88 | ——— P., 2/Lt. | 103 |
| ——— Francis, Major | 89 | Holdsworth, J. A., Lieut. | 51 | Horne, D. E. A., 2/Lt. | 126 | ——— R. D., 2/Lt. | 169 |
| ——— G. A. R., 2/Lt. | 168 | Hole, W. G., 2/Lt. | 16 | ——— H. F., 2/Lt. | 75 | ——— S. C., 2/Lt. | 109 |
| ——— G.E.M., Lt.-Col. | 64 | Hollamby, H. J., 2/Lt. | 55 | ——— O. W., Capt. | 76 | Hulbert, H. J., 2/Lt. | 94 |
| ——— J. O., 2/Lt. | 73 | Holland, A., Capt. | 24 | ——— W. G., Lieut. | 9 | Hull, G., Lieut. | 13 |
| ——— J. B., 2/Lt. | 117 | ——— C. B., 2/Lt. | 151 | Hornsby, H. R., Lieut. | 14 | Hullah, M. C., 2/Lt. | 13 |
| ——— J. S., 2/Lt. | 36 | ——— E. V., Lieut. | 170 | Horrocks, B. G., 2/Lt. | 87 | Hulls, A. R., 2/Lt. | 89 |
| ——— N. J., 2/Lt. | 137 | ——— R. P., 2/Lt. | 95 | Horseman, W. M., 2/Lt. | 15 | Hulme, J. B., Lieut. | 176 |
| ——— R. F., Lieut. | 156 | Holleran, O. C., Capt. | 170 | Horsfall, R. W., Lieut. | 41 | Hulse, W., Lieut. | 16 |
| ——— R. F. B., 2/Lt. | 36 | Holley, T. G., Lieut. | 150 | Horsfield, Wm., Lieut. | 11 | Humberstone, J. E., Capt. | 13 |
| ——— R. I. V., Lieut. | 156 | Holliday, C. E., 2/Lt. | 14 | Horsley, P. H., 2/Lt. | 28 | Humble, A. D., 2/Lt. | 112 |
| ——— S. J., 2/Lt. | 167 | ——— G. R., Lieut. | 35 | Horwood, J. C., Lieut. | 186 | ——— T., 2/Lt. | 156 |
| ——— T. L., Lieut. | 77 | ——— J., 2/Lt. | 21 | Hostler, A. C. V., 2/Lt. | 39 | Hume, Arthur J., 2/Lt. | 124 |
| ——— T. R. V., 2/Lt. | 161 | ——— J., 2/Lt. | 11 | Horton, John A., 2/Lt. | 84 | ——— R. C., 2/Lt. | 154 |
| ——— W., 2/Lt. | 119 | Hollingsworth, R. L., Lieut. | 166 | Houghton, D. L., 2/Lt. | 152 | ——— Ronald M. 2/Lt. | 73 |
| ——— W. R., Lieut. | 101 | Hollins, E. T., Lieut. | 96 | Houldsworth, J. F. H., Lieut. | 106 | ——— S. S., Lieut. | 153 |
| Hillam, A. W. M., Sub-Lt. | 144 | Hollis, A., Lieut. | 160 | Houlgrave, C., Lieut. | 174 | | |
| Hillian, John, 2/Lt. | 97 | | | Houlton, S., Capt. | 124 | | |
| Hillier, R. J., Capt. | 65 | | | | | | |

| | PAGE | | PAGE | | PAGE | | PAGE |
|---|---|---|---|---|---|---|---|
| Hume, W. M., Sub-Lt... | 144 | Ingham, C. R., 2/Lt. ... | 43 | James, C. P., Lt.-Col., | | Johnson, M. E. S., Major | 183 |
| Hummerston, H.S.,Capt | 136 | ——— H., 2/Lt. ... | 72 | D.S.O. ... | 72 | ——— P., 2/Lt. ... | 91 |
| Humphreys, A. W., 2/Lt | 12 | Ingle, A., 2/Lt. ... | 26 | ——— E., 2/Lt. ... | 31 | ——— R. F., 2/Lt. ... | 98 |
| ——— G. N., Lieut. | 146 | Inglesby, S. G., Lieut. | 189 | ——— F. E. S., 2/Lt. | 15 | ——— S., Lieut. | 127 |
| ——— L. B., Lieut. | 96 | Ingleson, W., Fl. Sub.- | | ——— G. C., Capt. | 98 | ——— S. M., 2/Lt. ... | 78 |
| ——— L. G., Lieut. | 131 | Lt. ... ... ... | 177 | ——— H. P., 2/Lt. ... | 37 | ——— W. D., Capt. | 23 |
| Humphries, E. A., Capt., | | Inglis, A. G., Capt. | 174 | ——— L. E., Lieut., | | ——— W., Lieut. ... | 189 |
| M.C. ... ... ... | 62 | ——— D. A., Sub-Lt. | 144 | M.C. ... | 92 | ——— W. C., Hon. Lt. | |
| Hungerford, S. A. H. | | Ingram, J., 2/Lt. ... | 137 | ——— L. R., Lieut. | 173 | and Qtmr. ... | 144 |
| Capt. ... ... | 184 | ——— L. J. W., Obs. | 164 | ——— M. A., Capt. | | ——— W. J., 2/Lt. | 173 |
| Hunt, A. S., 2/Lt. ... | 120 | ——— R. S. S., Capt. | 168 | M.C. ... | 61 | ——— W. W., Capt. | 140 |
| ——— B. P. G., Lieut | 150 | Inman, H. ... ... | 161 | ——— O., 2/Lt. ... | 50 | Johnston, B., 2/Lt. ... | 92 |
| ——— C. B., 2/Lt. | 75 | ——— T. E., 2/Lt. ... | 77 | Jameson, W. C., Sub.-Lt. | 181 | ——— B. L., Lieut. | 138 |
| ——— George, 2/Lt. | 96 | Insall, G. S. M., V.C., | | Jamieson, J. W., 2/Lt. | 102 | ——— E. W., 2/Lt.... | 109 |
| ——— K., 2/Lt. ... | 163 | 2/Lt. ... ... | 147 | ——— P., 2/Lt. ... | 120 | ——— G. B., 2/Lt. ... | 179 |
| ——— K. F., 2/Lt. | 149 | Insoll, F. N., 2/Lt. ... | 150 | Jardine, S. H., Lieut. | 189 | ——— G. D., 2/Lt.... | 67 |
| ——— O. G., Capt. | 24 | Ireland, J. W., 2/Lt. ... | 31 | Jarvis, J. F., Lieut. | 81 | ——— G. I. O'F., | |
| ——— R. E. B., Capt | 146 | Ireland-Blackburne, | | ——— K., Lieut. | 139 | Lieut. ... | 111 |
| Hunter, G. D., 2/Lt. ... | 152 | G. M., Capt. ... | 63 | Jasper, H., 2/Lt. ... | 47 | ——— G. N. S., Lieut. | 145 |
| ——— H. C., Lieut. | 163 | Irvine, A. C., 2/Lt. ... | 98 | Jay, T. W., 2/Lt. ... | 150 | ——— J. E., Capt. ... | 158 |
| ——— J., 2/Lt. ... | 91 | ——— C. G. S., Lieut. | 23 | Jeff, R. N. W., 2/Lt. ... | 155 | ——— L. J., Capt. ... | 109 |
| ——— J., Lieut. ... | 103 | ——— W. F., 2/Lt. | 109 | Jefferd, W. W., Capt. ... | 148 | ——— M. A. B., Lieut. | 185 |
| ——— Philip W. | | Irwin, H. G. W., Lieut. | 71 | Jefferson, G. R., 2/Lt. | 27 | ——— T. P., 2/Lt. ... | 112 |
| Lieut. ... | 133 | ——— H. J., 2/Lt. ... | 144 | Jeffkins, E. C., 2/Lt. ... | 172 | ——— V. H., 2/Lt. ... | 64 |
| ——— R. G., 2/Lt. | 114 | ——— N. F., 2/Lt. ... | 110 | Jeffreys, C. J. N., 2/Lt. | 88 | ——— W., Sub.-Lt. | 144 |
| ——— Stanley, 2/Lt. | 108 | ——— R. B. W., 2/Lt. | 60 | ——— M. D. W., | | ——— W., Major | 184 |
| ——— Sam S., 2/Lt. | 59 | ——— R. V., Lieut. | 166 | Lieut. | 189 | ——— W. A., 2/Lt. ... | 170 |
| ——— W. E., Lieut. | 13 | ——— S. S., 2/Lt. ... | 117 | ——— P. J., 2/Lt. ... | 91 | ——— W. S., Lieut. | 112 |
| ——— Wm. P., 2/Lt. | 55 | Isaacs, J. B., 2/Lt. ... | 175 | Jeffs, C. H., Lieut. | 156 | Johnstone, B. D., D.C.M., | |
| ——— W. T., 2/Lt. | 122 | ——— K. E., Lieut. | 189 | Jehu, W. J., 2/Lt. ... | 41 | M.M., 2/Lt. ... | 66 |
| Hunter-Blair, D. W. | | Isbell, A. T., 2/Lt. ... | 160 | Jenkins, A., Major | 108 | ——— G. R., 2/Lt. ... | 107 |
| Lieut. ... ... | 106 | Isbister, W. J., Capt. ... | 133 | ——— T. M., Capt. | 181 | ——— J., 2/Lt. ... | 153 |
| Hurley, Albert, 2/Lt. | 62 | Ivamy, W. J., 2/Lt. ... | 160 | ——— B. P., 2/Lt. ... | 168 | Joicey, E., Lieut. ... | 9 |
| Hurrell, J. N., Lieut. ... | 37 | Ivens, J., 2/Lt. ... | 168 | ——— E., Capt. ... | 67 | ——— Edwin, 2/Lt. | 102 |
| Husband, A. L., 2/Lt. | 16 | ——— J. P., 2/Lt. ... | 29 | Jenkinson, B. P., 2/Lt. | 85 | Jolliffe, B. G., Capt. ... | 18 |
| ——— C.E.P., Capt. | 132 | Ives, E., 2/Lt. ... | 80 | ——— T., Major | 186 | ——— C. J., Capt. ... | 54 |
| Huss, Thos. C. S., Lieut. | 73 | ——— F. J., Lieut.... | 25 | Jenks, J. L., Lieut. | 180 | Jones, A. B., 2/Lt. ... | 181 |
| Hustwitt, S. A., Lieut. | 162 | Ivey, T., Capt. ... | 187 | Jenner, P. C., Lieut. | 173 | ——— A. Basil, Lieut. | 119 |
| Hutcheon, Allen G. 2/Lt | 15 | Ivison, B. M., 2/Lt. ... | 94 | Jennings, C., Capt. ... | 7 | ——— Alex. D., Capt. | 19 |
| Hutcheson, W.B., Lieut. | 155 | Izod, F., 2/Lt. ... | 89 | ——— C. C., 2/Lt. ... | 104 | ——— A. D. R., Lieut. | 164 |
| Hutchings,V.R.L.,Lieut. | 121 | | | ——— E. D., 2/Lt. ... | 152 | ——— A. J., 2/Lt. ... | 188 |
| ——— W. M. M., | | Jack, G. W., 2/Lt. ... | 119 | ——— J. C. V., 2/Lt. | 98 | ——— A. M., 2/Lt. ... | 98 |
| Sub-Lt. ... | 145 | Jackman, J. R., 2/Lt. ... | 164 | ——— J. E., 2/Lt. ... | 173 | ——— A. R., 2/Lt. ... | 29 |
| ——— W. R., Capt. | 61 | Jackson, Lt. ... | 166 | ——— J. L., 2/Lt. ... | 81 | ——— A. R., Lieut. | 166 |
| Hutchins, A.J.A., 2/Lt. | 69 | ——— A., Lieut. ... | 120 | ——— L. H., 2/Lt. ... | 66 | ——— A. V., 2/Lt. ... | 162 |
| Hutchinson, C.A., Capt. | 84 | ——— A. R., Capt· | 22 | ——— L. N., Lieut. ... | 137 | ——— C. C., Capt. ... | 134 |
| ——— C. D., Lieut. | 155 | ——— A. T., 2/Lt. ... | 70 | Jenyns, C. G., Lieut. ... | 164 | ——— C. E. M., Capt. | 186 |
| ——— J., Capt. ... | 101 | ——— C. H., 2/Lt. ... | 88 | Jerrard, A., V.C., Lieut. | 161 | ——— David, 2/Lt. | 56 |
| ——— J. P., Lieut. | 14 | ——— E. A., Capt. ... | 54 | Jervis, B. A., 2/Lt. ... | 178 | ——— D. O., Lt. ... | 57 |
| ——— Miles, Lieut. | 99 | ——— F. H., Lieut. | 146 | ——— H. S., Capt. ... | 113 | ——— Ernest, 2/Lt. | 32 |
| ——— W.H.H., Major | 13 | ——— F. McN., 2/Lt. | 13 | Jessop, H. T., Capt. ... | 76 | ——— E., 2/Lt. ... | 83 |
| ——— W. J., Lieut. | 166 | ——— H. A., 2/Lt. | 90 | Jewett, F. F., Lieut. ... | 171 | ——— Evan, 2/Lt. ... | 96 |
| Hutchison, C. K., Capt. | 18 | ——— G. G., Lieut.... | 159 | Jimenez, A. J., Major ... | 84 | ——— E. C., Lieut. | 122 |
| ——— J., 2/Lt. ... | 11 | ——— G. G., Capt. ... | 75 | Joberns, A. J., 2/Lt. ... | 118 | ——— E. D., 2/Lt. ... | 119 |
| Hutson, H., 2/Lt. ... | 86 | ——— H. B., Major | 43 | Jobson, M., Major ... | 104 | ——— E. H., 2/Lt. ... | 181 |
| Hutton, J. L., 2/Lt. ... | 81 | ——— H. M., 2/Lt. | 47 | John, D. M., 2/Lt. ... | 173 | ——— E. H., Capt. ... | 134 |
| ——— T.W.M., 2/Lt. | 67 | ——— J. A., 2/Lt. ... | 80 | ——— J. H., Capt. ... | 45 | ——— E. H., Major | 10 |
| Huxley, H. W., Capt. | 53 | ——— J. B., 2/Lt. ... | 26 | Johns, R. A. P., Lieut. | 153 | ——— E. H., 2/Lt. ... | 81 |
| Hyde, E. P., 2/Lt. ... | 188 | ——— J. L., Lieut. ... | 131 | ——— R. C., 2/Lt. ... | 66 | ——— E. H., 2/Lt.... | 62 |
| ——— Herbert E. | | ——— J. V. R., Capt | 22 | ——— T. M., Lieut. | 149 | ——— E. L., 2/Lt. ... | 35 |
| Lieut. ... | 172 | ——— P. E., 2/Lt. ... | 78 | ——— W. E., 2/Lt.... | 171 | ——— F. B., 2/Lt. ... | 12 |
| Hyslop, A. L., 2/Lt. ... | 116 | ——— R. W., Lieut. | 30 | Johnson, A., 2/Lt. ... | 163 | ——— F. V., Lieut. | 139 |
| | | ——— S. C. F., Lt. | | ——— B., Capt. ... | 131 | ——— G. A., Capt., | |
| J'Anson, H., 2/Lt. ... | 101 | Col., D.S.O. | 69 | ——— C. S., Lieut. | 43 | M.C. ... | 30 |
| Ibbotson, H., 2/Lt. ... | 156 | ——— S. A., 2/Lt. ... | 97 | ——— E., Capt. ... | 43 | ——— G. Lewis, Capt. | 133 |
| Ibbott, W., 2/Lt. ... | 85 | ——— S. S. I., 2/Lt. | 40 | ——— E. F., 2/Lt. ... | 83 | ——— G. V., 2/Lt. ... | 87 |
| Icke, J., Lieut. ... | 71 | ——— W. E., Lieut. | 167 | ——— F. R., Lieut. | 171 | ——— H., 2/Lt. ... | 81 |
| Iles, R. V., Lieut. ... | 101 | ——— W. R., 2/Lt. | 169 | ——— F. W. B., Capt. | 100 | ——— H. B., Capt. ... | 133 |
| Ilett, F. C., Lieut. ... | 29 | Jacob, F. W., Lieut. ... | 120 | ——— H., Col. ... | 98 | ——— H. B., 2/Lt.... | 123 |
| Illingworth, C. F. W., | | ——— G. P. S., 2/Lt. | 21 | ——— H., 2/Lt. ... | 138 | ——— H. E., Lt. ... | 185 |
| 2/Lt. ... ... | 167 | Jacobs, A. H., 2/Lt. ... | 96 | ——— H. L., 2/Lt. ... | 26 | ——— H. F., 2/Lt. | 125 |
| ——— F. W., 2/Lt. | 153 | ——— G. S., Lieut. | 54 | ——— J. H., Lieut. | 163 | ——— H. G., 2/Lt. | 123 |
| ——— H. C. H., Capt. | 94 | ——— T. C., 2/Lt. ... | 67 | ——— J. W., Lieut. | 145 | ——— H. J., 2/Lt. ... | 48 |
| ——— O., Capt. ... | 42 | Jaggers, W. H., Lieut.... | 9 | ——— J. W. E., 2/Lt. | 35 | ——— J. C., 2/Lt. ... | 55 |
| Ince, W. H., 2/Lt. ... | 80 | Jago, J. W., 2/Lt. ... | 78 | ——— K. L., 2/Lt. ... | 137 | ——— J. W., Lieut. | 134 |
| Inge, R., Lieut. ... | 176 | James, C. E. H., Capt.... | 72 | | | ——— Leonard, Lieut | 97 |

|  | PAGE |
|---|---|
| Jones, Llewellin, 2/Lt., | 56 |
| ——— L. E., Capt. | 119 |
| ——— M. B., 2/Lt. | 32 |
| ——— Percy J., 2/Lt. | 39 |
| ——— R. G. M., 2/Lt. | 12 |
| ——— R. H. H., Lieut. | 8 |
| ——— R. L., Capt. | 10 |
| ——— S. E., Capt. | 44 |
| ——— S. L., Major | 139 |
| ——— S. T., 2/Lt. | 57 |
| ——— T. B., Lieut. | 30 |
| ——— V. E., 2/Lt. | 125 |
| ——— W. G., 2/Lt. | 63 |
| ——— W. G. S., Capt | 88 |
| ——— W. H., 2/Lt. | 157 |
| ——— W. O., Lieut. | 123 |
| ——— W. R., 2/Lt. | 55 |
| Jones-Lloyd, O. J. F., Lieut. | 164 |
| Jonsson, A. T., Capt. | 108 |
| Jordan, G. B., 2/Lt. | 55 |
| ——— Henry, Lieut. | 47 |
| ——— S. R., Lieut. | 178 |
| ——— T. C., 2/Lt. | 57 |
| ——— W. A., Capt. | 71 |
| Joseph, H. H., Capt. | 101 |
| Josephs, L. H.O., Capt. | 87 |
| Josland, A., 2/Lt. | 81 |
| Jotcham, W. E. S., 2/Lt. | 130 |
| Joule, A., Lieut. | 111 |
| Jowett, E., 2/Lt. | 40 |
| ——— H. E., 2/Lt. | 41 |
| Joyce, W., Lieut. | 147 |
| Joyes, W., 2/Lt. | 14 |
| Joynson, R., Capt. | 58 |
| Jubb, G. B., 2/Lt. | 85 |
| Judkins, O. V., 2/Lt. | 173 |
| Judge F., Capt. | 53 |
| Julius, S., Major | 186 |
| Jump, H., Capt. | 8 |
| Juriss, M., 2/Lt. | 128 |
| Justice, H. M., Lieut. | 180 |
| Kaizer, M. M., 2/Lt. | 152 |
| Kane, H. F., Capt. | 134 |
| ——— M.H.K., Lieut | 165 |
| Kantel, F. W., Lieut. | 153 |
| Karney, A. B. L., Rev. | 135 |
| Kay, E. O., Capt. | 70 |
| ——— H., Lieut. | 123 |
| ——— Harold Isherwood, 2/Lt. | 117 |
| ——— J. R., 2/Lt. | 59 |
| Kearney, P. W., 2/Lt. | 186 |
| Keating, O. J. F., Major | 98 |
| ——— W. F., Lieut. | 13 |
| Keay, R. A., Capt. | 136 |
| Keeble, Francis John, 2/Lt. | 168 |
| Keeling, E. H., 2/Lt. | 184 |
| ——— F. W., 2/Lt. | 96 |
| ——— John, 2/Lt. | 79 |
| Keen, S. H., 2/Lt. | 118 |
| Keene, H., Lyndon 2/Lt | 29 |
| Keighley, E., 2/Lt. | 42 |
| Keightley, G. S., 2/Lt. | 38 |
| Keiller, J. M. R., Capt. | 74 |
| Kelk, C. Kingston, Lieut | 49 |
| Keller, C. F., Lieut. | 158 |
| Kellog, W. B., 2/Lt. | 154 |
| Kelly, A., Capt., M.C. | 106 |
| ——— C. C., Lieut. | 87 |
| ——— C.Moore, 2/Lt. | 149 |
| ——— H., Major | 131 |
| ——— H. B., Lt.-Col. | 134 |
| ——— J. M., 2/Lt. | 173 |

|  | PAGE |
|---|---|
| Kelly, R., 2/Lt. | 167 |
| ——— R. J., 2/Lt. | 48 |
| ——— W., 2/Lt. | 62 |
| Kelsall, C. H., Lieut. | 51 |
| ——— J., Capt. | 71 |
| Kemble, A. F., 2/Lt. | 37 |
| Kemp, Fred, Lieut. | 165 |
| ——— H. T., 2/Lt. | 147 |
| ——— J. E., 2/Lt. | 170 |
| ——— N. H., 2/Lt. | 157 |
| ——— P., 2/Lt. | 164 |
| ——— W. J., 2/Lt. | 130 |
| Kempson, H. L., 2/Lt. | 109 |
| Kempton, F., 2/Lt. | 99 |
| Kendall, Sidney, 2/Lt. | 158 |
| ——— W. J., Lieut. | 32 |
| Kennard, C., 2/Lt. | 149 |
| Kennedy, A. K., Capt. | 136 |
| ——— C. A., 2/Lt. | 17 |
| ——— C. J., 2/Lt. | 148 |
| ——— F. E., 2/Lt. | 114 |
| ——— J., Major | 132 |
| ——— J. A. C., 2/Lt. | 109 |
| ——— J. O. N., 2/Lt. | 33 |
| ——— P. A., 2/Lt. | 118 |
| ——— W. H., 2/Lt. | 84 |
| Kennett, L. H., Lieut. | 22 |
| Kent, A. L., 2/Lt. | 113 |
| ——— G.C.H., Capt. | 94 |
| ——— J.A.V., Lieut., M.C. | 111 |
| ——— R. Leslie, Sub-Lt. | 177 |
| ——— T. J., 2/Lt. | 158 |
| Kent-Jones, D.W., Lieut. | 160 |
| Keppel, A. R., Capt. | 85 |
| ——— R. O. D., Capt. the Hon. | 18 |
| Ker, A. E., Lieut. | 123 |
| Kerr, A., 2/Lt. | 74 |
| ——— C., 2/Lt. | 148 |
| ——— S. J., 2/Lt. | 26 |
| Kert, L., Lieut. | 158 |
| Kettle, W. R. B., 2/Lt. | 128 |
| Kevill-Davies, H. S., Capt. | 106 |
| Kewley, B. H., Lieut. | 172 |
| Keyes, Cleveland, Major | 14 |
| Keys, S., 2/Lt. | 95 |
| Kidd, A. L., 2/Lt. | 159 |
| Kidder, W. S. G., Lieut. | 166 |
| Kier, J. N., 2/Lt. | 172 |
| Kiernander, O. G., 2/Lt. | 183 |
| Kilbourne, Watson H., Lieut. | 168 |
| Kilburn, Frank S., 2/Lt. | 15 |
| Killick, C. H. P., 2/Lt. | 170 |
| Killin, J., 2/Lt. | 179 |
| Killingback, H. C., Capt. | 87 |
| Killingsworth, H. L., 2/Lt. | 138 |
| Kilpatrick, W. J., Lieut. | 137 |
| Kilsby, M. J., Lieut. | 138 |
| Kinahan, J. H., 2/Lt. | 117 |
| Kincaid-Smith, M. A., Capt. | 103 |
| Kinder, M. Fitzgerald, Capt. | 121 |
| King, A. E., 2/Lt. | 129 |
| ——— C. H., 2/Lt. | 87 |
| ——— C. L., 2/Lt. | 49 |
| ——— C. L., Capt., M.C., D.F.C. | 175 |
| ——— C. M., 2/Lt. | 128 |
| ——— D. B., Capt. | 158 |
| ——— E. A., 2/Lt. | 22 |

|  | PAGE |
|---|---|
| King, E. S., 2/Lt. | 89 |
| ——— F. L., Capt. | 31 |
| ——— F. W., 2/Lt. | 171 |
| ——— G. G., S/Lt. | 125 |
| ——— G. H., 2/Lt. | 115 |
| ——— G. L., 2/Lt. | 98 |
| ——— G. P., 2/Lt. | 34 |
| ——— Harold, Capt. | 184 |
| ——— John P., 2/Lt. | 34 |
| ——— J. T., 2/Lt. | 91 |
| ——— P., 2/Lt. | 174 |
| ——— P. P., Lieut. | 61 |
| ——— S., 2/Lt. | 55 |
| ——— Wm., 2/Lt. | 67 |
| King-Smith, P. E., 2/Lt. | 94 |
| Kingdom, S. St. G. S., Capt. | 29 |
| Kingham, R. L., 2/Lt. | 172 |
| Kingsland, W. R., 2/Lt. | 158 |
| Kininmonth, D., Capt., M.C. | 19 |
| Kinloch, H. T., Capt. | 103 |
| Kinnes, J. R., Lieut. | 20 |
| Kinniburgh, R. C., 2/Lt. | 109 |
| Kippen, E. D., 2/Lt. | 117 |
| Kirby, F. B., Lieut. | 15 |
| Kirby, H., 2/Lt. | 152 |
| ——— L. L., 2/Lt. | 130 |
| Kirk, K. L., Capt. | 51 |
| Kirkcaldy, G. T., Lieut. | 73 |
| Kirkby, J. W., 2/Lt. | 99 |
| Kirkham F. J., 2/Lt. | 152 |
| Kirkland, F. A., Lieut. | 119 |
| ——— G., Lieut. | 138 |
| Kirkman, R. K., Capt. | 161 |
| Kirkpatrick, A.E., Major | 138 |
| ——— John., 2/Lt. | 142 |
| ——— S., 2/Lt. | 50 |
| ——— T. R., 2/Lt. | 69 |
| Kirkup, J. G., Capt. | 28 |
| ——— W. S., 2/Lt. | 100 |
| Kirkwood, C. H., Capt. | 182 |
| ——— H. S., 2/Lt. | 111 |
| Kirwan, C. K., 2/Lt. | 114 |
| Kissack, A. H., Lieut. | 55 |
| Kitch, A. W., 2/Lt. | 80 |
| Kitchen, E., 2/Lt. | 72 |
| Kitching, G. C., Capt. | 130 |
| Klingenstein, G., Lieut. | 149 |
| Knapp, F. R., Lieut. | 161 |
| Kneller, F. Kneller, 2/Lt. | 160 |
| Knight, C., Lieut. | 174 |
| ——— C. C., Lieut. | 154 |
| ——— C. G., Fl.-Sub-Lt. | 176 |
| ——— G. F., Lieut. | 149 |
| ——— H. W., Lieut. | 98 |
| ——— J. E. M., 2/Lt. | 22 |
| ——— N. L., 2/Lt. | 151 |
| ——— P. C., Capt. | 104 |
| Knight-Bruce, J. H. W., Capt. | 28 |
| Kniveton, F. M., 2/Lt. | 32 |
| Knott, H. W., 2/Lt. | J119 |
| Knowlden, W. E., 2/Lt. | 149 |
| Knowles, B. M., 2/Lt. | 94 |
| ——— M. B., Capt. | 151 |
| Knox, R. S., Lieut. | 107 |
| Knox Shaw, P., Major | 79 |
| Koop, C., 2/Lt. | 89 |
| Koplik, G. W., 2/Lt. | 44 |
| Krook, A. D. C., Capt. | 73 |
| Kruger, Max, 2/Lt. | 45 |
| **Labatt**, W. H. E., 2/Lt. | 166 |
| Labother, Lieut. | 182 |

|  | PAGE |
|---|---|
| Labouchere, A. M., Major | 75 |
| Lacey, G. Wm., 2/Lt. | 26 |
| Lacy, J. B., Lieut. | 171 |
| ——— R. S., Lieut. | 187 |
| Ladler, J., Lieut. | 139 |
| Lagden, F. C. W., 2/Lt. | 88 |
| Laing, J. D., 2/Lt. | 157 |
| ——— S. Van B., Capt. | 183 |
| ——— W. F., Capt. | 101 |
| Laird, D. A., Capt. | 131 |
| ——— F. M., 2/Lt. | 114 |
| Lamb, F. O., 2/Lt. | 41 |
| ——— F.W.M., Lieut. | 134 |
| ——— G. W., Lieut. | 34 |
| ——— H. L., Capt. | 129 |
| ——— J. M., 2/Lt. | 44 |
| Lambert, A., 2/Lt. | 27 |
| ——— C. J., Capt. | 20 |
| ——— F. W. M., 2/Lt. | 70 |
| ——— R., 2/Lt. | 36 |
| ——— S. C., 2/Lt. | 31 |
| Lambie, J. B., Lieut. | 46 |
| Lamble, A. B., Lieut. | 145 |
| Lamont, John C., 2/Lt. | 121 |
| ——— W., 2/Lt. | 162 |
| Lamport, A. J., Lieut. | 121 |
| Lanagan, A., Capt. | 136 |
| Lander, T. E., Lieut. | 180 |
| ——— T. E., Capt. | 176 |
| Landers, J., 2/Lt. | 125 |
| Landreth, T. A., 2/Lt. | 63 |
| Lane, C. W., 2/Lt. | 153 |
| ——— E. D., 2/Lt. | 123 |
| ——— F. O., 2/Lt. | 119 |
| ——— G. E. W., Capt. | 114 |
| ——— J. R. C., 2/Lt. | 35 |
| ——— L. C., | 162 |
| ——— T. W., 2/Lt. | 89 |
| ——— W. S., Lieut. | 145 |
| Lane-Davies, J. G., Capt. Rev. | 135 |
| Lane-Roberts, E.G., 2/Lt. | 46 |
| Lang, A., Lieut. | 186 |
| Langford, S. J., 2/Lt. | 16 |
| Langley, L., 2/Lt. | 27 |
| ——— R., 2/Lt. | 50 |
| ——— R. K., Lieut. | 130 |
| Langner, D. A. J., 2/Lt. | 12 |
| Langran, W. H., Lieut. | 39 |
| Langston, N., Lieut. | 83 |
| Lanham, F. W., Lieut. | 66 |
| Lansdale, E. C., Lieut. | 173 |
| ——— H., 2/Lt. | 175 |
| Lansley, H., Lieut. | 68 |
| Lanyon, T. S., 2/Lt., M.C. | 86 |
| Lapworth, C., Capt. | 69 |
| Larcombe, A. H., 2/Lt. | 67 |
| Larder, F., 2/Lt. | 47 |
| Larkin, E. P., Lieut. | 182 |
| Larrabee, E. P., Lieut. | 172 |
| Lart, E. L. B., Lieut. | 71 |
| Latham, Arthur S., Lieut. | 23 |
| ——— C., 2/Lt. | 62 |
| ——— H., 2/Lt. | 118 |
| Latimer, D., Capt., M.C. | 168 |
| Latta, A. Stuart, 2/Lt. | 72 |
| Lattimer, J. E., Capt. | 140 |
| Lauder, I. A., Lieut. | 122 |
| ——— J., Lieut. | 131 |
| Lauderdale, W. A., 2/Lt. | 64 |
| Laughland, N. A., 2/Lt. | 74 |
| Laurence, C., Fl.-Lt. | 177 |
| Laurenson, D. G., Lieut. | 9 |
| Laurie, K. S., 2/Lt. | 166 |

| Name | Page | Name | Page | Name | Page | Name | Page |
|---|---|---|---|---|---|---|---|
| Laverack, E., Capt. | 43 | Leigh, F. G., Lieut. | 29 | Liddell, A. R., Lieut. | 27 | Lodge, C. F., Lieut. | 150 |
| Law, B., 2/Lt. | 57 | ——— J., Lieut. | 100 | ——— H. H., 2/Lt. | 90 | ——— H. J., 2/Lt. | 36 |
| ——— C., Major | 93 | Leigh-Bennett, P. R., 2/Lt. | 183 | Lidiard, H. S., Capt. | 127 | Lofthouse, G., 2/Lt. | 51 |
| ——— C. B., 2/Lt. | 163 | Leighton, A. A., Sub.-Lt. | 144 | Liefeldt, A. W., Capt. | 141 | Loftus, W., 2/Lt. | 115 |
| ——— C. H., 2/Lt. | 80 | ——— Gordon, Lieut. | 142 | Liggett, M., Lieut. | 96 | Logan, G. C., 2/Lt. | 159 |
| ——— E. R., 2/Lt. | 152 | ——— J., Lieut. | 31 | Light, D. O., Lieut. | 89 | ——— J., Lieut. | 16 |
| ——— J. R., Lieut. | 159 | ——— K. A. W., Lieut. | 169 | Lightbourne, A. H., Capt. | 140 | ——— R. A., Capt. | 151 |
| ——— W. K., Capt. | 67 | ——— R. T., Lieut. | 155 | Lilley, W. D. N., Lieut. | 33 | ——— V. D. O., Capt. | 131 |
| Lawe, A. G., Lieut. | 168 | ——— T. W., Capt. | 133 | Lilly, H. H., 2/Lt. | 77 | Lomax, A. K., 2/Lt. | 161 |
| ——— F. W., Capt. | 44 | Leishman, W., Capt. | 71 | Lindley, A., Capt. | 172 | ——— C. N. L., 2/Lt. | 156 |
| Lawes, J. H., Lieut. | 44 | Leith, P. Fredk., 2/Lt. | 103 | ——— G. R. C. D., Lt. | 81 | ——— J. G., Lieut. | 10 |
| Lawrence, C. J., Lieut. | 139 | Leith-Hay-Clark, N., Lt.-Col. | 28 | Lindop, V. S. E., Lieut. | 146 | London, F. J., Lieut. | 94 |
| ——— C. W., 2/Lt. | 63 | Leithead, W. B., 2/Lt. | 32 | Lindsay, A. T. W., 2/Lt. | 160 | Lonergan, C. J., Capt. | 65 |
| ——— E. I., 2/Lt. | 24 | Leivers, F. A., Lieut. | 39 | ——— H. J., 2/Lt. | 90 | Lones, R. E., Lieut. | 126 |
| ——— J., 2/Lt. | 82 | Leman, L. L. L., Lieut. | 81 | ——— J., Capt., M.C. | 74 | Long, B. E., 2/Lt. | 84 |
| ——— S. C., Lieut. | 45 | Le Mesurier, H. F. A., Major | 56 | Line, W. W., 2/Lt. | 30 | ——— F. W., 2/Lt. | 10 |
| Lawrie, W., 2/Lt., M.M. | 20 | Lemon, A. B., Capt. | 45 | Lines, T. H., 2/Lt. | 153 | ——— G. R., Lieut. | 156 |
| Lawson, A. N., 2/Lt. | 25 | ——— G. H., 2/Lt. | 110 | Lingard, J. E., Lieut. | 152 | ——— H., Major | 131 |
| ——— F. G., Lieut. | 140 | Lennard, R. G., 2/Lt. | 28 | Linge, C. E., Capt. | 66 | ——— H. O., Lieut. | 148 |
| ——— P., 2/Lt. | 49 | Lennox, G. S., Lieut. | 140 | Lingwood, C. R., Capt. | 26 | Longdon, W. F., 2/Lt. | 12 |
| ——— R. G., 2/Lt. | 161 | Le Patourel, E., Lieut. | 184 | Linnell, H. G. B., Fl.-Sub.-Lt. | 157 | Longland, C. V., 2/Lt. | 50 |
| ——— T. D., 2/Lt. | 27 | Lepper, A. W., 2/Lt. | 86 | Linsley, F., 2/Lt. | 43 | Longmuir, J. B., 2/Lt. | 16 |
| ——— W. D., Lieut. | 120 | Le Ray, Hugh G., Lieut. | 11 | Lipp, G. R., Capt., M.C. | 132 | Longworth, T., 2/Lt. | 97 |
| ——— G. R. W., 2/Lt. | 120 | Leresche, G., Lieut. | 97 | Lipscomb, J. K., Lieut. | 124 | Lonsdale, V. O., 2/Lt. | 150 |
| Lawton, J. B., Lieut. | 149 | Le Roy, H. L., Lieut. | 163 | Lipsett, R. S., 2/Lt. | 171 | Lord, G., 2/Lt. | 13 |
| Lax, W. L., 2/Lt. | 17 | Lerwill, O., 2/Lt. | 147 | Lister, B. S., 2/Lt. | 153 | ——— T. V., 2/Lt. | 157 |
| Laycock, C., Capt. | 16 | Lescher, F. G., Major | 134 | ——— C. H., 2/Lt. | 102 | Loudan, S. M., 2/Lt. | 82 |
| ——— L. J. P., 2/Lt. | 82 | Leslie, D., Capt. | 137 | ——— E. A., Lieut. | 49 | Loudoun, L. G., Capt. | 169 |
| Lazarus-Barlow, A. J., 2/Lt. | 179 | ——— G., 2/Lt. | 119 | ——— G. D., Capt. | 83 | Lough, J. W., Lieut. | 25 |
| Lea, R. H. M., 2/Lt. | 92 | ——— H. H., Lieut. | 123 | ——— J., Lieut. | 176 | Loughbridge, J. A., Lieut. | 133 |
| Leach, A., 2/Lt. | 72 | Leslie-Moore, A., 2/Lt. | 188 | Litt, C. E. R., Capt. | 87 | Loupinski, J., Lieut. | 165 |
| ——— C. H., 2/Lt. | 75 | Lesley, J. W., Capt. | 90 | Little, A. H., Capt. | 133 | Lovatt, J. M., 2/Lt. | 91 |
| ——— J. M., Lieut. | 158 | Lesmond, C., 2/Lt. | 183 | ——— C. B., Capt. | 65 | Love, G. M., Sub.-Lt. | 144 |
| ——— R., 2/Lt. | 42 | Lester, G. E., 2/Lt. | 128 | ——— E., 2/Lt. | 75 | ——— H. K., Lieut. | 138 |
| ——— Wilfred L. W. | 118 | Letchworth, H. M., Capt. | 113 | ——— J. C., Lieut. | 140 | ——— J. H. A., Lieut. | 45 |
| Leadbitter, C. O., 2/Lt. | 18 | Lethbridge, E., Lt.-Col. | 187 | ——— J. W., 2/Lt. | 68 | Lovejoy, H. R., Lieut. | 136 |
| Leader, Leonard, Capt. | 60 | ——— H. W., 2/Lt. | 115 | ——— O. H., Lieut. | 179 | Lovell, C. E. A., 2/Lt. | 167 |
| Leahy, M. B., Civil Surg. | 131 | Leverton, H. S., Lieut. | 66 | ——— W. S., 2/Lt. | 33 | ——— G. B., Lieut. | 129 |
| Leathard, L. F., 2/Lt. | 27 | Leveson-Gower, J., Lieut. | 170 | Littledale, J. F., Lieut. | 86 | Low, W. T., 2/Lt. | 20 |
| Leather, V. S., 2/Lt. | 83 | Levett, E., 2/Lt. | 69 | Littlewood, J., 2/Lt. | 40 | Lowe, F. H., 2/Lt. | 33 |
| Leavitt, H. J., Lieut. | 162 | Levey, E., 2/Lt. | 84 | ——— S. C. T., Lieut. | 147 | ——— G. P., 2/Lt. | 92 |
| Leckler, A. N., 2/Lt. | 151 | Levy, J. M. D'Arcy, Midshipman | 176 | Living, C. H., 2/Lt. | 170 | ——— J. W., 2/Lt. | 83 |
| Lecky, R., Lieut. | 184 | Lewes, F. H. M., Capt. & Adjt. | 77 | Livingstone, W. E., 2/Lt. | 58 | ——— P., Capt. | 39 |
| Leckyand, Lieut. | 182 | Lewis, Archibald | 166 | Llewelin, L., Lieut. | 126 | ——— T. G., 2/Lt. | 126 |
| Ledgard, R., Capt. | 48 | ——— A. D. M., Sub.-Lt. | 177 | Llewellin, M. C., Capt. | 126 | ——— W. A., 2/Lt. | 16 |
| Ledger, H. G., 2/Lt. | 75 | ——— C. J., 2/Lt. | 50 | Llewellyn, W. E., 2/Lt. | 144 | ——— W. J. M., Lieut. | 9 |
| Lee, A. C., Lieut. | 153 | ——— C. S., 2/Lt. | 88 | Llewellyn-Davies, G., Lieut. | 176 | Lowes, E. J., 2/Lt. | 100 |
| ——— E. B., Lieut. | 160 | ——— D. F., Lieut. | 177 | Lloyd, A. C., Lieut. | 168 | Lowndes, R. C., Capt. | 185 |
| ——— F. G., Lieut. | 47 | ——— D. G., 2/Lt. | 161 | ——— C. B. E., Lieut. | 172 | Lowson, G. F., Lieut. | 116 |
| ——— Joseph J., 2/Lt. | 91 | ——— D. R., 2/Lt. | 124 | ——— E. A., Capt. | 57 | ——— J. H., Lieut. | 149 |
| ——— J. L., Capt., M.C. | 51 | ——— F. S. J. McK. | 73 | ——— E. A. L., 2/Lt. | 153 | ——— S. G., 2/Lt. | 76 |
| ——— M. C., Lieut. | 181 | ——— F. W., 2/Lt. | 12 | ——— E. R., Capt. | 60 | Loyd, E. E. F., 2/Lt. | 156 |
| ——— R. A., Lieut. | 15 | ——— G. T. M., 2/Lt. | 84 | ——— G. C., 2/Lt. | 38 | Luard, R. B., Lieut. | 169 |
| Leech, A. C., 2/Lt. | 76 | ——— H. G., 2/Lt. | 175 | ——— G. P., Lieut. | 86 | Lucas, A. S., Capt. | 116 |
| ——— C. J. F., Capt. | 10 | ——— H. M., 2/Lt. | 154 | ——— H. W. C., Capt. | 93 | ——— J. M., Capt. | 28 |
| ——— J. C., Capt. | 146 | ——— H. S., Lieut. | 139 | ——— J. P., Lieut. | 170 | ——— S., Lieut. | 90 |
| Leembruggen, R. A., Capt. | 133 | ——— H. T., 2/Lt. | 137 | ——— J. W., Major | 17 | ——— W. J., 2/Lt. | 45 |
| Lees, A., Capt. | 150 | ——— John S., 2/Lt. | 57 | ——— O. S., Major | 185 | Luff, R. G. R., 2/Lt. | 12 |
| ——— J. C., 2/Lt. | 149 | ——— M., 2/Lt. | 151 | ——— R. B., 2/Lt. | 188 | Luffingham, L. J., Lieut. | 89 |
| ——— P. R., 2/Lt. | 26 | ——— N. A., Major | 31 | Lloyd-Atkins, J. R., 2/Lt. | 120 | Lumley, A. F., 2/Lt. | 126 |
| Leeson, D., Lieut. | 146 | ——— R. G., 2/Lt. | 164 | Loch, A. C., 2/Lt. | 184 | Lumsden, A. C., Lieut. | 139 |
| Leeson-Ball, T. Major | 185 | ——— R. P., Asst. Surg. | 182 | Lochhead, A. G., 2/Lt. | 53 | Lunn, H. K., Sub.-Lt. | 144 |
| Le Fevre, F. E., 2/Lt. | 159 | ——— P. S., Lieut. | 181 | Locke, C. J., Lieut. | 176 | ——— J. J., 2/Lt. | 100 |
| Lefroy, C. B. H., Lieut. | 167 | ——— T. C., 2/Lt. | 114 | ——— G. H., Lieut. | 171 | Luscombe, L. H., 2/Lt. | 178 |
| Le Gallais, A., Capt. | 53 | ——— W. T. S., 2/Lt. | 169 | ——— H. M., 2/Lt. | 33 | Lusty, R. A., 2/Lt. | 69 |
| Legg, W., Capt. | 16 | Leybourne, E. A., Capt. | 101 | ——— P. J., Capt. | 138 | Luscombe, B. P., Lieut. | 10 |
| Leggatt, E. W., Capt. | 148 | Leyson, B. W. de B., Lieut. | 164 | Lockhart, F. R., Lieut. | 118 | Luther, A. C. G., Capt. | 85 |
| ——— C. W., Lieut. | 159 | | | Lockhead, R. O., 2/Lt. | 59 | ——— H. G., 2/Lt. | 175 |
| Legge, W., Capt. | 105 | | | Lockey, B., 2/Lt. | 174 | Luxmoore, F. L., Capt. | 160 |
| Le Grand, H. | 7 | | | Lockwood, G. F., 2/Lt. | 48 | Lycett, N. L., Capt. | 135 |
| Le Hunte, J., Lieut. | 69 | | | Loder-Symmonds, W., Lieut. | 93 | Lyle, A. M. A., 2/Lt. | 87 |
| Le Huquet, G., Capt. | 93 | | | Lodge, F. C., Lt.-Col. | 186 | Lymer, L., 2/Lt. | 52 |
| Leicester, G. W. F., Lieut. | 54 | | | | | Lynch, J. P., Capt. | 131 |
| | | | | | | ——— S. A., Lieut. | 109 |
| | | | | | | Lynch-Watson, H., 2/Lt. | 84 |

| | PAGE | | PAGE | | PAGE | | PAGE |
|---|---|---|---|---|---|---|---|
| Lynes, W. P., Capt. | 90 | MacDonald, Alex., Fl.-Sub.-Lt. | 177 | MacKay, Alex., Lieut. | 103 | MacMahon, C. L., Capt. | 43 |
| ——— W. S., Capt. | 71 | ——— A. T. C., Capt. | 132 | ——— A. R., 2/Lt. | 36 | ——— L. S., Lieut. | 137 |
| Lynn, F., Lieut. | 175 | ——— D. A., Lieut. | 163 | ——— D., Asst. Surg. | 182 | MacManus, A. A. L., 2/Lt. | 108 |
| Lyon, M. M., 2/Lt. | 104 | ——— D. C., 2/Lt. | 175 | ——— D. R., 2/Lt. | 51 | ——— G. E., 2/Lt. | 171 |
| ——— M. C. H. B., Capt. Hon. | 20 | ——— D. P., 2/Lt. | 151 | ——— E. A., Capt., M.C., D.F.C. | 169 | ——— O. B., 2/Lt. | 110 |
| ——— P. H. B., Capt. | 100 | ——— E. W., Capt. | 58 | ——— G. G. W., Lieut. | 49 | McMechan, J., Capt. | 59 |
| ——— P. W., Lieut. | 106 | ——— F. H. C., Lieut. | 139 | ——— J. E., 2/Lt. | 59 | McMeeken, G. S. P., Capt. | 19 |
| ——— P. W., Lieut. | 137 | ——— H. O., Lieut. | 154 | ——— J. R., 2/Lt. | 107 | McMichael, G. B., Lieut. | 156 |
| ——— W. J. G., 2/Lt. | 137 | ——— I. G., 2/Lt. | 105 | ——— J. W. M., Lieut. | 105 | McMicking, H., Lt.-Col. | 19 |
| Lyons, F. J. W., 2/Lt. | 99 | ——— J., 2/Lt. | 105 | ——— N. D., Lieut. | 17 | McMillan, A., Capt. | 112 |
| Lyster, P., Capt. | 10 | ——— J., Lieut. | 169 | ——— P. W., 2/Lt. | 73 | ——— C. D., 2/Lt. | 179 |
| | | ——— J. C., 2/Lt. | 64 | ——— W. B., Lieut. | 154 | ——— J. F., 2/Lt. | 65 |
| MacAllan, P. R., Capt. | 59 | ——— J. C. J., 2/Lt. | 174 | Macky, F. C. S., Lieut. | 113 | ——— R. E., Fl. Sub-Lt. | 177 |
| McAllister, A., 2/Lt. | 115 | ——— J. J., Lieut. | 171 | McKeag, V. M., 2/Lt. | 114 | McMinn, H. H., Capt. | 137 |
| MacAlpine, Ian F., Lieut. | 135 | ——— K. W., Lieut. | 155 | MacKechnie. W., 2/Lt. | 115 | ——— W., 2/Lt. | 53 |
| McAnally, A. R., 2/Lt. | 81 | ——— N., Lieut. | 19 | McKechnie, W. L., 2/Lt. | 116 | McMullen, J. R., 2/Lt. | 83 |
| MacAndrew, P. M., Lieut. | 20 | ——— Roy, 2/Lt. | 159 | McKegney, E. W., Lieut. | 60 | McMurtrie, G. D. J., Capt. | 39 |
| McAndrew, W., 2/Lt. | 23 | ——— R., Capt. | 129 | McKellen, F., Capt. | 28 | McNab, J. S., 2/Lt. | 108 |
| McArthur, G. A. D., Capt. | 132 | ——— R. A., 2/Lt. | 16 | McKelvey, M. T., Lieut. | 162 | MacNair, D., Capt. | 132 |
| MacArthur, R., Lieut. | 11 | ——— R. T. A., Lieut. | 178 | McKenna, H. P., Capt. | 60 | McNamara, J. F., 2/Lt. | 175 |
| MacArtney, W. F. R., Lieut. | 19 | ——— R. M., Lieut. | 173 | ——— J., A.D.C. & Major | 187 | McNally, Irwin, 2/Lt. | 81 |
| MacAskie, D. S. C., 2/Lt. | 148 | McDonnell, C. J., 2/Lt. | 79 | ——— J. C., Major | 183 | McNaughton, E. H. C., Sub-Lt. | 143 |
| MacAulay, A. C., Lieut. | 175 | ——— H. W., Lieut. | 139 | McKenny, C. N., 2/Lt. | 110 | ——— J. L., 2/Lt. | 65 |
| ——— G. J. R., 2/Lt. | 12 | ——— R. de Courcy, Lieut. | 82 | McKenzie, A., 2/Lt. | 105 | McNeal, H. S. D., Lieut. | 181 |
| McBain, J. M., Lieut. | 78 | McDougall, I., Major | 142 | ——— A., 2/Lt. | 91 | McNeile, J. H. | 18 |
| McBeath, W. J., 2/Lt. | 95 | McDowell, R., 2/Lt. | 127 | ——— E. G., 2/Lt. | 67 | MacNeill, I. D., 2/Lt. | 103 |
| MacBryan, J. C. W., Lieut. | 38 | ——— V. A. G. | 139 | ——— F. P., Lieut. | 141 | McNeill, K. D., 2/Lt. | 103 |
| McBryde, K., 2/Lt. | 12 | McElligott, J., 2/Lt. | 179 | ——— J. M., Capt. | 134 | McNicol, D., 2/Lt. | 74 |
| McCaffrey, W. P., 2/Lt. | 115 | McElnea, H. J., 2/Lt. | 113 | McKeown, C. J. W., 2/Lt. | 159 | McNish, J. A., 2/Lt. | 126 |
| McCallum, A. H. K., Lieut. | 151 | McElroy, C. H., Lieut. | 189 | MacKereth, J., Capt. | 169 | McPhail, A. G., 2/Lt. | 106 |
| McCallum, P., Lieut. | 136 | ——— H. F., 2/Lt. | 130 | McKerrell, A. D., 2/Lt. | 58 | ——— G. R., Capt. | 122 |
| McCann, A. F., 2/Lt. | 114 | ——— J. O., Capt. | 97 | McKerrow, W. A., Surg. | 144 | MacPhee, G. G., Lieut. | 161 |
| ——— A. J., 2/Lt. | 113 | McEntee, G. O., 2/Lt. | 152 | McKessock, R. R., Lieut. | 139 | ——— Roland, Lieut. | 170 |
| ——— Cecil, Lieut. | 161 | McErvel, J. E., Lieut. | 117 | McKie, J., 2/Lt. | 103 | McPherson, B., 2/Lt. | 161 |
| McCarter, W. H., Capt. | 133 | McEwan, J. G., 2/Lt. | 147 | ——— L. G., 2/Lt. | 91 | ——— D. B., 2/Lt. | 115 |
| McCarthy, J., 2/Lt. | 16 | ——— J. H. F., Capt. | 148 | ——— R. C., 2/Lt. | 11 | ——— J. M., 2/Lt. | 168 |
| ——— P., 2/Lt. | 114 | McEwen, J. A., Capt. | 87 | MacKinnon, A., Capt. | 26 | ——— R., Lieut. | 81 |
| McCaughey, F. H., Capt. | 134 | ——— P. A., 2/Lt. | 13 | MacKintosh, I. K., 2/Lt. | 74 | ——— R. C., 2/Lt. | 146 |
| McChleary, D., 2/Lt. | 112 | MacFayden, A., 2/Lt. | 184 | ——— J. D. V., 2/Lt. | 67 | McQuaid 2/Lt. | 54 |
| McChlery, W. R., Sub.-Lt. | 145 | MacFarlane, A., 2/Lt. | 117 | McKissock, C. W., 2/Lt. | 152 | McQueen, J. F. F. | 94 |
| McColl, A., 2/Lt. | 120 | ——— J. L., Lieut. | 155 | McKnight, Leo M., 2/Lt. | 98 | McQuiggan, A. J., Lieut. | 136 |
| McCombie, J. M., Lieut. | 187 | ——— W. K., Lieut. | 169 | McLachlan, A. E. W., 2/Lt. | 19 | McQuinn, W., 2/Lt. | 96 |
| MacConchie, T. Lloyd, Lieut. | 165 | McFie, J. A., Lieut. | 130 | McLare, W. M., Lieut. | 25 | McQuiston, T. E., 2/Lt. | 101 |
| McConnachie, J. S., Major | 132 | ——— J. D. A., 2/Lt. | 148 | McLaren, A. T., Lieut. | 20 | MacRae, A., Lieut. | 104 |
| McConnell, R. B., 2/Lt. | 59 | McGeachy, E., 2/Lt. | 13 | ——— James, Lieut. | 112 | ——— J. D. G., Lieut. | 180 |
| ——— S., Lieut. | 59 | McGeoch, W., 2/Lt. | 116 | McLaurin, D., 2/Lt. | 157 | ——— J. P., Lieut. | 158 |
| ——— S. B., 2/Lt. | 60 | McGeorge, W. B., Capt. | 104 | McLean, Alex. G., Lieut. | 106 | McSweeny, D. H., 2/Lt. | 80 |
| McConnell-Wood, A., Lieut. | 167 | Macghie, D. S., Lieut. | 179 | ——— A. J. H., Capt. | 112 | McTaggart, M. F., Lt. Col., D.S.O. | 106 |
| McConville, J., 2/Lt. | 185 | McGilton, D. J., 2/Lt. | 109 | ——— A. P., Capt. | 160 | MacTavish, D., 2/Lt. | 152 |
| McCormick, A. M., Lieut. | 134 | McGown, A., 2/Lt. | 136 | ——— G. D., 2/Lt. | 136 | McVey, J. S., 2/Lt. | 122 |
| ——— H., Lieut. | 118 | ——— J. C., Lieut. | 154 | ——— G. N., Capt. | 106 | Mabbett, R. W., 2/Lt. | 52 |
| McCovey, H. J., 2/Lt. | 79 | McGregor, A. H., Major | 53 | ——— I. C., Capt., D.S.O., M.C. | 133 | Maben, James, 2/Lt. | 58 |
| McCracken, E. C. J., Lieut. | 168 | ——— D. A., Capt. | 82 | ——— Murdo, 2/Lt. | 175 | Mace, C. A., 2/Lt. | 101 |
| ——— J., 2/Lt. | 74 | ——— J. F., 2/Lt. | 15 | ——— N. A., 2/Lt. | 91 | Mack, A. J., 2/Lt. | 13 |
| ——— W., Major | 112 | ——— J. R., Lieut. | 189 | ——— V. A., Lieut. | 138 | Mack, R., Capt. | 177 |
| MacCrea, P. C. S., 2/Lt. | 174 | ——— J. S., 2/Lt. | 20 | ——— W. A., 2/Lt. | 146 | Macky, J. B. B., Capt. | 28 |
| McCreary, A. T. S., Capt. | 186 | ——— R. R., 2/Lt. | 156 | ——— W. H., 2/Lt. | 92 | Maddison, E. J. C., Lieut. | 120 |
| McCrorie, A. W., 2/Lt. | 115 | ——— W. K., 2/Lt. | 74 | ——— W. L., 2/Lt. | 25 | Madeley, J. J., 2/Lt. | 90 |
| McCuaig, D. R., Major | 138 | McGroarty, E. C., 2/Lt. | 72 | McLennan, J., Lieut. | 74 | Madge, J. B. C., Lieut. | 155 |
| McCuish, A. C., 2/Lt. | 108 | McGruer, A. G., 2/Lt. | 107 | ——— J. E., 2/Lt. | 150 | Magee, E. A., 2/Lt. | 163 |
| McCulloch, A. F. G., 2/Lt. | 138 | McHugh, P., 2/Lt. | 54 | ——— J. McM., Lieut. | 173 | Magin, J., 2/Lt. | 86 |
| ——— I. M., 2/Lt. | 170 | McIlwaine, H. L., Capt. | 88 | MacLeod, A., 2/Lt. | 117 | Maggs, D. O. C., 2/Lt. | 85 |
| McCullough, J. D., 2/Lt. | 60 | McIndoe, G. E. B., 2/Lt. | 104 | ——— G. D., Lieut. | 163 | Magrath, C. G., Lieut. | 47 |
| McDermott, C. H., 2/Lt. | 186 | McInnes, John, Lieut. | 107 | ——— E. R., Capt. | 72 | ——— W. S., Fl.-Lt. | 177 |
| | | MacIntosh, D. R., 2/Lt. | 142 | ——— F. G., 2/Lt. | 104 | Mahaffy, J. B., 2/Lt. | 48 |
| | | ——— E. H. de M., 2/Lt. | 142 | ——— J., Lieut | 14 | Maguire, M. L., 2/Lt. | 180 |
| | | ——— F. G., 2/Lt. | 148 | ——— L., 2/Lt. | 73 | Mahon, B. E. S., Lieut. | 24 |
| | | ——— R. R., 2/Lt. | 153 | ——— Lachlan, 2/Lt. | 108 | Mahony, M. R., Lieut. | 173 |
| | | MacIntyre, C. C., 2/Lt. | 74 | ——— R., 2/Lt. | 58 | Main, R., 2/Lt. | 158 |
| | | ——— D. H., 2/Lt. | 148 | ——— R. W., Lieut. | 10 | Maitland-Heriot, A., Fl. Lt. | 181 |
| | | ——— J. A., 2/Lt. | 25 | McLoughlin, J., 2/Lt. | 47 | Major, F. C., 2/Lt. | 101 |
| | | ——— J. C., 2/Lt. | 48 | McLurg, J. E., Lieut. | 138 | ——— W. E., Lieut. | 46 |
| | | ——— W., 2/Lt. | 92 | | | | |

| Name | PAGE | Name | PAGE | Name | PAGE | Name | PAGE |
|---|---|---|---|---|---|---|---|
| Makeham, L. C., Capt. | 94 | Marsden, T. R., D.S.O., Lt.-Col. | 138 | Matheson, J., 2/Lt. | 20 | Mellis, C. G., Maj.-Gen., Sir, V.C., K.C.B. | 182 |
| Makepeace, I. W., Lieut. | 26 | ——— W., 2/Lt. | 80 | ——— R. K., Lieut. | 97 | Mellor, J. S. P., Lieut. | 187 |
| Makin, K. K., 2/Lt. | 40 | Marseille, R. K. G., Capt. | 80 | Mathew, C. G., Lieut. | 154 | Mellowes, H. A., Capt. | 64 |
| Makins, H. E., Capt. | 39 | Marsh, A. G. V., 2/Lt. | 44 | ——— H. C., M.C., Lieut. | 38 | Melvin, David L., Lieut. | 173 |
| Makinson, H., Lieut. | 95 | ——— G. R. T., 2/Lt. | 159 | Mathias, L., Lieut. | 184 | Menzies, C. D., 2/Lt. | 128 |
| Malby, R. C., 2/Lt. | 129 | ——— G. V., 2/Lt. | 64 | Mathieson, E. N., 2/Lt. | 120 | ——— Daniel, Lieut. | 122 |
| Malcolm, R. M., 2/Lt. | 102 | ——— J., 2/Lt. | 178 | ——— W. A., 2/Lt. | 20 | ——— J. F., Capt. | 77 |
| Malcolmson, J. C., 2/Lt. | 173 | ——— L., Sub.-Lt. | 188 | Matson, A. W., 2/Lt. | 160 | ——— R., 2/Lt. | 103 |
| Malkin, F., 2/Lt. | 36 | ——— Lewis, Capt. | 117 | ——— G., Lieut. | 35 | Meo, I., 2/Lt. | 11 |
| Mallabar, W. L., 2/Lt. | 131 | ——— R. M., 2/Lt. | 154 | Matterson, C. A. K., Capt. | 54 | Mercer, G. A., Lieut. | 16 |
| Mallace, M., Capt. | 59 | ——— S. S., 2/Lt. | 123 | Matthews, A. B., Lieut. | 185 | ——— H., 2/Lt. | 17 |
| Mallett, Donald, 2/Lt. | 165 | Marshall, A. F. W., 2/Lt. | 44 | ——— A. H., 2/Lt. | 31 | ——— W. T., 2/Lt. | 14 |
| ——— H. P., Lieut. | 167 | ——— A. M., Capt. | 137 | ——— E. V., 2/Lt. | 62 | Mercer-Smith, V., 2/Lt. | 164 |
| Mallinson, B. 2/Lt. | 33 | ——— C. C. B., 2/Lt. | 130 | ——— F., 2/Lt. | 151 | Mcredith, G. C., Capt. | 55 |
| ——— C. H., Capt. | 65 | ——— C. C. N., 2/Lt. | 76 | ——— G., 2/Lt. | 41 | ——— H. T. D., Lieut. | 72 |
| ——— R., Lieut. | 137 | ——— C. O., Lieut. | 25 | ——— J. S., Lieut. | 48 | ——— J. J., 2/Lt. | 161 |
| Malloch, A. C., Lieut. | 154 | ——— C. T., 2/Lt. | 97 | ——— J. A., 2/Lt. | 171 | ——— L. A., Lieut. | 105 |
| Mallous, C. G., 2/Lt. | 155 | ——— D., 2/Lt. | 51 | ——— J. H., Lieut. | 136 | Merrall, E., 2/Lt. | 99 |
| Malone, J. G., 2/Lt. | 109 | ——— G. E., 2/Lt. | 142 | ——— R., 2/Lt. | 130 | Merriman, G. V., 2/Lt. | 142 |
| Maloney, M., 2/Lt. | 188 | ——— H., Capt. | 35 | ——— S. E., 2/Lt. | 79 | ——— R. D., Lieut. | 184 |
| Malton, P. L., 2/Lt. | 66 | ——— J., 2/Lt. | 65 | ——— S. H., M.C., Capt. | 27 | Metcalf, R., 2/Lt. | 117 |
| Mance, J. D., Lieut. | 165 | ——— N. H., 2/Lt. | 165 | ——— T. F. V., Capt. | 62 | Metcalfe, J., Lieut. | 28 |
| ——— J. F., 2/Lt. | 31 | ——— R., Capt. | 169 | Matthewson, R. W. B., 2/Lt. | 157 | ——— L. W., 2/Lt. | 41 |
| Mandel, Oscar, 2/Lt. | 170 | ——— R. C., Capt. | 62 | Mattison, H., 2/Lt. | 111 | Metson, G. F., 2/Lt. | 168 |
| Mander, J. G. H., Lieut. | 29 | ——— S., 2/Lt. | 51 | Maude, J., 2/Lt. | 67 | Metters, H. H., 2/Lt. | 47 |
| Manders, T. C., Capt. | 88 | ——— T., Capt. | 72 | Maudslay, R. V., Major | 11 | Meyer, C. B., Lieut. | 136 |
| Manley, G. A. C., 2/Lt. | 159 | ——— T., Capt. | — | Maughfing, T., 2/Lt. | 98 | ——— J. V., 2/Lt. | 126 |
| ——— P. S., Lieut. | 173 | Marsland, T., Lieut. | 17 | Maule, H. S., Lt.-Col. | 184 | ——— O. F., Lieut. | 168 |
| Mann, F. A., 2/Lt. | 150 | Marson, H. W., Lieut. | 137 | Maunder, W. C., 2/Lt. | 36 | Meyers, V. H. L., Lieut. | 88 |
| ——— J., 2/Lt. | 24 | Marthews, L. G., 2/Lt. | 72 | Maunsell, Chas. F., Lieut. | 28 | Michell, P. C., Lieut. | 165 |
| ——— J. J., Lieut. | 19 | Martland, E. N. P., Lieut. | 133 | Mawer, A. L., 2/Lt. | 174 | Michelmore, R. F., 2/Lt. | 89 |
| Manners, C. M. S., Capt. | 183 | Marten, C. W., Lieut. | 46 | Maxfield, W. J., 2/Lt. | 25 | Middlebrook, N., 2/Lt. | 149 |
| ——— E. W., 2/Lt. | 102 | Martin, A. V. P., Lt.-Col. | 94 | Maxson, C. W., | 135 | Middleditch, R. H., Lieut. | 48 |
| ——— T. G., 2/Lt. | 122 | ——— A. W., Lieut. | 152 | Maxted, O. D., Lieut. | 151 | Middlemas, G., Lieut. | 19 |
| Manners-Smith, J. A., Lieut. | 155 | ——— D. A., Lieut. | 169 | Maxwell, E. C., Lieut. | 16 | Middlemass, R. W. H., Major | 185 |
| Manning, B. O'D., 2/Lt. | 18 | ——— E. C. de R., Lt. Col. | 52 | ——— G. A., Capt. | 49 | Middlemiss, G. A., 2/Lt. | 78 |
| Mansbridge, C., Lieut. | 52 | ——— E. P., 2/Lt. | 121 | ——— G. E., 2/Lt. | 147 | Middleton, A. H., 2/Lt. | 158 |
| Mansel Moullin, O., Lieut. | 146 | ——— E. T., Capt. | 185 | ——— K. G., Capt. | 95 | ——— B. L., Lieut. | 76 |
| Mansell, R., 2/Lt. | 97 | ——— G. C. R., Lieut. | 98 | ——— S. W., 2/Lt. | 108 | ——— C. de C., Capt. | 84 |
| Mantle, A., 2/Lt. | 33 | ——— G. M. K., Lieut. | 60 | May, L. B., Lieut. | 158 | ——— E., Capt. | 131 |
| ——— H. S., Lieut. | 172 | ——— J., Lieut. | 176 | ——— P. E., 2/Lt. | 21 | ——— G. V., 2/Lt. | 78 |
| Manzer, R., Capt. | 167 | ——— H., Lieut. | 7 | ——— R. G. S., Lieut. | 77 | ——— J. R., 2/Lt. | 150 |
| Mapleton, R. I., Lieut. | 107 | ——— J. D., Capt. | 186 | ——— T. A., 2/Lt. | 123 | ——— J. S., Lieut. | 33 |
| Mapp, C. H., 2/Lt. | 15 | ——— J. M. J., 2/Lt. | 60 | ——— W. E., 2/Lt. | 127 | ——— L. N., Lieut. | 53 |
| Mapplebeck, T., Capt. | 149 | ——— J. R., Lieut. | 140 | Mayhew, T. G., 2/Lt. | 43 | ——— R., Capt. | 129 |
| March, C. H., Lieut. | 150 | ——— J. S. S., Capt. | 182 | Maynard, C. E., Capt. | 27 | Midgley, C. W., 2/Lt. | 125 |
| Marchand, E. F., 2/Lt. | 158 | ——— L. W., 2/Lt. | 23 | ——— F. L., 2/Lt. | 14 | Milani, R. S., 2/Lt. | 163 |
| Marchant, E. A., 2/Lt. | 171 | ——— P. C. C., 2/Lt. | 159 | ——— H., 2/Lt. | 10 | Milburn, H. E., Capt. | 47 |
| ——— E. W., Lieut. | 89 | ——— R. E., 2/Lt. | 70 | ——— J. E., Lieut. | 88 | ——— O. L. F., Lieut. | 133 |
| ——— F. S., 2/Lt. | 59 | ——— R. V., Lieut. | 184 | ——— L. H., 2/Lt. | 13 | Miles, A. A., 2/Lt. | 160 |
| ——— G. A., 2/Lt. | 129 | ——— S. A., 2/Lt. | 21 | Mayne, H. G. L., Lieut. | 146 | ——— B., 2/Lt. | 83 |
| Marcus, G., Sub-Lt. | 145 | ——— S. T., 2/Lt. | 64 | ——— H. T., Lieut. | 146 | ——— C. S., 2/Lt. | 96 |
| Mardock, F. W., Lieut. | 176 | ——— T. G., Lieut. | 62 | ——— R. A., 2/Lt. | 160 | Milford, E., Major | 183 |
| Mardon, S. R., 2/Lt. | 40 | ——— W., 2/Lt. | 93 | Mayo, C. D., 2/Lt. | 19 | Millar, D., Lieut. | 141 |
| Mare-Montembault, M. J. J., 2/Lt. | 150 | ——— W. J., 2/Lt. | 88 | ——— F., Lieut. | 185 | ——— E. A., Capt. | 36 |
| Marfell, C., 2/Lt. | 61 | Martineau, C., Capt. | 29 | Mayor, A., 2/Lt. | 55 | ——— John, 2/Lt. | 19 |
| Margetts, C. F. M., Capt. | 71 | Martinson, W. F., Capt. | 76 | Meade-King, W. T. P., Capt. | 134 | ——— J. W., 2/Lt. | 70 |
| Mark, A. W. D., Capt. | 27 | Martyn, M. C., Lt.-Col. | 46 | Meaden, C. A., Capt. | 133 | ——— T. S., 2/Lt. | 153 |
| Markham, W. H. J., 2/Lt. | 25 | Mase, H. F., Lt. | 148 | Meadon, A. A., Capt. | 131 | ——— W. A., 2/Lt. | 18 |
| Marks, J. H., 2/Lt. | 88 | Maskell, G. N., Lieut. | 118 | Meaking, G. E. R., 2/Lt. | 146 | Millard, B. A., Fl.-Sub.-Lt. | 187 |
| ——— J. S., Capt. | 76 | Mason, A. E., Lieut. | 187 | Mearne, Colin, Capt. | 132 | Miller, A. D., 2/Lt. | 106 |
| Marlow, O. L., 2/Lt. | 90 | ——— C. G., 2/Lt. | 142 | Mears, H., Lt. | 183 | ——— A. H., 2/Lt. | 128 |
| ——— W., 2/Lt. | 12 | ——— H., Lieut. | 164 | Mecey, E. J., Lieut. | 83 | ——— A. L., Lieut., M.C. | 74 |
| Marple, G. W., 2/Lt. | 30 | Massey, G., 2/Lt. | 52 | Medlicott, H. W., 2/Lt. | 147 | ——— A. M., 2/Lt. | 170 |
| Marrion, J. F., 2/Lt. | 32 | ——— H. H., 2/Lt. | 64 | ——— R. F. C., Capt. | 142 | ——— A. W., Lieut. | 161 |
| Marriott, Reginald, Lt. | 53 | Massey-Cooke, W. E., Lieut. | 140 | Meggitt, W. G., Lieut., M.C. | 158 | ——— C. C., Capt. | 60 |
| Marris, E. N., Major | 124 | Masson, J. R., 2/Lt. | 58 | Meigham, S. S., Capt. | 133 | ——— David, 2/Lt. | 158 |
| Mars, W. S., Lieut. | 169 | Massy, B. E., Capt. | 54 | Meikle, T. J., Lieut. | 11 | ——— D. H., 2/Lt. | 115 |
| Marsden, C., Lieut. | 163 | Master, H. F. H., Capt. | 21 | Meiklejohn, R., Major | 28 | ——— F. K., Lieut. | 132 |
| ——— F. A., 2/Lt. | 86 | Mather, A. S., Sub.-Lt. | 177 | Mein, H. C., Lieut. | 19 | ——— I. R. F., Lieut. | 60 |
| ——— F. G., 2/Lt. | 41 | ——— E. E., Capt. | 133 | | | ——— R. M., Capt. | 103 |
| ——— J. W., 2/Lt. | 40 | ——— G. R., 2/Lt. | 87 | | | ——— R. S., Lieut. | 63 |
| ——— J. W., 2/Lt. | 25 | Matheson, A. M., Lieut. | 173 | | | | |

| Name | Page | Name | Page | Name | Page | Name | Page |
|---|---|---|---|---|---|---|---|
| Miller, R. T., 2/Lt. | 94 | Monypeny, R. W., Lieut. | 129 | Morrison-Bell, A. C., Major | 18 | Murray, A. M., 2/Lt. | 89 |
| ——— S., Lieut. | 187 | Montgomerie, F. D., Lieut. | 23 | Morritt, W. S., Lieut. | 65 | ——— A. R., 2/Lt. | 106 |
| ——— S., Lieut. | 133 | Montgomery, A. N., Lieut. | 101 | Morrogh, J. D., Major | 48 | ——— A. S., 2/Lt. | 112 |
| ——— S. S., Lieut. | 94 | ——— J., Capt. | 8 | Morse, T., Lieut. | 158 | ——— C., Lieut. | 189 |
| ——— W., Lieut. | 180 | ——— K. B., Capt. | 159 | Mort, J., 2/Lt. | 106 | ——— D. C. G., Lieut. | 154 |
| ——— Z., 2/Lt. | 169 | ——— R. N., 2/Lt. | 16 | Mortensen, W. M., 2/Lt. | 138 | ——— H. R., 2/Lt. | 57 |
| Miller-Stirling, A. E. S., Lieut. | 106 | Monteith, R., 2/Lt. | 109 | Mortimer-Phelan, 2/Lt. | 147 | ——— J. C. E., 2/Lt. | 107 |
| Millership, L. R., Lieut. | 94 | Moodie, A. M., Capt. | 74 | Morton, D. H., Capt. | 60 | ——— J. G., Lieut. | 139 |
| Milligan, A. D., Lieut. | 107 | ——— O., Capt. | 74 | ——— J., 2/Lt. | 109 | ——— P. S., Lieut. | 43 |
| Milling, H. B., Lieut. | 152 | ——— B. C., 2/Lt. | 153 | ——— J. D. M., Lieut. | 99 | ——— R. V., 2/Lt. | 175 |
| Millman, F. H., Capt. | 36 | Moon, R. C., Major | 122 | ——— J. G., 2/Lt. | 87 | Murton, H. S., Fl. Lt. | 164 |
| Mills, A. S., Lieut. | 180 | ——— W. J., 2/Lt. | 29 | ——— R. H., Lieut. | 108 | Musgrove, H. S., 2/Lt. | 167 |
| ——— C., Capt. | 136 | Moore, A., Lt.-Col. | 183 | Moseley, G., Capt. | 49 | Mussared, W. J., 2/Lt. | 154 |
| ——— D. W., Lieut. | 56 | ——— A., Lieut. | 165 | ——— R. A. D., Lieut. | 113 | Mutch, F. R., Lieut. | 53 |
| ——— F. G., 2/Lt. | 175 | ——— A. R., 2/Lt. | 94 | Moss, G. E., 2/Lt. | 122 | Myers, E., 2/Lt. | 119 |
| ——— H. J. F., Lieut. | 90 | ——— C. C., 2/Lt. | 52 | ——— S. C., 2/Lt. | 17 | ——— J. C., 2/Lt. | 35 |
| ——— J., 2/Lt. | 187 | ——— C. H. E., Capt. | 93 | Moss-Blundell, F. B., Lt.-Col. | 13 | ——— F. C. A., Lieut. | 138 |
| ——— J. F., 2/Lt. | 80 | ——— C. R., Lieut. | 173 | Mossop, Wm. N., Capt. Adj. | 41 | Nalder, R. F., Lieut. | 125 |
| ——— M., 2/Lt. | 45 | ——— E. E. J., Capt. | 59 | Mott, J. E., Capt. | 136 | Nantes, G. J., Major | 13 |
| ——— W. B., 2/Lt. | 118 | ——— E. S., 2/Lt. | 153 | Mottram, P., 2/Lt. | 105 | Napier, H., Lt.-Col. Hon. | 7 |
| ——— W. G., 2/Lt. | 115 | ——— H. S., Capt. | 132 | Mouat-Biggs, J. A., Lieut. | 47 | ——— J., 2/Lt., Sir | 181 |
| Miles, W. H., Capt. | 187 | ——— H. W. H., 2/Lt. | 31 | Mould, W. J., Lieut. | 73 | ——— L., Capt. | 107 |
| Millyard, T., Capt. | 87 | ——— L., 2/Lt. | 141 | Moulton, T., Lieut. | 55 | ——— W., 2/Lt. | 72 |
| Milne, A., 2/Lt. | 106 | ——— L. G., Lt.-Col. | 92 | Mount, W. J., Lieut. | 114 | Nash, C. P., Lt. | 135 |
| ——— C. G., 2/Lt. | 172 | ——— M., Lieut. | 154 | Mousley, E. O., Lt. | 185 | ——— E. L. F., Capt. | 132 |
| ——— D. W., 2/Lt. | 107 | ——— R. M., 2/Lt. | 110 | Moutrie, L., 2/Lt. | 127 | ——— F. M., 2/Lt. | 156 |
| ——— S. B., 2/Lt. | 27 | ——— R. S., Lieut. | 9 | Mowat, A., 2/Lt. | 105 | ——— G. E., Fl. Lt. | 177 |
| ——— W., Capt. | 20 | ——— T. S., 2/Lt. | 89 | ——— M., 2/Lt. | 105 | ——— J. F., Fl. Lt. | 113 |
| ——— W., Major | 121 | Moorhead, W. B., Lieut. | 31 | Mowlam, H. J., Capt. | 101 | Nathan, G. S. M., 2/Lt. | 28 |
| Milne-Thomson, A., Col. | 134 | Morant, N., 2/Lt. | 48 | Moxon, N. F., 2/Lt. | 173 | Nattrass, F. J., Capt. | 133 |
| Milner, J., Capt., M.C. | 36 | Morey, S. K., 2/Lt. | 70 | Moylan, F. E., Lieut. | 128 | Naylor, C. B., Lieut. | 171 |
| Milward, R., 2/Lt. | 79 | Morgan, D., Lieut. | 10 | Moyle, F. W., Lieut. | 69 | ——— F., 2/Lt. | 102 |
| ——— W. E., Lieut. | 64 | ——— F. N., 2/Lt. | 46 | Moysey, F., Capt. | 37 | ——— F. A., 2/Lt. | 75 |
| Mingo, E. W., Lieut. | 139 | ——— H. L., 2/Lt. | 68 | Mucklow, S. L., Lieut. | 174 | ——— G., 2/Lt. | 187 |
| Minifie, R. P., Fl. Com. | 160 | ——— H. L., Lieut. | 57 | Mudd, W. A., 2/Lt. | 38 | Neal, A. F., Lieut. | 16 |
| Miscampbell, A., Capt. | 68 | ——— H. T., 2/Lt. | 120 | Mudie, K., Lieut. | 51 | Neale, A. W., 2/Lt. | 69 |
| Miskin, W. L., Capt. | 184 | ——— J. B., Lieut. | 31 | Muff, W. R., 2/Lt. | 99 | Neame, E. G., Lieut. | 65 |
| Mitchel, G. W., Lieut. | 172 | ——— R. J., Capt. | 173 | Muir, A., 2/Lt. | 158 | Needham, E., Capt. | 123 |
| Missingham, W. S., 2/Lt. | 137 | ——— T. E., 2/Lt. | 16 | ——— J. C., Capt. | 132 | ——— Hayden, 2/Lt. | 43 |
| Mitchell, A. D., 2/Lt. | 142 | ——— T. P., 2/Lt. | 158 | ——— J. C., Capt. | 34 | ——— R. P., 2/Lt. | 81 |
| ——— A. P., Lieut. | 153 | ——— T. W. M., Capt. | 146 | Muirden, N. H., Lieut. | 164 | ——— T. H., Capt. | 122 |
| ——— F. H., Lieut. | 189 | ——— W. G., 2/Lt. | 157 | Muirhead, W. D., 2/Lt. | 41 | Neil, R. W., Lieut. | 139 |
| ——— H., 2/Lt. | 163 | Morland, W., Capt. | 187 | Mulcahy, M., 2/Lt. | 48 | Neild, Arthur, 2/Lt. | 77 |
| ——— H. B. O., 2/Lt. | 149 | Morison, R. B., 2/Lt. | 120 | Mulhall, H. F., Lieut. | 175 | Neill, J. W. F., Lieut. | 155 |
| ——— H. G., 2/Lt. | 58 | Morley, C., Capt. | 94 | Mullaly, J. C. D., Capt. | 143 | ——— P., 2/Lt. | 16 |
| ——— J.R.McC., 2/Lt. | 122 | ——— R. S., Capt. | 51 | Mullan, P. J., Father | 181 | Neilson, T. A., Lieut. | 59 |
| ——— J. V. R., Lieut. | 20 | Morlidge, A., Capt. | 27 | ——— H. P., 2/Lt. | 24 | ——— W., Capt. | 103 |
| ——— R. R., 2/Lt. | 91 | Morony, W. V., Lieut. | 60 | Mullis, F. L., 2/Lt. | 33 | Neish, F. H., Col. | 105 |
| ——— R. T. L., Lieut. | 106 | Morpeth, R. S., Lieut. | 122 | Mumford, G. W., Lieut. | 156 | ——— W., Capt. | 105 |
| ——— Sam, 2/Lt. | 33 | ——— S., Lieut. | 25 | Mummery, H. N. S., Capt. | 104 | Nelson, G. W., 2/Lt. | 106 |
| ——— T., 2/Lt. | 39 | Morrell, H. G., Capt. | 182 | Munday, J., 2/Lt. | 115 | ——— J. H., 2/Lt. | 58 |
| ——— W., Capt. | 131 | Morrill, T. J., Capt. | 43 | Mundey, C. B., Capt. | 186 | ——— J. W., Major | 187 |
| ——— Wm., 2/Lt. | 173 | Morris, A. A., 2/Lt. | 27 | Mundy, J. E., 2/Lt. | 127 | ——— R. C., Lieut. | 138 |
| ——— W. G., 2/Lt. | 11 | ——— B. A., 2/Lt. | 107 | Munn, L. S., 2/Lt. | 87 | Nesbitt, A. W., 2/Lt. | 101 |
| ——— W. T., Capt. | 104 | ——— C. A., 2/Lt. | 102 | Munro, A., Lieut. | 19 | ——— F.W.R., Lieut. | 101 |
| Mitchelson, J. K., Capt. Rev. | 135 | ——— H. O., 2/Lt. | 128 | ——— F. F., Lieut. | 122 | Neumann, C. W., Major | 182 |
| Mitchiner, H. G., 2/Lt. | 127 | ——— L. B. F., 2/Lt. | 149 | ——— J., 2/Lt. | 168 | Nevard, J. S., 2/Lt. | 23 |
| Mitten, R. C., Lieut. | 173 | ——— R., Lieut. | 136 | ——— J. G., Lieut. | 170 | Neville, D. A., Lieut. | 172 |
| Moberly, B. E., Lieut. | 140 | ——— V. C., 2/Lt. | 151 | Munroe, C. H. C., Lt. | 182 | ——— W. W., Capt. | 110 |
| Moffatt, F. B., 2/Lt. | 19 | ——— W. A., Lieut. | 66 | Murchison, R., 2/Lt. | 19 | Newbery, T. F., 2/Lt. | 118 |
| Mogridge, V., 2/Lt. | 142 | ——— W. F., Rev. | 135 | Murdoch, H. H., 2/Lt. | 60 | Newbold, J. W., Lieut. | 186 |
| Moline, R.W.H., Capt. | 123 | ——— W. H., Lieut. | 86 | ——— W., 2/Lt. | 136 | ——— L. A., 2/Lt. | 147 |
| Molloy, T. P. L., 2/Lt. | 149 | ——— W. P., 2/Lt. | 92 | Murphy, D. G. C., Lieut. | 126 | Newbury, G. G., 2/Lt. | 160 |
| ——— W. C., 2/Lt. | 20 | Morrish, D. R., Lieut. | 44 | ——— E. M., Capt. | 33 | Newcomb, C., Capt. | 184 |
| Molony, J. G., Capt. | 133 | Morrison, H. C., Lieut. | 137 | ——— G. G. D., Lieut. | 139 | ——— M., 2/Lt. | 157 |
| Molson, J. H., Lieut. | 140 | ——— H. St. J., Capt. | 109 | ——— J. P., Lieut. | 174 | Newcombe, L., Major | 49 |
| Monaghan, H. B., Lieut. | 172 | ——— J. B., Capt. | 130 | ——— L., Capt. | 181 | ——— S. F., Lt.-Col., D.S.O. | 179 |
| ——— M. J., 2/Lt. | 115 | ——— K. R. M., Lieut. | 140 | ——— L. W. R., Lieut. | 113 | Newenham, G. A., Lieut. | 152 |
| ——— P. J., Capt. | 143 | ——— K. S., Lieut. | 158 | ——— P. A., 2/Lt. | 78 | Newey, T., 2/Lt. | 172 |
| Monday, T. E., 2/Lt. | 61 | ——— L. S., Capt. | 138 | ——— T. F., Lieut. | 126 | Newland, N. C., 2/Lt. | 126 |
| Money, H., Lieut., M.C. | 75 | ——— R., 2/Lt. | 117 | ——— W. S., Capt. | 47 | Newman, C., Lieut. | 176 |
| ——— R.R.N., Capt. | 149 | ——— S., Lieut. | 120 | | | ——— Cyril, 2/Lt. | 32 |
| Monkman, Eric, 2/Lt. | 127 | | | | | ——— C. M., Capt. | 52 |
| Monks, C. A., 2/Lt. | 42 | | | | | ——— L. C., Lieut. | 57 |

| | PAGE | | PAGE | | PAGE | | PAGE |
|---|---|---|---|---|---|---|---|
| Newman, W. A., 2/Lt. | 121 | Nutter, R. U., 2/Lt. ... | 12 | Ormerod, E., Lieut. ... | 51 | Palmer, G. H., 2/Lt. ... | 154 |
| Newsholme, W. S., 2/Lt. | 83 | Nye, A. C., 2/Lt. ... | 21 | Ormiston, Peter, 2/Lt.... | 58 | ——— Harold, 2/Lt. ... | 51 |
| Newson, H. A., Lieut. | 113 | ——— G. J., 2/Lt. ... | 41 | ——— T., Major | 141 | ——— Jack M., Capt. | 144 |
| ——— H. M., Lieut. | 142 | | | O'Rorke, Rev. ... | 135 | ——— J. W. E., 2/Lt. | 120 |
| Newstead, C. W., Lieut. | 175 | Oakes, J., Lieut. ... | 34 | Orr, A. P., 2/Lt. ... | 53 | ——— K. R., Lieut. | 8 |
| ——— W. C., Capt., | | Oakley, R. S., 2/Lt. ... | 171 | ——— R. R., Capt. ... | 112 | ——— N. St. C., Capt. | 98 |
| M.C. ... ... | 40 | ——— W. E. B., Fl.-Sub-Lt. ... | 177 | Orr-Ewing, A. J., 2/Lt. | 156 | Panchaud, L. A., Lieut. | 84 |
| Newton, E. A., 2/Lt. ... | 179 | O'Brian, W., Capt. | 133 | Ortweiler, F. J., 2/Lt. | 157 | Panting, F. Owen, 2/Lt. | 41 |
| ——— G. E., Lieut. | 129 | O'Brien, C. R., Lieut. ... | 152 | Osborn, C. C. F., Lieut. | 153 | Papenfus, M.T.S., Lieut. | 166 |
| ——— H. M., 2/Lt.... | 52 | ——— J. F., 2/Lt. ... | 60 | Osborne, E. B., 2/Lt. ... | 64 | Papworth, A. S., 2/Lt. | 169 |
| ——— H. W. G., Lieut. | 38 | ——— P. A., 2/Lt. ... | 155 | ——— F. W., 2/Lt. ... | 178 | Paramore, L., 2/Lt. ... | 70 |
| ——— I. H., 2/Lt. | 127 | O'Bryne, A. J. O., 2/Lt. | 148 | ——— H. P., Lt.-Col. | 86 | Parfect, G. F., 2/Lt. ... | 30 |
| Niall, A. M., 2/Lt. ... | 8 | O'Callaghan, C. E., Lieut. | 113 | ——— J. E., Major | 139 | Parfitt, E., Capt. ... | 89 |
| Nichol, R. W., 2/Lt. ... | 148 | O'Carroll, A. D., Capt.... | 131 | ——— V. E., Lieut.... | 121 | ——— E. G., 2/Lt. ... | 12 |
| Nicholas, E. M., Lieut. | 164 | O'Connell, M.Wm., 2/Lt. | 114 | Osborough, A. H., 2/Lt. | 109 | Paris, A. E., Capt. ... | 16 |
| ——— T. C., Lieut. | 116 | O'Connor, O., Lieut. ... | 170 | Osgerby, R. W., 2/Lt. | 35 | ——— D. K., Lieut. | 152 |
| Nicholl, D. S. D., 2/Lt. | 12 | ——— R. D., Lieut. | 112 | Osgood, Edwin D., 2/Lt. | 23 | Parish, J., Lieut. ... | 39 |
| Nicholls, C. B., Capt. ... | 37 | Oddlafson, August, 2/Lt. | 128 | O'Shea, H. A., 2/Lt. ... | 168 | ——— W. G., 2/Lt. ... | 130 |
| ——— W. H., 2/Lt. ... | 138 | Oddy, E. A. H., 2/Lt. ... | 115 | Osmond, E. P., Lieut. | 181 | Park, C. A. R., 2/Lt. ... | 130 |
| Nichols, C. L., 2/Lt. ... | 10 | Oddy, N., 2/Lt. ... | 42 | ——— T. E., Capt., | 186 | ——— F. S., Capt. | 140 |
| ——— F. C., Capt. ... | 133 | O'Dell, W. H., 2/Lt. ... | 102 | Ostler, R., Lieut. ... | 75 | ——— S. M., Lieut. | 157 |
| ——— F. G., Lieut. ... | 44 | Odling, B. G., Lieut. ... | 148 | Oswald, G. A., Lieut. | 25 | Parke, J. E., 2/Lt. ... | 168 |
| ——— W. H., Major | 39 | Odom, G. C., Lieut. ... | 122 | Oswell, S. H., 2/Lt. | 82 | Parker, F. V., Capt. ... | 45 |
| Nicholson, D. A., Major | 107 | O'Donnell, A. B., Capt. | 29 | Oswin, P., 2/Lt. ... | 121 | ——— C., 2/Lt. ... | 57 |
| ——— E. B., Capt., M.C. ... | 20 | ——— T. F., 2/Lt. ... | 113 | Otter, R., Col. ... | 22 | ——— G. W., Lieut. | 36 |
| ——— G., Lieut. ... | 50 | O'Donoghue, J. H., 2/Lt. | 184 | Outran, J. L., Lieut. ... | 7 | ——— J., 2/Lt. ... | 28 |
| ——— G. H., Lieut. | 149 | ——— P. E., Lieut.... | 186 | Ovenstone, J. J., 2/Lt. | 61 | ——— J. K., 2/Lt. ... | 149 |
| ——— H. A., Capt. | 31 | O'Dowd, F. B., Lieut. ... | 134 | Overbury, G. E., 2/Lt. | 62 | ——— M. J., Capt. ... | 189 |
| ——— J. A., 2/Lt ... | 32 | O'Dwyer, J. E. A., Capt. | 188 | Overell, A. N., 2/Lt. ... | 42 | ——— N., 2/Lt. ... | 42 |
| ——— J. H., Lieut. ... | 27 | Oehl, G., 2/Lt. ... | 88 | Owen, A. L., 2/Lt. ... | 141 | ——— R. W. W., Capt. | 101 |
| ——— T., Lieut. ... | 47 | Oerton, Thomas, Lieut. | 36 | ——— D., Capt. ... | 157 | ——— S. J., 2/Lt. ... | 93 |
| ——— S., Lieut. ... | 187 | O'Farrell, W. R., Capt. | 178 | ——— D. C., Lieut.... | 13 | ——— W. B., 2/Lt.... | 117 |
| ——— T., Lieut. ... | 95 | Ogden, A., 2/Lt. ... | 21 | ——— G.C.F., Capt. | 176 | ——— W. B., 2/Lt. ... | 66 |
| ——— T. G., 2/Lt. ... | 19 | ——— C. E., 2/Lt. ... | 158 | ——— H. E., Lloyd, Lieut. ... | 139 | ——— W. B. H., Lieut. ... | 181 |
| Nicol, I. S., 2/Lt. ... | 13 | Ogilvie, S. S., Lt.-Col. ... | 93 | ——— H. H., 2/Lt. ... | 55 | ——— W. G., 2/Lt. ... | 129 |
| Nightingale, A. J., Fl. Lt. ... | 181 | Ogilvy, W. F., Lieut. ... | 170 | ——— H. W., Sub.-Lt. | 151 | Parkes, E. L., Lieut. ... | 16 |
| Nilen, F. P., Lieut. ... | 86 | O'Grady, W. de C., Lieut. | 139 | ——— J. C. F., Lieut. | 188 | ——— G. A. H., 2/Lt. | 154 |
| Nilson, A. C., 2/Lt. ... | 66 | O'Halloran-Giles, R., Lieut. ... | 9 | ——— L. D., 2/Lt. ... | 34 | ——— G. W., 2/Lt. ... | 14 |
| Nisbet, R. I., 2/Lt. ... | 27 | O'Hanlon, L. T., Lieut. | 58 | ——— L. V. D., Lieut. | 75 | ——— P. R., 2/Lt. ... | 129 |
| Nixon, G., 2/Lt. ... | 101 | O'Hara, D. H., 2/Lt. ... | 60 | ——— O. A., Lieut.... | 112 | Parkhouse, J. F., Lieut. | 60 |
| ——— J. G., 2/Lt. ... | 68 | O'Hare, O. J., 2/Lt. ... | 113 | ——— R. J., 2/Lt. ... | 161 | Parkin, G., 2/Lt. ... | 72 |
| ——— L. G., 2/Lt. ... | 158 | Ohrt, F. M., 2/Lt. ... | 159 | ——— R. O., Lieut. ... | 73 | Parkinson, J. A., Lieut. | 172 |
| Nobbs, C. H. F., 2/Lt. | 156 | O'Keefe, E. C. K., 2/Lt. | 141 | ——— T., 2/Lt. ... | 123 | ——— P., Lieut. ... | 179 |
| ——— H. G., Capt. | 128 | O'Keefe, L., 2/Lt. ... | 48 | Owens, G., 2/Lt. ... | 73 | ——— V. J., Lieut.... | 181 |
| Noel, J. B., 2/Lt. ... | 85 | O'Kelly, L. C., 2/Lt. ... | 136 | ——— James, 2/Lt. ... | 114 | ——— V. J., 2/Lt. ... | 138 |
| Noble, T. E., 2/Lt. ... | 73 | Old, R. M., Lieut. ... | 84 | Oxlade, E. R., 2/Lt. ... | 70 | Parks, G. C., 2/Lt. ... | 112 |
| ——— W., 2/Lt. ... | 105 | Oldfield, G. P., 2/Lt. ... | 93 | Ozanne, H. W., Capt. ... | 28 | Parr, F. S., Capt. ... | 146 |
| Nocton, V., 2/Lt. ... | 35 | O'Leary, D. A., Lieut. ... | 173 | Pack, D. H., Capt., M.C. | 32 | ——— H. O., Lt.-Col. | 183 |
| Nolan, J., Chap. ... | 135 | Olerenshaw, J., 2/Lt. ... | 172 | Paddison, R. M., Lieut. | 66 | ——— J. W., Lieut. | 103 |
| ——— J. G., 2/Lt. ... | 15 | O'Lieff, P. H., Lieut. ... | 161 | Paeo, A., Lieut. ... | 182 | ——— V. H., Major | 60 |
| Norcross, Bernard, Lieut. | 171 | Oliphant, G. W., Lieut. | 67 | Page, C. A. S., Major (A/Lt.-Col.), D.S.O. | 88 | Parrish, E. P., 2/Lt. ... | 82 |
| Norden, W. G., Lieut.... | 167 | ——— K.J.P., Lieut. | 93 | ——— R. A., Lieut. | 79 | ——— F. W., Lieut. | 92 |
| Norman, A. L., 2/Lt. ... | 99 | Oliver, D. C. M., 2/Lt. ... | 84 | ——— W. F., Lieut. | 57 | Parrott, A. E. H., 2/Lt. | 40 |
| ——— C. W., Lieut. | 9 | ——— F. G., 2/Lt. ... | 27 | Paget, G., Lieut. ... | 34 | Parry, C. F., Lieut. ... | 78 |
| ——— E. H., 2/Lt.... | 79 | ——— G., 2/Lt. ... | 102 | ——— O. L., 2/Lt. ... | 98 | ——— W., 2/Lt. ... | 57 |
| ——— G. R., 2/Lt. ... | 161 | ——— Henry, Lieut. ... | 105 | Paine, E. H., Capt. ... | 70 | ——— W. S., Sub.-Lt. | 145 |
| Norris, A. R., 2/Lt. ... | 69 | ——— R. C. D., 2/Lt. ... | 87 | ——— L. P., Fl.-Sup.-Lt. ... | 176 | Parsons, A. F., 2/Lt. ... | 91 |
| ——— Edwin J., 2/Lt. | 171 | Olphert, A. V., Lieut. ... | 110 | Pakenham-Walsh, L. H., Lieut. ... | 179 | ——— B. K., Capt. | 29 |
| ——— R. W., 2/Lt. | 61 | ——— W., Capt. ... | 145 | Palin, A. H., 2/Lt. ... | 87 | ——— C. St. C., 2/Lt. | 162 |
| Norrish, R. G. W., 2/Lt. | 12 | O'Malley, J. F., Lieut. ... | 113 | ——— G. W., Lieut., M.C. ... | 189 | ——— G., 2/Lt. ... | 95 |
| North, E. A., 2/Lt. ... | 52 | O'Mally, Cusack, Capt. | 133 | Paling, W. E., Lieut. ... | 69 | ——— J., 2/Lt. ... | 27 |
| ——— F. R., 2/Lt. ... | 66 | O'Neill, J. G., 2/Lt. ... | 60 | Palk, C. E., 2/Lt. ... | 52 | ——— J. C. L., 2/Lt. | 12 |
| Northey, H. G., 2/Lt. ... | 85 | Onslow, E. M., Lieut. ... | 28 | Palmer, A.E.P., Lieut. | 140 | ——— R. G., Lieut. | 185 |
| Northwood, G. W., Capt. | 139 | Openshaw, G. O., Capt. | 36 | ——— A. W., 2/Lt. ... | 158 | Partington, J. S., 2/Lt. | 96 |
| Norton, P. C., 2/Lt. ... | 157 | Oram, H.W.H., 2/Lt. ... | 95 | ——— C. B., 2/Lt. ... | 179 | ——— O. J., Lieut.... | 154 |
| Norvill, V. A., Lieut. ... | 154 | Orchard, A. F., 2/Lt. ... | 65 | ——— C. W., 2/Lt. ... | 147 | Partridge, A. T., Lieut. | 168 |
| Nottidge, P., Lieut. ... | 189 | ——— E.F.G., Lieut. | 33 | ——— E. A., Capt. | 13 | ——— E. G., 2/Lt. ... | 81 |
| Noxon, F. C., 2/Lt. ... | 51 | ——— W. D., 2/Lt. ... | 115 | ——— E. B., Capt.... | 20 | Pascoe, P. J., 2/Lt. ... | 26 |
| Nugent, T. C., Lieut. ... | 79 | Orde, M. A. J., 2/Lt. ... | 147 | ——— F., 2/Lt. ... | 34 | Pass, A. D., Lieut. ... | 178 |
| Nurse, F., 2/Lt. ... | 79 | Ordish, B. W. A., Lieut. | 149 | ——— F., Major ... | 141 | Patch, H., Capt. ... | 157 |
| Nutt, A. C. R., Major ... | 10 | Orford, E., Capt. ... | 37 | | | Patenaude, A. J., 2/Lt. | 163 |
| ——— A. H., Capt. | 70 | Organ, A. F., 2/Lt. ... | 148 | | | Paterson, A., Lieut. ... | 48 |
| Nuttall, H., 2/Lt. ... | 78 | Orgill, Philip, 2/Lt. ... | 123 | | | ——— C., 2/Lt. ... | 30 |
| ——— J. C., Lieut. ... | 167 | | | | | ——— J. R., Lieut.... | 103 |
| | | | | | | Patey, H. A., Capt. ... | 170 |

| Name | Page | Name | Page | Name | Page | Name | Page |
|---|---|---|---|---|---|---|---|
| Patman, A. C., Capt. | 48 | Peers, I. A., Lieut. | 163 | Phillips, P. A., Lieut. | 64 | Pond, Fredk., 2/Lt. | 88 |
| ——— G. H., Lieut. | 168 | Pegg, J. S., 2/Lt. | 120 | ——— P. L., 2/Lt. | 174 | Pont, E. S., 2/Lt. | 12 |
| Patmore, F. J., Lieut. | 187 | Pegge, E. E., Capt. | 94 | ——— R., Lieut. | 64 | Pontin, S. C. M., Lieut. | 164 |
| Paton, G. G. R., 2/Lt. | 11 | Peile, A. H., 2/Lt. | 159 | ——— R. E. G., Lieut. | 47 | Poole, A. A., 2/Lt. | 179 |
| ——— J. H., 2/Lt. | 120 | Peiler, M. F., 2/Lt. | 161 | ——— T. P., 2/Lt. | 107 | ——— B. C. H., Lieut. | 56 |
| Patrick, R. F. W., Lieut. | 105 | Peirson, G., Capt. | 7 | ——— V. G. M., Lieut. | 37 | ——— J. S., 2/Lt. | 90 |
| ——— W. D., Capt. | 161 | Pemberton, A. L., 2/Lt. | 161 | ——— W. A., Lieut. | 183 | ——— S. B., Lieut. | 32 |
| ——— J., Lieut. | 74 | ——— J., 2/Lt. | 57 | Phillipson, E., 2/Lt. | 51 | Pooley, H. R., 2/Lt. | 30 |
| Patten, A. G. B., 2/Lt. | 37 | Pendleton, W., 2/Lt. | 174 | Philpott, J. R., Capt. | 180 | Pope, A. D., 2/Lt. | 161 |
| Patterson, A. F. A., 2/Lt. | 149 | Penfold, F. S., 2/Lt. | 87 | ——— W. G., 2/Lt. | 127 | ——— C., Lieut. | 45 |
| ——— E. A., 2/Lt. | 76 | Pengilley, E. E., 2/Lt. | 31 | Phippard, F. H., 2/Lt. | 126 | ——— E. E. E., Capt. | 159 |
| ——— I. A., Lieut. | 10 | Penman, G., 2/Lt. | 58 | Phipps, W. G., 2/Lt. | 21 | ——— R. A. B., Lieut. | 170 |
| ——— K. S., 2/Lt. | 10 | Penney, C. M., 2/Lt. | 91 | Pickard, C. E., 2/Lt. | 102 | ——— J., 2/Lt. | 16 |
| ——— R. M., 2/Lt. | 12 | Penruddocke, N. F., Lieut. | 162 | Picken, J. C., 2/Lt. | 104 | ——— P. M., Capt. and Adj. | 90 |
| ——— W., Lieut. | 49 | Pentney, A. F., Rev. | 135 | Pickering, B. H., Lieut. | 23 | Porteous, J. D., 2/Lt. | 41 |
| Pattinson, J. F., Lieut. | 163 | Penwarden, H. G., 2/Lt. | 181 | ——— E. G., 2/Lt. | 44 | ——— J. S., 2/Lt. | 92 |
| ——— J., H., Lieut. | 102 | Peppé, C. G. H., Lieut. | 56 | ——— H. A., Capt. | 99 | ——— W. F., Lieut. M.C. | 118 |
| ——— T. S., 2/Lt. | 42 | Pepper, A. C., 2/Lt. | 151 | ——— W. J., 2/Lt. | 9 | Porter, A. C., 2/Lt. | 168 |
| Patton, G. E., Lieut. | 14 | ——— C. N., 2/Lt. | 41 | Pickett, A. C., 2/Lt. | 155 | ——— E. J., Lieut. | 130 |
| ——— W. F., Lieut. | 180 | ——— E., Lieut. | 41 | Pickford, E. W., 2/Lt. | 161 | ——— G. T., Lieut. | 147 |
| Paul, R. F., Capt. | 163 | Percival, B., 2/Lt. | 24 | Pickthall, H. C., 2/Lt. | 78 | ——— R. P., Capt. | 95 |
| ——— Sir R. J., Lieut. | 178 | ——— E., 2/Lt. | 152 | Pickup, H. J. | 92 | ——— S. B., 2/Lt. | 165 |
| ——— W. B., 2/Lt. | 39 | ——— R. L., 2/Lt. | 35 | Pidduck, E. W., Lieut. | 72 | Porteus, J., 2/Lt. | 52 |
| Pawsey, C. R., Capt. | 63 | Percy, F., Lieut. | 62 | Piesse, C. L., 2/Lt. | 21 | Portman, G. M. B., Capt. | 128 |
| ——— J. S., 2/Lt. | 62 | Pereira, A. E. W., 2/Lt. | 100 | Pighills, J. A., 2/Lt. | 52 | Potter, A. T., Lieut. | 68 |
| Paxton, A. G., Capt. | 98 | ——— F. V. C., Lieut. | 37 | Pike, A. B., Lieut. | 140 | ——— G. W. H., 2/Lt. | 15 |
| ——— J., 2/Lt. | 98 | Perham, W., Fl. Lieut. | 177 | ——— C.B.,Capt.Rev. | 135 | ——— H. W., 2/Lt. | 52 |
| Payne, A. C. J., 2/Lt. | 173 | Perkins, C. J. T., 2/Lt. | 111 | ——— E. A., Lieut. | 101 | ——— K. R., Capt. | 34 |
| ——— A. S., 2/Lt. | 117 | ——— G., Capt. | 189 | ——— P. R., Lieut. | 129 | ——— L. R., Lieut. | 183 |
| ——— H. E. A., 2/Lt. | 34 | Perks, G., Agent | 189 | Pilcher, A. M., 2/Lt. | 129 | ——— S., 2/Lt. | 30 |
| ——— H. S., 2/Lt. | 22 | ——— H., Capt. | 88 | Pill, S. V. P., Capt. | 134 | Potts, D., Lieut. | 131 |
| ——— J. M., 2/Lt. | 175 | Perrett, F. C., 2/Lt. | 63 | Pilley, E. A., Capt. | 85 | ——— J. P., 2/Lt. | 129 |
| ——— P., 2/Lt. | 171 | ——— R. E., Capt. and Adjt. | 130 | Pim, A. S., Capt. | 47 | ——— W. J., 2/Lt. | 175 |
| Peacey, R., Lieut. | 114 | Perring, J. H., 2/Lt. | 174 | Pinder, F. G., 2/Lt. | 147 | Poulter, C. G., 2/Lt. | 38 |
| Peachey, B. W., Lieut. | 80 | Perry, A. M., Sub-Lt. | 144 | ——— L., 2/Lt. | 64 | ——— W. F., Lieut. | 160 |
| Peacock, B., 2/Lt. | 27 | ——— B. B., Lieut. | 157 | Pineau, F. C., Lieut. | 174 | Pouncey, J. R., 2/Lt. | 70 |
| ——— F., 2/Lt. | 142 | ——— H., Capt. | 131 | Pinkerton, A. L., 2/Lt. | 149 | Powell, D., Lieut. | 189 |
| ——— N. L., Lt. | 186 | ——— P. P., Lieut. | 117 | Pinkney, M. R., 2/Lt. | 100 | ——— D. G., Lieut. | 156 |
| ——— J. W., 2/Lt. | 138 | ——— S. T. J. | 33 | Pinnick, L. W., Lieut. | 66 | ——— F. G., Capt. | 167 |
| ——— M. A., 2/Lt. | 156 | Perryman, H. M., 2/Lt. | 120 | Pinnington, E. A., 2/Lt. | 181 | ——— F. J., Major, M.C. | 159 |
| Peake, C. W. V., Lieut. | 62 | Peskett, R. F., Lieut. | 35 | Pinnock, A., Lieut. | 90 | ——— G. E., 2/Lt. | 51 |
| Pearce, C., 2/Lt. | 31 | Petavel, Paul Major | 66 | Piper, A. L., 2/Lt. | 75 | ——— J. F., 2/Lt. | 79 |
| ——— E., Lieut. | 117 | Peters, J. F. J. | 169 | ——— E. C., 2/Lt. | 69 | ——— T., 2/Lt. | 14 |
| ——— J. P., 2/Lt. | 75 | ——— S. F., 2/Lt. | 121 | ——— Percy, 2/Lt. | 31 | ——— H. T., Lieut. | 181 |
| ——— K., 2/Lt. | 38 | Peterson, G. G.W., 2/Lt. | 158 | Pirouet, E. K. G., Lieut. | 42 | ——— T. C. K., 2/Lt. | 128 |
| ——— L. W. C., Lieut. | 166 | Petley, R. E., Lieut. | 130 | Pirie, D. A., Capt. | 142 | ——— W., 2/Lt. | 64 |
| ——— W. H., 2/Lt. | 13 | Petit, G., 2/Lt., M.C. | 114 | Pitblado, C. B., Lieut. | 138 | ——— W. B., Lt.-Col. | 184 |
| Pearcy, G. S., Capt. | 30 | Petrie, W. R., Capt. | 105 | Pitman, R. C., Lieut. | 171 | Power, H. E., 2/Lt. | 174 |
| Pearse, L. H., 2/Lt. | 65 | Pettigrew, W., 2/Lt. | 61 | Pitt, W H., 2/Lt. | 62 | ——— J. F., Lieut. | 133 |
| Pearson, B. C., Capt. | 167 | Pettit, A. W. B., Lieut. | 137 | Pittar, G. P., 2/Lt. | 12 | ——— K. W., Lieut. | 10 |
| ——— D. H., Major | 179 | ——— S. L., Capt. | 181 | Pittard, R. S. R., Lieut. | 56 | Poweys, A. R., Capt. | 49 |
| ——— E., Capt. | 37 | Peverell,T.H.,Capt.-Adjr. | 104 | Pitts, F. B., 2/Lt. | 46 | Powl, S. R., 2/Lt. | 128 |
| ——— F. A., 2/Lt. | 88 | Phelan, R. S., 2/Lt. | 155 | Pitz, R. F., 2/Lc. | 44 | Pownall, J. W., 2/Lt. | 85 |
| ——— H. F., Capt. | 88 | Phelps, A., Capt. | 29 | Place, C. O., Lt.-Col. | 7 | Pragnell, F., Capt. | 78 |
| ——— J. M., Lieut. | 174 | ——— H. J., 2/Lt. | 34 | Plackett, C. H., Capt. | 85 | Pratt, A. B., Capt., M.C. | 62 |
| ——— L. H., Lieut. | 46 | ——— H. M. P., 2/Lt. | 30 | Plant, C. B., Lieut. | 125 | ——— A. R., 2/Lt. | 175 |
| ——— L. J., 2/Lt. | 147 | Philby, G. B., Lieut. | 38 | Platt, Percy, 2/Lt. | 50 | ——— H., 2/Lt. | 92 |
| ——— M., Major | 184 | Philip, D., 2/Lt. | 68 | Player, J. G., 2/Lt. | 63 | ——— O. S., Major | 89 |
| ——— R. W., Capt. | 134 | ——— G. H., 2/Lt. | 12 | Pleasance, M. D., Lieut. | 96 | Preston, A., Lieut. | 131 |
| ——— W. G., Capt. | 23 | ——— J. W., Capt. | 186 | Plews, J. C., Lieut. | 85 | ——— A., 2/Lt. | 170 |
| ——— W. N., 2/Lt. | 49 | Philips, G. P., 2/Lt. | 17 | Plimsoll, S. R. C., Capt. | 14 | ——— H., 2/Lt. | 40 |
| ——— W. O., 2/Lt. | 88 | Phillimore, G. W., Lieut. | 57 | Plowman, Paul, Lieut. | 72 | ——— J. T., Capt. | 35 |
| ——— W. S. L. M., Lieut. | 180 | Phillips, A., 2/Lt. | 127 | Plumb, R. H., Lieut. | 23 | Pretty, C. W., 2/Lt. | 43 |
| Pease, D., 2/Lt. | 19 | ——— A. W., Fl. Sub-Lt. | 177 | Plummer, J. E. B., Capt. | 33 | ——— H. J., 2/Lt. | 172 |
| Peat, R. W., Lieut. | 163 | ——— C. W., 2/Lt. | 76 | Pocock, A. N. D., 2/Lt. | 187 | ——— R. C., 2/Lt. | 172 |
| Peck, A. J., Capt. | 28 | ——— E. C. M., Lt.-Col. | 131 | ——— J. A., Lieut. | 185 | Price, H. W., Major | 185 |
| ——— J. N., Lt.-Col. | 34 | ——— E. S., Lieut. | 133 | ——— P. F., Major | 184 | ——— J. H., 2/Lt. | 152 |
| Peckham, C. W., Lieut. | 164 | ——— G. C., Capt. | 130 | Pollack, J., Lieut. | 110 | ——— L., Capt. | 89 |
| Peddie, F., 2/Lt., M.C. | 25 | ——— G. N., 2/Lt. | 15 | Pollard, A. M., Capt. | 131 | ——— O., Lieut. | 67 |
| Pedley, J. G., 2/Lt. | 42 | ——— J. R., 2/Lt. | 84 | ——— R. W., 2/Lt. | 30 | ——— P., 2/Lt. | 180 |
| Pedrick, F. B., Lieut. | 133 | ——— J. S., Lieut. | 118 | ——— W. H., Lieut. | 168 | ——— R., Lieut. | 143 |
| Peebles, A., Major | 37 | ——— K. McN., 2/Lt. | 100 | Pollitt, G. P., Lt.-Col. | 52 | ——— R. T., 2/Lt. | 113 |
| Peek, R. G., Lieut. | 9 | | | Pollock, J. B., 2/Lt. | 74 | ——— W., 2/Lt. | 59 |
| Peel, B. G., Major | 182 | | | ——— J.J.McE., 2/Lt. | 111 | ——— W. G., 2/Lt. | 65 |
| Peeling, H. V., 2/Lt. | 169 | | | | | | |

| | PAGE | | PAGE | | PAGE | | PAGE |
|---|---|---|---|---|---|---|---|
| Price, W. N., 2/Lt. | 98 | Ramsay, R. W., 2/Lt. | 73 | Rees, C. B. R., Lieut. | 49 | Richardson, G. T., Lieut. | 175 |
| Prichard, F. H., Capt. | 10 | ———— W. A., Lieut | 75 | ———— D. Ivor, 2/Lt. | 73 | ———— H. R., Capt. | 141 |
| ———— O. T., Capt. | 96 | Ramwell, J., Sub-Lt. | 145 | ———— E. C., 2/Lt. | 125 | ———— John, 2/Lt. | 26 |
| Priday, H. E. L., 2/Lt. | 68 | Randall, C. H., Capt. | 54 | ———— E. T., Lt.-Col. | 34 | ———— J. B., 2/Lt. | 171 |
| ———— N. H., 2/Lt. | 42 | Randell, W. B., 2/Lt. | 159 | ———— H., Brig.-Gen. | 7 | ———— J. P., Lieut. & Qmr. | 186 |
| Prideaux-Brune, F. K., Lieut. | 8 | Ranken, W. J. S., 2/Lt. | 122 | ———— H. R., 2/Lt. | 25 | ———— L. N., Lieut. | 108 |
| Prier, W. J., 2/Lt. | 162 | Rankin, C. D., Lt.-Col. | 131 | ———— W., 2/Lt. | 67 | ———— R. H., 2/Lt. | 156 |
| Priest, W. E. G., 2/Lt. | 100 | ———— W. A., Lieut. | 173 | ———— W. A., Capt. | 134 | ———— W. J., 2/Lt. | 101 |
| Priestly, H. E., Capt. | 131 | Rankine, A. C., 2/Lt. | 58 | ———— W. H., Lieut. | 111 | ———— W. M., Lieut. | 66 |
| Prime, H. L., 2/Lt. | 174 | Ransome, J. E. G., T/Capt. | 189 | Reeve, A., Lieut. | 34 | Riches, J. E., 2/Lt. | 92 |
| Pring, W., 2/Lt. | 106 | Ranson, A., Lieut. | 101 | Reeves, C. H., 2/Lt. | 118 | Richey, R. A., Lieut. | 111 |
| Pringle, R. M., 2/Lt. | 20 | ———— F. R., Capt. | 136 | ———— R., Lieut. | 12 | Richmond, A. H. D., Lieut. | 112 |
| Prior, E. G., Lieut. | 91 | Rasmussen, F. G. J., 2/Lt. | 11 | ———— W. A., 2/Lt. | 150 | Rick, J. H., Lieut. | 52 |
| ———— W. H., 2/Lt. | 30 | Ratcliffe, B. Lieut. | 39 | Reid, A., 2/Lt. | 74 | Rickards, A. R. M., 2/Lt. | 151 |
| Pristo, W. E., 2/Lt. | 91 | ———— T., Lieut. | 162 | ———— A. McK., Capt. | 121 | Rickard, H., Lieut. | 67 |
| Pritchard, R. J., 2/Lt. | 121 | Rathbone, C. E. H., Lt.-Col. | 151 | ———— C. W., Lieut. | 159 | ———— J., Lieut. | 131 |
| Pritchett, W., Capt. | 78 | ———— G. P., Lieut. | 98 | ———— G. C. W., Lieut. | 137 | Rickett, G. F., Lieut. | 129 |
| Profit, G. S. W., 2/Lt. | 77 | ———— H. J., 2/Lt. | 90 | ———— H. G., Lieut. | 176 | ———— W. H. A., 2/Lt. | 164 |
| Prothero, A. G., Major | 72 | ———— Leonard, 2/Lt. | 97 | ———— H. C., Lieut. | 93 | Riddell, L. H., Lieut. | 167 |
| Pruden, W. C., 2/Lt. | 158 | Rathborne, H. B., 2/Lt. | 71 | ———— J. E., Lieut. | 170 | Riddle, A. B., Lieut. | 188 |
| Pryde, R. M., Capt. | 109 | Ratliff, P. G., 2/Lt. | 162 | ———— J. F., Lieut. | 164 | Rideout, F. O., 2/Lt. | 43 |
| Pryce, F. M., 2/Lt. | 179 | Rattborne, C., Lieut. | 177 | ———— Kenneth, 2/Lt. | 104 | Ridgard, B. H., 2/Lt. | 64 |
| Pryor, J. W., Lieut. | 164 | Raven, C. H., 2/Lt. | 128 | ———— L. K., 2/Lt. | 109 | Ridgewell, L. P., 2/Lt. | 137 |
| Puckridge, H. V., Capt. | 165 | Ravenshaw, H. S. L., Brig.-Gen. | 7 | ———— S. E., Capt. | 51 | ———— S. C., 2/Lt. | 179 |
| Pugh, J., 2/Lt. | 175 | Rawden, C. H., Lieut. | 85 | ———— W., 2/Lt. | 146 | Ridgway, F. J., 2/Lt. | 68 |
| ———— J. A., Lieut. | 165 | Rawes, A. N., 2/Lt. | 12 | Reidy, F. J., Capt. | 26 | Ridley, C. A., 2/Lt. | 148 |
| Pughe-Evans, H., 2/Lt. | 157 | Rawlings, E. E., 2/Lt. | 47 | Reilly, H. L., Major | 180 | ———— C. B., Lieut. | 165 |
| Pulfer, L. H., 2/Lt. | 76 | ———— F. R., 2/Lt. | 61 | Rendle, G. A., 2/Lt. | 30 | ———— H. M., 2/Lt. | 102 |
| Pullin, A. H., 2/Lt. | 14 | Rawlinson, C. R., Capt. | 113 | Rennells, F. C., 2/Lt. | 84 | ———— P., 2/Lt. | 125 |
| Pulpher, L., 2/Lt. | 95 | ———— G. E., Lieut. | 126 | Rennie, H. R., 2/Lt. | 108 | ———— R. T., Capt. | 91 |
| Punchard, F. N., 2/Lt. | 184 | Rawson, Herbert, Sub-Lt. | 145 | ———— W. K., Lieut. | 120 | Riecke, A. F. M., Major | 11 |
| Purcell, V. W. W. S., Lieut. | 49 | ———— H. W., Capt. | 20 | Renshaw, H. W., 2/Lt. | 70 | Riffkin, R., 2/Lt | 174 |
| Puri, M. L., Capt. | 182 | Rawson-Shaw, K., Lieut. | 146 | Rethman, H. M. | 142 | Rigby, C., 2/Lt. | 80 |
| Purnell, A. W., 2/Lt. | 15 | Rayment, S. C., 2/Lt. | 78 | Reveley, P. T. A., 2/Lt. | 167 | ———— H. A., Lieut. | 138 |
| Purry, R. O., Capt. | 164 | Rawstorne, R. A., Lieut. | 178 | Reynard, C. H., 2/Lt. | 90 | ———— H. J., 2/Lt. | 40 |
| Purves, A. B., Capt. and Adjt. | 54 | Raymond, A. B., Lieut. | 153 | Reyne, G. R., Capt. | 183 | Rigden, B. L., Lieut. | 17 |
| ———— G., Lieut. | 115 | ———— L. B., 2/Lt. | 169 | Reynell, A. W., 2/Lt. | 148 | Riley, A. H., Lieut. | 42 |
| ———— S. S. B., 2/Lt. | 150 | Raymond-Barker, A. B. Lieut. | 149 | Reynolds, B. W., Lt. | 183 | ———— E. J., 2/Lt. | 166 |
| Purvis, W. B., Capt. | 97 | Rayner, A. E., 2/Lt. | 47 | ———— E. R. B., 2/Lt. | 12 | ———— F. B., Lieut. | 93 |
| Puryear, G., 2/Lt. | 169 | ———— C., 2/Lt. | 91 | ———— G. N., Capt. | 9 | ———— H. A., Lieut. | 64 |
| Pye, B. W., 2/Lt. | 35 | ———— L. S. P. H., 2/Lt. | 121 | ———— J. W., Lieut. | 36 | ———— R. R., Lieut. | 70 |
| Pym, F. G., Lieut. | 173 | Raynor, C. A., Capt. | 183 | ———— L. G. S., Major | 174 | Rimington, H. P., 2/Lt. | 84 |
| Pye, S., Lieut. | 93 | Rea, W. G., 2/Lt. | 18 | ———— T., Capt. | 85 | Ringer, E. C. S., 2/Lt. | 157 |
| Pyrke, L., 2/Lt. | 83 | ———— W. Q., 2/Lt. | 110 | ———— T. B., Lieut. | 121 | Ringham, H. T., 2/Lt. | 96 |
| | | Read, B. R. C., 2/Lt. | 116 | ———— W. J., Capt. | 90 | Rintoul, A., 2/Lt. | 138 |
| Quaintrell, A. E., 2/Lt. | 64 | ———— J. A., Lieut. | 189 | Rhett, R. B., Lieut. | 133 | Risk, J. B., 2/Lt. | 168 |
| Quayle, M., Lieut. | 63 | ———— J. F. W., Lieut. | 186 | Rhodes, C. W., Lieut. | 138 | Rissik, A. W. M., Capt. | 115 |
| Quigley, J. E., Lieut. | 133 | ———— L., 2/Lt. | 155 | ———— F. O., Lieut. | 120 | Ritchie, F. K. St. M., 2/Lt. | 142 |
| Quill, M. J., 2/Lt. | 70 | ———— R. J., 2/Lt. | 142 | ———— J. F., Lieut. | 67 | ———— J. N., Major | 13 |
| Quilter, E. G. C., 2/Lt. | 155 | Reader, R., 2/Lt. | 92 | ———— Tom, 2/Lt. | 124 | ———— T. M., 2/Lt. | 166 |
| Quine, A. H., 2/Lt. | 181 | Reakes, S. R. K., 2/Lt. | 14 | Riach, W. H., Capt. | 107 | ———— W. H., 2/Lt. | 31 |
| ———— R. H., 2/Lt. | 25 | Reay, R. H., Lieut. | 17 | Ribbons, A., Lieut. | 111 | Ritson, J. R., Major | 101 |
| | | Record, J. A. C., 2/Lt. | 22 | Rice, J. A. T., Capt., M.C. | 9 | Ritzema, J. R., Lieut. | 26 |
| Race, A., 2/Lt. | 99 | Reddie, Robert, Capt. | 34 | Rich, H. H., Lieut. | 184 | Rivers, S., Lieut. | 48 |
| ———— C., 2/Lt. | 35 | Redfern, L., 2/Lt. | 97 | Richardes, R. A. W. P., Lieut. | 188 | Robb, A. G., Lieut., M.C. | 59 |
| Rackett, A. R., Lieut. | 138 | Redgrave, W. T., Lieut. | 118 | Richards, A., 2/Lt. | 33 | ———— A. W., 2/Lt. | 58 |
| Radfield, J. J., 2/Lt. | 169 | Redhead, St. G., 2/Lt. | 46 | ———— C. R., 2/Lt., M.C. | 155 | ———— R. B., Lieut. | 118 |
| Radford, W., 2/Lt. | 63 | Redington, F. H. C., Lieut. | 120 | ———— C. S., 2/Lt. | 129 | Robbins, G., 2/Lt. | 118 |
| Radley, J. E., Lieut. | 175 | Redman, C. E., Capt. | 132 | ———— F. W., 2/Lt. | 115 | ———— W. A., 2/Lt. | 115 |
| Rae, G. R., Capt. | 183 | Redmond, M. Snowdon | 133 | ———— H. U., Lieut. | 62 | Roberts, A. D., Lieut. | 14 |
| ———— R. M., 2/Lt. | 24 | Redpath, H. S., Lieut. | 161 | ———— J., 2/Lt. | 57 | ———— A. K., 2/Lt. | 12 |
| Raggett, R. J., 2/Lt. | 109 | Reece, C., 2/Lt. | 152 | ———— J., 2/Lt. | 24 | ———— A. M., Lieut. | 166 |
| Raikes, J. F. C., Lieut. | 126 | ———— S. B., 2/Lt. | 163 | ———— J. D. M., 2/Lt. | 56 | ———— A. W., 2/Lt. | 42 |
| Railton, R., 2/Lt. | 100 | Reed, F. H., 2/Lt. | 174 | ———— J. Ivor, Lieut. | 73 | ———— C. L., 2/Lt. | 149 |
| Raine, H. E., Lieut. | 102 | ———— W., Lieut. | 187 | ———— R., 2/Lt. | 90 | ———— D. R. E., Capt. | 132 |
| Rainier, G. A., 2/Lt. | 163 | ———— W. J., 2/Lt. | 37 | ———— R. H., 2/Lt. | 32 | ———— E., Capt. | 41 |
| Rainsford-Hannay, A. G., Major | 17 | Reeks, Neville, Capt. | 187 | ———— R. J., 2/Lt. | 75 | ———— E., 2/Lt. | 46 |
| Raleigh, A. G., 2/Lt. | 46 | ———— V. R., Capt. | 185 | ———— R. J., Lieut. | 141 | ———— E., 2/Lt. | 164 |
| Ralston, K. B., 2/Lt. | 55 | Rees, B. E., Lieut. | 17 | Richardson, A. R., Lt.-Col. | 127 | ———— E, Capt | 85 |
| Rampling, H., Capt. | 167 | | | ———— D. D., Lieut. | 161 | ———— E. D., 2/Lt. | 70 |
| Ramsay, A. FitzG., Major | 8 | | | ———— D. H., 2/Lt. | 101 | ———— F. W., Capt., M.C. | 84 |
| ———— H. S., Lieut. | 137 | | | ———— G., 2/Lt. | 92 | ———— G. D., Lieut. | 100 |

| | PAGE | | PAGE | | PAGE | | PAGE |
|---|---|---|---|---|---|---|---|
| Roberts, G. T., 2/Lt. | 127 | Robson, F., 2/Lt. | 95 | Ross, J. A., Lieut. | 140 | St. Ledger, A., 2/Lt. | 70 |
| ——— H. E., 2/Lt. | 64 | ——— G. B., 2/Lt. | 66 | ——— L. J., 2/Lt. | 108 | Sabey, A. R., 2/Lt. | 170 |
| ——— H.G., Lt.-Col. | 51 | ——— H. T., 2/Lt. | 49 | ——— P. B., 2/Lt. | 98 | Sadgrove, K. H. O'R., Capt. | 72 |
| ——— H. J. W., Lieut. | 169 | ——— J. W., 2/Lt. | 68 | ——— P. M., Lieut. | 58 | Salisbury, O., Lieut. | 73 |
| ——— N., 2/Lt. | 117 | ——— L. S., Capt. | 20 | ——— R. Y., 2/Lt. | 127 | Salley, A., 2/Lt. | 13 |
| ——— P. A., Lieut. | 57 | ——— N. K., 2/Lt. | 107 | ——— W., Lieut. | 159 | Salmond, H. G., Capt. | 148 |
| ——— R. E., Lieut. | 83 | ——— T. A., Lieut. | 49 | ——— W. A. N., 2/Lt. | 106 | Salmons, H., 2/Lt. | 40 |
| ——— R. M., Lieut. | 153 | ——— W., 2/Lt. | 74 | Rothery, W., 2/Lt. | 156 | Salter, H. P., Sub.-Lt. | 177 |
| ——— T. H., 2/Lt. | 83 | Roche, S., 2/Lt. | 151 | Rought, C. J., 2/Lt. | 21 | ——— Y. W., 2/Lt. | 108 |
| ——— W. S., 2/Lt. | 179 | ——— W. J., Lieut. | 47 | Rounds, R. W. | 77 | Salvidge, A. T., Capt. | 33 |
| Robertshaw, P. S., 2/Lt. | 23 | ——— W. W., Capt. | 111 | Roussel, R., Capt. | 111 | Sampson, F. A., Lieut. | 30 |
| Robertson, A., Lieut. | 19 | Rochester, G., 2/Lt. | 169 | Routh, L., Lieut. | 131 | ——— H. W., 2/Lt. | 85 |
| ——— A. S., Capt. | 136 | Rochford, S. W., Lieut. | 170 | Routley, W. F., Capt. | 97 | ——— H. V., Lieut. | 64 |
| ——— A. W. M., 2/Lt. | 106 | Rockey, J., Lieut. | 176 | Rowan, A., Lieut. | 188 | Samson, H. W., Capt. | 58 |
| ——— Hon. B. F. R., Capt. | 9 | Rodger, J. C., 2/Lt. | 27 | Rowbotham, G. V., Capt. | 75 | Sams, F. D. H., 2/Lt. | 148 |
| ——— C. A., 2/Lt. | 80 | ——— K. M., Lieut. | 159 | Rowbottom, J., 2/Lt. | 64 | Samuel, J. R., Lieut. | 152 |
| ——— C. G., Lieut. | 139 | ——— W. H., 2/Lt. | 116 | Rowden, W. H., Lieut. | 133 | ——— F. D., Capt. | 89 |
| ——— C. T. A., Major | 106 | Rodman, F., Lieut. | 62 | Rowe, C. D., 2/Lt. | 31 | Samuels, F. A., 2/Lt. | 66 |
| ——— C. W., 2/Lt. | 96 | Rodney, C. C. S., Lieut. | 17 | ——— G. F., Lieut. | 100 | Rowe-Evans, C. B., Lieut. | 12 |
| ——— D., Lieut. | 134 | Rodwell, L. H., Capt. | 38 | Rowe-Evans, C. B., Lieut. | 12 | Sandbach, A. E. W., 2/Lt. | 22 |
| ——— D. B., Lieut. | 64 | Roe, W. R., 2/Lt. | 30 | Rowland, T., 2/Lt. | 56 | Sandeman, F. S., 2/Lt. | 107 |
| ——— F., 2/Lt. | 68 | Roebuck, E. de L. W., Lieut. | 36 | Rowlerson, G. A., 2/Lt. | 75 | ——— H. B., Capt. | 112 |
| ——— G., Capt. | 54 | Rofe, H. H., 2/Lt. | 174 | Rowley, C. S., Lieut. | 17 | ——— M. G., Capt. | 112 |
| ——— G. J., 2/Lt. | 107 | Roffe, H. F., 2/Lt. | 142 | Rowsell, G. W. N., Lieut. | 68 | Sanders, C. E., 2/Lt. | 119 |
| ——— G. M., 2/Lt. | 153 | Rogers, C. W., Lieut. | 182 | ——— V. N., Lieut. | 18 | ——— D. C. W., 2/Lt. | 146 |
| ——— G. P., 2/Lt. | 155 | ——— D. A., 2/Lt. | 27 | Royall, A. R., Lieut. | 47 | ——— G., Capt., V.C. | 41 |
| ——— H G., Staff Surgeon | 7 | ——— E. S., 2/Lt. | 32 | Roylance, C. K., 2/Lt. | 16 | ——— H. W., Lieut. | 89 |
| ——— J., 2/Lt. | 123 | ——— Fred. I., Lieut. | 167 | Royle, A. H., 2/Lt. | 25 | ——— J. W., Lieut. | 149 |
| ——— J. A. M., 2/Lt. | 158 | ——— G. F., Lieut. | 49 | ——— J., 2/Lt. | 46 | ——— R. E., Lieut. | 136 |
| ——— J G., 2/Lt. | 148 | ——— G. N., 2/Lt. | 183 | Rubinstein, R. F., Capt. | 61 | ——— W., 2/Lt. | 175 |
| ——— J. S., 2/Lt. | 104 | ——— G. W. H., 2/Lt. | 30 | Rudd, G. B. F., Capt. | 46 | ——— W. L., Lieut. | 90 |
| ——— N. C., Capt. | 70 | ——— H. G., Lieut. | 140 | Ruddock, H. W., 2/Lt. | 60 | ——— W. T., 2/Lt. | 37 |
| ——— R., 2/Lt. | 91 | ——— J. N., 2/Lt. | 101 | Rudge, G. M., Capt. | 100 | Sanderson, C. B., 2/Lt. | 172 |
| ——— R. S., 2/Lt. | 122 | ——— P. D., 2/Lt. | 91 | Rudman, Walter, Lieut. | 162 | ——— H. E., Capt. | 19 |
| ——— T., 2/Lt. | 30 | ——— R. P., Lieut. | 93 | Rumble, G. L., 2/Lt. | 116 | ——— J., 2/Lt. | 87 |
| ——— W., 2/Lt. | 63 | ——— S., 2/Lt. | 15 | Rundle, S., Lieut. | 67 | ——— O., Capt. | 8 |
| ——— W. C., Lieut. | 142 | ——— S. A., Capt. | 78 | Runnels-Moss, E. C. A., 2/Lt. | 12 | Sandes, E. W. C., Capt. | 185 |
| Robey, S., 2/Lt. | 118 | ——— S. E., Capt. | 142 | Rush, A. W., 2/Lt. | 157 | Sandiford, H. A., Capt. | 132 |
| Robins, L. I. O., Major | 72 | Rogerson, E. W., 2/Lt. | 47 | Rushton, E. R., Lieut. | 87 | Sandison, R. E. W., 2/Lt. | 123 |
| ——— S. M., Lieut. | 164 | ——— H., Lieut. | 154 | ——— P. C., 2/Lt. | 63 | Sandys-Thomas, C. J., 2/Lt. | 148 |
| Robinson, A., Lieut. | 64 | ——— J. C., Lieut. | 9 | Rushworth, H. M., Capt. | 155 | Sanford, S. A., Lieut. | 146 |
| ——— A., 2/Lt. | 20 | Rolfe, B. R., Lieut. | 173 | Russel, C. H., Lieut. | 66 | Sankey, I., Capt. | 52 |
| ——— A. C., 2/Lt. | 128 | ——— C. F., 2/Lt. | 69 | Russell, A. Scott, Capt. | 16 | Sargent, E. F., Lieut. | 92 |
| ——— A. D., 2/Lt. | 43 | ——— R. W. T., Lieut. | 126 | ——— A. L., Lieut. | 147 | Sarson, E. V., Col. | 13 |
| ——— A. K., 2/Lt. | 17 | Rollo, W., Lieut. | 103 | ——— D. J., 2/Lt. | 163 | Saunders, E. J., Lieut. | 55 |
| ——— A. Q., 2/Lt. | 54 | Rolls, J. A., 2/Lt. | 89 | ——— F. C., Lieut. | 167 | ——— J. A., Capt. | 115 |
| ——— A. S., Capt. | 135 | Rolph, E. G., Lieut. | 172 | ——— G. C., 2/Lt. | 171 | ——— J. T., Lieut. | 121 |
| ——— B. W., 2/Lt. | 161 | ——— J., Lieut. | 118 | ——— H. B., Lieut. | 147 | ——— P. C., Major | 185 |
| ——— C. R., 2/Lt. | 142 | Rolston, G. R., 2/Lt. | 123 | ——— H. V., Lieut. | 25 | ——— T. W., Lieut. | 32 |
| ——— D. E., Major | 23 | Rooke, W. E., 2/Lt. | 91 | ——— H. W., Lieut. | 176 | ——— W. J., 2/Lt. | 165 |
| ——— E., Lieut. | 180 | Root, H. W., Lieut. | 121 | ——— J. E., 2/Lt. | 21 | Savory, A. J., 2/Lt. | 154 |
| ——— E., Lieut. | 137 | Roots, H. Sydney, 2/Lt. | 70 | ——— J. J., 2/Lt. | 69 | Saward, N. C., Lieut. | 155 |
| ——— E. B., Capt. | 43 | Roper, D. A., 2/Lt. | 64 | ——— L. C., Lieut. | 30 | Sawrey, K. W., 2/Lt. | 15 |
| ——— E. M., 2/Lt. | 128 | Ropner, R., 2/Lt. | 122 | ——— L. W. E., 2/Lt. | 45 | Sawyer, E. V., 2/Lt. | 84 |
| ——— F. B., 2/Lt. | 169 | Rose, A. M., Capt. | 131 | ——— Thos. R., Lieut. | 17 | Saxon, H., Capt. | 69 |
| ——— H. E., 2/Lt. | 48 | ——— C. S., Capt. | 135 | ——— W. O., Lieut. | 152 | Saxton, R. C., 2/Lt. | 81 |
| ——— H. G., 2/Lt. | 157 | ——— Donald, 2/Lt. | 170 | ——— W. J., Lieut. | 17 | Sayer, C., Lieut. | 101 |
| ——— H. W., Lt. | 41 | ——— E. C., Lieut. | 11 | Ruston, R. M., 2/Lt. | 7, 14 | Sayes, J., Lieut. | 40 |
| ——— J., 2/Lt. | 109 | ——— F. C., Capt. | 35 | ——— A. F. G., Major | 16 | Scadding, Eric., Lieut. | 166 |
| ——— J., 2/Lt. | 27 | ——— F. L., 2/Lt. | 35 | Rutherford, D. W., Capt. | 180 | Scallen, H., Lieut. | 142 |
| ——— J. B., 2/Lt. | 147 | ——— Geoffrey, Lieut. | 165 | ——— G., 2/Lt. | 106 | Sclater, V. C., 2/Lt. | 179 |
| ——— J. C., Lieut. | 164 | ——— G., Lieut. | 155 | ——— H., 2/Lt. | 102 | Scanlen, W. A., Rev. | 135 |
| ——— J. D., Lieut. | 76 | ——— G. T., 2/Lt. | 70 | Rutledge, A. E., Lieut. | 36 | Scarborough, F., 2/Lt. | 155 |
| ——— J. P., 2/Lt. | 9 | ——— H. B., Lieut. | 93 | Ryall, A. G., 2/Lt. | 150 | Scarfe, C. G., 2/Lt. | 46 |
| ——— J. P., 2/Lt. | 59 | ——— J. B., Lieut. | 140 | Ryan, F. B., Capt. | 132 | Scarisbrick, C., Lieut. | 19 |
| ——— L. K., 2/Lt. | 15 | ——— P., Capt. | 7 | ——— J. J., Lieut. | 9 | Scarlett, J. C. D., 2/Lt. | 14 |
| ——— L. M., Capt. | 51 | ——— R. H., 2/Lt. | 171 | ——— T. F., Lieut. | 132 | Scharff, R. L., 2/Lt. | 169 |
| ——— N., Lieut. | 148 | Rose-Troup, J. M., 2/Lt. | 21 | Rybot, N. V. I., Major | 183 | Schneider, C., Lieut. | 77 |
| ——— R. W. G., Lieut. | 100 | Rosenbleet, A. M., Lieut. | 176 | Ryden, A., 2/Lt. | 55 | Schofield, H., 2/Lt. | 83 |
| ——— W. L., Capt., V.C. | 151 | Roser, W. C., 2/Lt. | 65 | Ryder, A. L. D., Lieut. | 22 | ——— J. A., 2/Lt. | 129 |
| Robison, H. J., Lieut. | 59 | Ross, H., 2/Lt. | 51 | Rylands, F., 2/Lt. | 93 | ——— J. F., 2/Lt. | 95 |
| Robotham, J. A., Lieut. | 117 | ——— J., 2/Lt. | 34 | Rylatt, A., 2/Lt. | 85 | Scholefield, E. R. C., Lieut. | 146 |
| Robson, C. C., Lieut. | 162 | ——— J. A., 2/Lt. | 65 | Rymer, L., 2/Lt. | 49 | ——— R. S., Capt. | 30 |
| | | ——— J., Capt., M.C. | 133 | | | | |
| | | ——— James, Capt. | 112 | | | | |

| | PAGE |
|---|---|
| Scholfield, J. A., Capt. | 95 |
| Scholtz, E., 2/Lt. | 157 |
| Schooling, G. R., 2/Lt. | 167 |
| Schoon, C. F., Lieut. | 90 |
| Schorn, F. F., 2/Lt. | 168 |
| Schreiber, R. T. B., Lieut | 151 |
| Sclanders, A. R., 2/Lt. | 104 |
| Scoby, H. H., Lieut. | 43 |
| Scott, A., 2/Lt. | 110 |
| ——— A. N., Capt. | 63 |
| ——— C. A., Capt. | 144 |
| ——— C. E., 2/Lt. | 86 |
| ——— C. H., Lieut. | 116 |
| ——— C. R., Lieut. | 138 |
| ——— D. L., 2/Lt. | 58 |
| ——— E. J. F., 2/Lt. | 45 |
| ——— E. T., Lieut. | 11 |
| ——— F., 2/Lt. | 104 |
| ——— F. G., Capt. | 90 |
| ——— F. N., 2/Lt. | 80 |
| ——— H. J. W., 2/Lt. | 100 |
| ——— J., 2/Lt. | 111 |
| ——— J. P., Lieut. | 114 |
| ——— J. Y., Lieut. | 22 |
| ——— R. A., 2/Lt. | 19 |
| ——— T. R., 2/Lt., M.C. | 13 |
| ——— V. R., 2/Lt. | 40 |
| ——— W., Lieut. | 112 |
| ——— W. A., Lt. | 163 |
| ——— W. D., 2/Lt. | 39 |
| Scott-Brown, N. A., 2/Lt. | 147 |
| Scott-Kerr, W. F., Lieut. | 163 |
| Scovil, M. A., Capt. | 140 |
| Scrivener, H. A., 2/Lt. | 170 |
| ——— H. K., 2/Lt. | 165 |
| Scrutton, H. U., Capt. | 188 |
| Scudamore, T. V. S., Capt. | 139 |
| Sealy, H. G., Capt. | 189 |
| Seaman, W., Lieut. | 47 |
| Searle, R. J., 2/Lt. | 169 |
| Sears, H., 2/Lt. | 27 |
| ——— R. L., 2/Lt. | 89 |
| Seath, C. P., 2/Lt. | 110 |
| Seaton, J. W. S., Lieut. | 65 |
| Sebright, J. H. K., Lieut. | 89 |
| Seccombe, G., Capt. | 143 |
| Seddon, A. D., Capt. | 23 |
| Selby, C. W. P., 2/Lt. | 147 |
| Sellars, F. M., Lieut. | 169 |
| Sen, E. S. C., 2/Lt. | 156 |
| Senecal, H. C., 2/Lt. | 171 |
| Senior, H. H., 2/Lt. | 171 |
| ——— T. W., 2/Lt. | 31 |
| Sergeant, G., Lieut. | 40 |
| Settle, M., Capt. | 98 |
| Settrington, C., Lord | 18 |
| Severn, FitzD., 2/Lt. | 77 |
| Sewell, J. H. B., Lieut. | 95 |
| Seymour, L., Lieut. | 163 |
| Shackleton, W., Lieut. | 175 |
| Shadbolt, G. G., 2/Lt. | 127 |
| Shadwell, L. M., 2/Lt. | 156 |
| Shakesby, C. V., 2/Lt. | 160 |
| Shakeshaft, A. J., Capt. | 186 |
| Shanks, W. Y., 2/Lt. | 114 |
| Shanley, H. J., Lieut. | 111 |
| Shannon, J. A., 2/Lt. | 181 |
| ——— J. H., 2/Lt. | 61 |
| Shapton, H. W., 2/Lt. | 31 |
| Sharp, C. C., Capt. | 155 |
| ——— E. E., 2/Lt. | 52 |
| ——— H. F., 2/Lt. | 17 |
| ——— S. R. C., 2/Lt. | 91 |
| Sharpe, F., Lieut. | 154 |
| ——— F., 2/Lt. | 35 |

| | PAGE |
|---|---|
| Sharpe, J. S., Lieut. | 46 |
| ——— S. A., 2/Lt. | 151 |
| ——— T. S., Capt. | 161 |
| Shaw, C., 2/Lt. | 126 |
| ——— E. B. B., Lieut. | 189 |
| ——— E. H., Lieut. | 95 |
| ——— F. S., 2/Lt. | 96 |
| ——— G. M., Lieut. | 159 |
| ——— H. M., Lieut. | 189 |
| ——— J. de B., 2/Lt. | 124 |
| ——— J. P., Lieut. | 87 |
| ——— J. W., Lieut. | 154 |
| ——— W., Lieut. | 126 |
| ——— W. H., Lieut. | 81 |
| ——— W. R., 2/Lt. | 45 |
| Shaw-MacLaren, T. D., Lieut. | 74 |
| Shawcross, E. L., 2/Lt. | 42 |
| Sheard, F. M., Capt. | 34 |
| Shearer, A., 2/Lt. | 102 |
| ——— T., 2/Lt. | 109 |
| Sheather, R. W. E., 2/Lt. | 21 |
| Shebbeare, F. W., 2/Lt. | 117 |
| Shedel, W. G., Capt. | 169 |
| Sheen, R. C., Capt. | 89 |
| Shell, W. H., Lieut. | 166 |
| Shelley, G., 2/Lt. | 75 |
| ——— V. B., Capt. | 98 |
| Shelton, F. E., Capt. | 45 |
| ——— L. J., Lieut. | 71 |
| Shepard, T., 2/Lt. | 150 |
| Shepheard, E. P. W., 2/Lt. | 92 |
| Shepherd, A. L. M., 2/Lt. | 149 |
| ——— A. S., 2/Lt. | 154 |
| ——— R. S., 2/Lt. | 38 |
| ——— W. E., Capt. | 99 |
| Sheppard, G. M., 2/Lt. | 61 |
| ——— H. J., 2/Lt. | 32 |
| Sheridan, F. S., 2/Lt. | 180 |
| ——— T., 2/Lt. | 64 |
| Shewen, W. N., Lieut. | 58 |
| Shewin, H. M., Major | 113 |
| Shield, T. L., Lieut. | 41 |
| Shields, P. R., Capt. | 80 |
| Shillington, T. C., Lieut. | 147 |
| Shipman, T. T., Lieut. | 168 |
| Shipton, G. A., 2/Lt. | 170 |
| ——— H. E., 2/Lt. | 71 |
| Shipway, W. G., Lieut. | 61 |
| Shipwright, A. T., 2/Lt. | 155 |
| Shook, J. K., Lieut. | 173 |
| Shore, J. L., Capt. | 54 |
| Shorman, L. E., 2/Lt. | 31 |
| Short, J. R., Capt. | 26 |
| ——— O. J., 2/Lt. | 63 |
| ——— W. P., Lieut. | 98 |
| Shorter, R. M., Capt. | 58 |
| Shott, V. B., 2/Lt. | 45 |
| Shreeve, F. D., 2/Lt. | 161 |
| Shubrook, A. W., 2/Lt. | 61 |
| Shufflebotham, J., Capt. | 72 |
| Shum, C. A. R., 2/Lt. | 150 |
| Shurrock, F. A., Lieut. | 41 |
| Shutt, F. J., 2/Lt. | 97 |
| Shutte, L. A., 2/Lt. | 103 |
| Sibley, S. J., Capt. | 159 |
| Siddons, J. T., 2/Lt. | 77 |
| Siems, F. W. M., 2/Lt. | 97 |
| Sieveking, L. de G., Fl. Lieut., D.S.O. | 177 |
| Sievers, R. F., Capt. | 130 |
| Silburn, L., Lieut. | 100 |
| Silcock, F. H., 2/Lt. | 130 |
| Silk, R. W., Lieut. | 174 |
| Sills, F. C., 2/Lt. | 128 |

| | PAGE |
|---|---|
| Silverwood, A. E., 2/Lt. | 78 |
| Sime, A. W., Lieut. | 139 |
| ——— T., Lieut. | 117 |
| Simmonds, W. A., Capt. | 70 |
| Simmons, D. A., Lieut. | 187 |
| ——— J. A., 2/Lt. | 38 |
| ——— W. R., 2/Lt. | 48 |
| Simms, P. J., 2/Lt. | 75 |
| Simner, P. R. O. A., Lt.-Col. | 41 |
| Simon, G. P., Lt. | 154 |
| Simonds, J. B., 2/Lt. | 70 |
| Simons, A. T., 2/Lt. | 165 |
| ——— F. L. C., 2/Lt. | 95 |
| Simpson, A., 2/Lt. | 90 |
| ——— A. A., 2/Lt. | 52 |
| ——— A. B., Capt. | 134 |
| ——— A. M., 2/Lt. | 74 |
| ——— C. J., Major | 105 |
| ——— E. H., Lieut. | 139 |
| ——— G., Capt. | 76 |
| ——— J. B., Lieut. | 105 |
| ——— L., Capt. | 85 |
| ——— R., Lieut. | 70 |
| ——— W. J. S., Lieut. | 88 |
| ——— R. W., 2/Lt. | 72 |
| ——— W., 2/Lt. | 122 |
| ——— W. L., Capt. | 37 |
| Simson, J. A., 2/Lt. | 174 |
| Sinclair, A. J., 2/Lt. | 62 |
| ——— A. S., 2/Lt. | 167 |
| ——— D. B., 2/Lt. | 170 |
| ——— E. H., 2/Lt. | 122 |
| ——— G. I., Lieut. | 17 |
| ——— L. R., 2/Lt. | 162 |
| ——— P., Lt.-Col., Rev. | 135 |
| ——— R. F., Capt. | 105 |
| ——— S. E., 2/Lt. | 119 |
| Singleton, E., 2/Lt. | 166 |
| ——— H., 2/Lt. | 99 |
| Sinkinson, F. G., 2/Lt. | 124 |
| Sisson, G., Lieut. | 15 |
| ——— J. A., 2/Lt. | 33 |
| Sitch, J. E., Lieut. | 174 |
| Skaife, E., Capt. | 56 |
| Skead, E. S., Lieut. | 141 |
| Skeet, C. H. L., 2/Lt. | 31 |
| Skene, A., Lieut. | 104 |
| ——— I., 2/Lt. | 51 |
| Skerrett, W. C., Capt. | 24 |
| Skill, H. J., Capt. | 89 |
| Skinner, A. H., 2/Lt. | 156 |
| ——— F. G., Capt. | 88 |
| ——— R. L. G., 2/Lt. | 162 |
| ——— R. T., 2/Lt. | 79 |
| ——— T. C., Lieut. | 118 |
| ——— W. H., 2/Lt. | 118 |
| ——— W. R. K., 2/Lt. | 155 |
| Slack, C. M., Capt., M.C. | 43 |
| ——— J. N., Lieut. | 100 |
| Slade, R. J., 2/Lt. | 146 |
| Slatem, S. S., 2/Lt. | 142 |
| Slater, G. B., Capt. | 128 |
| ——— K., Lieut. | 177 |
| Slatter, T., Capt. | 111 |
| Slattery, F. J., Capt. | 17 |
| Slaughter, G. H., 2/Lt. | 54 |
| Slavitz, S., 2/Lt. | 87 |
| Sleath, W. F., Capt. | 43 |
| Slee, F. D., 2/Lt. | 154 |
| Sleigh, H., Capt. | 68 |
| ——— T. W., 2/Lt. | 175 |
| Slipper, R. A., 2/Lt. | 162 |
| Sliter, E. D., Lieut. | 154 |
| Sloan, A. T., Major | 10 |

| | PAGE |
|---|---|
| Sloan, J. W. J., 2/Lt. | 121 |
| Sloane, D., 2/Lt. | 101 |
| ——— S. L. F., Capt. | 87 |
| Sloggett, A. J. H., Lt.-Col. | 115 |
| Sloper, G. O., Capt. | 24 |
| Sly, F. C., Lieut. | 186 |
| Smail, H. M., 2/Lt. | 66 |
| Smailes, E. B., 2/Lt. | 170 |
| Small, F. G. H., 2/Lt. | 117 |
| Smart, A. H., Lieut. | 69 |
| ——— F. L., Lieut. | 26 |
| ——— R. W., 2/Lt. | 88 |
| ——— W. P., 2/Lt. | 32 |
| Smedley, J. H., 2/Lt. | 46 |
| Smillie, T., 2/Lt. | 54 |
| Smith, Andrew, 2/Lt. | 109 |
| ——— A., Lieut. | 165 |
| ——— A. E., Lieut. | 124 |
| ——— A. F., Lieut. | 173 |
| ——— Arthur J., 2/Lt. | 78 |
| ——— A. McB., 2/Lt. | 44 |
| ——— B., Lieut. | 153 |
| ——— C., 2/Lt. | 148 |
| ——— C. F., Lieut. | 153 |
| ——— C. H., Capt. | 130 |
| ——— C. H., 2/Lt. | 48 |
| ——— C. R., 2/Lt. | 21 |
| ——— C. S., 2/Lt. | 99 |
| ——— C. W., Capt. | 98 |
| ——— D. Muro, Capt. | 134 |
| ——— E., Lieut. | 141 |
| ——— E. A. L. F., 2/Lt. | 157 |
| ——— E. F. H., Capt. | 116 |
| ——— E. Senior, 2/Lt. | 40 |
| ——— F., Capt. | 93 |
| ——— F., 2/Lt. | 166 |
| ——— F. G., Lieut. | 139 |
| ——— F. I., Lieut. | 63 |
| ——— F. J. K., Lieut. | 87 |
| ——— F. L., 2/Lt. | 156 |
| ——— F. P., Capt. | 132 |
| ——— F. S., 2/Lt. | 62 |
| ——— G., 2/Lt. | 126 |
| ——— G. B., Brig.-Gen. | 184 |
| ——— G. C., Capt., M.C. | 104 |
| ——— G. C., 2/Lt. | 137 |
| ——— G. F., 2/Lt. | 57 |
| ——— G. H., Capt. | 18 |
| ——— G. H., Lieut. | 49 |
| ——— G. H. B., Lieut. | 169 |
| ——— G. Johnston, Lieut. | 173 |
| ——— G. M., 2/Lt. | 155 |
| ——— G. Mackenzie, Capt. | 63 |
| ——— G. W., 2/Lt. | 40 |
| ——— H. B., Lt.-Col. | 184 |
| ——— H. E., Lieut. | 141 |
| ——— Hy. Edward, 2/Lt. | 79 |
| ——— H. M., Lt.-Col., D.S.O. | 86 |
| ——— H. Nelson, Lieut. | 29 |
| ——— H. T., 2/Lt. | 65 |
| ——— H. T., 2/Lt. | 51 |
| ——— Harold Worley, 2/Lt. | 53 |
| ——— I. C., 2/Lt. | 130 |
| ——— I. W., Lieut. | 16 |
| ——— J., 2/Lt. | 70 |
| ——— J. E., Lieut. | 137 |
| ——— J. F., 2/Lt. | 115 |

| Name | Page | Name | Page | Name | Page | Name | Page |
|---|---|---|---|---|---|---|---|
| Smith, J. G., Rev. | 135 | Sorley, J. T., Lieut. | 174 | Stanley, G. K., 2/Lt. | 11 | Stewardson, E. A., Lieut | 153 |
| ——— J. H., 2/Lt. | 52 | Sotham, E. G., Major, M.C. | 96 | ——— J. B., 2/Lt. | 93 | Stewart, A.D.L., Lieut. | 106 |
| ——— J. L., 2/Lt. | 165 | Souden, S., 2/Lt. | 104 | Stansby, J., 2/Lt. | 98 | ——— A. F., Major | 185 |
| ——— J. R. Leslie, 2/Lt. | 20 | Soutar, D. H., Lieut. | 107 | Staples, E. G., Capt. | 181 | ——— A.W.F., Capt | 59 |
| ——— J. Sercombe, Sub-Lt. | 177 | ——— Geo. C., 2/Lt. | 125 | Stapleton, H. E., Lieut. | 183 | ——— C. W., 2/Lt. | 105 |
| ——— L. A., Capt. | 153 | Souter, L. F., 2/Lt. | 183 | Stark, Conrad, 2/Lt. | 78 | ——— Douglas, Lieut | 148 |
| ——— L. Coleman, Capt. | 35 | Southern, Frank J., 2/Lt | 69 | ——— J. D., 2/Lt. | 58 | ——— D. J., Lieut. | 151 |
| ——— L. G., 2/Lt. | 172 | ——— H., 2/Lt. | 182 | Starkey, F. E., Lieut. | 116 | ——— G. A., 2/Lt. | 20 |
| ——— L. H., Lieut. | 181 | ——— Norman, Major | 13 | Starnes, D. S. B., 2/Lt., M.C. | 89 | ——— H., Lieut. | 54 |
| ——— L. H., Lieut. | 22 | Southon, H. G., Lieut. | 150 | Start, B. J., Capt. | 111 | ——— H. F., 2/Lt. | 32 |
| ——— L. H., Lieut. | 174 | Southorn, T. N., Lieut. | 153 | ——— D. M., 2/Lt. | 77 | ——— H. S., Capt. | 188 |
| ——— M. L. C., 2/Lt. | 183 | Sowerbutts, J. A., Lieut. | 115 | Startin, C. B., Capt. | 97 | ——— H. W., Asst. Surg. | 182 |
| ——— Norman, 2/Lt. | 175 | Sowerby, J., 2/Lt. | 25 | ——— J. S., Capt. | 184 | ——— John, Lieut. | 140 |
| ——— Noel A., Lieut | 162 | ——— J. P., 2/Lt. | 27 | Statham, Richard L., 2/Lt. | 71 | ——— I. A., 2/Lt. | 33 |
| ——— P. N., Capt. | 48 | Spackman, W.O., Lieut. | 184 | Stead, G. C., 2/Lt. | 154 | ——— J., 2/Lt. | 104 |
| ——— R., Capt. | 93 | Span, F. H., Capt. | 66 | ——— M.W.B., 2/Lt. | 158 | ——— John D., Lieut. | 74 |
| ——— R. B., 2/Lt. | 160 | Spargo, W. H., 2/Lt. | 33 | Stealey, E. T., Lieut. | 126 | ——— J.D.M., 2/Lt. | 152 |
| ——— R. E., 2/Lt. | 56 | Sparkes, C. P., Lieut. | 172 | Stearne, G. F., 2/Lt. | 30 | ——— J. H., Capt. | 109 |
| ——— Reginald Gilbert, Lieut. | 25 | ——— P. J., 2/Lt. | 58 | Stearns, H. D., 2/Lt. | 184 | ——— P., 2/Lt. | 188 |
| ——— R.H., 2/Lt. | 42 | Sparks, H. J., 2/Lt., M.C. | 160 | Stedman, A. R., Lieut. | 168 | ——— P. D., 2/Lt. | 40 |
| ——— R. H. T., Capt. | 42 | Speagell, H.M.D., 2/Lt. | 173 | ——— F., 2/Lt. | 152 | ——— R. J. G., 2/Lt. | 159 |
| ——— R. L., 2/Lt. | 111 | Spear, J. C., 2/Lt. | 119 | Steel, A. K., Lieut. | 121 | ——— R. R., Lieut. | 32 |
| ——— R.M., 2/Lt. | 157 | Spearpoint, H. D., Lieut | 154 | ——— G., 2/Lt. | 24 | ——— W., Capt. | 105 |
| ——— Robert Wm., 2/Lt. | 45 | Speedy, N., 2/Lt. | 43 | Steele, N. L., 2/Lt. | 181 | ——— W., Lieut. | 54 |
| ——— S., 2/Lt. | 187 | Speer, L.A.T., 2/Lt. | 86 | ——— T. Murray, Lieut. | 173 | Stewart-Cox, A., Capt. | 10 |
| ——— Sidney, Capt. | 132 | Spence, C., 2/Lt. | 68 | ——— W., Lieut. | 179 | Stewart-Murray, J. T., Capt. | 107 |
| ——— S. B., 2/Lt. | 137 | ——— H. F., Capt. | 87 | Steer, C., Rev., M.C. | 135 | Stewart-Smith, Dudley C., Lieut. | 73 |
| ——— S. C., 2/Lt. | 93 | ——— H. N., 2/Lt. | 68 | Steeves, D. T., 2/Lt. | 153 | Stickings, A. E., Capt. | 93 |
| ——— S. R., 2/Lt. | 97 | ——— R., Lieut. | 185 | ——— Gordon T., Lieut. | 160 | Stiles, R. A., 2/Lt. | 45 |
| ——— S. R., 2/Lt. | 72 | Spencelayh, V. C. H., 2/Lt. | 63 | ——— R. P., Lieut. | 139 | Still, J., Lieut. | 178 |
| ——— Vivian, Lieut. | 153 | Spencer, A., Lieut. | 122 | Steggall, G. E. A., 2/Lt. | 22 | Stillwell, J. G., Lieut. | 180 |
| ——— V. H., Capt. | 189 | ——— Cecil H., 2/Lt. | 113 | Stein, C. J., Capt. | 142 | Stirk, C. W., 2/Lt. | 49 |
| ——— W., 2/Lt., | 40 | ——— E. A., Lieut. | 10 | ——— Ian, Lieut. | 9 | Stirland, H., 2/Lt. | 77 |
| ——— W. C., 2-Lt. | 154 | ——— E. W., 2/Lt. | 22 | Steinberg, Roy D., 2/Lt. | 89 | ——— A., Capt. | 112 |
| ——— W. C. Lindsay, Lieut. | 107 | ——— Fredk. J. E., 2/Lt. | 94 | Stempt, L. F., Capt. | 14 | ——— A. C., 2/Lt. | 15 |
| ——— W. H., 2/Lt. | 97 | ——— John, 2/Lt. | 32 | Stenhouse, J. A., Lieut. | 131 | Stiven, R.W.S., Capt. | 53 |
| ——— W. R., 2/Lt. | 32 | ——— J. H., Capt. | 50 | Stenson, W., 2/Lt. | 120 | Stockley, C. H., Capt. | 183 |
| Smith-Masters, H. A., Rev. | 135 | ——— W.A.L., 2/Lt. | 155 | Stephen, A. M., Major | 15 | Stockman, E. J., Lieut. | 171 |
| Smithers, E., 2/Lt. | 161 | Spencer Smith, P., Lieut | 129 | ——— J. C., Lieut. | 73 | Stockwell, Lionel Geo., 2/Lt. | 175 |
| Smithwick, J. A., Capt. | 47 | Spensley, J. R., Lieut. | 131 | ——— J. T., 2/Lt. | 106 | Stogden, J., Lieut. | 94 |
| Smitten, Peter, 2/Lt. | 92 | Spibey, F. W., 2/Lt. | 71 | Stephens, C. H., Lieut. | 169 | Stokeld, F. E., 2/Lt. | 50 |
| Smurthwaite, A. S. T., 2/Lt. | 89 | Spicer, E. M., Lieut. | 64 | ——— D. E., 2/Lt. | 168 | Stokes, H., Capt. | 189 |
| Smyth, D. M., Capt. | 97 | ——— W. E. Hardy, Lieut. | 39 | ——— H. T., 2/Lt. | 43 | Stokes-Roberts, A. E., A/Lt.-Col. | 51 |
| Smyth, E. C., 2/Lt. | 112 | Spikesman, W. R., 2/Lt. | 30 | Stephenson, C.M., Lt-Col | 58 | Stokoe, J. S., 2/Lt. | 25 |
| Smythe, C., Lieut., M.C. | 157 | Spink, H. M., Capt. | 182 | ——— G. F., 2/Lt. | 43 | Stone, H. R., 2/Lt. | 128 |
| ——— Ingoldsby Lister, Capt. | 10 | ——— H. W., 2/Lt. | 85 | ——— Geo H., Lieut | 166 | ——— John L., Lieut. | 178 |
| Smythe-Osborne, J. G., Capt. | 56 | Spira, S., Capt. | 188 | ——— H., Lieut. | 186 | ——— R., 2/Lt. | 78 |
| Snadden, W. McN., Lieut. | 112 | Spiro, S. G., 2/Lt. | 158 | ——— L., Sub-Lt. | 144 | ——— R. Harris | 171 |
| Snape, J. A., Lieut. | 55 | Spite, J. L., 2/Lt. | 11 | ——— M. M., 2/Lt. | 79 | ——— W. J. G., 2/Lt. | 16 |
| Snell, W., Lieut. | 186 | Spooner, H. Father, Capt. | 186 | ——— W. S., Lieut. | 166 | Stonehouse, David U. | 37 |
| Snodgrass, H., 2/Lt. | 11 | ——— F. P., Lieut. | 120 | Sterndale-Bennett, J. B. Capt. | 57 | Stoneman, J. W., Lieut. | 13 |
| Snook, C. W., Capt. | 148 | Spratt, N. C., Lieut. | 146 | Steuart-Menzies, R., Lieut. | 18 | Stones, J. E., Capt. | 189 |
| Snow, S. R. E., Capt. | 178 | Spring, D. M., Capt. | 132 | Stevens, A. C., Lieut. | 176 | ——— W., Lieut. | 136 |
| Snowdon, G. C., 2/Lt. | 28 | Sprott, R., Lieut. | 110 | ——— B., Lieut. | 140 | Stopher, A. C., 2/Lt. | 187 |
| Snowden, Robt., Capt. | 139 | Sproule, E. R., Lieut. | 170 | ——— Charles F., Lt.-Col. | 10 | Storer, Samuel, 2/Lt. | 76 |
| Soames, C. E., Capt. | 21 | Sprowell, B. W., 2/Lt. | 94 | ——— E. G., 2/Lt. | 42 | Stormouth, S. L., Lieut. | 178 |
| ——— J. A., 2/Lt. | 56 | Spurge, F. J. C., 2/Lt. | 130 | ——— E. H., 2/Lt. | 153 | Storry, E. R., Lieut. | 67 |
| ——— R. M., Capt. | 133 | Squibb, H. M., 2/Lt. | 39 | ——— W. T., 2/Lt., M.C. | 22 | Story, D., Lieut. | 24 |
| Sole, S. G., 2/Lt. | 35 | Squire, E. A., 2/Lt. | 61 | ——— W. T., Lieut. | 46 | ——— J. C., Lieut. | 49 |
| Somervell, W. E., 2/Lt. | 147 | Stack, T. J., 2/Lt. | 60 | Stevenson, C. S., Lieut. | 84 | Stotesbury J. M. 2/Lt. | 127 |
| Somerville, D. H. S., Major, M.C. | 57 | Stace, R. E., Capt. | 185 | ——— E. A., 2/Lt. | 127 | Stott J. H. Lieut. | 50 |
| ——— G. B., Lieut. | 28 | Staff, O. H., 2/Lt. | 42 | ——— F., 2/Lt. | 43 | ——— J. N. S. Capt. | 146 |
| Somerfelt, Allister | 166 | Stafford, A., 2/Lt. | 39 | ——— F. B., 2/Lt. | 46 | ——— J. W., Sub-Lt. | 145 |
| Sopwith, G., Major | 99 | ——— F. W., 2/Lt. | 88 | ——— Gerald, | 131 | ——— Leslie Hamilton, 2/Lt. | 69 |
| Sorel-Cameron, Major | 107 | ——— Robt. H., 2/Lt. | 35 | ——— John F., Lieut. | 43 | Strachan, A. H., 2/Lt. | 113 |
| | | Stainton, E., 2/Lt. | 24 | ——— J. G., 2/Lt. | 156 | Stradling, C., 2/Lt. | 142 |
| | | Stair, J. J., Earl of, Major | 18 | ——— Ralph C. S., Capt. | 114 | Strang, A. R., Lieut. | 165 |
| | | Stalker, D., Lieut. | 103 | | | Strange, J. S., Capt. | 73 |
| | | Standage, A. K., 2/Lt. | 75 | | | ——— L. A. T., 2/Lt. | 151 |
| | | Standen, A. O., 2/Lt. | 14 | | | ——— M. H., 2/Lt. | 148 |
| | | Stanford, J., Lieut. | 10 | | | | |
| | | Stanier, F. A. H., Capt. | 87 | | | | |

## 215

| Name | Page |
|---|---|
| Stranger, Philip, 2/Lt. | 135 |
| Strangham, C. F., 2/Lt. | 189 |
| Strangward, F. L., Lieut | 173 |
| Strathearne, Wm. Miller, Lieut. | 170 |
| Strauss, A., 2/Lt. | 133 |
| Street, H., Capt. | 63 |
| Streets, Arthur H., 2/Lt. | 127 |
| Streight, J. E. L., Capt. | 138 |
| Strettell, E.F.D., 2/Lt. | 22 |
| Stretton, A.L.de C., Capt | 189 |
| Strickland, A. W., Lieut. | 178 |
| ———— D.de E., 2/Lt. | 11 |
| ———— W. A., 2/Lt. | 154 |
| ———— W. E., Lieut. | 13 |
| Stringer, Ernest, Lieut. | 189 |
| ———— F. H., Lieut. | 172 |
| ———— J. S., 2/Lt. | 170 |
| Strohm, E. C., 2/Lt. | 108 |
| Strong, A. H., 2/Lt. | 49 |
| ———— C. C., Capt. | 147 |
| ———— F. C., Lieut. | 126 |
| ———— P. J., 2/Lt. | 46 |
| ———— Robt., Sub-Lt. | 145 |
| ———— W., 2/Lt. | 42 |
| Stroud, Sidney Arthur 2/Lt. | 129 |
| Stroudley, A., Lieut. | 12 |
| Strover, E. J., Lieut. | 147 |
| Struben, H. M., Lieut. | 166 |
| Stuart, C. E., 2/Lt. | 156 |
| ———— J.A.G., Lieut. | 15 |
| ———— J.E.A., 2/Lt. | 137 |
| ———— Thos., 2/Lt. | 11 |
| ———— Wm., Lieut. | 179 |
| ———— W., 2/Lt. | 91 |
| ———— W. G., 2/Lt. | 144 |
| Stuart-Kelso, E. St. Brandon, 2/Lt. | 40 |
| Stubbs, H. B., 2/Lt. | 146 |
| ———— W., 2/Lt. | 46 |
| ———— W. H., Lieut. | 164 |
| Sturgess, T. M., 2/Lt. | 154 |
| Style, Oliver, 2/Lt. | 18 |
| Styles, W. B., 2/Lt. | 155 |
| Sugden, F., 2/Lt. | 41 |
| ———— J.E.W., 2/Lt. | 163 |
| Sugden-Wilson, W., Lieut | 146 |
| Sugrue, T., Capt. | 73 |
| Sullens, C. H., 2/Lt. | 89 |
| Sullivan, J., Capt. | 133 |
| ———— W., 2/Lt. | 92 |
| Sulston, H. E., 2/Lt. | 142 |
| Summers, G. D., 2/Lt. | 34 |
| ———— I. K., Capt. | 168 |
| Summerskill, J. H., 2/Lt. | 116 |
| Sumner, M. G., Lieut. | 94 |
| Surtees, W. M., 2/Lt. | 112 |
| Sutcliff, A., Capt. | 131 |
| Sutcliffe, A. H., 2/Lt. | 120 |
| ———— A. L., 2/Lt. | 156 |
| ———— C. A., 2/Lt. | 156 |
| ———— Geo., 2/Lt. | 68 |
| ———— J.E.T., Lieut. | 167 |
| Sutherland, A., Major | 183 |
| ———— A. M., Lieut. | 153 |
| ———— C. H., 2/Lt. | 19 |
| ———— F. H., Lieut. | 77 |
| ———— H. O., Lieut. | 24 |
| ———— J.L.C., Lieut. | 168 |
| Suthrien, G., Lieut. | 44 |
| Sutters, A. J., 2/Lt. | 92 |
| Sutton, M. F., 2/Lt. | 162 |
| Swain, A. B., 2/Lt. | 81 |
| Swales, M., 2/Lt. | 16 |
| Swallow, M.W.J., 2/Lt. | 83 |
| Swallow, S. H., 2/Lt. | 69 |
| Swann, J. H., 2/Lt. | 12 |
| ———— T. H., Lieut. | 172 |
| Swart, O. B., 2/Lt. | 159 |
| Swatman, C. M., 2/Lt. | 33 |
| Swaby, Geo. F., 2/Lt. | 67 |
| Swayne, H. D., 2/Lt. | 109 |
| ———— J. G., Lieut. | 38 |
| Swayze, W. K., Lieut. | 170 |
| Sweet, R., Lieut. | 184 |
| Swift, W. F., Lieut. | 96 |
| Swinburne, M., 2/Lt. | 24 |
| Sydenham, E. G., Capt. | 28 |
| Sydie, J. Errol, Lieut. | 165 |
| Syer, H., Major | 185 |
| Sykes, H. A., 2/Lt. | 116 |
| ———— I., 2/Lt. | 61 |
| ———— J. A., 2/Lt. | 14 |
| Symes, C. H., Lieut. | 100 |
| Tadman, R., 2/Lt. | 36 |
| Taggert, H. E., 2/Lt. | 111 |
| Tahourdin, V., Capt. | 54 |
| Tailyour, G. H. F., Major | 10 |
| Talbot, F. W., 2/Lt. | 157 |
| ———— H. E., Lieut. | 9 |
| Tallent, G. H. L., 2/Lt. | 179 |
| Tambling, H. G., 2/Lt. | 155 |
| Tannenbaum, H., 2/Lt. | 163 |
| Tansley, H. E., 2/Lt. | 163 |
| ———— V., Lieut. | 41 |
| Taplin, L., Lieut. | 138 |
| Tapping, A., 2/Lt. | 171 |
| Tarver, A. A., 2/Lt. | 118 |
| Tasker, W. T. B., 2/Lt. | 151 |
| Tate, J., Capt. | 132 |
| ———— R. S., 2/Lt. | 42 |
| Tatlow, A., Lieut. | 43 |
| Tatnall, E. W., Lieut. | 165 |
| ———— A. H., Capt. | 124 |
| Tattersall, H. V., 2/Lt. | 97 |
| Tayler, A. G. E., 2/Lt. | 92 |
| ———— H. M., 2/Lt. | 154 |
| Taylor, A., Lieut. | 184 |
| ———— A., 2/Lt. | 55 |
| ———— A., Lieut. | 156 |
| ———— A. L. T., 2/Lt. | 160 |
| ———— A. N., Lt./Col. | 184 |
| ———— A. O. D., 2/Lt. | 23 |
| ———— A. S., 2/Lt. | 26 |
| ———— C. D., 2/Lt. | 33 |
| ———— C. E., 2/Lt. | 86 |
| ———— D., 2/Lt. | 108 |
| ———— D. B., Lieut. | 109 |
| ———— D. H., 2/Lt. | 90 |
| ———— E. E., Lieut. | 171 |
| ———— E. H., Lieut. | 121 |
| ———— E. N., 2/Lt. | 79 |
| ———— F. F., 2/Lt. | 96 |
| ———— F. N. G., Capt. | 179 |
| ———— G. T., 2/Lt. | 32 |
| ———— G. T., 2/Lt. | 38 |
| ———— H. G., 2/Lt. | 188 |
| ———— H. G., 2/Lt. | 77 |
| ———— J., Lieut. | 38 |
| ———— J. A., Lieut. | 188 |
| ———— J. C., 2/Lt. | 148 |
| ———— Leofric, 2/Lt. | 50 |
| ———— L. B., 2/Lt. | 72 |
| ———— L. G., 2/Lt. | 169 |
| ———— L. G., 2/Lt. | 159 |
| ———— L. W., Capt. | 100 |
| ———— M. E., 2/Lt. | 144 |
| ———— N. J., 2/Lt. | 156 |
| ———— P. R., 2/Lt. | 127 |
| ———— R., Capt. | 139 |
| Taylor, R. A., 2/Lt. | 23 |
| ———— R. C., Lieut. | 158 |
| ———— R. E., Lieut. | 167 |
| ———— R. R., Lieut. | 189 |
| ———— S. H., 2/Lt. | 156 |
| ———— S. H., Lieut. | 98 |
| ———— T. H., Lieut. | 23 |
| ———— T. H., 2/Lt. | 28 |
| ———— W., 2/Lt. | 180 |
| ———— W., 2/Lt. | 24 |
| ———— W. C., 2/Lt. | 58 |
| ———— W. G. E., 2/Lt. | 80 |
| ———— W. H., 2/Lt. | 160 |
| ———— W. H., 2/Lt. | 92 |
| ———— W. H., 2/Lt. | 162 |
| ———— W. J., 2/Lt. | 119 |
| ———— W. R., 2/Lt. | 22 |
| ———— W. U. C., 2/Lt. | 84 |
| Teager, W. E., 2/Lt. | 38 |
| Teague, H. J. P., 2/Lt. | 122 |
| Tebb, H. G., Lieut. | 82 |
| Teeling, T. F., Lieut. | 58 |
| Telfer, H. C., 2/Lt. | 173 |
| ———— S., 2/Lt. | 118 |
| ———— V. A., 2/Lt. | 50 |
| Temperley, E., Lt.-Col. | 25 |
| Tempest, W. C., 2/Lt. | 164 |
| Templer, C. F. L., Lieut. | 61 |
| Templeton, W., 2/Lt. | 54 |
| Tennant, P. S., 2/Lt. | 175 |
| Tenney, F., Lieut. | 48 |
| Terry, J. M., 2/Lt. | 48 |
| Tetlow, A. R., 2/Lt. | 33 |
| Tew, D. McL., 2/Lt. | 70 |
| Thackrah, N. H., 2/Lt. | 160 |
| Thamer, O., 2/Lt. | 159 |
| Thatcher, A. R., 2/Lt. | 170 |
| ———— W. A. N., Lieut. | 39 |
| Thierens, J. P., Capt. | 133 |
| ———— V. T., Lieut. | 72 |
| Thin, J. A., 2/Lt. | 7 |
| Thomas, C., 2/Lt. | 171 |
| ———— C. H., 2/Lt. | 63 |
| ———— C. H., 2/Lt. | 176 |
| ———— C. H. G., A/Capt. | 93 |
| ———— C. S., 2/Lt. | 73 |
| ———— D. H., Capt. | 73 |
| ———— E. C., 2/Lt. | 56 |
| ———— E. H., Lieut. | 13 |
| ———— G., Lieut. | 162 |
| ———— G. H. de B., Lieut. | 142 |
| ———— G. P. F., Lieut. | 160 |
| ———— H., 2/Lt. | 174 |
| ———— H. W. M., 2/Lt. | 104 |
| ———— J., 2/Lt. | 61 |
| ———— J. T., 2/Lt. | 141 |
| ———— M. D., Lieut. | 17 |
| ———— R. W., Capt. | 113 |
| ———— W., Major | 186 |
| ———— W., Lieut. | 54 |
| ———— W. B., Lieut. | 59 |
| Thomason, W. L., 2/Lt. | 137 |
| Thompson, A., Major | 131 |
| ———— A., 2/Lt. | 158 |
| ———— Alex., Lieut. | 25 |
| ———— A. M., 2/Lt. | 50 |
| ———— A. N., 2/Lt. | 27 |
| ———— C. D., Lieut. | 155 |
| ———— C.W.M., Lieut. | 173 |
| ———— D. H., 2/Lt. | 14 |
| ———— E. L., 2/Lt. | 82 |
| ———— F. E., 2/Lt. | 45 |
| ———— F. G., Lieut. | 166 |
| ———— G., Capt., M.C. | 49 |
| Thompson, H. M., 2/Lt. | 21 |
| ———— H. S., 2/Lt. | 13 |
| ———— H. T., 2/Lt. | 68 |
| ———— H. W., 2/Lt. | 73 |
| ———— J. C., 2/Lt. | 64 |
| ———— J. C., 2/Lt. | 161 |
| ———— J. C., 2/Lt. | 24 |
| ———— L. E., Lieut. | 137 |
| ———— N. B., 2/Lt. | 100 |
| ———— P. E., 2/Lt. | 63 |
| ———— P. G., Capt. | 180 |
| ———— P. R., 2/Lt. | 50 |
| ———— Ralph, 2/Lt. | 43 |
| ———— R. C., 2/Lt. | 128 |
| ———— S., 2/Lt. | 32 |
| ———— Sidney, 2/Lt. | 155 |
| ———— S. F., 2/Lt. | 155 |
| ———— S. J., 2/Lt. | 30 |
| ———— W., 2/Lt. | 131 |
| ———— Wm. H., Lieut. | 142 |
| ———— W. T., Capt. | 131 |
| Thomsen, C. J., Capt. | 162 |
| Thomson, A., 2/Lt. | 106 |
| ———— A. B., Lieut. | 13 |
| ———— A. D., Capt. | 85 |
| ———— A. R., Capt. | 183 |
| ———— C. D., 2/Lt. | 103 |
| ———— D. A., 2/Lt. | 173 |
| ———— G. F., Lieut. | 164 |
| ———— H., 2/Lt. | 38 |
| ———— H. E., Lieut. | 164 |
| ———— H. G., Major | 181 |
| ———— J. W., Lieut. | 164 |
| ———— R.W.L., Lieut. | 174 |
| ———— W. R., Capt. | 122 |
| Thorn, J. C., Lieut. | 139 |
| ———— P. E., 2/Lt. | 21 |
| Thorne, A. C., Major | 183 |
| ———— D. S., Capt. | 16 |
| Thornhill, N., Lieut. | 31 |
| Thornley, S. C., 2/Lt. | 166 |
| Thornton, C. P., 2/Lt. | 151 |
| ———— R. A., Lieut. | 95 |
| ———— T., Capt. | 77 |
| ———— W., 2/Lt. | 49 |
| ———— W. R. Lieut. | 172 |
| ———— W. T., 2/Lt. | 68 |
| Thorp, A. F., Lieut. | 72 |
| Thorpe, A. H., 2/Lt. | 29 |
| ———— C. E., 2/Lt. | 168 |
| ———— G. L., 2/Lt. | 78 |
| Threadgold, T. C., 2/Lt. | 23 |
| Threlfell, G. R., 2/Lt. | 82 |
| Thresher, E. W., 2/Lt. | 175 |
| Thrush, H., Capt. | 52 |
| Thrustle, A. V., 2/Lt. | 44 |
| Thuillier, D'A. F., 2/Lt. | 114 |
| Thyne, T. P., Major | 70 |
| Tibbitts, G. D., Lieut. | 134 |
| Tibbetts, J. Lister, 2/Lt. | 149 |
| Tibbotts, A. H., 2/Lt. | 17 |
| Tickle, F. R., Capt. | 132 |
| Tidmarsh, D. W., Capt. | 151 |
| Tilbury, E. J., Capt., A/Major | 134 |
| Tildesley, T. E., Capt., M.C. | 98 |
| Tilley, H. W. V., 2/Lt. | 38 |
| Timmins, Leonard, 2/Lt. | 174 |
| Timmis, A. W., Capt. | 93 |
| ———— L. W., 2/Lt. | 158 |
| Timpson, N. M., 2/Lt. | 36 |
| Tingle, R. L. A., 2/Lt. | 41 |
| Tinney, W. C., 2/Lt. | 155 |
| Tinniswood, J. N., 2/Lt. | 16 |
| Tipton, R. J., Capt. | 179 |

| | PAGE | | PAGE | | PAGE | | PAGE |
|---|---|---|---|---|---|---|---|
| Tison, M., 2/Lt. | 167 | Tredwell, H. O., 2/Lt. | 62 | **Ubsdell,** A. R., 2/Lt. | 183 | Vines, C. H., 2/Lt. | 51 |
| Titterton, H. N., Lieut. | 189 | Tregear, F. C., Major | 183 | Udall, T. C. B., Capt. | 119 | Vipond, F. E., 2/Lt. | 154 |
| Tod, A. A., Major | 115 | Trembath, N. T., Lieut. | 175 | Underhill, E., Capt. | 132 | Voelcker, F. W., 2/Lt. | 86 |
| ——— A. R., Lieut. | 65 | Tremlett, G. W., Capt. | 88 | Unett, W. H., Lieut. | 85 | Vorley, C. A., 2/Lt. | 69 |
| ——— C. F., 2/Lt. | 11 | Trendell, C. J. W., 2/Lt. | 35 | Uniacke, D. P. F., 2/Lt. | 156 | Vosper, R. A., Lieut. | 165 |
| Todd, A., Lieut., M.C. | 151 | Treloar, W. N., Capt. | 178 | Upson, R. H., 2/Lt. | 152 | Vucovitch, T., 2/Lt. | 142 |
| ——— A. E., 2/Lt. | 110 | Tresham, W. H., 2/Lt. | 175 | Upton, D. F., Lieut. | 129 | | |
| ——— D. L., Capt. | 136 | Tresilian, C. S., 2/Lt. | 128 | ——— J. T., Lieut. | 9 | **Waddell,** D., 2/Lt. | 12 |
| ——— J., Capt. Rev. | 135 | Trevor, A. C. H., Capt. | 183 | ——— W. A., 2/Lt. | 82 | Wadden, G., Lieut. | 149 |
| ——— J., 2/Lt. | 12 | Tricker, W. R., 2/Lt. | 30 | Ure, Colin M. G., Lieut. | 16 | Waddington, C., Capt. | 63 |
| ——— James, 2/Lt. | 19 | Trigonna, A. S., Capt. | 114 | Uren, C. Trewhellan, 2/Lt. | 93 | ——— W. C., 2/Lt. | 44 |
| ——— J. A., Major | 19 | Triggs, H. T., Lieut. | 69 | Urie, W. A. E., Lieut. | 95 | Wadner, T., Lieut. | 90 |
| ——— R. F., 2/Lt. | 12 | Trollope, J. L., Capt. | 161 | Urquhart, A. M., 2/Lt. | 13 | Wadsworth, F. A. R., Lieut. | 119 |
| Todhunter, W. H., 2/Lt. | 62 | Troops, A., Lieut. | 77 | Urry, A. C., 2/Lt. | 82 | Wadworth, W., 2/Lt. | 80 |
| Tolkien, C., 2/Lt. | 26 | Troughton, L. H. W., Lt.-Col. | 116 | ——— R. T., 2/Lt. | 116 | Wagstaff, W., Lieut. | 45 |
| Tollemache, C. H., Lieut. | 81 | Trower, R. F., 2/Lt. | 11 | Urwin, T. A., 2/Lt. | 159 | Wahl, B., 2/Lt. | 43 |
| ——— D. P., Lt.-Col. Hon. | 81 | Trulock, J. C., 2/Lt. | 154 | Usher, C. L., Lieut. | 94 | Waine, V. J., Major | 136 |
| ——— E. A., Lieut. | 79 | Trusler, A., 2/Lt. | 11 | ——— C. M., Lieut. | 106 | Wainwright, B.M., 2/Lt. | 148 |
| Toller, W. S. N., Lt.-Col. | 78 | Tucker, G. L., 2/Lt. | 42 | Usher-Somers, C.E.,2/Lt. | 171 | ——— T., 2/Lt. | 122 |
| Tollett, G. W., Lieut. | 80 | ——— J. C., 2/Lt. | 73 | Ussher, J.F.H., Lt.-Col. | 140 | Waite, C. W., Major | 44 |
| Tolley, C. I. H., 2/Lt., M.C. | 124 | ——— N. O., Lieut. | 40 | Utley, Clarence | 99 | Wakefield Saunders, A., Lieut. | 90 |
| Tomley, W. P., 2/Lt. | 21 | ——— R. J., 2/Lt. | 39 | Utterson, A. T. Le M., Lt.-Col. | 46 | Walcott, E. P. M., 2/Lt. | 74 |
| Tomlinson, F. W., Capt. | 22 | Tuckett, H. S., Lieut. | 68 | | | Walden, H. F., 2/Lt. | 109 |
| ——— H., Capt., M.C. | 151 | Tudor-Hart, W.O., Lieut. | 147 | **Vacher,** W. E., Lieut. | 63 | Walding, T. W., Lieut. | 122 |
| ——— H. W., Capt. | 185 | Tudhope, E. D., Lieut. | 14 | Vagg, E. G., 2/Lt. | 144 | Waldram, H. G., Lieut. | 187 |
| Tomson, W. J. M., Lieut. | 148 | Tudway, Lionel, Lieut., R.N., D.S.C. | 187 | Valentine, J., Lieut. | 169 | Walgate, W. C., 2/Lt. | 43 |
| Tonathy, H., 2/Lt. | 20 | Tuffs, E. W., Lieut. | 99 | Van Baerle, P. E. H., 2/Lt. | 150 | Walker, A. P., 2/Lt. | 70 |
| Tonks, W., Capt. | 118 | Tullett, J., 2/Lt. | 82 | Vance, E., Lieut. | 108 | ——— A. W., 2/Lt. | 108 |
| Tongue, A. N., 2/Lt. | 95 | Tullis, J. N., 2/Lt. | 148 | ——— J. D., Lieut. | 165 | ——— E., Lieut. | 146 |
| Toogood, C., Major | 35 | Tulloch, Keith E., 2/Lt. | 148 | Van der Weyer, B. G., Major | 18 | ——— E. A., Major | 184 |
| ——— F. A., 2/Lt. | 43 | Tunbridge, G. C., 2/Lt. | 188 | Vane Tempest, C. S., Lieut. | 150 | ——— E. A., Capt., M.C. | 132 |
| ——— H. S., 2/Lt. | 29 | Tunnicliffe, E. C., Lieut. | 56 | Van Humbeeck,C., 2/Lt. | 86 | ——— F. C., Capt. | 129 |
| ——— J., 2/Lt. | 153 | ——— F. R., 2/Lt. | 98 | Van Nostrand, C. T., 2/Lt. | 147 | ——— E. G. S., Capt. | 162 |
| Toomer, J. C. J., 2/Lt. | 51 | Tupper, H., Capt. | 23 | Vans-Agnew, F., Capt. | 124 | ——— F. M., Capt., M.C. | 132 |
| Tooke, B. C., Lieut. | 176 | Turk, G. D., Lieut. | 75 | Vansittart, E., Colonel | 84 | ——— H. E., Lieut. | 118 |
| Toone, J. W., 2/Lt. | 147 | Turnbull, E., 2/Lt. | 27 | Van Someran, E. C., 2/Lt. | 36 | ——— H. S., Capt. | 107 |
| Toothill, Joseph, 2/Lt. | 104 | ——— G. I., Lieut. | 73 | Van Tilburg, J.A.,Lieut. | 166 | ——— J., Lieut. | 141 |
| Toovey, K. St. C. H. 2/Lt. | 24 | ——— J. B., Lieut. | 106 | Varah, G. I., 2/Lt. | 80 | ——— James, 2/Lt. | 43 |
| Topliss, R. H., Lieut. | 160 | ——— J. S., Lieut. | 68 | Vasey, W., 2/Lt. | 48 | ——— J. C., Lieut. | 170 |
| Torrance, G., Capt. | 132 | ——— J. W. E., Capt. | 101 | Vass, F. C., 2/Lt. | 84 | ——— J. E. M., Lieut. | 77 |
| ——— P., 2/Lt. | 53 | ——— M. R., McG., Major | 179 | Vaughan, B., 2/Lt. | 84 | ——— J. G. B., Capt., M.C. | 104 |
| Torrens, D. F., Capt. | 133 | Turner, A., Major | 82 | ——— D., 2/Lt. | 161 | ——— J. R., 2/Lt. | 13 |
| Torrington, Viscount | 188 | ——— C. A. C., Lieut. | 111 | ——— H. W., 2/Lt. | 21 | ——— J. W., 2/Lt. | 48 |
| Tottenham, R. C., Lieut. | 16 | ——— E. G., Lieut. | 165 | ——— R. M., Capt. | 60 | ——— M., 2/Lt. | 53 |
| Touchstone, G. R., Lieut. | 167 | ——— E. Lenten,2/Lt. | 38 | ——— Stanley, Lieut. | 23 | ——— P., Lieut. | 101 |
| Tounsend, F. H., Major | 40 | ——— E. S. F., Lieut. | 119 | ——— W., 2/Lt. | 82 | ——— P. L. E., Major | 9 |
| Towers, R., 2/Lt. | 52 | ——— G. F., 2/Lt. | 158 | Vautin, C. H., 2/Lt. | 181 | ——— P. S., Major | 38 |
| Towler, E. E., Lieut. | 72 | ——— G. M., 2/Lt. | 76 | Vaux, H. C., Capt. | 88 | ——— R. B., 2/Lt. | 41 |
| Towne, L. L. F., 2/Lt. | 161 | ——— H. P., 2/Lt. | 76 | Velho, S. F., Lieut. | 33 | ——— R. D., Lieut. | 148 |
| Townesend, E. J. D., Lieut. | 151 | ——— J., 2/Lt. | 124 | Vellacott, P. C., Major | 7 | ——— R. E., Capt. | 188 |
| Townley, D. C., Lieut. | 166 | ——— J. C., Lieut. | 148 | Veness, V. G., 2/Lt. | 138 | ——— R. H., Lieut. | 99 |
| ——— E. J., 2/Lt. | 50 | ——— K. K., 2/Lt. | 148 | Venter, C. J., Capt. | 168 | ——— R. S., 2/Lt. | 21 |
| Townsend, A. A., Lieut. | 188 | ——— L. J., 2/Lt. | 35 | Vereker, H. C., Lieut. | 176 | ——— S. H., Lieut. | 108 |
| ——— E. N., Major | 67 | ——— T. B., 2/Lt. | 106 | Vergette, R. G., 2/Lt. | 125 | ——— W., Lieut. | 176 |
| ——— H., 2/Lt. | 10 | ——— W., 2/Lt. | 164 | Verity, G. H., 2/Lt. | 55 | ——— W. J., 2/Lt. | 44 |
| ——— H. E., Lieut. | 163 | Turrell, J. W., Lt.-Com. | 144 | Vernon, H. R., 2/Lt. | 14 | Wall, A. M., 2/Lt. | 23 |
| ——— J. G., 2/Lt. | 123 | Turvey, A. E., 2/Lt. | 157 | ——— J. E., Lieut. | 113 | ——— H. R., Lieut. | 55 |
| ——— J. W., 2/Lt. | 41 | Tussaud, H. C., Lieut. | 166 | Vessey, J. O., Lieut. | 45 | Wallace, A., 2/Lt. | 50 |
| Townshend, C. V. F., Maj.-General | 182 | Tuxford, G., 2/Lt. | 91 | Vetch, D. M., Lieut. | 146 | ——— C. L'E., 2/Lt. | 128 |
| Tozer, W., Lieut. | 185 | Tweedale, G., Capt. | 95 | Veysey, G. C., 2/Lt. | 15 | ——— D., 2/Lt. | 19 |
| Tracey, H. A., 2/Lt. | 188 | Tweedie, G. S., Major | 19 | Viccars, Harold W., 2/Lt. | 64 | ——— J. F., Capt. | 40 |
| Trafford, E. B., Capt. | 18 | Twinberrow, J. S., 2/Lt. | 178 | Vick, C. W., 2/Lt. | 33 | ——— J. R., 2/Lt. | 17 |
| ——— W. E., 2/Lt. | 185 | Twiss, C. C. H., Lt.-Col. | 42 | ——— D. W., 2/Lt. | 61 | ——— P. M., Lieut. | 173 |
| Tragett, J. C. B., Capt. | 57 | Twist, T. F., 2/Lt. | 39 | ——— Horace, Lieut. | 164 | ——— W., Capt. | 183 |
| Tranchell, H. G., Lieut. | 182 | Tye, Harold, 2/Lt. | 51 | ——— W. W., 2/Lt. | 157 | ——— W. B., Colonel | 37 |
| Tratman, L. W. D. T., Lieut. | 166 | Tyer, Eric, 2/Lt. | 65 | Vickerman, F.H.D., Capt. | 7 | Wallace-Simpson, G., Lieut. | 176 |
| Trattles, R., 2/Lt. | 154 | Tylor, Cyril E., Lieut. | 162 | Vickers, E. R., Capt. & Adjt., D.C.M., M.C. | 91 | Waller, E. B., 2/Lt. | 12 |
| Travers, Gordon, 2/Lt. | 166 | Tyndale-Biscoe, N. E., Lieut. | 11 | ——— J. B., 2/Lt. | 175 | ——— Sydney, Lieut. | 67 |
| Treachman, B. A., Lieut. | 180 | Tysoe, C. G., Lieut. | 162 | Vidal, A. C., Capt. | 131 | Wallich, M. G. L., Lieut. | 21 |
| Trebilco, R. J., 2/Lt. | 76 | Tyson, G. D., Capt. | 32 | Villiers, A. H., 2/Lt. | 92 | Wallington, C. H., 2/Lt. | 75 |
| | | ——— J. D., Capt. | 112 | | | | |

| Name | Page | Name | Page | Name | Page | Name | Page |
|---|---|---|---|---|---|---|---|
| Wallis, C. E., 2/Lt. | 79 | Watkins, S., 2/Lt. | 56 | Welinker, S. C., Lieut. | 164 | Whitehead, Harry, 2/Lt. | 80 |
| ——— H., Capt. | 189 | Watkinson, A. V., 2/Lt. | 137 | Wellard, J. H., 2/Lt. | 95 | ——— H. H., Lieut. | 148 |
| ——— J. D., 2/Lt. | 188 | ——— W., 2/Lt. | 46 | Wellby, H. S., 2/Lt. | 157 | ——— H. R., 2/Lt. | 165 |
| ——— Percy, 2/Lt. | 43 | Watson, A., 2/Lt. | 152 | Wells, A. J., 2/Lt. | 38 | ——— M. J., 2/Lt. | 99 |
| ——— S. W., 2/Lt. | 30 | ——— C. H., 2/Lt. | 45 | ——— C., 2/Lt. | 71 | ——— W.H.N., Lieut. | 149 |
| Walmisley, E. A., 2/Lt. | 21 | ——— F. H. E., 2/Lt. | 181 | ——— D. P., Capt. | 136 | Whitehouse, C. E. L., Capt. | 71 |
| Walmsley, H. D., 2/Lt. | 65 | ——— F. W., Capt. & Adjt. | 23 | ——— E. W., 2/Lt. | 63 | ——— S. L., 2/Lt. | 157 |
| ——— J. H., 2/Lt. | 117 | ——— Guy, 2/Lt. | 60 | ——— G. A., Capt. | 170 | Whitehurst, C. W., 2/Lt. | 98 |
| ——— R. H., 2/Lt. | 17 | ——— G. P. H., Lieut. | 16 | ——— H. A. T., Asst. Surg. | 182 | Whiteley, R. F., Lieut. | 67 |
| Walpole, A., Sub.-Lt. | 145 | ——— H. S., Lieut. | 23 | ——— H. P., Lieut. | 169 | Whiteman, H. R., 2/Lt. | 13 |
| Walrond-Skinner, D. D., Capt. | 156 | ——— H. St. J. B., 2/Lt. | 98 | ——— N. B., 2/Lt. | 160 | Whiteside, H., 2/Lt. | 33 |
| Walsh, R. E., Lieut. | 16 | ——— J., Lieut. | 25 | ——— N. L., 2/Lt. | 140 | ——— H. S., Lieut. | 150 |
| Walter, C. G., Capt. | 69 | ——— J. F. J., Lieut. | 106 | ——— R. C., Lieut. | 16 | Whitfeld, G.H.P., Capt. | 167 |
| ——— J. S., Capt. | 21 | ——— J. H., 2/Lt. | 137 | ——— S. R., 2/Lt. | 161 | Whiting, Wm. C., 2/Lt. | 41 |
| Walthew, F. S., 2/Lt. | 131 | ——— J. L., Capt. | 67 | ——— Walter, Lieut. | 89 | Whitington, L. A., Lieut. | 137 |
| Walton, H. W., 2/Lt. | 51 | ——— L. C., Lieut. | 42 | ——— T. A., Capt. | 186 | Whitley, W. E., 2/Lt. | 43 |
| ——— L. S., 2/Lt. | 42 | ——— M. R., Lieut. | 93 | Welman, J. B., 2/Lt. | 180 | Whitlock, A. W., Lieut. | 30 |
| ——— M. J., 2/Lt. | 137 | ——— M. T., Fl.-Sub.-Lt. | 157 | Welsby, W. F., Lieut. | 17 | ——— H. H., 2/Lt. | 174 |
| Walters, A. J. C., 2/Lt. | 56 | ——— N. T., 2/Lt. | 160 | Welsh, W. A., Capt. | 68 | Whitney, R. T., 2/Lt. | 150 |
| Wand-Tetley, Lieut. | 93 | ——— N. V., Lieut. | 13 | Wenn, J. L., 2/Lt., M.C. | 87 | Whitrow, P. B., Lieut. | 84 |
| Wanstall, L., 2/Lt. (A/Capt.), M.C. | 88 | ——— S. H., Lt. | 61 | Wensley, J. H., Lieut. | 160 | Whittaker, B. K., 2/Lt. | 95 |
| Warbrick, H. J., 2/Lt. | 24 | ——— T. W. N., 2/Lt. | 127 | Wesson, J. S., Lieut. | 179 | ——— F. W., Capt. | 40 |
| Warburton, E., 2/Lt. | 79 | ——— W., Lieut. | 27 | West, C. H. L., Lieut. | 113 | ——— R., Capt. | 82 |
| ——— E. D., 2/Lt. | 151 | Watt, A., 2/Lt. | 104 | ——— W. G., Major | 66 | Whittall, F. K. B., Lieut. | 62 |
| ——— P., 2/Lt. | 65 | ——— A. G. M., 2/Lt. | 103 | Westby, F. H., Lieut. | 99 | Whittell, W. I., 2/Lt. | 41 |
| ——— S. E., 2/Lt., M.C., M.M. | 99 | ——— H. J., 2/Lt. | 81 | Westcott, G. F., Lieut. | 156 | Whittingham, H., Major | 15 |
| ——— T., 2/Lt. | 172 | ——— John A., Capt. | 92 | Westfield, C. J., Lieut. | 161 | Whittington, R. N., Capt. | 31 |
| ——— W., Capt. | 132 | ——— K. M., 2/Lt. | 179 | Westing, C. F., 2/Lt. | 160 | Whittle, O. L., Capt. | 148 |
| Warbutton, G., 2/Lt. | 117 | ——— W. H., 2/Lt. | 155 | Weston, G. A., Rev. | 135 | Whitworth, H., Lieut. | 158 |
| Ward, A., Lieut. | 180 | Watts, C. V., 2/Lt. | 32 | ——— P. O., Capt. | 182 | Whyte, A., Capt. | 20 |
| ——— A. A., 2/Lt. | 157 | ——— E., Capt. | 84 | Westwood, A. L., 2/Lt. | 85 | ——— J. C., 2/Lt. | 103 |
| ——— A. E., 2/Lt. | 115 | ——— F. H., Capt. | 15 | Wetenhall, J. P., 2/Lt. | 124 | ——— J. R., Lieut. | 97 |
| ——— A. H., 2/Lt. | 37 | ——— J. A., 2/Lt. | 48 | Whale, J., 2/Lt. | 63 | ——— R. Paisley | 165 |
| ——— A. O., 2/Lt. | 32 | ——— P., Lieut. | 144 | Wharrier, R. H., Capt. | 101 | ——— W.W., Lieut. | 14 |
| ——— A. P., 2/Lt. | 78 | ——— R., 2/Lt. | 149 | Wharton, C. E., 2/Lt. | 164 | Wickenden, H. J., 2/Lt. | 79 |
| ——— E. S., Capt. | 178 | ——— W. E., 2/Lt. | 157 | ——— H. A., 2/Lt. | 117 | Wickett, T. H., Lieut. | 153 |
| ——— H. E., Capt. | 22 | Waud, C. W. H. P., Lieut. | 21 | Wheatley, A. E., Capt. | 21 | Wickham, W. C., 2/Lt. | 121 |
| ——— H. K., Capt. | 131 | Waugh, Alec., Lieut. | 117 | Wheeler, F., 2/Lt. | 32 | Wicks, W. E., 2/Lt. | 123 |
| ——— H. S., 2/Lt. | 147 | ——— F. F., Capt. | 52 | ——— L. F., 2/Lt. | 156 | Widgery, H. J., 2/Lt. | 76 |
| ——— K. H. W., 2/Lt. | 90 | Wavell-Paxton, R. J., Capt. | 18 | ——— V., 2/Lt. | 128 | Wigan, A. P. C., 2/Lt. | 160 |
| ——— L. N., Lieut. | 158 | Waydelin, F. W., Capt. | 84 | Whelan, H. G., Lieut. | 113 | Wiggans, D. E., Capt. | 116 |
| ——— W. A., Lieut. | 54 | Weall, T. G., 2/Lt. | 121 | Wherry, J. H., Lieut. | 60 | ——— J. T. V. Capt. | 27 |
| Ward-Davis, W. L., Lieut. | 92 | Wearne, A., 2/Lt. | 138 | Whincup, H., 2/Lt. | 97 | Wiggett, A. J., 2/Lt. | 92 |
| Warden, G. W., Major | 23 | Weaterton, S., 2/Lt. | 25 | Whistler, L. G., 2/Lt. | 69 | Wiggins, H., 2/Lt. | 40 |
| Wardlaw, J. M., Capt. | 56 | Weatherill, G., 2/Lt. | 42 | Whitaker, G. G., Lieut. | 99 | Wigley, L., 2/Lt. | 155 |
| Wardell, J. M., Capt. | 48 | Weaver, J., Capt. | 164 | ——— H. G., Capt. | 72 | Wignall, G., 2/Lt. | 167 |
| Wardle, L. F., 2/Lt. | 128 | Webb, Charles, 2/Lt. | 125 | ——— J. A. C., Capt. | 18 | Wike, W., Major | 51 |
| Ware, D. R., 2/Lt. | 180 | ——— C. G., Capt. | 92 | ——— J. W., Capt. | 11 | Wilce, W. J., 2/Lt. | 39 |
| ——— G. R., 2/Lt. | 43 | ——— G. H., 2/Lt. | 56 | ——— S.G., 2/Lt. | 70 | Wilcox, C. H., 2/Lt. | 173 |
| ——— H. E. A., 2/Lt. | 155 | ——— G. W., 2/Lt. | 77 | Whitbourn, C. D., 2/Lt. | 84 | ——— A. J., Chap. | 180 |
| Warne, H. F. M., Major | 129 | ——— H. E, 2/Lt. | 49 | Whitbread, G. F., 2/Lt. | 89 | ——— E. N., Capt. | 127 |
| Warner, C. T., Capt. | 183 | ——— H. R., Capt. | 70 | White, A. J., 2/Lt. | 24 | ——— G., 2/Lt. | 31 |
| ——— W. E., 2/Lt. | 41 | ——— R. R., 2/Lt. | 66 | ——— A. M., 2/Lt. | 19 | ——— H., 2/Lt. | 40 |
| Warnock, Lieut. | 110 | ——— S. H., 2/Lt. | 84 | ——— D. C., 2/Lt. | 34 | Wild, F. J., 2/Lt. | 65 |
| Warr, A. E., Major | 20 | Webber, Maurice, 2/Lt. | 82 | ——— G., Capt. | 186 | ——— O., Lieut. | 82 |
| Warre-Dymond, G. W., Capt. | 66 | ——— N. V., Lieut. | 86 | ——— George, Major | 26 | ——— S. V., Sub.-Lt. | 144 |
| Warren, A. N., Lieut. | 115 | Webster, F. C., 2/Lt. | 53 | ——— H., Sub.-Lt. | 177 | Wilford, J. R., Fl. Sub-Lt | 177 |
| ——— A. P., 2/Lt. | 151 | ——— John, Lieut. | 164 | ——— H. E., 2/Lt. | 87 | Wilken, A. G., Capt. & Chap. | 140 |
| ——— D. F., 2/Lt. | 114 | ——— T. M., 2/Lt. | 155 | ——— H. P., Capt. | 126 | ——— W. A., 2/Lt. | 17 |
| ——— D. D., Lieut. | 45 | Wedgwood, F.C.B., 2/Lt. | 161 | ——— H. W., 2/Lt. | 37 | Wilkes, A. H. P., 2/Lt. | 14 |
| ——— F. S., Lieut. | 126 | Weeks, E. A., 2/Lt. | 65 | ——— I. H., 2/Lt. | 14 | Wilkie, H. J., Capt. | 58 |
| ——— M., 2/Lt. | 20 | Weighill, E. H., Capt. | 49 | ——— P. J., 2/Lt. | 91 | ——— J., 2/Lt. | 13 |
| Washington, J. N. C., 2/Lt. | 146 | ——— E. N. O., 2/Lt. | 80 | ——— P. R., Capt. | 162 | ——— J. F. McL., 2/Lt. | 74 |
| Wasley, V. B., 2/Lt. | 62 | Weir, Archibald, 2/Lt. | 54 | ——— R., 2/Lt. | 102 | ——— R. C., 2/Lt. | 19 |
| Waterhouse, Herbert, Capt. | 77 | ——— A. G., Lieut. | 146 | ——— R. E., 2/Lt. | 165 | Wilkin, B. O., 2/Lt. | 146 |
| Waters, C. B., Lieut. | 155 | ——— H. L., 2/Lt. | 109 | ——— R. W., Lieut. | 150 | ——— F. G. W., 2/Lt. | 114 |
| ——— H. E., 2/Lt. | 153 | ——— William, 2/Lt. | 104 | ——— S., Lieut. | 178 | ——— W. H., Capt. | 77 |
| Watkins, D., 2/Lt. | 15 | Welbourne, A. C., Lieut. | 86 | ——— S. G., 2/Lt. | 86 | Wilkins, H. O. D., Capt. | 154 |
| ——— H. Cyril, Lieut. | 73 | Welch, T. A. L., Capt. | 102 | ——— T. G., Capt. | 73 | Wilkinson, B. L., 2/Lt. | 12 |
| | | Welchman, P. E., Capt. | 172 | ——— T. W., Capt. | 181 | ——— D. F., 2/Lt. | 128 |
| | | Weld, D. S., Lieut. | 154 | ——— T. W., 2/Lt. | 154 | ——— D. S., Lieut. | 155 |
| | | Weldon, T., 2/Lt. | 85 | ——— W. D., 2/Lt. | 103 | ——— E., 2/Lt. | 95 |
| | | | | ——— W. E., 2/Lt. | 14 | ——— F. D., Lieut. | 23 |
| | | | | Whitehead, A. D., Lieut. | 150 | | |
| | | | | ——— F., 2/Lt. | 32 | | |

| | PAGE | | PAGE | | PAGE | | PAGE |
|---|---|---|---|---|---|---|---|
| Wilkinson, H., Capt. | 101 | Wilson, D. C., Major, | | Wischer, J. V., 2/Lt. | 152 | Wright, A. Y., Rev. | 186 |
| ———— H. M., Capt. | 55 | D.S.O. | 13 | Wisdon, A. L., 2/Lt. | 129 | ———— C. M., 2/Lt. | 78 |
| ———— J. R., Lieut | 50 | ———— D. W., Lieut. | 166 | Wise, D., Capt. | 113 | ———— D. C., 2/Lt. | 159 |
| Wilks, J. M., 2/Lt. | 63 | ———— E. J., 2/Lt. | 53 | Withers, H. G., 2/Lt. | 179 | ———— D. H., 2/Lt. | 111 |
| Will, G. K., Lieut. | 41 | ———— F. A., Lt.-Col. | 185 | With, P. M., 2/Lt. | 127 | ———— Ernest, 2/Lt. | 44 |
| ———— W. B. J., Lieut. | 62 | ———— F. C., Lieut. | 123 | Witherington, A. S., Lieut. | 14 | ———— E. F., Lieut. | 170 |
| Willcox, C. E., 2/Lt. | 35 | ———— H. B. B., Lieut. | 162 | Withers, K. G., Lieut. | 187 | ———— G. B., 2/Lt. | 178 |
| ———— W. T., 2/Lt. | 149 | ———— F. H., Lieut. | 150 | Witts, Chas., Capt. | 134 | ———— G. St. J., 2/Lt. | 50 |
| Wilies, A. H., 2/Lt. | 28 | ———— F. H., Lieut. | 141 | Witty, William, 2/Lt. | 96 | ———— H. W., 2/Lt. | 37 |
| Willey, B., 2/Lt. | 42 | ———— F. J. C., Capt. | 146 | Wodehouse, E., 2/Lt. | 56 | ———— J. W., 2/Lt. | 71 |
| Williams, Lieut. | 166 | ———— F. T., Major | 37 | Wolfenden, F., Capt. | 97 | ———— M. T., 2/Lt. | 86 |
| ———— A G., 2/Lt. | 83 | ———— F. W. B., | | Womersley, A. S., Lieut. | 95 | ———— M. T., Lieut. | 155 |
| ———— A. M., A/Capt. | | Lieut. | 185 | Wood, A. M., Capt. | | ———— P. L., 2/Lt. | 43 |
| M.C. | 81 | ———— G. E. H., Capt. | 143 | (A/Major) | 134 | ———— S. G., Lieut. | 83 |
| ———— C. D., 2/Lt. | 82 | ———— H., Lieut. | 117 | ———— A. S., Capt. | 49 | Wrighton, E., Lieut. | 78 |
| ———— E. Ll., 2/Lt. | 121 | ———— H. J., 2/Lt. | 27 | ———— A. W., Lieut. | 152 | Wrigley, E., 2/Lt. | 80 |
| ———— E. G., Capt. | 63 | ———— J., 2/Lt. | 41 | ———— C. L., Lieut. | 168 | Wylde, B. J. F., 2/Lt. | 81 |
| ———— E. J., Lieut. | 185 | ———— J. D., Lieut. | 140 | ———— C. W., 2/Lt. | 20 | Wylie, J. K., 2/Lt. | 110 |
| ———— F. C., 2/Lt. | 60 | ———— J. O., 2/Lt. | 101 | ———— F., Capt. | 96 | ———— Macleod, Capt. | 143 |
| ———— F. P. G., Lieut. | 185 | ———— J. R., Lieut. | 86 | ———— F. H., Lieut. | 141 | Wyman, J. B. H., 2/Lt. | 156 |
| ———— F. T., 2/Lt. | 57 | ———— L. G., 2/Lt. | 53 | ———— H. H., Lieut. | 168 | Wymer, G. P., Capt. | 94 |
| ———— G., 2/Lt. | 73 | ———— L. W., Lieut. | 100 | ———— J. A. V., 2/Lt. | 83 | Wyncoll, A. W., 2/Lt. | 163 |
| ———— G. B., Capt., | | ———— M., 2/Lt. | 125 | ———— J. C., 2/Lt. | 162 | Wyndham, J. R., Major | 93 |
| M.C. | 46 | ———— M.G., 2/Lt. | 168 | ———— J. H. A., Lieut. | 81 | Wynne, Albert, Lieut. | 56 |
| ———— G. E., 2/Lt. | 124 | ———— N., 2/Lt. | 166 | ———— J. L., Lieut. | 101 | ———— A. F., 2/Lt. | 159 |
| ———— G. E. E., 2/Lt. | 98 | ———— N. M., Capt. | 184 | ———— J. O., 2/Lt. | 172 | ———— G. C., Capt. | 85 |
| ———— G. G. R., Lieut. | 189 | ———— R., 2/Lt. | 80 | ———— J. S., 2/Lt. | 12 | Wynne-Eyton, R. M., | |
| ———— G. J., Observer | 180 | ———— R., Capt. | 116 | ———— P., Capt. | 182 | Capt. | 160 |
| ———— H., 2/Lt. | 97 | ———— R., 2/Lt. | 116 | ———— Ronald, 2/Lt. | 149 | | |
| ———— H., 2/Lt. | 31 | ———— R., 2/Lt. | 16 | ———— S. C., 2/Lt. | 118 | **Yacomeni**, W. McE., 2/Lt. | 24 |
| ———— J. R., Capt. | 33 | ———— R., Lieut. | 123 | ———— T. W., 2/Lt. | 46 | Yapp, G. H., Lieut. | 51 |
| ———— J. R., Capt. | 56 | ———— R. E., Capt. | 148 | ———— W. R., Capt. | 130 | Yardley, J. H., 2/Lt. | 12 |
| ———— J. R., 2/Lt. | 159 | ———— S. B., 2/Lt. | 43 | Woodacre, A., 2/Lt. | 96 | Yates, D., Lieut. | 123 |
| ———— N. E., Lieut. | 168 | ———— T., Lieut. | 189 | Woodcock, A. T., 2/Lt. | 43 | ———— G. A., 2/Lt. | 71 |
| ———— O. J., Lieut. | 100 | ———— T. C., 2/Lt. | 147 | ———— H. F., 2/Lt. | 24 | ———— J. A., Lieut. | 167 |
| ———— R. J., Capt. | 144 | ———— T. H., Lieut. | 109 | Woodfield, F. W., 2/Lt. | 181 | ———— L. W. P., Capt. | 60 |
| ———— S. G., 2/Lt. | 159 | ———— T. S., 2/Lt. | 160 | Woodford, A. F., Lieut. | 45 | ———— R. A., Lieut. | 165 |
| ———— S. H., Lieut. | 94 | ———— W., Major | 10 | Woodhead, W., 2/Lt. | 115 | Yearsley, K. D., Capt. | 185 |
| ———— S. M., 2/Lt. | 120 | ———— W., Lieut. | 109 | Woodhouse, C. M., Lieut. | 71 | Yeate-Brown, F.C., Capt. | 181 |
| ———— S. W., Lieut. | 155 | ———— W., A., 2/Lt. | 171 | Wooding, James, 2/Lt. | 168 | Yelland, W., 2/Lt. | 64 |
| ———— T. A., 2/Lt. | 49 | ———— W. K., Lieut. | 164 | ———— P. H., 2/Lt. | 17 | Yellowlees, J., Capt. | 39 |
| ———— V., Maj.-Gen. | 139 | Wilson-Browne, R. M., | | Woodland, P., Lieut. | 181 | Yelverton, C. N., 2/Lt. | 172 |
| ———— W. A., Lieut. | 55 | Lieut. | 148 | Woodman, K.C.B., 2/Lt. | 165 | Yendell, R. B., 2/Lt. | 125 |
| ———— W. A., 2/Lt | 12 | Wimble, A. S., Capt. | 7 | Woodrow, N. G., 2/Lt. | 36 | Yeo., H. A., 2/Lt. | 158 |
| ———— W. E., Lt.-Col. | 55 | Windebank, S., 2/Lt. | 65 | ———— W. H. V., 2/Lt. | 78 | Yeomans, F. L., 2/Lt. | 157 |
| ———— W. M., 2/Lt. | 73 | Winder, E., 2/Lt. | 96 | Woods, A., 2/Lt. | 76 | ———— J. H. M., Lieut. | |
| Williams-Taylor, T., | | ———— H. J., Lieut. | 10 | ———— Alex., Capt. | 117 | M.C. | 170 |
| Lieut. | 181 | Windle, B. C., 2/Lt. | 159 | ———— H. E., 2/Lt. | 26 | Yerex, Lowell, Lieut. | 170 |
| Williams-Thomas, F. S., | | Windover, W. E., Capt. | 174 | ———— J., 2/Lt. | 15 | Youens, H. St. J. E., | |
| Major | 178 | Windrum, C. H., Lieut. | 150 | ———— M. E., 2/Lt. | 150 | Fl.-Sub-Lt. | 177 |
| Williamson, A., 2/Lt. | 26 | Windsor, D. R., 2/Lt. | 57 | Woodward, E. G., Capt. | 96 | Young, A., 2/Lt. | 116 |
| ———— G. S., Lt.-Col. | 131 | ———— J., 2/Lt. | 179 | Woodyer, C. de Witte, | | ———— A. M., 2/Lt. | 19 |
| ———— J. C., 2/Lt. | 162 | Winfield-Smith, S. C., | | Capt. | 55 | ———— G. W., Lieut. | 93 |
| ———— T., Lieut. | 79 | Capt. | 186 | Wookey, H. C., 2/Lt. | 157 | ———— E. J., Lieut. | 21 |
| ———— W. M., Capt. | 85 | Wing, A., Lieut. | 31 | Woolcott, R., 2/Lt. | 44 | ———— E W., Lieut. | 17 |
| Willis, A., Capt. | 25 | ———— W. R., Flt. | | Woolley, C. L., Lieut. | 181 | ———— F., Major | 54 |
| ———— G. H., 2/Lt. | 92 | Sub.-Lt. | 177 | ———— D. B., Lieut. | 150 | ———— F. C., 2/Lt. | 76 |
| ———— N D., Lieut. | 172 | Wingate-Gray, A. G., | | ———— R. M., Capt. | 45 | ———— G. E., 2/Lt. | 57 |
| Willison, E., Lieut. | 43 | Lieut. | 161 | Woolliams, F. H., 2/Lt. | 152 | ———— G. W., Lieut. | 74 |
| Willmer, H. T., Capt. | 34 | Wingfield, E. N., 2/Lt. | 149 | Woolnough, C. W. F., | | ———— Hugh, 2/Lt. | 115 |
| Willmott, B. C. N., Capt. | 76 | ———— L. A., 2/Lt. | 147 | Lieut. | 117 | ———— Harry, 2/Lt. | 109 |
| ———— F. B., 2/Lt. | 159 | Winkler, M. H., Lieut. | 174 | Wooster, H. T. L., 2/Lt. | 82 | ———— J. G., 2/Lt. | 155 |
| ———— S. J., Lieut. | 27 | ———— W. O. B., 2/Lt. | 153 | ———— F. G. L., 2/Lt. | 61 | ———— J. H , 2/Lt. | 159 |
| Willock, G. W., Capt. | 59 | Winkworth, R. W., 2/Lt. | 31 | Worrall, W. R., 2/Lt. | 41 | ———— M. A., 2/Lt. | 116 |
| Willoughby, H., Lieut. | 70 | Winn, L. S., Lieut. | 117 | Worsley, R. S. L., 2/Lt. | 151 | ———— M. C. B. K., | |
| Wills, C. R., Capt. | 132 | Wise, S., Lieut. | 188 | ———— W., Capt. | 48 | Lieut. | 67 |
| ———— O. S. D., Lieut. | 34 | Winsloe, H. E., Major | 185 | Wotherspoon, G. W., | | ———— N. E., Capt. | 69 |
| ———— S. T., 2/Lt. | 152 | Winston, J.H.E., Lieut. | 49 | Lieut. | 104 | ———— R., Lieut. | 50 |
| Wilmot, E. P., 2/Lt., | | Winter, Lieut. | 131 | ———— H.C.F., A/Capt. | 36 | ———— S. H., Lieut. | 30 |
| M.C. | 158 | ———— A. E., 2/Lt. | 28 | Wotton, H. S., 2/Lt. | 22 | ———— T., 2/Lt. | 56 |
| Wilson, A. E., 2/Lt. | 34 | ———— F. C., 2/Lt. | 23 | Wray, C. B., 2/Lt. | 80 | ———— V. C. H., 2/Lt. | 76 |
| ———— A. I., Lieut. | 101 | ———— R. L. V., 2/Lt. | 111 | ———— W. S., 2/Lt. | 100 | ———— W , 2/Lt. | 24 |
| ———— C. B., Capt., | | ———— W. H., 2/Lt. | 157 | Wreford, C., 2/Lt. | 36 | ———— W. P., Capt. | 135 |
| M.C. | 176 | Winterbotham, F. W., | | Wren, H. L., Lieut. | 175 | ———— W. W., Capt. | 114 |
| ———— C. B., Lieut. | 147 | Lieut. | 154 | Wrigglesworth, E. H., | | Younger, J. E., Capt. | 10 |
| ———— D. A., Capt. | 132 | Wisbey, George W., 2/Lt. | 43 | Lieut. | 47 | **Zieman**, J. R., Lieut. | 163 |

www.ingramcontent.com/pod-product-compliance
Lightning Source LLC
Chambersburg PA
CBHW080400170426
43193CB00016B/2773